UTOPIA LOST

UTOPIA LOST

THE UNITED NATIONS AND WORLD ORDER

Rosemary Righter

A Twentieth Century Fund Book

The Twentieth Century Fund Press ♦ New York ♦ 1995

The Twentieth Century Fund sponsors and supervises timely analyses of economic policy, foreign affairs, and domestic political issues. Not-for-profit and nonpartisan, the Fund was founded in 1919 and endowed by Edward A. Filene.

Library of Congress Cataloging-in-Publication Data

Righter, Rosemary.
Utopia lost : the United Nations and world order / Rosemary Righter.
p. cm.
Includes biographical references and index.
ISBN 0-87078-358-0 :
1. United nations. 2. International organization. I. Title.
JX1977.R532 1995
341.23'1 -- dc20 94–33886
CIP

Cover Design and Graphic Illustration: Claude Goodwin
Manufactured in the United States of America.

FOREWORD

Sometimes it seems that the end of the Cold War has moved world statesmen from a chronic condition of justified professional apprehension in the face of a global nuclear standoff to one of acute personal uncertainty when confronted by morally vexing localized conflicts. At every level, those in the business of making and executing foreign relations are attempting to redefine their missions. In the process, the average citizen has come to see them less as watchmen in a divided and nuclear armed world than as routinely ineffective functionaries, an unfortunate combination of busybodies (always debating new and expensive problems) and handwringers (generally helpless when it comes to implementing solutions).

Indeed, the democracies, now that they have "inherited the earth," seem a trifle lost in the aftermath of the triumphs over Communist totalitarianism. The policies of the nations capable of action (financial, economic, military, and so forth) on an international scale in the post–Cold War world seem to result not in inaction, but rather in spasms of activity, often followed by ungainly retreats when negative consequences are encountered. It is oddly like the behavior of children who are suddenly able to move about, discovering, as a consequence, that "ouch," the stove is hot, and "oops," one can have nasty falls. But, of course, the great difference for contemporary nations and statesmen is that there are no "adults" ready to guide them—to instruct, for example, that one should neither dive headlong into an unknown pool nor into Somalia without first finding out how deep the water is.

Not surprisingly, the choppy seas of the 1990s have tossed the supporters of the preeminent international institution, the United Nations, from the highest of hopes to troughs of despair. In this context, the scholarship and experience of Rosemary Righter, chief editorial page writer of the *Times* of London, is especially useful in exploring the history and current state of the United Nations. Given the contemporary character of her analysis, Righter does an admirable job of placing recent events in a sensible context and of evoking the certainty of continuing change. And this is certainly appropriate. After all, over the last few years, we have started to understand that our notions of ideological rigidity, our dependence upon sovereignty, and even our definition of national economic interest must be rethought. Is it not inevitable, then, that our ideas about multinational organizations, especially the United Nations, should undergo similar reassessment?

Righter provides an in-depth survey of the history, operation, and recent activity of the United Nations. But the greatest strength of her work is that it asks the right questions about the future of the United Nations, and that it offers provocative answers by seeking to define the comparative advantage of the United Nations as a global actor. Her observations are symbolically timely as well, coming as they do virtually on the fiftieth anniversary of the founding of the United Nations.

It is fair to say that there would have been no United Nations without U.S. leadership. It still is true, Righter argues, that the United States has a unique role to play in terms of multinational, especially UN-led, action. Righter emphasizes, therefore, that American political leadership at any given time needs to think in terms of its leadership roles at the United Nations. For the Twentieth Century Fund, her work is one of a number of books we currently are sponsoring as part of broad exploration of the new foundations of American foreign policy. The Fund has explored *U.S. Policy and the Future of the United Nations* in a collection of essays edited by Roger Coate, looked at peacekeeping in Cambodia in a paper by Janet Heininger, explored America's struggle for democracy worldwide in Tony Smith's *America's Mission*, and the problems of ensuring peace in post–Cold War Europe in Richard Ullman's *Securing Europe*; in addition, the Fund is supporting ongoing work in this area by David Calleo, Michael Mandlebaum, Walter Russell Mead, and John Gerard Ruggie.

For most of its fifty years, the United Nations has seemed a frail reed to carry all these weighty hopes of humanity for world peace. Today, with UN peacekeeping missions in seventeen countries, the agency is playing a far larger role in world affairs than it was just few years ago. But no one would argue that it is yet what its supporters wish it to be. In fact, the surest lesson to be drawn from the past few years is simply that it is far too early to discern the shape of policy and delineate the roles of international institutions. What is undeniable is that debate about the significance of the United Nations in global politics has a new and sharpened relevance to all states.

In this situation, Rosemary Righter's book is especially welcome. She argues persuasively that the United Nations needs to do more than persevere; it must adapt to the extranational and subnational movements that are often central to contemporary international issues. While Ms. Righter shares the dismay of many at the performance of most of the specialized UN agencies, she also sees in them the potential for flexible, innovative responses to current problems. Her work highlights the impediments to change, but remains essentially optimistic about the future of the United Nations.

On behalf of the Trustees of the Twentieth Century Fund, I thank her for her contribution to our efforts to further discussion about the evolution of American foreign policy in a greatly changed world.

Richard C. Leone, *President*
The Twentieth Century Fund
October 1994

Contents

Foreword by *Richard C. Leone* v

Preface ix

Introduction The United Nations at the Watershed
Foreground 1
The Perspective 4
An Enterprise in Question 12
A Changing Debate 17

PART I: THE LAYOUT OF THE LABYRINTH

1. Utopia Invented
Wartime Beginnings 25
Collective Security 26
"A Layer of Peaceful Life" 31
More than the Sum of Its Member States 38

2. Boxes of Tricks: The UN Machine
The Consequences of Polycentrism 43
The Myth of "The UN System" 46
Chasing the Development Dollar 56
Dealing with the Consequences 63

3. The Politics of Illusion
Halls of Mirrors 67
The Impact of New States 72
The Fiction of "Nonintervention" 77
Rhetoric and Rights 81
Illusions of Control 87

PART II: THE WEBS OF IDEOLOGY

4. "New Orders": The Politics of Confrontation
Myth and Identity 93
The Third World Invents Itself 98
The Radicalization of the Agenda 105
"New Orders" as Declaratory Politics 109
The Power of Incantation 114

5. The Western Dilemma
Western Misgivings 121
Ideas, Bread, and Colonial Guilt 124
The Art of the Possible 134
"No Instructions, No Policy" 142

PART III: FROM REFORM TO REVOLT

6. Tinkering with Utopia
"Everything Has Been Tried" 155
Shutting the Stable Door 158
Design for Development: The "Capacity Study" 160

Political Fictions: "Restructuring" 168
Efficiency Is Not Enough 174
The View from Within 177
Impasse 181

7. Multilateralism for the Marketplace
Experimental Institutions 185
The Turbulent 1970s 189
Problems of "Adjustment" 196
Fire Engine and Hydrant 202

8. The Challenge from Washington
The New American Agenda 211
A Special Relationship 217
Style and Substance 224
The Washington Tea Party 231
Playing the Game 235

PART IV: BEYOND UTOPIA

9. Ways Ahead: The Options
Points of Departure 245
Opting Out 247
Structural Reform 250
Façade Management 253
Selective Action 255
The Options in Context 258

10. The Discriminating Buyer's UN
The Uses of Leverage 263
Transforming Development 267
Shaking Out the Bureaucracy 280
Humanitarian Challenges 289
Citizens' Causes 298

11. Another "New World Order"?
"The Scourge of War" 311
The Wind from the East 318
Under the UN Umbrella 325
A "Common Power to Keep Men in Awe" 329

12. An Improbable Phoenix
Security's Novel Dimensions 347
Global Stabilizers 362
The Shifting Paradigm 370

Notes 377

Index 401

About the Author 421

Preface

At an early stage in this study, the late Sir Robert Jackson remarked to me that of course I should never understand the United Nations, in the sense that insiders who have spent many years in its service understand it. And the insiders, he said, would join forces to reject an alien's perspective. Certainly any outsider must defer to such experience and knowledge as Jackson's, a man who had made a systematic effort to think through the problems and possibilities of the UN institutions with a view to their better functioning. But the thought necessarily follows: if the UN is only intelligible from within, how can it be useful, let alone accountable, to those it was created to serve? No organization sealed off from informed scrutiny can claim to be representative. Closed cultures are not dynamic. And an evaluation of the effectiveness of the global organizations must in any case be set within a larger perspective, one that considers the problems with which they are intended to deal.

Therefore, my scope is wide. This is not only a book about the United Nations, but about what multilateral institutions can contribute both to solving conflicts between nations and to promoting the world's economic welfare. It moves from the Utopian designs of the immediate postwar world to the piecemeal development of multiple different forms of cooperation in recent years. Adaptability and readiness to welcome competition, it argues, are key tests for all institutions. Yet Oscar Wilde once remarked that a map of the world which did not include Utopia was not worth looking at, and one is acutely aware, in the aftermath of the Cold War, that the rhetoric of "new orders" seems with us always. However vague, or even self-serving, such language embodies certain irreducible hopes of mankind.

The treatment of the United Nations is comprehensive in the sense that I have tried to look at all of the aspects of its work, treating the specialized agencies as an integral part of the grand design. Yet it is also selective, an anatomy rather than a history, focusing on those elements that help us to judge the relevance of the United Nations to political and economic life. Sometimes this leads to a severity of criticism. But to criticize an institution is not to question its original aims. The tendentious political games and fatuous programs of UNESCO concern us only because of the damage these inflict on the ideal of intellectual freedom it was intended to strengthen and defend. The shoddy machinery, the accretion of waste, the institutional paralysis represent wasted opportunity, the more galling given the undoubted importance of the UN's tasks and the urgency of the needs. That "reform" of the United Nations has been intermittently mooted since the late 1940s must be some indication of the magnitude of institutional transformation some parts of it will require if it is to be a player in the twenty-first century.

So wide-ranging a study has many sources and many debts. The early stages were generously supported by the Twentieth Century Fund, and I am grateful for the strong support and confidence expressed by its then director, the late Murray Rossant. Others whose encouragement from the beginning was of the greatest value include Peter Calvocoressi, Peter Galliner, Lord Nicholas Gordon-Lennox, Ambassador Henry Grunwald, Professor Sir John Hale, and Sir William Ryrie.

A wide variety of advice, information, and documentation came from within the United Nations secretariats, some of whose "insiders" were infinitely generous in sharing both their hopes and their frustrations, in illuminating the institutional labyrinths and in pinpointing the UN's systemic weaknesses. In Paris, for example, much valuable information came from members of the staff of UNESCO who unfortunately cannot be acknowledged. The same is true of the FAO in Rome. Their time, the trouble they took in procuring documentation, and the enthusiasm they expressed for a full investigation of the sources of the mismanagement and political manipulation pervading those unhappy organizations are reminders of how deep a vein of idealism runs through the United Nations civil service. Some information departments, particularly at the World Bank, the ILO and the UNHCR, proved magnificently that the UN can be open and accessible when its senior executives so determine. I am especially indebted to my extended conversations about the UN and its future with two of the most serious thinkers belonging to the "inside": the late Sir Robert Jackson and Maurice Bertrand. Among others, Sir Brian Urquhart, Francis Blanchard, and Shahid Husain offered particularly valuable insights. My thanks are due to the many senior staff members interviewed on an unattributable basis who will recognize their views on many pages. I have been severe about the caliber of much diplomatic representation to UN organizations, yet dozens of diplomats have given unsparingly of their time and often been first points of departure for particular areas of investigation. I have also had much help from UN departments of foreign services, notably those of Great Britain, the United States, and the Scandinavian countries.

Most important is my debt to Dragoljub Najman, not only for his knowledge of UNESCO, but for his infectiously enthusiastic vision of the possibilities of multilateral cooperation, and his pungent commentary on the state of the global enterprise.

Much of this research has involved primary sources, but there is of course a vast literature. I am particularly indebted to the librarians of the London Library and the Royal Institute of International Affairs.

Several readers have read individual chapters, and I am especially grateful for the comments of Shirley Hazzard. Invaluable advice on the manuscript have come from Peter Calvocoressi, Professor Pierre de Senarclens, Professor Brewster Denny, and Ambassador Morris Abram. The Twentieth Century Fund's publications director, Beverly Goldberg, and her deputy, Jason Renker, have been of the greatest assistance. The final stages of this work have coincided with my work as editorial writer at the *Times*, and I am indebted to its editors, Charles Wilson, Simon Jenkins, and Peter Stothard for their understanding and encouragement of what must have seemed an extraordinarily lengthy enterprise, and to them and my colleagues for the stimulus of editorial debates about the UN's relevance to political life.

William Righter has lived with this enterprise: as reader-in-residence, perceptive and witty critic, cajoler, and source of endless encouragement. My debt to him is limitless.

INTRODUCTION

THE UNITED NATIONS AT THE WATERSHED

FOREGROUND

The great cluster of global organizations grouped under the United Nations emblem ought, in theory, to be entering a golden age as the 1990s give way to the twenty-first century. The scope for multilateral diplomacy has broadened for a number of reasons, some positive and others negative. The collapse of communism in Eastern Europe and the dissolution of the Soviet empire, together with the surge of revulsion against dictatorships in much of the developing world and the end of apartheid, belong on the positive side of the scale. So may global economic integration, which has robbed sovereignty of some of its more destructive pretensions, and the growing social pressures for greater accountability on the part of those in power.

The obverse of these developments is greater political uncertainty. The abatement of the Cold War does not necessarily make for a more stable world. Realignments in Russian foreign policy, first to deal with the reality of economic decline and later as part of a quest for partnerships to help steady the course of headlong political as well as economic revolutions, have had directly benign consequences from Cambodia to the Middle East. But just as in Eastern Europe, the Soviet-imposed certainties symbolized by the Yalta agreement have disappeared, so elsewhere in the world the superpower balance may yet be seen to have restrained more conflict than the old bipolar rivalries inflamed. Proxy wars there were, in which superpower rivalries were played out at one remove, and they were brutally destructive. But governments may now calculate that attacks on their neighbors are less likely to invite superpower interventions, and the superpowers may in turn be under less compulsion to restrain their clients. Both Russia and the United States—the first perforce, the second by inclination—began the 1990s preoccupied with domestic problems. The term *superpower* may seem inapplicable to Russia in the mid-1990s, but may only await its redefinition. China's emergence as an economic giant and Asian superpower may be imminent; but in no country is the political landscape more shrouded in uncertainties.

This dramatic shaking of the global kaleidoscope would seem to call for precisely the type of institutions with universal reach that the UN provides, as well as creating the atmosphere in which its success might be guaranteed. Yet the greater the public need for global mediation and centers for cooperation, the sharper will be the assessments of the global organizations' capacities—and the greater the readiness to use alternative channels where the UN is judged inadequate. Flexibility and the ability to improvise will be at a premium, qualities never singled out by the UN's most ardent admirers. The United Nations has had a mercurial history in public and governmental esteem, but its future had never seemed less guaranteed than in the 1980s. The global organizations had come to be regarded, with a few exceptions, as hopelessly fossilized, incapable of adaptation. They owed too much of their remaining support to the special symbolism surrounding the blue and white United Nations emblem. Whether as an instrument for peace or as a champion of greater equity, the popularity of the UN traditionally had little to do with actual performance. This fidelity to symbol, wholly comprehensible to those who lived through World War II, tended to make the UN an object of faith rather than reason, and to insulate the affairs of its multiple institutions from the normal processes of scrutiny. For the diplomats who dealt with the UN and sat through its conferences, the quality of its performance had come to be discounted for a different reason. After periodic and unsuccessful attempts at reform, ineffectiveness had come to be accepted as "the price you pay for multilateralism." By the 1980s, however, the UN's symbolic magic was weakening, and the limits to tolerance of UN mismanagement and institutional infighting were being reached.

This creeping malaise had deep institutional and political roots that had not been seriously tackled when, in 1990, in one of the most startling shifts in the UN barometer since 1945, there was a dramatic resurgence of public confidence in its powers and of respect for its moral authority. The catalyst was the UN Security Council's unprecedentedly decisive response that August to Iraq's invasion of Kuwait. The UN's involvement in the Gulf confrontation was an important victory for international law and for the principle of collective deterrence. Yet this success was principally owed to determined national diplomacy (and American leadership), not to the UN machinery itself. Had the UN really changed, justifying the glowing optimism about its "renaissance," or was this simply the latest and most dramatic example of the gap between public perceptions (and hopes) and the real institutional character and potential of the United Nations?

The world had good reason to be astonished in the week following August 2, 1990. Less than twelve hours after the news reached Washington that President Saddam Hussein's forces were heading for Kuwait City, the UN Security Council convened in the New York dawn. After relatively brief debate, it voted unanimously to condemn Iraq's aggression and demand an immediate and unconditional withdrawal. The debate was as forthright as the vote. Only a few years earlier, Iraq's pretense that Baghdad had responded to a fraternal request from a new "free provisional government of Kuwait" might well have been used as a pretext for delay while a UN fact-finding mission was dispatched. Instead, it was swept aside as the transparent invention it was. Gone was the dreary charade of the veto. The Soviet Union, Iraq's principal armorer and close ally, was as insistent as the United States on immediate action by the UN. Even more remarkably, the Security Council decided from the start to act under Chapter VII of the UN Charter—the enforcement machinery, binding on all UN members, which gives the UN authority to deal, by force if necessary, with acts of aggression.

The next few days seemed to confirm the relaunch of the United Nations as the guarantor of peace through a system of collective security. The five permanent members of the council—the United States, the Soviet Union, Great Britain, France, and China—kept up informal contacts throughout the weekend. By August 6, Washington had secured the support of Moscow and Peking—and the cosponsorship of nine more of the council's fifteen members—for a further binding resolution. This imposed on Iraq the most comprehensive economic and financial sanctions brought to bear on any offending state since the UN's predecessor, the League of Nations, was founded in 1919. Only Cuba and Yemen abstained. Three days later, after Iraq, instead of withdrawing, declared an "eternal merger" with Kuwait, a further resolution unanimously declared its annexation null and void.

The pace was not sustained. By the time the Security Council brought itself to consider enforcing the embargo on trade with Iraq on August 25, President George Bush had already dispatched marines to defend Saudi Arabia, and Great Britain and the United States had ordered their navies in the Gulf to use force if necessary to stop sanctions-busting. At a moment when the UN's authority was being tested as never before, its secretary-general, Javier Pérez de Cuéllar, departed for Latin America on a preplanned tour, uttering from the distance of Peru veiled criticisms of the U.S. and British actions. The resolution that finally emerged authorizing naval enforcement of the blockade was a classic example of the kinds of verbal obfuscation that the UN had honed over the years to a fine art. Resolution 665 nowhere mentioned the words *enforcement* or *blockade*, preferring merely to invite states cooperating with Kuwait and with navies in the area to employ "measures commensurate to the specific circumstances."

The simple explanation was that the relatively painless stages of UN action were already past. The clearer it became that it would take more than "political will" and peaceful pressure to drive Iraq out of Kuwait, the more content was the Security Council to leave the United States to organize the response to Iraq's invasion. Diplomatically, 665 was a triumph for the allied coalition assembling in the Gulf; militarily, it was the point at which it became clear that collective diplomacy would not, after all, develop into collective security as envisaged by the UN Charter. Just as the naval blockade was to be enforced under the catch-all collective self-defense clause of the Charter, Article 51, instead of the never-used Article 42 under which the Security Council itself could take "action by land, sea and air" (including blockade), so the eventual military action to evict Iraq from Kuwait was to be taken by the United States and its allies as "states cooperating with the Government of Kuwait."

Yet the Security Council's decision to delegate military authority to a coalition detracted in no way from the importance of the precedent set. (In practical terms, strategic direction by the UN of the coalition's counteroffensive against Iraq would have been a military absurdity anyway, depriving the allies of the vital elements of surprise and military security, and of tactical flexibility.) For the first time since the Korean War—and the first time ever with the assent of all five permanent members of the Security Council[1]—the United Nations had shown itself prepared to go beyond purely verbal condemnation of unprovoked aggression. Iraq's invasion of Kuwait was a clear-cut violation of international law, but so had been its invasion of Iran a decade before. Then the Security Council had failed even to condemn Iraq squarely. Now, in a series of twelve resolutions, culminating on November 29 in the authorization of military action, the UN laid down a meticulous legal framework for compelling Iraq to disgorge Kuwait.

The UN's seal of approval enabled the Americans to assemble, and hold together, a twenty-eight-nation military coalition—extraordinarily wide, even if many were present only in token strength. By the time the counteroffensive began on January 17, 1991, fifty-four nations, nearly a third of the UN's membership at that time, were contributing financially or militarily to the effort in the Gulf. The Security Council's apparent firmness of purpose may have disguised much haggling behind the scenes, and the November authorization to use "all necessary means" to reverse Iraq's aggression may have required every ounce of American power, persuasion, and tenacity to achieve. But the fact that the United States and its allies attached so much importance to working within the Charter and clearly under the UN's express mandate gave rise to a new optimism about the possibilities of collective enforcement of international law, and a determination that this experiment must not be allowed to fail. For the first time in decades, powerful states were determined to use the United Nations rather than bypass it.

The United Nations emerged from the Gulf War in February with its reputation enhanced beyond anything that could have been imagined only a year earlier. At long last, faced with a clear threat to international security that could only have grown if appeased, the UN had lived up to that most emotive of the pledges in its Charter, the commitment "to save succeeding generations from the scourge of war." Aggression had been collectively defeated. The world seemed a safer place. Insofar as it was understood that the UN was "working" because the constraints on the Soviet Union's exercise of international power were now far greater than those on the democracies, that only enhanced expectations that the United Nations was embarking on a new era. The immense care with which each member of the coalition, Washington foremost, had justified every decision in the confrontation with Iraq in terms of the UN Charter confirmed its central role as legitimator.

Yet this deference gave a somewhat exaggerated impression of the UN's leadership in the Gulf and of its potential for leadership in the future. Few wars since 1945 had so indisputably come within the Charter's definition of threats to international peace, and few were likely to do so in future. Expectations matter, and the fact that the UN Security Council entered the 1990s with a success justified some degree of optimism. But the lessons of the Gulf in reality had everything to do with altered geopolitical equations. It remained to be seen where, in terms of its broader mission, the UN would fit. Because the Security Council had functioned relatively effectively, it was employed as the vehicle of choice, but Iraq's aggression would have had to be reversed even if the UN had been paralyzed. The UN had passed one extremely important test of its ability to function in an increasingly post-Communist world. But, as its checkered responses to armed anarchy in Somalia and the fighting that swept the Balkans were shortly to underline, this display of resolve served neither as a guide to the effectiveness of the machinery as a whole, nor in itself signified "the rebirth of the United Nations." A UN General Assembly which had seen nothing odd about declaring the 1990s an International Decade for the Eradication of Colonialism could hardly be said to be in touch with the political, economic, and social transformations in the world. Its specialized agencies and programs, which consumed the vast proportion of its money and personnel—theoretically to promote economic and social development—had a similarly ill-developed sense of relevance. As President Bush told the UN General Assembly in October 1990, nothing short of a "new compact" was needed "to bring the UN into the 21st century."

THE PERSPECTIVE

It is with this broader compact, and the prospects for its realization, that this book is concerned. A genuine revival of the UN would imply the successful addressing of a wide array of deeply embedded institutional ills, putting the UN organizations on a soundly managed basis and rendering them properly accountable. There are political diseases to be cured too: debates that have only the most tenuous grip on reality, manufactured confrontations, absurdly swollen agendas. Beyond that, purely governmental clubs that have habitually treated voluntary organizations with disdain, and commerce with hostility, have the smell of decay in a world where events are increasingly shaped by forces outside government. The UN, finally, has to learn to weave itself a place in the modern textures of multilateral cooperation, which are far richer and more complex than could have been envisaged in 1945. The collapse of the Iron Curtain has removed the familiar (and defeatist) excuse that the UN functions badly because it mirrors a world at loggerheads. For perhaps the first time, the UN has to justify the respect paid to it, or expect to be marginalized.

Three premises underlie this investigation. The first is that multilateralism, a shorthand term embracing all the multifaceted interactions across frontiers among governments, business people, and financial markets, research communities, and groups of private citizens, is an established, ineluctable, part of our lives. What was still a goal, even an ideal when the UN was founded in 1945, has become matter of fact, the consequence less of political or moral choice than of global communications, rapid technological change, and economic interplay. Business operates across frontiers. So does public opinion: instant news has given both publics and their rulers an understanding of the extent to which distant decisions or events affect them, to a degree that would have seemed improbable half a century earlier. In every country, this multilateral dimension to government and daily life has imposed strains on political and social systems that are rooted in the concept of national sovereignty. But these strains cannot be evaded. The concepts of sovereignty, and of national identity, are abidingly powerful touchstones for the emotions. Yet when, in practice, national power can be defined only in relative terms, what is left to decision is not whether we accept this phenomenon, but how well and by what means we can manage it. Multilateralism is transforming the nature of economic activity and forcing changes in our customary modes of policymaking, governance, and economic choice.

The second premise is that while multilateralism may be a fatality, this fact is not, of itself, enough to secure the future of the UN organizations created as the foundation-stones of international order after World War II. The rapid evolution of new forms of multilateral cooperation, sophisticated and flexible, has outflanked many of these global intergovernmental institutions. The ideals set out in the UN Charter and the Universal Declaration of Human Rights retain their resonance. The cooperative purposes laid down in the constitutions of the UN's specialized agencies continue to reflect felt needs. But the procedures, methods of work and programmed activities of many of these institutions invite no such respect. Thus the paradox: the greater the urgency and complexity of the multilateral agenda, the less tolerance there will be for organizations, formally dedicated to pursuing that agenda, whose activities yet seem only marginally relevant to the decisions governments take, to the workings of the global economy. The contrast between the success of the "international community" in the Gulf and its paralysis, four years later, before the genocidal massacres in Rwanda had a strong impact on publics increasingly impatient of failures, whether in preserving peace, preventing famines, or promoting prosperity. In the post-Communist world, there will be a premium on what works, and the malfunctioning of global machinery will, quite properly, come under closer scrutiny.

The long-standing defects of the UN are not confined to operational inefficiency. The rhetorical posturings of government delegates, the absurd and sometimes disgraceful political charades that too often pass for debate, and the destructive and corrupt systems of patronage and pork-barrel project funding have also contributed heavily to the decline in the credibility and effectiveness of UN secretariats. But there is a much larger issue: that of "universality" itself. The postwar concept of international order assumed universal participation in global organizations to be essential to civilized international conduct and the maintenance and development of the rule of law. The UN operates on the principle that more than 180 states, as disparate in size and wealth as Vanuatu and Germany, carry equal responsibility and weight. That system became close to unworkable over the years. Even where we accept that problems have global dimensions, does it automatically follow that they are most effectively tackled in such unwieldy forums? Finally, beyond the question of collective security, the relevance of purely governmental organizations to the actual global agenda is increasingly open to doubt.

Once put, as they have been with growing insistence since the early 1980s, these are not questions that are going to disappear. By its mere existence, the UN has undoubtedly contributed to the rapid evolution of multilateral cooperation since 1945, and failure to cure its sclerosis would be bound to have a negative impact on this development. But the lien these organizations exercise on the future will depend on the extent to which their services are deemed so indispensable as to compensate for the problems attendant on universality. The raised profile of the UN may whet political determination to address these questions, but cannot in itself resolve them.

The third premise of this book is that excessive fidelity to institutional molds will inhibit the development of international collaboration. This book is neither friendly nor hostile to the United Nations. One of the peculiarities of the myths that surround the UN is that a stance, for or against, is assumed to be the necessary starting point for analysis—as though people were made for institutions, not the other way around. The UN is not synonymous with multilateralism, just one of the vehicles for it. And in any realistic assessment of the complex fabric of international cooperation in the 1990s, the UN would emerge as only a small part of the whole.

This is partly because so much of that fabric is entirely or partly independent of governments. In the 1980s, thinking about the role of government began to be transformed. Within a remarkably brief span of years, ideas about what the state could and could not—and should and should not—do gained immeasurably in sophistication. The great tide of political liberation which transformed the political map of Eastern Europe at the end of that decade revealed an economic wasteland, transformable only through a painful process of radical restructuring. The plight of the republics of the former Soviet Union in the 1990s was, if anything, even starker. Nor were the richest and most powerful governments unaffected by technological change and the impact of free global capital markets. It became far clearer than before that although governments still make the laws under which they operate, the principal "actors" in the contemporary world—those whose decisions shape the way we live—are not necessarily governments.

This has large implications for policymakers, and the organizations they use when they need to act in concert. If global warming is to be controlled, for example, the DuPonts of the world matter at least as much as government departments. (In the case of chlorofluorocarbons, DuPont decided before the bureaucrats took action that producing chemicals that damaged the ozone layer was bad business in an environmentally conscious society.)[2] The business of legislation, national or international, becomes more complicated. In well-informed societies that have passed beyond the stage of being merely "policeable," governments are forced to be sensitive to public opinion.

Adjusting to a frontier-free world is not easy. Complaints that foreign investment encroached on sovereignty, commonplace in the Third World in the 1960s and 1970s, surfaced during the 1988 presidential elections in the greatest free-market economy of all, the United States. Migration is rapidly becoming an explosive issue. And in Western Europe in the early 1990s, governments were taken aback by the popular backlash against the Maastricht Treaty on European Union. An increasing proportion of economic activity and technical innovation takes place in a transnational world, operating across frontiers. But the institutions that governments have created to coordinate their responses to rapid economic and social change are *inter*national associations of sovereign states—associations, moreover, in which private enterprise and citizens' groups are disenfranchised as, in the democracies at least, they have long ceased to be in the national context.

Nowhere is respect for domestic sovereignty more deeply entrenched than in the United Nations. That alone has contributed to the marginalization of the global organizations. The UN machinery has lost much of its early dynamism. Where institutions lumber in the wake of rapid evolutions in the nature of power, and appear out of touch with the cross-fertilization of ideas, they eventually forfeit the claim to reflect the preoccupations of the international community which is their real, as well as theoretical, reason for existing. The UN—or at least the Security Council—will always have an audience in time of war. The shibboleth against intervention in a state's internal affairs, which has so handicapped it in dealing with the types of conflict that have cost most of the twenty-two million lives lost as a result of combat since 1945, may even be weakening. But the UN was intended to bring people together, not just to keep them from tearing each other to pieces. And here, the shadows cast by the global organizations on people's lives and the decisions of governments have shortened—for the healthy reason that there are competing channels, and for the unhealthy reason that they so seldom seem to be "about" the things that matter.

Insofar as this state of affairs has been attributable to ideological confrontations, North-South as well as East-West, these seem in the 1990s to be on the wane, although the destructive force of a resurgence of militant Islam should not be underestimated. The UN's bureaucratic inefficiency and openness to malpractice ought to be remediable. But the question that imposes itself is whether the UN's marginalization is the inescapable consequence of a model of cooperation that is becoming inoperative, and inoperable. The UN organizations may be doubly handicapped. In the first place, they fail to reflect the realities of power and influence because they accommodate on an equal footing the multitude of states that make up our politically fragmented world. In the second, they are absurdly exclusive, in the sense that they conduct their business with scant regard for the broader body politic of contemporary societies. It has to be asked how much energy we should put into keeping alive institutions that operate on such terms.

A bias toward keeping all channels open may be healthy, but not to the point of preserving organizations that may, by their existence, hold back the development of more effective coalitions and approaches. The business of containing frictions and managing interdependence cannot be left to moribund organizations. To pretend to rely on them, out of atavistic piety or political inertia, would be not only mistaken but perilous.

Our concern must ultimately be with tasks, not institutions. The primary question is how we are to manage the transition from the world of traditional polities, on which the architects of the United Nations based their designs—the world of nation-states in which it was assumed that domestic and international affairs could be neatly compartmentalized—to a world politically as well as economically transformed.

This book does not pretend to be a history of the United Nations, or for that matter of the political transformations that have been wrought upon it since 1945. It sets out to explore the institutional, political, and ideological dimensions of the malaise afflicting the global organizations, to see how and where problems have arisen, and why some of them have adapted better than others. Where it treats particular cases in some detail, its purpose is illustrative; policies toward the global organizations can only make sense in context. The aim is to identify the kinds of decisions that will need to be made both by UN executives and by governments, by reference to the problems that have beset these institutions and to past attempts to remedy them. This is necessarily an inductive rather than a thesis-driven exercise, an exploration of the UN's complex labyrinth that has the future rather than the past in mind. Rather than adopting a linear approach, it surveys the same terrain from different vantage points, internal and external.

We need more than one thread through the UN labyrinth, because the United Nations presents a palimpsest of different kinds of politics: those of its member states and (which does not necessarily or even frequently mean the same thing) of their permanent delegations to UN organizations; and those of the UN secretariats and, in particular, of their executive heads—functionaries who, within their domains, have been given powers to which most elected heads of governments cannot aspire.

Institutionally, the labyrinth is extremely complex, because the UN is not even centralized, let alone monolithic. This point is worth making at the outset because the UN is often thought of as a unitary system, and nothing could be further from the truth. An organizational chart of the UN could be drawn only by gross oversimplification, and even then it would mislead by suggesting that we are talking about a coordinated, or coordinatable, whole. The "political" UN in New York—so-called because it has responsibility for collective security although the vast proportion of its work, and expenditure, is devoted to economic and social questions—exercises no control, and precious little influence, over the more than thirty UN "specialized agencies," which have their own constitutions and governing bodies. Since 1945, UN bureaucracies have proliferated, to the point where there are now a hundred or so legally separate UN entities involved in almost every aspect of human activity. The machinery through which the UN's member governments have attempted, largely in vain, to control these bureaucracies have proliferated likewise. Parkinson's law has a flourishing global dimension.

There is not even a common understanding of what we mean by "the United Nations." My definition is the most comprehensive. It includes the Security Council, the General Assembly, and the organizations that are formally under the control of either the Assembly or the Economic and Social Council (most though not all of which are based in New York); the autonomous specialized agencies; and the international financial institutions, the International Monetary Fund and the World Bank, which are generally treated as though they belonged in a different world but are in fact UN specialized agencies.

Some of these organizations are relatively untouched by the most common symptoms of the UN disease—resolutions no sooner negotiated than consigned to the archives, studies and reports that nobody reads, paper targets and programs that have negligible impact on the well-being of the supposed "beneficiaries." Others are so distorted either by mismanagement or by misdirection—fulfilling their tasks inefficiently or assuming functions for which they were not designed and cannot perform—that they are probably incapable of reform. Some are indispensable, others have earned the right to be taken seriously, and still others have never made an impact or have ceased to do so and would, in a rational world, have been abolished. The purpose of attempting a guide through this labyrinth is to see where restructuring is needed—and where it is hopeless and alternatives must be found. Precisely because it takes multilateral cooperation seriously, this is a critical guide.

In dealing with such disparate organizations, generalizations obviously break down. Indeed, one of the purposes of this book is to show that they should, that it is appropriate and necessary to differentiate between these institutions, and that to treat them in terms of some more or less abstract "UN policy"—as Western governments have done in the past—is wholly meaningless. Different objectives require different strategies; different organizations justify different levels of expectation. To the question whether we should reform the global organizations, and what that would mean, there is no single answer. The pragmatic criteria are the ones that matter. The only general argument is that the UN should not be exempt from the rule that organizations justify their existence only insofar as they promote the smoother and more civilized handling of our affairs and, from time to time at least, enable things to happen that would not otherwise be achieved. Pragmatic criteria have too little been applied to the UN.

This book is divided into four main sections. Part I outlines the thinking that went, during World War II, into the creation of the UN and discusses the conceptual and structural contradictions—above all, the inherent tension between its affirmation of universal human rights and its insistence on nonintervention in a state's internal affairs—with which the UN was burdened from the start. It then reviews the two factors which aggravate what might be called its design faults: the multiplication of institutions and functions that render the UN machinery almost impossibly complicated; and the gulf between the uniquely rarified political climate in which it operates and the political and economic calculations that prevail outside its walls.

Part II examines the paralyzing impact on the UN of decades of political and ideological tension, as Cold War confrontations were exacerbated by the challenges mounted after decolonization by Third World politicians to the principles of individual liberty and economic liberalism on which the Charter was predicated. This section then discusses the failure by Western governments to react to these challenges in other than defensive, negative, and, ultimately, patronizing terms, the reasons for that failure, and the consequences for the UN and for multilateral cooperation.

Part III looks at the prospect for more positive global diplomacy in the light of two very different case histories of UN reform, on the ground that knowledge of what has been attempted in the past is indispensable to successful innovation in the future. First, it discusses the long and largely unproductive series of attempts at structural reform, elaborated at the UN in New York. It then turns to the more successful—because pragmatic and demand-led—efforts to modernize and adapt in the World Bank and the International Monetary Fund. The final chapter in this section discusses the beginnings of a revolution in thinking about the UN and its agencies. The catalyst for this transformation was the shock treatment adopted by the Reagan administration in the early 1980s, which was coupled with a taxpayers' revolt by the

U.S. Congress. Controversial as this U.S. policy was, it compelled a change of tone and pace in global diplomacy, forcing governments and secretariats alike to recognize the need for radical rethinking of the UN's roles.

Finally, Part IV sets out the options for policymakers, beginning with a schema of the kinds of approach that might be adopted to change the UN. It is addressed principally to Western governments. The choices, baldly, are to opt out of the organization entirely; to attempt structural reform from within; to continue with what has become a form of Western "façade management" (essentially by participating in the UN, the Security Council somewhat apart, in name only); and—the preferred approach—a strategy of positive discrimination. This would imply letting the worst-managed agencies wither on the vine instead of trying to reform them, and using the West's power of the purse, organizational abilities, and political influence to build up the parts of the UN most capable of good work. It looks at the scope for more selective policies in terms of the most urgent needs for cooperation, arguing that objectives should dictate institutional development, not, as in the past, vice versa. It then turns to the UN's role in collective security—a field in which, for most of its history, the UN has been forced to make the best of *ad hoc* improvisations, reacting to conflicts rather than preventing them, but where recent political trends could at last give its peacemaking, peacekeeping, and enforcement activities some real depth and importance.

Achieving a more orderly world, with rules of international behavior under which people feel safer and are encouraged to prosper, may not sound as grand as the "new world order" evoked by President Bush during the Gulf conflict. Certainly, it falls short of the Charter's vision of a global community equal in rights and united in aims. But it is an even taller order in a world of more than 180 states (with more perhaps struggling to be born, in the ethnic ferment generated by the collapse of the Soviet empire) than it was when the UN was created 125 wars before President Bush's clarion call of 1990. In any long-range assessment of multilateral organization, the possibility that the United Nations may prove to have been a transitional phase cannot be excluded. The final chapter touches on the changing attitudes to sovereignty and humanitarian intervention, to commerce and to multilateral cooperation itself, against which the UN's claims to "comparative advantage" will have to be set. Competition is healthy. It is time for the UN to be exposed to it.

In this huge field, there are certain areas that this book does not attempt to traverse systematically. Chief among these is the history of the UN's role in the containment of conflict and the postwar security system. Not surprisingly, given the importance attached to that dimension by the UN's founders—and the centrality to its place in public esteem of the UN's perceived successes and failures in keeping the peace—many books on the UN concentrate almost exclusively on what might be called Security Council affairs, UN efforts at mediation, and the history of its peacekeeping forces. Mine does not, and a word of explanation is called for. My main reason is that a textbook summary of UN peacekeeping would have added little to an analysis of the UN's potential. Despite the devices to which the more active UN secretaries-general have resorted to compensate for the nonfunctioning of the collective security system set out in Chapter VII of the Charter, the limits imposed by superpower confrontation left the UN only a marginal security role for most of its history. Many of the peacekeeping operations carried out under the UN flag have contained potentially dangerous situations; some have been indispensable; others have simply frozen conflicts. But the real collective security system of the postwar decades, insofar as it existed, was that of NATO and the Warsaw Pact in the industrialized world; and elsewhere, was left to spheres of influence, old and new, postcolonial and ideological.

The situation may now be changing, certainly to the point of making the Security Council more effective and the UN a more useful ancillary in the maintenance of peace. Chapters 11 and 12 address some of the implications of this changing scenario, which might in time lead to the development of a new multilateral security system. The resentments among smaller states of great power "fixing," palpable as early as the 1989 General Assembly, could yet force such a system to develop alongside the UN rather than within it, although superpower collaboration so evidently paid off in the Gulf that these resentments were at least temporarily stilled. Although the absolute priority attached by Mikhail Gorbachev's Soviet Union, and initially by Boris Yeltsin's Russia, to good relations with the United States could no longer be taken for granted by the mid-1990s, the prospects for multinational "policing" are still brighter than at any time since the onset of the Cold War.

The second omission is the UN's role in the development of international law, and the record of the International Court of Justice. The Court, a Charter body ranking with the Security Council and General Assembly, was for years enfeebled by the refusal of the Soviet Union and its satellites to recognize its jurisdiction, although most other states entered crippling reservations when accepting the Court's status. And even taking these difficulties into account, it still has to be said that the wheels of global justice have ground inordinately slowly. Some streamlining of its procedures has long been overdue. At the end of the 1980s, the Soviet Union declared itself prepared to submit to the Court's jurisdiction for a number of purposes. That reversal of policy, together with the interest of the newly post-Communist democracies in strengthening the writ of international law, might provide the incentive for a review. The Court might become a more important institution, charged with arbitrating disputes over governments' compliance with internationally agreed standards. At a conference in the Hague in 1989, a group of governments proposed to give it jurisdiction over environmental disputes; and the 1990s saw a revival, in response to the atrocities in former Yugoslavia, of interest in establishing a global tribunal for the judgment of war crimes. In general, however, it seems more likely that international standards will be embodied in national laws and enforced nationally. That is not least because the United Nations has, as the discussion in this book of its record on human rights indicates, developed an unenviable reputation for being vigorous in promulgating international norms but considerably less effective in enforcing them.

The reform of the international civil service is imperative if the global organizations are to function effectively—as those within the UN secretariats themselves know. That theme is present in most chapters and explicitly in sections of Chapter 6 and Chapter 10. If this important question has had a less than exhaustive airing, that is in large part because other reforms—management by objective, the development of serious systems for evaluating the organizations' performance and making them publicly accountable—would encourage better performance and would also entail a serious rethinking of staff terms and conditions of service. But it is also true that I have tried to focus less on the in-house problems of the institutions than on the purposes they might serve.

This book is less history than political critique: it attempts an anatomy of the UN's performance and potential. That has made a piecemeal, pragmatic approach essential, one that moves from analysis of the different institutional, procedural, and ideological dimensions of the UN's progressive marginalization, to an assessment of the varying capacities of the different parts of the machine to modernize and adapt, and finally to recommendations that take into account that variety, and the changing character of the multilateral agenda. In some cases, we need strategies for turning the clock back, concentrating "functional" organizations on their original roles. But we also face serious gaps in the frameworks of institutionalized international cooperation that must, inside or outside the UN, be addressed.

The purposes for which the global organizations were created—the peaceful settlement of disputes; economic, financial, and technical cooperation; the development of international law, including the safeguarding of human rights—remain on the agenda. Others—such as the preservation of the environment, humanitarian assistance to disaster victims—will require far more sustained effort in the future. The growth of networks outside the UN—and outside government—creates a margin for maneuver: We can concentrate on what works. The UN is not only not the linchpin of international order: it does not have to be. With so many channels for cooperation, we are freer than we would have been in previous decades to think about what it can contribute, and where else to turn. That is why our ultimate goal cannot be reform of the UN *per se*: even where we need intergovernmental institutions, we may not need the global institutions we have today.

AN ENTERPRISE IN QUESTION

Every salesman knows that goodwill is hard to build up and easily dissipated. The United Nations has always profited from an exceptionally intense "brand loyalty." People want it to work and are prepared whenever possible to give it the benefit of the doubt. A strong sense of relief that the UN had performed in a major crisis roughly as it was designed to do lay behind the dramatic revival in its reputation during the Gulf conflict. Relief, but also surprise, because popular (and official) disillusionment with the UN had never been deeper than it was in the preceding decade. Even governments were hard-pressed to say what the UN was "about." One incident may serve to illustrate the point.

In the late afternoon of October 25, 1985, the United Nations formally celebrated its fortieth anniversary in a solemn ceremony at its headquarters in Turtle Bay. This commemorative session was intended to be the climax of three weeks of tribute, in which sixty presidents and prime ministers, as well as over a hundred assorted royalty, military dictators, and senior politicians, had taken part and which Javier Pérez de Cuéllar, a man not normally given to hyperbole, had described as "one of the most extraordinary and important gatherings of world leaders in modern times." After speeches by the five permanent members of the Security Council, by India (representing the nonaligned movement), and New Zealand (for no discernible reason), that year's president of the General Assembly, Jaimé de Piniés of Spain, took the microphone. He was due to read a solemn declaration in which member states rededicated themselves to the UN Charter.

Instead, de Piniés produced some "purely personal" reflections. It was all he could do. There was no declaration to present. After fifteen months spent in desultory exchanges of papers and five in more or less concentrated negotiation, the drafting group charged with preparing it had broken up an hour earlier. So complete was the disarray that it had even forgotten to adopt the report in which it announced complete deadlock. An ambitious text on the purposes and principles of the Charter, which had originally been intended to involve no more than a few general statements of good intent, had to be abandoned.

Pérez de Cuéllar, whose idea this had been, was left with a public relations fiasco. In May 1984, when he had suggested to the committee preparing the fortieth anniversary that "nothing could be more valuable for the peace of the world than a firm recommitment by all Member States to their obligations under the Charter,"[3] he had added that this commitment would be better expressed in policies than in words and ceremony. He should have known better. The fortieth anniversary, he said, would be an appropriate moment for governments to ask themselves "what it is that the UN can and cannot do."[4] A working group was promptly set up to draft a text.

There may have been some hope that, as current affairs analysts never tired of saying in the mid-1980s, the developing countries had left behind the confrontations with the industrialized democracies that had plagued the UN in the 1970s. They were held to be less preoccupied with UN resolutions on new world economic or information orders than with surviving the impact of high interest rates, low commodity prices, and accumulated debt. There was some truth in this—but not at the UN. What followed was in the dreariest tradition of General Assembly politics. The first drafts of the proposed declaration were prepared under Indian chairmanship and included most of the standard UN agenda of contention, from Palestinian rights to demands for a new international economic order. The Soviet Union tried to add references to the victory over Nazism and fascism, objected as always to any reference to UN peacekeeping forces, and banged the drum for total nuclear disarmament. The European Community's draft, produced as a counterpoint "in order to help," was brief, elegant, and deadeningly anodyne.

The pattern of these negotiations also ran true to the habits of the 1970s. As usual, a nonaligned nations' text was taken as the basis for discussion and was then gradually diluted in a classic "damage limitation exercise" led by Great Britain and, later, the United States. Cuba and the Soviet Union then weighed in with amendments to radicalize the paragraphs on disarmament and the global economy. China tried for a clause demanding the withdrawal of foreign troops from sovereign territories (a reference to the Soviet occupation of Afghanistan) but did not press the point. The United States then led the battle to neutralize the statements on the world economy. The West Germans saved everybody's face on disarmament by disinterring some serviceable wording from the records of a 1978 UN conference. The British later claimed to have found a way around the Palestinian question so brilliantly ambiguous that the Syrians were insane to have scuppered it, while the Syrians muttered darkly about the perfidies to be expected from the authors of the Balfour Declaration. Time finally ran out. The Zambian chairman, Paul Lusaka, having appealed in vain to all to agree as "brothers in Christ," finally wheeled in the UN's legal adviser to stop the Soviet Union, Cuba, and Syria from pushing the document through by majority vote.

Clement Attlee overstated matters in 1946, at the UN's inaugural session. Neither for the British, nor for the 130-plus states then unborn, was the UN ever likely to become, as he said it must, "the over-riding factor in foreign policy."[5] But if one asks what it was, forty years later, that impelled governments which were quite capable of dialogue and even agreement in other contexts to persist at the UN with the agenda of known stalemate, Attlee would have had an answer. If the UN was to be "a living reality," he said in 1946, it must address and be seen to address "things that are . . . the concern of all and affect the home life of every man, woman and child." This was hyperbole too, but around a kernel of common sense. By the mid-1980s, the global organizations had largely abandoned Attlee's mundane criterion of relevance in favor of the politics of gesture. Since no negotiator in 1985 expected the least practical consequence to stem from the fortieth anniversary declaration, it was fair game for a nostalgic exercise in baiting the West.

The incident reflected, of course, a deeper malaise. Deadlock was, in fact, uncharacteristic of the UN, where governments had become adept at producing resolutions whose wording disguised the impossibility of reaching genuine agreement. In the view of Maurice Bertrand, then the senior inspector of the UN's small watchdog body, its Joint Inspection Unit, "lack of realism and mere talk" had come to play an essential role in the life of the global organizations, contributing to the UN's credibility gap with the public. A certain degree of "idealistic . . . vagueness" might, Bertrand conceded, blur the edges of confrontation, but "overdone, it ends up preventing the Organization from functioning." The UN was "very close to this type of situation."[6]

Bertrand's report, a devastating critique not only of the UN's malfunctioning but of the tasks it had assumed, had been prepared in response to Pérez de Cuéllar's call for clear thinking about what the UN could and could not do. It was ready in good time for the fortieth anniversary. Copies of it were sitting throughout these ceremonies, undistributed, in the UN's basement: it had, not surprisingly, fallen foul of the UN's top executives. Ironically, the report did much to show why the UN secretary-general's formulation of the problem was itself back-to-front. Instead of inviting reflection on what kinds of future cooperation would be needed, what actions absolutely required government decision, and where a global approach was indispensible—and *then* asking how the UN could contribute—he put the institutions first. And by 1985, while governments could still make good use of some of the organizations for specific objectives—such as combatting AIDS or negotiating a convention on torture—the point had long been reached where governments had ceased to turn to them naturally to iron out problems.

The "artificial climate of theoretical idealism," to quote Bertrand, still prompted politicians—at least when they turned up at the UN—to pretend otherwise. The fortieth anniversary was a case in point. Nobody reading the glowing speeches delivered on that occasion would detect that for most—and certainly for the most powerful—the UN was confined to the wings of the political stage. It was only the abortive effort to manufacture the statement of rededication to the Charter that exposed the lack of any accord about the "value" of the United Nations, and the degree to which, whatever uses the UN organizations might retain as safety nets and palliative, the sense of common purpose that had animated the original concept of a world order based on universality had evaporated—unless, that is, the parlous state of the UN's finances was taken to be a more accurate barometer of its standing than fortieth anniversary encomia.

Financial crises had periodically afflicted the United Nations ever since the 1960s, when the Soviet Union and France precipitated the first major political row over budgets by refusing to pay their share of the costs of the huge UN peacekeeping operation in the Congo. But the Western revolt over UN budgetary growth in the 1980s was qualitatively different. More was at stake than cash: The arguments over money were only the most conspicuous symptom of an erosion of confidence, and interest, in the global organizations. Diplomatic fictions and bureaucratic paper shuffling had pushed the UN to the fringes of collective endeavor. The multiplication of UN programs had led to a chronic loss of focus. As forums for debate, the UN organizations offered a miserable return on the investment of diplomatic and intellectual energies. Not only was ritualized confrontation endemic, but agendas persistently included proposals on which governments either were not prepared to act collectively or which, whatever they might say in UN meetings, they considered completely pointless.

Other than as a paper factory, the UN machine had become extraordinarily unproductive. Pérez de Cuéllar had acknowledged as much in his report to the General Assembly in 1983, saying that "the machine is running and the wheels are turning, but it is not moving forward." Western governments had taken to treating the UN bodies rather as they might old factories in smokestack communities. Reluctant to examine with any candor the diminishing returns on their investment, and convinced that not much could be done if they did, they found it simpler to go on providing the subsidies needed to keep the workforce employed and the plant ticking over, while looking elsewhere for growth centers in which to put new investment.

What happened in the 1980s was that it ceased to be entirely taboo to ask what good came of keeping such machinery running for its own sake. The idea that the UN would have to be reinvented if it was to justify its existence was an extreme position at the beginning of the decade. By the end, it was close to becoming received wisdom. Where the UN could be used, it was. Patience was, however, running out over the unproductive panoply of universality—the interminable conferences, mountainous paperwork, and laundry lists of activities that had only the most tenuous connection with the world outside. Governments were still reluctant to jettison the global organizations, however defective, but those with alternative clubs were conducting most of their multilateral business elsewhere. UN diplomacy had become synonymous with political and ideological rigidities—and with a massive waste of time. The hypocrisy of repeated commitments to general and complete disarmament, for example, had become embarrassing: junior officials were sent to sit through meetings on the subject. For purposes of policymaking, the UN's highest common factor was set too low to be of interest.

Political will does not exist in a vacuum. The UN, created in large measure to ensure the peaceful management of change, was lagging far behind the game. Governments could not be expected indefinitely to take seriously global machinery that appeared overwhelmingly to operate for the benefit of its international staff, armies of consultants, and conference-goers. Within UN secretariats as well as among governments, the diagnoses of what ailed the UN were increasingly severe, and were no longer confined to discussing managerial defects. Skepticism about the UN was reinforced by the contrast between the inertia described by Pérez de Cuéllar and the dynamism of competing forms of multilateral cooperation. At the governmental level alone, there were by now several hundred non-UN organizations. Some were insignificant but others, such as the European Community, were acquiring a supranational dimension far more ambitious than anything the UN was designed to offer. With the growth of organizations involving restricted numbers of countries—such as the Group of 7 summits of the leading industrialized democracies, the Organization for Economic Cooperation and Development, the Conference on Security and Cooperation in Europe, and regional organizations in Latin America and Asia—many governments found that the global bodies fitted only incidentally into their scheme of things.

That the UN should loom less large on politicians' horizons than in 1945 was not entirely sinister. Where collective security was concerned, for example, the UN Charter stipulated that nations should bring their disputes to the UN only when other local means of peaceful settlement had been exhausted. And even before the UN's membership more than trebled from the original fifty-one countries, it was obvious that not all issues were sensibly tackled on a global basis (for example, whaling). Even where the global dimension was evident, there was much to be said for regional pacts that, if successful, could serve as an example to others and spur them to action. The problem was not so much that the UN was perceived by the 1980s as a forum of last resort, but that even in this capacity, it inspired scant confidence. And the less governments benefited from the UN's "practical activities," the less Western politicians were inclined to put much effort into overhauling UN agencies and the more Third World governments used them as showcases for ritual "solidarity."

It is in this sense that the UN has reached a watershed, and that is why the changed political conditions of the 1990s will not alone guarantee the future of the massively complicated global enterprise the UN has become. To say that the UN is not assured of a future does not, of course, mean that the global institutions will not still be in place in the twenty-first century, or that today's recruits to the international civil service will not complete their careers within its walls. Governments may occasionally be impelled by singularly flagrant evidence of corruption and mismanagement to insist on a housecleaning. But the forces of institutional inertia should never be underestimated. Even where they have lost the authority implicit in the initial vision of the UN as the conscience of the world, the global organizations simply by existing provide an inexpensive palliative for uneasy consciences, alibis when governments do not want to act. It is easier to leave them be than to pick up the surgeon's knife or send for the undertaker. On being told of the death of President Calvin Coolidge, Dorothy Parker is said to have asked: "How do they know?" The demise of any institution is still harder to verify.

There are still individuals and groups, particularly those belonging to the generation for whom the creation of the UN was a singular rite of passage from totalitarianism and the horrors it generated, who are ready to argue that we must "stand by the UN" in all its manifestations and whatever its inadequacies, because without its myth-making aura there can be no rule of law. For them, the very existence of institutions with universal membership constitutes such momentous progress, such a force for good, that to insist that they should, either figuratively or literally, give value for money is to demonstrate an irresponsible lack of commitment to an ideal that self-evidently outweighs the sum of its parts. Where such people admit the existence of problems, they tend to see the solution in terms of revivalism: a recovery of fervor by governments, an exercise of will to "strengthen" the United Nations.

But that is to confuse the myth with the temple. The UN was indeed a great imaginative enterprise. If, however, we are to address the serious question of what we should be trying to achieve today in terms of international cooperation, deconstruction may be a more promising approach than revivalism. That process began in the 1980s, although the diagnoses do not yet converge. Given the wide range of UN organizations and the many perspectives—those of the diplomat, the international civil servant, the businessman or banker, the campaigner—from which the UN is observed, perhaps they never will. Nonetheless, common to all the arguments that have begun to surface is a sense that these institutions no longer satisfy contemporary needs. At the risk, therefore, of moving ahead of the necessary context and example, these arguments may be worth summarizing.

A CHANGING DEBATE

The first shift in the debate has to do with the question of "fault." Previous generations of international civil servants took refuge in the argument that the United Nations was, after all, no more than an expression of the collective will of its member states, a "mirror of humankind." Governments, in turn, accused the secretariats (with some justice) of drawing up programs that reflected neither the priorities for cooperation nor the actual capacities of the organizations. Today, this pattern is beginning to be reversed. The more intelligent diplomats and politicians are increasingly embarrassed by their failure to "use" the UN effectively for such obviously global purposes as the control of drug trafficking or protection of the environment, where concerted action is urgent and step-by-step agreements ought to be possible. Equally, a minority of UN bureaucrats is prepared to acknowledge that the secretariats have abused their agenda-setting powers, and expanded the range of their activities for reasons that have far more to do with buying the support of government X for a director-general's reelection or with interagency rivalry than with their ability to make an impact on the problem in question. This growing recognition that it is up to the heads of UN organizations to "sell" their services intelligently, and to win governments' assent to decisions needed in the common interest, is particularly important because the political procedures at the UN inhibit innovation. The huge volume of past resolutions can always be brought into play: Some government will always be able to lay its hands on a forgotten text that makes a fresh approach to any problem inadmissible.[7] Intelligent backstage management by the secretariats is indispensible.

The second area of debate concerns what should be expected of the United Nations. There are those, heavily represented in Western foreign ministries, for whom the UN exists chiefly to prevent, contain, or resolve armed conflicts. For them, the UN has an irreplaceable function as a safety net, and it is merely a bonus if its other activities help to improve the *quality* of peace. The other school of thought maintains that the UN's security role is inseparable from the task of promoting international cooperation in a wide range of fields—building that new dimension of peace that the UN's founders saw as distinguishing their creation from the more narrowly "political" League of Nations. Bringing the nations together for positive tasks constitutes, in this view, an integral part of the business of keeping them peacefully apart.

This debate, too, is changing its character, due to growing awareness that social and economic breakdown can constitute serious threats to peace. This has been particularly obvious in Africa, where entire communities have been displaced within their own countries or forced to flee over international boundaries. Refugees from famine, guns, or anarchy, they are victims of new kinds of strife whose roots lie in political cruelty, incompetence, or corruption, in extremes of poverty, in the stifling of individual creative and economic potential, and in land hunger. In 1987, Mikhail Gorbachev, in the article that formally reversed Soviet policy toward the UN (and will be discussed in some detail in Chapter 11), insisted on the need to include in the concept of "collective security" these broader economic, social, and environmental dimensions.

By 1991, the French idea of a limited humanitarian right to intervene in a state's affairs was beginning to gain public support. For all the problems that beset the first experiments in armed humanitarian intervention, in Somalia and in Bosnia, these ideas seem likely to gather momentum—inside or outside the UN.

The most fundamental debate concerns the role of the United Nations in the protection of human rights and the development of international law. This is where the proclaimed purposes of the UN touch the lives of individuals most closely; and in no area is its performance more inadequate. This debate directly addresses the basic premise on which the UN was founded—that there are inalienable individual rights that have universal validity and which governments are bound to respect. These assumptions are embodied in the UN Charter and expressly formulated in the 1948 Universal Declaration of Human Rights. The Charter is accepted by all UN member states; the Declaration is acknowledged to have acquired the force of customary law. But the premises were challenged in the Cold War by Communist governments, citing Leninist tenets about the primacy of the state. Third World politicians in turn insisted that individual rights must be subordinate to the task of nation-building and stressed collective economic rights. Finally, there is a school of political scientists, Western or Western-educated for the most part, which contends that the imposition of the "Judeo-Christian model" is incompatible with respect for cultural pluralism. Nothing has divided the UN more bitterly than this issue—and the confrontation has, as was demonstrated at the 1993 UN Conference on Human Rights in Vienna, outlasted the Cold War.

An important aspect of the problem, of course, is that the Charter itself is ambiguous. There is a contradiction between the principle, which is the foundation of international human rights law, that the "international community" has a legitimate interest in the way governments treat their subjects, and Article 2.7 of the UN Charter, which prohibits interference in the internal affairs of states. The UN's human rights machinery, intended to bridge that gap, lacks credible enforcement procedures, and the UN has lagged far behind public opinion in imposing elementary standards of decent conduct. The gap between what governments say and what they do, and the impunity with which regimes have curtailed or suppressed such basic rights as free speech and a free press, freedom of assembly, and freedom to choose a form of government, have done more than anything else to bring the UN into public disrepute. The UN has scored some successes; governments have proved sensitive to international condemnation (particularly in the rare cases where Western governments have been prepared to link trade and aid to human rights). But the record falls far short of the promises contained in the Charter. Private citizens' groups—Amnesty International, national human rights committees, the Helsinki watch groups that played such a crucial role in Eastern Europe in the 1980s, and the relatively new and highly effective Human Rights Watch—have captured the public imagination as the UN never has. Even governments are more in awe of Amnesty than they are of the slow-moving UN commissions and committees. There will be no clearer test of the UN's relevance to a world progressively more impatient of dictatorship than the steps it takes toward squaring this hapless circle.

For the UN's organizations to carry out the mandates assigned to them in 1945 was a demanding brief. It was made harder by the Cold War, the tremendous expansion in the UN's membership and consequent loss of homogeneity, and the play of East-West rivalries on colonial and postcolonial resentments. The difficulties of operating multinational bureaucracies made it no easier. Some organizations—the Bretton Woods duo, the International Labor Office, and, to a lesser extent, the World Health Organization—made a passable success of tempering their activities to the increasingly complex cross-currents of conflicting national self-interest and ideological allegiances while retaining their greatest asset, the ability to act as catalysts for ideas and aids to policymaking. But these were exceptions. Faced with the clear need to adjust both its activities and methods of operating, much of the UN machinery has instead been clogged by conceptual paralysis, administrative incompetence, and an almost total inability to establish priorities.

Reforms limited, as they have been in the past, to improving the efficiency of the UN will resolve none of these fundamental problems. Doing the same things slightly better is no substitute for rethinking the agenda. There is still little sign of that. The more fragile governments perceive the UN to be, the more nervous they are of a thorough overhaul, for fear that failure would fatally weaken it. They can, after all, make a case for passivity: the most inefficient global body may still serve, in extremis, as a vehicle for averting conflict or (in rare instances) mobilizing responses to aggression. It may manage to mitigate the effects of war by providing peacekeeping forces and humanitarian assistance. But the UN organizations created, in the words of the Charter, to "harmonize the actions of nations" and promote positive cooperation between them can fulfill their functions only insofar as they command respect. And in these spheres, for all the goodwill toward the Security Council, the UN entered the 1990s in the position George Kennan once described as the most dangerous for any institution: too many of its lovers were uncritical, and its critics were too often unloving.

Even though the UN was almost constantly in the headlines in the 1990s, the types of debate outlined above still engaged only a tiny minority, for the most part professionally involved with the UN either as diplomats or as international civil servants. Most of its work has become so remote from ordinary citizens, and enters so little into the calculations of politicians or of the agents of global change outside government, that its affairs are conducted in a near vacuum. Because too few of those who understand what is wrong believe that a more effective UN could "make a difference," the pressure for reform is slight.

There is an analogy between reform of the UN and the restructuring of national economies. Governments generally have to be convinced that there is no alternative before they embark on radical surgery—and even then the decisions are usually made long after the process should have begun and implemented less than resolutely. Tinkering with the UN will do no good. If the UN has reached a watershed, it is not in the last analysis for want of deciding what it "can and cannot do," as Pérez de Cuéllar put it, but because organizations of states, formally wedded to absolute respect for national sovereignty, are out of step. As we shall see, aspects of contemporary multilateralism inevitably blur the edges of sovereignty. Modernizing the UN will thus involve far more than streamlining—however indispensible it may be to shake out its bureaucracies.

Yet, at the same time, the circumstances for regenerating certain aspects of global cooperation ought to be propitious in the 1990s, and at least some UN organizations should be capable of catching the tide. There are several grounds for optimism. The apparent readiness of both Washington and Moscow to use the UN as one of the vehicles of diplomacy may be a passing phase. But even partial recourse to the UN provides an opportunity to rethink collective security. In a world in which the typical conflict is undeclared and/or internal, and the UN's conventional peacekeeping techniques fit only a minority of cases, such rethinking is in any case overdue.

The bloc politics that have been a dreary feature of UN debate appear to be on the way out, at least in the old East, South, West format. Constructive engagement in the UN forms part of the post-Communist world's insurance against political uncertainties; and for Russia, its neighboring republics and the Eastern Europeans alike, the International Monetary Fund, the World Bank, and the General Agreement on Tariffs and Trade regime are important assets in the hard task of modernizing their economies and integrating them with the outside world. The collapse of the "Eastern bloc" will inevitably disrupt old, ritualized allegiances and voting patterns. The myth of the "South," like nonalignment, required East-West rivalry as its foil. The "North-South" divide was of course a misnomer: it was a South-West divide, exploited by the East. Some pessimists anticipate that ideological divisions will be replaced by a *genuinely* North-South divide between "haves" and "have-nots." But the real world fits less and less readily into such neat divisions. Countries such as Mexico can no longer be counted even as reliable members of the "South" and even India, for so long a standard-bearer of Third World solidarity, is developing a robust streak of pragmatism. And in the poorest countries, the great wave of nationalism that accompanied decolonization has passed its euphoric phase; the demythification of sovereignty has begun and, with that, there may gradually be less inclination to use the global organizations as an anti-Western grandstand. Where states have a genuine stake in the outcome of a negotiation, the Uruguay Round of the General Agreement onTariffs and Trade (GATT) talks revealed a new determination to put practical self-interest before theatricals. There is no "Third World interest." The breakup of the Soviet empire produced a resurgence of nationalism from the Baltic to Mongolia and—accompanied by vicious fighting—south to the Illyrian Coast; but for states in the throes of headlong change, functioning global institutions are a source of stability and external support.

Finally, in what constitutes as profound a political mutation as the collapse of communism, countries of all political hues are questioning the efficacy of state *dirigisme* and central planning. And this coincides with the growing importance of problems such as environmental management, which ought to cut across conventional political and ideological allegiances, although Third World "solidarity" was going strong in the United Nations long after developing countries had abandoned the pretense in non-global diplomacy, and the UN will be its last bastion. Taken together, these trends could eventually begin to depoliticize the UN's "technical cooperation" programs—though it will take more than mere depoliticization to make them worthwhile.

It would be too much to say that the prospects for the United Nations are thereby transformed. The problems discussed in this book are deeply ingrained. Some political obstacles will be removed by a new and constructive attitude in the Kremlin, assuming that it is sustained, but the UN's institutional defects will not thereby be eradicated. A burst of energy in the Security Council no more constitutes the "rebirth of the UN" than the UN's failure to prevent dozens of wars between 1945 and 1990 justified its demolition. The fact is that the pacesetters of multilateral cooperation in the 1990s, the Bretton Woods institutions apart, are outside the UN. The competition has flourished at least partly because most UN organizations provide too little scope for the kinds of interaction that would convert political agreement into workable programs. The rigidity of much of this universal machinery and the low caliber of its output cast further doubt on its ability to meet the needs of the twenty-first century. The picture varies of course: the "regulatory" agencies such as the Universal Postal Union operate systems that can work only on a global basis and would, to borrow the cliché so often used of the UN in New York, have to be invented if they did not exist. The rest—and in particular those parts of the UN that were created to promote exchanges of ideas and to encourage cooperation for social and humanitarian ends—cannot in the long term survive unless both governments and their publics take them seriously. That is even truer of the machinery for conflict resolution.

Utopia Lost is a deliberately Popperite title,[8] indicating a distaste for comprehensive blueprints, which are, in any case, part of the UN disease. With their lack of realism as to goals, and imprecision about ways to reach them, the UN's international development decades and millennialist strategies promising health, food, or jobs for all by the year 2000 are in part to blame for the indifference with which their activities are viewed. Improvement is likely to come about on a piecemeal basis. The only proposals that have much chance of placement on a crowded international agenda are those that meet the politician's question: "How do I get from here to there?" This does not mean that getting international machinery to work better, inside or outside the UN, is an easy task. Piecemeal does not mean cosmetic. It requires selectivity; and that, in the context of the UN, has nothing but radical implications.

In his classic reflection on Utopianism, Karl Popper commented that "it is easier to reach a reasonable agreement about existing evils and the means of combating them than it is about an ideal good and the means of its realization."[9] The Soviet Union and the United Nations had one thing in common. Each was constructed "with the desire to build a world which is not only a little better and more rational than ours, but which is free from all its ugliness: not a crazy quilt, an old garment badly patched, but an entirely new coat, a really beautiful new world."[10] The very all-embracing nature of Utopian designs makes them singularly hard to adapt; the notion of adjustment is contrary to the spirit of the original enterprise. In rethinking the grand design of 1945, however, the United Nations should fare better than communism, for the founders of the UN had what was for Popper the saving grace of Utopianism: "reason . . . responsibility, and . . . a humanitarian urge to help."

I

THE LAYOUT OF THE LABYRINTH

1. Utopia Invented

Wartime Beginnings

The United Nations was intended by its founders to be far more than "a method for carrying on relations between states,"[1] the somewhat dry encapsulation of the functions of its interwar predecessor, the League of Nations, offered by Sir Alfred Zimmern. The replacement of Covenant by Charter, of "high contracting parties" by "we, the peoples," betrays something of the expectations vested in the new organization. To a far greater extent than the League, it sought not only to ensure stability—if necessary by requiring states, under Article 43, to put armed forces at the disposal of the Security Council—but to systematize the promotion of change. The Charter was consciously innovative, and nowhere more so than its explicit concern with the rights of individual citizens to humane and equal treatment under the law.

A more complex, and more consciously ambitious undertaking than the League, the UN was intended not just to be an "an addition to the machinery for managing human affairs,"[2] but an organization that added value to the sum of its membership. Although the Treaty of Versailles had explicitly made the connection between peace and "social justice," the League remained primarily "a point of convergence between Power and Law,"[3] which sought to deal only with a small part of the field of international relations. It co-opted some preexisting international organizations and acted as umbrella for much useful "technical work," as it was called, but the new concept of "functional cooperation" was far more all-embracing.

By the time governments assembled in San Francisco in 1945 for the final negotiations on the UN Charter, the British and American drafters believed, with some justification, that they had evolved a comprehensive blueprint. In the UN Security Council they had created a highly structured containing device both for crisis management and—a breathtaking ambition—for operating collective security machinery to ensure that force would be used only in the general interest. Here the five "veto powers," President Franklin Delano Roosevelt's "global policemen," were given special status. The smaller powers were compensated by equal participation in building "a working peace" through economic and social cooperation. The United Nations was not only to be proof against past failures to keep the peace, but harbinger of the world of Roosevelt's Four Freedoms.[4]

The creation of a "successor" organization to the League had not, however, been a foregone conclusion. In the early years of the war, there was considerably more Anglo-American agreement on international systems for cooperation in the economic and social fields than on the desirability of a global security organization.

Even before the U.S. entry into the war, what stands out in the discussions and agreements between President Roosevelt and Winston Churchill is their joint determination to secure the expansion of the postwar economy on liberal internationalist principles. Despite Churchill's reluctance to tamper with imperial preference, the idea of nondiscriminatory, open trading practices was even built into the Lend-Lease Agreement. The fifth principle of the Atlantic Charter of August 1941,[5] calling for "the fullest collaboration between all nations in the economic field, with the object of securing for all improved labor standards, economic advancement and social security," established such cooperation as a major war aim. And within weeks of the bombing of Pearl Harbor, the U.S. Treasury Department was pressing for a conference of the "United Nations" to establish an international monetary stabilization fund, an idea that it rapidly followed up with a plan for an international bank to finance postwar reconstruction.

These moves considerably predated the commitment to a new global organization. Roosevelt's initial predilection was different, favoring the creation of a number of separate international organizations scattered around the globe, each dedicated to a particular task and with no reference to any central body. Early planning for postwar cooperation concentrated on deciding what activities needed to be collectively organized; the institutional forms were to be shaped according to functions. The arguments as to whether international economic and social cooperation should be institutionally integrated or polycentric continued right through the war and were never perfectly resolved. And when it came to international security, Roosevelt needed a considerable degree of convincing that a world organization was desirable.

In summer 1941, Roosevelt had insisted that Churchill delete a reference to "effective international organization" from his draft of the Atlantic Charter. Eventually, Roosevelt reluctantly agreed to include in the final text a phrase envisaging a "wider and permanent system of general security" but only on the understanding that this might be contemplated in some indeterminate future, *after* the Allies had disarmed the Axis and set up their own global policing system. Churchill himself, who had his own reasons for skepticism, initially preferred a system of regional organizations for security to a global forum. It was this, ironically, that edged Roosevelt toward a world organization: his secretary of state, Cordell Hull, suspected that the probable consequence of the Churchillian model would be to draw the U.S. once again into the old European "entanglements."

One consequence of these initial hesitations was that, by the time planning for a global security organization was seriously under way in 1943, specialized agencies were already in an advanced state of formation. The United Nations security system that had finally emerged was a curious cross between Roosevelt's "Four Policemen" and a global organization.[6] And the total design for postwar cooperation was an amalgam of his concept of independent "functional" organizations with his ultimate conviction that a "United Nations organization" was needed to solder Allied unity.

COLLECTIVE SECURITY

Not until the Moscow conference of October 1943 did the Allies formally assert "the necessity of establishing at the earliest practicable date a general international organization . . . for the maintenance of international peace and security." And it took a further Allied meeting, the December 1943 Tehran conference, before Roosevelt took the idea sufficiently seriously to ask Hull for a draft Charter. But various proposals dealing with both the security and the economic dimensions of such an organization had been crossing the Atlantic in both directions for some time. Hull had already set up an Informal Political Agenda Group of advisers after the Moscow meeting, including persons outside government. This group drew up an outline for Roosevelt's approval by February 1944. That formed the basis for the blueprint presented by the Americans to the Dumbarton Oaks conferences, the critical inter-Allied negotiations on the United Nations Charter, which took place between the United States, Great Britain, the Soviet Union, and then, separately, between the first two and China in the summer of that year.

Three times as long as the Covenant of the League and much more ambitious in its range, the UN Charter may have seemed a more expansive and optimistic document. It was in fact a hybrid between the conventional and the novel, the precautionary and the expansive. The provisions of what must have appeared its most resolutely utopian dimension—a system of global security—were in fact ultraconservative. Obsessed with the failures of the League, the drafters were set on creating a disciplinary system based on Allied military power.

The interwar experience of serious military aggression—in Manchuria, Ethiopia, the Rhineland—had left the Charter's architects with few illusions about the readiness of governments to have their feet held to the fire in a crisis. Political will had proved a nonexistent asset in keeping the peace. The apparent clarity of the guarantees of collective action contained in the "enforcement" articles of the covenant—X and XVI—had early been undermined by a series of resolutions in which states set out their reservations about the automaticity of military cooperation, and by the failure to conclude a draft treaty in the 1920s, sought by France to fill what it rightly saw to be gaps in the drafting. The League procedures had been straightforward, but when it came to implementation, too much was felt to have been left to political discretion. The Charter's architects had accordingly put enormous effort into devising a system that would prevent governments from vanishing like the Cheshire Cat just when joint action became vital. It rested on the precise delineation of explicit legal obligations, a body capable of enforcing their observance, and carefully developed procedures for determining what constituted a threat to the peace.

Above all, where "effective measures for the prevention and removal of threats to the peace" were concerned, the "principle of sovereign equality" proclaimed in Article 2 of the Charter was firmly subordinated to the disciplines of military power. In deliberate contrast with the League, the new security system created exceptions to the exercise of "sovereign equality" in the hope of securing Great Power commitment to joint action. The coping-stone of this structure was the Security Council, whose five permanent members had the right to veto decisions, and whose six rotating members were to be elected under Article 23 of the Charter, on the basis of their ability to contribute to collective security. Once the Security Council decided on enforcement action, all of the UN members were obligated to provide forces and facilities on request. The American insistence on China's inclusion in the "Big Five" was something of an aberration, but in every other respect the whole emphasis of the Allied formula was to guarantee the UN's effectiveness by clearly correlating responsibility and power.

When, in an early instance of its enduring penchant for optimistic fictions, the UN information department described the Security Council's powers as "those of a supreme war-making organization," it was no doubt overstating the case.[7] Nevertheless, under Chapter VII of the Charter, the Security Council was empowered to declare war on war, if necessary by using force "to maintain or restore international peace and security," and to muster the necessary troops. The existence of these powers was intended to have a strong deterrent effect and, by giving it the means to mobilize an international military or policing contingent, to give states the strongest possible incentive not to test the Security Council's authority. Practical arrangements were to be made by a Military Staff Committee (MSC) of the five permanent members.

One of the most persistent of the myths trotted out to explain the UN's failures "to maintain international peace and security" is that the Security Council reflected starry-eyed Rooseveltian illusions about Great Power unity and was therefore crippled at birth. Instances of starry-eyed American thinking in this period can, of course, be found: in November 1945, for example, the then U.S. secretary of state, James Byrnes, suggested that the inter-American regional organization was a model of cooperation comparable with the "effort of the Soviet Union to draw into closer and more friendly relations with her central and eastern neighbors."[8] Roosevelt may have underestimated the *degree* of Soviet aggressiveness. But his essential judgment was that for straightforwardly geopolitical reasons the Soviet Union had to have a key role. The arguments in 1944 and 1945 about the permanent members' rights of veto were so intense and protracted precisely because the veto was expected to be used.

Implicit in the veto provision was the recognition that although no international organization could prevent, or survive, war between the superpowers, the superpowers could use such an organization to prevent or contain conflicts among other states—while at the same time conceding that their own conduct would be subject to international scrutiny. The principal flaw in these arrangements was that the Security Council was designed less for mediation than for policing. Where the peaceful settlement of disputes was concerned, it could only recommend, not enforce. The UN's much-emphasized "teeth" were designed to compel states by using sanctions or armed force to adopt the path of peaceful settlement. It was ill equipped to influence the forms that such settlements might assume, or to intervene in the early stages of a dispute.

The stipulation in Article V of the Covenant of the League that unless expressly stated otherwise, council decisions must be unanimous may not in practice have been a vital factor in the League's indecisiveness at critical moments—the absence of the United States and the reluctance of Great Britain and France to be drawn into military commitments were certainly more pertinent—but it was firmly believed that the new organization must not be hobbled by objections from the parties to a dispute. The veto was reckoned, correctly, to be an advance on the League's consensus rules—which had been ruthlessly exploited by Japan in the Manchuria case. The Security Council operated under rules that were inherently more flexible. The Charter provided a mechanism for great power cooperation while, at the other end of the scale, preventing the majority from committing the UN to action that, without the economic and military muscle of the major powers, it would be incapable of undertaking. That any effective enforcement depended on five-power agreement was a matter of fact rather than a statement of principle. Had Article 23—which required the remaining members of the Security Council to be chosen "in the first instance" with regard to their capacity to contribute to collective security—not been systematically ignored, the veto might have been more reticently used and less often required.

Napoleon is said to have remarked that good constitutions should be short and vague. In one sense, the drafters of Chapter VII of the Charter proved him right. The very detail with which enforcement mechanisms were set out was to provide, once any element failed to function, an excellent alibi for inaction. This had happened by 1948. The Military Staff Committee set up under Article 47 was forced to report to the Security Council that it had reached insurmountable deadlock on the size, positioning, and provisioning of the forces it had been intended to control—an admission of rare frankness in UN annals that did not however prevent the committee from meeting regularly over the next four decades, only to decide the agenda for its next session and adjourn.

The drafting of Chapter VII had given such satisfaction to the legal experts who had labored to make it leak-proof that the importance of that "failure" has been exaggerated ever since. There is no compelling evidence that the impotence of the Security Council should be traced to this chink in its armor, or that the drafters were mistaken. From the Korean War, which broke out in 1950 (when Stalin's great blunder in boycotting the Security Council over the exclusion of the People's Republic of China admittedly simplified matters), to the present, the absence of a formal great-power command has not prevented collective military action whenever political agreement could be mustered for it. It could also be argued that the UN's military operation in the Congo in the early 1960s would not only have been hopelessly politicized if the MSC had controlled it, but would never have got off the ground. Paradoxically, the more dispersed *ad hoc* arrangements for peacekeeping adopted, under the secretary-general's authority, because of the MSC's inoperativeness made action easier—enabling the Soviet Union to dissociate itself from operations that it would certainly have blocked under the joint command system. But the absence of a joint command removed a potentially important standing council for superpower consultation; and while its effective demise did not make UN military enforcement impossible, the reality of superpower confrontation that it reflected made a systematic approach to collective security impossible.

At the same time, the Charter's security provisions, more realistic than those of the League, did establish a number of useful principles, not least by treating peace as a state of affairs rather than as an ideal, and by recognizing that states are unlikely to disarm unless they feel safe to do so. The limits to the founders' optimism were, moreover, candidly acknowledged. The Charter's Chapter VII hedged the collective security bet quite heavily. The important insurance was contained in Article 51, which, by acknowledging "the inherent right of individual or collective self-defense," left the door open to traditional responses to aggression where the UN failed.

The real wishful thinking came later, as attention shifted to disarmament. This was contrary to the original plan. One of the salient features of the Charter was that—once again with the interwar years in mind—it stressed security rather than disarmament. The hope was that, once it was established that, in the words of the Preamble, "armed force shall not be used, save in the common interest," national forces would be reduced because they had come to represent a diminishing return on investment. It was in this spirit that the General Assembly was expected to discuss the "principles" of disarmament: and these principles were assumed to embrace the UN's need to be able to call on adequate forces. Deliberately reversing the priorities of the League, the Charter linked the prospects for disarmament firmly to collective regulation of disputes rather than to international negotiations on force reduction, relying on sanctions against illegal action rather than abolition of the military capacity to misbehave.

This was not the only important lesson to have been drawn from the failure of the League to prevent war. The League had suffered from its association with the Treaty of Versailles: Germany, in particular, saw it as an alliance of victors against vanquished. A critical feature of the Dumbarton Oaks negotiations was the determination of the United States and Great Britain not only to separate the Charter from the postwar peace treaties, but to ensure that the new organization was in place before these were drawn up. This prescient decision also suggests that nobody, not even Roosevelt, was wholly confident that the unity of the United Nations—which owed its name to the "United Nations" alliance against the Axis—would much survive the end of hostilities.[9] Pessimism about Soviet intentions varied in intensity—Churchill was later to write that he had for much of the war felt "bound to proclaim my confidence in Soviet good faith in the hope of procuring it"[10]—but there was enough of it around to generate an Anglo-American sense of urgency about creating the UN.

As Ruth B. Russell notes in her authoritative reconstruction of the drafting of the Charter, the British and Americans at first hoped that a commitment to postwar cooperation would contain Stalin's territorial ambitions and then, later, as the Red Army mopped up central Europe like a sponge, that the existence of an international organization might help to mitigate the consequences. At the least, they hoped that it "would facilitate collective rather than unilateral decisions, by providing the procedures and machinery for international action. It would also be valuable, in case of future aggression, in keeping the record straight. If states were not obligated to settle their disputes peaceably and to collaborate in maintaining international security, Soviet or any other aggression would not be illegal or politically 'immoral.'"[11]

The pressing need felt by the American and British negotiators to get the show on the road is demonstrated by the trouble they took to settle the shape of the new organization with the Soviet Union at Dumbarton Oaks, to work out in some detail with Moscow the structure of the Security Council and its relationship with the General Assembly, and to devote part of the crowded and contentious agenda at Yalta to patching up disagreements over the use of the veto.

By the time the San Francisco conference opened on April 25, 1945, their persistence had paid off. The momentum for a United Nations was too great to be arrested, even by the severe stresses in East-West relations by then evident. The Soviet Union, which had surrounded Berlin on the day the conference opened, hardly presented itself as an enthusiastic convert to the multilateral approach. It was only as a special gesture, in response to Roosevelt's sudden death, that Stalin consented to upgrade Soviet representation at the conference to foreign minister level. But Moscow was not, when absolutely pressed, prepared to sabotage the enterprise, although Stalin's attitude to the legal and diplomatic niceties that members of the UN were expected to observe was well illustrated when, two weeks into the meeting, members of the London-based Polish government-in-exile were arrested in Moscow. The absence from San Francisco of Poland, one of the "United Nations," symbolized the unsavory state of affairs in Soviet-occupied Europe and helped to explain why such doubts as there were about the viability of the United Nations centered on the difficulty of shackling the demon of aggression, whose features were so vividly present. The relatively unfamiliar task of giving coherent expression to the business of making the United Nations a positive "center for harmonizing the actions of nations"[12] appeared comparatively uncomplicated and uncontroversial.

"A Layer of Peaceful Life"

The Allied drafters of the Charter anchored the system for collective security clearly and firmly to political reality. They took similar precautions at Bretton Woods in 1944, when they created financial organizations to ensure monetary stability, to provide some of the capital needs for the reconstruction of Europe, and to regulate in broad terms the operation of open trading and financial markets. In this sphere, too, the interwar experience decisively influenced negotiations. All present were keenly aware that by the time the League had convened a conference to fight protectionism in 1927, the patterns of economic nationalism had been set, and that it had been on a national, piecemeal, and unsatisfactory basis that countries had emerged—partly thanks to the spur of rearmament—from the Great Depression of the 1930s. In the interest of firm international leadership, therefore, votes in the International Monetary Fund and the International Bank for Reconstruction and Development were calculated to correspond to financial weight. But a persistent thread running through the many blueprints elaborated, mostly in Washington and London, between 1940 and 1945 was the need to distinguish between the methods required to manage the politically controversial business of collective security, and those that would best promote the activities that, because they yielded positive benefits, were expected to unite governments (and technocrats) of all political persuasions.

In the Charter's Chapter IX, which dealt with economic and social cooperation, the Allied drafters thus produced the very model of grand design unencumbered by precision as to means: Napoleon would have found little fault with these pages. Here, with a view to compensating the smaller powers in the realm of hope for their unequal standing in the critical financial and security fields, they set out goals that were utopian, and consciously so. Here, the Charter reached beyond the notion of a compact between states to concern itself, quite explicitly, with individual rights. The League had provided for the protection of certain minorities, provisions that had been widely understood at the time as a means of preserving the stability and territorial integrity of the multi-ethnic states that came into existence with the dissolution of the Ottoman and Austro-Hungarian empires. Other than that, its explicit concerns for human rights work were confined to the human rights clauses in the mandates system, the 1926 Slavery Convention and—through the International Labor Organization (ILO)—workers' rights. Otherwise the Covenant placed human rights "solely within the domestic jurisdiction" of states. Under Article 56 of the Charter, UN members pledged themselves "to take joint and separate action in cooperation with the Organization" to promote "universal respect for, and observance of, [individual] human rights and fundamental freedoms for all."

In this chapter, too, were set out generous assumptions about cooperation in "nonpolitical" fields, in which a melioristic optimism about common purposes overrode drafting caution. These were the expression, at the end of an ideological war, of the Western part of the Alliance's determination to "win the peace." (For the next four decades, until it began to rethink its foreign policy under Mikhail Gorbachev, the Soviet

Union was to treat this entire aspect of the United Nations with contempt, regarding it as useful only as a weapon with which to inflame anti-Western sentiment.)

The inconsistencies in the *organizational* provisions for achieving these social goals were to do the UN lasting damage. Basic disagreements—between those who sought a centralized system for cooperation and those who favored clusters of autonomous organizations—were never clearly resolved. The care that had been taken to ensure workable decision-taking in the financial and security areas was not felt to be essential to economic and social cooperation. The first article of Chapter IX firmly stated that this was to be "based on respect for the principle of equal rights and self-determination of peoples." And the open-endedness of the arrangements reflected the drafters' impression that here, instead of guarding against the repetition of failure, their task was to build on earlier success.

For the League had had its successes. First and foremost a political covenant that had taken under its wing preexisting international organizations such as the Universal Postal Union, it had, somewhat as an afterthought, developed an ancillary and limited economic and social brief in fields such as hygiene, leprosy, workers' rights, the suppression of slavery, and drug trafficking. These "functional" organizations and subdivisions had largely survived the League's eclipse. The Charter's drafters therefore sought both to build into the UN a melioristic philosophy and, by creating independent specialized agencies charged with particular sectors, to ensure that cooperation in these "functional" domains was insulated from political pressures. Economic and social advancement was thus clearly established as a major aim of the United Nations—a political commitment, part and parcel of its innovatory concern with individual human rights (which, interestingly, created no problems for Stalin)—and carefully compartmentalized.

Structurally, all these organizations were superficially similar: Each had a permanent international secretariat governed by a board elected from the membership and, ultimately, by a universal assembly. To link them as a UN "family," an Economic and Social Council (ECOSOC) was set up. A "Charter" body, legally on a par with the Security Council, ECOSOC was to review the agencies' activities, convene international conferences where it saw fit, and make its own studies and reports to the General Assembly on economic and social issues.

This curious interweaving of a central council and a network of purpose-built agencies, wholly autonomous but "brought into relationship with the United Nations"[13] through mutual agreements that each was to work out with ECOSOC, was intended to resolve the wartime arguments over the integrated versus the sectoral approach to economic cooperation. On one side had been those, Cordell Hull among them, who argued that because health, education, food production, and trading networks were interrelated with macroeconomic issues, sectoral compartmentalization could not in practice work. Advocating a more centralized and integrated approach, they had cited the findings of a committee that the League had set up in 1939—on the edge of its extinction as a political organism—to look into more effective forms of economic cooperation. Headed by Stanley Bruce, the Australian representative to the League, it had come down on the side of centralization and coordination, proposing a central committee for economic and social questions that would include ministers of commerce, transport, and so forth, among its members.

On the other was a widely held conviction, strongly supported by Roosevelt, that the International Labor Office had proved its usefulness when the League had foundered and that too close an association with a central organization would leave the world without lifeboats in the event of shipwreck. This school argued that the League had been only too centralized prior to the Bruce Report: Its social units were centrally controlled by the League's political governing bodies, which even determined the budget of the much larger ILO. Polycentric, autonomous agencies would be better insulated from political tensions. Cordell Hull began preparations for a general international economic conference in January 1943, which he hoped would ensure integrated treatment of these issues. His efforts were promptly undercut by Roosevelt, who, without even consulting Hull, decided to call another on long-term food problems. This took place at Hot Springs, Virginia, in May and June 1943, and led to the establishment of the Food and Agriculture Organization, the first of the post-League generation of specialized agencies.

The basic doctrines of functional cooperation were worked out by David Mitrany, a Romanian-born British academic, in a paper he published in 1943.[14] Part of a series of studies organized by the Royal Institute of International Affairs to stimulate official Anglo-American thinking on the postwar order, it had considerable influence on both sides of the Atlantic. Mitrany's theme was simple. The world's political culture, based on the nation-state, was centrifugal, a fact that no purely political organization, however perfectly designed, could alter. The international division of labor, on the other hand, bound people and countries together socially and economically. The only way to reconcile the political with the "material" cultures was through purpose-built organizations that would attend "to common needs which are evident, while presuming as little as possible upon a global unity which is still only latent."

The League, Mitrany argued, had died of inanition: The negative function of keeping states apart was an inadequate cement for common interest. What was now needed was "not a promise to act in a crisis, but . . . action that will avoid the crisis." Every cooperative activity would be "a layer of peaceful life." The result would be "a working peace" that, by bringing people actively together, would gradually erode the meaning of frontiers by developing common activities and interests.

For Mitrany, the form organizations took would be dictated by the nature of their particular activity. Some, like the Food and Agriculture Organization then under discussion, would be advisory bodies, helping to coordinate national policies. Others would be executive agencies with autonomous tasks and powers (and able, eventually, to generate enough revenue from the common services they provided to become self-supporting). Some would be universal—but not all, because not all countries would automatically be drawn to a particular area of activity: Switzerland, for example, would have no immediate interest in international shipping regulation.

Interestingly, Mitrany was no advocate of the exercise of sovereign equality when it came to running these organizations. Indeed, he insisted that it was "not in the nature of the method that representation on the controlling bodies should be democratic in a political sense, full and equal for all." It might be ideal, but it would not work. A nation, he believed, should exercise control in proportion to its ability to contribute to an organization's activities; only *benefits* would be common. Small states might not direct the agencies' policies, but would gain access to services they could not hope to mount or to maintain on their own. A major attraction of organization-by-objective for Mitrany was that it created specific and carefully defined spheres in which states would be ready to accept the leadership of others where "it rested on evident practical claims and was coupled with practical benefits." "Specific functional arrangements, which would not steal the crown of sovereignty while they would promise something for the purse of necessity," might well succeed in taming "that most disruptive and intractable of international principles, the principle of state equality." Conceding that "the idea of an equal voice and the demand for it will die hard, in spite of its hollowness in all past experience," he argued that power was a fact of life, but that issue-linked international cooperation would harness power to common ends, and under some degree of common control. Success in these areas would produce "genuine equality, based upon a sharing of positive rights and duties."

Mitrany was equally insistent on the independence of the new agencies. Their success, he argued, did not even require the existence of an "over-all political authority"; and no central organization could in practice develop the expertise to issue them with directives. Coordination would arise naturally where it was needed. Ideally, the agencies should be widely dispersed geographically, so that "people in many parts of the world would have before their eyes a piece of international government in action."

Mitrany's ideas, in their deliberate departure from the centralized, if in practice loosely coordinated, structure of the League, tracked closely with Roosevelt's. But his vision of polycentric clusters of functional cooperation had a further dimension: these networks would, he believed, shame the politicians into cooperating. As meteorologists, doctors, labor leaders, or agriculturalists increasingly collaborated in evidently indispensible tasks, the habits of international cooperation would gradually spill over into the political arena, crowding out the dangerous antagonisms and cross-purposes of competing sovereignties.

As to the proper role of the state, the views of the functionalist school, of which Mitrany was the most influential wartime advocate, were somewhat ambiguous. In one sense, the whole concept of sectoral cooperation radiated faith in state planning—a faith reinforced by the perceived success of Great Britain's social and economic mobilization for war, which both helped to inspire and had already begun to create the organizational basis for the British postwar welfare state. This vein of social meliorism was deepened by the admiration Mitrany and his colLeagues felt for some wartime Allied activities. Preeminent among these was the Middle East Supply Centre. Originally no more than a logistical backup service, it had, for purely military reasons, set out to make North Africa self-sufficient in food and eventually expanded into a network of regional cooperation that extended as far as Persia and dealt not only with agricultural policy but with road transport, locust control, the distribution and rationing of goods, and the development of reliable statistics. Other wartime organizations had been created to control supplies of raw materials and coordinate merchant shipping; and in 1943, the United Nations Relief and Rehabilitation Administration was formed to cope with the chaos left by the retreating Axis armies.

But while Mitrany envisaged the development of intergovernmental organizations that would jointly construct and manage roads, railways, and (remarkably) research laboratories, and regulate vital supplies including those of key commodities, even he foresaw limits to governments' readiness to undertake this kind of joint management. It would be vital, he warned, to distinguish clearly between agencies restricted by the nature of their area of competence to offering governments advice, and those to which governments would be prepared to relinquish executive authority. It would also be important to "avoid the over-zealous tendency to change advisory bodies into executive ones or extend their field of operation beyond their assigned and natural scope." Half a century later, that warning has a prophetic ring.

Part of the attraction of functionalism was, however, that ultimately it was not *dirigiste*, or state-centered. In order to lure states into increasingly complex webs of common interest, the agencies for functional cooperation would need to be intergovernmental. Superficially, their division of functions might appear to correspond to the ministries of national governments. But they were intended to bring together what the UN Charter was to term "we, the peoples." Eminent specialists, on their staffs and among national delegations, would inch states toward what Mitrany called "the social century," in a process that would benevolently modify the meaning of the word *Realpolitik*. As academic doctrine functionalism looked, if not to the withering away of the state, at least to the erosion of nationalism and national sovereignty. Since this was to be achieved by reinforcing the stake of nonpolitical actors in international cooperation, it was bound in the end to challenge the monopolies of state power (provided that the state did not move first to absorb these "nonpolitical" activities within its spreading ambit). It was in this sense that the new organizations, given "a wide freedom of continuous adaptation in the light of experience," would create "a growing measure of social equality."

These ideas have been summarized because they exercised a profound influence on the shaping of the United Nations. They suffered, inevitably, in translation into politicians' language. Key caveats—above all, that juridical equality should not be taken to mean voting equality if these organizations were to be coherently run—were set aside.

The United Nations that emerged in 1945, however, was an uneasy hybrid of these and other ideas, simultaneously conceived as a unified "system" and organized polycentrically. This was partly because, from 1943 onward, individual organizations—for agriculture, disaster relief, and monetary and trade management—were being put in place while the UN Charter was still in gestation. It also reflected continuing indecision. The U.S. State Department's first "Draft Constitution" for a global organization, in June 1943, gave the agencies maximum autonomy. Yet only three months later, another State Department "Charter of the United Nations" subordinated them totally to General Assembly control. The most detailed set of proposals, independently produced that autumn by an Anglo-American group of economic experts, was the one serious attempt to reconcile the need for overall cohesion in economic and social policies with the sectoral division of labor.

This group took it as read that there would be a world political organization. What they felt it needed was an "economic wing" to keep the international economy under review, to alert governments to dangerous trends, and to persuade them to pursue consistent and mutually reinforcing national economic policies. This body, they believed, should also coordinate the activities of the international agencies with sectoral responsibilities. They therefore proposed the creation of an international advisory economic staff.

Once the Moscow conference of October 1943 had settled in principle for an international security organization, these ideas were further developed by a State Department economic committee. It came up with a proposal for an Economic Council, parallel to the global political body, technically competent and established at a very high political level—high enough to handle problems beyond the scope of individual technical agencies and to deal effectively with political leaders. It would coordinate broad policy and rule on conflicts of jurisdiction between the global sectoral agencies, whose policies, senior appointments, and budgets it would have authority to review, and whose activities it could veto if they strayed outside their mandates. With governments, it could only hope to use persuasion, but its composition would give it weight. It would have fifteen members, nominated from among groups of countries: two each from the two countries of "principal economic importance"; one each from the next two; four from the next eight countries in line; and only five from the third group of all other countries. They would vote as independent experts, and decisions would be taken by simple majority.

In what is a sketch, not a history, of the thinking that went into the preparation of the Charter, this particular blueprint stands out. Not only was it the high-water mark of the integrated approach to economic and social cooperation; it was also the only wartime plan that addressed the question that was to dominate the debates over the reform of the UN in succeeding decades: how to relate the United Nations to the sectoral agencies. The Economic Council survived, but in name only.

Hull's Informal Political Agenda Group retained the idea of an economic council but subordinated it to the General Assembly of the United Nations, thus markedly diminishing its prestige, and gave it no authority over the specialized agencies. For fear of linking the fate of these agencies too closely to that of the council they had thus emasculated, they changed their original draft, which had integrated the agencies with the world political organization, and substituted an arm's length relationship. From there it was only a modest step to the formula agreed at Dumbarton Oaks, under which the Economic and Social Council's members were to be elected by the General Assembly without weighting in favor of the economically powerful. The council was to have consultative and advisory powers only.

A State Department resumé on the choices involved in creating a United Nations organization, prepared for Hull in August 1943, had pointed out that a decision had to be reached as to "whether the agencies thus separately created will operate as independent members or whether they will become component parts of a comprehensive international organization." The draft presented to the San Francisco conference tried, in effect, to accommodate both approaches. Failure to be clear on this point has plagued the United Nations ever since.

Structurally, United Nations economic and social cooperation was organized along functionalist lines for what started out as a carefully separated and fairly neatly delineated set of tasks. The founders took bodies like the Universal Postal Union, which had existed prior to the League, as well as some of those created by the League, and freed them, along with the ILO, of central control. Alongside these they set three major new specialized agencies with broad social mandates in education, health, and agriculture, which were also fully autonomous.[15] And they adopted as "United Nations" organizations the International Monetary Fund and the International Bank for Reconstruction and Development, the financial institutions set up under the 1944 Bretton Woods agreements. All of these were invited under the UN Charter to negotiate the terms of their relationship with the "political" UN, rather as sovereign states might consent to join a confederation.

Conceptually, however, the Charter endowed the infant United Nations with the fiction that these links constituted a system, by devising a nonbinding formula under which the agencies would be coordinated from the center by the UN General Assembly and ECOSOC. This fiction was justified on the perfectly sensible ground that some central body must set broad priorities for international cooperation and provide a policy forum capable of cutting across different sectoral interests. Yet means were not matched to ends. Both the General Assembly and ECOSOC (whose representative roles were so loosely defined that each could, and did, make recommendations to each other in a circular ritual) were intended to fulfill these functions. They were expected to coordinate the agencies' activities, although the agencies were not accountable to them. They were given power to initiate special programs, conferences, and reports on particular issues that they felt the agencies were not addressing, but they had no powers to make the agencies pay any attention to what was proposed. In addition to its special responsibility for monitoring human rights, ECOSOC was empowered to draft conventions and to establish new specialized agencies. The "center" was thus positively encouraged to expand into the realm of functional cooperation—a temptation to which it was to succumb the more readily because it was not in fact a center.

The Charter's ambivalence in the economic and social spheres was important because it was in its meliorist vein that the United Nations most clearly marked out new territory. A major and enduring element in its appeal is its claim not merely to regulate the conduct of states toward each other, but to press the claims, material and moral, of the citizen against the state. And at San Francisco, the Dumbarton Oaks draft was considerably amplified in this direction. The fifty governments of the "United Nations" added new words to the Charter's preamble and to the first article setting out the purposes of the organization, which gave much more prominence to the UN's role in furthering people's material well-being and promoting the observance and protection of their individual rights.

The San Francisco conference, taking place as it did against a background of daily revelations of Nazi and Japanese atrocities, revealed what a profound shift the experience of international economic crisis, total war, and the Holocaust had produced in the demands made of international organizations. The amendments committed the UN to "promoting and encouraging respect for human rights and for fundamental freedoms for all without distinction as to race, sex, language, or religion."[16] In terms far more specific than the Dumbarton Oaks draft, the final version of Chapter IX on economic and social cooperation set out such goals as "higher standards of living, full employment . . . solutions of international economic, social, health and related problems . . . international cultural and educational cooperation." It was at San Francisco that ECOSOC was charged with protecting "human rights and fundamental freedoms."[17] An optimistic secular humanism, egalitarianism, and confidence in common purposes survived two months of committee meetings and was even reinforced in the process. The Charter that emerged was a ringing affirmation of the inalienability of individual rights and a statement of mutual human solidarity. It was also not without inconsistencies.

"In the Charter," Clement Attlee was to say as he welcomed ministers to the first United Nations General Assembly in London a year later, "we see the freedom of the individual in the state as an essential complement to the freedom of the state in the world community of nations."[18] This already raised interesting questions. States, under the Charter, were being asked to respect claims against the state. Yet for all the explicit recognition of citizens' individual rights, the United Nations was nonetheless an organization of governments. Exhorted to protect citizens everywhere, the United Nations was enjoined to the respect of sovereignty and, in Article 2.7 of the Charter, was prohibited from intervening "in matters which are essentially within the domestic jurisdiction of any state." None of these factors necessarily made the aims of the Charter unrealizable: They simply provided constitutional alibis for inaction. But the Charter also conveyed a misleading impression of the competence and authority of the United Nations Organization with regard to the agencies for sectoral cooperation, by suggesting that there was indeed a global hub and that the spokes were firmly attached to it. This systemic fiction, which built frustration right from the start into the proceedings of the General Assembly and of ECOSOC, was accepted by ministers of the states which had been involved throughout the drafting process. The British foreign secretary, Ernest Bevin, told that first UN General Assembly that ECOSOC's responsibilities "to carry on the great war against poverty, misery and disease" were on a par with those of the Security Council in its sphere.[19] In practice, it was equipped to do little more than comment on the battle. But encouraged by such exhortations and "by the loose language of the Charter, the infant Ecosoc began by pursuing every social and economic objective in sight, with an extravagant faith in the virtue of words and resolutions and in the value of proliferating committees and commissions."[20] It is hard to see what else could have been expected.

The case for polycentrism will be discussed more fully later on. It is obvious that—given the all-embracing functions postulated for the United Nations under the Charter—a wholly centralized system could have created a bureaucratic monster quite as uncontrollable as the collection of bureaucracies that developed under autonomous management. There was sense in the idea that agencies with specialized tasks would be the best judges of their own needs and performance, and were therefore best left to govern themselves. But there was little sense in pretending that this arrangement constituted a system. And sectoralization, in practice, also put the United Nations out of step with two great postwar trends: the integration of economic activities both nationally and internationally, and the growing impact of social issues on political security. Heroically—and imaginatively—the UN Charter sought to reconcile the need for stability with the need to promote change. That contradiction was already a sufficient challenge without the addition of organizational ambiguities.

More than the Sum of Its Member States

The ambitious roles assigned to this new network of global organizations, and the opening to global debate of a wide range of areas that governments had traditionally considered their domestic concern, put a premium on the independence, as well as the quality, of UN administrators. Here again, the founders broke with the precedents set by the League of Nations. The League was a covenant between "high contracting parties" to act together for given purposes, an offshoot in this respect of the diplomatic traditions of the Concert of Europe it was intended to replace. Its secretariat had never been intended to be more than an administrative convenience and neither had, nor was intended to have, a distinct institutional identity or powers of initiative. The quality of the League's civil service, modeled on Whitehall, was extraordinarily high—even though, during the 1930s, the politicization of appointments had begun to erode standards. But its size, at under a thousand, gives some indication of the limits governments set to its functions. The League's secretariat discharged these with some distinction and with the necessary guile of all good civil servants, but it could not be said to have had a life of its own.

The founders of the United Nations, by contrast, agreed to "establish an international organization."[21] The distinction, reflecting general determination to construct cooperation and security on something more solid than political goodwill, was crucial. Both the United Nations and the organization are referred to throughout the Charter, the

not trusting in altruistic govts.

latter more than two dozen times. And to give the United Nations, as *organization*, a voice and responsibility of its own, the Secretariat was accorded the status of a Charter body, putting it on a par with the Security Council and ECOSOC.

The secretary-general owed his appointment (and reelection) to the Security Council, where any one of the five permanent members could veto a candidate. Once in office, however, he was "responsible only to the Organization." The secretary-general was not only "the chief administrative officer." He and his staff—over whose appointments he had, unlike his League predecessors, sole power—had a distinct legal identity. And, in still more significant contrast with his counterpart in the League, he was expected to initiate debate and, where necessary, propose courses of action. This he could do in broad terms through his reports to the General Assembly, and Article 99 gave him powers to "bring to the attention of the Security Council any matter which in his opinion may threaten the maintenance of international peace and security."

The pattern was repeated throughout the specialized agency network, creating an ambitious international civil service under chief executives whose powers, in their own domains, paralleled those of the secretary-general. Its members were expected to treasure their independence and most were accordingly employed, at least in the early decades, under contracts that gave them a security of tenure not unlike that of academics—and which were intended to protect them from improper pressures by governments.

The creation of an independent and dynamic civil service was, once again, the outcome of careful thought. Faith in the civilizing power of organizations geared to promote the exchange of ideas and knowledge ran high in 1945; but even then it was recognized that governments might, in practice, use these forums to advance their short-term and not necessarily enlightened national goals rather than to pursue peace, development, and the promotion of human rights. The secretariats were intended, as that of the League had been unequipped to do, to make these organizations "work" even when governments were reluctant to assume their responsibilities. They could not make final decisions, but they were expected to use their considerable powers to initiate and persuade, so "harmonizing the actions of nations." The central role given the civil service recognized that although governments pay lip service to common long-term interests, they make policy within shorter time frames and in the light of narrower political considerations. The job of the secretariats was to nudge governments in the right direction, by presenting proposals that would align the two more closely.

The UN's chief executives thus had the politically sensitive tasks of discerning where progress could be made on the basis of real, rather than paper, agreement; of deciding when negotiations might effectively be pursued and when they were better quietly shelved; of preparing cooperative activities, where feasible; and of drafting conventions where governments would agree to be bound by them. The chief executives' considerable agenda-setting powers, and the scope for creative management given to the international civil service, were critical to the UN's development—not least because, even in 1945, the range of activity of the new organizations outstripped the capacity of all but the best-endowed governments to monitor them.

The very comprehensiveness of the founders' vision had ensured that, from the start, the United Nations Organization and the agencies formally affiliated to it embraced three distinct types of function—some of which were in practice a good deal less susceptible to joint global management than was supposed. At the simplest level there were the "service" organizations of the nineteenth-century type, exemplified by the Universal Postal Union. Then there were the large specialized agencies with broad mandates in sectors such as food, education and culture, health, labor, and, under the Bretton Woods agreements, money and finance. And there was the United Nations Organization itself, whose task it was not only to maintain international security but to provide a sort of global watch in economic and social affairs; to oversee the process of decolonization; to deal with humanitarian emergencies and to promote human rights; to develop a corpus of international law (for which purpose the International Court of Justice, adapted from a preexisting body, was given full status as an organ of the Charter); and to serve as world forum. The skill with which the executive heads exercised their functions was the more crucial because each of these types of cooperation required differing degrees of commitment to joint action. Governments at San Francisco could not foresee how the UN would increase in complexity, but they already understood the importance of a civil service equipped to impart a degree of realism and intellectual discipline to the new enterprise.

The seventy-eight tons of paper that went, at San Francisco, into the final drafting of the Charter and the statutes of the International Court of Justice produced, if not a coherent system, a document of considerable moral resonance. It broke new ground: in the detail of its provisions for the collective use of force; in the explicit connectives it drew between peace and material well-being; and perhaps above all in its determination, through a global organization, to encourage states to respect not only other states, but their own people. The United Nations was intended to be a hair shirt for governments which, because they themselves had made it, they had committed themselves to wear—at least on public occasions.

That the Charter of the United Nations was all-embracing was its architects' special pride; that it confronted the real world of sovereign recalcitrance and power politics was their source of hope. That it was curiously schizophrenic, in its assumption that states must be disciplined against aggression but were naturally drawn together in cooperation, struck nobody as particularly inhibiting. "They thought they had provided for everything. The ensemble looked, in fact, coherent. The hope that the peace would be guaranteed in the short term and solidly constructed in the long term could well have appeared justified."[22] And, by the time the first United Nations General Assembly convened in London in January 1946, the "United Nations" had taken out extra insurance. In order to keep the United States in the United Nations, they had decided to place the UN in the United States.

It was not a time for caution. Speaking for the United States in London that January the U.S. secretary of state of the day, James Byrnes, inserted what was intended to be a realistic note into a speech primarily designed to stress Washington's wholehearted commitment to the new organization. "Let us beware," he said, "of the die-hard optimists as well as the die-hard unbelievers. Let us not think that we can give over any and every problem to the United Nations, and expect it to be solved. Let us avoid casting excessive burdens upon the institutions of the United Nations, especially in their infancy."

But he went on to set the following "priorities" for action: "to build a lasting system of peace and security capable of meeting the stresses and strains of the future, and to promote through more effective international cooperation the economic and social well-being of the peoples of the world. In the months ahead we must concentrate on these tasks."[23] His words undoubtedly felt "right," but it is hard to envisage priorities less precisely defined than those of building a safe and prosperous world. Byrnes's was a model of the inflationary rhetoric that was to become routine. The prospects for effective international cooperation were adversely affected from the start by systematic exaggeration of the potential of the United Nations—a group of organizations endowed with small budgets, even less legislative authority, and limited resources of manpower.

However contradictory and loosely connected its various structural elements, the United Nations created spaces for multilateral mediation that were, in the already dangerously tense circumstances of 1945, a considerable and necessary achievement. The "temple of peace" was still, as Winston Churchill remarked in his speech at Fulton, Missouri, in March 1946 (better remembered today for its vivid invocation of the "Iron Curtain" descending over central and eastern Europe) designed but not yet built. It remained, as he said, to make sure "that its work is fruitful, that it is a reality and not a sham, that it is a force for action, and not merely a frothing of words, that it is a true temple of peace in which the shields of many nations can some day be hung, and not merely a cockpit in a Tower of Babel."[24]

Churchill, who had been a minister at the time of the Versailles Treaty, reminded his audience of the "high hopes and unbounded confidence that the wars were over and that the League of Nations would become all-powerful"—a mood "painful to contrast" with the lack of confidence and hope in "the haggard world" of 1946. This time, he insisted, governments must be certain that collective security would work before they "cast away the solid assurances of national armaments for self-preservation": the United Nations must first be equipped with an international armed force. He went further: in a pitch for Anglo-American military cooperation and a joint stance by the "Western democracies" against Soviet expansionism (an early airing of the principles underlying NATO), he argued that far from being inconsistent with those countries' "overriding loyalties to the world organization," such cooperation was "probably the only means by which that organization will achieve its full stature and strength."

This suggests that in some politicians' heads, the concept of security through the UN was being modified within two months of the opening of the first United Nations General Assembly. Its broad purpose—to proclaim (and enforce) universal rules and common values as bastions against governments' aggression and domestic misconduct—was not in question. But there was already some sense that, for all the stress on building for the future that characterized postwar planning from the mid-Atlantic meeting between Roosevelt and Churchill in 1941 to the San Francisco conference, the United Nations was strangely ill-constructed for the actual tensions of the post-1945 world. This sense, which soon became acute with the onset of the Cold War, was to be further reinforced by the consequences of decolonization.

The United Nations Charter and the constitutions of the specialized agencies were drawn up by, and for, states for the most part sufficiently mature and confident in their national identities to afford to take some liberties, for common and mutually beneficial ends, with the precious fictions of national autonomy. But they were drawn up on the eve of the greatest expansion in history of entities calling themselves nation-states, and those who came later to "hang up their shields" saw the UN, by contrast, as an affirmation of that autonomy. Nationalism, not cooperation, became the quite unintended cement of common purpose as these states gained a numerical majority. Nor was this the only sense in which the United Nations was to prove a regressive influence. It sought to provide—again, in Churchill's formulation—protection against the rise of tyranny, yet it accentuated the role of the state. On the eve of a postindustrial revolution whose dimensions were barely discernible in 1945 and whose implications for the nature of government had yet to be grasped, the governmental bias of the United Nations gave too little scope to the communities which made up "the peoples of the United Nations." That these elements of political and social obsolescence were inadvertently built into the design was to prove quite as important, in determining whether it would be a "force for action" or "a cockpit in a Tower of Babel," as the ideological and political strains that Churchill identified so clearly that day in Fulton.

2. Boxes of Tricks: The UN Machine

The Consequences of Polycentrism

In setting out to design a network of institutions for postwar order, the UN's architects assumed that the creation of organizations custom-made for different forms of cooperation would simplify the tasks ahead. Nobody foresaw that in the following decades, this principle would be carried to such extremes that the United Nations would acquire a complexity beyond the grasp of all but a handful of specialists, and quite beyond the control of national bureaucracies. The necessary precondition for control is understanding how machines work. The United Nations today defies logical analysis.

The complexity derives not just from the increase in the the number of UN organizations, but from the fact that each UN specialized agency has expanded the range of its activities far beyond anything envisaged in 1945. Nor do the problems end there, for perhaps the most extreme example of institution-building run riot is the United Nations in New York. While primarily focused on collective security, its original remit allowed for an economic and social dimension. This represented, from the start, a curious compromise with the notion of cooperation by sector, which was the rationale for the autonomous specialized agencies. And today that secondary dimension has expanded to absorb most of the "political" UN's budget and staff. Aside from the five regional economic commissions, which report to the Economic and Social Council, the UN has formal responsibility for fifteen other organizations and programs ranging from the major, such as the UN Development Program (UNDP), to the obscure and scantly funded, such as the UN Research Institute for Social Development. In addition, the General Assembly has created numerous "special bodies of the United Nations" charged with tasks such as advancing the status of women, disarmament research, human settlements, disaster relief, or the rights of the Palestinian people. To list the main units and types of functions[1] is to give only a taste of the proliferation of these activities.

Under the original concept of functional cooperation, few of these would have existed. Through ECOSOC, the UN in New York was certainly given the general task of overseeing economic and social matters. But the business of cooperation in these fields was to be assumed by the specialized agencies—in particular by the new generation of organizations that had sectoral responsibilities, but whose functions were expressed in terms that went far beyond the technical. The model for these major new agencies—the World Health Organization (WHO), UNESCO, and the Food and Agriculture Organization (FAO)—was the International Labor Office (ILO), which had been created in 1919 to remedy "conditions of labor . . . involving such injustice, hardship and privation . . . as to produce unrest so great that the peace and harmony of the world are imperilled." The constitutions of the World Health Organization and UNESCO, in particular, explicitly expressed the belief that success in the "nonpolitical" spheres would promote greater harmony in the political. The WHO's asserted that "the health of all peoples is fundamental to the attainment of peace and security"; UNESCO's declared that "since wars begin in the minds of men, it is in the minds of men that the defenses of peace must be constructed."

By the 1990s, there were sixteen of these specialized agencies, including the Bretton Woods institutions but excluding the General Agreement on Tariffs and Trade (GATT), and the GATT was in the process of being transformed into a new World Trade Organization.[2] Under the umbrellas of the larger and more ambitious, in addition, a large range of autonomous bodies had sprouted—between ten to twenty of them created by each of the big four. And well before then, it had become clear that the orderliness of this division of labor was deceptive. The "sectoral" approach was always vulnerable to inflation, to the creation of new units for each "new" problem, just as it offered obvious scope for interorganizational rivalries.

The hope had been that, despite their autonomous status, the specialized agencies would still look to New York for general guidance and coordination — even though ECOSOC had no powers to impose its views and the secretary-general of the UN was not, and was never intended to be, *primus inter pares*. In the absence of prime minister or cabinet or means of agreeing priorities between different kinds of activity or expenditure, the UN sprouted principalities whose powerful executive heads were sovereignly indifferent to external pressures either from New York or from the capitals of member states. Coordination was to become an obsession in New York. But New York contracted the same disease of organizational proliferation. Partly in an effort to assert itself as the center that it was not, the General Assembly in turn created, under its own or ECOSOC's aegis, a multiplicity of bodies dedicated to "functional cooperation."

The agencies had, and have, sound reasons for defending their autonomy. Not only were they intended to establish identities so distinct, and activities so self-evidently useful and neutral, as to render them proof against political earthquakes; they were intended to function as social and political shock absorbers. The notion that "practical" and "political" questions could be separated in watertight compartments looks remarkably innocent today—and as outmoded as the parallel idea that domestic and international policies can be segregated. For many of the smaller technical agencies, such as the International Civil Aviation Organization, autonomy has been an important factor in retaining a high degree of ideological neutrality. But in practice, through most of these "nonpolitical" parts of the UN, all kinds of political pressures have built up, influencing the work of the UN General Assembly in ways the founders never intended. The politics of debt, food, oil, and aid have shaped the political landscape and become some of the sharpest points of international confrontation.

Politics is not what it seemed in 1945; it has become quite as charged a matter to "bring nations actively together," as David Mitrany put it, as it is to "keep them peacefully apart." Both the progressive integration of international economic life and the deliberate effort to involve governments, through the UN, in a much broader range of cooperation than had been attempted under the League of Nations, have contributed to the emergence of economic and social politics. Yet the more ambitious the UN has become in these domains, the more marginal has its real impact been: a paradox this chapter will start to explore.

These tendencies may also have been accentuated by the UN's patchy record in conflict containment and settlement. For most of the UN's first half-century of existence, it was all too apparent that peace in the industrialized world was been maintained through military alliances and nuclear deterrence. In the Third World, most major conflicts were fought, and settled, largely outside the UN even where, as in the agreements on Afghanistan and southern Africa of the late 1980s, the UN was accorded a subsidiary diplomatic or peacekeeping role by the powers concerned. The UN's peacekeeping missions, useful and appreciated though these small-scale military deployments often were, represented not so much collective security in action as *ad hoc* palliatives for the failure to find political resolutions to conflicts, or face-saving devices for exhausted combatants. For much of its history, therefore, the UN's claims to public esteem rested heavily on successes in the "nonpolitical" arena—the eradication of smallpox, the relief of famine.

The United Nations has had some success in persuading the broader public that it had another face—the UNICEF Christmas card face—to compensate for paralysis in the Security Council and the acrimony of General Assembly debates. This was the "real UN," whose multiple technical and specialist organizations, ignored by the media and inadequately supported by governments, beavered steadily away for the good of humankind, greening deserts and inoculating children and animals, protecting workers and improving parcel posts, training teachers and administrators, spreading knowledge, and making sense of change. UN propaganda has made large claims to this effect: in reviewing its first thirty-five years of operation, the UN Development Program boasted, for example, that if "one single generation has changed the world in a way that all the others could not," it was due to "an international cooperative effort in which the United Nations has from the start played a leading role."

This attractive self-portrait has never withstood very close examination. Useful studies and effective programs do occasionally emerge from the UN's many beehives. But since the 1960s at least, those who sit through UN conferences or digest the advice of its experts have had a more jaundiced view. The global organizations have accumulated a reputation for unreadable reports and working documents, for make-work programs and a scattershot approach to problems that deprives their work of impact, for consuming vast quantities of governments' time in the elaboration of declarations of blinding banality, for "strategies" that discredit the meaning of the word, and for duplicative effort beyond comprehension or control. Yet the theoretical appeal of functional cooperation—the idea that the UN exists to make things happen and not merely to prevent them—has survived to a remarkable degree. Although these organizations were created in a climate of greater faith in the efficacy and desirability of state planning and intervention than is now current, the concept of linking across frontiers for particular purposes has not been invalidated.

The fiction of neatly parceled areas of activity is attractive for several reasons. It reassures those for whom the thought of a coordinated, centralized system of cooperation conjures up the specter of "world government." The arguments for tackling tasks piecemeal are if anything magnified by the poor performance of individual agencies. However aware they are of the problems of institutional proliferation, pragmatists argue that scrapping the fleet in favor of one all-purpose monster vessel would merely magnify existing problems—and that to duplicate activities is a form of insurance against the worst incompetence. There is also an built-in tendency to assume that even the worst-run agency is capable of reform, capable in principle of providing essential and irreplaceable service. Doubts about the UN's performance have, finally, been balanced by the growing public awareness of the value of cooperative approaches to refugee crises, natural disasters, environmental degradation, and poverty—the UN's "natural" social agenda.

But as confidence in the UN agencies' handling of these issues has declined, the vivacity and destructive impact of interagency rivalries have come to attract more scrutiny. The African famine of 1984–85, where the UN conspicuously failed to sound the alert, brought the problem briefly but dramatically into the public eye. This was the second African famine in just over a decade. On paper, the FAO had made immense progress in the intervening years, promoting land reform, food security strategies—and early warning systems. There had also been, again on paper, unprecedented efforts to coordinate the activities of the different UN organizations that claimed to be involved with food and agriculture—no fewer than twenty-seven of them, according to the World Food Council (WFC) of agricultural ministers, which had been created in 1974 in the wake of the earlier famine to bring some coherence to their activities. The FAO statistical machinery had all the relevant data. But only the World Bank had subjected these data to proper analysis—concluding as early as 1981 that even without drought, Africa's decade-long decline in food production would tip it into crisis within the decade.

When drought struck, the UN proved about as fleet and adaptable as a dinosaur. The tired joke that if UN paper were edible there would be no starvation acquired a new and bitter point. Western governments moved much more rapidly to initiate programs of emergency relief and humanitarian assistance, which had long been commonly acknowledged to be one of the UN's most irreplaceable functions. To stir the UN machine into action, the secretary-general was compelled to set up a special temporary unit in New York, mainly to cut across the elaborate UN demarcation lines—a unit with which the FAO's then director-general, Edouard Saouma, refused to cooperate until forced at least to pretend to do so by the failure of his efforts to set up a rival emergency operation. The temporary unit, when it got into its stride, performed effectively; but hundreds of thousands died whose lives could have been saved had the UN's emergency alert systems worked properly, and had its bureaucrats not put turf warfare before saving lives. Rivalry between UN bureaucracies was exposed as a problem with more than theoretical implications.

What is more, as the postmortem revealed, there was little that governments could do about this. (Even efforts to secure a change of management at the FAO in 1987 failed: Saouma was elected for a third term of office—and with the support of many of the African governments whose people the FAO had failed in the 1984–85 crisis.) The apparent impossibility of overhauling existing UN structures has, paradoxically, encouraged the formation of new ones—at the cost of rendering the UN still more complex and ungovernable. As the machinery has multiplied, it has spun even further out of control. The United Nations has come to resemble an astronomical phenomenon in which new parts constantly break off and spiral away, self-propelling fragments in an exploding nebula, either as new agencies or as boxes within boxes, self-contained in a complex that is not so much centrifugal as inchoate.

The Myth of "The UN System"

Efforts to make the UN work as the system that it is not have plagued it ever since its foundation. The freedom of the UN's specialized agencies to disregard admonitions from New York has never been accepted there. The General Assembly and its second, third, and fifth committees, the Economic and Social Council, and palimpsestic layers of coordinating machinery have produced neither workable forums for linking policies and activities nor administrative tidiness. "Common system" procedures for staffing and program formulation have reduced the flexibility of the most effective UN organizations without improving the efficiency of the worst run. The obsession with systematic coordination has if anything increased the difficulty of understanding how, and for what purposes, the UN operates. As the Bertrand study of 1985 commented:

> The problems of management and functioning of the System as a whole ultimately take up an undue proportion of the work schedule of delegations and secretariats. The way in which the mill operates becomes much more important than the quality of the flour it produces. In order to overcome the difficulties inherent in the complexity of the whole, delegations are forced not only to learn how the machinery conditions the interplay of influence, but also to follow closely the most trivial administrative matters.[3]

By the 1980s, as a result, in addition to hundreds of intergovernmental committees concerned with making the parts cohere, there were more than sixty different pieces of interagency coordinating machinery. Hundreds of senior UN officials do nothing except attend coordination meetings and "observe" the meetings of the councils and general conferences of other agencies. Few suffer from any illusions that these efforts have the faintest impact on overlap and duplication. Most see their jobs in terms of keeping tabs on territorial "poaching" by rival agencies, and of maintaining the claims, profiles, and "special expertise" of their own. World Bank officials, generally franker about the politics of the United Nations than most bureaucrats, describe these expensive and time-consuming exercises as "purely political."

At the "overview" level in New York, the ratio of time consumed to results achieved is poorer still. An inaptly named Administrative Committee on Coordination (ACC), consisting of the heads of the specialized agencies under the chairmanship of the UN secretary-general, meets for thrice-yearly "summits." These serve principally as occasions for long and generally inconclusive arguments over territory—unless common interests are perceived to be threatened: in 1986, the UN barons were, for example, virtually unanimous that the Bertrand report on UN reform should be buried. Where the ACC does reach a decision, it is open to the governing executive boards of the agencies—generally on the recommendation of the chief executive concerned—to reject its recommendations. The secretary-general has powers only of persuasion, and these have rarely been decisively exerted. Most secretaries-general have in practice been either incompetent in administrative matters or uninterested in them. Both Kurt Waldheim and Javier Pérez de Cuéllar relied on reading from prepared texts, the latter betraying both innocence and incompetence when, at his first meeting, he accidentally read out the guidance notes in the margin that warned him where, and from whom, to expect difficulties.

The ACC's brief, unfulfilled, is in any case limited to administrative housekeeping. Policy is theoretically taken care of by the governmental bodies—ECOSOC and the General Assembly's economic and social committees. The Committee for Program and Coordination (CPC), which operates under the joint auspices of the Assembly and ECOSOC, is charged with eliminating duplication of the different UN organizations' programs and preventing them from working at cross-purposes. A further committee of experts elected from member states, the Advisory Committee on Administrative and Budgetary Questions (ACABQ), reviews budgets and financial management. In the early 1990s, there was a further attempt to bring these various efforts together, and involve the heads of the specialized agencies directly in coordination, through joint meetings of the ACC and the CPC. The fact remains that the conclusions of all these bodies can be, and generally are, ignored by the specialized agencies (and even by New York-centered organizations that are, as the agencies are not, formally accountable to them).

The essential futility of much of their work has not prevented them from expanding. As early as 1960, ECOSOC appeared to Gunnar Myrdal to have "sunk to a level of unimportance which must appear almost scandalous."[4] Its agenda even then was unmanageable, but it went on steadily adding to it, creating more commissions, committees, and expert groups in a trend-setting example of the empire building that it was part of its function to keep in check. As policy forum, ECOSOC has drowned in paper and the weight of its procedures. Twenty-two bodies reported to the council in 1947; by 1987, the number had grown to nearly sixty. The Joint Inspection Unit (JIU)[5] calculated in 1983 that, not counting reports from the specialized agencies and papers for its own subsidiary bodies, the representatives of the council's fifty-four member states were expected to absorb nearly 4,000 pages of documents. Secretariat sources acknowledge that 95 percent of this is repackaged from previous years; most of it, unsurprisingly, remains unread.

The delegates respond in kind. Each year, council meetings produce a further 2,500 pages of records, resolutions, and official statements. In 1983—one year after the council had solemnly decided to cut documentation and to "focus its attention on a limited number of carefully selected policy issues"—it issued 148 requests, of which more than a third were for new reports. The JIU commented that "the Secretariat appears as the main supplier and as the main target of the Council's decisions." Serious efforts at pruning began only in the 1990s. On the insistence of the Japanese, who objected to paying the bill, ECOSOC's annual summer session in Geneva, treated by most delegates as a delightful respite from the New York summer, was finally canceled. And in December 1993, further solemn undertakings were made to repackage ECOSOC's agenda and end the practice of discussing in plenary subjects that had already been exhaustively aired in its committees. *Finem lauda*: all these good intentions remained subject to objections from any participating state. And in addition to its fifty-four elected members, all UN member states, the representatives of all the bodies reporting to it, and a clutch of accredited nongovernmental organizations have the right to speak—all swelling the torrent of words.

The selection of priorities has proved as impossible for ECOSOC as for the General Assembly's economic and social committees and its plenary sessions, which go roughly over the same ground, with the same diplomats largely repeating their ECOSOC speeches. The creation of the United Nations Conference on Trade and Development (UNCTAD) in 1964, a direct bid to take over from New York as the global economic policy forum, was a response not only to Western "hegemony" in the international financial institutions but to the ineffectiveness of ECOSOC (whose reputation for unfocused rhetoric it rapidly surpassed). The "coordinating" bodies occasionally managed to put problems that needed tackling on the international map. But they had neither the intellectual coherence nor the power over budgets to improve policymaking or to oil the administrative machinery. While it was true that the agency heads resisted from the start all attempts to control their activities, the chaotic proceedings in New York made their obduracy remarkably easy to justify from an early stage.

The years of debate and multiplication of committees in New York had one unintended result: They further complicated the picture by taking the "political" body into the "functionalist" business on its own account. By 1984–85, two-thirds of the $10.6 billion budget of the UN and its agencies (excluding the Washington-based international financial institutions) was spent under New York's expanding umbrella. Political activities, including peacekeeping forces and conference services for the "forum of negotiation," the General Assembly—which was itself increasingly devoted to economic and social issues—then accounted for less than 12 percent of New York's spending: three quarters went toward economic, social, and humanitarian activities. The massive expansion of UN "peacekeeping" in the 1990s—costs increased from $700 million in 1991 to around $4 billion in 1993—gave the impression of a sea change. But peacekeeping was always, in both the financial and the administrative senses, largely "off budget"—backed by a tiny core UN staff and funded out of budgets drawn up for each operation and paid for on a separate, and differently calculated, scale of assessment. The routine of UN activities continued to be overwhelmingly weighted to the social and "development" spheres.

Despite appearances, none of this vast expansion implied a centralization of UN activities. What happened was that programs and funds multiplied until the UN was responsible for dozens of units of varying size and degrees of autonomy, spread out from Tokyo to Santo Domingo but also occupying skyscrapers in Turtle Bay that now dwarf the political headquarters. Their remits ranged from population or the environment to narcotics, multinational corporations, and disaster relief, and many were involved in major programs of direct technical assistance. Functionalism had done a reverse takeover.

The more the UN in New York built up its own battalions, the less capable its policy bodies became of providing an interdisciplinary framework: it became even more difficult for the UN to put brakes on interagency rivalry when it was competing in the game itself. But that capacity was always in doubt. In a polycentric structure, in the first place, national governments were always liable to speak with different voices on the same subject in different forums; fragmentation of tasks into more and more units merely exacerbated this tendency. But there was a more important reason. The deceptively simple division of labor masked, from the first, a profound confusion about what these organizations were for—and for the good reason that there could be no single answer, because governments were prepared to go much further in accepting international management in some fields than in others. The vital distinction between "advisory" and "executive," between promoting cooperation and setting out to regulate national conduct, rapidly became blurred.

The cooperative enterprise was certainly more modest than the wartime enthusiasts for joint action had hoped. There were no UN shipyards or railway companies (the sort of common venture, such as Ariane and Esprit, which took the European Community thirty years to put in motion). Barring the odd exception, such as the powers of the International Atomic Energy Agency (IAEA) to police nuclear energy stations, or the World Health Organization's role in combating epidemics, governments had generally been disinclined to relinquish real executive powers to the UN agencies. And this was just as well, since, had the agencies been global ministries, their sectoral demarcations would have been not only artificial, but farcical. The UN's organizational structures would have been comparable to a country governed by separate parliaments for agriculture, education, and industry, whose legislators did not recognize the authority of the other and whose rival civil services—the secretariats—were barely on speaking terms.

Having agreed that member states would sacrifice some degree of sovereignty under the Charter—to the Security Council, not to the UN *qua* organization—in the interest of common security, the founders set out to assert the authority of member states over the functional organizations all the more emphatically. Where secretariats drafted conventions, it was for the agency "parliaments" to debate them—but for national governments to ratify them. UN agencies were inverse images of national structures: Their "parliaments," generally biennial assemblies to which all the relevant national ministries sent delegations, acted out a fiction of setting policy. But these "parliaments" were not, of course, legislatures. And beyond the duty to inform policymakers, and the freedom to encourage action by others, most agency work had nothing in common with the functions of a ministry or with the execution of policy. The UN bodies stopped well short of Mitrany's—and even Roosevelt's—dream of "pieces of international government in action."

But as to just how far short they stopped, and what the roles of the secretariats were, there was considerable ambiguity. Broadly, the agencies followed two totally different models, although the distinctions were not always clear-cut.

The first had developed in the nineteenth century, as outgrowths of technological change that for the first time made the national unit too small for successful administration. The Universal Postal Union and International Telegraph Union were set up because governments could not operate these services efficiently without common international rules. Agencies were needed to draw up regulations and common standards and to monitor their application. The second model, pioneered by the ILO, had a much broader purpose, combining efforts to improve material welfare with a broad concern for social equity and the promotion of human rights and freedoms.

Only within strict limits can it make sense to box all human activities into neat parcels. These limits had been observed in the nineteenth-century experiments, and the sectoral approach made eminent sense for the clutch of similar UN service organizations set up to deal with such matters as civil aviation, merchant shipping and marine pollution, atomic energy, or the protection of intellectual and industrial property.[6] All of these have been relatively successful and uncontroversial—not because their activities are not politically sensitive (atomic energy, the allocation of radio frequencies, and patent protection all involve important conflicts of interest) but because they deal in matters that governments know must be managed in common. Because they know that they have a serious stake in the successful outcome of negotiations in these bodies, governments tend to address them at a high level of technical competence and to make sure that agreements reached are thoroughly feasible and practical. When, for example, Third World claims in the 1970s to ownership rights over the geostationary orbit threatened to paralyze a crucial conference on the allocation of radio frequencies, several Western governments provided preconference assistance to developing countries to ensure that their delegations were technically competent to deal with the agenda—on the shrewd principle that nothing makes for the politicization of debates like inadequate grasp of technical issues.

The secretariats of these organizations are not immune from jobbery. But they are comparatively small, have correspondingly less room for unqualified placemen, and, since their functions are relatively well understood by the specialists who attend their meetings and sit on their governing bodies, governments are less liable to dump incompetent friends or awkward enemies in their secretariats. The vested interest in their efficient operation is strong enough to keep management reasonably honest and—as international bureaucracies go—unpadded. The likelihood that governments will turn to them in an emergency is correspondingly higher, as is the probability that solutions to the crisis in question will be found. When the South Korean airliner, KAL 007, was shot down by the Soviet Union in 1983, it provoked a high-profile storm at the Security Council. North of the border, the International Civil Aviation Authority went quietly to work. Within eighteen months, with the full assent of the Soviet Union, it had succeeded in drawing up new regulations governing civilian flights over or near militarily sensitive areas.[7] (This is a clearer case than the more publicized success of the IAEA in bringing scientists together to handle the aftermath of the Chernobyl nuclear disaster in 1986; because in 1983 Soviet-U.S. relations were appalling, and *glasnost* and "new political thinking" undreamt of.)

There is a world of difference between joint management of technical change and common services, and the kinds of cooperation involved in promoting economic and social change. Where decisions impact on political structures and social customs, sovereign sensitivities are rapidly engaged. The capacity and enthusiasm for joint management diminish accordingly. The four great UN agencies, the ILO, UNESCO, the FAO, and the WHO, were structured much as were the UN's "service industries," but their tasks were qualitatively different. They were intended to be the principal means by which the UN met the goals of Article 55 of the UN Charter—"higher standards of living, full employment . . . social, health and related problems; and international cultural and educational cooperation." These were extraordinarily delicate missions, because the level of consensus that existed, say, for strengthening postal services could not be presumed to exist for women's education. UNESCO could not construct peace in the minds of men, as it was charged to do, by regulation; WHO could not even promote a system of basic health care without running up against problems of social inequality. Above all, the sectoral approach to such broad purposes was, to put it mildly, inhibiting.

In this "new generation" of agencies, the Bretton Woods institutions were to come closest to justifying the high expectations of the 1940s. But this was in part because an interdisciplinary approach was required to maintain monetary stability, facilitate the expansion of trade, assist countries with balance-of-payments difficulties, and promote capital investment; and this was implicit in the Bretton Woods agreements. These defined the purposes of the World Bank and the International Monetary Fund (IMF) fairly rigorously, but left them scope to redefine their methods as circumstances changed. The UN's big four agencies of social change, by contrast, were expected to address themselves within their specializations to problems that cannot in real life be neatly compartmentalized. You cannot isolate farm production from roads, transport, and the availability of market outlets; or treat environmental degradation without considering population pressures and energy needs; or consider nutrition in isolation from purchasing power; or make much impression on illiteracy where there are too few opportunities to use the skills acquired. It could be argued that, if you attempt to do so, you promote disaggregation rather than integration, obstructing rather than furthering social and economic well-being. A fragmented approach to problems that are essentially interlinked tends to be ultimately destructive.

The original, and sensible, answer to this structural difficulty was that, for all the ambitions proclaimed in the Charter and in their individual constitutions, these agencies were not intended to "deal" with these issues in the sense of being directly involved in policy execution. They were there to help governments to help themselves and to persuade them to help each other. With the exception of the WHO, always a hybrid that combined promotional and educational activities with a "service" obligation to control epidemics and organize the personnel needed to tackle the main killer diseases, they were conceived in nonoperational terms. And the WHO's first director-general was extremely clear about its "operational" limits:

> WHO is not a supra-national health administration. It cannot act in place of and for the national health authorities in any area of public health. Its only role is to use all possible means of international cooperation in order to provide certain essential elements which those authorities need to promote the health of their peoples. The rest is up to each individual nation.[8]

Even at the level of essentially intellectual outputs, strains occurred: the ILO, UNESCO, and the FAO clashed almost at once over their claims to be responsible for agricultural education. But as facilitators and catalyzers, their sectoral specialization made a degree of sense.

Aside from the question of standard-setting, more prominent in some agencies than in others, some essential tasks were common to the old and the new types of agency. Both were to provide governments and other "consumers" with statistical data—rudimentary or nonexistent in 1945. They were to be fact finders—clearinghouses through which governments and specialists obtained access to pertinent research. Although they could commission research themselves, their basic job was putting research bodies in touch with each other and, as it has been well put of the FAO, "making the world aware of the scope and content of agricultural research and stimulating its application to agricultural development."[9] They were to gather in one place a collective memory, to produce reports and publications and see that they reached those who needed them. Their standing, if not as centers of excellence (bureaucrats were never expected to be at the cutting edge of research), as authoritative bodies able to marshal the world's most distinguished specialists, would enable them to accelerate the exchange of ideas and experience. As "universal" meeting places (though in fact their memberships vary) they could promote the harmonization of national policies where appropriate and propose international standards where these were needed and there was a prospect that governments would accept and abide by them.

At their best, the agencies performed, on small budgets, some or all of these services, but the tendency to dissipate energy in a multiplicity of underfunded and dubiously relevant projects appeared early on. By 1949, ECOSOC was appealing to the agencies to limit their projects "to those for which there exists a practical possibility of implementation." A year later, it attempted to set out criteria to encourage more rigorous selection. These were urgency, feasibility, scope of expected benefits, need for the UN to act, and ability to take on the task; likelihood of demonstrable results within a reasonable period; and the capacity of states to take up where the UN left off.[10] UNESCO's research into "how the artist lives" continued, unchecked by any such considerations. By the 1970s, this proliferation of activities had seriously eroded the quality of much UN work. This tendency was not just the product of intellectual indiscipline allied to permissively vague mandates. For most agencies, it was integral to the pursuit of empire.

In certain manifestations, this virtually universal empire-building phenomenon may be a logical and quite positive response to the artificiality of sectorally divided mandates. When the International Atomic Energy Agency began investigating the uses of radio isotopes, food irradiation, and mutation breeding in agriculture, industry, and medicine, for example, it was enlarging its "field," but in ways perfectly consonant with its expertise. The trouble, even then, is that such programs then become embedded. In the IAEA's case, 20 percent of its technical assistance budget was going into agriculture by the 1990s—yet by then, quite aside from the obvious need to concentrate more heavily on its central missions of making nuclear safeguards effective, it could be argued that the technology the IAEA had to offer was much less pertinent and cost-effective than the fast-developing new approaches involving biotechnology and chemistry.[11] Equally, not all overlap is unhealthy. In the prediction of natural disasters—which, if timely, can limit damage and suffering—the scope for joint action by the World Meteorological Organization, the Food and Agriculture Organization, the UN Environment Program, and, importantly, non-UN organizations such as the U.S. Climate Analysis Center has yet to be adequately developed. Similarly, debates between agencies, such as the argument in the 1980s between UNICEF and the World Bank and IMF over the social consequences of structural economic reform programs, can be useful forms of cross-fertilization. And this is bound to be true of some of the most intractable challenges of the twenty-first century, environmental management first and foremost.

But carried to extremes, and when each agency is primarily concerned to assert its "unique competence," it is liable to lead to the sort of territorial and bureaucratic infighting that impels fifteen different UN organizations to involve themselves with ocean management—and to such extreme fragmentation of effort that the impact of these multiple small-budget activities is minimized. Territorial rivalries have led the most ambitious agencies to cast their nets wider and wider, and to dissipate their limited funds in thousands of programs with a few dollars attached to each.

The 1985–86 draft program of UNESCO might serve as example. It spread UNESCO's activities over no fewer than fourteen "major programs." The first, a "reflection on world problems and future-oriented studies," clearly distorted its mandate, staking a claim to all human enterprise by virtue of its "intellectual" brief. The eighth, almost equally sweeping, was to elaborate "principles, methods and strategies of action for development." The tenth, the most concrete of these three examples, was to cover "the human environment and terrestrial and marine resources." Yet for these three all-embracing enterprises, UNESCO proposed to spend less than $28 million a year—less than half the budget of an average British university. The implications appear more clearly at the level of particular projects. Under UNESCO's politically contentious thirteenth program for "peace, international understanding, human rights and the rights of peoples," one and a quarter staff were to supervise an enquiry into "the effective exercise of human rights in specific social and economic conditions." This was expected to improve research, training, and information on the relation between the exercise of human rights and scientific and technological progress, and to improve access to human rights by disadvantaged groups, all for $60,000 a year plus staff costs. This subprogram in turn justified a study on "the debate created by the new biomedical research and its implications for women," costing $5,000.[12] The lack of intellectual focus behind these grandiose designs was underlined by the derisory sums attached to undertakings whose tentacular reach stretched far beyond the confines both of UNESCO's mandate, and of the "practical possibility of implementation" stressed by ECOSOC decades earlier.

Proliferation of activity is highly effective in one respect: as camouflage. One of the few concrete results of the efforts that began in 1984 to reform UNESCO is that it is easier than is the case with many agency budgets to see how, in theory, it spends its money—at least where the regular budget is concerned and despite a catchall "participation program" that still, in the 1990s, provides the director-general a discretionary fund open to considerable manipulation. The budgetary presentations of other agencies, including those of the UN itself, are much less precise. Agency heads defend their programs by arguing that they simply reflect the will of member states. But, even leaving aside the paralysis of the forums through which member states may express that will (to be discussed in the next chapter), it is hard to see how any governing body could be expected to make sense of a program that, not counting the sections in the UNESCO example just cited covering general policy and direction, "general" program activities and administrative and support services, is broken down into 13,014 separate paragraphs.

Complexity, the enemy of accountability, is a weapon manipulated by all civil servants. The skills that accompany long familiarity with a brief can be highly effective against politicians whose time frames are short and horizons wide. Traditionally, complexity is used as a protective shield against ministerial folly or, at worst, as a means of obstructing change; but at the United Nations it has doubled as an offensive weapon. Unnoticed phrases buried in a budget, $15,000 for a small "program activity," slip through assemblies otherwise preoccupied—and establish "precedents" for much-expanded future strategies. Protest is then futile: The secretariat can claim merely to be carrying out the instructions of member states, including governments that now object but failed to vote against the original proposals. The director-general can counter any suggestion that the new departure might be outside the mandate, for was it not mandated in year 19XX? Or that the program is bound to lead to confrontation, for was not the principle behind it accepted by consensus? Since the international civil service, unlike the national, does not have to contend with a single minister with the authority to decide that he or she is not going to be tricked a second time and to issue instructions accordingly, the process is virtually unstoppable.

Complexity has a third use. Governments that claim to take seriously the principle of member states' control of UN activities prepare for general conferences by combing through the small print. Once assembled, they spend the time left over from negotiating resolutions—the bulk of which will have no practical impact on the agency's activities—in haggling with other delegations over the excision or amendment of potentially awkward little innovations in the printed program. Since the process is likely to be made the more drawn out by the fact that certain delegations will have been martialled in good time by the secretariat to swear in the name of peace and progress that the item in question is the embodiment of their most profound hopes for the future of the organization, there is little time left for more constructive activity.

Complexity is a formidable extra weapon for directors-general. They have in any case enormous discretionary power, deliberately built into their organizations' constitutions to enable them to shrug off improper pressures from member governments. They are expected to report to their governing bodies on the organization's activities, but the reports may take any form they please. They "propose" programs and budgets to their members for decision, but do so secure in the knowledge they will suffer only minor modifications. Until the "taxpayers' revolt" in the 1980s began to force changes to budgetary committee procedures, they could also be confident that expansionary budgets would be carried by the Third World majority. In most cases, financial controls are still weak; and the major contributors have no option, short of withdrawal, but to pay up. Scrutiny of the agencies' activities is rudimentary. External auditors verify that money has been spent, that the books square, but conduct few value-for-money evaluations. Most assessment of the effectiveness and impact of programs is internal. With the notable exception of the World Bank, the only organization to take evaluation seriously, the relevant reports go to the director-general, not the governing bodies, for decision, and the findings may see the light of day years late or not at all.

In theory, directors-general can be dismissed, but since in most cases this requires a vote by two-thirds of the membership at the organization's annual or biennial assembly, in practice they are secure at the very least for the duration—from four to six years—of their terms of office. In some agencies they are required to "consult" their executive boards over the most senior appointments, but otherwise have absolute power to hire, fire, promote, and demote staff. (There is a UN appeals procedure, first internal, ultimately before an ILO tribunal, for aggrieved international civil servants, but it takes an average of three years, and while the tribunal may order compensation or recommend reinstatement, a director-general may reject the latter without giving reasons.) All these factors, together with the patronage inherent in their powers, give them ample latitude, while maintaining the fiction of the civil servant's subservience to his political masters, to set the agencies' agendas.

It is an arrangement based on trust. A director-general inhabits a world with boundaries that are essentially invisible. With a duty to innovate—particularly in the major "social" organizations—and to encourage orderly change, he can exercise a creative influence on government thinking. He can choose his means; but if the agency's long-term reputation is to be enhanced he must concentrate on those activities for which there is almost universal support and a will to cooperate, or those in which there is a real prospect of bridging conflict. The measure of an agency's worth is the degree to which it is felt to be indispensable, the speed with which governments will turn to it in difficulty. The job requires imagination, modesty, administrative skill, and political and intellectual independence. Amadou Sedou, an experienced diplomat from Niger, remarks that it takes a philosopher king to rule "the last of the world's absolute monarchies." Since, unlike the absolute monarch, the term of his rule is fixed—and since he is eligible for reelection—the actual incumbent is likely to possess the skills and temperament not of a philosopher, but of a machine politician.

It is hardly surprising that, in office, executive heads are tempted to invert the servant-master role. The parliamentary forms foster the "ministerial" fiction, promoting delusions of grandeur. Some resist; others are carried away by *folie de grandeur*. Richard Hoggart recalls how, as UNESCO's assistant director-general for culture, he accompanied the newly elected Amadou Mahtar M'Bow on an official visit to Indonesia. They attended a ceremony arranged by the then deputy prime minister, Sultan Hamengku Buwono IX, at his palace in Jogjakarta. As the sultan was arriving, M'Bow flew into a rage: He had discovered that his chair had been placed a few inches behind the sultan's. Hoggart narrowly averted M'Bow's stormy departure by moving behind the chair and nudging it surreptitiously into parallel position. Edouard Saouma, director-general of the FAO for nearly two decades, once called off a visit to Canada when the prime minister declined to meet his plane in person. And on a visit to Denmark, he scandalized the Scandinavians by objecting vehemently to the existence on his schedule of a meeting with their national FAO committees. "I didn't," he said, "come here to meet *farmers*." The pleasures and perks of a ministerial existence are certainly sufficient to make the voluntary relinquishing of these jobs an extreme rarity. Even those, like Javier Pérez de Cuéllar and Saouma himself, who first took office publicly insisting on their intention to serve a single term, tend to stay on. (Saouma's clinging to office for three terms was a particularly blatant case, since as a delegate for Lebanon he had been instrumental in changing the FAO constitution to prevent directors-general from serving a second term. Once elected, he had the constitution changed again, obtained agreement that the change could apply to the existing incumbent, and successfully ran two singularly ruthless reelection campaigns.) The cases of Halfdan Mahler of the WHO and Bradford Morse of the UNDP, both of whom decided without external pressure to retire, are much-cited rarities.

Unlike those of ministers in democratic countries, the perks are not balanced by accountability. Some directors-general are certainly pressed to stay on because their performance in their jobs has been outstanding and their skills felt to be urgently needed. A notable instance in the 1990s was Arthur Dunkel of the GATT, although this was principally out of governments' fear of changing horses in the middle of the difficult Uruguay Round of trade negotiations; and in the end it was left to Dunkel's successor, Peter Sutherland, to bring a fresh charge of political energy to the final stages and to bang down the Round's concluding gavel in December 1993. But more often, there is an inverse correlation between performance and tenure. Only rocklike Chinese resistance prevented Kurt Waldheim, who quite apart from his lies about his war record presided over one of the UN's worst periods of politicization and drift, from winning a third term as UN secretary-general. M'Bow, the most obviously disastrous and corrupt of the UN chief executives, was only squeezed from office with the greatest difficulty, and after thirteen years . One explanation is that, since the 1950s, so many UN organizations created to promote exchanges of ideas have involved themselves actively in the business of Third World economic development. Their executive heads have become not merely ministers, but patrons. Ministerial pretensions have been given undreamed of scope, and pork-barrel politics have found a multilateral dimension.

Chasing the Development Dollar

For the bureaucrat seeking to expand his agency beyond what David Mitrany had called its "assigned and natural scope," to build its prestige by claiming for it executive rather than purely mediating and informational roles, "field programs" began in the 1960s to offer brave new worlds. For the machine politician, the tissue of small direct aid projects, operated outside regular budgets and subjected to even less scrutiny than headquarters activities, provided a major new area of patronage. By 1983 technical assistance, at first conceived as a modest outgrowth of their core activities, had expanded to the point where UN agencies employed between them 1,200 staff in 612 separate offices in 130 countries.[13] Visiting teams of UN experts poured through national ministries: the vast proportion of the "field program" expenditure consisted not of capital investment but of fees paid to experts preparing reports or supervising projects. The UN monarchies—particularly the larger ones—had become empires.

Rival empires, each fighting at one end for larger slices of donor finance, at the other for the ears of ministers in the "recipient" countries that had to be persuaded to "buy" an agency's particular brand of assistance as a matter of national priority, and thus unlock the funds required. Empires that, by acquiring spending power, greatly increased their control over governments by their potential patronage, as member states became clients/supplicants.

This cycle of dependence requires some explaining. To outward appearances, where the specialized agencies were concerned, Third World governments exercised their sovereign choice. They requested assistance and the agencies complied. Technical assistance was in theory demand-led, and the agencies' role was neutral. Theory occasionally reflected reality, and the case for using the agencies' expertise to fill out the yawning manpower gaps in newly independent countries seemed overwhelming. But in practice, particularly in the countries that stood most in need of such assistance, the very paucity of administrative skills laid their governments wide open to manipulation because they relied heavily on the agencies to "suggest" what their needs might be.

This was where the UN's sectoral divisions became deadly. Agencies competing for a larger share of foreign aid money pressed different ministries (which themselves had the competitive instincts of all spending departments) to argue for priority for "their" projects. The agency salesmen dreamt up most of these projects, coached their clients, and—back at headquarters—presented their agency's activities in a particular country as reason enough for cooperative behavior by its delegate when votes came to be counted. The neutrality of UN advice, which was what the agencies claimed made their assistance programs superior to those of the national aid departments of donor governments, suffered accordingly.

Funds for these activities derived from three principal sources. Western governments, particularly those without the personnel to administer their foreign aid programs bilaterally, provided "funds in trust," appointing a UN organization as executing agent. The World Bank awarded contracts for specific programs. The third source was the UN in New York, in particular the UNDP.

The UNDP is a good example of the UN's tendency to undergo curious institutional transformations. It was set up in 1965 as the amalgamation of two earlier experiments, a UN "extended program of technical assistance" (EPTA) and a "Special Fund" that provided preinvestment surveys and training on the premise that "investment—public and private—will not venture into the unknown." The aim of this amalgamation was to reduce the already alarming proliferation of separate UN assistance programs and, through an integrated approach, to help governments to develop the skills to use capital investment productively.

The agencies had a stake in its working otherwise. EPTA had simply allocated them fixed shares of its budget, based on the agencies' previous levels of activity rather than developing countries' needs. The more hard-headed Special Fund, which included the UN secretary-general, the World Bank, and the IMF on its board but pointedly excluded the agencies, had put equal emphasis on promoting private and public investment, and had resisted "the idea that it should be a pie for the specialized agencies to carve up."[14] It was in the agencies' interests to push the new organization to follow the EPTA route. At first, they encountered obstacles.

The UNDP adopted country quotas as a device for allocating funds, basing them on per capita gross national product and population size, with extra weighting for the poorest. Within these quotas, governments were to submit requests for assistance. Its first director, Paul Hoffman, who had administered the Marshall Plan, encouraged his deputy, Arthur Lewis, to turn down recipient governments' more ludicrous spending proposals, and emphasized that he, as director, was free to select the most competent body to carry out a project, from private enterprise if he chose, and that the agencies had no monopoly.

Lewis, a Nobel laureate in economics, had been one of the three authors of a 1951 UN report that called for an international development agency with an annual budget of $3 billion—but that also, with a candor the UN was not to repeat until the World Bank finally made the same obvious point publicly in 1989, acknowledged frankly that money would be wasted where governments were corrupt or bent on sustaining privileged elites. To qualify for assistance, the report said, governments must redistribute land and give farmers incentives, provide mass education and training programs, end discrimination based on race or caste, and allow for democratic choice. Foreign aid, it warned, could sustain "corrupt or reactionary cliques whose regimes might otherwise be overthrown by the people. . . . Members of the United Nations will not wish to have any hand in fastening such governments on peoples."[15] Lewis never managed to introduce the faintest shadow of political conditionality, but he did in the early years display some toughness both in turning down proposals and in focusing on those likely to encourage productive investment.

This promising start was not sustained. The interdisciplinary approach suffered because Hoffman failed to involve the World Bank as closely as he had originally planned. The Bank, fearful for its triple-A rating on world capital markets, was reluctant to become involved in grant-based projects linked to "country programs" over which it had no influence, and was anyway discovering that its soft-loan affiliate, the International Development Association (IDA), established in 1960, was making heavy demands on its personnel. The bias toward sending in foreign experts to tackle problems reasserted itself because it offered the fastest route to growth in "output"; and Hoffman, in his eagerness to expand the UNDP, gradually acceded to pressures from the specialized agencies. Once again, it became virtually automatic for them to be given executing authority for projects within their areas of competence. Only exceptionally did the UNDP's own resident representatives, sent to capitals to help governments sort out their spending priorities, establish authority with ministers. Most of the "resreps" were treated by the agencies' teams of visiting experts as people who booked hotel rooms and hired limousines or land rovers.

The outcome of this attempt to put development aid on a country-programmed basis and to bring some interdisciplinary coherence to UN activities in the field was bizarre. Donor governments provided money to the UNDP, which handed it to specialized agencies, which, having pocketed a 14 percent administration fee, hired consultants who arrived, at a cost that by the 1980s was around $100,000 a year, at the "request" of the recipient. A more circuitous route from A to B would be hard to devise. Far from decreasing interagency competition, it intensified it. By 1985 UNDP money, which at its peak never accounted for more than 3 percent of official development assistance, was being spent through twenty-nine "executing agencies" of the UN, and another eight "participating" UN organizations.

The bureaucracies of the unfortunate recipient governments had to deal with each of these. The result, according to a survey by the World Food Council, was to burden Burkina Faso, a poor country decidedly short of skilled administrators, with 340 separate aid missions in a single year. In addition to the UN organizations and programs, it had to contend with twenty or more bilateral government donors and a large clutch of nongovernmental organizations. Such countries ought to have been able to look to the UN agencies for impartial advice, rather than contend with them as aid salesmen.

Almost from the moment, as early as 1952, when it became clear that the center of gravity was shifting to "operational activities," repeated attempts were made to curb the destructive consequences of agency salesmanship. Not least of these was the abuse of technical assistance as a pork barrel to obtain votes for a director-general's policies or for his reelection—an abuse all the more discreditable in view of the genuine need for high-quality technical assistance, particularly among the poorest microstates and in sub-Saharan Africa. The remedies proposed down the years included five-year country planning exercises, increased formal coordinating powers for UNDP representatives at country level, and much talk about decentralization of responsibility and the need "to stop the endless cycle of outside experts and technology and build instead indigenous capacities that would stick."[16] But none of these attempts, which will be reviewed in Chapter 6 in the context of efforts to reform the UN, made more than marginal impact. It is remarkable, given that the whole purpose of technical assistance was to enable countries to stand on their own feet, that the UN was twenty-five years in the business before building "indigenous capacities" returned to the forefront of UNDP concerns.

But by then the UNDP, whatever its policy, was severely handicapped by its surrender to the agencies; it had become banker to feuding sectoral interests. The artificial divorce of technical advice and capital investment—which the UNDP had been created to marry—had produced, one voluntary organization told the Organization for Economic Cooperation and Development (OECD), a "butterfly" approach to Third World problems: thousands of "mini-projects working on mini-objectives."[17] A report in 1986 to the UNDP governing council's working group on coordination of technical assistance drily observed that "the different mandates of the various organs of the United Nations system do not appear to be conducive to joint programming" and that any significant improvements would "require major changes in attitudes, mandates and structures" of the agencies.[18] Mere *aggiornamento*, modernization of the existing arrangements, would in other words not be enough.

The need to restore some coherence to this chaotic scene had also, by this time, drawn the World Bank, so reluctant to be involved in 1965, into major programs of training, technical cooperation, and expert assistance. Intended to ensure the more effective use of project aid within "policy frameworks" at country level, the cost of those activities had reached $1.5 billion a year by the 1980s, outstripping the combined outlay on technical assistance of the rest of the UN. Ironically, the UNDP now began, belatedly, to focus more on macroeconomic analysis and policy dialogue, in an attempt to improve on the "laundry list of opportune projects" that had passed in many developing countries for a UNDP "program cycle." And it was turning increasingly to the World Bank and to the private sector to get things done.

In the harsh economic climate of the 1980s, moreover, some Third World governments had begun to discover that there was no such thing as a free consultant, that they "paid" for them whether the money came in grant form out of their UNDP allocation, out of bilateral aid from individual donor countries, or indirectly through the interest they paid on World Bank loans. *Does Aid Work?* a report in 1986 to the intergovernmental task force set up by the Bank/Fund Development Committee, reinforced the skeptics. It estimated that there were "150,000 or so external advisers, consultants, seconded expatriates, and other "experts" at loose in the developing world, and that their cost (anything up to $150,000 per person, adding up to an estimated total of between $8 billion and $15 billion a year) was "a rising source of irritation" to the presumed beneficiaries. The report observed that they were often forced on recipients as a condition of aid (sometimes they *were* the aid) and that, while many, notably among these provided under bilateral aid programs, were highly competent, "the quality and relevance of some UN experts is a recurring theme."[19] Careful to point out that training and expert assistance from all sources had greatly increased "institutional and human capabilities throughout the Third World," it nonetheless concluded, in impeccable bureaucratese, that "few would disagree that the programming and operating processes of the UN's technical cooperation leave much to be desired." A top UNDP official put it more bluntly. "The agencies' *droit de seigneur* has got to stop. Their concept of 'partnership' is that we provide the money and they decide what happens to it. We have no control, at best a monitoring role, and no sanctions if they ignore the time frames and objectives of a particular undertaking—and they know we have none. The idea that they have automatic first call on UN funding is a recipe for inefficiency—and corruption."[20]

The length to which agencies will sometimes go to extract their "share" of UNDP finance was illustrated during the 1985 conference of the FAO, when the secretariat mobilized speaker after speaker from developing countries to castigate the UNDP for reducing its funding for agriculture. The governments of these same countries had, in fact, been responsible for this situation: under the country programming system, UNDP allocations for a particular sector are made in accordance with a government's stated priorities. When, after listening to days of condemnation, the unfortunate UNDP representative tried to point this out, his microphone was simply cut off. (The same man tried, six months later, to deliver a mild protest to a UNESCO Executive Board about persistent failures to implement projects on time. This provoked a tirade from M'Bow, culminating in the assertion that "I permit nobody to criticize anything whatsoever"[21]—a remark with sweeping implications that drew no formal protest from any Western government.)

By 1988, excluding the Bretton Woods agencies, the budget of the UN for "operational activities" had reached $3.7 billion a year, and they accounted for half its 50,000 staff.[22] Yet the management of these funds continued to deteriorate. This was a direct consequence of the UN's absurdly complex patchwork, with its largely artificial distinctions between "funding" and "executing" agencies, between technical cooperation and capital development. This does not mean that successful programs of technical assistance—some of them with lasting impact—were not carried out by UN agencies. Nor does it mean that there were no instances of cross-sectoral successes. Rice scientists and WHO water disease experts worked together at the International Rice Research Institute. The Special Program for Research and Training for Tropical Diseases (TDR), jointly funded by the World Bank, UNDP, and the WHO, has been a hugely effective example of the UN as "catalyst." The tentative breakthrough in developing a vaccine for malaria, announced by Colombian scientists in February 1994, was speeded up by TDR financing of field tests in Tanzania.[23] But it does mean that bureaucratic competition, overlap, and cross-purposes—both in the field and at the different headquarters—have made dealing with the UN a nightmare for donors and recipients alike. It has meant wasted personnel, pointless activity, and plummeting credibility.

The UN, as the World Bank and successive chairmen of the OECD's Development Assistance Committee never tire of impressing on the major Western donors, is not alone in failing to coordinate and to keep the interests of the recipients in mind. Sometimes as the result of mistaken judgment, too often in the pursuit of overseas contracts for underemployed northern industries, generally with the complicity of ruling elites and occasionally, and scandalously, in connection with the pursuit of lucrative arms sales, "cathedrals in the desert" have been built by everyone in the development game. And empire-building is not confined to the UN either. The spectacle of private charities squabbling over "their" patch of infinite misery is one of the more dispiriting features of emergency relief operations. But instead of mitigating these national and interorganizational rivalries, the UN hunts at the head of the pack, adding to chaos and indiscipline instead of serving as a coordinating focus for the activities of these multiple actors.

A veteran official with years of experience in the multilateral aid business from Sudan to South Korea summarized some of the consequences in a letter to the *Economist*.[24] He cited a South Korean government official's complaint that UNDP was reluctant to assist with advanced technology that would help his country's position in "donors' markets"—that "they are willing to help, providing that we do not progress." He criticized UN "institution-building projects" for creating "new bureaucratic entities," diverting "scarce trained staff towards prestigious activities of doubtful priority because of higher salaries, equipment support and other fringe benefits, such as overseas fellowships and study tours, usually associated with UNDP involvement." These and other failings to which he also referred, such as the "disgraceful monuments in the Sudan, completely equipped 'ghost factories' which have never been used," are of course also found in bilateral aid—though without the important "perks" factor. But special to the UN is "the lack of individual accountability in UN practice and the importance attached to smooth relations with the host government [which] means that public relations focus on project objectives, rather than visible results." The UN's internal vetting procedures, its value-for-money assessments, are so rudimentary that the task force on aid effectiveness that produced *Does Aid Work?* decided not to use evidence from specialized agencies because it was both difficult to obtain and simply not comparable with the data available from donor governments and the World Bank. (The report's author, Robert Cassen, concluded that in any case, UN activities were "so marginal that they did not affect the picture.")[25]

If their positive impact on developing countries has been "marginal," the effect of field activity on the agencies themselves has been of critical importance. The central problem is not the failure rate of specific projects, or the probability, as many economists inside and outside the UN believe, that its approach "increases countries' dependence on outside aid rather than enhancing their self-reliance." The record (insofar as there *is* one) is obviously mixed. As the UNDP official quoted above acknowledges: "Even a poor agency will do a good job in one country; the best do much better." The real issue is the structural deformation generated by these activities, both in the field and at headquarters. By the 1990s, according to the Nordic UN Project,[26] extrabudgetary resources—reflecting the scale of the agencies' technical cooperation programs—funded 58 per cent of all FAO activities, 54 percent of the WHO's, 41 percent of the ILO's, and 32 percent of UNESCO's. And because these activities were outside the regular budget, governing bodies had virtually no controls over where, and how, the money was spent. Technical assistance (including the WHO's substantial field programs under its regular budget) now exceeds spending on their core functions: it has become the tail that wags the dog. In the field, this same UNDP official observes:

> The whole system perpetuates the "export experts" game, jobs for the boys. The agencies now employ armies of field wallahs, whose career is expertise but who are often not in touch with their specializations because nobody in the UN is ever sacked. The pressure is always to ensure that there is another job for the expert, whether it is needed or not. Projects are routinely extended to fit his needs; local counterparts are not properly trained to take over. Studies are put in train as part of this "make work" attitude; and often all the government gets out of them is a report which tells it that it has a problem—which it knew it had in the first place. And yet the whole point of technical assistance is that the expert is supposed to be working himself out of a job.

Excessive concentration on "development" also blurs priorities at headquarters. The policy context is not neglected in all agencies, but the drive to launch new "practical" programs accentuates sectoral tunnel vision. The larger goals of cooperation are obscured. The temptation to play to the Third World gallery is increased when agencies have a stake in ministers "selecting" their services, and the UN becomes increasingly the "property" of the client states that form the voting majority of its membership but contribute little to financing it.

Worst of all, and in the worst cases, the politics of development has corrupted the agencies' vital function of accumulating and analyzing information. What trust is to be placed in statistics put out by UNESCO, when it claims to have helped within a mere four years to make fifteen million people literate? This is a number that, on UNESCO's budget, could barely be counted, let alone placed in serious literacy programs and schools. Yet the claim was made, and ironically at a time when UNESCO was reporting serious underspending of its small grants program for literacy teachers because it had been unable to locate enough candidates. Almost equally meaningless was UNICEF's boast in 1992 that oral rehydration therapy (ORT), a cheap soluble remedy for diarrhea, was saving a million children's lives a year. This was not only a highly optimistic guesstimate; UNICEF had no evidence that the children so "saved" did not die later of other illnesses.[27]

Agencies defend their field programs as the means by which they keep in touch with reality. Dr. Jacques Diouf, the Senegalese who successfully campaigned to succeed Saouma as director-general of the FAO in 1993, argued in his campaign literature that the FAO "cannot simply be an 'International Academy of Agriculture' in a world plagued by famine and hunger . . . without field activities and regular experience of local realities through concrete projects, FAO cannot be a 'Center of Excellence in Action' nor can it have concrete impact."[28] But the reality is a good deal less worthy than this makes it sound. In practice, in the experience of one of the rare consultants willing to risk future contracts by consenting to be quoted on the subject, reports from the field are regularly doctored with the purpose of "keeping on the right side of the people in Rome." Where the reports are honest, he adds, they tend to be "very much edited" in-house if they do not provide the desired picture.[29] The picture has more to do with enhancing future fund-raising than with the relevance or impact of the project in question. The FAO's research and statistical activities are still judged indispensible by most governments; but their reliability must be undermined by this injection of falsified data. The FAO has become known in the agricultural world as "the elephant's graveyard"[30]—a reference to the large number of superannuated lifetime "experts" it spends so much of its energy recycling through the Third World. As it has immersed itself in the consultancy business, the FAO has become increasingly irrelevant to policy formulation.

The polarization of UN member governments into client and donor camps was possibly unavoidable. It grew sharper, however, as developing countries came to view UN agencies as providers rather than advisers. Arguments over which programs to fund, which would have occurred anyway, became steadily more politicized.

The extent of the damage varied. The smaller "service" organizations fared best because they continued to respond to needs common to industrialized and developing countries, and kept roughly within range of their constitutional mandates. The WHO and the ILO, although they increasingly tended to cover the waterfront with units that were each too small and inadequately staffed to make a serious impression on their particular area of activity, made efforts in the 1970s and 1980s to group some of these according to priorities established by their directors-general. The UN's own regional commissions, one for each continent, succumbed to proliferation, assuming too many gigantic tasks and assigning too few people to them—a classic example was the allocation, by the UN Economic Commission for Latin America (ECLA) of a staff of just three people to handle the environmental problems of the entire subcontinent.

Most importantly, growing interagency competition made solid interdisciplinary debate on economic or social policy virtually impossible: Questions of turf, of "special competence," got in the way. In 1985, for example, the World Food Council, the only body in the UN composed of ministers, met in Paris to discuss policies to address Africa's agricultural crisis. Their draft communiqué praised the Office for Emergency Operations in Africa, the temporary unit set up by the UN to coordinate famine relief, for its efforts in promoting *both* relief and rehabilitation. The WFC's director, Maurice Williams, got an anxious telex from New York: would ministers kindly excise the word *rehabilitation*? It would offend the FAO, which would not tolerate any questioning of its leading role in organizing Africa's longer-term recovery.

The overall effect is to diminish the value of the agencies as working forums in which different approaches to problems can be discussed, and clear distinctions made between issues on which governments need to devise common policies, and areas such as education, with which governments deal at national level while profiting from exchanges of experience and timely advice.

DEALING WITH THE CONSEQUENCES

None of this happened without governments' assent and even pressure. The whole notion of what "assent" and "pressure" mean in UN contexts is intimately connected with the question, which will be discussed in following chapters, of what controls can be and have been asserted by the nationally sovereign member states. But the original impetus behind the UN's expansion into "field activities" was, quite genuinely, demand. The fledgling governments of newly independent countries urgently needed help in filling the gaps left by departing colonial administrators, and it suited both sides that they should call in what was expected to be politically neutral advice.

It took some time for these UN programs to evolve into a top-down, self-generating industry, controlled in practice not by national administrators or by the plethora of UN "field offices," but by decisions made at a comfortable distance in agency headquarters. It took time for them to assume such dimensions that they became the key to the political life of many UN agencies. Only gradually did Third World governments come to view UN organizations as sources of extra pocket money—even then largely symbolic, since the actual sums involved were always a small proportion even of official aid and constituted a minute proportion of domestic and foreign investment, and since most of the money was spent on the salaries and costs of expatriate experts and UN headquarters "backup services." And it took time for Western governments so far to forget the original purposes of the UN's roles in "functional cooperation" that they frequently defined "reform" in terms of more "practical work in the field"[31]—even while acknowledging that the value of much of this work was suspect.

It was not until the 1980s that people began seriously to question not just the quality of the product but the appropriateness of UN involvement in this whole range of activities. A report by the OECD in 1987 sought to address the more fundamental question, which was the conflict between the sectoral approach to development, cornerstone of the UN method, and donor governments' commitment to pursue a more coherent and integrated approach to development financing. That commitment, it pointed out, was inconsistent with existing practice. The donors damaged their credibility by *voluntarily* funding the interagency competition they deplored through direct grants to individual agencies, "the dangers of which are in principle recognized."[32] These grants had grown from $292.2 million in 1979 to $412.8 million by 1985 (and were to grow by half as much again by 1992). The report called on Western governments to recognize that "the issue that is on the table is whether UN agencies are an efficient and effective instrument for channeling resources for the promotion of development."

The issue was, of course, wider still. It concerned the overall role of the UN in economic and social affairs. By the time *this* was clearly on the table, however, enlarging debate beyond discrete questions of efficiency and coordination, it was also apparent that no agency was likely to welcome reforms that would reduce either the agencies' independence or their "visibility."

The OECD blamed Western donor governments for failing the UN. Their lack of determination and unity in pursuing reforms, their adoption of different, and inconsistent, positions in different agencies, and their evidently contradictory habit of slipping voluntary contributions to competing agencies while publicly animadverting on the need for coordination in development cooperation, had assisted its slide into irrelevance, mismanagement, and empire-building. But the OECD also recognized that these UN activities had acquired such a life of their own that it would be virtually impossible to effect change from outside. Even if donors united, the force they could apply to the immovable object would be eminently resistible. Since, the report argued, it was "perfectly rational" for UN secretariats to resist external pressures, the momentum would have "to come from within" for real changes to take root.

It did say, however, that the donors, "by virtue of their status as the main source of funds," were well placed to support internal efforts at reform—and that there was now a new climate, a new degree of plain speaking about the problems inside and outside the UN. And while admitting that "the trouble is that the [UN] structure is one which promotes self-defence which is of a largely negative nature," the OECD pointed out that governments too were guilty of negativism: that "the agents of reform within the system have repeatedly found themselves bereft of backing at the last moment, even from groups which might have been expected to support the reforms in question."

Why, given the OECD's optimistic conclusion that shifts in the attitudes of the secretariats and of some developing countries could be exploited by the West to secure a profound rationalization of the UN's activities, did it stress that the West would nonetheless have to rely on movement "from within," and to be content with supporting rather than initiating reforms? The basic reason was that Western governments did not begin to exercise the requisite influence at the critical early stages of decisionmaking.

Agendas for meetings were prepared by the secretariats. So were the agencies' budgets and programs of work. These documents, in theory "drafts" presented to governments for decision, were in practice vast printed texts that could be modified only marginally in the conferences of "governing bodies" of the full membership, which assembled for up to six weeks ostensibly for the purpose of deciding on the next two years' activities. The UN appeared, *strictu sensu*, ungovernable. The UN secretariats had, furthermore, become masters of imprecise description; obtaining a clear picture of the intentions of all too many of the bureaucracies had become a highly specialized art—and the virtual absence of any timely evaluation of their activities deprived governments of the ability to assess the value of continuing them. As a result, the vast majority of delegations arrived at these assemblies ill equipped to do more than rubber-stamp the secretariats' blueprints: they did not know what was going on.

The smokescreens that the agencies had thrown over their activities, in other words, had become so impenetrable as to convince most governments that they did not know enough to reassert control of them—and, eventually, that as things stood they did not care enough to make the considerable efforts required to do so. A kind of *apartheid* developed between UN secretariats and the delegations of their "governing" bodies of member states: the agencies took on a life of their own, functioning virtually independently of the interminable boards and conferences theoretically convened to dictate their policies. With millions of pages of documentation submitted for their "consideration," even the best organized of the UN's member governments had become slow to read and slower to act even on the few items genuinely presented for scrutiny and capable of modification. Cancellation of even the most obviously unproductive program or conference had become, for practical purposes, impossible.

There is a case for the extraordinary executive independence of the UN secretariats. The UN's founders were not mistaken in believing that the directors ought to have a positive, creative role in working out where governments needed to cooperate and how they might be persuaded to do so. The functions of the UN secretariats were distinctly intended to include innovation: putting ideas into governments' heads. But this degree of independence was open to abuse. Once a UN agency, in the great rush of decolonization, took to playing to the gallery of Third World rhetoric and ignoring the elementary discipline of matching means and ends, and to reaching well outside its mandate, there was little governments could do about it.

Institutional complexity was not however the only factor rendering the UN ungovernable. When they drew up the Charter, the founders had made large assumptions about the coherence of the international body politic. These assumptions, optimistic even in the circumstances of 1945, began in the 1960s to have less and less bearing on political reality. The political disaggregation of the postwar world, and the emergence of a numerical majority of countries whose governments had only tenuous claims to represent their people, contributed heavily to the malfunctioning of UN organizations.

"There is," a senior UN official remarked in 1987, "a pervasive sense of falsehood about the enterprise, a perception within and outside that the UN just isn't plausible."[33] That sense of implausibility, while it may temporarily be modified by greater optimism about East-West cooperation in the field of collective security, is rooted in the erosion of the UN's original claims to represent accurately the will of the "international community." In assessing the prospects for the reinvention of the UN, particularly as a set of forums for "harmonizing the actions of nations in the attainment of . . . common ends,"[34] this evolution, and its causes, are of cardinal importance.

3. The Politics of Illusion

Halls of Mirrors

Normally rational beings undergo strange metamorphoses in the assemblies of the United Nations. Constrained in the world outside to act in accordance with David Mitrany's truism that "sovereignty is nothing where it cannot be enforced," within the UN walls diplomats and politicians overcompensate for the frustrations of the limits of power. There, sovereignty becomes paramount, so mighty a principle that the most microscopic state commands, on a basis of parity with the mightiest, the oceans, the moon, and outer space; and the political leaders of small islands like Madagascar assert, without irony, their right to be party to negotiations on the reduction of the superpowers' batteries of intercontinental ballistic missiles.

In a sense, this is as it should be. The United Nations was founded on the principle of the sovereign equality of unequal sovereignties, and its various assemblies foster an illusion of shared global management operating through parliamentary processes. Their legislative authority is, as we shall see, largely nonexistent; but the parliamentary fiction, with its resolutions and negotiating formulas, sustains a shadow play in which real shapes are distorted and myths take on a life of their own.

The politics of illusion operates at many levels. First, and most obviously, it affects the kinds of discussion that can take place in UN forums. When what governments say bears only the most tenuous relation to their intentions or capacity to act, what passes for debate is bound to acquire a considerable artificiality. And the rituals attaching to the primacy of sovereign equality come seriously to inhibit any government tempted to put substance before form.

Second, it has contributed to the marginalization of the United Nations by generating an "international community" that represents neither the actual balances of political and economic power, nor even the distribution of the world's populations. African states, which together contain just over a third of China's population, have over fifty votes to China's one. The resort to alternative clubs by the UN's more powerful nations has, ironically, merely confirmed the sanctity of the one-nation, one-vote principle for the dozens of newly independent states created in the postwar wave of decolonization. The less "real business" there is to transact, the more important the shadow play becomes: At least it has the merit of projecting onto a global stage the essential myth of sovereign dignity and autonomy.

Third, it occasionally provides governments with the fictions they need to extricate themselves from military confrontation. This use of the politics of illusion is widely viewed as justification, in itself, for the UN's existence. But since 1945, many of the bitterest conflicts have been at least partly civil wars; and here the UN is inhibited by the doctrine, solemnly laid down in its Charter, of nonintervention in the internal affairs of states. It can be overridden by a Security Council decision, assented to by the five veto powers, that international security is threatened. But ever since the Congo operation of the early 1960s exposed the necessarily interventionist character of collective enforcement operations, the existence of the doctrine has created an immense gap between the UN's theoretical and its actual capacity to promote the peaceful settlement of disputes. The "humanitarian" interventions of the early 1990s in northern Iraq, Somalia and former Yugoslavia, which will be discussed in Chapter 12, may mark a fresh departure. But in different ways, each of these operations underlined the constraints on the UN when the parties to a conflict withold their cooperation.

Similar contradictions have eroded the UN's performance in the protection of human rights, singled out as a major UN aim at the founding San Francisco conference in 1945. It is in this area that the politics of illusion most appears as the politics of deception, and the original concept of universality is most thrown into doubt. Finally, the rhetoric employed by governments creates the impression that they control the machinery of the UN secretariats. This too is an illusion: in most UN agencies, the governing bodies—whether executive boards or conferences of the whole membership—have proved incapable of setting strategy. The halls of international discourse serve not for policymaking but as platforms for a kind of declaratory politics. The UN has often been called the "mirror of mankind." Leaving aside the question whether, in a democratic world, gatherings of governments can provide a less than wholly accurate reflection, the image completely misrepresents the actual conduct of governments in UN forums, and the distinguishing characteristics of the rhetoric they employ, there as nowhere else.

Looking back on his time as British ambassador to the UN, Sir Anthony Parsons recalls the moment, early in October, when the heads of state have departed and the UN General Assembly settles into ten weeks or more of speeches, resolutions, and committees to deal with the nearly 200 items on its agenda.[1] "In the debating chambers, a dense pall of stupefying boredom settles over the proceedings," as each day some forty speakers follow one another to the rostrum to speak on the same subject, and "the audience declines in numbers and morale" until by evening "only a sparse scattering" of delegates remains. Plenary debates, in particular, proceed in almost deserted auditoria—for the very good reason that, far from representing opportunities for "world opinion" to coalesce as states exert influence on one another, they are in no sense debates. When their sense of sovereign dignity compels more than 180 speakers to take the microphone, it could hardly be otherwise. The set speaking order, moreover, is fixed by the secretariats and can be disturbed only for a right of reply. This means that on the rare occasion when a speech actually reflects something said by somebody else, it is likely to be distanced from the earlier intervention by anything from days to weeks.

The leaden pall that hangs over these *pro forma* utterances is intensified by the fact that 10–20 percent of a typical speech will be spent congratulating the president of the conference on his brilliant election (in practice, uncontested, since the vote rotates by region on the principle of Buggin's turn, and relations with the organization's chief executive help determine which individual is preselected), and around half devoted to painting a flattering portrait of his nation's achievements. Most of the rest will rehearse issues that are being "debated" in identical language by the UN's seven committees or, in the case of the agencies' general conferences, by the commissions into which they generally subdivide.

"Behind the scenes," Parsons records, "there is vigorous lobbying as delegations bargain for their pet resolutions," which in the closing days will be brought to a comparatively animated plenary for ceremonial reiteration, and endorsement either by vote or by "consensus"—a procedure presented by its advocates as the acme of constructive compromise but recognized by most participants as a ruse for disguising unbridgeable disagreement.

These resolutions—thousands are passed in any one year—are the real "business" of UN conferences, and the object of intense activity. Small "representative groups" will meet, for weeks and often through long nights, to negotiate—with pauses to consult their particular geographical constituencies—texts of quite stunning opacity. By the time the last comma and all the preambular "considering," "deploring," or "noting" paragraphs are in place, the resolution is likely to have been deprived not only of much of its original purpose but also, particularly if "consensus" has been sought, of all real meaning. At this point, it is ready for adoption by the entire membership in plenary session.

Resolutions are the lifeblood that nourishes the central illusion that, through its parliamentary procedures, the UN exercises legislative authority. Like the speeches in plenary, they influence member states only rarely and cannot in any case bind them. Nor, in practice, are they instruments of government, even when specifically addressed to an organization's programs. Most such resolutions are drafted by the secretariats to provide formal sanction for activities of their own devising, and they are adept at manipulating negotiations over resolutions that threaten to constrain them, ensuring that the final version is so watered down that its impact on the organization's activities is negligible. (Even at the UN in New York, where the fiction of member states' control is most energetically sustained and the secretariat insists that all its activities spring from the directives of the Assembly, the secretariat has such latitude either to bury a proposal in a working group or to press energetically ahead that its discretion is almost total in practice.) Almost nobody outside the conference in question, and not everybody inside, will read the resolution.

Translated at considerable expense into the UN's six official languages, many of these texts then achieve virtually eternal life as a preambular reference to almost identical resolutions that will be equally minutely negotiated at subsequent conferences. A handful, cited by secretariats when it suits them, and by member states wishing to demonstrate the utter impossibility of new approaches to a particular topic, will be given a more substantial airing. The sheer number of resolutions witnesses to the psychological need of diplomats to show results for the weeks they spend closeted together. But the fervor that goes into their negotiation has a more serious justification. Resolutions bind nobody, but like the Chinese water torture, they slowly penetrate the collective skull, promoting (or, all too often, obstructing) a common approach to a particular question and effecting a slow mutation in the terms in which it is discussed. They can nudge governments toward accepting a convention outlawing torture—or toward bestowing international respectability on the equating of Zionism with racism, or the free flow of information with Western domination. Such mutations matter.

In "Waffle, but Still Worthwhile?" Parsons acknowledged that "to the uninitiated, this maelstrom of spoken and written words may well appear to be a grievous waste of time, money, and effort" (which is how it also appears to many of the initiated). But his final verdict was positive for three reasons. First (a consideration that applies to New York, but not to the UN's other gatherings), because "the General Assembly provides a unique meeting place for world leaders," enabling foreign secretaries to cram in bilateral chats with allies and meetings with ministers that might be politically awkward to arrange on each other's territory. Second, because "all major powers obliged to conduct global foreign policies are forced . . . to examine annually every single one of their policies and to restate them in public," an exercise that he thought not only "a valuable discipline for foreign offices" but an opportunity for governments to measure the international acceptability of their policies. Third—and again, the argument applies principally although not exclusively to New York—because such assemblies serve to remind governments what kinds of behavior, whether military adventures abroad or repression of their citizens at home, exceed the tolerable, and produce "a long term climatic effect on governments' attitudes towards themselves and others."

It is not self-evident that the first function, generally met in the first ten days to three weeks, requires an annual UN General Assembly of around three months, plus supplementary sessions, or that major powers do in fact go through the meticulous self-scrutiny Parsons describes or discuss their conclusions with any great candor. As for the salutary procedures of collective shaming, they are counterbalanced by the shamelessness with which politicians denounce in scapegoat governments—a cast of villains that has remained remarkably constant over the years and is led by Israel, South Africa, and, of course, the United States—actions that they match or exceed at home. But even leaving aside some of the questions raised by Parsons's comfortable conclusion, it is a statement of faith in the UN's potential rather than its actual value.

There is a rich tradition of fatuity in all parliamentary rhetoric: the U.S. Senate is one of its finer exponents. But the remorseless addiction to grandiose fictions displayed by diplomats and politicians at UN gatherings is still in a special class. The fatuity, in functioning national parliaments, is moreover largely confined to the debating stage: at the point of legislation, precision takes over. In the UN's world of pseudodecisions, by contrast, the all-consuming air of unreality that characterizes the speeches attains its apogee in the resolutions. In the search for "consensus," language is frequently contorted to disguise the fact that no genuine discussion has taken place or that no agreement has been reached. Such fictions do indeed induce "a long term climatic effect on governments' attitudes towards themselves and others"—but not in the sense that Parsons found so encouraging.

What Maurice Bertrand has called "the artificial climate of theoretical idealism"[2] manifests itself all too frequently in sheer escapism. Analyzing the 1980 General Conference of UNESCO in Belgrade, Pierre de Senarclens, who was at the time director of its already controversial human rights division, remarked on the almost perfect inverse correlation between the "abstract, moralistic and rhetorical" quality of a speaker's discourse and the "repressive political system and conflict-ridden national environment" in the country that he represented. Senarclens cited as an example the Lebanese delegate, his country then gripped by a singularly vicious civil war, holding it up to international delectation as

> a mixture of civilizations, of cultures, of religions, of sects united to form a single nation . . . a country which constitutes a unique example of a place where

> the civilizations of east and west join . . . giving to the world torn by conflicts and rivalries an admirable example of coexistence . . . this example, this Lebanon, this object of beauty, illuminated by the hopes of the human race.

It manifests itself, too, in hypocrisy. By 1980, Western governments were fully aware of the damage inflicted by confrontational policies and aberrant management of UNESCO's then director-general, Amadou Mahtar M'Bow. Yet when M'Bow was unanimously reelected at the Belgrade conference, an entire day was set aside at considerable expense to permit member states to offer their congratulations. And Western governments—prominent among them the United States, which had halfheartedly sounded out allies on the possibility of finding an alternative but given up on finding that there was no stomach for the fight—fell over one another to pour forth eulogies rivaling the almost mystical effusions of M'Bow's African brothers. It was open to them to vote against his reelection; it was open to them at least to say nothing.

Finally, it manifests itself in an assault on the values that the United Nations was intended to uphold. President Sekou Touré of Guinea, whose bloodthirsty repression of political dissent and contempt for human rights had forced a mass exodus by those of Guinea's educated elite lucky enough to escape murder, was welcomed to that same general conference by M'Bow with these words:

> Your people, inspired by your example, learned to clear the paths towards the future with their own hands. In this way the most profound aspirations of your people towards liberty and justice were gradually expressed in your policy and you yourself became the living symbol of their renewed pride.[3]

Hypocrisy on his part, or genuine admiration?

It is a world that Lewis Carroll would have appreciated. Some of the games are played with a certain effrontery. A delegate from a country whose deliberate policy is to deny women education, or the basic right to own property, incur debt, or inherit wealth, will be inspired by the world of the global forum to plead most eloquently for an ambitious program for the advancement of women, to which he will declare his head of state to be singlemindedly dedicated. And not only will he plead for it—he will get it drafted in the most grandiloquent terms and world-circling scope, with a few thousand dollars attached to it (and some of that quite possibly earmarked to provide a secretariat job for one of his countrymen).

This routinization of the unreal permeates UN forums, creating peculiar standards of decorum, lapses from which are rare, and ill received. In 1985, for example, it was considered grossly inappropriate of Eugene Whelan, a former agriculture minister of Canada, to use the platform that was his as president of the World Food Council to state that Africa's second famine in a decade meant that "we have failed." Cutting through the collective hypocrisy is difficult. The diplomat who insists in private, walking one of the endless corridors with which all UN conference centers are graced, that he or she wishes for nothing so much as to see a perennial bone of irreducible contention excised from the overloaded agenda, or an obviously unproductive program canceled, will rise in public to denounce in passionate terms proposals calculated to produce such a result.

After exposure to a certain number of such conferences, the familiar justification that these gatherings are an accurate reflection of a troubled world wears extremely thin.

Far from being its mirror, these unproductive proceedings are a distortion of reality. The image these UN conferences more readily call to mind is that of the halls of mirrors in amusement parks, in which thin men become fat, short men become tall, and gestures are gracelessly exaggerated.

The consequences of this phenomenon, to those outside the charmed circle, are obvious. Even if these forums do not reflect the political will of member states—whose representatives, outside them, behave with a far finer sense of the reciprocity between obligations and benefits and a distinctly keener appreciation of the realities of economic and political power—they certainly *affect* political will. In 1987, a senior official in the U.S. administration attempted to explain why the United States had not used the exceptional attention that its withholding of American dues had temporarily assured for its views, in order to progress beyond its largely negative demands for "reform." His assessment revealed a pessimism that is widely shared but rarely articulated in public. "The problem with a positive agenda is that you can never tell in the UN what will come out at the other end. The best proposal can have disastrous results. The environment is not yet good enough to take major initiatives."

This pessimism has four related sources: a lack of confidence in the secretariats (the focus of repeated calls for reform); a growing awareness that the UN's hundred or so legally separate entities are not a "system" and that nothing sensible can be achieved by attempting to treat them as such; a sense that to commit imaginative effort to a world of pseudosolutions and illusionist politics is to empty good ideas of any force or authority; and a suspicion that the "politicization" of the forums—the insertion of divisive and irrelevant considerations into discussions of primary health care, women's advancement, and so forth—is so bound up with the political and organizational contradictions of the UN that it cannot be dismissed as a waning legacy of the 1970s, "the silly season of postcolonial Third World hubris."[4]

If the first two factors present formidable obstacles to reform, the political contradictions tempt even the most convinced multilateralist to seek other avenues for cooperation. The folk memory of weeks wasted trying to get rid of a single small subcommittee or evidently ineffective activity is further burdened by recollections of speeches dedicated not to the result but to the primacy of the ritual.

THE IMPACT OF NEW STATES

The artificiality of these rituals is intimately connected with the growing heterogeneity of the UN's membership. The number of states more than trebled between 1945 and 1990, when the break up of the Soviet empire added more than twenty almost overnight. Both the League of Nations and the United Nations were in some respects created in revolt against the elitism of the nineteenth-century European concept of a "concert" of sovereign states, but they also reflected their "concert" pedigree by assuming a working level of comparability between the members of the successor organizations. The challenge confronting the architects of both organizations was—as was well understood at the time—"to make the transition from the directorate of the Great Powers to an international system in which the smaller states could have an active voice without frightening away the Powers or affronting the formal principle of state equality."[5]

This, as the drafters of the collective security provisions of the UN Charter recognized, required some device such as the five-power veto to redress the balance between the realities of power and the artificialities of sovereign equality. Otherwise, the universal forums would become sideshows, as decisions that mattered came once again to be taken in closed circles by the major powers. The Charter, in addition, required members to be "able and willing" to carry out the obligations it imposed, including that of contributing to collective defence.

The question of what constituted an effective "sovereign state" had troubled the League of Nations. It rejected Liechtenstein's application for membership on the ground that it had "chosen to depute" some of the attributes of sovereignty, but accepted Luxembourg's. More generally, and with paralyzing effect, it sought to balance the requirements of its least and most powerful members by establishing the rule of unanimity.[6] The United Nations, on the other hand, operated, outside the collective security field, on the basis of majority vote. In addition, it responded to the post-colonial explosion of new states by effectively abandoning all standards of qualification for membership. The Soviet-sponsored United Nations resolution 1514 of 1960, which came to be known as the Anti-Colonialist Charter, jettisoned the traditional criteria of statehood—a functioning government, the capacity to enter into relations with other states, a clearly defined territory, permanent population and the capacity to support it—forthrightly declaring that "inadequacy of political, economic, social or educational preparedness should never serve as a pretext for delaying independence." A newly independent state's application for UN membership was referred to the Security Council where, in theory, it was subject to the five-power veto. In practice, this safeguard came to be considered politically unrealistic. The Security Council's Standing Committee on Admissions was, at its most active, no more than a rubber stamp. The obdurate opposition of the United States excluded the People's Republic of China from membership until 1971, but the UN never failed to admit a single applicant—not even Tuvalu, with its 7,000 inhabitants—on the grounds that it could not carry out the Charter's obligations.

By the 1980s, the Balkanization of the former colonial empires had swollen the membership of the United Nations Organization to 159; some agencies had even larger memberships. A quarter of the UN's member states by now numbered fewer than a million inhabitants; few had all or even many of the attributes of the nation-state in the nineteenth-century meaning of the term. A further fifteen tiny entities still figured as states-in-waiting on the list of the UN decolonization committee in New York. The question was whether such a body could lay claim to functioning as an association based on parity between its members—whether it could claim to be an "international community."

Differences in size, wealth, population, and political and social experience are not insuperable barriers to association. But there may be a question of degree. By the mid-1980s even committed internationalists were prepared to argue that the UN's heterogeneity had exceeded the limits of the possible. It linked:

> super-sovereign or suzerain states at one end of the political spectrum whose dominance in large areas adjacent to their borders effectively cancels the sovereignty of a dozen or so supposedly independent members of the UN . . . micro-states . . . most of them impecunious, unstable and in no position to defend themselves against external enemies or internal mafias . . . states, in Africa for example, which lack the coherence to function as states, and yet others, in the Middle East for example, whose leaders equate statesmanship

> with gangsterism. A world which comprises suzerain states and micro-states, anarchic states and gangster states, is not a community of any kind, least of all one amenable to the rule of law.[7]

Once a country had been admitted to membership of the UN, the Charter was unambiguous. "The Organization is based on the principle of the sovereign equality of all its members" (Article 18.1) and "each member of the General Assembly shall have one vote" (Article 2.1). In the UN General Assembly, a two-thirds majority was required for "important questions," such as Security Council recommendations for the admission (or suspension) of members, trusteeship questions, or the budget; otherwise, a simple majority sufficed. The pattern was similar in most other UN organizations although there were exceptions. (Weighted voting operated in the International Monetary Fund and the World Bank, and, to differing degrees, in some of the organizations created after the expansion in the UN's membership, notably the UN Industrial Development Organization and the International Fund for Agricultural Development, with its unique group system of Western, OPEC, and Third World oil-importing states.)

The possibility that the proliferation of new states might undermine the UN's viability as forum was raised as early as 1965, following the admission of the Maldives and the Gambia, by U Thant, the then UN secretary-general. He suggested the introduction of associate membership. Four years later (in UN terms, a relatively rapid response) the Security Council appointed a committee of experts that "examined proposals from the United Kingdom and the United States and issued an interim report summarizing these, but then ceased to operate."[8] The British had proposed that what had come to be known as the microstates should voluntarily renounce the right to vote or to stand for election to UN committees, and in return pay only nominal fees. The United States had suggested free associate membership, without vote but with "appropriate rights" in the Security Council and ECOSOC. Both proposals, in the opinion of the UN's Legal Counsel, were difficult to reconcile with Articles 2(1) and 18(1) of the Charter, an objection raised against all subsequent proposals, such as joint membership of groups of island states.

The truth is that the very existence of the UN served to promote what a Senegalese prime minister, Mamadou Dia, once called "micronationalism." However inadequate and apt to collapse in foul weather was the umbrella of collective security it had erected, the UN had taken some of the risks out of statehood. The activities of its trusteeship and decolonization committees encouraged the smallest territorial entities to catch the postcolonial tide. It was through the UN, in effect, that the doctrine of self-determination declared its independence from mundane considerations of functional viability. The best-laid schemes of the departing colonial powers—for federations and other forms of association between new countries whose frontiers had been shaped by "alien rule and historical accident"[9]—collapsed under the pressures of the struggle of these new states to become the nations that many of them manifestly were not.

The fact that by the mid-1980s a simple UN majority could be comfortably assured by the votes of governments representing populations of under five million—even excluding the half-dozen Western states in that category—illustrates the growth of this postwar micronationalism. Many of these states were culturally, linguistically, and ethnically fragmented; some were landlocked, and others spread over scattered island archipelagos; all too many, according to a 1985 study of the problem entitled *Small Is Dangerous*, had "too few financial resources to enable them, ever, to be self-sufficient."[10] And for these flag-and-anthem states, internally weak and vulnerable to foreign intervention, membership in the UN was both a form of insurance, and a vital expression of their national and international legitimacy as equal members of the global community. The UN authenticated and bolstered their claims to statehood.

This new majority affected the development of the United Nations forums in two ways. The first was to change the nature of what the voting majority expected from international organizations. The new national elites, from large countries as well as small, used the UN to bolster their prestige as they set about asserting power in the institutionally weak domestic frameworks of what Gunnar Myrdal once termed "soft states." For them, the precise, practical value of the world of declamatory politics was that it affirmed their legitimacy as rulers, and demonstrated to others the "integrity" of their nation's statehood. Forums intended to encourage governments to cooperate across frontiers, and to relinquish some of their national autonomy for specific purposes, became arenas for the affirmation of nationalism.

Second, the one-state, one-vote principle vested authority in the global forums equally in governments capable of executing decisions, and those that ranged from weak to dysfunctional. It was impossible to take issue with a principle so evidently democratic. But it produced gross distortions: microstates with a combined population of fewer than 90 million could out vote states representing the other 4,900-plus million. And it created the absurd situation in which Western governments providing three-quarters of the UN's regular budgets could be out voted by a two-thirds majority of states that together paid less than 1 percent. However, what mattered more than either size—both Norway and Singapore carry considerable authority within and outside the UN—or wealth was the erosion of the sense of common purpose, which relied on some degree of comparable capacity to participate. Voting democracy took precedence over working democracy, and resolutions became the principal measure of the UN's "output."

The problem was not just that the disparities between, say, India and the Comoros were so great that it was difficult to identify common interests and prosperity. It was the devaluation of the UN and its agencies as places for "harmonizing the actions of nations," as UN conferences were transformed by the new majority into worlds of make-believe. The ringing language of an International Development Strategy, or a resolution calling for general and complete disarmament, or pledges to bring food or health or jobs to all by the year 2000 threw comforting veils over the unworkability of "debate" between so many participants and the paucity of agreed, achievable, specific decisions. Allusions to the "international community" proliferated; the community, like the mirage of a great oasis in the desert, receded. The UN and its agencies became less and less responsive to the needs either of India or of the Comoros.

This was not immediately apparent, although the myth of sovereign equality created difficulties even before the major explosion in the UN's membership. Writing in 1962, Conor Cruise O'Brien observed:

> Those who depict the Assembly as an anarchic collection of small countries, constantly voting down, with vindictive glee, the great responsible powers, are wide of the mark. Most of the small countries have to exercise considerable discretion in the way they vote, because of their ties—very often coercive ties—with this or that great power. Great powers get crushing majorities against them . . . only when they do something [his example was Suez, in 1956] very strange indeed.[11]

But a decade later, the "crushing majorities" were being mustered in favor of proposals, such as the resolution equating Zionism with racism, that were clear candidates for the "very strange" category and bore more than a trace of "vindictive glee."

What was actually significant about this development was that, paradoxically, as their numbers grew, the small states exercised their independence as voters less and less. Great power influence weakened considerably at the UN, but microstates came to exercise, if anything, still more "discretion"—in the service of Third World solidarity. The "tyranny of the majority," of which John Scali, then the U.S. representative to the UN, complained in 1974 after governments representing less than a fifth of global trade and investment voted through a Charter of Economic Rights and Duties of States, tyrannized the majority itself: breaking ranks became unthinkable.

In theory, the new concept of the "South" conferred collective power on the powerless. But it had a strongly negative impact on the *effective* exercise of sovereign equality. As the UN became an arena for bloc politics, the hundred-plus members of the Non-Aligned Movement or the nearly 130-strong Group of 77 into which the developing countries had clustered adopted a shopping-list-plus-solidarity approach in order to arrive at a common negotiating platform. Countries could thus find themselves committed to package resolutions in which certain elements were, quite frequently, inimical to their national interests. The display of national autonomy presented by the formal roll-calls of the UN votes was deceptive: The show was increasingly stage-managed by small groups of diplomats—either the most militant individuals, or diplomats working under instructions from the most militant capitals.

The shopping list approach itself so inflated the range of issues coming to the vote that ministers in Third World capitals, ignorant of the existence of many resolutions and incapable of paying attention to all but a handful of them, increasingly directed their ambassadors to "vote with the Group of 77" throughout a particular conference. The result is that although, in relation to their gross national product, small states spend fortunes on their missions at New York and in Geneva, the missions do not fulfill the function of enabling them to assert their claims to a hearing and to fair treatment under common rules—one of the most important advantages of multilateral diplomacy. Their actual participation in UN debates is rarely commensurate with these outlays. "If you look down from the roof of the UN Development Program in New York," a UN official commented in 1986, "you will see the roof of Uganda House, bristling with the most sophisticated telecommunications equipment. It is difficult to see what purposes it serves, when the Ugandan government is barely able to control its own capital, never mind master the arcana of the Second Committee."[12] What was true of Uganda was even more true of much smaller states.

The combination of equal voting rights with bloc politics—a phenomenon the end of the Cold War has by no means caused to disappear, since that mainly affects the "East–West" dimension—threatens the demise of the global forums as centers for debates on any but the narrowly utilitarian and technical questions dealt with by regulatory agencies. The reiteration of fixed formulas mires the UN in yesterday's agenda. Some of the more absurd manifestations of the politics of illusion—such as the pointless decision in 1988, against which only the United States dissented, to declare the 1990s the International Decade for the Eradication of Colonialism—could be avoided by resorting to secret ballots. But most governments shy away from the thought. Many Western governments, including that of the United States, see the open vote as a means of establishing, as a

British diplomat put it, "what governments which say they are sympathetic, moderate, or even on our side are prepared to do about it." Third World leaders of countries like Algeria or India exploit it as a demonstration of their international "influence." And for the small states, the ritual of the vote reminds the world of their existence. Even when Third World diplomats discreetly urge their Western counterparts to recognize and assist the "silent majority of moderates" attempting to curb the excesses of UN demagoguery, they resist the suggestion that secret ballots would free them from the thralldom of the voting bloc. The game of "showing the world where we stand" is the main stock in trade of UN assemblies. Shadow has become substance.

THE FICTION OF "NONINTERVENTION"

Explanations exist at many levels for the reluctance of governments to break through these ritual barriers and explore the possibilities for establishing better debating mechanisms. The most important may be that, when governments assert that the United Nations is indispensable, they mean it only in the narrowest of political terms. They mean that the UN has to be there for the wholly exceptional case, such as the Cuban missile crisis, when time must be bought and face saved to interrupt the momentum of threat and retaliation. This is the minimalist justification for the UN. It holds that, while the balance of terror between the superpowers may be the primary guarantee against world war, the UN provides a fail-safe mechanism—that it is, in some combination of the mystical and the ultimately practical that T. S. Eliot would have understood, a fragment we have shored against our ruin, a "ritual at the brink."[13]

To characterize this view as "minimalist" is not to deny the importance of this role. It is widely acknowledged that the opportunity offered in 1962 to Khrushchev by the "international community" to cover his losses with dignity may have averted war; and in a case like that, even "may" justifies the UN's existence. There are instances where governments which needed to stop fighting would have found it more difficult to do so without first using the Security Council, as Pakistan did in 1965, to berate their opponents,[14] or without drawing, as did Iran in 1988, on a Security Council resolution. It can be, and often is, argued that to fulfill its purpose as insurance company, the UN does not have to function well. It suffices for it to exist. Even if its broader purposes of fostering cooperation between countries have fallen into desuetude, it can still prize warring states apart.

But this apparently simple function is as fraught with contradictions as the rest. The UN's political paradoxes do not end with the acting out of sovereign equality. Almost equally hallowed is the doctrine that nothing in the Charter "shall authorize the United Nations to intervene in matters which are essentially within the sovereign jurisdiction of any State."[15] The UN's loss of credibility has been closely allied to the evident nonsense of this absolutist separation of "domestic" and "international" concerns. The taboo that customarily rules out of order even discussion of wars, tyrannies, and disasters unless they clearly impact on other states, began to weaken in the 1990s. But it remains the general rule. The UN has begun since the end of the Cold War to intervene in cases where the disintegration of states has led to famine and/or war; but most governments remain extremely reluctant to support UN action against murderous regimes. The "there but for the grace of God" club of delinquent regimes still closes ranks when the myth of absolute sovereignty appears threatened. And this severely limits the UN's practical utility as an insurance company.

It is worth reemphasizing that Chapter VII of the Charter, its enforcement machinery, was the great pride of the drafting teams in the 1940s. It rested on two assumptions: five-power cooperation in a "firefighter's role," and acceptance of the need for collective efforts to "maintain *international* peace and security" (italics added). No one anticipated the conflicts which were to prove typical of the postwar decades—internecine battles, generally in developing countries although fought with the weapons of East and West, and most frequently confined within the frontiers of a given state instead of spilling across frontiers. The degree to which Article 2.7 would inhibit action by the Untied Nations had not been foreseen. The constraints were was demonstrated as early as 1947 by the Indo-Pakistani dispute over Kashmir. At partition, Kashmir, whose Hindu maharajah ruled a population that was 80 percent Moslem, had declined to join either India or Pakistan. But when faced with a revolt near the Pakistan border, supported by Pathan tribesmen from the other side, the maharajah appealed to India to help. At the UN, Pakistan pleaded the principle of self-determination; India, having swiftly got the maharajah to agree to accede to the Indian union, argued that since the ruler had made his decision, the matter was now India's internal affair. With the armies of Pakistan and India now confronting each other, the international threat to the peace was obvious. But by the time these legal arguments had been duly considered by a UN fact-finding mission, and the desirability of a plebiscite agreed, the best the UN found it could do was to establish a cease-fire line and place UN observers along it—observers who were still in position nearly fifty years later. Armed force had won out over self-determination, and the UN had entered in only after the fact, armed not with the majesty of enforcement machinery but with a modest safety net. A full-scale war between India and Pakistan had been averted, but peace had not been brought to Kashmir.

The founders intended to create a balance between sovereign rights and the claims of the individual against the state. The nonintervention clause in the Charter, easily and repeatedly invoked, weights the scales firmly in the favor of the state. Largely because of the incompatibilities between the UN's peacekeeping role and the taboo against intervention, the "ritual at the brink" has become part of the diplomatic armory governments use to avoid taking action in cases of conflict. The test case that determined whether the United Nations could, in the interests of peace, override the taboo was its lengthy military and civilian intervention in the Congo. That operation, more than any other, exposed the contradictions in the Charter and the limits to the power of the United Nations as an *organization* charged with international security. Until the Somalia operation more than thirty years later, this was the nearest the UN came to assuming a supranational role for the purposes of restoring the internal peace of a country, and its lessons were taken by subsequent UN secretaries-general to be profoundly negative.

On the surface, there was little at first about the Congo episode to indicate that the UN's offers of peacekeeping forces would plunge it deep in the country's internal affairs. The crisis began in July 1960 within a few days of the Congo's independence, when part of the army mutinied against white officers. Troops from Belgium, the outgoing colonial power, promptly intervened, claiming to protect the white population, but also and hardly coincidentally taking over Elizabethville, the main city of the richest province, from which Belgium's protégé Moise Tshombe then felt it safe to declare the province's secession as the independent state of Katanga. The young Congolese government, headed by Patrice Lumumba, appealed to the UN; and the Security Council, with masterly vagueness, authorized "such military assistance as may be necessary." The sequence of events seemed simple enough.

It was not, however, as Thomas Franck has pointed out, quite the whole picture: Lumumba's cabinet had appealed not only to the UN, but to Ghana. It had also, critically, asked Washington for military assistance. The UN secretary-general, Dag Hammarskjöld, who had already helped to redraft the Congolese appeal to the UN, was determined to preempt U.S. involvement: he believed that it would both upstage the UN in a vital test for the establishment of its peacekeeping authority and risk a superpower confrontation in Africa. Using his powers under Article 99 of the Charter, he convened the Security Council and presented a plan for an international force to assist the (anarchic) Congolese armed forces, take over law-and-order duties, assure essential supplies to the civilian population, and restore the "integrity" of the Congo. "Of this episode," wrote Franck, "it is fair to say that the Secretary-General essentially wrote the Congolese request, conceived the UN response, convened the Council, prompted the resolution by which he was empowered to act, and helped ensure its adoption."[16] Hammarskjöld thus deliberately plunged the UN, Charter-bound as it was not to intervene in domestic politics or policies, into the mission of defending the integrity of the Congo: a mission that it could not carry out without intervening massively in domestic politics.

Within two months Lumumba—who had raised the specter of superpower involvement for the second time by seeking Russian logistical aid to end the Katangese secession—was overthrown by Colonel Joseph Mobutu. The smooth operation of the coup was facilitated by the fact that Andrew Cordier, Hammarskjöld's representative, had closed the radio station and the airport in the interests of "public order." Lumumba was then "protected" by UN troops in a form of house arrest from which he subsequently escaped, was captured by rival Congolese, and in the conspicuous absence of UN efforts to continue its protective duties, was transported to Katanga and murdered.

The UN was now not only in the business of keeping order in a country four times the size of France and of ending the Katangese secession (tasks that remained unaccomplished when it retreated in 1964). It was in the business of inventing a government. This it had done, by August 1961, in the name of a new prime minister, Cyrille Adoula. It was not exactly a spontaneous outgrowth of national consensus.

> We brought the members of parliament back from all over the country, wherever they had fled into the bush, to their villages. It was not easy; some of them were really afraid; in some cases we used force. And when we had them in Leopoldville, Mahmoud Khiary [a Tunisian member of the UN's core political team] put them in the old university and said: "You're not getting out of here until you choose a government. No beer, no women, no exit." And they didn't believe him, until they looked out of the window and saw the UN troops rolling out the barbed wire. So they produced a list of ministers, and Khiary went through it with a great red pencil and crossed out three or four as Belgian agents. And sent it back, and they came up with some new names, and Congo had a government.[17]

This eyewitness account by a senior UN official hardly squares with Hammarskjöld's description of the UN's role in the Congo as one "of utter discretion and impartiality." It does indicate what kinds of improvisations were required to create a semblance of respect for "national decisions" in a case where there was, at the time, no "nation" to decide. The awkward truth was that had the United Nations's considerable military and civilian forces—the latter amounted to the provision of a shadow civil service to assure education, health, and basic administration—adhered to the letter of nonintervention, it would have made a nonsense of their presence.

From the start to its equally untidy finish, the UN Congo operation was resolutely interventionist. Of its many errors, that was not one of them. Militarily it was, to put it kindly, inconclusive: with the departure of the UN forces in 1964 the Congo immediately erupted again into civil war, and the Stanleyville rebellion was in the end put down with the help of European mercenaries, Belgian paratroopers, and Belgian and U.S. logistical support. But in retrospect, the Congo operation set the pattern for the rest of sub-Saharan Africa in two ways. First, the UN intervention affirmed the primacy of stable boundaries over "national" self-determination. This was an important principle to establish in a continent where colonial boundaries divided nations, and nation-based boundaries could only have replaced colonial ones at the cost of multiple wars and potentially almost infinite political fragmentation. Second, its civilian operation, a virtual, if temporary and benevolent, recolonization, set a precedent for the "ventriloquization" of states on the point of collapse, but also pointed to the wisdom of keeping the process discreet. Internationally, however, by exposing the UN's limits, it also set the pattern of UN peacekeeping efforts for the next three decades along more modest lines, confining them to the interposition of small noncombatant forces with tightly limited mandates between armies that needed an excuse not to fight.

For Conor Cruise O'Brien, who as the UN's representative in Katanga in the opening phase had a ringside seat, the moral of this tale was clear: where the UN was forced to operate in conditions involving force, it was essential to distance the office of the secretary-general from controversy—for example, by appointing an executive officer who reported directly to the Security Council. He had a point. Even had Hammarskjöld not been "killed" fairly early on in the Congo affair—he perished in a mysterious air crash—he could probably not have lasted much longer. The Russians perceived him as personally implicated, and Lumumba's overthrow and death had made them fiercely hostile to Hammarskjöld and to the whole operation. What O'Brien had in mind was not that the UN should not become involved in a country's internal affairs, but that if it did "the spiritual authority of the Secretary-General" should not be weakened by the inevitable resorts to stratagem that would follow.

> The Goddess Athena must not be seen kicking the Eumenides on the shins or feigning ignorance of the whereabouts of Orestes. As the man responsible for a major peace-keeping operation may be forced to perform the equivalents of these actions he can no longer, when he returns to the stage, properly play the part of the Goddess Athena.[18]

The moral that many UN officials drew was that the UN's prestige mattered more than its effectiveness (an odd inversion, since the prestige of most organizations depends on the results they achieve). Hammarskjöld's successors—distinguished, like most of the UN's other chief executives, by a horror of delegating any real authority—were inclined neither to designate independent scapegoat executives nor to surrender the role of goddess. They consequently shied away from controversial initiatives. When the Iran-Iraq War broke out in 1980, Kurt Waldheim understood the dangerous implications of the Security Council's failure to condemn Iraq's aggression. But even when it became clear from his private soundings that governments were not prepared to respond, he made no serious public effort to shame them into displaying the even-handed respect for the rule of law that was indispensable if the UN was to have subsequent standing in the affair. Member states not only acquiesced in such passivity; they were delighted to be let off the hook. They too invoked the preservation of the UN's "prestige" to justify inaction. Even in 1987, when the five permanent members at last began to draft a Security Council resolution to end the Iran-Iraq war, Sir John Thompson, Britain's permanent representative, was privately worried that such an initiative would "damage the UN" if the combatants failed to respond.

If neither conventional international wars like that between Iran and Iraq, nor the open intervention by Libya in Chad's long-running civil war in the 1980s, inspired UN secretaries-general to use their powers under Article 99 of the Charter to mobilize the international community, the far more numerous cases of "internal" war were comfortably submerged within the doctrine of nonintervention. The conflicts in Nigeria, Cambodia, Angola, and Sudan, the violent tyrannies and massacres in Uganda, Ethiopia, and Burundi, which might under a more robust interpretation of the UN's role have been deemed thoroughly destabilizing to regional peace, were allowed to run their course. It was left to the UN High Commissioner for refugees, the International Committee of the Red Cross, and the Oxfams of the world to mitigate their tragic human fallout as best they might. In the legally crystalline case of Indonesia's aggression against East Timor, where international law, rights of self-determination, and gross violations of human rights were all at issue—and where the strategic interests of the great powers, although they existed, were not so acute as to be decisively inhibiting—the United Nations did less than the decently minimal.

The embarrassments and criticisms to which the UN had been exposed in the Congo had left deep scars. Rather than risk accusations that it was acting inconsistently with the Charter by intervening in "internal" conflicts, it was safer to do nothing: there is no recipe against inconsistency like inertia. But inertia, of course, exposed the broadest inconsistency of all: that between talk and action. As debates, in the General Assembly and above all in the Security Council increasingly reflected the prospect that votes would not be followed by action, the moral authority of the UN—its principal strength—was weakened in the eyes of governments and, importantly, of the public. At the UN, governments continued to reiterate the sacred Charter doctrine that armed force should not be used except in the collective interest, and to call for disarmament; but in practice they relied on the tested combination of national armies and military alliances. When, in the late 1980s, progress began to be made toward resolving some of the century's murderous "little" wars, the fictions of a UN role were duly, and in some instances usefully, dusted down; but by then there was no disguising its ancillary nature. Abruptly called upon in the 1990s to reinvent collective security to deal with a host of disparate threats to peace, the UN had neither the machinery nor the force of precedent to steer it. Each improvisation put an untested organization publicly on the line. Illusion had long been a refuge of sorts. But the uses of illusion are limited.

RHETORIC AND RIGHTS

In its commitment to uphold the rights of the individual, the United Nations was, rightly, believed to represent a departure from all previous models of international organization. In no area of its activities has the gap between rhetoric and action inspired greater public disillusion. On paper, the record is not unimpressive: the Universal Declaration of Human Rights of 1948, the two 1966 conventions that codify it, and the elaboration of conventions such as those on asylum, the prevention of statelessness, genocide, and torture are important achievements. The undertakings of the Charter with respect to human rights were bound to encounter obstacles. As Professor Theo van Boven, a former director of the UN Human Rights Center in Geneva, put it in 1984: "It would be unrealistic to assume that forces drawing benefit from the maintenance and continuation of present power structures and power relations would be willing to abandon . . . their privileged position on behalf of the enslaved, the exploited and the underprivileged."[19] The UN was here embarked on the inherently self-contradictory enterprise of setting standards for the behavior of states, while adhering to the principle of nonintervention in their internal affairs. Finessing the contradiction required not only an exceptional moral weight on the part of the standard-setting authority, but time in which to win governments' assent to norms of conduct that would then be codified and universalized.

The legal contradiction between sovereign rights and the principle that states may be held to account for their treatment of their citizens is not insuperable. The key precedent was set in the nineteenth century, when the Great Powers reached agreement on the abolition of slavery. Where the rights of workers to freedom of assembly and tolerable working conditions was concerned, the International Labor Office (ILO) made considerable headway between the wars. The effectiveness of ILO conventions has, of course, always been uneven—in the 1990s, China's *laogai* system of forced "reeducation through labor" is as great an affront to basic human rights as were the gulags Stalin established in the 1930s. And the ILO has itself diluted the impact of its conventions by multiplying their number—a manifestion of the UN disease of inflationary rhetoric that puts promulgation before enforcement. But the ILO has the advantage of a tripartite membership: joint "peer groups" of governments, employers, and representatives of organized labor vet observance of its conventions. It thus avoids the serious, structural contradiction that has blighted the human rights performance of the rest of the UN machinery. This is that meetings of United Nations organizations are gatherings of "we, the peoples" only in the most ruthlessly collectivist sense.

The constitutions of the UN and the specialized agencies are fine expressions of liberal ideals and benign purposes centered on individual rights. They assume a common concern for the "four essential human freedoms . . . of speech and expression . . . worship . . . freedom from want . . . freedom from fear," enunciated by Roosevelt.[20] But the guardianship of these rights (the equal status of which is in any case disputed) has been assigned to governments—which lead the way in violating them. This paradox, inherent in the UN's structure, became steadily more relevant to its loss of moral authority as more and more governments came to swell its ranks whose claims to represent and to be accountable to their citizens ranged from the questionable to the absurd.

International assessment of the way governments treat their people is a radically subversive departure from historical concepts of international "order," which had assumed that what governments did within their borders was their own affair. Sovereignty is threatened by the notion that citizens have claims against the state and the right to invoke universal norms and conventions in pursuit of them. The UN Charter was not without its ambiguities on this score. Article 56 pledges all member governments "to take joint and separate action in cooperation with the Organization" to promote the social and economic well-being of their citizens and "universal respect for, and observance of, human rights." But the linked preceding article sets these aims and actions in the context of "peaceful and friendly relations among nations based on respect for the principle of equal rights and self-determination"—a consideration that gently restores sovereignty to its pedestal. Not surprisingly, governments that become the object of attention take the international inspection of their record to be highly detrimental to "peaceful and friendly relations among nations."

Given the sensitivity of the most improbable regimes to public opprobrium, human rights ought however to have been an area in which the reduction of UN debates to largely descriptive and declamatory exchanges inflicted only limited damage. The reluctance of states publicly to repudiate widely accepted standards of conduct, even if they routinely violate them, made it possible to draw up the Universal Declaration of Human Rights in 1948, and enabled it to acquire, over the following decades, the force of international customary law. By 1966 its essential provisions had been incorporated into two covenants, one on political, the other on economic and social rights. On these cornerstones were built an array of covenants and declarations: on racial discrimination, apartheid, torture, and genocide, the rights of women; and, more controversially, because closer to a concept of group rights as distinct from individual rights, of children and minorities. The formal international machinery to monitor compliance kept pace: the UN's Human Rights Commission and its cumbersomely named Subcommission on the Prevention of Discrimination and Protection of Minorities (important because it had powers to consider complaints brought by individuals as well as states) were joined by two committees of independent jurists. To these, parties to the 1966 covenants were required to submit periodic reports on their performance—reports on which the committee could then decide to hold public hearings. The Third Committee of the UN gave human-rights questions a routine annual airing.

All this constituted progress, however limited. But it was progress increasingly marred by what could kindly be called double standards in debate, and by an increasing tendency to concentrate on the elaboration of new rights while putting relatively little effort into pressing states to respect their existing engagements. Veterans of international human-rights negotiations have been too ready to assume that while the UN could light a torch in the darkness, it would be foolhardy to flash it around too aggressively. This would, after all, in the words of one country's leading international law expert, imply "getting governments to agree to powers and institutions of which they would be afraid."[21] Progress has in other words been thought to be sustainable provided there are no serious sanctions and the UN's member states can be confident that they will only be called to account verbally. Even to this, the secretariat itself set limits: Van Boven himself was dismissed by Pérez de Cuéllar for his excessive candor in naming offending governments. Between the democratic minority's reluctance to name offenders, and the majority's efforts to hijack agendas for political purposes such as attacking Israel or the United States, the United Nation's claim to provide a civilizing and protective bulwark against oppression was gradually eroded through the 1970s and 1980s.

Veterans of the UN's human rights debates, whether from the secretariat, diplomatic missions, or even human rights bodies that view them as the only means of pressuring governments directly, tend to dwell on the progress—and to accept that some degree of double standard is inevitable in intergovernmental bodies. Outsiders tend to note the extent to which governments continue to get away, quite literally, with murder and to conclude, in William Buckley's extreme formulation, that "the United Nations is the most concentrated assault on moral reality in the history of free institutions, and it does not do to ignore that fact, or, worse, to get used to it."[22] William Scranton was more diplomatic, but scarcely less pessimistic when in 1976 he told the Third Committee—which he was one of the few heads of mission to bother to attend on a regular basis—that "today the only universality one can honestly associate with the Universal Declaration of Human Rights is universality of lip service." He charged the UN with being "long on declarations and so short on implementation," spending "so much energy recognizing rights and so little providing remedies for the wronged." Compliance with human rights standards, he said, was measured "by vote-gathering ability," and "justice delayed, as it is by slow and easily obstructed United Nations procedures, becomes mass murder condoned."[23]

Occasionally, the reproach is brought home by the victims. In the 1980s, President Corazon Aquino of the Philippines and President Yoweri Museveni of Uganda came to the General Assembly to castigate the UN's members for abandoning their peoples to injustice and murder—actions that were considered by many of their Third World colleagues to have been needlessly "divisive," almost verging on bad manners. Even Western governments have subordinated "the peoples" to *raison d'état*. A French foreign minister, Claude Cheysson, once famously asserted that French denunciations of human rights violations were "general, universal and indiscriminate," but the citizens of Gabon and a number of other Francophone African dictatorships would have considered him parsimonious with the truth. Richard Schifter, President Reagan's envoy to the Human Rights Commission (speaking, he emphasized, as a private citizen), put it frankly:

> We have not made a major issue of the human rights record of the People's Republic of China, not during the Carter years and not since . . . not for lack of sympathy for the brave souls who came forward a few years ago to put posters on Democracy Wall but because we did not think it was in our national interest to speak up. Nor have we made a major public issue of the status of women in Saudi Arabia. . . . It is a perfectly understandable and wholly defensible aspect of our conduct of foreign policy.[24]

Perhaps. And there is also a natural tendency to single out "soft" targets where pressure will have a visible effect: Mexico is a softer touch than, say, Syria. But it puts the United States in a poor position to argue against the double standards of other, less powerful states. When President Reagan gave President Sésé Séko Mobutu an elaborately chalorous welcome at the White House, as loyal ally (and head of a state richly endowed with strategic minerals), the United States proclaimed in effect that the suppression of dissent and imprisonment of political opponents, for which it was rightly attacking Cuba at the Human Rights Commission, were of less consequence in Zaire. Cheysson's boasts invite a wry response, when set against François Mitterrand's reception of Sekou Touré (or Valéry Giscard d'Estaing's long friendship with Emperor Jean Bédel Bokassa, even if revelations of a massacre of schoolchildren did finally prompt the French to display their customary efficiency in removing him). Great Britain's welcome for Kenya's Daniel Arap Moi, at a time when his tampering with the constitution, abolition of the secret ballot, and imprisonment of critics were drawing worldwide protest and warnings of "a danger of totalitarianism" from Kenya's Roman

Catholic bishops, emboldened him to return to Nairobi and dismiss press reports as "dirty words" and detainees as "pigs."[25] And the flabbiness of British policy was shown up a few years later, when Western donors finally suspended aid to Kenya and Moi reluctantly agreed to legalize oppposition parties and hold an election. When Western leaders contend that quiet persuasion is the best recipe for "friends," it carries little conviction: they are taken, generally correctly, to mean that with this particular country, they have bigger fish to fry.

To such "realism" in the conduct of foreign policy, the UN ought to be a counterweight. Exposing as they do the venality of governments and the cowardice of bureaucrats, human rights issues are rightly perceived by ordinary people as touchstones of their faith in the UN—precisely *because* they reflect the central paradox of its creation. The United Nations, a global forum of states, exists to modify the behavior of those same states. Progress over human rights is thus a key measure of the extent to which the UN is fulfilling the purpose for which it was created.

Formally, respect for human rights law and its corresponding machinery has held up remarkably well. By the mid-1980s, only Iran had openly repudiated the Universal Declaration and its covenants—telling the UN's Third Committee in 1984 that they were products of the "secular understanding of the Judaeo-Christian tradition" and had "no validity" in the Islamic republic.[26] (This denunciation, which must be taken at face value, also provided a convenient pretext for Iran's refusal to admit a UN human rights investigator into the country. And it was followed in 1989 by one of the most remarkable *international* violations of human rights and respect for law committed by any country since 1945: Ayatollah Khomeini's *fatwa* against the author Salman Rushdie—an incitement to murder the citizen of a foreign state solely because of the contents of a novel he had written.)

In practice, the record has been less impressive. Scott Sullivan, commenting for *Newsweek* on the Human Rights Commission's thirty-ninth session in 1983, registered the shock which commonly afflicts outsiders at such meetings:

> Most discussion dwells on only three subjects: Israel and the Palestinians, the Pinochet government in Chile and the sins of "colonial and racist regimes in southern Africa." Western delegates are proud of slipping resolutions on Iran, Poland, Cambodia and Afghanistan into the record. . . . The entire first two weeks of the current six-week annual session were set aside for Middle Eastern and southern African issues. A Western initiative on religious freedom was allotted a half day and another on abuse of psychiatric detention one day. . . . The annual spectacle of its partial, partisan debates must be repugnant to any serious advocate of human rights and dignity.[27]

Alexander Solzhenitsyn, reacting similarly, characterized the UN in his Nobel address as a place where the peoples of the world were delivered up to the designs of governments. And Ben Whitaker, after years spent on the UN subcommission, had this to say:

> In no part of the UN's work is reform more overdue. . . . Widening public knowledge of abuses will no longer tolerate double standards, politically selective hypocrisy, and stonewalling by cynical tactical alliances. The most

> urgent necessity, for the sake of the UN's credibility as well as for the victims, is to give some practical reality and meaning to the ever-growing rhetoric of covenants and declarations.[28]

The lead of the secretary-general, Whitaker concluded, was awaited. That was in 1983. Three years later, the secretary-general abolished a meeting of the subcommission—the nearest thing to a hair shirt tolerated in the UN—as one of his first measures to cut the UN budget.

By the 1980s, however, the entire theoretical underpinning of the Charter and the Universal Declaration had come under sustained attack from the voting majority. The new challenge went far beyond the question of double standards. In the context of Third World demands for new economic and communications orders in the 1970s, a formidable trend developed, away from individual rights and toward collective rights. What had hitherto been thought to be the moral consensus of the UN collapsed. Rights to peace, to development, to sovereignty over natural resources—the "new rights of solidarity"—could be and were advanced in the context of social justice (and were supported in that spirit by some Western liberals). But their essence was to involve the state as spokesman and incarnation of "peoples's rights" and to attack the Western emphasis on democratic liberties as at best outmoded, but more generally as an irrelevance or even as a tool in its conspiracy to perpetuate global inequality. The collectivist revolt is encapsulated in Resolution 32/130 of the 1977 General Assembly:

> The international community should accord . . . priority to the . . . mass and flagrant violations of human rights of peoples and persons affected by situations such as those resulting from apartheid, from all forms of racial discrimination, from colonialism, from foreign domination and occupation, from aggression and threats against national sovereignty, national unity and territorial integrity, as well as from the refusal to recognize the fundamental rights of peoples to self-determination and of every nation to the exercise of full sovereignty over its wealth and natural resources.[29]

More will be said in Chapter 4 about the implications of the "new rights." What matters here is that their enunciation, by governments most of whose domestic arrangements are models neither of social equality and economic opportunity, nor of civil liberty, and whose common denominator is their leaders' reluctance to relinquish power voluntarily, lent a decidedly Orwellian tone to the United Nations—and diverted attention from areas on which there might be agreement to those in which no compromise was possible. They served to unite artificial groups; they also served to alienate Western governments. By putting in question the liberal assumptions of the Charter, they threw into particularly sharp relief questions about the "plausibility" of universal organization. Above all, they flaunted the primacy of the state. To the governments that advocated them, the essential virtues of collective human rights were, first, that they diverted attention from the violation of individual rights and, second, that they justified the assimilation of human rights to sovereign power.

The collectivization of human rights was a natural outgrowth of the illusion, fostered by UN resolutions committing "the international community" to evermore ambitious goals, that governments controlled far more of human endeavor than they did, could, or should. It could, of course, be argued that it would be a still greater fallacy to suppose that the UN organizations, which are governmental in membership and work through governments, could develop an international language predicated on anything other than state power. Governments make the laws and set the policy frameworks within which societies operate, so where is the illusion? But that would, also, be to argue that there can be no such thing, internationally, as the rule of law.

ILLUSIONS OF CONTROL

The UN's halls of mirrors not only distort the conduct and international status of states: They reflect them back upon themselves, giving them a wholly exaggerated idea of the impression their debates and resolutions make not just on the outside world, but on the UN's own machinery. Governments behave as though the UN secretariats were neutral entities, existing to carry out their will, and the secretariats naturally encourage the illusion. Behind the looking glass, the machine functions by the simple method of putting words into the mouths of member states and adapting their meaning to its purposes. Governments lost in the filaments of their own negotiating bodies are ill positioned to control the labyrinthine secretariats: the bureaucrats are infinitely better equipped to set the terms of the argument. Major donor governments complain that the one-state, one-vote principle subjects them to a form of taxation without representation; but in practice neither minority nor majority controls the machine or knows in other than vague terms what is there to be controlled. Institutions shape debate, not vice versa.

The illusion of all-permeating, all-powerful government, of which the UN is both principal advocate and first victim, takes it into realms of political and economic unreality in which the hubris of governments nicely complements, and serves, the empire-building ambitions of the secretariats. Ironically, the assumptions about the proper range and scope of government involvement in economic activity and social engineering fostered in the UN have become more ambitious as the majority of its member states have found it increasingly difficult, at home, to master the techniques of sustainable economic development and to assimilate technological change. A steady verbal and conceptual inflation, afflicting all but a handful of UN agencies, has led to the definition of tasks in terms that greatly exaggerate governments' actual commitment to cooperation or joint management, and to programs that suffer from conceptual elephantiasis and fiscal starvation.

It is one thing to agree to regulate air traffic, and quite another to seek a universally acceptable definition of the "responsibilities of the artist," or of "youth." Grandiloquent statements of commitment may mask "divergent views on how even agreed common interests are best pursued in an international and multilateral context."[30] One effect of the expansion of the UN's membership and activities is that distinctions between paper targets and what is possible have become blurred. An example is the relatively modest concept of a "development decade." The first decade was conceived in the early 1960s as a set of relatively modest proposals for cooperation; the second and third "decades" that followed inflated the enterprise, producing international development strategies that were essentially declamatory, and grounded in North-South confrontation.

The cumulative effect of this combination of international *dirigisme* and rhetorical overkill has been disastrous. Bertrand's report in 1985 for the Joint Inspection Unit commented that "the world-wide scale of all these undertakings; the gulf between the ambitions and the means; the lack of a transmission belt between the offices at headquarters and the responsible national services within each country; the inability to define modest objectives within the stated time-limits, raise doubts whether in the long run most of the activities have any connection with reality."[31] The reference was to the UN's "field programs" of technical assistance, but the strictures have wider application.

The irony of this looking-glass world is that as public faith in the competence of governments as economic and social managers declines, and as governments individually accept the limitations of centralized planning and state ownership, at the UN these same governments still combat any effort to modify its programs to take account of these realities.

One reason is that when it comes to rendering UN institutions more responsive to the concerns of those in whose interests they were designed—people as well as governments—even governments committed to reform will be deterred by two important factors. The first is that policy control has become a myth. Agendas are prepared by the secretariats and modified only marginally by governmental delegations. When resolutions have any real bearing on programs of work, the secretariats have generally drafted them with a view to ensuring that "governing bodies" disturb their activities or working methods as little as possible. In attempting to assert control, moreover, governments have multiplied their handicaps by adding almost obsessively to the number of committees. When in 1987 an intergovernmental commission was created in New York to try to streamline the governance of the UN Organization, its opening meeting established that no member knew how many intergovernmental committees there were. The secretariat, asked for enlightenment, could only say that the number lay between 110 and 200.

The more crowded the agenda, moreover, the harder it is to identify the scope for reforms. Member states can be counted on to add to a conference's workload by introducing procedural wrangles and hardy political perennials. Some secretariats, such as the FAO's, have become masters of the art of drafting contentious resolutions calculated to derail debates. In this sense, powerful and powerless states are equally caught in a charade; safely imprisoned in the square-bracketed subparagraphs of disputed resolutions, they have neither time nor negotiating opportunities to look at the grand design.

The second is that the disparities between the UN's members, in organizations that stress sovereign equality, have made of that principle almost an end in itself. Detached from the realities of political and economic power, juridical equality becomes the enemy of purpose. Here political paralysis compounds organizational defects: The less governments believe in the workability of the forums, and the less they value the UN's activities, the less energy they are inclined to give to clearing the great thickets of frozen resolutions and obsolete or irrelevant programs, in order to identify areas in which the UN organizations might have comparative advantages over other forms of intergovernmental cooperation.

Experiments have not been encouraging. In 1984, for example, the Scandinavians proposed a streamlining of UNESCO. The idea was that it should cut its activities back and focus on tasks where a universal approach was essential and intergovernmental agreement a precondition for success, and where it had a good track record or a genuine prospect of making an impact. Under the financial pressure caused by U.S. withdrawal, the majority "conceded" these principles—and continued to argue that every fragment of UNESCO's hopelessly dispersed and undisciplined program fell within the guidelines.

UNESCO's undertakings, from its lofty "reflection on world problems and future-oriented studies" to its "study of the problems of armaments and their consequences in UNESCO's fields of competence" and its promotion of government policies for "interpersonal communication" retained, even under acute crisis, their grand *dirigiste* sweep. And when M'Bow's successor, Federico Mayor, claimed in 1990 to have refocused UNESCO, the medium-term plan turned out on close inspection to be an astute repackaging of almost all the old items, shorn of most of the overarchingly ambitious rhetoric of the M'Bow era.

"L'Onu pour quoi faire?" was the headline given by the impeccably *tiers-mondiste Le Monde* to its article marking the occasion of the UN's fortieth anniversary. The question was still pertinent to its fiftieth. The difficulty of reaching what must obviously be varied answers to that question is compounded by the erosion of the sense of common purpose with which the United Nations began. By the early 1980s, the old *status quo* powers were more comfortable than they admitted with the UN's increasing irrelevance to economic and political diplomacy; they were content with its safety-net residual function. And many of the aging oligarchies of the "new" countries had come to prefer the rhetoric of economic and social change to the reality. They, too, within a narrower rational compass, had interests in preserving the *status quo*. Effective UN intervention to improve the quality of national policies, to uphold human rights, or to mediate internal disputes might, with unpredictable results, strengthen rival actors on the domestic stage.

Such inertia was compounded by an almost total breakdown of dialogue in the UN's forums. By the 1980s the political channels had been choked for two decades by North-South confrontation, by the politicization of what should have been debate, and by the Third World attempt to structure all UN activity within the ideology of "new orders"—a phenomenon quite distinct from the persistent intrusion into unrelated debates of such political causes as the Arab-Israeli conflict. Where the need to improve the efficiency of the UN secretariats was concerned, some of the same points were made by developed and developing countries alike. But there was little agreement as to the purposes a more efficient UN might serve. And these divergences—often actively fostered, in the Western view, by the UN's theoretically neutral secretariats—had become so acute that they rendered the questions of incompetence and inefficiency wholly secondary to the UN's political crisis. Before we turn to the question of UN reform and its reasonable objectives, it will therefore be necessary in the next section to look at the ways in which "new order" politics blighted the political prospects for more effective multilateral cooperation inside and outside the UN framework.

II

THE WEBS OF IDEOLOGY

4. "New Orders": The Politics of Confrontation

Myth and Identity

"Politicization," in the broadest sense, was not an unfortunate by-product of the Third World campaign to use its majority at the United Nations to dominate and transform the international agenda. It was its driving force. The proponents of the "new international orders" were the spiritual children of Ghana's first president, Kwame Nkrumah, whose admonition to his African and Asian peers, "Seek ye first the political kingdom," captured the heady optimism of triumphant anticolonialism. In subordinating UN business to an overarching framework of confrontation, their paramount aim was the assertion of the new states' collective political will.

For the more moderate among the politicians, intellectuals, and diplomats articulating the rights of the global "underclass" against the entrenched balance of political and economic power, the Western tradition of case-by-case diplomacy was artificial in the first place, and wholly incommensurate to the needs of a period of rapid change. For the more radical, it was politically suspect. They accused the West of maintaining the separation of politics and economics in international relations as a device to perpetuate its "hegemony." To address problems piecemeal and in "technical" terms, while it might appear a neutral method, favored incremental adjustments that left the international structures intact.

The campaign for "new orders" necessarily rejected the piecemeal approach. It insisted on the seamless nature of the webs linking trade, aid, the monetary system, social welfare, disarmament, and the flows of information and cultural influence—all within the framework of the sacred struggle against colonialism, neocolonialism, and racism. Nor, for all its resort to the language of a global New Deal, was the Third World challenge utilitarian in essence. Western diplomats who treated Third World demands as raw material for the delicate processes of gradual concession either failed or refused to recognize that these processes were themselves the ultimate focus of attack. The aim was not goods, but power and a place under the sun, even if this was cloaked in claims to distributive justice.

In the early 1980s came the virtual economic collapse of most African and even a number of Latin American countries, under the impact of gigantic accumulated debt coupled with recession in their Western export markets. It became fashionable to dismiss the North-South confrontation of the previous two decades as a passing phase, now superseded by more pressing practical matters. The "new orders" rhetoric looked dated almost to the point of quaintness—particularly after 1989, when the disappearance of the Berlin Wall deprived Third World "nonalignment" of its meaning and the "South" of the opportunistic support of the Soviet Union and its satellites. The Third World's enduring taste for paper victories at the UN, and its collective attachment to the formulas of the 1960s and 1970s, could be ascribed, Western politicians suggested, to the reflexivity of United Nations procedures and, above all, to the requirements of face. In the real world, nebulous ideas about the sovereign equality of the self-evidently unequal could carry only so much mileage. Men would want their crust of bread on the last day—and for many countries, the 1980s looked remarkably like the last day.

They did want the bread. Individual governments, tempering the wind to the shorn lamb, had always adjusted their rhetoric in bilateral dealings. And, by the 1980s, even regional groups were prepared *in extremis* to admit some domestic responsibility for their problems, as did the Africans now bidding for greatly increased aid. A political mutation had nonetheless taken place and reached far deeper than these essentially tactical maneuvers.

The "new orders" might be no nearer realization than they were when it had been the turn of the West, swayed by its anxiety over the price and supply of oil in the 1970s, to go through the motions of flexibility; but the old assumptions about the purposes and forms of international cooperation had been destroyed. It was no accident that, at the United Nations, in votes that reflected Third World solidarity rather than any given country's trade or aid relations with the West, the Third World as a bloc continued to affirm its undying fidelity to the "irreducible" demands of an era that appeared to practical people to have receded. What was at stake was the Third World claim that the historic transformation of the world by decolonization had irrevocably changed the shape of the negotiating table, the nature of international politics, and the purposes of the United Nations as the forum through which that transformation found universal expression.

The ninth summit of nonaligned heads of government, held in Belgrade in September 1989, reveals the tensions in this period between economic realism and political myth-making. Denying that "prejudice or dogma" had ever been a feature of the movement, their final declaration stressed the importance to North-South negotiations of "concordance rather than confrontation." But they also affirmed that "fifteen years after its proclamation, the New International Economic Order remains a difficult but valid goal."[1] And three years later, the continuing vitality of the politics of confrontation was demonstrated during the UN Conference on Environment and Development, at Rio de Janeiro in 1992. In the environment, as we shall see in Chapter 10, a rich new vein of "solidarity" has been opened for mining.

Politicization had penetrated far beyond the practice, so exasperating to the West, of bringing up the Palestinian cause during debates on primary health care. The true, and more consequential thrust of Third World strategy was to impress on every debate, whether it dealt with plant genetic resources, the preservation of the cultural heritage, or the peaceful uses of outer space, the imprint of its arrival on the international stage. The countries in question had one major comparative advantage over the established arbiters of international relations: Poor in resources and organization, they were rich in number. To exploit this advantage, they had to concentrate on intergovernmental forums, and pursue through them an enlarged role for the state in economic and social affairs. Their campaign thus called into question traditional liberal ideas about the limits to government intervention. It focused on the United Nations and sought to transform its cluster of organizations, created in the West's image as vehicles for managing change through incremental steps agreed after exchanges of ideas in a spirit of mutual compromise. This "seamless web" approach to international relations, in which each item on the agenda was weighed in relation to the overall political struggle, rejected and dislocated the functionalist character and compartmentalized structures of the United Nations.

The demands for radical change were not therefore confined to questions of substance—like the redistribution of wealth, control over the World Bank and the International Monetary Fund (IMF), or the recognition of state sovereignty over information. Far more important than any individual component of the "new orders" was the business of interring the claims of the "old," and establishing sovereign equality as a fact far more significant than the demeaning realities of economic dependence.

This meant that every subject, every negotiation was political. Success was not measured in terms of agreements reached or missed, because agreement was not in the end the name of the game. Success was measured by Third World ability to keep up the pressure, to continue challenging the "Western" method of whittling broad areas of confrontation down to a negotiable minimum, and above all to make sure that the agenda was set in its terms. The posture of confrontation was more important than any concrete gains that might accrue from compromise. The discrete negotiation is liable to expose conflicts of interest within any grouping of states, never mind one in which more than a hundred made it an article of faith to speak with a single voice. The more specific the issue, the more it is likely to encourage traditional calculations of immediate national advantage—and weaken the collective will. The Third World penchant for broadening agendas and insisting its political dimension, ingrained by the 1980s, thus rested on expediency—the broader the goal, the easier to maintain solidarity—as well as conviction.

Daniel Patrick Moynihan recalls a reception at the UN in 1975, following Henry Kissinger's speech to the Seventh Special Session on the New International Economic Order (NIEO). Kissinger, who was preoccupied by shuttle diplomacy in the Middle East, did not turn up to read the speech, but its seriousness was nonetheless universally recognized at the time. It set out proposals on trade, compensation for commodity price fluctuations, and a multilateral investment trust, grain reserve, and energy institute. This went far further to meet NIEO demands than anything on offer from the Europeans. At the reception, Moynihan records, Senator Jacob Javits told the assembled UN ambassadors that if the U.S. proposals were not discussed in good faith in a positive spirit, an opportunity would be lost and might not recur and that "this was the time for the developing nations to judge whether development was more important to them than ideology." At this, the Pakistan ambassador "raised the question whether the United States intended to deprive the developing nations of their ideology—and, if so, whether it would in truth be a fair exchange."[2] Moynihan was one of the few who understood at the time what the question meant.

This is not to say that the "South" possessed or possesses a coherent ideology: the myth of solidarity was sustained through anticolonial symbolism and a widely shared insecurity of identity. The tenets of the "new orders" were not bargaining positions in the Western sense; they were not "tradables." They were articles of faith, beside which material concessions—for example, promises by Western governments in the 1970s to convert earlier loans to the poorest countries into grants—were almost an irrelevance. By treating the NIEO as a negotiation like any other, Kissinger's specific proposals threatened the integrity of Third World revolt: it was not entirely surprising that some governments at the nonaligned summit in Colombo the following year "argued for the addition of 'Kissingerism' to the litany of evils against which [the movement] must guard."[3]

What Third World leaders had set out to do in the 1960s was to act out the consequences of the history they had lived through: to take their liberation seriously. The West, which had assumed that the new states would be just like the old states, only poorer and weaker, joining a club in which the rules were clearly established, was slow to understand the nature of the challenge. Dismissing as completely unrealistic the Third World claim that the great upheavals that were altering the political map had rendered these rules obsolete, the West continued to seek some sort of "constructive" accommodation through negotiated concessions. Governments wedded to traditional assumptions about the empirical constraints on the exercise of power were naturally tempted to treat as irrelevant the view of power and its uses evolved by the leaders of the new states, many of which were so small or so poor that they could hardly have come into existence as sovereign members of the global fraternity, had empirical considerations been uppermost.

The Soviet Union, inherently conservative in its attitudes to the rule book and its perceptions of sovereign power, treated the "liberation politics" with extreme reserve until it recognized the strength of its anticolonial mythology. It then welcomed the new polarization, and learned to exploit it. To the extent that Moscow understood the damaging implications for international cooperation, it must have reasoned that it had everything to gain thereby. The whole postwar thrust of Soviet policy toward the UN, an essentially Stalinist line faithfully perpetuated for four decades by Andrei Gromyko, first as its permanent representative to the UN and then as foreign minister, was profound suspicion of the UN's meliorist functions. The collapse of a common framework for dialogue served its purposes both in this sense, and by providing a political platform for a spoiling operation against Western governments in which it was no longer so isolated as it had been during the 1950s.

After 1987, when the Soviet Union under Mikhail Gorbachev reversed Gromyko's policy and set out to exploit the United Nations for economic as well as political ends in a far more activist and basically constructive spirit, this policy proved a difficult legacy. The Soviet Union found itself in an embarrassing position. It was attempting to establish pragmatic bases for cooperation without abandoning a language of solidarity that was inimical to pragmatism—seeking, in other words, to use the UN in ways that required the cooperation of the industrialized West, while retaining its rhetorical credentials as a champion of Third World demands for "justice." These demands, meanwhile, had crystallized in terms impregnated with borrowings from Marxism, which made it more difficult for the Soviet Union to repudiate them. Just as the United States, given the moral strand in American thinking about the world and its emphasis on freedom and equality, found dealing with the inversion of these values by Third World spokesmen exasperatingly difficult, so the Soviet Union had to struggle with the rigidities of a collectivist rhetoric it could not too openly abandon. Even after the dissolution of the Soviet Union at the end of 1991, Russian policy at the UN continued, other than in security affairs, to betray an element of uneasy ambivalence.

It was, of course, in the name of liberty that the leaders of the Third World's "huddled masses" set out to repudiate Western concepts of liberal democracy. Asserting their liberation and their rights, not as the projection of individual freedoms but as the transforming triumph of a new global collectivity, they spoke a new language, alien to the West, based on the rights of states and of "peoples." A moralizing mentality found an alternative morality for which the language of the Communist world was a natural medium. This borrowing of idioms was largely superficial. If a group of underpaid and discontented army officers decided they were the Marxist saviors of their country, this implied neither an understanding of Marx nor, necessarily, adoption of the Soviet socialist model. But an affinity, once asserted, could be exploited, and the language of collectivist thinking actively shared.

On the international stage, this loose alliance put the United States, a fervent supporter of the decolonization process, into the dock with the old colonial powers—encouraging it to identify the North-South confrontation with the conflict between East and West. The breakdown in common language was an integral part of the North-South stalemate. The United Nations, fulcrum of the Third World's claims, suffered from the near-total incompatibility of purpose with which it was now approached. The normative and political claims of the "new orders" challenged the liberal philosophies concerning the relationships between state and citizen, state and marketplace, and state and state with which the UN's founding texts were imbued. They thus assailed the touchstones of Western loyalty to UN organizations.

Confusion about Third World objectives persisted into the 1980s. Two decades of ideological skirmishing, with battle never conclusively joined, left illusions on both sides: among Westerners, that the era of "new orders" was over; among developing countries, that sovereign equality was immutably established as a principle against which the West might occasionally struggle, but which would survive as the decisive factor in international affairs once the passing fit of "Reaganism" had subsided. Outside the UN, the Third World began to shrink; but at the UN, its leaders calculated that since their traditions would prevent the Western countries from simply walking away from the negotiating table, they would live with its altered shape. Accumulating evidence that, spiritually at least, the West was abandoning the global forums and settling the problems of international cooperation elsewhere, had little impact, for two reasons. The first was that, in Third World eyes, when it came to actual decisions the West had always treated the UN as somewhat optional. The second was that, perversely inverting the original purpose of universal forums, continued confrontation had become the cementing element of Third World unity. Merely by offering a target, Western participation served a real purpose.

Western expectations that hard times would render all this talk obsolete reckoned without the importance of such fictions, or the degree to which, the further the goal of "real" independence receded, the more psychologically and even politically necessary the fictions became. The possibility that incompatible world views might render universal organizations unworkable continued to be unthinkable, and in that sense Third World assessments were justified. Western countries continued to act as though the UN remained a place where bargains might be struck and interests reconciled, and where "moderates" would ultimately win the day for a new pragmatism. Meanwhile, conscious of the evident gap between countries' needs and the ability of the UN to address them, they focused on poor performance and mismanagement in the secretariats. It was intellectually less taxing, and since these defects had by now become painfully evident to Third World "moderates," they hoped for support.

The prospects for UN reform—and, indeed, for the reinvention, in any forum, of effective international dialogue—depend not only on restoring some coherence to the activities of UN organizations, where the bureaucracies seized on the limitless ambitions of the "new orders" to expand their reach far beyond their capacity, but on the reinvention of a common language. This was starkly laid out, in 1987, by the International Labor Organization's then director-general, Francis Blanchard, in a report on "the future of multilateral cooperation":

> In the necessary overhaul of the international organizations, agreement must first be reached on a number of basic issues relating to their purpose and function. If these organizations are to work properly, they must have an irreducible and ineluctable core of common interests, which each country must serve to the best of its ability within the international system. If this is not acknowledged and respected, the political viability of the system is threatened. That would appear to be the situation today, when tensions have brought into the open the deep divisions between the Members of the United Nations.[4]

Blanchard traced these tensions firmly to the "opposition, discord and ideological conflict" that had accompanied the search for a new international economic order. "The lure of the words" had, he said, "fallen far short of the will—or even the ability—of the international community to achieve this order." Yet at the same time, he argued that the clock could not be turned back to the UN's early days. "The postwar world order no longer exists," he said: ways had therefore to be found to marry "two opposing views of the role" of the UN.

The development of "new orders" politics—and their continuing, almost addictive attraction for politicians and diplomats who have come to think of confrontation as almost synonymous with Third World identity—is thus central to the UN's prospects. Its history is far from concluded. The challenge to Western power, and Western values, has profoundly affected the integrity of the international civil service, rewritten the conventions of global diplomacy, and locked the UN in cross-purpose.

THE THIRD WORLD INVENTS ITSELF

The speed with which decolonization occurred threw the institutions devised at Bretton Woods and San Francisco off balance. The United States, in particular, had intended the outcome: decolonization was one of its postwar aims. But most countries had assumed in 1945, as Brian Urquhart recalls,[5] that it "would take a hundred years." It did not, and the new states rapidly transformed UN organizations, making claims on them which they were not built to anticipate and to which they adjusted clumsily. Almost overnight, the world was composed not only of many more states, but of new kinds of states. The United Nations is often given credit for the rapid realization on a global scale of the charter's principle of self-determination, but a glance at the timing and the map reveals the extent to which the process was random, unplanned, reactive rather than positive. The borders of many of these new countries, sawing through ethnic and linguistic ties, yoking under the fine charters of independence, multiple loyalties, and traditions in conditions of economic vulnerability, made little sense except as a reminder of the disaggregation of old empires. The new world flowed pell-mell into the vacuum of the old.

To emphasize the precipitate retreat of the colonial powers is not to say that there was no force in the anticolonial tide. Serious, sometimes violent struggles for independence started in Indochina and India as early as the 1920s, and were prosecuted after World War II by the Indonesians, Kenyans, or Algerians with a vehemence that etched domestic scars on the weakened colonial powers. But often, the new sovereignties emerged from the conjunction of demands by a small, Western-educated elite with the exhaustion of European governments preoccupied by the postwar reconstruction of their battered economies. For many of the new states, untidy and even illogical accidents of history, the *nation*-state was still to play for. In Africa, the Balkanizing legacy of the nineteenth-century "scramble" produced states either geographically minute and seriously overpopulated like Burundi, or vast tracts of landlocked desert lacking either the resources or the critical concentrations of population to move beyond precarious subsistence. For these, as for a multiplicity of casual small appendages of empires staking their claim to a discrete identity, the United Nations (and, for some, the Commonwealth), legitimized and made absolute the achievement of an almost accidental statehood. The UN was the insurance and proof of their existence.[6]

The West unleashed this process out of a mixture of design and necessity, but had not foreseen the consequences. Its designs for the United Nations had made provision for security in a "steady-state" world, which largely equated peace with the maintenance of the postwar equilibrium. Even the trusteeship machinery was better equipped to deal with what international lawyers call state succession than with a great surge of liberation movements. The UN agencies created for international cooperation, however progressive their constitutions, were structured for the harmonization of policy between governments with developed institutions and administrative capacities—"responsible" in the sense that they were capable of executing any agreements they might reach.

Had the West responded more sensitively to the early formation of Third World groups within these forums, it might have recognized that they were a logical response to national institutional fragility and diplomatic inexperience, and found it natural that newly established governments should seek to use UN organizations, where they had at least theoretical parity, to proclaim the arrival of the postcolonial world. Some kind of effective grouping was needed to cope with the rapid expansion of UN membership, from 51 to 159 within four decades. By the late 1950s and early 1960s, these groups showed signs of forming along regional lines in Asia, Africa, and the Arab world (Latin American organizations having existed for some time). They could possibly have become a useful form of collective representation. The formative phases of the nonaligned movement, antipathetic to the concept of the "bloc," offered the West opportunities for dialogue that, through hostility or the conviction that it interfered with bilateral treaty systems and was irrelevant to multilateral diplomacy, it chose to ignore.

It is true that the rhetoric that characterized the "Third World's" first official manifestation, the "Afro-Asian" meeting at Bandung in 1955, did not help. There, twenty-nine Third World leaders (predominantly from Asia and the Arab world, plus three from Africa and, somewhat anomalously, politicians from Turkey, Japan, and China) adopted ten principles for international relations heavily indebted to Indian Panchshila traditions of nonviolence. But the keynote was set by Indonesia's flamboyant President

Sukarno, whose speech of welcome evoked the common Afro-Asian struggle against colonialism, racism, and nuclear confrontation in language reminiscent of Lenin's Anti-Imperialist League or the 1927 Comintern Congress of Oppressed Nationalities and gave the emerging theme of solidarity an anti-Western ring.

The Bandung principles—peaceful coexistence, respect for territorial integrity, mutual nonaggression and noninterference in each other's internal affairs, and commitment to equality and mutual benefit as the ground of international relations—formed a rough basis for the doctrine of nonalignment. But the Bandung meeting was anything but a gathering of the nonaligned: Pakistan confronted China with impassioned denunciations of the dangers of communism; members of the Southeast Asian Treaty Organization (SEATO) and Baghdad Pact were prominent. Western perceptions of Bandung as an anti-Western gathering owed much to sensitivities about anticolonialism and the Cold War—President Eisenhower viewed it as a straightforward Soviet bid, through China, to expand its tentacles into the Third World. There was enough anti-Westernism in "positive neutralism" to encourage the Soviet Union and China to invoke the "spirit of Bandung" when they later promoted the Afro-Asian Peoples' Solidarity Organization as a Third World propaganda front. But John Foster Dulles's excoriation, in 1956, of the emerging theory of nonalignment as "an immoral and shortsighted conception"[7] was still a cold warrior's overreaction.

"Nonalignment" was to develop its distinctive characteristics only some years later, as a counter to the Russo-Chinese bid to capitalize on Bandung. Invitations to the inaugural meeting of the nonaligned movement in Belgrade in 1961 stressed equidistance, and pointedly omitted both China and members of Western military alliances who had been present at Bandung. For Josip Broz Tito, the movement's animator, "uncommitted countries" meant just that. Communist Yugoslavia might be, but it had been expelled from the Cominform and was seeking to maintain a safe distance from the Soviet Union. His insistence that the movement was not, and did not wish to be, a third "bloc" was solidly grounded in Yugoslavia's national interest. Tito and his cofounders, particularly Jawaharlal Nehru, intended to achieve more than mere neutralism: they believed that a positive moral stand against Cold War blocs would constitute a basis for some kind of collective security. Nonalignment's professed determination to act as a stabilizing factor in East-West confrontation—through "moral violence," as Sukarno put it—brought a global dimension to Belgrade that outweighed for the time being the anticolonial evangelism of most of the African participants.

There existed, at least in these early years, a promising basis for relations between the West and this loose conjunction stretching from Cyprus to Indonesia (Cuba was the only Latin American participant at Belgrade). It would have married reasonably enough with President Truman's "Point Four" strategy for the containment of communism through economic and technical cooperation. It would, to be sure, have required some skillful Western footwork to counter the commitment by members of the movement to close all foreign military bases: but seemly euphemisms such as "cooperative defense arrangements" in strategically critical cases would probably have done the trick. Otherwise, little in the movement's inherently declaratory platform—peace and disarmament, self-determination, sovereignty and territorial integrity, economic cooperation between Third World countries—need have inhibited cooperation. Some of the same themes were to be found in the regional organizations that sprouted in the same period in Africa, Latin America, and the Arab world, and inspired no particular dread.

Yet nonalignment was treated in Western capitals with a mixture of distrust and indifference that nourished in it the forces of militancy.

Perhaps, at the time, this was inevitable. The West Europeans, who might have been sensible to the charms of genuine nonalignment, were still preoccupied with economic recovery, the consolidation of NATO, and experiments with new regional structures such as the European Free Trade Area or the translation of Jean Monnet's dream into the European Economic Community. In addition, the impassioned condemnations of the old colonial order touched raw nerves, coinciding, as they did, with the crisis in the Congo, France's national agony over Indochina and Algeria, and Britain's efforts to temper national dignity to the "wind of change" Harold Macmillan sensed blowing through Africa.

It was not until the 1970s that the Western world began to treat the nonaligned movement as an interlocutor. By then it had lost much of the spirit of nonalignment. In the economic sphere, too, its members' ambitions far exceeded their early, modest goals of securing more aid and expanding their share of world trade through improved access to Western markets: With the formation of the larger Group of 77, the Third World had evolved a genuinely anti-Western stance.

The existence of the United Nations forums, in which Western governments were captive audiences, added to the incentives to elaborate common claims—and thus accelerated the process of Third World organization. By 1956 the Arab and Asian countries already accounted for forty-six of the UN's seventy-nine members—a simple voting majority required only the support of either a handful of Latin Americans or the Soviet bloc to attain the two-thirds required for "important questions." The Latin Americans, then as now spiritually aloof from the Fanonesque postures of Bandung, had never classed themselves with the "*damnés de la terre*" (having, for the most part, successfully suppressed their own indigenous "*damnés*"), and, because the Soviet Union posed no threat to them, were lukewarm about nonalignment. They were, however, happy to make common cause with the new majority to press their increasingly radical economic agenda at the UN.

By 1960, sustained Third World demands for a Special UN Fund for Economic Development (SUNFED) had prompted the West, determined that any such fund should be under donor control, to establish the International Development Association (IDA) as a special soft-loans wing of the World Bank. In the same year, the first United Nations Development Decade was launched, setting a 5 percent annual growth target for developing countries and (loosely) committing donors to allocate 0.7 percent of their GNP to assist in its achievement. The following year, the United States publicly abandoned Truman's anti-Communist rationale for giving development aid. In a speech to the U.S. Congress in April 1961, President Kennedy announced that from then on the United States would provide, "not in order to contain the spread of communism, not just because other nations are doing it, but because it is right." The Peace Corps fanned across the globe.

But the horizon was shifting as fast as the West thought it discerned its shape. During that same summer of 1961, even before the first nonaligned summit in Belgrade, Argentina called for comprehensive negotiations, outside the General Agreement on Tariffs and Trade (GATT), which was considered a Western club, to give the developing countries a new trade deal. The express purpose was to create exemptions from GATT's basic rule of equal treatment for all traders—a rule from which, Argentina argued, the rich benefited disproportionately—in order to give newcomers preferential terms.

In 1962, at Tito's urging, Gamal Abdel Nasser convened an economic summit in Cairo. The platform elaborated there stressed the "reparations" theme, demanding more aid and better outlets and prices for exports, and reiterated Argentina's demand for a global conference to deal with North-South economic relations. In a sense, the politics of redistribution came to the rescue of the young nonaligned movement, which Tito was experiencing some difficulty in keeping alive and faithful to its founding ideas. The second nonaligned summit in 1964, also in Cairo, was largely prompted by Tito's determination to preempt an Afro-Asian meeting, which the increasingly and embarrassingly belligerent Sukarno and Algeria's president, Ahmed Ben Bella, planned to convene the following year—on the tenth anniversary of Bandung—with a much more radical anticolonial agenda that had little time for the peaceful settlement of disputes.

The Cairo summit, divided on much else, united in calling for a "new international economics [sic] policy." It was followed by a long period of drift: it was not until the Lusaka summit, in 1970, that the movement acquired the machinery to ensure its institutional continuity, and even then it was still in danger of running out of political steam. At the UN, however, the anticolonial theme combined with the radicalization of the economic agenda to give the nonaligned a sense of cohesion and purpose—and the second theme brought the Latin Americans (none of whom joined Cuba as non-aligned members until the late 1970s) into play. Many Third World governments became convinced that their concerted pressure had been responsible for a transformation in Western attitudes at the beginning of the 1960s. This was partly an illusion, but no less important for that. Paul Mosley has pointed out that where aid was concerned, they were pushing at an open door:

> This decade was the high-water mark of idealism concerning what overseas aid could achieve. . . . It was the decade in which most countries first began to formulate a policy towards the Third World, and in which an institution, the Development Assistance Committee of the OEDC, was set up to coordinate the efforts and policies of the Western donor nations. It was a period of substantial multilateralization of aid. . . . It was the end of the 1960s before one saw any signs of feedback [as failures implanted the beginnings of doubt].[8]

But at another level, concerted pressure was pushing the West further than it wanted to go. Governments that were happy "because it is right" to give aid to countries that couldn't make a living out of exporting sisal were far less happy with the germination of demands that the West pay considerably more for sisal. Compensating countries for their miserable earnings from the marketplace was one thing; rigging the market was another. It was widely expected that aid would fill gaps in the new countries' requirements for capital and expertise and enable them to integrate successfully and relatively rapidly with the international market economy. Faith in national planning happily assumed that the planners' ultimate mecca was the liberal free market; support for international cooperation assumed mutuality of interest. It was therefore thoroughly disconcerting, just at the high tide of Western enthusiasm for assisting developing countries to join the global club, to discover that influential voices were beginning to reject its rules.

Yet at the General Assembly in 1962,[9] knowing full well that its Third World promoters saw it as a way to effect a sea change in the nature of international bargaining and to alter the rules in favor of the new majority, the West agreed to hold a once-off United

Nations Conference on Trade and Development (UNCTAD) in 1964. With speed born of its awareness of the incipient revolt, the West then pushed through the International Monetary Fund a Compensatory Financing Facility to help exporters of commodities deal with sudden price fluctuations. Despite this effort to draw the thorn in advance, the West approached the first UNCTAD on the defensive, aware that it was more than an effort to counter the impotence of the Economic and Social Council, and anxious to protect the role of the GATT. The principle of mutuality of interest was under attack, together with Western assumptions about the purposes of "development."

The commodities issue loomed large: a major purpose of the conference was to get Western nations to raise their prices across the board as a matter of equity. But the 1963 General Assembly had made it clear that the agenda was still wider. The Latin Americans had obtained nonaligned support for a resolution sponsored by seventy-five states (including, in a single-minded expression of national interest, New Zealand), that called for international action to supplement Third World development efforts—and that specifically asserted the need for a new international division of labor. This demand for structural change in the developed world to "make room" for newcomers, which prefigured the New International Economic Order, also marked the formal incarnation of the Group of 77 as a voting bloc.

The Group of 77 was never monolithic. It arrived at a common platform via regional meetings, and the differences between the Latin American members and the Afro-Asian majority were symbolized at the 1964 UNCTAD by the establishment of four theoretically separate negotiating groups—East (meaning Soviet bloc), West, Afro-Asian, and Latin American. Even then, Afro-Asian caucuses tended to be riven with conflict, reflecting the wholly disparate economic interests of countries in highly varied stages of economic and political evolution. The Group of 77 nonetheless came together with impressive solidarity at the 1964 UNCTAD. Against initial Western opposition, it voted through, by 83–20, a proposal to establish UNCTAD as a permanent secretariat, charged to prepare and service periodic conferences in an explicitly North-South mold.

On the strength of this alone—the first UNCTAD did little more than create an institution that the Third World perceived as its very own—the Group of 77 proclaimed a "new era."[10] From this point, the most violent internal disagreements on strategy and priorities would be secondary to solidarity—itself a victory of a sort, and a source of rapid radicalization. The UNCTAD formula, which accepted the existence of "blocs" for negotiating purposes, spread through the rest of the UN and helped to create both the illusion of collective strength and an atmosphere of triumphant, collective, revolt. By symbiosis the UN, which emanated from ideas that had their roots in the Enlightenment, was to be converted into a tool for challenging them. That first UNCTAD may have produced little in the way of negotiation, but it still gave the new "bloc" more than a sense of itself: it gave it a theory. At least, Raúl Prebisch did so.[11]

Prebisch, the first secretary-general of UNCTAD, had been a former governor of Argentina's central bank and then a director of the UN's Economic Commission for Latin America (ECLA). His ideas dominated the process of welding Afro-Asian anticolonialism with a radical platform for economic "liberation." At the 1962 nonaligned economic summit in Cairo, where he had been prominent among the Latin American observers, he had actively pressed Argentina's demand for the UNCTAD conference. He was appointed ECLA's secretary-general by U Thant, the new UN secretary-general, who, as rapporteur to the founding meeting of the nonaligned in Belgrade, had supported

Tito's parallel ambitions for a world trade conference and a new international organization for development. For Prebisch, UNCTAD combined the two. Radical, persuasive, and highly intelligent, he proceeded to convert into an agenda for this new organization the "center-periphery" theory of international economics that he had developed in the Latin American context.

According to Prebisch, the laws of the market (and the dominance within them of Western-based multinational corporations) reduced the developing countries to perpetual subservience to the industrialized world. These laws condemned the "periphery"—countries heavily reliant on the exports of raw materials—to earn less and less for its goods, while paying more and more for the manufactures of the "center." This was ineluctable because growth in the center's demand for commodities would not keep pace with increases in supply as "development" pushed up the Third World's productive output. The Third World's rising demand for Western manufactured goods, meanwhile, would push up prices. Even without assuming ill will, a free market would thus amount to the freedom of the few to exploit the many. Given the persistent divergence between North and South, it was illusory to assume any spontaneous correction of the balance.

In the interest of social justice, governments must therefore agree to countervailing measures. These should include the stabilization of commodity prices at rates that ensured adequate incomes for the producers, possibly by index-linking them to the cost of manufactured imports; zero tariffs in the North for goods processed and manufactured in the Third World (to assist them to industrialize and escape their dependence on primary commodities); and automatic flows of finance to the South—not because it was "right," in Kennedy's sense, but because it was owed as compensation for the accumulated Western privilege and prosperity built on tropical sweat.

As description, Prebisch's analysis was too close to the truth to be dismissed out of hand, as many Western conservatives sought, and seek, to do. The failures that beset subsequent efforts to establish effective commodity agreements (including, in the mid-1980s, the collapse of the London tin market) testified to the inelasticity of demand for key commodities. While wildly fluctuating prices *ipso facto* go up as well as down, the trend seemed set downward, as the growth rates of the 1950s and 1960s faltered and as the North developed synthetics and other substitutes. Not all the white elephants that littered Africa three decades after Prebisch launched his theory were attributable to governmental folly; the difficulties of industrializing in nations too poor or too small to establish domestic markets were greater than even he had realized, and Western trade barriers merely compounded them.

As prescription, however, Prebisch's theory was explosive and in many ways destructive. Prebisch himself did not lay all the blame for Third World poverty on the laws of the market. As stern a critic of domestic injustice and inequality as he was of the inequities he perceived in the impersonal operations of the international market, he exhorted Third World governments to reform land tenure, invest in education, and reduce internal income gaps between rich and poor. It was not his fault if the Group of 77 governments heard only what they wanted to hear—that external factors were to blame for poverty, that state planning on a global scale could redress these, and that trade, supported by automatic transfers of capital (at a time when development was still widely believed to be a matter of cash flow and worries about "absorptive capacity" lay in the future) could be the route not merely to growth but to "catching up." His theory was destructive, ultimately, because it launched international economic negotiations down a dead-end road; and because it lent itself to the evolving "bloc" approach, in which blanket demands would be made with little regard for the quite different needs of individual developing countries. It lent itself to conspiracy theory. It led to the New International Economic Order.

THE RADICALIZATION OF THE AGENDA

Two strands thus came together to transform multilateral politics at the global level: a distinctive political identity through the nonaligned movement, and the center-periphery economic theories developed by Prebisch (which were adopted as dogma by the "South" as a whole, although they were principally relevant to Latin American economies and reflected their governments' deep-rooted paranoia about the regional "hegemony" of the United States).

The process was more ragged than it sounds, and necessarily so. The leaders of the nonaligned movement, still a fragile project in the 1960s, were uneasily conscious that it had been founded as an expression of antipathy to bloc politics. They responded positively to the constitution of the larger Group of 77 partly because, in a period of political drift for nonalignment, it articulated easily identifiable grievances, and partly because it seemed to represent the "third force" that had never been absent from Tito's or Nehru's ambitions. But it took some years for them to absorb "redistribution politics" as a natural extension and expression of the campaigns against colonialism and racism.

The doctrinal radicalism of the Latin American *dependencia* school implied not only a degree of economic *dirigisme* undreamt of in the Bretton Woods philosophy, but a level of confrontation for which many governments were still unprepared. In the years after the first UNCTAD, Latin American and African governments made rare common cause to argue within the group in favor of relatively modest proposals that the West would have to take seriously. The first ministerial meeting of the Group of 77 in Algiers in 1967 produced a common statement of Third World grievances and demanded financial "transfers," debt relief, and preferential Third World access to Western markets to close the gap between poor and rich countries; but there was violent disagreement over strategy. At this meeting, the militant group, mostly Arab and North African, which argued for the total restructuring of international economic relations, was outnumbered. The proponents of tough negotiations within existing bargaining conventions won the day, partly because the continuing enlargement of the Third World "agenda" at the UN, notably with the creation of the UN Development Program in 1965 and a UN Industrial Development Organization a year later, had reinforced their position.

The "moderate" strategy made little headway in the negotiations with the West at the 1968 UNCTAD, however—at least in terms of Third World expectations. Rightly or wrongly, the developing countries believed their demands for creating buffer stocks in key commodities, for swifter and easier transfers of technology, for more aid, and for systematized debt relief to be both coherent and reasonable, "an invitation to the rich to join us in the battle against underdevelopment." What they got was the Generalized System of Preferences, a Western concession of "special and differential status" under the GATT that would allow them to retain their own trade barriers while gaining greater access to industrialized countries' markets. The concession was in fact large—large enough to provoke a mercantilist backlash that led to the erection of nontariff barriers against Third World imports. But as a political response, it seemed paltry. The outcome of the conference thus strengthened what might be called the Algerian faction against the "realists."

Algeria had always maintained that political independence was only a first step toward demolishing the structures of Western dominance. It now claimed that it was vindicated in its contention that, since the problem was born of geopolitical injustices, the Third World should attack the structure of North-South relations before proceeding to specific negotiations that, without a changed climate, would in any case be doomed to fail. Two events in the early 1970s reinforced these arguments and brought closer an outright confrontation with the West.

The first was Libya's unilateral decision in 1970 to extract higher royalties for its oil from foreign companies. Meeting virtually no opposition to the first rise, it continued to ratchet them up and, to Third World observers, thus exposed the falsity of Western doctrines concerning the decisive role of free markets in determining commodity prices. The second was the floating of the U.S. dollar in August 1971 and, with it, the disintegration of the international monetary system established at Bretton Woods. President Nixon's decision, reflecting the strains of the Vietnam war on the U.S. economy, also signaled the end of a period of growth that had, in two decades, transformed the global economy. The "old order" seemed ripe for a decisive attack.

A second front was now opened by President Luis Echeverria of Mexico. At the third UNCTAD conference in 1972, he called for the elaboration of a Charter of the Economic Rights and Duties of States—a code of international economic conduct expressed as a bill of rights. This proposal gave a new political dimension to the *dependencia* theory of economics. It challenged not only the postwar economic order, but traditional ideas about what properly constituted "rights" going back to the Enlightenment. By postulating rights of *states* rather than of individuals, the proposed charter, which Echeverria said should "supplement" the Universal Declaration of Human Rights, marked not an extension, but a break. Echeverria was serving notice that the Third World was no longer content with the pragmatic management of the *status quo*: through political will, a new global design must be established according to new moral and legal norms.

Western governments somewhat absentmindedly let Echeverria's resolution pass. So peripheral did this proposal appear to the serious economic difficulties with which they were then grappling, that Western diplomats expected it to join the hundreds which ministers present to international conferences—to be politely applauded, converted into resolutions, and then interred. They seem not to have grasped that it represented not a further demand, but a departure from all previous modes of demanding; that this was not an economic platform but a challenge to the moral basis of liberal economics. Or that it had particular force when the monetary disarray in the "North" gave new edge to the language of resentment. The Western powers could now be presented not only as the manipulators of the international system, but as the incompetent manipulators of an unworkable structure. Or that, in postulating a new set of moral codes based on people's rights and the supremacy of the state, Echeverria was inverting the sense of a whole series of ideas about self-determination, freedom, and equality that had evolved in the West in the context of progress toward the expression of individual rights through parliamentary democracy.

It was precisely in its challenge to these concepts that Echeverria's speech caught the Third World tide. And this was underlined only three months later, when the nonaligned foreign ministers, meeting in Georgetown, issued a Declaration that attacked the operations of the free market not only in goods but in ideas: the revolt against "cultural imperialism" was integral to a challenge that assaulted Western ideas as much as Western power.

The catalyst that fused these disparate elements into a militant political platform was the fourth nonaligned summit, in Algiers in September 1973,[12] which articulated the demand for a New International Economic Order. Algiers transformed Third World approaches to international negotiation. The goal ceased to be convergence and compromise; the policy of offering "invitations to the rich" was declared bankrupt and interred. The Third World claimed its political kingdom.

Even at this stage of collective organization, "Third World" essentially meant Africans and Asians, with strong OPEC participation; Latin American membership of the movement was still limited to Cuba, Salvador Allende's Chile, and Peru. But "the largest international gathering in history" outside the UN, proudly greeted as such by President Houari Boumedienne, still managed to assemble seventy-five governments, fifty-four of them represented by heads of state. And Boumedienne made the most of the host government's drafting prerogatives to include in the texts to be debated elements of all previous agendas, including those that particularly concerned Latin American leaders. The summit declarations were intended to focus on the "real" issue of colonialism: the legal, economic, and trading structures that, whatever flag was unfurled over government offices, condemned the "South" to permanent dependence.

In ebullient mood (symbolized at its most effervescent by Idi Amin's offer to march the Ugandan army into South Africa, and at its most aggressive by its characterization of Zionism as a form of racism), the summit set out the main lines of the New International Economic Order, agreed a "program of action" to implement it, and decided to give top priority at the next UN General Assembly to Echeverria's charter. For the first time, this nonaligned gathering imposed itself on skeptical leaders in both East and West as a major political event—even before the Yom Kippur war, the OPEC oil embargo and quadrupling of oil prices that swiftly followed it. Leonid Brezhnev, disturbed by the potential for a poor-versus-rich alignment, hastened to congratulate the summit on its "anti-imperialist program." By the following year Kissinger was describing the movement as a "pillar of our foreign policy." Algiers set the stamp on Third World approaches to international negotiations so firmly that subsequent developments were, if not footnotes to the Algiers declarations, at least extensions of them.

Much of the "program of action" was in fact the old UNCTAD agenda, but it was set within a framework which transfigured it. The "contents" of the NIEO, and of the New World Information Order that was later to evolve as its companion, have been exhaustively analyzed since 1973 and subjected to considerable scholarly polemic as to their "real" radicalism. Slogans rather than "orders," both of them contained enough internal contradictions to fit almost any interpretation; it was the sum, not the component parts, that constituted their radicalism. That so much attention has been paid to these far from consistent declared aims is a tribute to the change of atmosphere their prosecution wrought in almost all global assemblies. What matters about the Algiers summit is not whether the propositions formulated there were coherent—they were not—but that it established Third World solidarity as a galvanizing political principle and provided it with its sacred texts. Derogation from the scriptures in the pursuit of national self-interest became unthinkable: heresy might be entertained in private, but public departures from the faith were inconceivable. Not until 1979 did a Third World government (Costa Rica, which rapidly withdrew under pressure) formally seek to place the economic costs of high oil prices on a UN agenda.[13]

The summit condemned in ringing terms the "imperialism" which imposed on developing countries "political, social and economic structures which encourage alien domination, dependence and neo-colonialism" and which it held accountable, without qualification, for the gap between rich and poor. Imperialism, it stated, not only passively blocked progress but, through its "transnational and monopolistic" companies, practiced economic and political aggression against countries seeking to escape domination. The successes of OPEC (a source of considerable excitement, it is often forgotten, even before they impinged on the Western consciousness) revealed the escape route: "organized concerted action" by exporters, not just to obtain better remuneration for commodities but to force the West to accept that it could no longer run the world its way.

Even such a celebration of solidarity as the Algiers meeting had to resolve tensions among participants. The declarations point in several directions. The most serious cleavage, then and later, was between those, like Algeria, who saw the battle in North-South terms and those, notably among the poorest countries, who were seduced by Julius Nyerere's vision of a union of the poor, relying on collective self-sufficiency to break the chains of northern domination. These ambitions were reflected in decisions, no less sacred in the years that followed for being unimplemented, to double South-South trade, to cut mutual tariffs at least to the level of those imposed against northern goods (they were generally much higher), and to mobilize independent lines of credit through the creation of a Third World financial institution.

The political thrust was, however, directed against the North (which, since it was the actor on stage, meant the West). None of the familiar demands of the 1960s was dropped; those for more, and more automatic, "transfers of resources" and nonreciprocal trading concessions were simply stated more uncompromisingly. But the essence of breaking the yoke of imperialism lay in assaulting market forces. Producers' associations were to improve terms of trade, increase governments' bargaining power vis-à-vis multinational corporations, and change the rules that governed the latter's operations.

Foreign investment was singled out for particularly radical treatment. It should, the summit decided, be authorized and controlled by governments, conform with national plans, and, before applications for licenses could be considered, guarantee miracles in the way of developing indigenous technological capacity, creating jobs and generating foreign exchange. Quite how even the most well-intentioned applicant was to meet these criteria was uncertain, given that no external investment was to be permitted in "strategic sectors"—which included mining, raw materials, public services, communications, banking, insurance, and commerce. Reinvestment was to be subject to the same restrictions. And for investment already in place, the summit agreed on the "limitless" sovereign right of states to nationalize and/or expropriate; compensation would be decided in accordance with national laws. This, said Boumedienne, symbolized "the determination of our peoples to put an end to unequal treaties and to reject an international law of bygone times which reflects imperial interests." Nations had an absolute right to recover their assets without being penalized "by those who, logically, owe them reparations."

Ironically, this forthright assertion of governments' sovereign right to ignore international law was coupled with demands for international legislation: the summit called for mandatory codes of ethics for multinationals, and codes aimed at speeding up the transfer of technology to the developing world. The summit's attitude to the Bretton Woods institutions was equally inconsistent. It rejected the premises of the 1944 agreements, with their emphasis on encouraging the play of market forces and intervening just enough to temper the imperfections of free markets and to provide a minimum of security against unforeseen shocks or the consequences of national miscalculation. But, simultaneously, it called for increased finance for the IMF, the World Bank, and IDA and demanded that the West give developing countries equal power in their councils—power that would enable them to elaborate a new and "equitable" international monetary system. "Equity" implied the creation of new liquidity, and the allocation of loans from the global reserves to Third World governments on the basis of their development needs rather than the size of their IMF quotas. Algiers both rejected the rules of the club and demanded the commanding voice on its committees.

Liberation, Boumedienne reminded his audience, "begins with the decolonization of the mind." Here the Algiers summit took modest initial steps, but opened up large horizons. Agreements were reached to cut mutual postal and telecommunications tariffs, build up national media, and improve communications circuits "inherited from the colonial past" so that countries could exchange news about their "achievements." More explicit ambitions to control the flows of global information were reflected in a plan to draw up codes of conduct regulating the use of satellites. The larger goal, as set out in the communiqué, was to transform not only the flow but the content of news, information, and entertainment.

Third World leaders had begun to reason that, to break the chain of dependence, they must use information for nation-building; for this, domestic information systems would have to be shaped in a new mold, free of alien values and thus able to mobilize the masses behind the government and against "ideological domination." From that starting point, the assertion of national sovereignty over international news flows was a natural progression.

"NEW ORDERS" AS DECLARATORY POLITICS

A case can be made for the "new orders," as political platforms. Radical shifts in power tend to be achieved not through incremental adjustments but by the Luthers nailing their theses in revolt to the church door, questioning not just the way the Pope governs but his right to govern at all.

The new politics was logical in its way. It was born of the developing countries' conviction that their problems could not be tackled successfully in isolation from the international context, and their growing awareness of the limited nature of their freshly minted sovereignty. It was fostered by governing elites in societies where the state—sometimes for ideological reasons but often for lack of robust alternatives—played a dominant role as arbiter and organizer of all activity, as the impersonation of the collective good. It flourished on the illusion that, given solidarity, the evident justice of global redistribution would triumph: was not OPEC already demonstrating that the free market was a fraud perpetrated by the "transnationals," that the "real" market price of oil had been many times what was being paid for it? It was sustained by the conviction that without solidarity, nothing would change. And it played on social and political shifts in the West itself, where economic planning and the postwar creation of welfare states had moderated the internal operations of the free market and increased the roles of governments.

It has often been pointed out that the tenets of the "new orders," ranging between the inchoate or loosely inspirational and the relatively precise, hardly amounted to a rational system. That may be true, but it is not relevant, because what mattered to their proponents was the affirmation that the "rationality" of market forces, which mocked their sovereign equality and contaminated their societies with "alien" values, could be countered by the collective will. There has never been a majority that did not seek to use it. The size—and novelty—of the Third World majority at the UN convinced many otherwise quite realistic governments that solidarity was indeed strength, and that the moral claim of three-quarters of mankind to share power with the privileged minority could be enforced. The political framework had changed, so the laws of economics must conform.

Article 1 of the UN declaration[14] of 1974, in which the NIEO was formally launched as a platform, essentially dismisses the entire framework of international law and practice as an "unequal treaty," a device whereby the wealthy impose their liberal philosophies and free-market doctrines of competition on the socially vulnerable and economically uncompetitive. "The gap between the developed and developing countries," it asserts, "continues to widen in a system which was established at a time when most of the developing countries did not exist as independent states, and which perpetuates inequality." The links between wealth and power, in other words, are incompatible with the rights of states to equal opportunity. This hostility to market principles stemmed not only from the conviction, after two decades of rapid global growth, that they favored the rich, but from recognition that a system based on such principles was inimical to the achievement of global structural change by political *fiat*. And it was on this point that moderates and radicals united—on this point, and on the cardinal principle of national sovereignty.

For all the rhetoric about world order, the campaign was not remotely supranational in spirit. A revolutionary stance abroad was integral to building national unity at home. It was equally true that the revolutionary content of these doctrines was for international, not national consumption. To many of their advocates, the main attraction of new international orders whose moral and legal norms were predicated on collective rights was that they enhanced the role of the state—and thus helped to legitimize the ruling structures of these countries. When these self-styled revolutionaries set out to break the monopolies of Western power—raising in their cause the standard of the oppressed, championing pluralism and equal participation against the old evils of monopoly capitalism and imperialism—their ultimate aim was to concentrate domestic power more firmly in their own hands. The new orders were inherently conservative in the important sense that they buttressed national authority.

These two unifying factors, coupled with awareness of their own weakness as individual actors, enabled developing countries to maintain solidarity in support of a declaratory manifesto in which the revolutionary sat uneasily with the reformist, rejection of the international system with complaints about its malfunctioning, and complaints about the inequity of a system that allegedly created one law for the rich and another for the poor with demands that in order to redress the balance, there should indeed be two sets of rules, under which the poor would be given special treatment. An underlying, common resentment, for which colonialism, neocolonialism, racism, apartheid, Zionism, or *dependencia* became almost interchangeable code words, sustained unity even on issues where some states (the Latin Americans on Palestinian rights, for example) were indifferent.

When Third World governments blamed their poverty on Western "dominance," this was not however merely a cynical attempt to shift the blame for poor economic performance at home. To the South's negotiators, automatic transfers of capital and technology and due reparations for the iniquities of colonialism and the inequities of neocolonialism were a logical corollary of sovereign equality. Only the more radical (and better endowed) were prepared to attack aid itself as a form of "repressive tolerance," but all could support a platform that questioned the altruism of aid programs, the validity of the economic models on which Western concepts of "development" were based, and the value of cooperation on existing terms. "Collective self-reliance" meant different things to different governments—autarcky and delinking from the "North" for some, collective pressure against the West for others—but both camps could exploit it as a potent political slogan. The Marxist and Soviet terminology in which their claims tended to be couched was largely coincidental; its main significance was that it gave both Western and Communist governments an exaggerated impression of the "class war" element in what was quintessentially a nationalist revolt.

In 1973, the "oil weapon" was added to the arsenal of moral and economic arguments. Here too, somewhat in defiance of the laws of economic gravity, a unified political stance was assembled. The solidarity front so painstakingly and triumphantly constructed by Algeria at the 1973 summit had drawn some inspiration from OPEC's successes in dealing with the powerful Western oil cartels. But the quadrupling of oil prices that autumn surpassed the summit's wildest expectations of "producer power"—and created the potential for a serious rift between OPEC and hard-hit Third World oil importers. The speed with which Boumedienne acted at the United Nations in January 1974 to secure a special session that summer on raw materials and development reflected his belief that the Third World must rapidly be rallied behind OPEC—before the West could exploit economic hardship in oil-importing developing countries. He calculated correctly that, in public, no member of the Group of 77 would characterize OPEC's coup as other than a triumph.

By launching the NIEO and Echeverria's charter in an atmosphere of North-South confrontation, that session generated a wave of Third World optimism about Western vulnerability and the prospects of forcing through an agenda for radical change. OPEC became so important as a symbol of opportunity that immediate economic costs were discounted; the "blackmail card," as it was characterized by exasperated Western diplomats, was to be treated as a trump long after it became clear that it was unplayable. (The Saudis, as Bernard Nossiter has pointed out,[15] never intended to play it; but this did not diminish its importance so long as the West believed that they might.) Equally, although the economic fortunes of OPEC governments were closely linked to the prosperity of the West and the stability of its banking system, they nonetheless maintained their total formal identification with the campaign for a "new order," recognizing in group solidarity a major source of support for the Arab campaign against Israel.

By conventional standards, this united front was too artificial to endure. It proved far more resilient than most observers anticipated. This was principally because the Third World campaign was based on concepts of national interest far more intangible than those that had traditionally informed diplomacy. Had the "new orders" been no more than a new window-dressing for old demands for more aid or better terms of trade, their appeal would have been ephemeral. They survived both negotiating deadlock and the tensions operating between historically, culturally, and economically diverse states because the politics of gesture provided outlets for the existential affirmation of identity.

The campaign for "new orders" rejected not only the assumptions of common purpose on which, as the ILO's 1987 report cited earlier stated, the "political viability" of the UN rests, but the common language without which no international negotiating relationship can survive. Nothing brought this conceptual rift more starkly into focus than the drive for a New World Information and Communication Order. The NWICO, as it was gracelessly labeled, directly attacked freedoms regarded by the West as universal. "Decolonization of the mind," as Boumedienne had put it, rapidly assumed the dimensions of thought control. In the name of diversity and plurality, governments set out to "nationalize" truth. Information became a commodity to be used for purposes of state. "The activities of imperialism," the seventy-five governments at Algiers had declared, "also cover the cultural and sociological fields," imposing "cultural alienation and imported civilization" on developing societies. Independence was unattainable without a "repersonalization by constant and determined recourse to the people's own social and cultural values which define it as a sovereign people."

Something obviously had to be done about the underdevelopment of Third World communications, and it was natural for governments to resent their countries' dependence on Western-based media for international news and entertainment. But "repersonalization" meant far more than a natural ambition to build up media that responded to national needs and enabled countries to reach the outside world with their news directly rather than through foreign intermediaries. The advocates of the NWICO attacked not only the dominant position of Western-based media, but the model of a free and independent press that they represented. "Repersonalization" included the rejection of the free flow of information in favor of a new model, in which the state would use the media to mold an "authentic" collective consciousness and to mobilize the masses behind the task of nation-building.

As a doctrine of positive manipulation, in which the state became the arbiter of what its citizens *ought* to learn of their world, this differed qualitatively from simple censorship. Journalists, in the words of Ramazani Baya, Zaire's minister of information, should be "steeped in the ideals of the Party . . . and aware of their responsibility to lead the masses to adhere to the national will."[16] There could be no such thing as a neutral fact: the least fragment of information acquired an intentional, purposive element. "Constructive" debate might be permitted, provided it was within the context of national values determined by the state, whose rights in the matter were unquestionable. As a Tunisian minister put it: "The government is the guarantor of stability, and security; and it is also the main catalyst for development, the entrepreneur responsible for the vast proportion of investment. If one accepts that role, it must be given the fullest opportunity to muster community support through the media."

The rhetoric of the NWICO stressed its commitment to freedom: freedom from domination by the Western "monopoly" of information channels, from the distortions of the market; freedom to express the plurality and diversity of cultures and the sovereign will of peoples. To be effective, national controls required the complement of international regulation. The more moderate opponents of "cultural imperialism" viewed the contamination of their societies as the unintended result of the free flow of ideas; the more radical saw the international media as part of a conspiracy to "support the existing system of domination and nullify all critical and reflective abilities, therefore all capacity for revolution."[17] The NWICO asserted the absolute right of states to regulate the content of news and its transmission internally and across national frontiers. But the campaign for international regulation had a further purpose. States were already, in practice, capable of "protecting" their publics from the culturally inappropriate, "irrelevant," or embarrassing fact. The larger goal was to win international recognition of the principle that information should be subject to the state.

The introduction, at UNESCO and then at the UN in New York, of the concept of "information sovereignty," compelled Western governments to engage in a debate on the role of the media which they passionately believed had no place in intergovernmental forums: the very act of arguing over the proper role of the press constituted an unacceptable degree of state intervention. There was, moreover, nothing to negotiate because there was no scope for compromise. There is an unbridgeable gulf between those who, like Lenin, view the media as servants of the state, and those who, for all the tensions between government and media in the freest democracies, believe that a well-informed citizenry is the best defense against the abuse of power, and the power of the state in particular—and that a free press is therefore indispensable.

More clearly than any other single issue, the demand for a NWICO impressed on Western governments the extent to which the majority of the UN's members rejected the values, presumed in 1945 to be universal, which the global organizations had been founded to protect and spread. The extent to which the meaning of freedom was being reinterpreted was underlined by Third World claims that it was in the causes of plurality and freedom that they rejected the free flow of news and ideas embodied in the UN Declaration of Human Rights and in UNESCO's constitution.

The need for a richer and more diverse flow of information and cultural exchange was unquestionable, and there was some foundation for many of the complaints about international reporting of Third World affairs. The sensitivities of small nations about preserving their cultural identity were wholly comprehensible. But the crux of the controversy was that the proponents of a "new order" meant just that—an *order*. They sought assistance to build up their national media, but their principal goal was a charter committing all governments—and notably those whose media circulated internationally—to ensure that their media respected internationally determined rules of conduct and served the cause of "international understanding." In other words, states were to regulate both the flow and the content of information.

The campaign had both East-West and North-South dimensions. The Soviet Union exploited it to justify its jamming of foreign broadcasts (obtaining at UNESCO an international declaration, with large potential implications for the technology of the future, that direct satellite broadcasts required the prior consent of the receiving state). More generally, it used the NWICO debate to throw a veil of respectability over its refusal to honor its commitments under the 1975 Helsinki Final Act to permit "the free and wider dissemination of information" across frontiers. Third World advocates of NWICO borrowed from Eastern bloc theories that states had a duty to "respect the sovereign rights of other states" by preventing the media from "interfering" in their internal affairs.[18] At Baghdad in 1980, nonaligned ministers called for a charter that would incorporate "the right of every nation to develop its own information system and to protect its national sovereignty and cultural identity; . . . to use its means of information to make known worldwide its interests and aspirations," and to resist "the distribution of false or distorted information which may cause harm to its interests or jeopardize friendly relations between states."

These were not ambitions lightly to be relinquished in exchange for a few journalism training courses and the odd million dollars for national news agencies. The perfect expression of confrontation politics, the campaign for a new information order manipulated Western perceptions of the value of pluralism so skillfully that, in a mistaken attempt to divert its energies into genuinely pluralistic modes, the West accepted the concept and then tried to resist the regulatory connotations that were inseparable from it. In the process, North-South relations were seriously damaged—and the developing countries discovered a wonderfully potent source of solidarity. As the conference of African governments, convened by UNESCO at Yaoundé in 1980 to elaborate communication policies for the continent, declared: "If information organs are systematically used to strengthen national unity, mobilize energies for development and greater participation by popular masses in communication, and reinforce African solidarity and combat all that divides the African continent and prevents it from asserting itself in all its dignity, this will be a means of liberation and an expression of our peoples' freedom." The idea that the new media should be employed in the struggle for a new economic order introduced a new perspective to the conduct of international negotiation.

THE POWER OF INCANTATION

As vehicles for sensitizing Western governments to some of the developing world's most intractable problems and keenly felt resentments, the politics of the new orders were effective. As weapons in the struggle to produce radical change in the global economy, they had only marginal impact. As an approach to international negotiation, they were counterproductive. As a prescription for reinforcing the authority of United Nations forums, they were disastrous.

On the economic front, the record was mixed. Cooperative deals, like the Generalized System of Preferences and the IMF's compensatory finance and oil facilities, were struck to meet some grievances. But when governments translated the assertion of their sovereign rights into restrictive national legislation, much-needed foreign direct investment dried up. Shadows of other possible initiatives, such as energy price indexing or the special drawing rights (SDR) link, flickered across conference tables creaking under the weight of interlocked agendas presented as an indissoluble whole. Special help for the poorest countries was promised, and global mechanisms for food aid were set in place (as they almost certainly would have been without the "new orders"). An unworkable Common Fund for commodities was laboriously negotiated, with a price tag of a few hundred million dollars rather than the billions sought by developing countries. The "oil weapon," that great tide in Third World affairs, swept Western governments into the uncertainties of stagflation and compelled the industrialized world to make structural adjustments. The result was to depress markets for Third World goods—hardly the most promising route to transforming the international division of labor in favor of the poor. Brutus believed that he was taking the current of fortune at the flood, but he went down to defeat at the battle of Philippi. As the tide receded, the oil-importing majority in the developing world discovered themselves stranded with unpayable debts and the worst slump in commodity prices since the 1930s. The interdependence of the global economy, demonstrated with peculiar brutality, brought home to all governments the impossibility of devising policies in isolation and strengthened the case for multilateral approaches. But it was a Pyrrhic victory for the Group of 77: the arteries of international negotiation had been hardened by the rituals of bloc votes on bloc agendas.

If the main impact of the call for a new economic order was to paralyze international debate, the insidious rhetoric of NWICO cast a longer shadow. Third World citizens were culturally impoverished rather than enriched as governments asserted, in the classic formulation of a senior Singaporean minister, that freedom of the press was not an absolute value but "a means to an all-embracing end—the integrity and independence of our country; its security, its prosperity; the eradication of anything that would sow seeds of social, racial and religious conflict"[19]—and proceeded to legislate accordingly. A nonaligned news agency pool was created, which by 1987 had acquired ninety-eight members and was circulating three thousand items a day, but much of this output, slipshod where not evidently sanitized, failed to make an impact on an already saturated world market. It was easier for governments to put into practice their ambitions for "nation-building" media than to control the price of coffee. But the fact that the "international community" had determined that government "guidance" was morally respectable did not render publics any more amenable to this sort of mobilization. Nor did NWICO have a discernible impact on the "friendly relations between states." At the end of 1986, declared by the UN to be the International Year of Peace, forty-one countries were fielding 5.5 million combatants in thirty-six armed conflicts around the globe.[20] Insofar as matters had improved by the 1990s, the principal factor was great-power cooperation in dispute settlement.

The revolution in international negotiating procedures, which began with the formation of the Group of 77 and the creation of UNCTAD, initially had the merit of enabling countries that were individually of small account to insist that their concerns be taken seriously by the more powerful actors. There was enough matter common to a sufficient number of developing countries to make discussion of "development" a useful international undertaking, and there were certain ways in which Gamani Corea, UNCTAD's second secretary-general, was not being wholly fanciful when he said that it had been "an instrument for stirring the conscience of the world."

Some reorientation of the United Nations to reflect Third World interests was inevitable and necessary. For the British historian Sir Michael Howard, the principal achievement of the UN by the end of the 1980s was that although it had "failed in its primary task" of collective security, it has "eased the transformation of the world from a Eurocentric to a truly global system" and enabled "the smallest and least considerable of its members to feel themselves part of a world community."[21] Perhaps only from the distance of an Oxford college and the perspective of a military historian could this have seemed to have taken place "in a remarkably orderly and amicable fashion." Allied to the "new orders" packages of nonnegotiable structural demands, the principle of solidarity became destructive not only of Third World interests, but of the only forums in which they could use their solidarity to articulate them.

Because the strategy of confrontation depended, critically, on the authority commanded by the United Nations and its place in international decisionmaking, "strengthening" the UN became an obsession with the nonaligned. It figured on the agenda of every summit. The terms in which it was discussed—the constant themes were "democratization," equal participation, universality, charter revision to enlarge the Security Council and break the five-power veto indicate; however, that "strengthening" meant reinforcing the power of the numerical majority. The purpose, as Tito had put it at the 1973 Algiers summit, was "to make the UN an effective factor in the struggle to create a new international regime."

Tito himself believed that "results will not be achieved either by imposing solutions, not by the game of majority vote, but by concerted solutions." But for most of those Third World governments that had an evolved UN policy (many went no further than the idea of solidarity) the test of the UN's "strength" became the degree to which resolutions and UN programs reflected the "new orders" agenda, and the positions of the nonaligned or Group of 77 negotiators. When the 1974 UN General Assembly closed, after voting through large segments of the Algiers summit declarations virtually verbatim as UN resolutions, the assembly president for that year, Algeria's foreign minister Abdelaziz Bouteflika, asserted that the battle of the agenda was won, and that "the only thing left now to decolonize is the [UN] secretariat."[22] It was in this spirit, in the following year, that developing countries approached an exercise aimed at restructuring the UN "to make it more fully capable of dealing with problems of international economic cooperation and development."[23] For Western negotiators, this meant making the UN more efficient; but for the South, it meant establishing the General Assembly's preeminence over the World Bank and the IMF in international financial and monetary policy, and subordinating the other specialized agencies to the broad political determinants of the new orders.

"Decolonizing the secretariat," a symbiotic process assisted by the anxiety of agency heads to empathize with the new majority, weakened both negotiating procedures and the quality of the international civil service. Even where UN posts were not, as often happened, allocated as a favor to a particular minister or influential delegate, their "equitable geographical distribution" came to outweigh the competence of applicants. There were also constant pressures to enlarge all committees, however specialized. And the founders' vision of a community of equal sovereign states was invoked, together with the principles of self-determination and universality, to justify the inclusion of dependencies as small as the Pitcairn or Cocos islands (populations respectively under one hundred and five hundred) in the list of potential "nations" monitored by the UN Decolonization Committee. The secretariats elaborated programs to reflect the "new orders" platforms—sometimes, as at UNCTAD or UNESCO, going beyond anything formulated in debate. The UN's potential was progressively eroded, not because of the concentration on the "North-South dialogue" but because dialogue was never seriously joined and because it gradually became apparent, even to the most sympathetic Western governments, that dialogue was not, ultimately, the purpose. The effect of the "new orders" was to elevate symbol over substance to the point that it was not only conservative Western governments, but the most avowedly liberal, for whom the definition of a successful UN conference became one in which there was no agreement.

In 1980, after months of committee work, a formula for "global negotiations" on the world economy hovered within reach at the UN—provided the Group of 77 dropped its insistence on the General Assembly's right to take the final decisions on agreements negotiated within the IMF and the World Bank. The Chinese argued, in vain, that the Group of 77 should accept the terms of reference as a basis to start talking, for two reasons. Terms that all sides found unsatisfactory had the merit of reflecting a desire to compromise; and in any case, developing countries were going to need whatever boat lay to hand in the fresh economic typhoon that was blowing up. Manuel Pérez-Guerrero, Venezuela's veteran North-South negotiator (and Prebisch's successor at UNCTAD), muttered angrily that the Chinese had failed to understand even the basic principles of the debate.

He was right. The point of the long drawn out battle for "global negotiations" was to establish the theses of the NIEO: that all negotiations must be linked and comprehensive, and that they were political in nature—hence the primacy of the General Assembly. To accept the Western condition (designed to protect the independence of the World Bank and IMF) that different issues should be discussed in the "competent" agencies would be to abandon the argument about power. Victory for the Group of 77 could therefore be won only by holding out, by maintaining its fidelity to the dogma, enunciated in Colombo in 1976, that "new, concrete and global solutions cannot be brought about by piecemeal reforms and improvisations."[24] A similar sense of priority had characterized a conference of the UN Industrial Development Organization a few months previously. On that occasion, the Group of 77 had voted through, against the entire OECD, a resolution that called for a $300 billion fund for industrial development, to be managed by the developing countries, and for good measure condemned capitalism as responsible for colonialism, racism, and imperialism.

Thomas Weiss, a sympathetic commentator who as a senior UNCTAD official from 1975 to 1985 was closely involved with critical phases of "new orders" diplomacy, questions whether many Group of 77 governments really welcomed concrete successes. "On no issue," he says, "is there not at least a significant number of countries that would be taken aback if somehow the North suddenly agreed to G77 demands," and he takes commodities to illustrate the point.[25] The original demand, at the 1974 UNCTAD, for an Integrated Program for Commodities made little headway, and the South focused increasingly on the Common Fund. Agreement, on a scaled-down basis, was finally reached in 1980. Several European governments promptly signed and Norway, with the OPEC Special Fund, offered to pay the least developed countries' membership contributions. Yet not only did the major Third World producers turn out to be extremely reluctant to commit themselves; even the poorest, whose costs were to be covered by others, "had to be pursued by members of the UNCTAD secretariat or other high-level missions to persuade them to sign on the dotted line." Governments were evidently indifferent to a fund that "had been fully and sometimes bitterly advanced as part of the southern cause."

Once the Group of 77's bluff had been called, Weiss comments, "the North-South dialogue was exposed as a bit of international theater while the real business of national interests on raw materials was being negotiated elsewhere." Within the theater, he points to a consistent pattern of support for ideas originating with the South or with sympathetic members of the secretariats, of rejection for those from the North, and of "manifestly non-negotiable proposals" frequently couched in abusive language—indicating not merely indifference to concrete results, but even a "hidden agenda": the desire to fail. Failure served many interests: those of the Group of 77 negotiators who found their professional *raison d'être* in the games of square brackets; of inept or corrupt governments seeking international explanations for local misery; of those governments, more intelligent, that hoped to use failure at the UN to extract concessions in bilateral negotiations or within the EC's Lomé framework; and of the articulate handful of genuinely radical politicians sincere in their confrontation with the West. Stalemate guaranteed

"Southern" solidarity in a coalition of more than 120 states as diverse as Sudan and Singapore—a coalition so fragile that the compromises necessary to achieve agreement threatened to unravel the process whereby joint demands were formulated.

The politics of solidarity have been a defining force in shaping UN organizations, and remain therefore an important consideration when it comes to assessing the UN's future. It proved so durable, so proof against experience in the world outside the UN, because governments did not have to believe their own rhetoric to be faithful to it. For many, the sense of achievement at having maintained the coalition, allied to a continuing conviction of the justice of the cause, outweighed the advantages of compromise in forums that, for most, appeared to have only the most tenuous connection with the daily business of domestic government. The greater the differentiation between Group of 77 members' circumstances and politics, the more symbolic importance was attached to unity at the UN. The more individual governments adopted, by necessity or conviction, more pragmatic policies outside the multilateral arenas, the more psychologically necessary the antidote of incantatory theater within them became.

Between 1980 and 1987, the commodities price index declined by an annual average of 5 percent. The longer perspective was no more encouraging: commodities represented 17 percent of global exports, as against 30 percent in the 1960s, and the Third World market share in commodities exports had fallen. To deal with the implications—particularly for countries that would continue to be heavily dependent on commodities trade—of what were clearly long-term trends, UNCTAD itself finally suggested "a more pragmatic and flexible approach." Presented to a preparatory meeting for that year's seventh UNCTAD conference by the head of UNCTAD's commodities division, Havelock Brewster, it emphasized changes in domestic policies, more sharply focused international negotiations geared to issues such as processing and market access, and recognition "that not all commodities are amenable to the same type of action." Commodity agreements, he said, could work only with adequate financial backing and when price levels were "market-related and compatible with dynamic market conditions." Uncertainty about the Common Fund was inhibiting alternative forms of cooperation. A deadline should be set for obtaining the ratifications necessary to bring it into force and, meantime, other "less comprehensive" approaches should be explored. For UNCTAD, it was the beginning of a delicate reversal out of an economic and political dead end, an acknowledgement that the Common Fund and the Integrated Program for Commodities (IPC), the twin pillars of its strategy, had limited relevance to the real predicament of most developing countries.

Brewster was vehemently attacked by the Group of 77, collectively and individually, for "abandoning" sacred texts—and for suggesting the need for domestic policy adjustments. Brazil, angrily rejecting the possibility that it was a "relic from a Utopian era," insisted that implementing the IPC was simply a matter of "sufficient political will"; Nigeria rejected "any new thesis"; Indonesia insisted that the old strategies were "relevant and valid"; and Ethiopia's Medhin Getachew, speaking as chairman of the Group of 77, intoned its "surprise, deep concern and disappointment" at UNCTAD's "underlying approach." Within days Kenneth Dadzie, UNCTAD's new secretary-general, had run for cover, with a statement affirming UNCTAD's full commitment to the IPC and the Common Fund.[26]

This reaction, so contrary to Third World interests, was a classic example of the intellectual and procedural rigidities of "new orders" politics. Individually, governments might be aware of the absolute need for a fresh approach to commodities. But the negotiating packages assembled by the Group of 77 tended to reflect the most radical positions and, once formulated, to be treated as inviolable sacred texts: No government could derogate from them publicly. The UNCTAD program was particularly sacrosanct because it reflected the widely held Third World belief that UN organizations existed to tilt the balance of political power and advantage southward. Commodity price management was symbolic of a much broader commitment to state intervention.

Similar factors lay behind the Group of 77's resistance to proposals, first formulated by the United States and then by the Western "Group B" in 1984, for reforms of UNCTAD—for an end, as the United States somewhat bluntly put it, to "its pursuit of artificial resolutions and decisions that chase the myth of global solutions." Thus formulated, the goal was understood to be a direct attack on Third World ambitions for structural change, and was met by a categorical Group of 77 refusal to countenance any review of UNCTAD's role "that would prevent us from using the UNCTAD forum *as a political forum* for bringing about changes in the system, even though such changes are not found acceptable in the short run to a particular group of countries."[27]

By the 1980s, any attempt to return the multilateral agencies to cautiously incremental programs, to confine negotiations to areas in which agreement was both urgent and possible, to stress the technical nature of their respective mandates, or to break away from the rhetoric of vague international development strategies and the litanies of the new orders was liable to be interpreted as an attack on multilateralism itself. For the Group of 77 to abandon its insistence on the contemporary relevance of "new orders" resolutions was felt to be tantamount to admitting the bankruptcy of three decades' effort at collective identity building, and the complete absence of any prospects for radical change.

Even housekeeping reforms, of the kinds being advanced in this period at UNESCO, the FAO, UNCTAD, and the UN itself, were treated by many Third World spokesmen as matters for "concession" or (as they put it at UNESCO's 1985 General Conference) "sacrifices." Anything at all far-reaching immediately brought into the open fundamental incompatibilities between Western donors, wedded to utilitarian criteria, and Third World governments, for whom the priority was to establish UN organizations—all UN organizations—as political vehicles dedicated to effecting a revolution in intergovernmental relations. Within the suspended animation of constantly reiterated formulas, faith in the utility of multilateral cooperation was damaged on both sides by recognition that there was little agreement as to the meaning either of utility or of cooperation.

Had UN secretariats in the two previous decades seen it as their duty to separate out the negotiable from the declamatory, to assist in bridging bridgeable gaps, and to provide the quality and type of staff papers in order to clarify the scope for common action, the impasses of the 1980s might have been less formidable. Some did, and a number of agency heads made strenuous efforts to insulate their agencies from ideological confrontation and the profound sense of cross-purpose that underlay it. Halfdan Mahler appealed to the World Health Assembly in 1983 to avoid political "minefields" that could "blow up our organization." Francis Blanchard, arguing that it is "inescapable for the West to consider problems—such as the social consequences of debt-related adjustment policies—which it has neglected," insisted that it was possible to elaborate the international dimensions of policy without rhetorical confrontation. "It would," he said, "have been so easy for us to produce a new international social order. But both instinctively and because of hard analysis, I've been diffident about embarking the ILO on grandiose enterprises: such as the NIEO—unfortunate, hypocritical, a non-starter."[28] Too many allowed the UN's greatest potential, its ability to promote mutual tolerance, to be diverted into the manufacture of "grandiose enterprises" in the name of tenets that alienated their basis of support in Western countries.

That alienation was treated by some UN heads with total contempt: even in 1985, when the United States had already left UNESCO and he was faced with British withdrawal, UNESCO's Amadou Mahtar M'Bow told a press conference in Geneva: "What does it matter if some governments are not satisfied with UNESCO's evolution? They had better understand that the world has changed since 1945."[29] The truth is that the radicalization of debate was extremely seductive to UN officials for two quite different sets of reasons.

The first was that many of the most talented believed that the UN, if it was to have a genuinely catalytic role, had a duty to be constructively subversive of the existing system, fostering the collective uneasiness that prepares official minds for change. Since the forces favoring the *status quo* were to be found in the wealthy states that benefitted from it, they argued, partisan involvement with the "new orders" by UN secretariats was a healthy and appropriate counterweight to the realities of political and economic power. The second was less high-minded. Third World governments wielded the votes; and Third World demands enlarged the agencies' potential for increasing their activities—and their budgets, which they could count on the majority to vote through. When Western governments, in the 1980s, began to reverse decades of passive resistance and to demand that the UN put its house in order, the bias toward the numerical majority was so ingrained in secretariat thinking that the natural reflex was to summon Third World support against an attack on "multilateralism."

"International organizations," Blanchard reminded governments in his 1987 report cited earlier, "are far from being deeply rooted in contemporary consciousness. Public opinion is at best skeptical or indifferent, at worst biased or hostile." While he argued that "no representative section of opinion questions the legitimacy of the United Nations system," he acknowledged that, if the agencies were "being left on the sidelines," it indicated "a gap of some sort between felt needs and the system's ability to meet them; an indication, no doubt, that the international agencies are lagging behind the pace of change in the world."[30] The ultimate irony of the politics of the new orders was that, dedicated to radical change, they had cocooned the UN in a warp of rhetoric that marginalized the very agencies they relied on to transform the political order.

5. THE WESTERN DILEMMA

WESTERN MISGIVINGS

The Gulf War of 1990–91 generated, particularly in the West, such a wave of public confidence in the UN that optimistic statements about its revived potential became almost obligatory for politicians. The Rio "Earth summit" of 1992 attracted a record number of Western heads of government—a significant fact not least because many of these politicians would undoubtedly have been advised a few years earlier to steer clear of the summit's contentious and unmanageably copious agenda. The "green vote" may have counted for something, but the real pressure on them was to be seen to be taking global diplomacy seriously. But official optimism was otherwise carefully centered on collaboration within the Security Council; when it came to the prospects for "revitalising the UN system," circumspection prevailed. And this circumspection had its source in the perceived gap between the world of the UN and the world outside.

UN diplomacy still conjured up for Western governments an image of impotence before the demands of an intransigent majority, of Western negotiators consistently outvoted or reduced to improper compromise by the Byzantine procedures of "damage-limiting" consensus. This is the debilitating legacy of the new orders politics. When George Bush, in an uncharacteristic burst of rhetorical hyperbole, figured forth his own "new world order" in 1990, what was uppermost in his mind were not the global dimensions of multilateralism, but the vistas of cooperation between the major powers opened by the collapse of communism. The Clinton administration started out in 1993 by setting up a U.S. commission[1] to advise it on ways of "improving the effectiveness of the United Nations"—a brief as revealing as it was familiar—only to receive sharply conflicting advice from its members as to the reliance that could sensibly be placed on global diplomacy.

It would be misleadingly simplistic to characterize these divisions as nationalist versus multilateralist. The image of the UN as a place where the powerful are rendered impotent is shared by those liberals who, in the West as well as the Third World, argue that the old order is genuinely defunct, that Western foot-dragging only delays the inevitable surrender to the "international community" of the rich countries' politically and morally unsustainable positions of privilege. In this view, the UN projects the future on our screens even if, in today's world, the diminution of East-West conflict may appear to have further tipped the North-South balance in the North's favor. It is shared, from another perspective, by those who argue that the collective assault by the majority of the UN's members on many of the ethical, legal, and organizational principles on which Western conduct of international relations is based removes the common ground essential to global cooperation—and thus makes of the UN a burnt-out case.

But does this impotence, or loss of influence, reflect reality? And insofar as it does, to what extent is it due not to the dethronement of the West within the UN, but to its abdication—its resort to reactive and even evasive tactical maneuvering, its quiet abandonment of any attempt to sustain coherent diplomatic strategies? We have examined the challenge to the original concept of the UN's role—and to Western interests in it—articulated through the politics of the new orders. It is time to look at the factors that over the years prompted Western governments, by and large, to give so much ground at the UN, and to ask what realistic alternatives they had—and have.

It could be argued, with strong supporting evidence, that at the height of the politics of confrontation, when Western governments most needed to defend the UN's original purposes, they were disinclined to do so. And the less they did so, the less incentive there was to make these organizations work. A UN official charged in the late 1980s that "the organizations are dissolving and the best Western governments have done is to organize themselves as, at the crudest level, accountants. They talk about cost and value for money. But intellectually, they have put them into receivership." A Western official responsible for UN affairs responded that this was, in essence, where the organizations now belonged. "It is reasonable," he said, "to put in enough effort to maintain them in some state of order, since abolition is not an option, and that in itself is exceedingly difficult. But you have to accept that policy reflects the fact that it is simply impossible now for any of us to think ourselves back into the language of the late '40s or early '50s."[2] What this suggests is that the incompatibility of views—political, managerial but above all ideological—about those original purposes has become so great that it is pointless to pretend that there exists, still, the minimum level of common ground that would make it possible to invest the concept of universality with any serious set of meanings.

One effect of the Third World assault on "the language of the late '40s and early '50s" was to engender such degrees of pessimism as this—a pessimism that particular UN "successes," whether in conflict resolution or agreements to limit damage to the ozone layer, would address only superficially and that runs far beyond frustrations with managements or committees. To review the critical issues in new orders politics from the Western viewpoint is to see how sharply they affronted both of the liberal strains of thought that found expression in the UN Charter and the Universal Declaration of Human Rights. The first strain, which might be termed classical, traces its descent from the Enlightenment through Tocqueville and John Stuart Mill; it is the liberalism that holds that individual well-being may be rationally organized in a free society and between free societies, and whose nineteenth-century political exponents argued for "legal or administrative reforms tending in the direction of freedom or democracy."[3] The second, also represented in the Universal Declaration, is a more recent political phenomenon, opposing to the calculations of power the moral case for redistributive policies and carrying, in the period with which we are concerned, strong connotations of welfare state politics. It is in the defense of values and philosophies deriving from both these traditions—of individual rights, and of the melioristic gradualism of liberal social engineering—that the West has had greatest difficulty in responding to the polarization of the global forums.

But if Western governments can justly be charged with abdicating their responsibilities, it is also necessary to acknowledge the growing conviction of the majority of

Western policymakers, at the least since the early 1970s, that no purpose could be served by robust opposition in these forums to stances that were fundamentally alien to Western interests and ways of thinking. Was, and is, that assumption correct? The record of too many UN debates, in which the slightest move by a Western government to reroute discussion is liable to end in the thickets of procedural impasse as the regional voting blocs assert themselves, suggests the affirmative.

A senior Western ambassador to the UN disagrees—on the ground that

> the cards at the UN are stacked, contrary to appearances, rather heavily in favor of the West. The Charter and rules of procedure were largely written by the United States and the UK. In any negotiation, we hold the bargaining chips because we have the money and power. We are exceedingly defeatist if, having written the rules of the game, we aren't prepared to play it; and feeble if we can't win it.

The West's failure, he contends, is one not of competence nor even of power but of imagination: "A great deal of mental labor goes into our conduct of UN affairs, but nothing we could dignify with the name of thought. We work hard at managing it, but we have yet to think how to use it."[4]

Such claims to inbuilt advantage look more convincing in the abstract than they do during late-night drafting groups, or when, as happened in 1982, four out of six weeks available for technical negotiations on the allocation of radio frequencies at a conference of the International Telecommunications Union (ITU) had been spent fighting against the exclusion of Israel from the ITU. It is not self-evidently easy, as a small minority, to uphold the original purposes of organizations conceived for the defense of liberties that are under assault by the majority; and even when it comes to improving the organizations' effectiveness, the ease with which secretariats can muster allies to oppose attempts to rationalize their programs or to improve evaluations of their impact can reduce bold ideas to forgotten footnotes. But they have enough substance to suggest that the paralysis of Western policies toward UN organizations cannot just be ascribed to minority status. On the few occasions when Western governments have acted with even some degree of cohesion and tenacity, they have made an impact.

Allied to the power of the purse, the diplomatic skills and organizational backup at the disposal of Western governments ought to give them considerable leverage with UN secretariats, about whose operations they are equipped if they choose to be far better informed than most of their Third World counterparts. And, for all the essentially destructive exploitation by the voting majority of the egalitarianism built into the enterprise, the UN's founding documents do work in the West's favor. The concept of multilateral cooperation is profoundly rooted in a liberal internationalism, based in common adherence to the rule of law, which is largely Western-inspired. And "development" itself implies a degree of convergence, through the progressive integration of societies and economies and the challenge this poses to the despotic monopolies of power.

If the cards are stacked, if the West does have certain assets, why has it played them reluctantly or not at all? Some of the more general answers to that question have already been explored. The purpose here is to review some of the specific constraints on Western policymakers—and the extent to which the West's wounds have been self-inflicted.

The constraints fall under three main headings: ideological, procedural, and organizational. The first will lead us back to human rights. It cannot help but do so: their defense and promotion lie at the heart of the West's commitment to global organizations, and inform its attitude to multilateral cooperation for economic development. The tensions between the principles of the UN Charter and the claims of a moral relativism adapted to the diversity of the UN's membership have been an important feature of Western debate about policies toward these forums. Under the second, we will explore the practical difficulties of "forum management" and the temptations to resort to damage limitation. The third concerns the management, in Western capitals, of UN business. Together, they provide the context in which the Reagan administration set out to effect a seachange in multilateral diplomacy by challenging what it saw as the capitulation of the West; just as they raise, today, the larger question of whether there can be such a thing as "Western" policies toward global organizations.

Ideas, Bread, and Colonial Guilt

It was, paradoxically, their sense that the West held all the cards that initially persuaded many thoughtful Western internationalists that the Third World's success in setting UN agendas and asserting the claims of small countries to equality vindicated the existence of global forums. Here, the individually powerless could make their concerns felt, could argue their case for assistance in meeting the needs of their citizens uninhibited by the political tensions of the donor-client relationship, could assert in all their poverty "the dignity and worth of the human person."[5] Here, they could remind Western governments of the responsibilities of power, whether military or economic. Short term, their demands might conflict with Western interests in the economic field, but in the longer view there could be no incompatibility between their accelerated economic development and the West's prosperity in an interdependent world. The very fact that the decisions that counted—and that often directly affected other countries—were made between East and West or, particularly in the economic field, within Western clubs was felt to increase the importance, as a counterweight, of places in which these countries could attempt to influence the global oligarchy and draw it into a process of consultation.

If the "new" countries and the old but economically laggard civilizations brought to these debates new cultural and political perspectives, this too was to be welcomed. They enriched international understanding in the best traditions of liberal democracy. And these traditions, in turn, would influence them. The UN was "a great educational institution," according to one Western diplomat who believes that it still is: "Working by talk and compromise, it helps delegations to understand realities and accustoms them to democratic processes." The tinge of *noblesse oblige* in the suggestion that governments need such "education" was balanced by the belief that the UN's forums served to remind Western governments of their obligations of respect for the cultural autonomy and national interests of their "partners." Even the mammoth and necessarily inconclusive UN sessions largely devoted to nuclear disarmament could be justified on the ground that universal participation in debate furnished the powerless with compensatory fictions—fictions that, in an unequal world, were necessary lubricants of global diplomacy.

The rise to prominence of economic issues seemed to be a further "balancing factor." The "New Deal" tenor of early debates was perfectly consonant in Western minds with the cultural and historical connections between civil liberties and material progress. The Universal Declaration itself included a wide range of social and economic "rights" that encapsulated most of the aspirations of the postwar welfare state. The Third World pressure for special funds and programs and the remarkable expansion in international technical assistance during the 1960s were logical concomitants of decolonization. The needs of countries catapulted into political independence with often rudimentary experience of administration and severe shortages of both capital and skilled manpower were so glaring as to constitute, at least to the ex-colonial powers, a reproach. Both bilaterally and through the UN, "aid" became a flourishing form of diplomacy. The first UN Development Decade was launched in 1960 in a climate of considerable optimism that, given politically neutral infusions of assistance and carefully constructed development plans, developing countries could rapidly reach the point of "takeoff." The shift in nomenclature, from "backward" or "underdeveloped" to "developing," heralded the heyday of meliorism. Purposes were assumed to be common; arguments centered on the quantity of external assistance and even here, without necessarily agreeing to pay the bills as presented, Western governments did not dissent in principle. To flourish in a period of rapidly rising productivity and technological change, capitalism—or, more accurately, the free-market mixed economy—required expanding markets, which a massive increase in the purchasing power of the new nations could supply.

Only gradually, as Third World leaders reinterpreted the language of the Enlightenment to press the radical and essentially collectivist claims of the new orders, did the world of "multiple voices" appear in an alien guise—as a world in which the right to disagree, defended by Voltaire, lost the connotation of individual rights that constitutes its force.

It is not easy to trace the beginnings of the UN's loss of innocence, but they have more to do with a growing conceptual gulf than with shifts in voting majorities. Ironically, it was the high rates of economic growth achieved by most of the new countries in the 1960s that triggered divergence. The concept of development planning—implying as it did a large measure of state intervention—remained common ground, but in the West, questions began to be asked both on the Right and the Left about *who* was benefiting from the flows of Western capital, while in the South not only the possibility but the desirability of attempting to "catch up" within an international environment set and controlled by the West became central issues of debate. The landmark texts were Robert McNamara's 1973 Nairobi address and the Prebisch/Echeverria/NIEO theories discussed earlier. At Nairobi, McNamara pledged the World Bank to address "absolute poverty," which he defined as "a condition of life so degraded by disease, illiteracy, malnutrition, and squalor as to deny its victims basic human necessities" and "so limited as to prevent realization of the potential of the genes with which one is born."

Behind that speech lay an acknowledgment that official aid was creating a thin layer of relative affluence from which "some forty percent of the peoples of developing countries" were excluded. McNamara's new World Bank strategy, "redistribution with growth," was intended to bring pressure to bear on the new elites. When he asked: "Are we to tolerate such poverty, when it is in our power to reduce the number afflicted, by failing to fulfill the fundamental obligations accepted by civilized men?" the question had a double edge. The mirror image of the Third World's collective mythologization of sovereignty was an increasingly skeptical Western scrutiny of the commitment of Third World leaders to "the dignity and worth of the human person." As each challenged the legitimacy of the other's declared values, development became highly political. The Third World insistence on the primacy and collective nature of economic and social rights was more than a little defensive; in demanding the restructuring of an unjust and repressive international order, its leaders were bolstering their self-respect by turning the West's concern with justice back on itself.

While each side accused the other of double standards, Western governments presented a disunited front that reflected differences of opinion within and between their societies. It was offensive as well as alarming to be told by those who arrogated to themselves the moral authority of the "international community" that values and freedoms that Westerners believed to be universal were merely "Western" or, worse, that they were mantles thrown over the immoral defense of privilege and power. It was doubly offensive when the assault came from those whose claims to represent and speak for their people were, to Western eyes, somewhat fraudulent. But the facts of inequality were also inhibiting, as were traditions of intellectual tolerance. While ultimately convinced that defence of these principles was in the genuine interest of all citizens, once the voting majority insisted on their "reinterpretation" not all Western governments had the same readiness to go into battle as the conscience of the world. "We are not missionaries," a West German diplomat told a group of Third World UN delegates dealing with information issues. "We cannot force any country into accepting the liberties so dear to our hearts. The question of freedom in any country must be decided by its people."[6]

Such scruples made it difficult to construct coherent Western policies out of broadly shared beliefs. Although in private most diplomats were more cynical, most governments agreed, at least in public, with Jeane Kirkpatrick's testimony to the U.S. Senate in 1984 that "it is not enlightened or generous or responsible . . . to be, or seem to be, indifferent to what transpires in great international fora . . . to act as though we did not care about decisions in international bodies. It is our duty to try in all appropriate ways to strengthen freedoms and human rights and to promote the values of the Charter." The source of much Western division has lain in differing estimates of the "appropriate." For the West, might not promoting "the values of the Charter" mean standing by the Voltairean principle of respect for difference? Western diplomats balanced on a permanent trip wire as they sought to act out a proper respect for cultural and political pluralism without falling into the relativist trap and endorsing principles that violated individual liberties. It was in this sense that the confrontation over Third World demands for a New World Information Order, the basic tenets of which were discussed in the last chapter, posed exceptional difficulties for the West.

The free flow of ideas and knowledge is a principle on which there can be logically no ground for compromise. It might have been expected to unite the West more than any other issue at the UN. Yet the Western response was both hesitant and dissonant, both at governmental and nongovernmental levels. There was a tendency to start from the "realistic" position that encroachments on intellectual freedom were a fact of life about which the West could do nothing; then to look for a "consensus" that would avert confrontation; and finally to take refuge in the assertion that UN resolutions bound nobody anyway.

"Freedom of information," of which press freedom was an important constituent, had been proclaimed in a much-quoted resolution of the UN General Assembly in 1946 to be "a fundamental human right and . . . the touchstone of all the freedoms to which the United Nations is consecrated."[7] It was UNESCO's *raison d'être*. Its international dimension had been stated in singularly uncompromising terms in Article 19 of the Universal Declaration of Human Rights, which spoke of "freedom to seek, receive and impart information through any media and regardless of frontiers." From the earliest years of the UN's history, however, it had been a disputed right. Governments proved incapable even of discussing freedom of information without seeking to ensure that the media, in particular, "merited" their freedom. Even back in the 1940s, efforts by the United States to strengthen governments' commitment to the principle of the free flow of information boomeranged, eliciting a flurry of proposals at the UN for codes of ethics, rights of reply for states, and legislation to prevent "false or distorted reports likely to injure friendly relations between States."[8] Nothing was more alien to Western values than the idea that the media should be dictated to by governments, yet UNESCO's constitution, in careless language that would later be exploited by the proponents of "information sovereignty" and the right of governments to use the media for purposes of state, committed states to "employ" the means of communication to promote peace and international understanding. In defending the free circulation of facts and comment in UN forums, Western governments were inhibited by their shared belief that, apart from laying down laws of libel, privacy, confidence, or national security, governments had no business discussing the content of news and the conduct of the press. The entire debate was therefore out of order. Once other governments brought up the subject, however, there were principles at stake: Was not one of the purposes of UNESCO, in particular, "to promote plurality by reminding governments that they had a duty not to infringe freedom of information"?[9] The West's irresolution in the face of the campaign for a new information order was, given its connotations of thought control, remarkable; but it was partly attributable to an excessive anxiety to give the developing countries the benefit of the doubt.

Third World spokesmen attracted considerable initial sympathy by harping on two themes: Western dominance and the right to cultural sovereignty. In the early 1970s, developing countries did indeed depend on the major Western-based media for the bulk of their international news. They found allies in the West ready to support their contention that Western-based (or even Western-style) media, chiefly in the entertainment but also in the news fields, failed to reflect their priorities and swamped them with alien material. To remedy the problem of "dependence," it seemed reasonable that the West, bilaterally or through the UN, should assist in the development of national media. It even seemed reasonable that, where private news organizations (and commercial markets that would make these viable) were underdeveloped, states might be assisted to build up publicly owned media in the hope that they would exercise their proprietorship with discretion—although increasingly strident Third World attacks on the principle of the free flow hardly justified optimism.

Western opposition to Third World efforts to legitimize control of the media on grounds of political and cultural sovereignty was moreover nuanced by the "cultural imperialism" thesis, synonymous for some West Europeans with the preponderance of the American media. As late as 1982, by which time the regulatory goals of the proposed "new order" were fully evident, France's minister of culture, Jack Lang, demonstrated the limits of Western solidarity on this issue at a UNESCO conference in Mexico, launching a violent public attack on the United States for defending "the freedom of the fox in the barnyard" in order to promote American cultural imperialism. And eleven years later, in 1993, France's successful demand for an *exception culturelle*, to protect the French film industry from international competition, came close to shipwrecking the GATT Uruguay Round when all other hurdles in this seven-year negotiating marathon had been surmounted. There were many, less dramatic occasions in UNESCO and at the UN in New York when Western negotiators, to show their understanding of the resentment of the "South," borrowed the Third World's language.

None of this made policy coordination any easier and it was only after a decade of delicate fencing, promising Western aid in return for "reasonable" language, that the West united in concluding that principles were at stake on which no compromise was possible—and that the tactic of trade-offs had in any case failed. By this time, however, the earlier search for conciliatory language had seriously eroded the scope for a principled stand. The West had agreed to acknowledge Third World "aspirations" for a new information order, provided that it did not involve binding rules and was seen as "an evolving and continuous process." This phrase, the pride of its Western negotiators, was supposed to guard against regulatory encroachments on press freedom. The advocates of the new order concluded that it had now been endorsed in principle, and "evolution" toward prescriptive definition was merely a matter of time and persistence. If it was legitimate for governments to discuss an "order," it followed that it was proper for them to consider the content of information and the media's role. When, in 1987 at the UN's Committee on Information, the U.S. delegate argued that the whole concept was "alien" because "the word 'order' connotes political and economic systems inherently opposed to freedom of opinion and expression,"[10] she was repudiating a formula that the United States had accepted nine years earlier. By the time a new UNESCO director-general had committed himself, in 1988, to removing this apple of discord from the organization's agenda, it had infected debate in New York.

Western governments' handling of the demands for a new information order illustrates the kinds of double standard that afflicted their policies at the UN during this period. Half-acceptance of the thesis that the media were indeed resources that governments in the throes of nation-building might understandably seek to mobilize had its political parallel in the argument, widely employed by Western liberals, that desperately poor, politically fragile, and culturally "unsophisticated" societies could not "afford" democracy. With its unspoken assumption that the best hope for lesser breeds was to replace colonial paternalism with a home-grown version of the same and its more or less explicit rejection of the possibility of universal values, this argument acquired respectability through reference to cultural pluralism. The literature of human rights theory is enormous and highly sophisticated; what concerns us here is the political impact of a certain line of argument. Postcolonial guilt and the excesses of Cold War rhetoric produced among many Western intellectuals a pronounced reaction, one of the symptoms of which was a tendency to treat the defense of democratic rights—whether in the Eastern bloc or the developing world—as "right wing," ethnocentric, and arrogant. (After the collapse of communism in Europe, Russian and East European intellectuals said how extraordinary they had found the liberal abuse heaped on Reagan for calling the Soviet Union "the evil empire." This was, for them, simply a statement of fact.)

As Pascal Bruckner has pointed out, almost nobody actually read Frantz Fanon's essays on *The Wretched of the Earth*,[11] which took the liberal intelligentsia by storm when the book was published in 1961, the year of his early death. But everybody read the preface in which Jean-Paul Sartre melodramatically summoned to ultimate confession a Europe (and "that super-European monstrosity, North America") that was morally "at death's door." Hailing Fanon as a standard-bearer of the Third World's intellectual emancipation, in a "wide-awake world that has run our falsehoods to earth," Sartre condemned Western humanism as "nothing but a tissue of lies, a perfect justification for pillage." The bankruptcy of a culture that had subjugated mankind in the name of a universal civilizing mission had, he argued, left the West with a single hope of salvation, "the very Christian sentiment of guilt."

Fanon's essays, themselves, were remarkably free of such breast-beating. In all their radicalism, they were distinctly products of the "Western" culture that Sartre so eloquently accused the colonizers of "branding" on subject peoples. Their passionate preoccupation was the danger that new elites would betray the movements for independence by slipping into colonial shoes, neglecting the countryside, and stifling the "free flow of ideas from the people up to the government." His penetrating analysis of "the pitfalls of national consciousness" conjured up the image of one-party states developing into "tribal dictatorships" that, "powerless economically, unable to bring about the existence of coherent social relations," would "not create a state that reassures the ordinary citizen, but rather one that rouses his anxiety." With an elite "preoccupied with filling its pockets as rapidly as possible but also as prosaically as possible, the country sinks all the more deeply into stagnation. And in order to hide the stagnation . . . the bourgeoisie can find nothing better to do than to erect grandiose buildings in the capital and to lay out money on what are called prestige expenditures." Leaders who derived their "moral power" from their struggle for independence would "become the general president of that company of profiteers impatient for their returns." To maximize the privileges of its elite, the young state would steadily increase its indebtedness to and dependence on the old colonial power. Neocolonialism, Fanon bleakly predicted, was something the countries' leaders would themselves create—while presenting themselves to the people as the bulwark against colonial and neocolonial exploitation.

That it was to take nearly three decades before Fanon's preoccupations were frankly discussed shows how deeply Western debate had been penetrated by a combination of false humility and Sartrean "guilt." False humility borrowed the language of Third World radicals to argue that, yes, the central place accorded by liberal theory to individual rights was indeed a product of the historical evolution of Western society and that the West should not presume to inflict its "individualistic bias" on societies in which family, clan, or community were the "relevant" measures. "The Chinese," as Alain Peyrefitte confidently proclaimed in a classic formulation of this kind of moral pluralism, "have no need of liberty; they have never known it and it is alien to their culture."

Such assumptions increasingly permeated Western policy, and not only within UN forums. Looking back, just after massive student demonstrations in June 1987 had forced the government of President Chun Doo Hwan to promise open presidential elections in South Korea, Abe Rosenthal discussed their impact on U.S. policy toward that country:

> American specialists kept telling South Korean democrats not to push hard, warning that Korean traditions and Confucian heritage were incompatible with democracy, you see. The South Koreans did not see. Year after year

> opposition leaders were jailed and beaten and year after year students battled in the streets for a free political system. They did not seem to think freedom was antithetical to Confucian values, or maybe didn't care if it was.[12]

Guilt nourished a bread-before-freedom school of thought, which further complicated the notion of respect for pluralism. Without delving into Sartrean introspection on the West's forfeiture, through exploitation, of its claims to civilized values, this school argued that in insisting on the primacy of individual liberties, the well-fed West demonstrated an insensitivity to the daily exigencies of poverty that bordered on the obscene. Among both governments and development theorists, there grew up a considerable body of support for claims by Third World leaders that, without state intervention to secure their peoples' "positive" rights such as those to food, development, and international realignments of wealth and power, "old rights" were meaningless abstractions. In the belief that it thereby identified itself "with the underprivileged," the Dutch government of 1973–77 formally welcomed the New International Economic Order, announcing that "the maintenance of the colonial power structure can no longer be accepted by the developing world."[13] And in 1977 Charles Yost, who had been U.S. permanent representative to the UN in the early 1970s, took the Carter administration to task for harming U.S. human rights policy by concentrating on "political and civil rights, where its own traditions are clear and its performance, at least recently, excellent, while minimizing economic and social rights which, to a large part of mankind that is never sure where its next meal is coming from, are far more urgent."[14] Such considerations hedged with the spirit of compromise much Western discussion of collective rights.

This postcolonial *noblesse oblige* did not exactly accept double or incompatible standards; it simply supposed that developing countries could not be expected to recognize and practice democratic liberties until they had become prosperous and politically mature. Such "realism" was not incompatible with Western efforts to nudge their leaders in that desirable direction, provided they neither attached to the exercise extravagant hopes nor underestimated the cultural and economic barriers. Meantime, policy had to be based on the insurmountable fact that the international language of states did not amount to a language of peoples, whatever the preamble to the UN Charter might proclaim.

This argument could be persuasively put. For Edgard Pisani, a minister in both Gaullist and socialist French governments and the European Community's development commissioner in the early 1980s—a man who describes himself as "*tiers-mondiste* but not out of penitence"—the West's mistake "is to talk about human rights as though they were revealed truths, not a continuing struggle. It is absurd to demand that countries observe rights which their people have yet to conquer—even if this leaves me accused of relativism. And until they do, we go against history in opposing the arbitrary powers of the state."[15] Pisani puts in a nutshell a view widely held in chanceries—and in international boardrooms, where it provides a convenient rationalization for the endemic practice of bribing corrupt Third World officials in order to win contracts. An "evolutionary" approach that accepts without excusing, it seeks historical justification for finessing the principles of the Enlightenment—and of the UN Charter—to fit the requirements of practical politics. It might be said to reflect a distinctively European (and particularly French) attitude to the management of relations with unpalatable Third World governments—although Europeans would argue that U.S. policy, as opposed to rhetoric, was not dissimilar. For many years, there was not much to choose between the United States and Europeans when it came to a "strategically important" dictatorship like Sésé Séko Mobutu's Zaire.

Such a stance is not incompatible with the odd abstention on UN resolutions that affront Western democratic sensibilities, assuming as it does that civil liberties are so deeply embedded in Western societies that their governments can afford to allow for the expression of less enlightened perspectives. It assumes that liberty, like prosperity, is geographically and culturally specific—and, most conveniently for policymakers but perhaps most speciously also, that rights, rather like prosperity, are earned.

The apparent respect for other countries' priorities and cultures implied by such Western scruples may serve practical political ends, but can also, under the guise of tolerance, lend respectability to the apparatus of state repression. It is little comfort to individuals who attempt to combat such repression to learn that they and their countrymen may be deemed by the West not to have progressed far enough with their "continuing struggle" to justify the outside world's putting its weight in the scales "against history." Pluralism of this sort undermines such advances as have been made under the UN in codifying the rights of individuals to live under the rule of law and to choose their forms of government. The bread-before-freedom argument also has limitations even in its own terms. The hungry farmer might with good reason take the old-fashioned view that respect for civil and political liberties offered him his best chance of extracting a fair price for his crops from the state marketing board, or of combating the corruption and social injustices that deprived him of material security. He might even be prepared to trade a bit of sovereignty for the prospect of some form of external sanction against official abuses of power.

It was only gradually—and this was one of the effects of new orders politics—that the consequences of this relativism began to be apparent, and to upset what might be called, paraphrasing Stalin, the doctrine of freedom in one country. The campaigns for new economic and information orders did not, in fact, so much reject the universal applicability of norms and rules as insist that the rules themselves be altered to take into account new realities—notably, that "respect for difference" added a new cultural dimension to the barriers sovereignty erected. What the campaigners sought in effect was Western endorsement of collective bargaining rights—rights stemming from the requirements of sovereignty and the aspirations of "peoples." As these demands unfolded, the struggle involved in finding ways to contain this revolt against what they saw as the basic principles underlying the Charter, without in the process compromising their own principles, largely accounted for Western government's frustration with United Nations debates. The effort to accommodate incompatible points of departure produced a new school of theorists of human rights, many of them Western or Western-educated, who sought, either within the UN or in active cooperation with its secretariats, to incorporate Third World ideological platforms into "rights of solidarity." The method was to move from the notion of innate individual rights to dynamic processes whereby rights evolved—a subtle but decisive shift from Pisani's formulation—in response to the needs of society.

As presented in summary form by Stephen Marks,[16] an American then working for UNESCO's human rights division, the theory assumed an alliance between human rights and social progress. Crudely put, it ran thus. The "first generation" of human rights, rooted in the Enlightenment and internationally influential thanks to "the privileged position [of] Western Europe and North America," were negative—"freedoms from" state controls over opinion, conscience, religion, movement, the right to own property, and so on. Because "the freedom of the first generation had meant for the majority of the working class and peoples of conquered lands the right to be exploited and colonized," nineteenth-century social upheavals led to a second generation of "economic, social and cultural rights," influenced by "socialist and Marxist writings," and "characterized by the intervention . . . of the state . . . *claims*—rather than freedoms."

The anticolonialist revolution then took the process a stage further, "giving a privileged status to self-determination and non-discrimination," and articulating rights that dealt with "planetary concerns" such as peace and development. The realization of these rights required concerted action by all states and also—his example was the concept of the common heritage of mankind—benefited "the peoples of the Third World, being that segment of mankind which has been excluded in recent history from the benefits of precisely those domains over which the economic domination of the North has been so successfully exercised."

So starting from the premise that human beings have needs, this theory argued that where people could not satisfy them through self-help, they had the right to claim them "through the social process." Needs that a society recognized entered the body of that society's values. "International society" in turn recognized certain "standards" as human rights. With a nod to the "problematical . . . temptation to believe that a desirable proposition is a human right and to rely on the slightest evidence, such as a resolution of the General Assembly, to prove it," Marks argued that "UN resolutions occupy a crucial role in the norm-creating process." And this was particularly true of the "rights of solidarity," for while most of these had an individual dimension, their novelty resided in their collective claims and the international dimension of demands for their recognition.

The premises, once granted, opened out almost limitless vistas—"the right to disarmament . . . the right to international cooperation . . . the right to the satisfaction of basic needs regardless of the level of development of the country. . . ." The concept of "third-generation rights" weakened the authority of the Universal Declaration and the two 1966 covenants that codified it in two ways: first by implying (as its liberal advocates recognized, although they denied intending it) that the "old" rights were outmoded; second by dilution. Once "rights" were postulated that were so vague as to be unenforceable, the entire argument about human rights shifted to the political plane—and reflected the concerns of politicians with the exercise of power.

The "right to development" is a case in point. It is often presented as a down-to-earth concern removed from the abstractions of civil and political rights; but it is of course highly political. It makes sweeping assumptions about the purposes of government, and the capacity and will of the state to order economic and social life. And the idea of a "right to the satisfaction of basic needs regardless of the level of development of the country" reaches further into the absurd, since while citizens may well stake claims the state is incapable of meeting, they cannot realistically claim that simply by demanding, they establish these claims as rights. To the peasant who cannot make his needs known, or call the state to account if they are not met, the right to development may be a more meaningless abstraction than the civil rights he is conscious of being denied. But the postulation of these new "rights" presented Western governments with an awkward political dilemma: Who could reasonably object to a "right to development"?

In practice, the texts of this "right" negotiated in UN bodies in the 1970s and 1980s served to codify the demands of the 1975 NIEO Declaration. These included the duty of states to promote the NIEO, to "formulate international development policies," to "eliminate the massive and flagrant violations of the human rights of peoples" perpetrated by *apartheid*, colonialism, foreign domination, and so on, and, reflecting Soviet concerns, to "achieve general and complete disarmament."[17] The language of rights was being used to promote a political agenda. It suited that agenda that the new "rights" took the spotlight off governments' violations of established rights, and the momentum out of efforts to improve monitoring and enforcement. More importantly, they provided moral justification for policies that—in the name of social progress, cultural autonomy, or economic imperatives—abridged individual rights.

The proliferation of new "rights" also deflected the UN and some of the major "functional" agencies from the pursuit of the negotiable and the promotion of standards that were capable of being implemented. When McNamara talked about the importance of meeting "basic human necessities," he was thinking of what active, concrete steps could be taken, and which changes in national policies would help people realize their "individual potential." Paradoxically, the codifying passion that gripped so many UN secretariats and bulked out conference agendas, principally served to blur objectives such as these, and reinforced the inertia of conservatives of both North and South by making action dependent on unattainable ideological compromise. UN studies and programs increasingly reflected this emphasis on ideology. Both as forums and as sources of advice, the effectiveness of the major UN organizations was correspondingly impaired.

For Western policymakers, the question of whether to treat the erosion of the primacy of individual rights as a vital interest or a matter for token gestures presented itself at three levels. First, given that the International Monetary Fund (IMF), the World Bank, and regional development banks, the Lomé Conventions and other channels for economic cooperation existed, they had to decide how much importance to attach to the UN's frameworks for "global bargaining." Second, they needed to assess the threat posed to democratic societies by international legitimation of rights and obligations that they could not themselves accept. Finally, they had to weigh the degree of self-interest, however enlightened, that might be served by active participation in organizations of decreasing efficacy. There was little obvious gain to be had from sitting through "debates" in which Western policies were vilified as repressive, the freedoms dear to Western societies as hypocritical, self-serving, or outmoded, and the laws by which Westerners expected states to conduct their affairs as inequitable. In a world of irreconcilables, did arguing the case simply endow the opposition with magnified status? The natural temptation was to reply that it all depended on the instance—and the readiness with which Western Europeans tended to yield to that temptation was a major source of transatlantic friction over UN policy.

In a classic exposition of Washington's frustrations with its allies at the UN, Kenneth Adelman, then a member of Jeane Kirkpatrick's team in New York, argued that there was no alternative to the active defense of principle: "No matter how tedious the UN's rhetoric or unreadable its resolutions, it does influence the climate of international opinion. It thus helps to shape the context in which the 'real world' of international politics takes place. Many of us feel that a war of ideas is being waged both in the UN and outside it, and the believers in liberty had best act or risk losing by default."[18] He accused "some, if not many" Western governments of treating the UN as a place "where the Third World's goodwill can be earned 'on the cheap' . . . by 'giving them' a resolution, a vote or a sympathetic speech," assuming meanwhile that the United States would carry the opprobrium of standing up for Western values and interests. "They will abstain on, or even support, resolutions which call for measures which they have no intention whatsoever of complying with . . . abstain on resolutions that contain language they regard as unacceptable or even offensive." Yet even Adelman took the view that the UN was indeed "a Third World forum" in which "the prevailing political arithmetic . . . means that the West will usually be forced into a reactive and defensive posture," in which the West's only hope of convincing the majority to abstain from "extreme resolutions" was to be "unified in opposition."

This description of Western conduct was not inaccurate. But it was not entirely, as Adelman suggested, dictated by cynical opportunism. Scruples of the kind we have been discussing entered in and nuanced the portrait. No Western government, moreover, including that of the United States, felt at ease with the prospect of a monolithic "bloc" approach to every issue. In addition, Adelman's case was heavily influenced by his concentration on the UN General Assembly debates and resolutions, on ideology rather than activity; and the UN's *activities*, the mediation of disputes and the promotion of peaceful change, provided scope for genuine differences of perspective. But Adelman argued that, for policy purposes, these differences should not be insurmountable—given "basic agreement on the importance of and proper role for the UN." Western policy should be based on the proposition "that unity in defence of Western principles was the only adequate response to problems discussed at the UN."

THE ART OF THE POSSIBLE

The professionals respond to this language of principle by asking how it is to be translated into the politics of the forum. Diplomats and bureaucrats responsible for "forum management" have considerable contempt for political appointees who ignore the weight of precedent and the need to "carry the majority," and who fail to recognize that the name of the game is compromise. When accused of allowing the UN to become "a Third World forum," they reply that in practice, there was no alternative. As a group, they attach importance to nursing Third World sensibilities, not just out of a sense that this is honorable compensation for the West's wealth and power but because, as they see it, the whole business is otherwise simply inoperable.

At its crudest, they are up against voting strengths. Member states who between them pay less than 2 percent of the costs can muster the necessary majority to decide on policy—and on operating budgets, until the withholding of U.S. dues led after 1986 to gentleman's agreements at the UN and some specialized agencies on informal weighting of budgetary decisions. But this merely dramatizes one aspect of the problem (and, since two-thirds of the UN's total budget is voluntarily financed, too much stress on budgets also distorts it). More insidious is the use of voting majorities to deny or abridge a government's right to present its case in debate. Procedures that close debate are regularly exploited, both by Group of 77 radicals and by secretariats through the use of tame delegates. The device was used in 1985 to prevent the United States explaining to ECOSOC its opposition to a blanket resolution on African debt, in 1987 to rule "out-of-order" attempts by the United States and the United Kingdom to put reform on the agenda of an Food and Agriculture Organization (FAO) council, and on many other occasions. Such abuses—perfectly legal—of Roberts's Rules make something of a mockery of admonitions to Western diplomats that they should stay and fight their corner.

A Swiss veteran of derailed agendas and aborted debates argues that the situation is not as hopeless as either the "arithmetic" or the results make it sound. He points out that the considerable atmospheric pressure that builds up at all meetings in favor of producing "an outcome" should give the West, which is not normally the *demandeur*, a natural advantage. Admitting that once a conference starts the West is eminently outvotable, he insists that far more could be done beforehand, by *démarches* in capitals and in secretariats, to influence both agenda and outcome. Western defeats on procedural motions are, he contends, the result of carelessness:

> When it comes to playing the game, the Third World is far cleverer. They take it seriously and they send their "experts"—always a few, always from the same small clutch of countries. They are based generally in New York, sometimes in Geneva, and they are specialists on *procedure*. They know the bible on this. And we either don't have such specialists, or we don't send them to such conferences because we are naive enough to believe we are there to address a *subject*. Taking it seriously means something different to us. And we are fools.[19]

All this does however imply that, beyond tactical clumsiness or negligence, there is a fundamental dissonance about objectives. When it considers an issue important, the West can muster impressive negotiating teams, and prepare the ground meticulously—as it has consistently done, for example, for conferences on the allocation of frequencies at the ITU. But in assessing an "issue," the West is liable to focus relatively narrowly on the ostensible subject matter, whether it is locust control, strategies to reduce post-harvest losses, the UN convention against torture or the 1993 treaty banning chemical weapons. Briefed on the "matter" to hand, its negotiators are unprepared for its diversion into unrelated political channels or its absorption into an overarching framework of demands for global restructuring. They are conceptually as well as numerically handicapped. Experts on locust control are rarely masters of parliamentary tricks.

In the 1970s, the great age of UN special conferences, this pattern was repeated constantly. The decade for women was launched with a long battle over resolutions on the rights of Palestinians and the struggle against racism (including Zionism). The Habitat conference of 1976 became similarly engaged, and the Western experts on low-cost solar energy and slum upgrading dispatched to Vancouver were ill equipped to cope. Even the International Labor Office's (ILO) World Employment Conference in the same year, a model of meticulous secretariat preparation that opened with a gentleman's agreement to keep politics off the agenda, was partially hijacked by condemnations of Chile and a decision—which clinched the U.S. withdrawal a year later—to seat the Palestine Liberation Organization (PLO). Prepared for the discrete issue, Western negotiators were confronted repeatedly by the "seamless web." Their proposals for stricter pollution controls at the first international environment conference in Stockholm in 1972 were attacked as a plot to prevent the Third World from developing its industries (a conspiracy theory that still had life in it twenty years later, at the Rio "Earth summit.") The first population conference in Bucharest was confronted with a Group of 77 assertion, as it was later summarized by the UN General Assembly, that population growth was a problem only in view of "inequitable economic structures and relations of dependence and exploitation."

These were the years during which the West's "problem-solving" approach to international organizations, based as it was on the old-fashioned tradition of limited concessions to achieve results to everybody's advantage, pushed it toward "damage limitation" in an effort to diminish the triumph of rhetoric over substance. The same Swiss diplomat says, approvingly, that when it came to dealing with "political" debates in technical forums—such as "health in the Israeli-occupied territories at the World Health Assemblies"—his government's policy was simply "not to speak to it, to let the Arabs and whoever else have their say and get to a vote as fast as possible, in order not to lose precious time." Since the resulting resolution inevitably contained a clause ensuring that it came up at the next World Health Organization (WHO) assembly, this tactic was arguably less "practical" than it sounds. But it says something about a professional cast of mind averse to "wasting time" over the hardy perennials of political confrontation, even in the face of accumulating evidence that, to an articulate minority of Third World radicals able to muster majority votes, this had become the central purpose of such gatherings.

The concern goes beyond "wasting time," however. Western diplomats are wary of engaging in the negotiation of some acceptable form of words every time ideological questions are imposed on "technical" discussions. To do so, many of them argue, involves defending Western principles in an "inappropriate" context—and in the process, letting "extraneous matter" take center stage. A certain *déformation professionelle* is here in evidence. Diplomats accredited to the UN from Western governments are conditioned by training to advance national interests, not values—to carve acceptable compromise from unpromising material, to chart the incremental steps by which international business is carried forward. Negotiation does not preclude the holding of strong principles, but it does mean finding ways to bridge differences without requiring any party to sacrifice (or be seen to sacrifice) those principles, in order to reach agreement. Where it serves this purpose, diplomats are perfectly capable of animadverting on ultimate truth, but it is not their preferred mode; where there is no advantage to be gained of a perceptibly concrete kind they incline to view declaratory utterance as time-wasting and ultimately embarrassing. Some national traditions of oratory disguise this better than others. The British make an almost comical virtue out of "plain man's common sense"; the French excel at dressing national interest in the garb of *liberté*, *égalité*, and *fraternité*: but both have their sights set firmly on results. Wars of words may be the necessary accompaniment to action, but somewhere at the end of the process the criterion of productivity enters in.

This cast of mind is firmly established in most Western ministries. From a Western perspective, "to think ourselves back into the language of the late '40s or early '50s" would thus imply some degree of real optimism that the UN, to quote Article I of the Charter, was again capable of providing effective vehicles "for harmonizing the actions of nations" in the pursuit of "common ends." Western diplomats do not on the whole expect that pursuit to require them to rethink the moral universe every time they bend their attention to the future of the rubber market or, even, of the Middle East. And they take seriously the idea that successful negotiation involves mutual advantages, a perspective that ill equips them to deal with demands from which there is no fallback position or to wrestle over statements of principle that they believe to be irrelevant to the business at hand.

Western governments tend therefore to respond to a "difficult" agency or an excessive quotient of rhetoric by downgrading the level of representation—or by sending a veteran "technocrat" who is deemed to have built up a personal network that will enable him to massage his conegotiators into a state of reasonableness. This creates other problems, as Douglas Williams has noted:

> The same delegate . . . reappears year after year at the meetings of a particular body within which he becomes a one-man institution. Frequently he identifies himself far more with his cronies on the body concerned than he does with the policies or even the interests of his own government. He becomes a predictable force in favor of the *status quo* and of agency power.[20]

The *status quo* may involve acquiescence in policies contrary to Western interests, pursued by the agency as a result of earlier "consensus" decisions, or in institutional practices in dire need of reform. Foreign offices are aware of the problem. A senior European foreign service officer describes as one of his main headaches the existence of

> special interest lobbies, too much long-term collusion between departments which have their own people who liaise with a particular agency and have been for years and know everybody there, a cozy life which they are quite prepared to defend, if necessary by sabotaging instructions aimed at making our policy more coherent and robust. Even if we give them speeches to read, they have ways of indicating to delegates that while this is the official line, they understand the difficulties that will create and the need to find a "realistic" accommodation.[21]

The sheer length of board and conference sessions, with their emphasis on negotiating the small print of resolutions, tends in addition to blunt the antennae with regard to moral absolutes—and to serve as a further temptation to lower the level of representation. This is something of which UN secretariats often take advantage, tailoring agendas so that controversial issues arise late in the proceedings—after ministers have gone home. This greatly diminishes the chances of being seriously challenged; at worst, the program in question will be lightly modified by the permanent representatives or "technicians" left behind.

Dragoljub Najman, who dealt with governments as UNESCO's assistant director-general for external relations until dismissed by the increasingly paranoid Amadou Mahtar M'Bow in 1983, recalls that René Maheu, M'Bow's predecessor as director-general from 1961 to 1974, considered UNESCO's Executive Board far too intellectually high powered and actively involved for comfort.

> The solution was simple. We slowly extended the length of the meetings, to three weeks, then to five weeks, and increased their frequency. Nobody of real calibre is going to give ten weeks a year of their lives to a place like UNESCO. So gradually we got a Board of placemen and retired civil servants, happy to be in Paris on their *per diems*, and after that we could run it as a rubber stamp affair.

This situation was only reversed, and then only partially, when Western governments belatedly recognized in the 1980s that they had a disintegrating organization on their hands and that although M'Bow, as chief executive, was principally responsible, their own neglect had contributed to the crisis.

Even where boards and policy committees are not rubber stamps, the apostles of damage limitation can produce evidence that the penalty for too robust a stance is loss of influence—since the majority can easily vote the offending government off the committee in question. Just one of many examples was the ousting of Canada from the FAO Finance Committee in 1985 for persisting with demands for greater transparency and accountability, leaving North America unrepresented. But this happens because a "difficult" Western government cannot count on peer support; with rare exceptions, the pressures for consensus are such that the delegation that stands on principle is liable to find itself friendless.

As defined in the Oxford dictionary, *consensus* is wholly admirable: suggesting "agreement, sympathy, common feeling," or "concord . . . in achieving a common purpose." It sums up the object of multilateral cooperation. The breakdown of consensus in this sense, both between states and between states and secretariats, cannot but be gravely damaging to universal organizations. But the deification of "consensus" as a form of linguistic subterfuge, a diplomatic device to mask the absence of the real thing, has compounded the UN's problems.

The "consensus" procedure at United Nations conferences resembles an enormously elaborate mating ritual that ends with the pretence of a consummation that has not taken place. Drafting groups, "friends of the president of the conference," contact groups—their names and degrees of formality vary—are formed with the sole purpose of finding some wording that all governments can agree to live with, even though there is no accord on the matter at hand. The impenetrable result is then presented to plenary. Once accepted by consensus, up to two dozen delegates then take the floor to explain why, had it been put to a vote, they would have voted against it, and the precise meaning—which does not of course appear in a text the whole purpose of which is imprecision—which they intend, for their part, to attach to it. Years later, by which time the resolution is simply recorded as something that all have accepted, the more persistent will still be taking the floor to remind everybody that they did not really agree and only joined the "consensus" under certain conditions—and cannot therefore assent to a program based on a different interpretation.

Its advocates point out that this charade saves the minority—the West—from the humiliation of being outvoted; that it clears the way for action by an agency; that it buys temporary peace and spares the West to fight again another day; most convincingly, though the instances are rare, that it terminates fruitless debate. The price is high. "Consensus" creates fictions which, by suggesting that there have been negotiations where none have been held, or that progress has been made where none is possible, can be thoroughly counterproductive. It saves governments from the effort or embarrassment of stating their real positions, but makes a mockery of debate. And as a method of rendering inaction respectable (another of its uses), it is inordinately time-consuming. Since in theory the UN exists to render certain services, it wastes not only time but reservoirs of commitment. Western governments' readiness to accept toned-down versions of Third World language, provided there are no "financial implications" attached, negates the purpose of negotiation and makes it harder the next time round to recoup the territory apparently yielded. It may buy peace for the moment, but at the price of deepening the atmosphere of confrontation later, when dissenting governments appear to retreat from a commitment that they did not consider themselves to have made. The process has greatly contributed to public disillusionment, as UN forums have come to be seen as places where difficult decisions are avoided.

Western governments understand perfectly well that this fake consensus has become, in a European diplomat's phrase, an "*oreiller de paresse*—a barely coded way of saying we don't give a damn." They are also aware that they ought to give a damn, for two reasons. First, imprecisions can be exploited by secretariats to press ahead with activities that lack genuine governmental support. This is easy enough in any case: When the UN General Assembly alone annually adopts resolutions adding up to a quarter of a million words, even if many of them are "repetitious and meaningless appeals"[22] to the secretary-general or the world at large, some phrase in one of them can generally be produced as evidence of authorization—but it is still easier when the words have been deliberately fudged. Second, although resolutions have no binding effect, governments can and do cite them in support of national policies that may be repugnant. This is where Western delegations feel themselves to be subject to blackmail: the alternative to assenting to a resolution after doing everything possible to void it of content is to stand on principle, at the risk that the majority will then vote for a text that is far worse—and that will still have the imprimatur of "the international community." Asked by a skeptical *New York Times* journalist whether it was worth losing an entire night's sleep over the wording of one phrase in a nonbinding resolution, Ambassador Barthold Witte, who as head of the West German delegation spent weeks at UNESCO's 1980 general conference resisting Third World efforts to set guidelines for the media, replied: "I spent years in prison because nobody stopped a certain government from using language like this."

The rewards for perseverance are all too often, however, a text that, although watered down, is still inimical to Western values or interests. The resolution for which Witte fought so hard was accepted by consensus. The applause was spoiled only by an outburst from the Afghan delegate—who then sensibly sought political asylum—to the effect that it legitimized Soviet control over his country's press. Lord Nicholas Gordon-Lennox, stating Great Britain's formal reservations, described it as "equivocal, insufficient, and inadequate"; its list of principles governing a new information order omitted "such fundamental principles as the right to freedom of thought, opinion and expression, the free circulation of information and ideas, freedom from censorship and arbitrary government control" and concentrated "too much on the rights of countries—that is, governments—and not enough on the rights of individuals."[23] Yet such was the addiction to consensus that no government that concurred in the British assessment—not even that of the United States or the sturdy Witte—could be found to join Great Britain in a negative vote. Faced by a Group of 77 ultimatum that if there was a single no, they would vote through their original text, the United Kingdom bowed to pressure from other Western delegations who argued that sufficient conditional verbs had been inserted to draw the resolution's teeth. It was a classic instance of damage limitation.

Consensus is often presented by Third World spokesmen as a concession to the minority, permitting it to influence majority opinion. Instead of complaining that it has become a spider's web for their entrapment, they say, Western governments should produce more "positive initiatives" for negotiation, instead of waiting for secretariats or the Group of 77 to produce drafts that they then try to water down. Western diplomats say, citing a long series of examples, that such efforts would be wasted because in the end the Group of 77 will agree to negotiate only on its own texts. Time and again, constructive approaches from the West are discredited solely because of their origin. If Third World governments are genuinely interested in arresting the decline in Western support for the UN, they argue, they could prove it by putting forward ideas that Western governments could seriously support.

Blackmail, like voodoo, requires a consenting victim. The trouble with damage limitation is that it consumes principles: each "consensus" encourages further pressure and, by providing evidence that the West will give way rather than lose in a vote, strengthens hard-line negotiators against conciliators. Much of the new "reasonableness" that Western diplomats claimed to discern in Third World conduct in the 1980s was ascribable to more robust Western tactics. Where there was greater Western willingness to let issues go to the vote, it had a salutary impact. At the UN General Assembly and even at UNCTAD, the Group of 77 was by 1987 prepared to remove some of the NIEO sutras from texts in order to arrive at an agreed "assessment" of the world economic situation. But the factor that weighed most heavily was that Third World negotiators—and their governments—were aware that under the Reagan administration, U.S. financial support for the UN was, at least temporarily, in the balance; and also that among a small but influential minority of Western governments, the idea of nonparticipation in UN organizations had ceased to be unthinkable.

The argument that absentees have no influence has always weighed powerfully against withdrawal from any UN organization, although by the end of the decade the continued influence of the United States and Great Britain in UNESCO, after their withdrawals in 1984 and 1985, could not fail to be noted. Selective nonparticipation, in a debate, a vote, or a conference, has always been a tactical weapon available to any government. Yet even such tactical nonparticipation has been treated as practically taboo. Western governments have shied away from taking a leaf out of the Third World procedural book and moving cloture of debates, because for them it would have different consequences. If they then, as was inherently likely, lost the ensuing vote their options, depending on the gravity of the issue, would be to withdraw from debate, and possibly from the meeting. There is no reason to suppose, however, that the impact of such decisions would be nil. Prior warning to influential Third World capitals that a group of Western governments would refuse to participate in debates if a particular proposal was put forward, or if there were no serious response to plans for reforming an organization, could—once it became clear that action would follow—have the required impact. To refuse to participate in a single negotiation is a much less radical step than total withdrawal; and a more determined Western stance at UNESCO, for instance, earlier in its descent into confrontation, would probably have averted the American and British departures.

All this may sound contrary to the spirit of the Charter. UN organizations cannot, however, function properly without universally accepted procedural rules, and respect for minority opinion. For the West to insist on this point—above all in the 1990s, when it would have the support of many of the new Eastern European democracies—would do more to promote the purposes of the UN than any amount of verbal flannel unsupported by serious political commitment. Discussing alternatives to damage limitation, a

Norwegian official dismissed the possibility of even selective nonparticipation on the ground that it exploited the West's "unfair advantage." He meant that while the industrialized democracies had other forums, such as the OECD or the East-West forums of the post-Communist world, to retreat to, UN organizations offered the Third World their only platforms for influencing Western policy. But he conceded that the West's reluctance to play its cards had won it little gratitude or the UN much respect. The West was increasingly taking its serious business elsewhere in the belief that confrontation followed by verbal fudge had reduced dialogue at the UN to a charade, and this reduced the usefulness of the global forums to the developing countries, too.

Hitting a punching bag for want of a live adversary is an exercise of which the pugilist tires. No sooner had the United States withdrawn from UNESCO than a senior Russian diplomat was insisting that the United States must be brought back—not, he said, primarily for financial reasons, but because it was politically essential. Two years later, in a remarkable speech to UNESCO's executive board that was one of the earliest indications of a shift in Moscow's thinking about the UN, the Soviet delegate not only demanded serious reforms at UNESCO but suggested that it was time "to start a search for the most efficient solutions instead of the most acceptable wordings." Governments, he said, should "look for what unites us, not what separates. Perhaps all of us, me included, should think over the problem of eradicating from our practice stereotyped images of each other, which have often led to unnecessary and futile arguments, hampered comprehension of the counterpart's proposals and eventually caused damage to our common cause. . . . It is necessary to withdraw confrontation from the cooperation sphere."[24] The speech was intended to be accepted as a Russian olive branch (and the mission took the almost unprecedented step of making the text available, translated into French and English). Not a single Western representative responded; by the summer of 1987 there was almost no commitment to or belief in the possibility of genuine reform at UNESCO. In the years that followed, the new democracies in Eastern Europe began to tip the balance of debate in this most ideological of the UN's specialized agencies. But in the parallel task of institutional reform the principal driving force was to be the goal of bringing the United States and Great Britain back into the organization.

Gunnar Myrdal once remarked that when the UN and its agencies were founded, there was a genuine expectation even among "sober minds" that they would not only be efficient but "would in time develop into a real world community, founded on the will of the peoples and on the general enforcement of law and common decisions arrived at by due procedures"—adding drily that "as usual . . . the propaganda had its greatest effect on those who made it."[25] By 1960, he already found the UN "lost in empty, hostile controversy and the building up of tactical defence positions of *non possumus*."[26] Western governments began in the 1980s to realize that by allowing themselves to be traumatized at the UN—whether by misplaced liberalism, by their membership of the numerical minority, or by ritual obeisance to the idea of a "real world community," they had compounded the damage inflicted by the Third World's collective revolt.

But they were ill organized for the elaboration of more activist policies. Disaffection had for some time been translated into Myrdal's *non possumus*. As a French diplomat put it in the mid-1980s, "We are not ready to destroy the UN. We believe, widely, that it no longer responds to its mission. But we shouldn't try to reform it before we redefine its mission, decide what its aims should be. So we should start by redefining objectives, then redesign the structure accordingly, then bring the two together, dialectically, with what exists."[27] But he saw no evidence then that Western bureaucracies were capable of such a task—nor any incentive for them to gird themselves to it.

"No Instructions, No Policy"

In the early 1990s, the incentives were abruptly created, as the climate of international affairs warmed dramatically. The dissolution of the Eastern bloc permitted a new degree of diplomatic mobility in the conduct of Western policy. At the UN the Group of 77's solidarity, already eroded by the widening gap between its richer and poorer members, was further weakened when it no longer became possible to play one side in the Cold War off against the other. Instead of "tolerating inanition in a mothballed organisation,"[28] Western governments came under pressure from their publics to "make the most of the UN." Yet translating these calls for "Western leadership" at the UN into practical initiatives remained anything but easy. Even at the Security Council, the old habit of passing resolutions without following them through—more than forty of these were passed concerning the former Yugoslavia alone between 1991 and the end of 1993—reasserted itself before the glow of the UN's success in the Gulf War had faded.

And for the broader UN, the old problems of institutional complexity, pork-barrel politics, the ingrained disproportion between ritual and substance, and internal resistance by vested interests to reform remained. All these were disincentives to upgrading the quality of attention paid to global diplomacy in Western capitals. There was a further problem, also of long standing. This is that Western policies toward the global organizations are also constrained by the way these policies are formulated—or fail to be formulated—at the national level.

For governments, there are three stages involved. They have to make the policies, translate them into working mandates for delegations, and maximize their impact. A large part of what follows will be the testimony of insiders as to where, and why, the circuits fail to connect.

The problems begin with governments' skepticism as to the utility of the kinds of long-term assessment without which policies, as opposed to tactical game plans, cannot be formulated. In the letter to President William Tubman of Liberia with which he prefaced his landmark study of the UN's machinery for development cooperation, Sir Robert Jackson enumerated the sources of resistance to reform: senior UN officials, pleading constraints of time; specialized agencies which, "supported by governments . . . have now become the equivalent of principalities"; and "the Cabinets of member states."[29] Yet to suggest to any Western official or minister that *cabinets* might devote serious attention to reform of the United Nations is to invite a gently raised eyebrow and some elegant phrases about ministerial priorities. Jackson reported that his "enquiries revealed example after example where Departmental Ministers have advocated policies in the governing bodies of the particular Agency which concerned them . . . which were in direct conflict with [their] government's policies towards the UN as a whole." These inquiries must have been probing indeed to discover, beyond platitudes, the existence of these policies, let alone their content.

The lack of strategic planning and clear directives from capitals is a fact of life with which UN delegations have to contend, both on the "political" scene in New York and in the supposedly "technical" agencies. Asked why the European Community seemed to have so little collective influence in Turtle Bay, a senior European ambassador replied: "No instructions. No policy."

The twelve members of the European Community, he added, worked very hard at coordination.

> We have some three hundred meetings during each General Assembly, four to five a day, many starting before 8 AM; we talk to each other, in fact, so hard we have no time to talk to anybody else. But since we almost never get timely instructions and since, more seriously, the Community has not addressed the question of what it wants to do at the UN, we might be better off recognizing that our real influence depends on our personal use of our time, as individuals.[30]

Many Western diplomats compare their situation unfavorably with that of Third World colleagues who, "at least, can always get on the line to their president or foreign minister; we would generally be lucky to get through to the head of the UN desk, and even he would not expect to be called out of office hours." A respected and experienced Scandinavian representative to the FAO echoes this theme.

> The essential fact is that our politicians—even in an avowedly internationalist country like mine—don't need the UN. Not needing it, they are ignorant. They look to us, the bureaucrats, to resolve for them the only question which matters: that is that we can't get rid of our aid funds without the UN. And that's an administrator's paradise: it's such a neat method to write a cheque to the UN Development Program. As to how the money is spent, we are on our own: and we do not necessarily render ourselves popular at home by saying that funds should be blocked because money is being wasted or misappropriated.[31]

This is not to say that there isn't a sizable government bureaucracy dealing with UN affairs in most Western countries. The U.S. State Department's coordinator for refugees has over a hundred people working full-time on international refugee problems; of these, a large proportion monitor the UN Relief and Works Agency and the office of the UN high commissioner for refugees. The manpower devoted by the United States to UN affairs is wholly exceptional, but the global estimate by Gérard Blanc[32] of fifteen thousand to twenty thousand bureaucrats and experts employed on UN affairs in national administrations could well be an understatement.

Even so, none manages to keep abreast. The British permanent representative to the clutch of UN organizations in Geneva complains that in Switzerland alone there are fifteen thousand UN meetings a year. (Great Britain maintains an exceptionally large mission in Geneva, with more than thirty staff plus a separate ambassador and staff for disarmament negotiations; but that is still inadequate.) One direct consequence of this is the junior level of much governmental representation in UN committees—a problem frequently identified as central to the UN's loss of relevance. Another is that many of these meetings operate in a policy vacuum: given the workload, it could hardly be otherwise. To carry home the documentation churned out in the course of a single UN agency's general conference, a delegate would be lumbered with some eighty kilos of overweight. Even Western governments find it physically impossible to attend all meetings, never mind to ensure that their representative is fully briefed and sufficiently expert. Many of them achieve so little that they encourage foreign offices in the view that, as one Western diplomat put it in 1989, "the UN isn't real diplomacy." On the rare occasions where decisions are taken that require governments to follow through—either at national level or to support or monitor the consequent activities by the agency in question—the workload in capitals is further increased.

This proliferation of activity has two major consequences. The first is that UN affairs come to be considered as so arcane that there is little contact or discussion between bureaucrats who deal with other international aspects of national policy in a particular field and those who deal with it in the UN. "Those not directly involved with the UN and its family regard the whole thing as too Byzantine to understand and too irrelevant to reality to be worth serious consideration," says a British official with long experience. "They consider their colleagues involved with the UN as a cross between burglars' advocates and the High Priests of some esoteric mystery."[33]

High flyers do not, as a result, relish postings to their UN departments or, New York somewhat apart, to UN missions. "Nobody likes being posted here," says a long-serving staff member of the U.S. State Department's International Organizations (IO) division, "except to the UN Policy department which is considered a plum—provided you stay close to the other policy bureaus and so long as it's no more than a two-year tour. Anything more is considered a health hazard."[34] The upshot, he says, is that a lot of the IO career staff are drawn from outside the foreign service—not necessarily a bad thing, but liable to accentuate the divorce between UN affairs and national policy.

IO is at least well endowed with staff. The size of U.S. dues and voluntary contributions to the UN means that it accounts for around a third of the State Department's budget, giving it "the clout which comes from being the nearest thing State, as a whole, gets to being a spending agency" and involving, between Washington and the missions reporting to it, some six hundred people. In London, a senior official of the Overseas Development Administration, the aid wing of the Foreign Office, complains that he has "three men and a boy to deal with policy towards the FAO, the UNDP and [prior to British withdrawal] UNESCO." Canada, which takes the FAO more seriously than most, allocates less than eight man-years to it.

> Compare that with the manpower the FAO can muster to block any of our efforts to ask awkward questions or press for reforms, and you will see why no government can control an agency. We know that there are a lot of things we should be doing, but we don't have the manpower, and if we trebled it things would be no different. We have to accept that we are not in the business of paying a dog and barking ourselves.[35]

The second consequence is that most of these bureaucrats consider themselves fortunate if they can keep abreast of the paper mountains crossing their desks. Even those who insist that they aim beyond damage limitation, to promote specific and positive actions, concede that they give little space to the long term. The often sophisticated arrangements within most Western bureaucracies for interdepartmental coordination on UN affairs are geared to preparing the next round of briefing material and attempting—with limited success—to ensure that their country's policy statements in the many UN bodies that are likely to be dealing with similar subjects are consistent.

The process involves satisfying three quite different domestic constituencies. Foreign ministries, which—outside the domain of collective security—rarely consider anything to do with the UN to be worth the adjustment of bilateral policy, must be satisfied that a position taken there will not offend important allies or client states. (French UN policy has for years been virtually a sub-branch of its Francophone African desk, spiced with a pinch of declaratory *tiers-mondisme* and more than a trace of Gaullist U.S.-baiting.) Treasuries must be assured that it will not involve extra spending. And domestic pressure groups, such as farm lobbies at the GATT or the pharmaceuticals industry at the WHO, must be taken into account. Once all parties are satisfied, there is a strong incentive to stick with the formula, if only because fifty to sixty different national entities may have been involved, and because adjustment to fit the circumstances of a particular agency would open up the process with respect to others. The dispersal of activities within the UN thus finds its reflection, even in the most well-organized governments, in a reactive and unimaginative management of complexity that leaves little time, energy, or inclination for work on strategic overall objectives.

In the absence of a radical simplification of UN business, it is easier to criticize this state of affairs than to see an alternative. Western governments are aware of its deadening effect, but argue that there are no shortcuts. British officials, who operate a system that divides up responsibility for different UN agencies between "lead departments" coordinating work through a Foreign Office committee system, say their main preoccupation is to clamp down on too much fraternization between these lead departments and the agency concerned. They stress that "coherence" is a key objective, but admit that it is not always obtained. A Canadian diplomat points out that it is all very well to talk about the larger horizon, but that strategies are worthless without detailed briefing and tactical preparation:

> To be effective in any one of these agencies you need a strong sense of the substance, some fairly detailed knowledge; and you must have mastery of the procedure and sensitivity to the dynamics of different groups; and you must be well-informed as to where and through which mechanisms the secretariat is likely to cut the ground from under you. Lose on any of these fronts and the most enlightened ideas will make little dent.[36]

All of this gives an impression of meticulousness that fits ill with the complaints by delegations that they operate without a policy framework or even, for much of the time, instructions on the matters to hand. The Scandinavian FAO representative mentioned above is quite blunt about it: "Most representatives to these organizations do not reflect their government's thinking—because there isn't any. My instructions are those which I write here, and turn around in the capital, which I take care to visit three or four times a year to make sure that they come back to Rome in the terms I want and need."[37] And he was one of the least cynical of the permanent delegates to the FAO in the mid-1980s: his position was untypical in that he belonged to a group that was actively trying to instigate a far-reaching review of the functioning of the FAO and its future direction, under the umbrella of what was later to be known as the Camberley

Group. He was therefore attempting to obtain—if necessary by writing them himself—instructions that assisted him in pressing, on his government's behalf, for reform.

His remarks, as the representative of a country where, exceptionally, a committee of agricultural experts and bureaucrats from the agricultural and foreign ministries meets regularly in the capital to discuss the FAO, illustrate a widely shared frustration. Many delegates feel that they can hardly be expected to be taken seriously either by other missions or by secretariats in the all too apparent absence of ministerial interest. He agrees with other Scandinavian career officials who say that when their ministers repeat that the UN is "the cornerstone of our foreign policy," they are wholly sincere—"in the sense that *having* a foreign policy, in tiny countries like ours, is almost an embarrassment and the UN offers a way out." But ignorance and indifference can coincide with the most "progressive" attitudes.

From the politician's angle, the worse a UN agency is run, the less incentive there is to get involved. In 1978, when the late Baroness Hart, a committed internationalist on the left wing of the British Labour Party, was minister for overseas development, she was approached by a group of editors appealing for government action to confront the challenge to press freedom at UNESCO. She yielded to persuasion, but not before saying: "Gentlemen, I will give you just three minutes to show me why I should ever set foot in that useless institution."

The indifference or even, as in this case, the distaste of politicians where UN matters are concerned helps to explain why professionalism—represented by detailed tactical briefs—may coexist with a political limbo of policy oblivion. That explains why governments can point with pride to meticulous coordination of "positions," why delegations may still complain of the lack of clear policies, and why both of them can be right. The UN's low priority rating also means that the time frame in Western capitals tends to be much shorter than that of the UN secretariats—or even of developing countries. By the time desk officers begin serious preparation for a particular meeting, the agenda will have been set—and the nonaligned or Group of 77 will in all likelihood have gone through their own complicated coordinating processes months before. Exchanges of information between Western capitals prior to the UN General Assembly, which starts in September each year, tend to start flowing only at the end of July, by which time most politicians are on holiday and unreachable. The opportunity to bring the West's undoubted influence to bear before the session opens, whether in other capitals or on the General Committee, which sets the Assembly's agenda, will have been lost, and Western delegations will be left to fall back on the familiar routine of holding the line on the other parties' terms.

The failure of Western governments to exploit their superior capacity to anticipate and to persuade, subjects them to the very rigidities of interbloc negotiation of which they complain. "The fact is that for all our superior organizational ability, our performance is little different from the G77's," according to a Danish diplomat with wide experience of specialized agencies. "The only areas in which we consistently make a serious effort are on senior appointments and money. The combination of the G77's inability to handle the UN on a policy basis, for lack of information, and our inertia rooted in a well-founded paranoia, makes for gridlock and, on our part, ultra-conservatism."

He meant by this that, to a large extent, Third World governments handle UN affairs as an extension of their preoccupations with solidarity, and "as recipients."

> *Their* ministers can use the UN: as providers of aid. They can sell that in their constituencies—and they do have them, however undemocratic—and in their internal fights with rival ministers. But of course there it is volume that counts: they are not concerned with aid effectiveness. So their main preoccupation with any agency will be increasing its budget as a demonstration of collective power and in the hope of building prestige at home. *Our* ministers, unconvinced by the value for money this spending represents, and rightly so, put a premium on stopping the bandwagon. So when we criticize the bureaucracy, we talk volume too: cut the bureaucracy, cut the budget. It's the wrong measurement; and it also means that when we push for more accountability and clear priorities we are suspected, not without reason, of budget-cutting by another route—at which point a secretariat can mobilize a Pavlovian "no" from the G77.[38]

UN officials in turn complain that, where they introduce new ideas or try to scrap old program lines, they get little cooperation from the West. One recalls that, after months of delicate negotiation to obtain assent to the abolition of the UN's regular Report on the World Social Situation (once assailed by Daniel P. Moynihan[39] as "a totalitarian tract" in which, due to the absence there of dissent, the well-being of Communist Czechoslovakia was rated higher than that of the United States), the matter came up to the Third Committee. The delegate for the Philippines unexpectedly sprang to its defense in the usual high-flown terms. Not a single Westerner spoke. The report was reprieved. When the official asked the British afterward why they had done nothing, he was told that it was not "worth offending the Philippines."

This kind of sophistry gives Western diplomacy a bad name. The British were as aware as the UN official that "the Philippines" almost certainly neither knew nor cared about the report in question. The delegate was probably playing the local stage without reference back to Manila—and if by some miracle he was acting on instructions, it was hardly likely that the Philippines would have thought it "worth offending" Great Britain on such a matter. Dismay at the West's apparent inability, above all collectively, to say what it wants is a fairly constant theme among the more knowledgeable Third World diplomats. Ivo Margan of Yugoslavia, chairman of a "temporary committee" of UNESCO's Executive Board set up in 1984 to attempt to stave off the U.S. departure through an agreed program of reforms, came out of the first round of meetings saying that it was difficult to know what to do, since "they haven't asked for anything beyond a few housekeeping measures." Two years later, at a private dinner in Paris, a group of Asian, Latin American, and African diplomats urged Western ambassadors to get their governments to say publicly and formally that they could not accept M'Bow for a third term at the head of UNESCO. That, they said, would clear the way for *their* governments to argue within the Group of 77 that a new candidate must be found, acceptable to all parties. By this time, such a statement would have been consonant with the policy of every remaining Western member of UNESCO, including France. It was not forthcoming.

UNESCO may admittedly have been in a somewhat special bracket at this stage. By 1986, Western policymakers and diplomats took the view that if the Third World was not prepared to pull its chestnuts out of the fire there, the West was under no obligation to do it for them, and that its governments were quite adequately aware that M'Bow's reelection would alienate from UNESCO the last shred of Western support. But the basis for Western support—unanimous—for Javier Pérez de Cuéllar's reelection in 1986 as UN secretary-general was equally flabby. As the ambassador of one of the West European veto powers explained in private conversation: "It's true that his administrative talents are zero and that he is the last man to cope with financial crisis. But his political antennae are good and besides, it's Africa's turn and since the Africans couldn't agree on a candidate there was no alternative."

A bit of context shows how extraordinary an admission this was. In the late summer of 1986 two top UN jobs fell vacant: the UN secretary-generalship, and the managing director's job at the IMF. The second was a closely and seriously fought battle between supporters of two superbly qualified candidates, the Dutch finance minister Onno Ruding and the eventual victor, Michel Camdessus, then governor of the Bank of France. Finance ministers met to discuss the appointment; nobody doubted that the issue was consequential. Pérez de Cuéllar, by contrast, was virtually nodded through—despite his own insistence that he was not seeking a second term, and the fact that he had just had heart bypass surgery—at a time when the UN clearly needed a secretary-general of quite exceptional dynamism to sort out its financial and political crisis.

The sorry excuse that "the Africans couldn't agree" was just that. "If the world had to wait for the Organization of African Unity to make up its collective mind, Africa could stop the world," was the comment of a former Ethiopian diplomat who had been active in founding it. In 1991, when African countries came up with not one, but eight candidates, the Security Council considered them all. And there is, in any case, nothing in any UN procedural document, never mind the Charter, to require either continental rotation or endorsement by a regional group. Had the Big Five felt strongly about finding a good candidate (for which there is no evidence) without offending the Africans, they could have sought one out. No search for a suitable candidate, African or otherwise, was undertaken. The nearest thing to a candid explanation came from a senior U.S. official: "We want Pérez to stay because we want a weak secretary-general in order to reassert the control of the UN by member states." This remark betrayed a certain innocence. The secretary-generalships both of Pérez de Cuéllar and of Kurt Waldheim before him—years of drift and pervasive jobbery—provided ample evidence that a weak incumbent was more likely to be overruled and bypassed by his UN barons than to be "controlled" by member states. And it was far from the whole truth.

The deference to regional rotation outlasted the Cold War, pointing to a degree of fatalism about management at the UN that casts doubt on Western claims that, precisely out of concern for its efficient running, they take at least senior jobs seriously. Often it betrays lack of foresight. At worst it displays cynicism. The director-generalship of the World Health Organization fell vacant in 1988, at a time when governments were agreed that the WHO would need to display considerable political acumen, and exploit all its standing, if it was to get governments to acknowledge, and tackle, the spread of AIDS. Knowing this, the outgoing director-general, Halfdan Mahler, had appealed a year ahead of the election to WHO's executive board to form a search committee. Yet nothing was done, although all the candidates were known to be wholly inadequate—partly because the Japanese, second-largest contributors to the UN budget and underrepresented in senior posts, were lobbying furiously for Dr. Hiroshi Nakajima, one of the WHO's regional directors. Despite virtually universal misgivings, he was duly elected.

After a disastrous first term, Dr. Nakajima then proved impossible to dislodge; against the objections of every major donor country except Japan, he was reelected in 1993.

Appointments are a telling indicator of governments' readiness to think ahead. There is not much merit in governments' complaining of the UN's complexity if opportunities to provide effective leadership of its organizations are neglected. Failures to secure strong and efficient management significantly weaken the familiar argument that the UN is so "unmanageable" that Western governments can do no more than struggle patiently with the minutiae in the hope of keeping the monster within bounds. The triumph of attention to trivia over strategy is admittedly hardly a monopoly of UN diplomacy, any more than the UN has a monopoly over absurd projects (there was once a committee in Brussels that spent more than two years trying, unsuccessfully, to negotiate a common European Community standard for teddy bears' eyes). The West's lack of strategic policy formulation is, however, the less excusable because it does have the means to orchestrate serious thinking about global organizations. A "Geneva Group," cochaired by the United States and the United Kingdom, was formed in the 1960s in order—in the interests of all the UN's members—to improve the quality of management and introduce proper budgetary controls. Comprised of the eleven governments that individually contribute 1 percent or more of the budgets of the major specialized agencies, this informal committee was originally intended in addition to concern itself with "program development"—with what the UN does with its money.[40]

This wider function was rapidly allowed to lapse. Even though collectively its members contributed nearly three-quarters of UN funds, until the early 1990s they came up with little more than a patchy insistence on zero budgetary growth, an even more fragile commitment to opposing third terms for UN chief executives, and some collective work on methods for streamlining UN budgeting techniques. Officials maintained that, since the Group had no official standing and could at best hope to persuade UN secretariats and other governments of its views, this was about all that could be expected. More pertinently, the common ground between its members was nowhere near great enough to permit the coordination of larger policy questions.

Whatever channels are employed, the principal obstacle to more creative approaches to overhauling the UN is not the obvious diversity of outlook among Western governments, but their shared folk memory of repeated failures to secure value for money, program, or management reforms. The years of confrontation accustomed Western policymakers to the idea that what the UN was "about" was an unending round of conferences—and that it was unrealistic to aspire to more than an "acceptable" outcome, whether from a conference or from proposals for reform. But it is also true that Western politicians, however ready to record their attachment to the UN "with all its faults," have for decades considered it too minor a part of the agenda to justify the effort to put the faults right. Because the source of skepticism is not entirely institutional, it is not clear that either of the two major evolutions in thinking about the UN since 1980—first the American attempt, initiated by the Reagan administration, to alter the matrix of Western policy assumptions toward the global organizations, and then, after 1989, the shift in Moscow's attitude to multilateral diplomacy—will greatly alter the political scale of priorities.

The enormous growth of demands on the UN's security apparatus does not, in the view of most policymakers, in itself require far-reaching institutional changes in the way the whole machine operates. If anything, the West was beginning in the 1990s to be more selective in the attention it gave to the specialized agencies than during the years when the collective security dimension of the UN was marginalized. And in the economic and social fields, the enormous task of assisting the peaceful transformation of the former Soviet and East European economies in the early 1990s appeared to most Western governments by far the most serious challenge for multilateral policy—a challenge to which only the Bretton Woods institutions seemed obviously relevant.

Most foreign and economic ministries, moreover, have been organized on the premise that the vital issues are "Northern." For almost all of the UN's history, strategic arms control, economic relations, and monetary stability have been treated as essentially East-West, or intra-Western, matters. The ready assumption is that close cooperation between the United States, Europe, and Japan—and beyond that, the handling of what were for decades called East-West relations—are what matter in the final analysis; and that without that, no amount of global diplomacy would make much difference, either to the West or to the rest of the world. "The question," says a British government policy planner, "is how much energy, money, manpower we want to put into the UN, when it is obviously in our interest to put our best people into NATO and the European Community. There is a much wider range of multilateral avenues—the Western economic summits, the Group of 5 at the IMF, the EC—than there was in 1945; and many of them are closer to home, and to our interests. Don't look for honour: remember the old saying that the sun never set on the British Empire because God couldn't trust the English in the dark."[41]

Granted the paramount importance of intra-Western cooperation, to which at the end of the 1980s was added the management of changes sweeping through Eastern Europe, the attractions of relying on an essential regional, and largely "Northern," framework for multilateral cooperation and leaving the rest to bilateral diplomacy have been magnified by the intractability of the problems that beset the global institutions. Yet the most blinkered Western policymaker is compelled—by the global consequences of environmental mismanagement, by the dangers of nuclear proliferation, by the challenge of mass migration and its roots in poverty and social disintegration—to acknowledge limits to the "congenial club" approach. Western coordination of responses to drug trafficking, or terrorism, may be vital, but it can be only one part of the jigsaw. To identify Western interests in expanding markets that operate in conditions of political stability, in the orderly integration of developing economies with international markets, it is not necessary to "look for honour."

Nor can bilateral diplomacy alone—even for governments like that of the United States, let alone those of smaller Western countries whose interests may be global but whose bilateral reach is limited—guarantee orderly international relations. Bilateral channels may seem the most economical way to address specific issues, but decisions thus reached may have knock-on effects, which need to be considered in a multilateral framework. Modified insularity, even that which groups the leading economic and political powers, may not always be adequate. Effective multilateral cooperation may not require, and in some instance might be incompatible with, a global approach; but the wider world does not thereby cease to exist.

The search for new relationships between bilateral and multilateral diplomacy, and for ways to exploit new forms of multilateral cooperation and new groupings, is quickening. It is one aspect of the much-needed reassessment of the contribution the United Nations can make to a world of more complex international connections than existed in 1945. The task for Western governments is to find ways to put an accurate, unsentimental but unprejudiced price on the global organizations. This implies greater willingness to recognize that institutions that are not worth managing well are arguably not worth sustaining at all, and to sort out the indispensable from the accumulated baggage of global multilateralism.

But in the most hard-headed assessment, even honor might enter in. One of the sources of the West's claim to global influence is its perceived commitment to cooperate with weaker states to promote economic well-being and human rights, as well as to prevent or contain conflicts. And that implies that it will do neither to dismiss the global organizations as "Third World forums," nor to accept the rules of the game invented by the architects of Third World solidarity. In the course of the 1980s, the prospects for a less defeatist, *faute-de-mieux* approach began to improve. However criticized by the United States's allies, the withholding by the Congress of U.S. dues to the UN concentrated minds. "Attitudes are changing," a senior U.S. official suggested in 1988, "impelled in developing countries by U.S. pressures and by hard times on the economic front." But, he added:

> The final outcome will be a matter of what we ourselves do. There are opportunities, but they are yet to be grasped. The test will be whether we can pursue objectives, over a period of years, with some consistency—in the recognition that for most of our governments, these are basically secondary issues. The Secretariats have resisted reform *because* they know that to us they *are* secondary, and also because they are consistent and we are not. So they gamble, like Khrushchev, that "we will bury you"; and over the years we have proved them right.

The long history of efforts to reform the United Nations and its agencies provides, however, nothing but ground for skepticism. The incentives to summon and concert energies for a fresh analysis, and to pursue objectives with the tenacity this official rightly identified as essential, ought in theory to be created by the growing importance of multilateral diplomacy. The institutional and political obstacles we have been discussing are, however, so formidable as to give ground for doubt that even clearly articulated goals for reform, consistently pursued, would succeed in modernizing and adapting the global organizations to the needs of the twenty-first century.

Western politicians and diplomats, in particular, continue to be inhibited by two factors. The first is their sensitivity to the charge that criticism of the UN is coterminous with a "retreat from multilateralism," a return to the narrow pursuit of national self-interest. The second is that the global organizations have proved remarkably reform-proof. No one who has been exposed to the various drives to reorganize and restructure the UN contemplates reembarking without a shudder. It is against the background of a profoundly dispiriting record of failure that fresh policies will have to evolve. To embark for a fourth time along the routes taken by the three principal abortive attempts to "reform the system" would be a disservice not just to the UN but to the development of multilateral cooperation. Understanding the past, and the reasons for previous failures, is therefore indispensable to any assessment of the UN's future potential.

III

FROM REFORM TO REVOLT

6. TINKERING WITH UTOPIA

"EVERYTHING HAS BEEN TRIED"

In the late 1960s, Sir Robert Jackson described the UN as "probably the most complex organization in the world." The whole edifice, with its multiple governing bodies, different headquarters whose "administrative tentacles thrust downwards into an extraordinary complex of regional and sub-regional offices, and finally . . . into field offices," invited the question: "Who controls this 'Machine'?" Jackson concluded:

> The evidence suggests that governments do not, and also that the machine is incapable of intelligently controlling itself. This is not because it lacks intelligent and capable officials, but because it is so organized that managerial direction is impossible. In other words, the machine as a whole has become unmanageable in the strictest sense of the word. As a result, it is becoming slower and more unwieldy, like some prehistoric monster.[1]

His words have lost none of their immediacy. Practically since its inception, proposals for reform have washed over the UN like tides. They have generally left the beach even more littered with debris than before, a new committee here or new organization there giving the impression of improved order while actually complicating the terrain. Underlying the more ambitious proposals—those that have gone beyond routine housekeeping—have been the constant tensions: between the concept of centrally directed order, and the polycentric fashion in which the UN actually operates; between the pursuit of efficient negotiating and governing procedures, and the claims of sovereign equality. Efforts to improve the former have exposed without mitigating the UN's structural malformations. Attempts to reconcile the latter have been caught by the political undertow almost before they surfaced.

There have been three main cycles of reforms. The first was mainly concerned to devise stoplight controls over the expanding secretariats, by introducing orderly programming, reporting standards, and methods for evaluation of UN activities. The second sought to adapt the UN to its new "developmental" roles. The third, while overtly institutional in focus like the others, was political. In the context of the Third World challenge to the ideas that had animated its founding constitutional texts, it attempted to enable the UN to function by focusing on methods of dialogue that would circumvent increasingly profound disagreements about the scope and purpose of universal organizations. All to some degree relied on the exercise by UN headquarters in New York of powers over the agencies that it did not possess.

Efforts at reform have paid scant attention to "outsiders": the UN has never had a customer-conscious culture, and has been reluctant even to bring voluntary organizations and foundations, its closest constituencies, into its internal deliberations. The debates on reform have chiefly involved two sets of actors: governments, or rather national bureaucrats; and the secretariats, or experts co-opted by them. Each has had distinctively different sets of aims, which could loosely be described as governability and serviceability. And each group has tended to blunt the creative energies of the other.

At governmental level, most of the periodic drives for reform have been *ad hoc* responses to crises (generally financial), or have been aimed at bringing the UN's multiplying bits of machinery under some semblance of political control. A sense of collective impotence emerges from the remarkably constant preoccupations of intergovernmental committees, from ECOSOC's appeals to the agencies in the 1940s to the streamlining efforts of the Group of 18 four decades later and the revivalism of the Nordic group in the 1990s. Terms like *coordination*, *rationalization*, *the elimination of overlap* echo down the years. The orderly division of labor has been a Holy Grail, whose pursuit has spawned new bodies and bureaucratic layers behind which the goal has continued to recede. The pleas for readable, relevant documents, flexible forward-planning, for monitoring of programs in order to avoid the repetition of failures, for transparent budgeting and greater accountability—all aims that make sense in themselves—reflect the frustrations of national bureaucracies dealing with the not merely ungovernable but, increasingly, incomprehensible.

While there have been piecemeal improvements in areas such as budget presentation and approval, the outcome of these efforts has principally been to complicate the intergovernmental machinery without increasing the effectiveness of policy control. That is not surprising, since governments, however united in their desire to regulate the secretariats' activities, have been unable to agree on certain key questions—such as the purposes of control or the appropriate mechanisms to employ. Negotiations have therefore tended to degenerate, losing grand designs in the small print of procedural modifications—and, of course, requests for documentation. The perennial arguments about budgets have reflected serious political and ideological cross-purposes. From the early 1960s, Third World insistence on expanded remits for the organizations, or on enlargement of the policymaking bodies to reflect the UN's expanded membership, convinced "Northern"—Western and Soviet-bloc—countries of the need for more effective financial tourniquets. Even during the Cold War, there was always a degree of East-West solidarity about money. This was, however, strictly limited to regular UN budgets: the Soviet Union, which contributed almost nothing to emergency relief, the care of refugees, or the expanding technical assistance programs (all paid for by voluntary contributions, with the Western industrialized countries providing over 90 percent)[2], was happy to stress the moral obligation of imperialism to finance Third World development.

The second set of actors has, on paper, turned in a more impressive performance. Expert groups, bringing together members of the secretariats, co-opted diplomats acting in their personal capacity and the occasional academic, have come up with ambitious blueprints for reform. These proposals, even when presented in the numbing bureaucratese that Richard Gardner, the principal author of one of the more readable, has called the UN's seventh official language, have at least touched on the issues from which governments recoil, such as the conditions for effective policy dialogue and the longer-term objectives of UN programs. A few individuals in this second group—Jackson in 1969, the Joint Inspection Unit's (JIU) Maurice Bertrand in 1985, or the International Labor Office's (ILO) Francis Blanchard in 1987—have diagnosed the causes of the organization's sclerosis with clarity and precision, and focused accurately on the relations between means and ends. The JIU, created in 1968, has pursued the question of staff quality with a tenacity demonstrated by no government.

At the same time, as Jackson pointed out, the UN "has more than its fair share of 'experts' in the art of describing how things cannot be done." They exercise a vigorous purchase in what, as early as 1969, he discovered to be a "bureaucratic undergrowth which now strangles action" and which made of the UN "a disproportionately old and bureaucratic organization" lacking "any sense of urgency."[3] The UN's severest critics and most committed reformers are to be found within its offices or closely connected with them. Yet UN managements have also proved past masters at converting "reforms" into new jobs and increased spending. Displays of energetic implementation have masked the successful emasculation of any threat to sectoral prerogatives or bureaucratic habits. As any politician will testify, this state of affairs is not unique to the UN: it is simply more serious because in national administrations ministers ultimately possess real power over the bureaucrats, if they insist on exerting it. Governing bodies composed of many theoretically coequal masters cannot speak with a single voice—hence the comparative ease with which, in the global organizations, the secretariats manipulate them.

Officials can also quote chapter and verse to argue that, in the words of one UN assistant secretary-general, "practically everything has been tried."[4] Since the 1950s, all aspects of the UN—its finances, its programming and planning techniques, its coordinating machinery, its procedures for internal and external audit and evaluation, the roles of its governing bodies, and its debating and negotiating mechanisms—have been subjected to recurring bouts of scrutiny.

Some of the recommendations are as relevant today as when they were drafted. But so few of them have been implemented that it would be more accurate to say that everything has been thought of, rather than that everything has been tried. Glimpses of broader horizons have been rapidly obscured in the fog of compromise. There has been a considerable degree, moreover, of collusion between diplomats and senior bureaucrats with common interests in the defense of the *status quo*. The search for "consensus," whether between governments or between governing bodies and secretariats, has deprived innovations of whatever coherence they originally possessed. Only on the territory of "realism"—of small incremental changes that do not offend, because they do not threaten anyone—have both casts of actors tended to meet.

A classic example of collusion was the "reform" that in 1978 created a UN director-general for development and international economic cooperation. For reasons that will be discussed later, the holder of this exalted post was in practice powerless to improve the UN's contribution to either objective. The creation of the post suited the UN in New York because it appeared to acknowledge the appropriateness of its involvement in these issues. Because in practice the director-general lacked the power to threaten their autonomy, the UN agency heads were happy with the arrangement. It pleased the West because it appeared to commit the UN to better coordination; and Third World governments, because it emphasized the importance of development assistance. The solution was classic, finally, in its stress on administrative tidiness. The problem with UN reform has not been so much the absence of ideas as their dilution to fit institutional molds. "When your house is crumbling and on the verge of collapsing, you cannot content yourself with plastering over the cracks in the walls and putting fresh paint on rotten beams."[5] Marten Mourik's verdict on the miserably inadequate reforms with which he was involved as Dutch ambassador to UNESCO from 1978 to 1985 could be applied to most attempts to overhaul the UN. But the more hopeless the state of the structure, the more daunting it is to embark on fundamental repairs. Those like Jackson or Bertrand, who declared the structures dangerous, paradoxically accentuated anxiety that anything more radical than continued patching would destabilize the whole edifice. The gulf between what they presented as minimally necessary and what was assumed to be "realistic" was so great that they generated hostility and, worse, embarrassment.

Yet these past efforts do not count for nothing. They have steadily broadened the agenda for reform. They have made it progressively harder for either governments or secretariats to claim that the UN's shortcomings are the inescapable consequence of the difficulties of multilateral cooperation. Even if their cumulative effect has been institutionally counterproductive, adding scales to Jackson's "monster" and reducing flexibility, successive failures have helped to demonstrate the futility of tinkering and half-measures. The record of reform in the first five decades of the UN's existence offers some guide to the prospects for a fresh approach. To accept that "everything has been tried" would not only be to concede that the UN's obsolescence was irremediable; it would discount the possibility of mobilizing the considerable reserves of idealism and competence still to be found in the secretariats.

SHUTTING THE STABLE DOOR

The recurrent efforts to oil the machine have focused on New York. This is not only because capitals persist in taking the UN's political headquarters as the center of a "system," but because foreign offices tend to stir themselves only when confrontations invade the General Assembly and its committees, or when financial crises put in jeopardy even the UN's capacity to mediate in armed conflicts.

The UN was plunged into the first of these financial crises in 1965, when the Soviet Union and France refused to pay their assessed shares of the expensive peacekeeping operations in the Congo and Cyprus. Their action compelled governments to face two facts. The first was that, quite apart from the huge expansion in the peacekeeping budget, the UN's general expenditures had spun out of control. The second was that it was far from clear where the money went.

Just how unclear is indicated by the fact that the *ad hoc* committee established to tackle the crisis was asked for two reports. One was to establish the real financial situation: nobody knew what it was. The other was to propose planning and regulatory frameworks for future spending. Inflation was sweeping the UN. Spending on economic and social activities had nearly trebled in a decade. The number of meetings and conferences had doubled in six years: there were over two thousand a year in New York, over four thousand in Geneva, and some eleven hundred in the UN's regional economic commissions. Every year, eight hundred million pages rolled off UN presses and copying machinery in New York and Geneva alone. Delegates to a single session of the Economic and Social Council in 1965 had been expected to wade through eleven thousand pages of documentation. Yet for all this documentation, no breakdown of expenditures was available, and forward planning was virtually nonexistent. In terms of the most basic management techniques, the UN belonged in the Dark Ages. So alien was the notion of budgetary control that several of the committee's own members (those, in a prefiguration of things to come, from the Third World) argued that it was "not practicable" to adopt predetermined spending limits "or to define in advance a rate of growth" for the UN.[6]

The *ad hoc* committee presented the 1966 UN General Assembly with around fifty recommendations. These were intended to provide governments with full information on the programs of UN headquarters, its dependencies, and the specialized agencies; to coordinate UN activities; and to ensure that money was well spent. Each UN entity was to be required to draw up six-year programs, with more detailed two-year budgets in which each organization would set out "what it hopes to accomplish within definite points of time" and present costed alternatives for governmental decision. The committee called for standard methods of budget presentation, to enable governments to compare programs and costs and to reveal overlapping activities between different organizations. It was hoped that secretariats would consult governments when drawing up these "program budgets," enabling them to find out in advance what spending levels were proposed, and so to control cost overruns and compel the secretariats to relate activities clearly to objectives.

Once this "systemwide" machinery was in place, it was hoped that governments would be able to coordinate the whole—including the UN's burgeoning technical assistance programs. Where these were concerned, the committee called for "harmonization" of UN actions at country level. The newly created UN Development Program (UNDP) was to assist governments to draw up national plans; to guarantee coherent development programs, the specialized agencies were requested to inform UNDP in advance of their proposed activities in particular countries.

In addition, the committee proposed that the organizations should evaluate their activities regularly—and make the findings available to their governing bodies. It suggested the establishment of a common panel of external auditors to inspect the books of all UN organizations, to certify the accounts and also to report on administrative performance. Its most important innovation was, finally, to propose the creation of a UN Joint Inspection Unit (JIU) to investigate "all matters having a bearing on the efficiency of the services and the proper use of funds."[7]

The underlying motive of this last proposal was partly political. The setting up of a totally independent corps of inspectors would, it was hoped, convince France and the Soviet Union that the UN's spending was being rigorously scrutinized, and thus persuade them to contribute to a special fund to resolve its financial crisis. Since their refusals to pay for the peacekeeping operations were politically motivated, this gambit not surprisingly failed. But the JIU, modeled on such national bodies as the General Accounting Office of the U.S. Congress and the French *Inspection des Finances*, with full rights of access to UN files, established a potentially important precedent—although with only eleven inspectors, it was a very small watchdog, and its effectiveness was gradually weakened as governments nominated underqualified candidates to fill vacancies. When the JIU began work in 1968, the UN's chief executives greeted it with a hostility quite out of proportion to the threat it posed—but quite in tune with their general resentment of external scrutiny.

Because this package passed the UN General Assembly in November 1966 without difficulty, its efforts were considered a major success. Indeed, by the standards of later intergovernmental committees, it was a relatively smooth-running affair. Its origins in financial crisis may have helped to concentrate minds, but far more important was its compactness by UN standards and the fact that, of its eight members, five were major contributors to the budget. The Third World minority argued strongly against any notion of budget-capping: spending, they said, should be geared to needs, and since their needs were infinite, it was inappropriate to regulate the pace of the UN's future growth. But they conceded the desirability of ensuring that the money was well spent. (Twenty years later, even this proposition, with its connotations of accountability, was considered controversial.)

The success was more apparent than real. A decade later, biennial budgets, related in theory to six-year plans, had become common UN practice. But standardized budgets, programs that set clear, time-limited objectives, and coordination within countries of UN technical assistance remained pious hopes. Evaluation had yet to be taken seriously. The fact that governments proved powerless to enforce the implementation of these basic reforms exposed their incapacity, even in the mid-1960s, to control the UN's activities. The horses had already bolted.

The 1966 reform was one of many unsuccessful attempts to bring the specialized agencies to heel by appealing to organizational logic. The committee somewhat naively assumed that agency heads could be persuaded to pay attention to ECOSOC and the General Assembly, on which they relied neither for funds nor votes. In addition, instead of asking whether it was healthy for the UN to expand into new fields for which it had not been designed, the committee contented itself with devising controls to mitigate some of the untidier consequences of this expansion. It would perhaps have been heresy at the time to throw doubt on the growing involvement, both of the "political" UN and of the specialized agencies, in providing technical assistance to the newly independent countries; and in practice, UN governing bodies were incompetent to form a judgment either on the urgency of demand for these services, or on the quality of the agencies' performance. But the committee was so concerned with audit and evaluation precisely because there were already widespread doubts that these activities were being properly planned or competently carried out.

Design for Development: The "Capacity Study"

Three years later, the massive study[8] by the team under Sir Robert Jackson of the "capacity" of the UN to promote Third World development brought in an authoritative, and damning, verdict. The defects it uncovered applied, moreover, not just to technical assistance but to the whole gamut of UN activities. Jackson had been commissioned by the Governing Council of the UN Development Program to assess the ability of the UNDP and the specialized agencies to handle the aid money flowing through the UN, and their capacity to make effective use of double that sum within five years. Jackson said flatly that the job was already beyond them and that nothing short of a comprehensive overhaul of policymaking, financial controls, and field organization would render them capable of tackling it.

Jackson spoke with considerable authority. His wartime experience had included the defense of Malta, the highly complex and totally successful operation to make the British-controlled Middle East self-sufficient that so inspired David Mitrany, and the launching in 1993 of UNDRA, the UN Relief and Rehabilitation Administration set up to assist the recovery of devastated European countries as World War II ended. In all these operations, he had demonstrated a remarkable ability to juggle political, logistical, economic, and organizational considerations and bring coherence out of chaos. The Capacity Study drew on this experience to show why the UN, as then organized, could never hope to meet the demands being made of it.

Jackson had no quarrel with the fact that "development cooperation" had become the UN's predominant function. He believed that "partnership" between the UN and the newly independent countries could make up for the political stalemate of the Cold War years, and prove that "the UN can, and does act." An energetic UN presence in the Third World, creating the conditions for investment and building up national skills, could, he thought, "mean a decisive move towards a peaceful and creative world." But he did not believe that the partnership was working effectively. His diagnosis extended well beyond the narrower considerations of technical competence and project-planning mechanisms to indict "the great inertia of this elaborate administrative structure which no one, it seems, can change." Rationalization, he argued, had become "imperative."

The essence of Jackson's remedy was to combine greater policy control at the center with the maximum possible decentralization of operational decisions. A central "brain" and fund-raising entity was, in his view, vital to interdisciplinary coherence. But the "institution-building" effort must be locally controlled. Development, after all, did not take place in remote UN headquarters in New York, Geneva, Rome, or Paris, but in the farms, villages, and cities of the "developing" world.

This apparent platitude was the reference point for the study's forthright condemnation of the UN's "top-down" approach to development assistance, in which projects were more frequently devised with reference to the services and experts available at various UN headquarters than in response to the recipient country's needs. Interagency rivalries aggravated this bureaucratic tendency. In theory, governments approached the UNDP for assistance with a project in a particular sector—agriculture, education, or health—and the UNDP called in the specialized agency concerned. In practice, as we have seen, each agency sold its pet schemes to individual ministers in recipient countries, thus claiming through them a larger slice of the UNDP cake and expanding its own operational empire.

The UNDP had its representatives in the "field," but so did the major agencies, a situation that is "not conducive to the best interests either of the country's development or of the UN development system" and that "merely adds to diffuseness and bewilders the government." The obsession of individual agencies with their spending "capacity" added a further dimension because, rather than surrender unspent funds to the UNDP at the year's end, they pressed national ministries to agree to patently unviable projects. Jackson identified "dead wood" in a fifth of the large number of projects his team surveyed. Of those that proved disastrous failures, he remarked that the causes generally "lay in the origins of the project and should have been foreseeable." Quality was routinely sacrificed to quantity.

Despite excellent individual examples of effective cooperation, the cumulative effect of the scattered and often incompatible activities of UN organizations had been to complicate governments' lives. In connection with the disbursement of dozens of small grants, they had to deal with twenty major UN agencies and a number of virtually autonomous

UN units. Overall, UN intervention had been unsatisfactory, involving little transfer of knowledge, poor application of science and technology, and heavy reliance on foreign experts of uneven quality "who occupy a kind of sacrosanct position at the heart of the operation."

What was strikingly original was Jackson's insistence that the consumers' interests should henceforth be paramount. The UN's approach should be geared to helping governments decide for themselves, within a framework of national development plans, what they needed in the way of external assistance. To eliminate agency salesmanship, they should channel their requests through a single UN representative within the country; and at the center, they should have at their disposal the services of a single interdisciplinary policy planning team.

This implied the wholesale disruption of existing practices. But these were demonstrably unsustainable. The UN's inefficiencies were already being exposed, Jackson pointed out, by the World Bank and its soft loans wing, the International Development Association (IDA). They were providing similar services at a higher level of competence, within a framework of efficient management and an integrated approach to a country's needs, which produced "tangible results at reasonable cost." Because developing countries felt happier with organizations not subject to the World Bank's system of voting weighted according to financial contribution, and because some activities could not of their nature meet Bank criteria for returns on investment or direct impact on GNP growth rates, Jackson nonetheless believed that the UN should continue to be involved in operational activities. But he predicted that if by 1975 the UN bodies had failed thoroughly to restructure the way they went about their business, governments would have to consider turning investment preparation over to the World Bank—reducing the operations of UN agencies to reflect their inability to deliver. The UNDP would become, "by sheer force of circumstance, a junior partner of the World Bank."

Given coherence, Jackson saw no reason why international organizations should not operate efficiently. Had not the wartime United Nations Relief and Rehabilitation Administration he had directed moved supplies "on a scale and at a rate unsurpassed by any military organization in World War II, as well as dealing with over eight million displaced persons"? But the polycentric structure of competing autonomous agencies, created by "accidents of history," was "inimical to efficiency." To bring the agencies under control, governments would have to centralize the UN's strategic policymaking. Under the existing rules of polycentric autonomy, thirty governing bodies with countless committees were responsible for the UN development effort. To tinker with this palimpsestic nightmare of conflicting authority would be pointless; major political decisions had to be taken. And if donor governments were prepared to provide more money for multilateral development aid but "not willing to take action to reorganize the present 'non-system,'" they had better find "other channels" through which to funnel the cash.

The logic of this analysis, as Jackson recognized, led beyond the organization of technical cooperation: it implied the overhaul of the policy framework for multilateral cooperation in economic and social affairs. He therefore proposed, as a long-term objective, radical changes to decisionmaking at the UN. The Economic and Social Council should be gradually reinforced, to serve as "a one-world parliament for economic and social progress." It should have the power to decide the specialized agencies' budgets and be responsible for reviewing their policies. The agencies' individual governing bodies would then confine themselves to technical questions and details of administration and management. A UN director-general should be appointed, equal in rank to the secretary-general, to oversee all economic and social questions. Within this policy framework, all "operational activities" should be the responsibility of a single organization that would control the specialized agencies' field programs and absorb the special-purpose entities, such as UNICEF and the World Food Program, which had proliferated under the UN's own umbrella.

So comprehensive a challenge to the autonomy of the specialized agencies would, Jackson acknowledged, be bitterly opposed. For the time being, a start could be made where technical cooperation was concerned. It would however be impossible to impose order within chaos without, at the very minimum, a central body to deal with policy, research, and funding; direct links between this center and the "field"; and a coherent interdisciplinary approach at field level. What was needed was an International Development Authority, with a compact headquarters staff, working in partnership with individual countries where the bulk of its manpower, administrative authority, and operational decisionmaking would be located. The authority would draw on the agencies, as appropriate, for scientific and technical advice.

Even this more restricted goal was, Jackson said, unattainable in the short term. Although he insisted that his aim was effective *decentralization*, the plan would largely cut the agencies out of the picture—and he knew that any threat to their decisionmaking (and empire-building) powers would undoubtedly engender implacable resistance.

That left two options for immediate action. The first was to induce the agencies to cooperate as members of an interagency "headpiece." The second was to force them to do so, by making their technical cooperation programs dependent on a central funding authority. Jackson was under no illusion that the first would work. He recalled receiving a letter back in 1948, when he was UN assistant secretary-general in charge of agency coordination, from Lord Boyd Orr, then director-general of the Food and Agriculture Organization (FAO). It expressed the hope that Jackson "would be able to do what I have been clamoring for in the last two years—bring the heads of the specialized agencies together, and try to get a coordinated drive." Experience since then had shown that "circumstances and attitudes are not conducive to collective direction." And with the growth of field activities, "political pressures" from their different constituents—he did not mention the secretariats' imperial ambitions—had made it "impossible for them to subordinate sectoral interests to a collective policy." In any case, there were so many of them that the "headpiece" would be too unwieldy to take "the swift and decisive action essential for operational control."

Pending the creation of an International Development Authority, Jackson therefore set out a scheme to provide a pivot for technical cooperation, based on "the power of the purse." The UNDP should be reorganized to do the job. It had worldwide field offices; these should be strengthened. It was already the conduit for the bulk of multilaterally channeled funds for technical cooperation; this could, he thought, give it the necessary leverage. The UNDP administrator could be given the task of assessing the global sums available and allocating them among countries. The UNDP would give governments a rough estimate of what multilateral aid they could expect over a five-year period. Armed with this "indicative planning figure," the government, in close cooperation with the UNDP country officer, would then draw up a "country program," setting out its main objectives and outlining projects for which it required external funding. These country programs would be approved by the UNDP's Governing Council, but it would be left to the administrator, or the country representative, to approve individual projects—and to decide with the government who should execute them. There would be no guarantee that UN agencies would be selected.

This decentralization of development planning to country level was not merely a device to counter agency objections to central spending controls: it reflected Jackson's conviction that only at local level could projects be firmly subordinated to overall objectives. To improve the quality of the advice available to governments, he proposed the creation of a UN Development Service, specially trained in a UN Staff College—a small core of experts in program management. UNDP headquarters would be responsible for fund-raising and answerable to donors for project execution (which would give it a supervisory role over agencies and other executing agents). Gradually, Jackson hoped, it would become the focus of thinking about development policy within the UN.

To be effective in the "field," Jackson argued, the UN needed a "brain." "The greatest constraint of all" on the UN's capacity to promote development was, he believed, that there was "no group which is constantly monitoring the present operation, learning from experience, grasping all that science and technology has to offer, launching new ideas and methods, challenging established practices, and provoking thought inside and outside the system." UNDP headquarters would therefore need to create a program policy staff—the brain. This would be backed up by a technical advisory panel, to which the specialized agencies were to second top-grade specialists (and pay for them). A computerized information bank would collate the statistics, scientific and technical information, and evaluations of programs, from all UN organizations with economic and social data gathered at country level.

Finally, the UNDP's procurement and contracting office would be free to identify the most efficient contractors inside or *outside* the UN. The agencies would lose "the virtual monopoly of execution that has been theirs in the past." Competition would provide "a vital incentive for them to improve their operational efficiency," and compel the UN to become more outward looking. And this was essential: it could never be effective unless it adopted "a true universality, mobilizing the best brains, knowledge and facilities wherever these can be found." If competition meant slower growth in the agencies' operational activities, this would "permit a better balance between their operational and their constitutional functions." The horses were to be conducted back to their stables.

Curiously, he applied a much lighter touch to the UN's "own" funds and agencies. Pending some future amalgamation, they were simply to cooperate with the UNDP by pooling information about their activities through a "development resources panel"—a fact that did little to endear his proposals to the specialized agencies. But this was not because Jackson intended to make New York the UN's operational hub. On the contrary, his proposals not only stressed devolution of responsibility to country level, but envisaged moving the restructured UNDP out of New York. The report suggested either Washington—for better harmonization, via the World Bank, between capital investment and technical cooperation; or Geneva, where it would be close to the majority of the agencies.

This might well have mitigated the resentments of the "principalities," as he called them, toward what they alleged to be a takeover bid from New York; but the proposal, put forward with uncharacteristic hesitancy, was never seriously considered. Twenty-five years later, Jackson regretted this keenly. Gesturing at the ring of UN skyscrapers, which by then dwarfed the original secretariat building, he expressed his conviction that stripping New York back to its political functions would be a first and indispensable step toward restoring sanity.

The ghost of this particular report has haunted every subsequent foray into the UN's administrative morass and influenced every prescription. Its peculiar resonance derives from the vividness with which it depicts a human enterprise progressively dehumanized by its self-defeating complexity—and from its unflinching focus on the needs and interests of those for whom the great machine, in theory, exists. The Capacity Study was interpreted, and resisted, as an attack on "functional autonomy"—and so, in its ultimate goal of unitary formulation of economic and social policies and budgetary decisionmaking, it was. The questions it raised could not, however, be silenced merely by objections to the particular model it put forward.

Because Jackson speaks largely through the voices of the governments and bureaucrats wrestling with the machine, the report's publication made it infinitely more difficult for either to plead ignorance and indifference. It is with constant, detailed reference to the experiences, prejudices, and frustrations of its inhabitants that the report illuminates the "administrative jungle," exploring the gaps between theory and practice, paper objectives, and actual achievements, contrasting the dedication and good sense of many individuals with the senselessness of their administrative environments. It is through concrete examples of the short-circuiting of good intentions by political infighting, conflicting institutions, and administrative slovenliness that it focuses on the unworkability of the UN's sectoral monopolies.

In its exposure of the agencies' pretense of deference to the governments whose ministers they manipulated (and of ministers' collusion in the game), and in its criticisms of "evaluations" of UN spending, which certified that experts and equipment arrived on time but did not ask what they left behind them, the study's constant benchmark is not the search for administrative tidiness but the well-being of those "assisted." It pays the UN "nonsystem" the respect of treating it as a collection of organizations like any other, subject to normal criteria of assessment. These characteristics raise it above the run of committee reports, even if at the end it comes down to putting forward relatively modest proposals to deal with the problems in what it sees as a politically accessible way, confining itself to the UN's "operational" role. What the report does is to raise the question whether UN organizations as then (and still) interrelated can collectively summon the authority and coherence to improve the quality of governments' policies.

And yet its influence, for three reasons, was probably counterproductive. The first and most obvious is that it was only half-heartedly implemented, falling victim to precisely the kind of tinkering that Jackson had warned would be fatal. By sketching in the eventual goals of genuine reform Jackson had, however freely he conceded that they were for the time being unattainable, enraged not only the agency heads but even the UNDP administrator, the veteran Paul Hoffman. And the half-measures that were adopted following the report's publication had the effect of entrenching the agencies' prerogatives.

The second reason is that the realism with which the study analyzed the managerial and structural defects of "the machine as a whole" deserted it when it came to assessing the potential of global machinery—however brilliantly organized—to effect the day-to-day business of economic development. Jackson's conviction, as he put it in his covering letter to President Tubman, that the UN could "do the most constructive job in the history of the world," led him to overemphasize the importance of project-based technical cooperation. While the report stressed that "projects" must—as they were not—be part of coherent policy frameworks, and that these could ultimately derive only from the decisions of individual governments, its tone and principal recommendations conjured up the image of a UN machine primarily geared to directing a vast network of field programs that would transform the developing world. Third, this emphasis accentuated the UN's southward shift of gravity. It exacerbated the already-pronounced tendency of Third World governments to judge UN organizations by their ability to come up with extra dollops of finance—rather than by their proficiency as centers providing impartial data and technical expertise and their utility as neutral territory for debates and for occasional progress toward intergovernmental agreements.

What came out of the Capacity Study was arguably the worst of all worlds. Its main thrust was formally endorsed in 1970, both by the UNDP's Governing Council and by what was rather portentously known as the "Consensus" of the UN General Assembly. The five-year country programming cycles were adopted, whereby recipient governments formulated their requests to the UNDP on the basis of anticipated resources. But UNDP headquarters retained responsibility for all but minor operational decisions, with the result that the UNDP resident representatives never acquired the discretionary powers that would have made them respected interlocutors at country level. (Nor did they acquire, as a group, the necessary competence; the idea of a "development service" and a Staff College to train one remained on paper.) In practice, the UNDP "resreps" continued to be the whipping boys of the specialized agencies, which circumvented the notion of integrated programming by persuading "their" ministers to insist on priority for projects in their sectors. "Country programming" became the assembly of laundry lists. In these circumstances, the allocation to governments of what amounted to entitlements made it harder for UNDP headquarters or local staff to veto ill-conceived projects: the money was, in a sense, "theirs." "Project approval became an open chequebook game," recalls Maxwell Finger; "It was a question of 'what Lola wants, Lola gets.'"[9]

UNDP officials say this is an exaggeration, but admit that it was difficult to resist the combined pressures of agencies and "beneficiaries"—particularly when the resident representative had so little real power that he relied on maintaining good relations with the government concerned. Whereas World Bank country missions had, as Jackson noted, already started to assess not only what strategies were needed but whether the government was likely to carry them through, the UNDP continued largely on the basis of discrete projects that were never seriously linked to overall objectives.

Matters were exacerbated by the fact that UNDP headquarters failed to develop the policy "brain" that Jackson had considered indispensable—and continued for another two decades with the collusive tradition of automatically allocating to the specialized agencies projects that fell within their "jurisdiction." The concept of the UN as development agency gradually took hold; but the number of warring fiefdoms actually increased, and Jackson's firm ideas about devolved responsibilities, direct accountability, and greater professionalism thus remained largely dead letters. Unable or unwilling to challenge the agencies' monopoly rights, the UNDP itself got into the business of setting up special funds in order to attract donor finance that it could keep under its own control.

Because donor governments made their pledges annually, the principle of five-year planning cycles—an idea that anyway made for excessive rigidities—came to mean little. Twice, in the mid-1970s and in 1982, the UNDP was forced to cut back its "indicative" projections by as much as 45 percent when pledges fell short of its projections. And the pledging system itself, an unintended effect of the reforms, helped to reinforce quantity as the measure of success. In 1986, in his first annual report as UNDP administrator, William Draper gloried in the large number of current projects—5,275—and the fact that a third more had been approved in 1985 than in the previous year. By then, as Draper proudly claimed, no fewer than thirty-six agencies were involved in UNDP projects. Partly in consequence, administrative overheads absorbed 27 percent of spending.[10] By the time Draper retired in 1993, the number of UNDP projects had increased further, to more than fifty-nine hundred. Since there had been almost no real growth in the volume of UNDP funding between 1970 and 1993, what this implied was an ever more scattershot approach.

Most important of all, the key condition for success in this attempt first to order and ultimately to reverse the polycentric autonomy of the specialized agencies was not fulfilled. Jackson had anticipated opposition, and aimed to neutralize it by giving the UNDP increased power over a larger purse. He had assumed that the recommendations of the then-unpublished Pearson report on development[11] for major increases in Western development aid would be accepted, and also that a far higher proportion would henceforth be channeled multilaterally, via the UNDP.

This principle was fully endorsed by Western governments when they discussed the Capacity Study. In practice, they ignored it. The UNDP "share" of UN spending on technical assistance dropped from 65 percent in 1968 to 38 percent in 1980. Donor governments allocated larger and larger sums to other UN units or special programs, whose numbers continued to increase, or to "trust funds" attached to specialized agencies. The UNDP's influence over, and ability to coordinate, the spending of the UN as a whole on technical assistance declined in proportion to its loss of capital share.

Well before the 1990s, as Jackson had predicted, the World Bank's technical assistance outweighed the UNDP's both in quantity—averaging $1.2 billion a year in the 1980s, as against $0.9 billion for the UNDP—and, partly because of the Bank's insistence on "policy dialogue" and competitive tender, in quality. And in-depth investigation by the Nordic countries concluded in 1991 that there had been a "migration of tasks" to the international financial institutions, with the expertise of the World Bank in sectors such as education and the environment surpassing anything available in the "specialized" agencies of the UN.[12] The UN's technical assistance did not wither away, but its reputation declined even among recipient governments. And this affected the standing of the UN in general—the more acutely, because by now the notion that this was what the UN was largely "for" was deeply entrenched. This perception owed much to the Jackson report.

The hostility that the report aroused, when it was published and even into the 1980s—"just the sort of plan which *would* be dreamt up by a naval officer"[13] is one of the kinder versions of in-house dismissal—was, at secretariat level, predictable. It is less easy to see why Western governments, whose voluntary contributions financed UN technical assistance, put so little into reforms with which they openly agreed, based on a diagnosis in which they concurred.

One reason was undoubtedly their fear that a successful assault on the autonomy of the specialized agencies might, as an unwelcome side effect, erode the independence of the World Bank and the International Monetary Fund (IMF). Even had he not been too much of a realist to attack these "Western" citadels, Jackson was preoccupied with what worked. It would not have occurred to him to suggest, in the name of some theoretical symmetry, weakening the authority of organizations he considered efficient. But his long-term ideal for economic cooperation, involving as it did the elevation of ECOSOC to a "parliamentary" role and the appointment of an economic supremo for the UN, did suggest that key policy issues would be determined in New York, not Washington. Jackson may have seen the financial institutions as partners rather than subsidiaries in the new structure; Western governments knew that developing countries were unlikely to take the same view.

There was a second, tactical consideration. Western governments had taken to using voluntary contributions to the agencies' "operational" budgets as informal bargaining chips. They hoped thereby to keep the growth of regular budgets, to which their contributions were mandatory, within bounds. The heads of these agencies knew this, knew that they could always secure voting majorities for large increases in these core budgets, and extracted their pounds of flesh. Although the West had agreed within the OECD's Development Assistance Committee that these payments, essentially Danegeld, were an inefficient way of providing aid, they increased exponentially in the years following the Jackson report. (They had the special attraction for donors that trust funds could be "earmarked" for particular projects, and donors could expect to be favorably treated in related procurements of equipment and recruitment of experts.)

But the fundamental problem was that Jackson's working model assumed that, once the UN was reorganized, governments would trust to its efficacy and corporate intelligence. Since they were not prepared to do so, they prevaricated. Ready enough to criticize the existing situation, the West supported coordination as a device to improve efficiency. Prepared as they might be intellectually to endorse an integrated approach, however, Western governments declined to take the decisive political steps to achieving it. The grand design for a central structure—with "brain" and information bank, central funding authority, organized links between the public and private sectors, and serious field coordination—required, moreover, a degree of accord as to the purposes of the UN's development "partnership" enterprises that, by 1970, was already evaporating. This was not just because Western governments were unwilling to confine themselves to exercising broad policy control in the UNDP Governing Council, leaving detailed management to UNDP field offices. Third World governments were already beginning to argue that the levers of power that mattered were not those directing technical cooperation, but those that governed the international financial and marketing systems.

Jackson's great visionary project had assumed no quarrel with its strategic objectives. These cross-purposes condemned his study to the limbo of half-measures. Since this outcome left them free to play off rival offers on the supposition that they would net more cash that way, it suited recipient governments better than they pretended. In these conditions, it was easy for the specialized agencies to protect their sectoral monopoly interests. Integrated "country programming" remained a charade and the UNDP's operations, as Jackson was to comment seventeen years later, "a travesty of the Capacity Study."[14]

POLITICAL FICTIONS: "RESTRUCTURING"

Although the fate of the Capacity Study suggests that there were no terms on which a global reform of the UN was possible, the new politics of North-South confrontation ironically prompted a further attempt only a few years later. In 1974, when Jackson's report had barely had time to gather dust, the General Assembly—this time on the initiative of the developing countries—called for a new expert group to put forward "proposals on structural changes within the United Nations system so as to make it fully capable of dealing with problems of international economic cooperation in a comprehensive manner."[15] It was to report to the Assembly's seventh special session on development in 1975. Kurt Waldheim, in full electoral campaign for his second term, endorsed the political impulses at work: reform would enable the UN "to work with the necessary degree of speed, effectiveness, and cohesion towards the establishment of a new international economic order."[16] Demands for institutional efficiency had been replaced by demands for a UN geared to the acceleration of political change.

The twenty-five "experts" (half of them ministers or diplomats) nonetheless produced a report that assumed that member states were genuinely concerned to overcome negotiating blockages, and that the "comprehensiveness" they sought had to do with organizational structures rather than with the changing politics of international economic relations. The group—whose rapporteur, Professor Richard Gardner of Columbia University, strongly influenced the outcome—echoed Jackson's theme of coherence between development policy and operations, and linked this to the problem of establishing workable negotiating processes.

The main emphases of the Gardner report,[17] as it came to be known, were the need for stronger central direction of the UN's research, analysis, development cooperation, and—in the first attempt to surmount the problems of interbloc confrontation—the desirability of small subject-based groups for resolving arguments about policy.

To reinforce the "center," it too recommended the appointment of a director-general for development and international economic cooperation, not coequal with the secretary-general, as Jackson had proposed, but second to him only in rank. He would be assisted by a research and policy unit, "composed of outstanding professionals" seconded from organizations inside and outside the UN, and an advisory committee of the heads of the specialized agencies and regional commissions (which was intended to provide the collective leadership that Jackson was certain they were incapable of giving). The director-general would be responsible for a single United Nations Development Authority (UNDA), whose administrator would report to him. This would merge all the twenty-four separate UN operational units (except, for no stated reason, UNICEF) under one umbrella—although they would remain sufficiently distinct to permit "earmarking" of aid funds for purposes such as population, the environment, or narcotics. Its board, equally balanced between donors and recipients, would meet once a year at ministerial level to provide broad policy guidance, and would report to ECOSOC.

ECOSOC itself was to be reorganized. To avoid duplicated debate, most of its plethora of subcommissions would be abolished. The revamped council would also review the plans and budgets of all UN organizations as well as their operational activities. Most importantly, it would set up small negotiating groups with full-time chairmen, to work for up to two years on particular controversial issues. Membership of these groups, with some deference to geographical balance, would be drawn from countries particularly interested in the subject under discussion. Once they had reached unanimous agreement, they would present their proposals to ECOSOC and the General Assembly—which could vote on the package but not attempt to renegotiate it. This amounted to a form of bicameralism, a revolutionary departure from the rigidities of universal negotiating forums—and a particularly subversive proposal coming, as it did, at the high tide of majoritarian UN politics.

The Gardner report also broke the taboo on abolishing any part of the UN machinery. Referring back to the unimplemented Havana Charter of 1948, it advocated the establishment of an International Trade Organization and—logically but, given the Third World's fierce attachment to "its" organization, astonishingly—recommended the parallel phasing out of UNCTAD. UNCTAD's nontrade functions would be assumed by the General Assembly, ECOSOC, and the new policy secretariat. In a similar spirit, it suggested that the recently created UN Environment Program's operations should be absorbed by the UN Development Authority, and its policy functions by ECOSOC. Finally, it recommended that the specialized agencies be "gradually redirected" toward their original research and standard-setting functions. The new UNDA should be free to contract out where it chose—to government agencies, universities, private contractors, and regional commissions among other possibilities.

Even though the group also recommended a redistribution of the voting rights in the World Bank and IMF, the general tenor of its report was thoroughly out of tune with the *zeitgeist*. Fifteen of its members were from the Third World, among them such ardent advocates of a new international economic order as Venezuela's Manuel Pérez Guerrero, a former UNCTAD secretary-general. Yet it was singularly unaffected by "new orders" politics. Stolidly, the group set out functional priorities for the UN, and proceeded to devise institutional responses to the needs it identified. These depended heavily on central controls and unified policymaking. But the group also had the wisdom to acknowledge the tensions between "working democracy" and "voting democracy" that Mitrany had foreseen half a century earlier, and to seek a formula to resolve them.

Much of this was eminently sensible. But the seventh special session, to which the group's report was presented, was a highly charged political event, intended by Third World spokesmen to transform the whole international vocabulary of economic relations. Nothing could have been more alien to the Gardner group's pragmatic concerns with more effective cooperation, and as a result the report was given short shrift. Once its existence had been formally noted, an *ad hoc* intergovernmental committee of the entire UN membership (itself a rejection of the Gardner concept of working through small groups) was set up to review its proposals.

The contrast between this new group, whose members spoke (at least in theory) for their governments, and the Gardner group, whose members had been free to concentrate on what might help those governments work together, illustrates the gulf that was developing between "insiders" and politicians. The 1975 resolution that set up the new *ad hoc* committee, under the chairmanship of the Ghanaian ambassador Kenneth Dadzie, defined its tasks in accordance with the prevailing ideological trend. It was so to reorganize the UN as to make it "more responsive to the requirements of the provisions of the Declaration and Program of Action on the Establishment of a New International Economic Order [NIEO] as well as those of the Charter of Economic Rights and Duties of States."[18]

This was a project not to reform the UN, but to transform it—and to transform it moreover into a vehicle through which the majority could realize its goal of revolutionizing the international economic, financial, and trading systems. The declaration on the NIEO had been, as much as anything, a declaration of rupture with liberal concepts of "development": the thirty-four articles of the 1974 Charter, as Pierre de Senarclens has pointed out, had put forward "an absolutist concept of sovereignty while tearing down the frontiers between the rule of law and the arbitrary will of governments."[19]

A UN that "responded" to these manifestos for North-South confrontation would necessarily be a radically different enterprise.

The tension between the intergovernmental committee's political terms of reference, based as they were on documents that were not accepted by the West, and the institutional dimensions of its remit, was maintained through the two fretful years of horse-trading between negotiating blocs before it produced its report. Each bloc approached the process with different and mutually incompatible ends, and the first victim of this dissent was the Gardner report. Objections by developing countries prevented its use even as a basis for the committee's deliberations. Where its ideas survived, they were adapted to fit the predominantly ideological preoccupations of the Third World majority, or used by the defensive Western minority as shields against the "politicization" of the negotiations.

The Group of 77 had two major aims in "restructuring" the UN. In the first place, they sought to confer supreme authority for policymaking and negotiations on the two forums they felt most confident of controlling, the General Assembly and UNCTAD, and to oblige other bodies (including, in particular, the Bretton Woods institutions) to respect their decisions. Their second goal was to increase the UN's funding for development. They therefore supported the idea of a director-general for development, on the ground that this would increase the prominence of development aid and, therefore, put pressure on the West to make more money available. But they opposed the consolidation of policymaking and institutional authority that had been, to its proponents the point of creating the post.

The United States and the European Community were determined to disregard the terms of reference and to use the occasion for more traditional purposes. As ever, they were out to obtain improvements in administration, budget presentation and personnel policies, and to reduce overlap and duplication of activities. The United States, however, was more alive than the Western Europeans to the destructive impact of interbloc confrontation, and therefore supported the Gardner report's proposals for the creation of small negotiating groups. Here it met not only vehement opposition from the Group of 77, for whom the idea was an assault on their majority status, but some hostility from the West Europeans, who claimed to prefer the "flexibility" of "consensus" involving all member states.

The fact was that the representative group formula, intended to provide an effective route to serious multilateral discussion of issues of substance, appeared at the height of ideological confrontation to entail some risk of preemptive concessions by the West. The implicit bargain was that the majority would accept some diminution of sovereign equality in return for a commitment by the paying minority to negotiate in good faith. But the origins and terms of reference of this particular committee suggested to some Western governments that "good faith" might involve acceptance of the premises of the NIEO and the 1974 economic Charter. Both the United States and the EEC (which presented the two major Western papers for the committee) were attracted by the idea of a single UN Development Authority—but not by the Group of 77 condition that in return for such a rationalization, they should promise to increase their overall funding to the UN's development efforts.

The final report[20] emerged after an infinity of haggling on December 14, 1977. A compromise text that papered over continuing disagreements, it was too imprecise to be capable of implementation. The statements of reservation and interpretation that festooned it reflected, moreover, basic disagreements about the purposes of institutional reform. The "restructuring resolution," 32/197, by which the General Assembly adopted the committee's report on December 20, was treated by virtually every delegation as a great leap forward. This was not so surprising: the most insignificant document is liable to be so acclaimed by those responsible for its negotiation, and in the North-South stalemate of 1977, the fact of reaching agreement mattered more than the content, or the degree of fudge required to get there. What is more curious is that the illusion that "the UN had accepted the most ambitious internal reorganization plans since its inception"[21] persisted even after the delegates went home.

On paper, there were certainly some gains. A director-general for development and international economic cooperation was duly appointed, charged in the most grandiloquent terms with providing "effective leadership . . . in the field of development," with coordinating a UN-wide multidisciplinary approach to development problems, and with the efficient management of all its operational activities. But that decision was so diluted by compromise as to deprive it of impact. The incumbent was appointed by the UN secretary-general rather than elected by the membership, and given the inadequate rank of under-secretary-general. Ken Dadzie, chairman of the *ad hoc* committee, to whom the job went, was from the outset kept at arm's length by Waldheim, who had no intention of permitting a rival center for decisionmaking. He was deprived of any influence even over the Department of International Economic and Social Affairs in the UN secretariat in New York. As for the agency heads, they saw no reason to take seriously a unit with a professional staff of fewer than a dozen.[22] They treated Dadzie as a minor flunkey, and his successor, the Frenchman Jean Ripert, met with similar treatment.

The New York secretariat was extensively reorganized, in order to make it capable of the new "systemwide" interdisciplinary approach, to strengthen its research capacities and to enable it to monitor all UN activities. An office for Program Planning and Coordination was created to investigate problems of rivalry and overlap. The real distribution of power, as between the agencies and New York, remained as before. The principle of a single governing body to control operational activities was accepted, but no action was taken. The UNDP country officers were now formally designated by the UN secretary-general as the UN's sole representatives, with the fine title of "resident coordinator." That made them officially responsible for "field coordination," but they still had no powers to compel the agencies to cooperate—and the agencies countered by increasing the size of their missions.[23] The nearest approximation to a unified approach to UN development activities was the agreement that governments would announce their voluntary contributions to all the "operational agencies" at a single annual pledging conference.

For internal coherence at the policy level, the reform package relied on that unsatisfactory old workhorse, the Administrative Committee on Coordination (ACC), in which the secretary-general met with heads of agencies twice a year. This now sprouted subcommittees to deal with personnel, administration, budgetary matters, and "substantive questions"—such as the coordinated preparation of their separate programs and "joint planning" of longer-term strategies. The agency heads continued to pay little more than lip service to the ACC, attending its meetings principally in order to ensure that nobody was poaching on their patch.

The net effect of these modest innovations was to create a number of UN jobs, and to produce at the price of greater institutional complexity some minor irritants for agency heads. They made no real impact on coordination either at the level of policy planning, where the agencies continued to formulate strategies independently, or in the field. They failed to produce the "integrated approach to development" for which the General Assembly ritually and unconvincingly continued to call. In 1982, a sympathetic analysis concluded that, while it was too pessimistic to say that "restructuring has advanced many careers but little else," the UN was no more "efficient and cost-effective" than before and "the changes which might have had a truly significant impact . . . were either discarded . . . or have yet to be acted upon."[24]

The whole long-drawn-out business did, however, have one "significant" consequence: contrary to the intentions of the Gardner group, it reinforced the claims of the General Assembly, UNCTAD, and even ECOSOC to be centers for binding political and economic negotiation, ascribing to them an authority that they did not, and could not, possess. In that sense, the Group of 77 won.

In designating the General Assembly the "principal forum for policymaking and the harmonization of international action" on economic and social matters, resolution 32/197 reflected the Group of 77's determination to translate their voting strength in global forums into a real negotiating weapon. ECOSOC was to be reorganized to make it the principal vehicle for devising "solutions" to these questions and monitoring progress in implementing them. UNCTAD, far from being phased out, was to be the main forum for detailed economic negotiations. Western governments, thankful to have avoided specific reference to any General Assembly authority over the Bretton Woods institutions, accepted these proposals as a gesture to Third World demands. They had no intention of translating them into reality. But the rhetoric alone was enough to lock the UN into the long, sad charade of "global negotiations" in which nothing was negotiated, but which absorbed enormous amounts of time and energy, and further diminished the UN's credibility. The emphasis on "negotiation" and "decision" reduced the prospect that UN organizations would be used for exploratory dialogue or to identify issues around which policies might converge. It also made it even less likely that the idea of using small working parties to iron out controversies would be adopted: the greater a forum's pretensions to decisionmaking, the more insistent would be the pressure to involve all sovereignly equal member states.

The "restructuring exercise" purported to be a comprehensive overhaul of the UN "family." This was misleading: it was little more than a collection of organizational modifications, which erected fictions of central control without touching the sectoral prerogatives that made such control an impossibility. Negotiated in New York, adopted in New York, such impact as it had was almost entirely limited to New York. Its premises were unrealistic. No reform that depended on the voluntary relinquishing by the agencies of any part of their autonomy stood a chance. The agency heads had, furthermore, good reason to be skeptical of "coordination" by New York, where the "political" UN had itself generated so many special programs, units, and funds that it could hardly claim to be a model of coherence.

The UN's policymaking capacities were, in theory, strengthened. In fact, by setting its debating forums the objective—the fundamental reshaping of international economic relations—on which there was the least prospect of agreement, the 1977 resolution increased the chances that they would be used for political shadow boxing while actual decisions were taken elsewhere. Most seriously, the opportunity to institute workable negotiating machinery was missed. The whole exercise was vitiated by its concentration on adapting the UN to accommodate the ambitions of its numerical majority. The tensions between the requirements of dialogue and the claims of sovereign equality were resolved by a paper "consensus" in which universality won a decisive victory over practical considerations of what could be made to work. The process set back by years—not least by creating the fiction that the question had been addressed—serious examination of the kinds of multilateral cooperation for which global organizations were indispensable, and of the reforms that might succeed in inducing all governments, including those able to conduct their international business through other channels, to take the UN seriously. The Third World's refusal to contemplate a "bicameral" negotiating structure reduced the prospect that governments would conduct such a review in future. If anything, the outcome increased the "ungovernability" of the UN identified by Jackson.

Efficiency Is Not Enough

The UN creates its own microclimate. Diplomats can work for hours to reach agreement on whether the "debt situation" should be described as something to be debated in a "spirit of shared responsibility," or "responsibilities," and emerge feeling that they have made a vital contribution to international dialogue.[25] They are also apt to ascribe the failure of even longer marathons, such as the reform efforts of the 1970s, to lack of political will. Samuel de Palma, U.S. assistant secretary for international organizations for part of that period, recalls of the "restructuring negotiations":

> We couldn't find a consensus anywhere, because it was being dealt with by middle-level bureaucrats, with nobody behind them and no government interest at the bottomline. So we got all those nice papers and had nowhere to go. Our Secretary of State's eyes glazed over after ten minutes: as an issue it just didn't compare with the Middle East. All of us were working with huge national bureaucracies not paying much attention—and facing massive resistance from the people who were, in the agencies and at the UN.[26]

But this begs the question. How relevant were these "nice papers" to making the UN more usable as an instrument of national policy? Even the Jackson report, for all its intellectual clarity, was curiously out of tune with what politicians of both North and South were beginning to perceive as the determining factor in their attitudes to UN organizations: the flexing of Third World voting muscle. His conclusions, in consequence, had little real resonance for Third World diplomats and politicians, who increasingly insisted that "international cooperation" must involve the redistribution of political and economic power—or for those in the West who feared that, left to the UN, it might.

By the time the restructuring negotiations were under way in the 1970s, these political tensions had moved from the wings to center stage. Diplomats dutifully trod the familiar territory of negotiating reforms. If ministers' eyes glazed over, this did not necessarily denote a failure of political will, or even political indifference. They were simply by then all too keenly aware of the political impossibility, in the absence of shared objectives, of negotiating any agreement that would make a real difference either to the UN's efficiency, or to the uses they could make of the global bodies. Apart from a polite but lukewarm commentary on President Carter's report to the U.S. Congress on the matter, the major British Foreign Office review of UN policy in 1978 devoted a mere twelve lines out of its thirty-eight pages to the outcome of the restructuring process. It clearly expected that it would have no more than a marginal impact on the UN's increasing "capacity for duplication and overlapping of responsibilities."[27]

In the late 1970s, the question of overlap and duplication again became the focus of Western policy, but in a far more piecemeal, agency-by-agency approach, which combined a dogged pursuit of efficiency with efforts to curb the politicization of debates and programs—notably at the ILO and UNESCO. As belief in the availability of a "systemwide" approach receded, realism appeared to dictate a strategy limited to curbing particular abuses, within existing frameworks. These efforts increasingly assumed the form of a taxpayers' revolt: "zero real growth" in budgets, sustained battles to cut costs and programs. They therefore encountered stiff resistance both from Third World governments and from secretariats—to the point where reasoned demands that organizations give better value for money were resisted as disguised attacks on multilateralism.

The extent to which this "realism" had become accepted dogma was illustrated in 1984, when Jean Gerard, then U.S. ambassador to UNESCO, remarked that if the reforms being negotiated in that organization resulted in it doing the same things more efficiently, the situation would be even worse. Her comment was seized upon, by Western "moderates" as well as M'Bow's spokesmen, as evidence that the United States was not serious about reform and was simply bent on departure. Washington's diffidence about putting forward more far-reaching proposals for change, and the serene duplicity with which Gregory Newell, then assistant secretary for international organizations, persisted throughout that year in placing on record his friendship and even admiration for a director-general Washington knew to be both incompetent and corrupt, suggests that it was indeed not serious. But those who so interpreted Ambassador Gerard's remark revealed that they themselves lacked the "seriousness" to assess the real nature of UNESCO's crisis.

Diplomats might say privately—as one European did in a confidential note to colleagues—that nothing short of a frontal lobotomy would bring UNESCO's ambitions into line with its capacity and mandate and enable it to recover respectability on more modest terms. In public, they restricted themselves, with few exceptions, to calling for minor rationalizations—merging the odd subprogram, trimming three days off the interminable biennial General Conference, or "inviting" the director-general to "continue" to account for certain highly suspect expenditures (such as the lump sums paid in cash at his discretion for "scholarships") on which no proper accounting had ever in fact been provided.

UNESCO's long flirtation with disintegration was exceptional for the publicity its later phases attracted, and for the unscrupulousness with which M'Bow mustered resistance to any reforms that ventured beyond the cosmetic. It was also exceptional in prompting the withdrawal of three states—the United States, Great Britain, and Singapore—and the firm commitment to withdrawal, in the event of M'Bow's reelection for a third term in 1987, of such pillars of multilateralism as Denmark, the Netherlands, and half a dozen others. But in other respects it was typical of the history of UN reform—above all in demonstrating the degree to which, in the absence of policy review, efficiency can make things worse.

Oiling the administrative wheels of an institution may improve its mechanical functioning—yet fail in the more crucial task of equipping it to tackle more effectively the problems it was created to address. The FAO under Edouard Saouma functioned relatively efficiently, in its own terms: but the terms were the wrong ones. A country could, for example, suffer considerable damage by going all out for food self-sufficiency—one of the concepts most energetically pushed by the FAO—if the objective of feeding its people was more likely to be attained by a combination of growing its own food and earning the foreign exchange required to import what it could not, without serious ecological stress, raise itself. And if the only outcome of reforms is to send an organization careering more energetically down the wrong alley, the business of reform itself becomes discredited. Ministers are then unlikely to give the process the political attention without which significant improvements in the policies of an institution are unlikely to be secured from the "outside." The efforts by Western diplomats to tackle deep-seated problems at the level of efficiency drives, however understandable in the absence of political agreement on more ambitious targets, were self-defeating because they failed to address the defects that had eroded "political will" in the first place.

The question apparently raised by the UNESCO case was whether, in the absence of cooperation from an organization's top management, governments could achieve serious changes in policy or the quality of programs by any means less radical than threatening to withdraw. The real problem, as the Dutch diplomat Marten Mourik concluded, was that nothing in the history of UN reforms suggested that governments had discovered any way of revitalizing UN institutions, other than by changing the management. And at UNESCO, they had not seriously attempted to look for a way. Since even the Western governments had operated in a near-vacuum of policy, in the sense that they had made little effort to reach agreement on what they wanted UNESCO to do, they had no basis for anything more than incremental tinkering—and an ill-orchestrated campaign to change the director-general.

In fact it was only the prospect of mass desertions in the event of M'Bow's reelection in 1987, making UNESCO's collapse inevitable, which forced a change of management and gave the organization a chance of reform. And the decisive factor in securing M'Bow's reluctant departure was the Soviet Union's determination to salvage an organization that served its national interests—but only so long as Western governments remained in the club. It was Soviet diplomats who, at the eleventh hour, told M'Bow that he must withdraw his candidacy and that they would not take no for an answer and informed his Francophone African supporters that they would refuse to countenance any attempt to sabotage the orderly election of his Spanish challenger, Federico Mayor.

Down the road in Rome, two days after the UNESCO vote of November 7, the limits of Western influence in the absence of threats to withdraw seemed to be conclusively demonstrated. Edouard Saouma easily secured reelection for a third term as director-general of FAO, defeating a well-qualified African candidate, Moise Mensah, who was supported by almost all the Western governments as well as the Organization of African Unity. There were massive last-minute African defections to Saouma's camp, by delegates whose governments had firmly committed themselves to Mensah. The West's defeat was underscored by the fact that at the FAO a number of governments, led by Canada, had put considerable energy into persuading Third World capitals that reform of the FAO was indispensable, was in their interest, and depended on Saouma's departure. They had also worked far harder than they did in the case of UNESCO to find a serious challenger for the job.

The two cases had one thing in common. Western governments, after some years of trying to negotiate—against Third World and secretariat obstruction—agreements on programs of administrative reforms, came to accept the truth of the old Dutch proverb that "lenient surgeons leave stinking wounds." But that led not to the development of more coherent, ambitious strategies, but to revolt. In UNESCO, the more extreme case because of the challenge its policies in areas such as communications and human rights presented to Western values, revolt took the form of actual or projected withdrawals. Both instances suggest that it is an illusion to expect governing bodies to remedy their incapacity to govern these organizations—and therefore, that if policy impasses are to be surmounted and new strategies charted, the impetus for change has to come from inside the secretariats themselves. The clearer it is to UN managers that their survival depends on the quality of service they provide, and on their ability to persuade governments of different political persuasions that the wares on offer are attractive and worth supporting, the more likely is such "reform from within." And the duty to innovate would, paradoxically, justify greater politicization in the secretariats—not in the familiar sense of jumping onto political bandwagons, but in the virtuous sense of developing an institutional capacity to twitch the political levers that mean something to governments and their publics. It would mean constant reference to needs and demands. This is what Dag Hammarskjöld had in mind when he said that "the United Nations is, and should be, a living, evolving, experimental institution" and that "if it should ever cease to be so it should be revolutionized or swept aside for a new approach."[28]

THE VIEW FROM WITHIN

Yet this brings us full circle back to Jackson's lament that the UN is "unmanageable in the strictest sense of the word"; that it is "so organised that managerial direction is impossible." To many politicians, government officials and workers in private voluntary organizations who deal regularly with the UN machine, the idea of the impetus for change coming from within is simply risible. Over the years, the concept of an "international civil service," a creation of which the League of Nations was, to the end, justly proud, has been gutted of most of the elementary disciplines of a career bureaucracy. So ingrained are slipshod UN management, political pressures on appointments, and the neglect of career development that the whole concept of an international civil service now needs to be rethought, a subject that will be discussed in Chapter 10.

Under the right conditions, however, the evolutionary impetus identified by Hammarskjöld as indispensable to the UN's survival could revive—agency by agency if not systemwide. As Jackson also pointed out, there are hundreds of civil servants with the commitment and capacity to innovate trapped within the UN's prematurely fossilized bureaucratic carapace. Any extended contact with the UN secretariats reveals widespread anxiety about the debilitating impact of managerial drift, ill-conceived programs, interagency rivalries, and inept or corrupt personnel policies. Where UN insiders blame governments for the hypertrophic disorder within secretariats, it is most typically for settling for less than they should, for insufficient toughness in demanding high standards of performance and accountability.

This is less evident to outsiders than it might be, because the United Nations speaks to the world through a tiny handful of official spokesmen and agency heads. The most competent of these tend to keep their heads down, while the complacency or arrogance of others gives an impression of monolithic bureaucratic resistance to change that is accurate enough in terms of practical outcomes, but misleading as an indicator of staff attitudes. Highly stratified hierarchies frustrate the talents of a substantial minority of civil servants. Given a system that disciplined or fired incompetents and gave talent its proper scope, and in which loyalty to a UN organization ceased to be coterminous with loyalty to its chief executive, they would respond as well as most workforces to management by objective. Many of them are more bitter than external critics about the imperviousness to reform of the structures in which they work, because in a daily, routine way they live with the consequences. They of all people are aware that the UN's failures to achieve its potential cannot be divorced from questions of leadership, vision, and basic competence within the secretariats; they are well placed to understand the connections between quality of output and "political will."

The degree of openness with which they ventilate their ideas and frustrations differs from house to house. As a rough rule of thumb, the greater the institutional paralysis, the less tolerance there is of dissent. It spoke volumes for Blanchard's ILO that its press office was decorated with blow-ups of uncharitable press cartoons. By contrast, the large public relations department at the Food and Agriculture Organization spent much of its time during Saouma's eighteen-year reign complaining to news editors about "hostile" articles, the information for which had often been provided by the organization's own demoralized staff. Like civil servants everywhere, UN staffers are in addition conditioned to the language of camouflage. Much skill goes into crafting reports whose layers of generality and official optimism are designed to protect failures from scrutiny—and to avoid offending member states by unduly candid assessments of disastrous "field projects." Many are inhibited by their oaths (and feelings) of loyalty from public expression of their disquiet. And, although senior managers rightly complain that well-merited dismissals are absurdly difficult to secure, criticism carries genuine risks. Particularly if it is written down or made public, it may result in nonpromotion or transfers, sometimes to the "nonjobs" that, in most UN organizations, are in plentiful supply. With an increasing proportion of the younger talent recruited on short-term rather than permanent contracts—no bad thing in itself—unscrupulous managements have used the threat of nonrenewal to stifle excessive zeal.

Occasionally staff concerns find a public platform. This happened at the Palais des Nations in Geneva in December 1985, during a meeting cosponsored by the UN and a group of religious foundations as part of the UN secretary-general's summons to "reflection" in the UN's fortieth anniversary year. The theme "Is universality in jeopardy?" may have been designed to elicit condemnations of the Reagan administration's policies toward the UN. What took place was a confrontation between the secretary-general's representative, Robert Muller, and past and serving UN staff members. Condemning the UN's bureaucratic sclerosis, its irrelevance to the process of reconciling national policies, and its "incoherent, remote and inefficient" operational programs, they maintained that a serious review of the UN's contribution to multilateral cooperation was long overdue.

Pérez de Cuéllar's choice of Robert Muller to take charge of the anniversary celebrations had been enough to confirm internal skepticism about the seriousness of his call for a reevaluation of the UN's role. A UN assistant secretary-general proud of his authorship of uplifting works on the power of faith and "the great mysterious journey of human fulfillment and cosmic consciousness unfolding on this planet," Muller's thirty-eight-year career with the UN had been marked by a pronounced aversion to mundane practicalities. When, for example, he had been responsible for coordinating the activities of the specialized agencies, he had drawn up a "checklist of human concerns" to assist him, which began with "our relations with the sun" and ended with "spiritual exercises of interiority, meditation, prayer and communion with the universe, eternity and God." He had pinned this helpful flowchart to his office wall.[29]

Evidently shocked by the frankness of the discussion at Geneva, Muller retorted that the solution was to "get out of the trough of pessimism," remembering that the UN is a mirror of humanity and that "we are in the kindergarten of planet management." It was futile, said this televangelist manqué, to demand fundamental reforms. The secretariat had done so much: it had set up UNCTAD; it had proposed an international development tax. And it was absurd to complain about the degradation of staff quality; nobody was hired today without a doctorate and two to four languages (a claim without the remotest substance). "In 38 years," he complained, "I have heard nothing but reform."

Havelock Brewster, head of UNCTAD's commodities division, replied that staff members had "been offering suggestions as to how the secretariat at the highest level might assist governments. With some surprise, I found Muller's reply devoted to praise of the secretariat." Nothing, he went on, could have illustrated more clearly the UN's tenuous grip on reality.

> Can he not be aware that in large numbers of countries, the attitude to the UN borders on ridicule; that this year the UN was seen to be stranded, immobilized, while millions starved; that the developing world is in economic decomposition while the International Development Strategy is an exercise in hypocrisy and there is chaos in the negotiating functions of the UN? That there is overlap and incoherence among its 32-odd agencies about which Ecosoc does little and the office of the Director-General for Development and International Economic Cooperation does heaven knows what? Is it credible, in these circumstances, to meet here as the board of a mutual adoration society?

Muller left the meeting early. Brewster was considered by his colleagues to have laid his career on the line—a comment in itself on the UN's intellectual climate. Brewster's heresy was not so much that he emphasized the irrelevance of much UN activity. That had by then become commonplace even among the UN's staunchest apologists. Muller's more celebrated contemporary, Brian Urquhart, for example, has acknowledged the bureaucratic "elephantiasis" of the UN and ridiculous methods of operating in which "cockeyed ideas from member states or other sources begot studies which produced reports which set up staffs which produced more reports which were considered by meetings which asked for further reports and sometimes set up additional bureaucratic appendages which reported to future meetings" in a "self-perpetuating" process.[30] Where Brewster trespassed was in violating convention by openly attributing responsibility for the UN's malfunctioning not to member states, but to the secretariats. Yet that view is shared, privately, by many insiders. Few of them look to governments to remedy matters, because they do not think them capable of coherent strategies. They believe that the responsibility to initiate, and the capacity to convert ideas into action, lies within the house.

A survey of UN staff in Geneva a year later, conducted by their own association, revealed that 80 percent thought that "a profound reform aimed at modifying the way in which the United Nations secretariats operates is necessary"; 60 percent said that either the secretary-general or staff members themselves should take the initiative, while only 19 percent thought that the impetus should come from member states. Thirteen proposals, drawn up on the basis of this survey, centered on three overriding preoccupations: the need for better overall policy direction, for the elimination of political patronage and cronyism from recruitment and promotion procedures, and for stricter evaluation of programs. "Most staff members," the report stated. "are concerned about the lack of impartiality and effectiveness of the controls on United Nations activities, as well as the wastage, duplication and lack of credibility of the Organization that this entails."[31] They felt themselves to be operating in a policy limbo: only a third of those polled claimed to be regularly informed of the activities of their respective divisions—never mind wider UN issues, on which less than a quarter claimed to be briefed.

In some organizations, this lack of vertical information flows is deliberate, and is compounded by the absence of communication between different divisions. The FAO, under Edouard Saouma's direction, concentrated power within the "cabinet" by placing strict limits on interdepartmental consultations at lower levels—between rural development and forestry, for example. And the pervasiveness of patronage is suggested by the fact that UN staff polls repeatedly record that only a small minority believes recruitment and promotion to be based on merit. There is widespread scorn for administrative systems that proliferate petty controls—a desk officer can be required to obtain up to a dozen "visas" of approval from different offices in order to invite a single expert to a two-day seminar—but that pay markedly less attention to the overall performance of staff or the impact of programs. The author of a path-breaking FAO survey on the carrying capacity of land, published in 1985, said that it took him twenty years—"sixteen to get permission to start, four to carry it out." And although the survey demonstrated its method with a study of Africa, most African delegates to that year's FAO conference had neither seen it nor been told of its existence.

Many of these anxieties are common to all large bureaucracies. But a significant number of UN civil servants have in addition come to believe that their organizations are not merely inefficient but are, in broad strategic senses, out of touch both with the real limits of their capacities and with the changing profiles of the external world's needs—that they are doing the wrong things. Such uneasiness can surface even among the most outwardly subservient senior *apparatchiks*. One of these, having defended the FAO's programs in Africa in 1984 for a solid forty minutes, abruptly requested anonymity, and said: "We are ruining Africa. Just as my generation blames the missionaries and colonials for much that is wrong there, I tell my children that they will look back and say that we, the new colonials, ruined Africa with food aid, ensuring that in the next century it will be a totally dependent basket case. Why do we push it? It buys governments' votes. We are in the power business, not the business of food."[32]

Senior managers refer in their turn to the tenacity with which departments resist efforts to disband them or refocus their work. They also point out that the right of staff to inspect their own dossiers—and the existence of rebuttal procedures for unfavorable reports on their performance—has made a mockery of proper staff assessment. They are quite right that it has become infinitely easier to offload incompetent staff somewhere else than to fire them—although the UN's top management is largely responsible for this state of affairs, since dismissal procedures do exist. Javier Pérez de Cúellar's decision to rely on attrition, when acute insolvency coupled with a Group of 18 recommendation forced him in 1986–87 to promise to cut UN staff by 15 percent, was typical of the UN's approach to personnel questions. Ken Dadzie, then secretary-general of UNCTAD, complained that he was all in favor of using cuts to produce a leaner and more capable organization—but that to do the job properly and match skills properly with tasks he needed to fire about 25 percent, and then recruit 10 percent. This, however, would have involved paying compensation—and when he put this to Pérez, the secretary-general refused even to contemplate approaching member states with a request to finance this long-term investment in quality. (In fairness it has to be said that rejuvenating UNCTAD would not have been top of any Western government's wish list; but in fairness it must also be said that this consideration had probably never entered the UN secretary-general's head.) That decision, Dadzie commented, forced him to part with younger, better-qualified staff as their short-term contracts expired, and to keep on the securely tenured dead wood.

The lack of "any sense of urgency" about overhauling the machine, of which Jackson had complained, has been evident at the highest level. Even under the pressure of extreme financial and political crisis, Pérez de Cuéllar could summon little enthusiasm for broad policy matters outside the security sphere. An incident in October 1987 says much about the sense of priorities on the thirty-eighth floor at Turtle Bay. The secretary-general called to his office the executive heads of the agencies, who had gathered in New York for the regular meeting of the Administrative Committee on Coordination. He informed them that he had proposed a meeting of ECOSOC at ministerial level in his annual report, that it would have to be carefully prepared, and that he would need their help in devising a promising agenda and coordinated position papers. He had called them in, he said, to listen to what they had to say. Barber Conable, Michel Camdessus, and Francis Blanchard[33] pledged their organizations' resources; William Draper, less enthusiastic, said that he had quite enough to do administering the UNDP. At this early stage of the meeting, a note was brought in for the secretary-general. He rose, explaining that with great regret he had to leave: he was due to preside at a ceremony in memory of Danny Kaye.

IMPASSE

The UN will be condemned to relive this history if governments do not remember it. All of the three programs of reform outlined in this chapter had practical merits—at least as they were conceived, if not as they were left half-implemented by governments and secretariats. Yet cumulatively, their effect has been to expand the UN without enhancing its capacity to adapt—and the same fate could attend later proposals, such as the Nordic countries' rehearsal in the 1990s of the themes covered by Jackson. The blueprints were flawed by their underlying assumption that the UN must be restructured to do the same things better, or to do more. Governments in turn, while constantly stressing their concern to control this expansion, distrusted the existing machinery so much that they were constantly inventing units and specialized agencies to perform new functions—population control, environmental protection, the promotion of industrial development, or the coordination of disaster relief—high on the current political agenda. The focus of reform remained institutional and remarkably inward-looking; the appropriateness of the UN's involvement in an ever-widening range of issues was seldom questioned.

The talk about "priorities" meant little more than reordering what existed or adding to it. Reforms intended to streamline the UN thus compounded its complexity. The secretariats, as has been said, bear considerable responsibility for these failures; but it has to be added that when UN executives *have* put forward creative ideas—as Blanchard did in his 1986 report to the ILO conference on fostering self-help in the "informal employment sector," on which twelve hundred million rely—governments give them scant attention. This betrayal, too, is keenly felt: even if UN civil servants do not expect governments to initiate reforms, they resent their failure to encourage the process. The mutual distrust between governments and secretariats is one of the major obstacles to regenerating and adapting Jackson's "prehistoric monster."

In consequence, by the 1980s the UN had assumed functions that were far beyond the competence of any collection of intergovernmental organizations in almost every field. In most of its forums, the negotiating agendas had far outstripped the readiness of governments to commit themselves to agreements. Mahatma Gandhi once advised his followers in the 1920s that "it would . . . save a great deal of time and trouble if we cultivate the habit of never supporting resolutions . . . if we have not either the intention or the ability to carry them out."[34] Such resolutions had become the stock in trade of most UN conferences. Some of them had in addition—such as many of those on the Middle East—exacerbated regional tensions and diminished the UN's capacity to mediate in conflicts, just as inflated objectives had helped to marginalize its role in international cooperation. And the Security Council was infected with the same disease, passing resolutions not as a prelude to action, but as substitutes for policy. The UN was ripe for reassessment.

The problem of obsolescence had become widely acknowledged, even if opinions differed as to its causes. Some analysts, like Brian Urquhart, traced it back to the original, 1945, design. In his view: "The UN was a beautiful Western concept constructed to deal with the problems of the early 1930s, and in this beautiful Rolls Royce we're now bumping over all sorts of uncharted and unexpected terrain, with a whole lot of problems which the vehicle wasn't constructed for at all."[35] Urquhart had in mind the sleight of hand involved in invoking a Charter that was intended to deter aggression across frontiers, in order to deal with internal conflicts or with threats arising from the competition between great powers' spheres of influence. But the wider implication of this reading of UN history is its assumption that there was no alternative to using the vehicle, however ill fitted it might be for the job.

As Urquhart himself well knew, in a competitive world in which other forms of multilateral cooperation were flourishing, this had long ceased to be the case. The problem was not that governments were using the UN less, resorting to regional groups or coalitions of countries with particular interests in common: that was a perfectly healthy development. What mattered was that the UN had come to be perceived as virtually unusable even for those purposes where the global dimension was inescapable. The critical question was whether the UN had become ineffective in spite of, or because of, its expansion to deal with "problems which the vehicle wasn't constructed for." By the 1980s, it was gradually becoming clear that further overhauls of the vehicle were pointless, in the absence of clear-headed reassessments of the terrain it could properly aspire to cover. Only through a radical stripping down of the machine coupled with a redefinition of its functions could the UN hope either to improve its efficiency or realize its potential as an "experimental institution." Criticisms that had hitherto been largely confined to committee rooms and the small print of amendments to budgets had begun to crystallize into a much larger political phenomenon, a sense of system failure.

It seemed clear, too, that the last place to look for such a reassessment was the UN's Turtle Bay headquarters. That was where the fidelity to old agendas, and the rituals of intergovernmental committees, were most deeply entrenched. And in the senior echelons of the New York secretariat, there was a deeply ingrained tradition of attending to the façade rather than to the substance of reforms: it had always sufficed in the past, and the UN's top management had become deeply conservative. Brian Urquhart recalls that in 1983 he became aware that "the ideologically hostile climate in Washington" would produce a "critical" assault on the "fat and flabby UN secretariat," riddled as it was with "political appointments, rotten boroughs and pointless programs." He suggested to the secretary-general that he should "get ahead of the game" by calling in a respected international figure "to stalk through the jungles of our administration, put the fear of God into its inhabitants, and recommend serious changes and improvements." The idea "scared the timid souls in our administration, and it was shelved."[36]

The anecdote is telling in two ways. Urquhart had been with the UN from the beginning and was by then its most influential under-secretary-general. His commitment to, and knowledge of, the UN, was not in question. But it was not primarily because the UN was operating inefficiently that he was moved to recommend such action. It had done so for most of his career, and Urquhart belonged to the majority school of thought, which accepted a degree of inefficiency as the price worth paying for multilateralism. He recommended urgent action when he did because he realized that the "hostile" U.S. Congress was on the verge of a taxpayer's revolt. The point was to "get ahead of the game": a tactical maneuver anticipating a political crisis. The second point of note is that, in recommending that the UN bring in somebody to shake up the bureaucracy, Urquhart recognized that only an "outsider" could lend the exercise credibility. The man he suggested was Robert McNamara.

McNamara had been the architect of the World Bank's conversion in the 1970s from conventional lender to active partner in policy dialogues with borrowers. He was a leading exponent of the thesis that multilateral cooperation must justify itself by results. And his shake-up of the Bank—the first of several—had been recognized both by admirers and critics as evidence that the immobilism that gripped the UN headquarters and most of the specialized agencies was not, of itself, proof that international governmental organizations were incapable of adjusting to changing demands.

The World Bank and the International Monetary Fund had figured prominently in "new order" demonology as bastions of conservatism and symbols of Western hegemony. For Third World spokesmen, one of the principal aims of the UN "restructuring" exercise of the 1970s was, as we have seen, to bring the Bretton Woods institutions under the control of the "democratic" General Assembly. Demands for reform of the system of weighted voting, which gave donor governments ultimate control of both institutions, have resurfaced regularly since then.

Yet the transformations that these allegedly conservative institutions have undergone since their creation suggests that the global organizations are not reform-proof, that they can in the right circumstances, and with intelligent management, meet the test of adaptability. The record of these two organizations, therefore, is not only central to any consideration of the future potential of global intergovernmental cooperation: it puts the "crisis of multilateralism" in a different and more promising light. It is an important part of the jigsaw that has to be assembled in assessing the "experimental" potential of UN organizations, in the more hopeful but also more turbulent climate ushered in by political and economic liberalization in much of the Third World, and above all by the great changes that swept Eastern Europe and the former Soviet empire after 1989.

7. Multilateralism for the Marketplace

Experimental Institutions

For half a century, the most striking exception to Western policies of damage limitation at the United Nations has been the determination of all Western governments to shield the International Monetary Fund (IMF) and the World Bank from "political" control by the UN General Assembly. There is no question that they have seen this duo as more important to international order than any part of the UN except the Security Council, and their independence as a vital interest on which no compromise was possible. Throughout the protracted North-South wrangles at the General Assembly in the late 1970s and early 1980s over "global negotiations" on a New International Economic Order (NIEO), the ultimate sticking point was the West's insistence that there could be no question of diminishing the autonomy of the two Bretton Woods institutions, or of subjecting them to the world of gestural politics.

To diplomats from developing countries, this confirmed at the time the need for an NIEO. They ascribed the West's attachment to both organizations to its determination to retain control of the global levers of money and finance. This interpretation stemmed from an exaggerated, almost romantic view of the roles of the IMF and the Bank. They are not the supranational treasury and bank some of the poorest countries imagine them to be and, while their resources dwarf those of the rest of the UN put together, the proportion of global financial flows managed by them is negligible. But they have acquired unique authority as mediating institutions, and this has been a constant factor in the controversies that have at different points surrounded them.

They have been attacked, separately or together, from an impressive range of angles. NIEO ideologues have seen them as the agents of neocolonialism; development lobbies have accused them of imposing alien economic and social models on Third World communities; conservatives have seen in them the accomplices of state control or, even, communism. Environmentalists have with increasing effect charged the World Bank with massive despoliation of the earth's resources. But however fierce (and sometimes just) the criticism, it has not been on the ground of inconsequentiality. Their influence, while it is often exaggerated, is real, and their policies are considered by both critics and supporters to matter. They are, moreover, linked into political and economic circles where decisions are taken: they operate, in the broad sense, in the marketplace.

If this degree of influence makes it difficult to recall that they are specialized agencies of the United Nations, so, more importantly, does their record of keeping their roles and performance under constant internal review. Both have had periods of drift. But neither has ever lost more than temporarily the capacity to transform itself which Dag Hammarskjöld considered so vital. A single example symbolizes the contrast between the outlook in Washington and the inertia of much of the rest of the UN. In 1987, an intergovernmental commission in New York took all year to agree on the procedures it would adopt for a review intended to reduce the number of UN intergovernmental committees—a review that, not coincidentally, ended a year later in North-South deadlock. In roughly the same period, the World Bank reorganized its entire bureaucracy—a process that involved the formal resignation of every employee, the reassessment of each, and the negotiated departure of about one in ten, and that put its policy research and operational activities on an entirely new footing. Nobody could claim that this fundamental overhaul was perfectly managed, or that staff morale was not shaken or—as was acknowledged in 1992 when the Bank's activities were further reorganized—that it got everything right. But it was radical, it was strategically well aimed, and it was carried out at lightning speed. Yet the financial and political pressures on the United Nations that year to put its house in order were far greater than any on the Bank.

There are a number of explanations for this superior adaptability. In the first place, the Bank and the IMF have on the whole been well managed, and staffed by people of high caliber expected to turn in commensurate performances. (In contrast with the rest of the UN, the financial institutions made "efficiency, competence and integrity" the "paramount consideration" in hiring, as Article 101 of the UN Charter required, with geographical origin figuring only as a secondary consideration.) They have also been responsibly governed by their executive directors: whatever confrontations were being ritually pursued by foreign ministers and diplomats elsewhere in the UN, it has been common ground between the finance ministers of North and South that decisions in the Bretton Woods boards should be taken on merit. Third, the institutions have used their continuing ability to attract talent to build up analytical expertise, making them important (some would say dominant) sources of policy advice. This in turn has been central to their capacity to use their own lending as catalysts, mobilizing finance from commercial banks, governments, and, to a lesser degree, private direct investment. The prestige and responsibilities they have built up have, finally, compelled them to scrutinize their own performance more rigorously than is the practice in other UN agencies: repairing the façade has never been an option.

History has also compelled them to adapt. The intentions of the drafters of their founding charters, the 1944 Bretton Woods agreements, were balked at a very early stage. The original plan envisaged a triad of organizations to underpin a free, open, and stable financial and trading system. The IMF was to provide supervision and safety nets for monetary management that would prevent governments taking the kinds of unilateral protective measures that had so damaged the interwar economy; the Bank was to promote postwar recovery; and an International Trade Organization (ITO) was to create nondiscriminatory rules for the expansion of international trade in a progressively more open world economy.

The first two were created at Bretton Woods, but the third element in the plan aborted. The ITO, whose charter was negotiated in Havana in 1948, had been intended to regulate tariff barriers, international business practices, investment, and commodity agreements. The regulatory implications of this agenda proved too ambitious for the U.S. Congress, and in 1950, rather than face its certain defeat, President Truman withdrew the U.S. administration's request for ratification of U.S. accession. The ITO was shelved: it was pointless without the participation of the government then producing two-fifths of global output. It was to resurface, in modified form, only after more than four decades, as the World Trade Organization provided for in the 1986–93 Uruguay Round of trade negotiations. Part of its remit, the promotion of nondiscriminatory trade agreements, was assumed by the Geneva-based General Agreement on Tariffs and Trade (GATT). The GATT, which started life as a stopgap arrangement pending the establishment of the ITO, maintained a curiously provisional identity, half agreement, half organization, semidetached from the UN. This did not preclude considerable successes in cutting tariff barriers and other obstacles to international trade; its "provisional" status was in many ways helpful. But its relatively limited mandate placed a heavier onus on the other two, Washington-based, organizations.

The IMF was created to oversee a stable system of international payments, based on fixed exchange rates with currencies pegged to a gold-convertible dollar. Its resources came from the quotas members paid on joining, which determined the number of votes they mustered on its board and the value of the drawings they could make, at need, on its funds for balance-of-payments support. Above a certain proportion of quota, borrowing governments were required to make policy commitments to stabilize their economies. The International Bank for Reconstruction and Development (IBRD) was intended to provide capital loans to enable war-devastated Europe to rebuild its productive capacity. It was only peripherally conceived as a development agency, much less as the World Bank, the name by which it came to be known. It raised its capital from government subscriptions of paid-in and callable capital, from the sales of its own securities and from net earnings and repayments. Using its callable capital as guarantees, it borrowed cheaply on commercial markets and lent the money at slightly higher but still attractive rates to governments or government-guaranteed enterprises.

The history of both organizations has been one of piecemeal adaptations, some of them unforced innovations, others dictated by circumstances. The Bank was confronted by the need to reinvent itself early on, when the enactment of the Marshall Plan in 1947 more or less put it out of the European reconstruction business. As for the IMF, it has had to redesign itself twice: first, when the Bretton Woods system of fixed exchange rates collapsed following President Nixon's abandonment in August 1971 of the dollar's convertibility against gold; and again in the 1980s, when the insolvency of middle-income debtors threatened the international financial system. Both managed to turn crises of identity into opportunities, adapting to changing demand. As the end of the century drew near, the wheel turned full circle, confronting both afresh with the remit with which the Bank started: the "reconstruction" of Europe—east of what used to be the Iron Curtain.

Ironically, it has been through the Bank and the IMF, not the rest of the UN, that Third World governments have in practice exercised their greatest leverage on the West. The very fact that in the IMF and Bank the developing countries do not have, and therefore cannot exploit, a one-state/one-vote majority has encouraged mutual accommodation. Second, however they may differ in emphasis, both institutions are inherently multidisciplinary and are consequently untroubled by the sectoral distortions of focus and consequent special pleading that plague the other UN specialized agencies. Third, and paradoxically, their image as "status quo" organizations has given their chief executives considerable leeway to argue for innovation and generosity on the part of their Western shareholders. Recipient governments periodically inveigh against both organizations for excessively rigid diagnoses and prescriptions, but they have often been effective advocates of new and ever radical departures from the orthodoxies of development cooperation. Serious dialogue among governments has been sustained, finally, by the fact that each organization has a relatively small "in-house" board of directors representing member states individually or, for the smaller states, in groups. Meeting in semipermanent session, these have proved far more effective than the system of "permanent representatives," which obtains elsewhere in the UN in maintaining working contact between governments, and between them and the institutions. Like their boards, Bank and IMF committees are small enough for proper debate, while their executive directors are closely enough involved with the work of the institutions to develop the necessary degree of camaraderie, and of loyalty to the enterprise.

In the 1990s, the authority and flexibility of the IMF and the Bank will again be tested. If they are to maintain their influence in the context of the liberalization of financial and capital markets, the progressive horizontal integration of production, and the emergence of potentially mercantilist regional trading blocs, both will need to make further changes—in their relations with each other and with the commercial world. After 1989 they were already, through the Brady plan for debt reduction, being drawn into closer relations with the commercial banks, as goads and as guarantors for debt-reduction schemes. Both were searching for ways to improve on the traditional pattern of formal consultations between donor and recipient governments, which looked increasingly inadequate as tools for sustaining economic reforms in developing countries, and for averting economic disaster in the ex-Communist world. The Bretton Woods institutions also face the challenge of finding ways to draw in the private sector more actively. Beyond practical considerations of efficiency, a larger philosophical question is assuming increasing importance: in a world shifting decisively to market economics, what ought to be the role of organizations that lend either directly to governments, or under government guarantees?

Debates on the role of foreign aid in reviving productive investment and sustainable development will intensify in the 1990s. That is partly because the requirements for external finance in Eastern Europe will compete with Third World claims. Donors and creditors who accept that countries must be assisted to implement long-overdue policy reforms or to grow their way out of debt will increasingly insist on their legitimate interest in the policies adopted; and political conditions have been added to the economic conditionality of the 1980s, as standards set for to Eastern Europe are applied to the developing world. Another reason is the growth of private sector finance available (unevenly) to developing countries—from 13 percent of their overseas borrowing in 1989 to 40 percent in 1994.

Already in the 1980s, both institutions had become involved with broad-based lending for economic reforms and balance-of-payments support to the heavily indebted—involving discussions with governments in which the distinctions between macro- and microeconomic management had become blurred in ways which their founders were far from anticipating. That, too, has stimulated fresh debate about their respective future roles. It is in this context, with its implications for the future, and inevitable, reorganization of international development cooperation that the record of the Bretton Woods organizations is important. Three principal cycles are discernible in their evolution. The first important departures from their mandates were made by both, if for different reasons, in the 1970s. In the decade that followed, two contradictory pressures—severe criticisms by the Reagan administration on the one hand, and the urgent demands created by the near collapse of many Latin American and African economies on the other—propelled them into designing and promoting explicitly market-orientated reforms that put lending into an overall context of economic "adjustment." The third phase, an outgrowth of these policy interventions, was taking shape as the 1980s ended. In 1989, the World Bank published a report on the future of sub-Saharan Africa that candidly drew attention to the continent's "crisis of governance" and the near impossibility of economic development in the absence of democratic freedoms and the rule of law. This was the first report by a UN agency to tackle the political dimension of development since the 1950s; the Bank's efforts to address failures in economic policy had drawn it into the domestic politics of the countries it advised. At the same time, a clearer understanding of the intractability of the problems faced by many developing countries—among them, Western trade barriers against their exports—raised the question whether the Bank and IMF could function effectively without involving themselves more actively in the industrialized world's debates on monetary and trade policy—debates which affected the global marketplace.

Their history is significant for the United Nations as a whole, and not just because the professional standards they have maintained challenge the theory that global or near-global organizations are condemned to be inefficient. It is significant because the road they have taken, instead of leading inward to a rarefied form of political discourse, has led into the world outside—a world not only of international finance, but of small manufacturers, farm laborers, and newly urbanized poor. Their relationship with these forces has been imperfect, improvised, and sometimes arrogant; but it has nonetheless enabled them to resist the obsolescence that has afflicted their fellow institutions. In an important sense, these pillars of free-market orthodoxy have been the radicals of the United Nations.

THE TURBULENT 1970S

The sister organizations had, from the start, certain characteristics in common. From the moment they were installed in their neighboring Washington headquarters, they deliberately set out to cultivate reputations as ultraconservative institutions. Frankly elitist, they set out to build their authority on the basis of high levels of technical expertise and formidable analytic capacities, and they remained relatively immune from politicization. Political patronage intervened only, and importantly, in the choice of their executive heads: although nothing in their statutes so stipulates, the presidency of the Bank was, and remained, in the "gift" of the United States; and the managing director of the IMF was by convention European. They also had in common a certain immunity from Cold War confrontation because, although the Soviet Union signed the Bretton Woods agreements, it declined to provide the national economic data required of its members by the IMF and therefore did not join that institution—or the World Bank (with whose objectives it had in any case little sympathy) since Bank membership is open only to members of the IMF. They were, and remained until first China and then the former Eastern bloc countries sought membership, solidly "Western" free-market institutions.

After initial collaboration while both were building up their staffs, however, they took what amounted to a corporate pride in emphasizing their separate identities. The IMF's priority was necessarily to ensure that it was taken seriously by central banks and finance ministries. That conditioned its ability to promote consultation on international monetary policies, to safeguard stable exchange rates and set rules for international payments, and to encourage the elimination of foreign exchange restrictions. The IMF's economists, drawn mainly from central banks, concentrated on national and global economic forecasting, the careful surveillance of monetary policies, exchange rates and currency liberalization, and the provision of technical advice to members in balance-of-payments difficulties who needed to draw up stabilization programs. Until the mid-1970s, drawings on the IMF's credits were, almost exclusively, by the industrialized countries—and were made available, on a short-term basis, strictly in support of these broad objectives. The IMF's was, consciously, a policing role.

Once its reconstruction role in Europe had been largely overtaken at the end of the 1940s, the World Bank stuck to banking. It spent the next decade establishing its triple-A rating on the capital markets through its extreme prudence in lending. It lent principally for investments in infrastructure—ports, roads, power, and telecommunications—with high economic rates of return. Its customers were its most creditworthy shareholders, principally in Western Europe and Japan; only a sprinkling of loans went to Latin America. Less creditworthy countries were (somewhat paradoxically) expected to look to private investment. To help them to mobilize it, the Bank's legally separate International Finance Corporation was created in 1956.

It was not until the late 1950s that Eugene Black, its president from 1949 to 1962, altered his view that concessionary-lending simply undermined financial discipline. In 1960, partly in response to demands at the UN for a grant-making agency, partly because of India's foreign exchange crisis, and partly because the United States was determined to spread the "aid burden," the Bank's Western shareholders created the International Development Association (IDA)—a fund to which they subscribed capital, replenishing it at approximately three-yearly intervals, to be lent by the Bank to the poorest countries at zero interest and fifty-year repayment terms.

The IDA launched the Bank for the first time into development lending, but the credits initially differed from normal Bank loans only in their terms: most financed infrastructure and were expected to yield high, quantifiable rates of return. They were administered by the same staff. Involvement in these countries did however hasten the broadening of Bank expertise: to its skills in preparing and evaluating the projects it financed, it added capacities for statistical and economic analysis as it became involved in assessing of the microeconomic strategies of its borrowers.

Contact between the Bank and the IMF in this period was regular but formal, mainly intended to ensure that, within their respective areas of responsibility, they were not giving governments conflicting advice. This emphasis on separate development, carefully nurtured in-house, assumed a new and public dimension when, in the 1970s, the World Bank dramatically altered the whole thrust of its lending.

The McNamara revolution was unexpected. When he arrived at the Bank in April 1968, Robert McNamara brought from his earlier career at the Ford Motor Company a reputation for hard-nosed efficiency and a predilection for statistics. As U.S. defense secretary during the Vietnam War, he had become notorious as the man to introduce the "body count" into the language of American strategic planning. That McNamara increased the volume of Bank and IDA lending, from $934 million a year in 1968 to an annual $12.3 billion in 1981, when he departed, was consistent with this reputation. The crusade he launched in 1973, to make the alleviation of "absolute poverty" central to development cooperation, was not. It altered the character of the Bank, and with it the terms in which development aid was discussed, for good.

McNamara employed his enduring passion for statistics as a tool, almost a battering ram, to convince skeptical ministers, both donors and recipients, that the poorest people in developing countries were an unexploited asset, "human capital": helping them was not just morally imperative but far more efficient than relying on overall growth targets and waiting for benefits to "trickle down." The Bank's underlying orthodoxies—export-led growth, infrastructure development—remained unchanged, and it continued to be the butt of ritual condemnations at the UN General Assembly and in UNCTAD, where Third World spokesmen castigated both Bretton Woods institutions as the handmaidens of neocolonialist exploitation. But in Washington, Third World members of the Bank's executive board came to view it as a serious ally, and McNamara as their most persuasive champion in the West. Not all Third World capitals gave an enthusiastic welcome, however, to his poverty strategy. It was consciously anti-elitist: the new emphasis on providing the poor with basic health care, nutrition, and education, and on investing in slum upgrading, population planning, and rural development threatened, at least potentially, to erode the privileges of the governing circles.

The classic exposition of the new approach was furnished by the Bank's chief economist, Hollis Chenery, in *Redistribution with Growth*. This book, which stressed the importance of assisting the poorest and most powerless to participate much more actively in economic life, strongly influenced all subsequent thinking on development. The thesis, simply put, was that development was impossible unless it harnessed the energies of all members of a society, and meaningless unless they benefited. This required direct action to improve the health, skills, and purchasing power of slum-dwellers and subsistence farmers and, to encourage self-help, their participation in decisions affecting them. The links between economic empowerment and democracy were difficult to ignore.

To equip the Bank to undertake this new type of lending, McNamara gave it a complete structural overhaul, setting up regional departments with their own technical teams. Through what were politely termed "policy dialogues," the Bank explored the implications of the new strategy with governments, while, in order to demonstrate that such lending was within the terms of the Bank's charter, its research departments calculated the "economic rates of return" on education or training programs. Infrastructure projects began to place somewhat more emphasis on feeder roads linking villagers to markets than on the satisfactorily conspicuous superhighways, which ministers derive pleasure and electoral profit from declaring open. The markedly labor-intensive techniques involved in promoting small-farm technologies and rural development generated an important change in the Bank's methods: it became increasingly involved in technical assistance. By the end of the 1970s, although this would continue to be unacknowledged in the arguments elsewhere in the UN about the respective functions and powers of the UN Development Program (UNDP) and the other specialized agencies, the Bank had in effect already assumed the functions of the proposed UN Development Agency, which was the subject of so much fruitless negotiation in New York.

During this same decade, the International Monetary Fund was twice compelled to reinvent its functions, first to deal with the collapse of the Bretton Woods system of fixed exchange rates, and then, in 1973, to respond to the consequences of the quadrupling of oil prices. It was difficult enough to rewrite the IMF's rules for a world of floating exchange rates. It took its member governments five years, from 1973 to 1978, to draw them up, and three years of work by a committee of twenty failed to lay the bases for international monetary reform. The new rules equipped the IMF with a potentially useful tool for improving macroeconomic cooperation. It was required to monitor each country's macroeconomic policies on a regular basis, submitting the resulting reports to peer scrutiny by the IMF's executive directors. Designed to provide early warning of balance-of-payments difficulties, the scheme increased the IMF's leverage over countries running deficits; but not over those in persistent surplus.

The problems of handling floating currency rates were exacerbated by the disequilibria created first by the surge in oil prices and then by the recycling of petrodollar surpluses. The impact of sharply higher oil prices on developing countries' balances of payments placed on the IMF demands it had not been designed to meet. The IMF improvised, with limited success. It attempted to stabilize the international payments system (and to strengthen its capacity to influence global liquidity) by creating the special drawing right (SDR), a form of supranational currency whose value was calculated in terms of a basket of the five main currencies. Efforts to develop the SDR as a new global reserve currency were however resisted both by the Group of 5 on whose currencies it was based, and by the so-called Group of 10 governments (of eleven industrialized countries, including Switzerland, which was not an IMF member), and supplies were firmly restricted. This Western determination to control the international monetary system, coinciding as it did with the debates on a new international economic order at the UN, came under sustained attack at the IMF. The Group of 24 which dealt with monetary affairs on behalf of the Group of 77 in Washington, eight countries each from Asia, Latin America, and Africa, demanded a link between the creation of SDRs and their own needs for external finance.

The cost of oil had meantime increased these needs dramatically. The IMF's traditional short-term borrowing facilities, designed to help governments over temporary balance-of-payments difficulties, were irrelevant to the emerging long-term structural deficits of the oil-importing developing countries. The IMF devised various expedients to reduce this evident mismatch between its facilities and the needs of its members. It introduced one extended financing facility, with conditions attached, to provide support over three-year rather than twelve-month periods, and another to compensate countries for sharp drops in commodity prices or major crop failures. A trust fund financed from the sale of part of its gold holdings and a temporary fund financed by OPEC loans were set up to help countries most severely affected by escalating oil bills.

But throughout the 1970s the IMF remained marginal to the massive recycling operation, lending well under $3 billion a year for most of the decade while the commercial banks assumed center stage. The IMF was capable of meeting a much larger proportion than it did of developing countries' needs for external finance; the problem was that their governments were not prepared to accept the conditions governing its standby credits. They complained that its formulas for economic stabilization—credit controls, cuts in public spending, currency devaluation, and trade liberalization—imposed intolerable deflationary pressures and failed to distinguish between domestic mismanagement and externally generated crises. Global inflation and low or negative real interest rates meantime increased the attractions of borrowing heavily on commercial markets. By 1978–79 there was a net flow of resources to the IMF from developing countries.

Some of this criticism was political grandstanding. The IMF's stabilization packages were not as uniform as they were asserted to be. Nor were all oil importers in the same boat, since the prices of some commodities boomed in the mid-1970s. An IMF study in 1980 of the recent cocoa and coffee booms[1] found that governments had rushed to spend the windfall revenues, often wastefully, with the result that their reserves were in no better shape when the booms ended. And a World Bank study, covering a wider range of commodities, found that because they continued spending at these levels when the boom was over, most found themselves in a weaker balance-of-payments position afterward than before. The argument that countries needed more time, and more flexibility, to adjust their economies, while correct, had to be set against evidence that many were borrowing in order to *avoid* adjustment. Even in 1979 and early 1980, when all the storm signals were hoisted—oil prices had again increased, by 130 percent, commodity prices were dropping sharply, there was stagflation in the industrialized world, protectionism was on the increase, trade was stagnating, and commercial bank loans were drying up—most oil-importing developing countries still continued to pursue expansionary fiscal and monetary policies.

Whatever the merits of the economic arguments, the political reality was that the IMF's relations with these countries, which formed 85 percent of its membership, had deteriorated to the point where it was unable to exert much influence. Governments would not turn to it unless desperate. By the time they did so, agreements were the more difficult to reach because of the severity of their economic problems. Negotiations frequently broke down. And at the first sign that the immediate crisis was easing, they put IMF-imposed policies into reverse. The IMF's negotiators were failing to persuade governments that economic stabilization was in their interest, or that budgets that far exceeded revenue and absorbed a disproportionate share of gross domestic product were unsustainable. The conflicts between the IMF and its clients were over objectives as well as time scales. Governments argued that stabilization programs were damaging their development prospects and that Western economic theories about equilibrium were designed to cramp their evident needs for rapid growth and keep them in a state of subservience to the industrialized world. The sources of their problems, they argued, were essentially international, and the IMF was not only neglecting this dimension but was, as President Julius Nyerere of Tanzania put it in 1980, acting against their interests, as the agent whereby "powerful economic forces in some rich countries increase their power over the poor nations of the world."

By the end of the decade, people within the IMF recognized that if it was to lay the intellectual and political foundations for dialogue with governments whose policies were unsustainable, it could no longer rely on short-term injections of liquidity to address their problems. Clearly, it had to take the constraints of underdevelopment into account in setting conditions for macroeconomic management, and develop its capacity to use its own lending to mobilize additional finance, either from commercial banks or from governments. If its standby programs were to win acceptance, it had to lessen their heavy stress on demand management.

From a different perspective, but for some of the same reasons, the Bank was also being forced to take stock by the end of the 1970s. The limitations of its Articles of Association, which legally required it to lend for specific projects rather than balance-of-payments support, were becoming obvious, whether in terms of tackling poverty or of improving countries' overall economic performance. Too many projects were failing, and the root cause was not defective Bank project planning, appraisal, and supervision. Some projects, particularly in Africa, had indeed been inappropriate or badly designed; but what was causing most projects to fail was the appalling policy environment in which they were being implemented. In countries whose governments were either corrupt or incompetent themselves, or exerted feeble control over bloated bureaucracies and loss-making state enterprises whose bosses had powerful vested interests in inefficiency, the catalytic effect of the most successful individual projects was limited. In addition, the rapid growth in the Bank's lending, and the demands for detailed micromanagement engendered by its antipoverty strategies—rural development was a completely different kettle of fish to dam building—were straining its management capacity. The Bank's celebrated environmental disasters, such as the Polonoroeste scheme in Brazil, exposed weaknesses both in its relations with governments and in its own management. The Bank was not short of economic analysts and it had well-developed mechanisms for discussing overall policies with governments. But there was only a tenuous connection between this economic work and its actual project lending decisions.

In a "project-driven organization," where managers are under pressure to disburse funds, loans had been going ahead even where national policies made failure—waste of the investment—highly probable. In the words of Stanley Please, a former senior Bank executive and expert on Africa, "In country after country, and year after year, the Bank had continued . . . to have active, and in most cases, rising programs of project lending to agriculture and industry in the very countries in which it was asserting to governments that their policy frameworks were distorted—not marginally distorted, but distorted in major ways."[2] That in many cases this meant money down the drain was confirmed by the Bank's Operations Evaluation Department, the only serious and independent body of its kind in the United Nations. In sub-Saharan Africa, it found that no fewer than half of its rural development programs had failed. The Bank's poverty strategy had proved that, given appropriate supporting policies, small farmers could be helped dramatically to improve their productivity and prosperity. But no farmer was going to continue investing in improved seeds and fertilizers if governments held down the prices paid for his crops, if he could not get harvests to market, or if there was nothing to buy with the profits.

Just as the IMF was being drawn to the conclusion that it must look beyond crisis management and pay attention to supply side measures to build up countries' productive capacities, the Bank was coming to terms with the need to introduce some overall policy conditionality into its lending. It was becoming clear that unless loans were tied to policy reform, even successful projects were likely to remain "islands."

The Bank had another reason to emphasize the vital role of policy reforms. Its internal assessments of the impact of its poverty strategy suggested that, in what were inescapably areas of social policy, there were limits to what externally generated and externally managed reforms could achieve. At one level, the poverty programs had been a success. They had highlighted the needs and the economic potential of the poorest and demonstrated that policies aimed at improving their well-being could make economic sense. But the McNamara experiment had also revealed the problems inherent in working through governments, as the Bank was obliged to do, to reach the "grass roots." Formal projects were better at reaching the poor than the "absolutely poor," the small farmer than the landless laborer, the primary-school children than the street children. The Bank came fairly rapidly to acknowledge that except through nutrition and informal education, and occasionally by upgrading slums, it could not realistically pretend to reach the bottom 15–20 percent. Nor was this the only problem.

Programs designed to reach the poor entail a multiplicity of interconnected activities, small-scale in terms of their components, whose success depend on intimate understanding of local cultural, political, and institutional obstacles. "We discovered," a Bank vice president was to comment some years later, "that these projects were too poorly designed, and bound to be, because we are too remote, we cannot hope to understand the detail. Where we failed, it was often because we ignored the local frameworks, and the resistances." With some schemes, above all in rural development, too much had been attempted at once, putting great demands on local government services—when the more such schemes were needed, the weaker these services were likely to be. Others "created hostility among government agencies and the moment we left they killed the project."[3]

The twin objectives of creating a rapid demonstration effect and building up local capacities tended to conflict. The use of expatriate managers and advisers speeded things up, not least because they had more clout with the authorities, often producing results that ensured the beneficiaries' enthusiastic participation and encouraged governments to adopt similar schemes; but reliance on such "shortcuts" made it less likely that after the foreigners left, the locals would be equipped to take over.

International developments clinched these arguments, forcing both the Bank and the IMF to adopt new strategies. The combination of a further 130 percent rise in the price of oil in 1979–80, followed by recession, resumed global inflation and high real interest rates, brought the debt crisis to a head. Project lending became impractical: many governments were unable to put up the counterpart finance they were required to muster in support of Bank projects. In 1980, the Bank began to provide rapidly disbursable balance-of-payments support for governments committing themselves to policy reforms. These "structural adjustment loans" were modest at first, but by the late 1980s they constituted a quarter of its total lending, and two-thirds of its loans to sub-Saharan Africa.

The case for giving priority to policy reforms in future Bank lending was put by Elliot Berg, one of the Bank's senior economists, in a report requested by the Bank's African executive directors and issued in 1981.[4] Its theme was the economic and humanitarian tragedy shaping in the sub-Saharan continent, but its implications were more general. Berg argued that the responsibilities of national governments must be squarely addressed: skewed government policies were the core of the problem. In Africa, he stated bluntly, "A reordering of post-independence priorities is essential." The continent was awash with unproductive state bureaucracies; its survival depended on reversing governments' "persistent bias" against agriculture and on removing the multiple constraints they had set on economic activity.

The report was harsh on donors as well as Africans, acknowledging the disadvantages with which Africa had embarked on independence—shortages of manpower, lack of infrastructures and basic statistics, political fragility, and "insecurely rooted and ill-suited institutions." It recommended a doubling of Western aid. But its review of the accumulated costs of distorted policies made it clear that without fundamental policy changes, aid, even where it continued to flow, would not reverse economic disintegration. It also argued that external assistance should no longer mean the invasion of the continent by armies of expatriate experts (whose share of Africa's aid receipts was already, in some estimates, between $3 billion and $4 billion a year). This of course implied that the Bank, by now the biggest multilateral provider of technical assistance, would have to undertake a major reassessment of its own methods. Technical assistance was unavoidable in some circumstances, the report concluded. But if a project depended for its success "on finding a manager who possesses abilities far superior to the average" available in the country in question, it was quite simply "badly designed." The high cost of expatriates and the growing competence of local technicians were "lowering the threshold of acceptability" for expatriates' services: policies would have to change.

The reassessments made by both institutions pointed to two needs. They would have to develop a more closely complementary relationship between their respective functions as advisers to developing countries. And there had to be a serious effort to coordinate all sources of external finance—commercial loans, bilateral as well as multilateral aid, and foreign direct investment—within agreed policy reform frameworks. The early 1980s were not, however, conducive to orderly and measured progress from analysis to reorganization.

PROBLEMS OF "ADJUSTMENT"

In 1982, as finance ministers and bankers assembled in Toronto for the annual joint meeting of the 151 members of the Bank and the IMF, Mexico told its creditors that it could not pay the interest on its $90 billion foreign debt. The global banking system was threatened with collapse. Jacques de Larosière, the Fund's managing director, responded by reinventing, overnight, the concept of IMF conditionality: it would now operate for creditors as well as debtors. Working with Paul Volcker, then chairman of the U.S. Federal Reserve Board, he summoned the major commercial bankers to a meeting at the Federal Reserve in November. There, he told them that he would work out an IMF stabilization package with Mexico—on condition that they came up with $5 billion in new loans and set about restructuring the old debt.

The plan averted the immediate crisis: the banks accepted the logic of the argument that, without substantial new lending, well beyond the IMF's means, neither Mexico nor the other large middle-income debtors would be able, with or without policy reforms, to meet their obligations in the short term. The IMF assumed a new, indispensable role, marshalling debtors and creditors down roads neither wished to travel. In the following two years the IMF lent $22 billion in support of radical programs of retrenchment and policy reform in seventy countries—linking each package to fresh lending from governments and (for the richer countries) commercial banks, which provided between four and seven times as much as the IMF itself.

De Larosière's strategy moved the IMF from the fringes to the center of crisis management. But it did not make much dent on the underlying problems. IMF standby credits remained relatively short term and for several years, unforced commercial lending dried up and with it, much foreign direct investment. The short IMF cycles, ideal for liquidity crises but not for economic collapse, created politically embarrassing reverse flows: in the drought year of 1984, net repayments to the IMF by African governments amounted to $400 million. In addition, its relations with debtor governments remained subject to constant crises. The IMF typically continued to set tight conditions for public sector deficits, money supply, exchange rates, and other macroeconomic "performance indicators." It also typically insisted on sharp cuts in state subsidies. Its system of monitoring compliance every three months created further strains: if a government failed to perform under any one of these indicators, its IMF credits were liable to be suspended or even terminated—and with them, the backing loans provided by governments or commercial banks. On the other hand, the new approach bought time, both for the debtors and for the banking system, and it established the principle of joint responsibility for debt management, which was all the more essential given the transitional, short-term nature of the funds the IMF was able to make available. It gave donor governments a chance to adjust to the fact that many debtors were in fundamental economic disequilibrium, and that since their problems had to do with more than illiquidity, they would need sustained help to grow their way out of debt.

The IMF's decisive, and speedy, reaction to the Mexico crisis was politically courageous because both the IMF and the Bank were at this juncture under attack from their most important shareholder, the United States. Within a month of President Reagan's inauguration in 1981 his budget director, David Stockman, had opened fire on the World Bank, calling for the renegotiation of a 1979 agreement to double its capital, and a halving of the U.S. contributions to IDA, which he accused of "supporting state planning efforts." Meanwhile Donald Regan, the new U.S. treasury secretary, declared that the United States opposed any increase in governments' quotas to the IMF and, even before de Larosière took action in 1982, conservatives in the U.S. Congress were accusing it of "bailing out the banks," which had lent so profligately to Third World governments during the 1970s.

The White House itself had ordered an interagency review of all U.S. aid expenditure, and instructed the Treasury to conduct an enquiry into the policies of the World Bank and the smaller regional development banks. This was to explore all options, including the downgrading or suspension of future U.S. participation. Senior U.S. officials indicated that while these were in progress, the development banks should expect less U.S. funding; and that their entitlement to U.S. support would depend on the compatibility of their policies with U.S. national interests. Finally, just before the 1981 Bank/IMF meeting, Regan and the new U.S. secretary of state, Alexander Haig, jointly announced that from now on the Third World should expect less foreign aid, and President Reagan, in his address to that session, exhorted developing countries to discover "the magic of the marketplace." At the very moment when the Bank and the IMF needed to exercise maximum leverage with their clients, they faced the prospect of deep cuts in their funding.

The Treasury inquiry, under the direction of Beryl Sprinkel, the new under-secretary for monetary affairs, was not completed until February 1982. An early draft, widely leaked, asserted that "in the area of multilateral assistance . . . the election of the Reagan administration means a break with the past."[5] U.S. officials did nothing to discourage speculation that the administration's objective was to "break the Bank."

The Treasury set out four criteria on which multilateral lending was to be judged. It must contribute to "free and open markets, private enterprise, limited government involvement and [provide] public assistance to the truly needy." Sprinkel's Treasury team sifted some three hundred World Bank projects to determine whether the Bank was supporting state intervention—its yardstick being whether, in the United States, these activities would have been undertaken by the public or the private sector. (Since, in the event, only 8 percent failed this somewhat curious test, the team concluded that the Bank was "essentially agnostic with respect to the question of ownership.")

The team also reviewed, at length, a wide range of criticisms of the development banks, from the Left as well as the Right, *inter alia* that they were immune to their shareholders' political control; that they were bailing out the banks; that they benefited Third World elites and failed to reach the poor; that they "support extravagant and imprudent government policies, foster inflation, discourage private investment, and buttress the forces of statism." It looked thoughtfully at a number of propositions: that development banks were simply not needed in a world best left to the private sector (and to bilateral aid, which donors could more readily control); that all U.S. contributions to IDA should be terminated by 1985: and that, should the World Bank fail to reflect U.S. policies in its lending, the United States should prohibit it from raising capital in the U.S. bond markets.[6] All this reflected considerable congressional hostility to both the Bank and the IMF—ascribable partly to the political climate, but also to budgetary pressures and to the steep increases in U.S. contributions to the multilateral banks, which had risen from $700 million in 1970 to $2.3 billion in 1980, and were eating into the totals available for high-profile bilateral aid.

The Treasury's final report was something of an anticlimax. It endorsed in ringing terms the irreplaceable role of the development banks in dealing with "market imperfections," and the quality and value for money of their services. The World Bank's poverty programs received high ratings, and its investment in education, health, and other "welfare" programs was judged to be "capital investment important to a country's development." The nationalistic and unilateralist themes that had earlier been in evidence were considerably softened, the American national interest being defined, impeccably, as the promotion of "a more stable and secure world." The report recommended that the United States should seek to increase its influence in the multilateral banks, but there were, after all, to be no "abrupt shifts" in policy, only "an evolutionary process" in which the United States would attempt "to build an international policy consensus" around its proposals for change.[7]

The main thrust of these proposals was to persuade the banks to use their leverage more effectively, tying loans to national policies that would encourage domestic savings, promote the private sector, and "encourage individual incentives in a free market environment." Hardly revolutionary even in 1982, such objectives were to become the commonplaces of the decade. It also proposed concentrating multilateral assistance on the neediest countries, through a tough policy of "graduating" countries as they developed from soft loans to hard, and eventually to the commercial markets. But although the report was hardly the frontal assault on the principle of multilateral lending that had been anticipated, it did, as it conceded, seek to maximize U.S. influence while minimizing U.S. contributions, "getting more for less." It proposed that U.S. contributions of paid-in capital to the development banks should be reduced and eventually phased out; and that its contribution to IDA—even though this was the vehicle for helping the "neediest" countries—should be sharply reduced. The immediate consequence was a sharply reduced U.S. contribution to IDA—replenishments for which, even under the Carter administration, had been blocked in the U.S. Congress. But over the next few years, the idea of stopping U.S. contributions was more or less abandoned.

The spectacle of the Bank and the IMF besieged by budget-cutting congressmen, Treasury free-market evangelists, and conservative think-tanks accusing them of international "welfarism" did much for their public image outside the United States. Third World governments adopted the argument, advanced by Western governments in the preceding decade when they were under attack for neocolonialist, capitalist bias, that the development banks should be kept free of political pressures. Even in Washington, the Treasury report had a positive effect: by dealing head-on with congressional suspicions that had been accumulating during the McNamara years, it left the Bank and the IMF in a stronger position with the United States. The following year, the U.S. Treasury dropped its opposition to the increase in the IMF quotas.

But the inquisitorial atmosphere in which the inquiry was conducted forced the World Bank onto the defensive at a sensitive point. It was finding it difficult to develop its new reform-based lending strategies; and it changed management when the Treasury review was in mid-course. McNamara's successor, Tom Clausen, formerly the Bank of America's chief executive, was a well-intentioned man with an uninspiring line in homely metaphors whose instincts were to appease the Bank's U.S. critics. His maiden speech in 1981 emphasized the Bank's dedication to "effective price incentives, improved market signals" and export performance; and its opposition to "misguided subsidies that benefit the rich in the guise of helping the poor." He appealed to Congress to recognize that "an IDA cheque is not a welfare cheque" and promised much more active World Bank partnership with private investors. But at the same time, Clausen proved hypersensitive to developing countries' complaints that the emphasis, in the new structural adjustment loans on realistic exchange rates, deregulation, price incentives for producers, and the reform or elimination of inefficient parastatal corporations subjected them to IMF-type conditionality.

The result was drift. Many of its own executives now felt the Bank to be a "hobbled giant," [8] hovering uneasily between conflicting views about its real areas of comparative advantage—an assessment borne out by the creation, that year, of a dozen task forces to define "the future role of the Bank." Its real problems were due not to failure of political nerve, but to the fact that it was technically ill equipped to carry out policy-based lending. It was one thing to articulate the intellectual case for structural adjustment, but quite another to enforce conditionality on governments whose borrowings from the Bank, in the case of all but a handful of the poorest countries, represented only a small percentage of their foreign exchange receipts. Early experience with structural adjustment lending had been discouraging. Agreements had frequently been only partially implemented. Most governments had cut expenditure because there was no alternative, but there had been "little progress if any in improving efficiency because sectoral changes are politically even more difficult than across-the-board belt-tightening."[9] Governments found it easier to fudge medium- and long-term reform programs than they did the monetary targets set by the IMF. And little progress had been made in persuading donor governments to use their bilateral aid to support structural reform programs.

In theory, the World Bank's machinery for coordinating aid to individual countries, the Consultative Groups, should have been capable of bringing the donors into line. The principle was that Bank economists, together with the recipient government's planners, drew up a profile of economic strategy and its needs for external finance. This was then reviewed with donors, meeting in Paris, roughly on an annual basis. Where they existed, the Consultative Groups were an improvement on the round tables operated for the same purpose by the UN Development Program. Preparatory work was more serious, and the Bank's teams had more expertise and influence than their UNDP counterparts—and were unhampered by the UNDP's practice of channeling 90 percent of its technical assistance through competing UN specialized agencies. But the Consultative Groups, meeting only once a year, were still no counterweight to the steady pressures on recipient governments' spending ministries exerted by individual donors.

The pattern, according to an experienced World Bank country officer, was fairly consistent: "The donors insist that we take the lead with internal policy reform and demand that we go and tell the president, with the full support of the donor community, what needs to be done. So we do. Then the finance minister convenes a meeting with all

Western ambassadors and the World Bank—and the support evaporates as they compete to offload their turn-key factories and new urban hospitals." In 1986, Ernest Stern, then the Bank's senior vice president in charge of operations, privately rebuked ministers at the OECD's Development Aid Committee. As part of reform programs agreed by the Bank and supported by donors, all sorts of pet donor projects would be canceled—only to "re-emerge phoenix-like to again plague the decision-making process and undermine the resolve of the recipient government's decision-makers." At that point, he said, it was very difficult for the Bank to intervene. To get the government to change its mind a second time could be "politically sensitive and very time-consuming." It was high time for donors "to subordinate [their] views of what is attractive to the country's judgment of what is required and can be afforded; and cease to take advantage of the weak central institutions by persuading individual ministers to accept investments which would not pass agreed criteria."[10]

The Bank itself, however, was feeling its way. The volume of policy-based lending was increasing rapidly, both under a new "special facility" for Africa and in support of the plan, put forward by James Baker as U.S. treasury secretary in 1985, for stepped-up World Bank and commercial lending to enable the fifteen most heavily indebted middle-income countries to grow their way out of debt. But because different teams were involved with lending for projects, and with drawing up structural reform programs, governments were receiving conflicting advice from the Bank itself. The result, according to a senior World Bank executive, was that

> decisions were being referred higher and higher on a centralized basis, with the front line decisions at country level being modified en route. The result was that we tried country assistance strategies, adjustment programs, lender-focused management, but we didn't follow through in execution because the staffs remained separate. The technical and program people were meeting only at vice-presidential level.[11]

If donor governments talked with two voices, simultaneously demanding the adoption of economic reform programs and undercutting their objectives with bilateral aid, it was partly because they were not convinced that the programs worked out by recipients with the Bank and the IMF, sometimes in tandem, *were* reflecting "the country's judgment."

Implicit in the prominence given to the World Bank in the Baker plan for debt management was the view that, without official finance, the commercial banks could not be coaxed into further lending. This brought the Bank's performance under fresh scrutiny, and doubts about its flexibility, effectiveness and the rigor of its conditionality crystallized as Clausen presented his last budget in 1986. Its five largest shareholders—the United States, Japan, West Germany, France, and Great Britain—abstained from adopting it.

It was this that triggered the Bank's second complete overhaul under Barber Conable, who took over from Clausen soon after the budget vote. A veteran congressman, Conable was aware that a campaign to cut the Bank's salaries and more than six thousand staff was again gathering momentum on Capitol Hill. He also knew that when Clausen departed, he left the Bank under fire from many directions. It had been criticized, by Paul Volcker among others, for failing to give the IMF adequate support in debt management. Despite the publication in 1985 of a report on "poverty and hunger," as a result of which staff were instructed to evaluate the probable impact on poverty of all new loans, the Bank was suspected by development lobbies of abandoning its concern for poverty under pressure from free-market conservatives.

Its environmental record was under still more serious attack. Well-documented reports by Western environmental groups on the cultural disruption and environmental degradation created by three major Bank-financed programs—the Amazon development scheme in northwest Brazil, the resettlement of hundreds of thousands of farmers from overpopulated Java in outlying Indonesian islands, and the huge Narmada Dam hydroelectric and irrigation scheme in India—had turned these loans, and the Bank's general approach (or lack of one) to environmental questions, into a *cause célèbre* on Capitol Hill.

Restoring donor confidence was imperative because in order to sustain its credibility as a catalyst for economic reform, particularly in cash-starved Africa, the Bank was going to need a sharp real increase in IDA funds, whose replenishment was currently being negotiated. It would, in addition, soon hit its lending ceiling for IBRD loans unless it obtained an early increase in its capital base.

Conable first called in an external management team. In December 1986, he reinforced it by setting up a steering committee composed of energetic middle-management staff and three external advisers—the chairman of the Bank of Tokyo's board, a former Colombian finance minister, and Robert McNamara—to plan a complete reorganization of the Bank. This committee was in turn backed by three task forces dealing with policy and research, operations, and finance. The committee reported in April 1987.

The Bank, it said,[12] had failed to chart a strategy for helping borrowers to deal with "economic volatility, resource scarcity and a frayed consensus in the international arena." New techniques were required "in virtually every sector in which the Bank operated." As "policy adviser, cofinancier and crisis manager," it "must be tailored to reinforce integration at the country level rather than fragmentation," to promote "tightly disciplined economic management," and a "better informed debate on policy issues." It could not meet these needs through "discrete investments in productive capacity": it must concentrate on policies, aid coordination, cofinancing, and the generation of ideas.

The Bank must develop the intellectual authority to fill the vacuum in relations between developing and industrialized countries, and to assess and help to bridge the contradictions between domestic policymaking and the external environment. This would involve two changes. As "a knowledge-based institution," it was top-heavy in construction engineers and desperately short of economists; this would have to be reversed. Second, it needed to get rid of "the embarrassing amount of bureaucracy" complicating its relations with developing countries. Individual country directors should be given full responsibility both for reform-based lending and for projects, aid coordination, and cofinancing.

This analysis was accompanied by detailed plans for restructuring the Bank, which Conable accepted in May. He left their implementation to the steering committee, on the ground that senior managers, who had vested interests to protect, should be kept out of the picture. Less wisely, Conable himself remained aloof. The committee decided that maximum equity and flexibility would be achieved by dismissing almost the entire staff and inviting them to apply for "reselection." What followed was in some respects a casebook exercise in how not to reform a large bureaucracy. Virtually every division of the Bank was abolished. The new structure was created by proceeding from the top and inviting each level of management to pick the team under it—a game of musical chairs that was dubbed "cascading cronyism." Bank activity, predictably, came almost to a halt: with one in ten about to be made redundant, nobody was willing to leave town without first establishing a niche in the new system. Conable himself earned headlines as a bungler by failing to retain the services of the Bank's brilliant treasurer, Eugene Rotberg, to whom he offered the key job of handling the Bank's debt strategy, but at a level commensurate neither with the importance of the task nor with Rotberg's reputation. An exaggerated concern to make room for new talent cost the organization people whose experience it needed.

But in others it was exemplary. Within six weeks, forty-eight hundred staff had been reassigned and the whole exercise was completed in four months. Integrated country departments, each with its own technical staff, were created within four regional divisions. Accountability for performance rested with country directors in a simplified and decentralized decision-making structure. Policy planning and research were separated from operations, with a view to "ensuring that we are not simply articulating policy to justify what we are doing, but providing independent and imaginative thinking about questions to which we do not yet have answers." In addition to new regional environmental divisions, a department for environmental policy was created and embarked, within months, on an environmental review of all Bank projects and a detailed survey of environmental problems in thirty seriously affected countries. Staff cuts, in contrast to a concurrent exercise at the United Nations, were achieved not through attrition but by severance payments. (These payments, however, while effective in cutting out deadwood and people whose skills no longer matched the Bank's needs, were in some case wildly overgenerous. The overall costs were so high that the Bank had to trim its plans to hire economists, environmentalists, and policy analysts in their place.)

The reorganization greatly strengthened the Bank's ability to design and monitor economic reform programs; to coordinate external aid from other sources; and, potentially, to put pressure on donor governments and commercial creditors to support credible reform packages with aid, reschedulings, and debt forgiveness. By 1989, it was able to report that in Africa, seven-eighths of the increases in Western bilateral aid was being spent in support of structural adjustment programs. Finally, it was better equipped to work with the IMF: the institutional framework appeared to have caught up with contemporary demand.

Fire Engine and Hydrant

Western governments remain extremely attached to the orthodox division of labor between the IMF as the provider, under strict conditions, of temporary injections of liquidity, and the Bank as long-term development lender. So do the governments of developing countries, who suspect that as the roles of the two organizations converge, they will be caught in a vice of "cross-conditionality." Such convergence is, however, unavoidable in the context of Third World debt: cross-conditionality reflects the legitimate interest of donors and lenders in borrowers' policies. Where debt overhang was a key constraint on growth, it was as pointless for the World Bank to insist (as Conable did as late as 1988) that it was "not a debt-settlement agency," as it was for the IMF to insist that it was required, like Justice, to remain blind to the social and political side-effects of its stabilization programs. Officials in both organizations were driven to acknowledge the impossibility of an absolute distinction between stabilization and recovery measures: when it came to putting out a fire, there was, as one senior Bank official put it, "an essential symbiosis between the fire-engine and the hydrant."

The IMF's own review of its lending policies, launched in 1987 by its new executive director, Michel Camdessus, acknowledged the special, and novel, problems of long-term intervention in national policymaking. Programs had to be politically feasible if governments were to be persuaded to approach the IMF earlier and agreements were then to hold. By 1988, IMF officials were conceding that "overregulation" put "too many constraints on authorities to adjust" and that it might be better to conduct its national economic assessments less frequently and to shorten its lists of performance indicators. Camdessus, a veteran of Paris Club debt reschedulings, also recognized—as had de Larosière before him—that governments would only accept IMF medicine in conjunction with longer-term finance. In 1984, de Larosière had appealed to commercial banks to "think long," rewarding countries that accepted reforms with reschedulings so that they could plan their strategies "without a sword of Damocles over their head."[13] But the pattern in the 1980s was for the commercial banks to reduce their exposure while that of the official creditors—the financial institutions, governments, and export credit guarantee agencies—increased. Despite the reluctance of donor governments to transfer accumulated debt risks to the taxpayer, the management, and reduction, of Third World debt had become an inescapable priority for intergovernmental cooperation. And the management of economic reforms had become an inescapable part of resolving the debt crisis.

Successful management presented an organizational challenge—and an ideological conundrum. Market-based reforms depended on convincing governments, in the words of a senior World Bank executive, that "the government is not benign, that their state machinery is almost uniformly too big and too unmanageable, and that we are offering wholly non-ideological advice in telling them to withdraw from whole sectors of economic activity."[14] But the route to the "magic of the marketplace" required careful mapping—and involved politically unpopular reforms that could only be carried through by determined policymakers. Governments also found it politically easier to cut back on basic health and education than on spending that benefited the powerful urban middle classes—with the result that the pain of reforms was seen to fall most heavily on the poor. Charting new strategies therefore required a far more politically intrusive "dialogue" with borrowers. However evident it might appear that "the issue of development is the role of the state, and the principal task for multilateral organizations is to help governments to address the institutional implications of rolling back the state," any such definition of the organizations' role suggested an unprecedented degree of official outside intervention in domestic politics and social as well as economic policy. Anti-*dirigisme* thus paradoxically implied, at least initially, highly active roles both for governments and for their foreign advisers, and the development of new forms of multilateral economic diplomacy in which the distinctions between the Bank and the IMF would inevitably become blurred.

From the viewpoint of Western governments, fearful for the stability of the international banking system, the most urgent testing ground for this new, frankly interventionist economic diplomacy was Latin America. In the mid-1980s, it also seemed to be the most intractable terrain. The root causes of the debt crisis, the accumulation of years of unsustainable borrowing, were massive distortions of economic policy, mostly by various types of dictatorships. Most of the major debtors had unwieldy and inefficient public sectors and overvalued exchange rates that, largely because of hyperinflation, were nonetheless accompanied by massive capital flight. The income gaps between their urban elites and large landowners and the poorest peasants and *favela*-dwellers were higher, on average, than anywhere in the world. But the complexity of these societies limited the impact of external advice, and the investments required seemed likely far to exceed anything the multilateral institutions could hope to provide, or even to generate indirectly. As one gloomy (too gloomy, it was to turn out) Bank official said of Argentina in 1988:

> You talk to the government and you will fail. Argentina has the economists; and the wealth. But it also has the labor unions, the army, the oldest and most archaic industrial structure in Latin America. States within states operate both in the public utilities and in the provincial governments. The railways alone run a deficit which is 2 percent of GNP. Provincial governments effectively print their own money and force central government to bail them out. The layers of vested interest permeate the society: and the Peronist legacy makes any scaling-down of social entitlements politically explosive. You cannot simply require the government to bring the budget into line with its resources without analyzing these questions; and they cannot be answered at the level of aggregates and performance indicators.[15]

And when, a few months after this conversation, the Bank went ahead with a $1.2 billion loan to Argentina *before* an IMF program had been agreed, there was a furious row; Britain and other Europeans accused the Bank of bowing to political pressures from the United States and of agreeing to lend on inappropriately soft terms.

The dilemma for both organizations appeared at this stage to be that "adjustment fatigue" in developing countries was coinciding with debt fatigue among creditors, creating a dangerously volatile situation. Donors, distrusting the pressures on the Bank for quick disbursement, insisted that IMF programs must first be in place. But so many IMF programs had failed when countries reneged on the conditions it had set that commercial banks no longer saw the IMF seal of approval as a guarantee of security for fresh lending. New leverage, on both debtors and creditors, was needed. In 1989, the creditors gave way, at official level: the U.S. treasury secretary, Nicholas Brady, announced a "plan" that, though far from thoroughly thought through, gave the go-ahead for debt-reduction negotiations—and a major role for the Bank and IMF in bringing the commercial banks around to the idea.

By itself, the scheme had only limited potential to make the positions of middle-income debtors manageable; debt reduction carried the risk of choking off future commercial credits and would require complex negotiation. The plan also carried the risk of being seen as a substitute for economic reforms that remained indispensable. Yet its timing turned out impeccable—because it chimed with a political sea change in Latin America as dramatic, in its different way, as the conversion to market economics in Eastern Europe. Within a couple of years Mexico's economy seemed well on the way out of trouble, and by 1993 even Argentina had defied the pessimistic prognosis quoted above to turn its economy around—and under a Peronist president at that. Chile, which had a head start on reforms, achieved growth of 10.3 percent in 1992, and although this rate was halved in the two subsequent years by depressed export markets, the country was considered unequivocally to have turned the corner. Latin America's debt problem was by no means "solved," but exports were booming, inflation in many countries was under control, and of the major Latin American debtors, only Brazil had yet to carry out a serious overhaul of the gamut of economic policy. It was a rare instance of serendipitous conjunction between economic necessity and democratic regeneration. To the surprise of both the Bank and IMF, and of many in the donor community, they had turned out in most cases to be pushing on an open door.

A much tougher and more inconclusive struggle to make sense of aid policies lay ahead in sub-Saharan Africa. The IMF consciously altered its strategy for the subcontinent in 1986, launching its own growth-orientated series of subsidized loans to governments poor enough to qualify for IDA credits. The new IMF "enhanced structural adjustment facility" (ESAF) required governments, assisted by staff from both Bank and IMF, to draw up annually updated three-year policy framework papers, in return for loans disbursed over three years and repayable, practically interest-free, within ten. The framework papers set out new approaches to dialogue, detailing the macroeconomic and structural policy objectives, the action proposed and the finance required. They provided details of public investment plans and, "to the extent that information is available," the roles of other UN and bilateral aid agencies. They included analyses of the "social implications of the program and . . . steps . . . to ameliorate the possible adverse short-term effect of the adjustment program on vulnerable groups"[16]—an acknowledgment of criticisms that IMF conditionality bears most heavily on the poorest. The papers were to be reviewed by the executive directors of both the Bank and IMF.

The sums involved in such programs were not large—some $9 billion between 1986 and 1990. Their virtue, in the IMF's view, was that the accompanying plans provided a clear framework within which other bilateral and multilateral aid could be channeled, stimulating generous Paris Club reschedulings and more debt forgiveness, generating external investment, and making better use of available funds. The verdict on the first experiments was mixed. Their weakness was that the plans tended to become purely Bank-IMF documents with only token national input. But the elaboration of policy frameworks did ease the pressures on government administrators, while strengthening their hand with external donors and aid agencies. Much was learned in the 1980s, moreover, and by the time the ESAF was relaunched in February 1994, with a fresh pool amounting to $8.87 billion, its work had attracted wide approval not just among donors but among developing countries, many of which contributed to its replenishment—and, as generously, approved the addition of Armenia, Georgia, Kyrgyztan, Tajikistan, and Macedonia to the list of countries eligible for ESAF loans.

Most of the ESAF loans went to sub-Saharan Africa, where by the end of the 1980s the majority of governments had committed themselves, out of desperation more than conviction in most cases, to far-reaching economic reforms. Some were beginning to show results. Multilateral dialogue had gained considerably in sophistication. The severity of the obstacles to reversing years of economic mismanagement, in a continent where "austerity" easily translated into hunger and rising infant mortality, was better understood. The donor community had come to recognize how long it would take to rectify distortions of the kind described in a 1987 Bank study, which calculated that because the economic cost of inputs into Tanzania's state-owned industries was five times greater than the value of outputs, the country would become richer overnight simply by closing the factory gates. Donors had also found that second-best programs with political backing were more promising than the best accompanied by mere lip service.

Yet at the decade's end, although sub-Saharan Africa had received more aid per head than any other region and although some governments at least had embarked on radical policy changes, most black Africans were poorer and hungrier than they had been at independence. Returns on investment had shrunk from 30 percent in the 1960s to a derisory 3 percent. Its share of world trade had halved since 1970, an economic loss equivalent to the cost of servicing the continent's debts—which had rocketed, from around $6 billion to nearly $140 billion. The total wealth of black Africa, with a population twice that of the United States, was barely greater than that of Belgium. And in thirty years, their numbers would double. Africans themselves were increasingly aware that Africa's decline would never be reversed without political reforms.

Sub-Saharan Africa: From Crisis to Sustainable Growth,[17] the report published by the World Bank in 1989 and alluded to at the beginning of this chapter, broke new ground for the United Nations by addressing Africa's political ills squarely—ending the taboo on mentioning internal politics that had made official discussion of development, not only but principally in Africa, so artificial. Authoritarian rule, it said, had allowed Africa's elites to "serve their own interests without fear of being called to account." Its bureaucracies had been politicized and corrupted, its judicial systems destroyed, its lawyers browbeaten, human rights violated, and debate stifled through press censorship. Politicians had siphoned off fortunes into overseas accounts; and foreign donors and investors had colluded in this, with the result that aid had "expanded the opportunities for malfeasance." Even more important than the waste of money had been "the profound demoralization of society at large," and a loss of confidence so great that "ordinary people see government as the source of, not the solution to, their problems." Entrepreneurship was stifled by red tape and corruption, and the continent was wasting its "best-trained minds, many of which are in exile or under-utilized," while importing some one hundred thousand expatriates at an annual cost of around $5 billion. (Five percent of these expatriate salaries, the report drily noted, would increase the amount available for each primary pupil's schoolbooks from 60 cents to $5 a year.)

Given that under its articles, the World Bank is not allowed to take political factors into account in making loans, this excursion into forbidden territory had to be justified. The report argued its case on three main grounds. The first was that without "political renewal" to reverse the breakdown of Africa's institutions and restore the popular legitimacy of governments, economic reforms could not be sustained. Rotten political environments could not, it said, "readily support a dynamic economy." Africa needed not only less government, but better government, accountable and open to the talents. Social and economic collapse could be averted only by "a determination to respect the rule of law, and vigorous protection of the freedom of the press and human rights." The second was that, even if reforms took hold, Africa would need increasing external aid until the early part of the next century. Other equally poor regions had made better use of foreign capital, and donors knew it. Fresh sums would not, and should not, be made available for "military spending, luxury consumption and capital flight."

Finally, Africa could not hope to achieve even modest prosperity by 2010 without average annual growth of 5 percent, implying a rise in productivity that would be impossible without "releasing the energies of ordinary people by enabling them to take charge of their lives." Even that rate of growth would be inadequate unless Africa's unprecedentedly high rates of population growth could be slowed. What was needed was a revolution in social attitudes. And this made the case for political reforms: change on such a scale could come about only with the consent and understanding of the governed. A grass-roots revolution was needed "to transform Africa from an expensive and difficult place to do business into an efficient one"; and "the fundamental objective of improving human welfare" could not be met unless people were freer to take their own decisions—and free to hold their rulers to account.

The report, at once the most severe and most humane to have been published by any international institution, was a logical outgrowth of the 1980s. Encouragingly, it had been prepared after exceptionally intensive consultations with African intellectuals, professionals, and businessmen; and they had insisted on the vital importance of the political dimension. The World Bank was at last giving proper weight to regenerating Africa's political institutions—bureaucracies, the judiciary, and the institutions of civil society. The African Capacity Building Foundation, set up two years later, began actively to invest in creating and strengthening policy units and training institutes and launching specialized courses to build skills in short supply. The report also prefigured the coming debates of the 1990s: when Western governments were introducing political conditions so openly into their provision of aid to the emerging democracies of Eastern Europe, the taboo on mentioning tyrannical misrule in countries like Malawi or Zaire was as intellectually unsustainable as it had long been morally discreditable.

What was beyond dispute was that Africa would, in the 1990s, have to go through changes as wrenching as any in Eastern Europe, and in conditions of acute poverty for the great majority. Structural adjustment was an ugly, intimidating phrase for policies that were both unexceptionable and theoretically straightforward: governments must spend within their means, stop meddling with prices, dismantle supports for inefficient state enterprises, and give private initiative enterprise space to grow. But in Africa, it was already obvious that turning these economies around would take years, perhaps decades.

By 1994, twenty-eight African governments were at least committed to structural reforms. A report published by the Bank that year was able to record that growth had picked up since 1986 in fifteen of these, and agricultural production had doubled. But most governments still put up fierce resistance to privatization—less than a fifth of Africa's state enterprises had been sold off—and, even more critically, to switching spending to the rural poor. Kenya, for example, had sold almost none of its state industrial portfolio by 1990, and spent none of its investment budget for education that year on primary schools: 75 percent of it went to universities. And not a single country looked as though it had turned the corner; even Ghana, Africa's star reformer, remained critically dependent on continuing aid and was attracting almost no foreign investment.

This suggests that in Africa at least, the Bank should be more selective, seeking to influence governments by example. That would mean concentrating its efforts on a small number of governments wholeheartedly committed to reform, and complementing policy reforms with determined advocacy, where necessary, of large-scale debt forgiveness. Envy might breed emulation, where across-the-board adjustment programs create an absolute fraternity of sullen government elites.

Greater selectivity may also be required to address the decline in the quality of its lending performance during the 1980s. This was recognized by Lewis Preston, who took over from Barber Conable in 1992, and ordered a further reorganization of its lending operations after the Bank's evaluation department reported that the proportion of projects with "major problems" had doubled since 1981, to 20 percent overall and to a quarter of all agricultural loans. Even though average real returns on investment were still 16 percent, this deterioration gave ammunition to critics, inside the Bank as well as outside, who had long argued that far too much emphasis was being placed on increasing the volume of loans and that quality was suffering. Lending portfolios in India, Nigeria, Turkey, and Brazil (where a third of eighty-one projects, together worth $10.7 billion, were judged failures) were rapidly overhauled, with projects redesigned or canceled. In May 1993, Preston pledged that "on-the-ground benefits—rather than loan approvals" would now be the "measure of success,"[18] even if in some countries that meant less rather than more lending. He accepted the sensible conclusion, for too long brushed aside, that in countries with "serious implementation problems . . . continued lending adds to debt without producing commensurate benefits." And in two further overdue reforms, more responsibility for lending decisions was shifted from Washington to the Bank's sixty-plus resident missions, and staff were instructed to simplify projects and match them more closely to the borrowers' capacities to implement them.

The irony is that this necessary refocusing coincided with unprecedented Western pressures on both Bank and IMF to take a far more expansive, and more "political" role in Eastern Europe, the republics born of the dissolution of the Soviet Union and, above all, in Russia. The fact that Western governments put so much emphasis on multilateral action to prevent an economic meltdown with clear implications for their security had much to do with their own internal difficulties at a time of deep Western recession. But it also emphasized the degree to which the Bretton Woods institutions, in contrast to the UN's other specialized agencies, had entered the 1990s well integrated into the heart of global policymaking. And this was a tribute to their internal dynamism, and their ability to recognize and attempt to rectify mistakes. By 1994 both were under heavy attack, particularly in Washington, for having "failed" the reformers in Russia by failing to disburse funds sufficiently rapidly. But much of this criticism was both opportunistic and ill founded. Russia, along with most its ex-Soviet neighbors and the former Communist countries of Eastern and Central Europe, was faced with levels of hyperinflation that would tear at the sinews of any society. Both Russia and Poland had tried gradualist strategies of reform in the 1980s, which had turned out macroeconomic disasters. Poland, which took the enormous political risk of "shock therapy" in January 1990, was by 1994 on track for 4 percent growth. Russia, in much graver political turmoil, could hardly be said to have embarked on reforms before 1993, when President Boris Yeltsin reappointed Yegor Gaidar as deputy prime minister in charge of the economy—and even then, the "war of the laws" between government and the Russian parliament made it impossible for most of that year for Gaidar to block the pell-mell creation of credit by the Russian Central Bank.

The defeat suffered by Gaidar's reformist group, Russia's Choice, in the December 1993 elections rapidly led to a furious argument in the West. Some economists, and politicians, believed that lack of adequate Western aid at critical political junctures had "lost Russia," by dooming the efforts of Gaidar and his able finance minister, Boris Fyodorov, to capitalize on their initial successes in freeing prices and privatizing Russian industries. Others maintained that fiscal stabilization—which still eluded Russia—was an essential prerequisite to making use of large-scale foreign credits. Russian inflation at the end of 1993 had been reduced, but still stood at an annual 900 percent and was set to rise again. As an internal Bank/IMF memo of the time somewhat drily noted, experience elsewhere in

Eastern Europe suggested that such a gradual approach to the reduction of inflation was "not an effective way of minimizing economic hardship or maximizing political support": it was sufficient to compare the Czech Republic with Ukraine. The risk, as they saw it, was that financial assistance without policy conditionality would encourage vested interests to seek to maintain an untenable *status quo*, increase capital flight, and prolong the period of reduced, and appalling living standards for most of the population.

Western politicians had, however, publicly committed themselves, individually and through the Group of 7, to massive and rapid assistance to the Yeltsin government—which most Russian bureaucrats had interpreted as meaning that the IMF and the Bank would waive conditionality. It relieved Western governments of some embarrassment, early in 1994, to blame the Bretton Woods institutions for holding back.

Yet it is no good asking rule-based institutions to tear up the rulebook at the behest of their shareholders, even of the largest shareholders. Through no particular fault of the reformers, Gaidar's team was unable to muster the institutional power to force through a credible reform program; the December elections had demonstrated just how powerful and entrenched the old order remained. And Russian reformers were themselves, by 1994, counseling against abandoning the West's economic leverage by pouring in money without waiting for reforms.

The short answer to "political aid," aid aimed at shoring up a particular government, is to make it bilateral, but this was not an answer Western capitals wished to hear. The strains these arguments seem likely to impose on Western multilateral cooperation will be discussed later. What seems pertinent here is that these fresh controversies about the roles of these two global organizations were so fierce precisely because they were considered essential to any coordinated strategy for the post-Communist world. The same could not be said for most of the UN's other specialized agencies.

The organizations that have already proved capable of change are those that stand the best chance of adapting further. The patterns of reinvention we have discussed in this chapter have been securely anchored because policies have been demand-led and, to a large degree, internally generated rather than imposed. There are lessons here for the rest of the UN, where reforms have characteristically stemmed from concern about the functioning of the "system," instead of concentrating on the functions it might perform. The reliance of the Bretton Woods organizations on the confidence of the capital markets, without which they cannot operate, helps to explain this distinctive concentration on function. So does their historically greater integration in national financial and economic policymaking, not only in developing countries. The influence of IMF economists on the agendas of the Western economic summits is one instance; the role of the Group of 5 and the Fund's Interim Committee another. And the joint Bank/IMF Development Committee, while only advisory, is by far the most effective multilateral channel for North-South consultation on broad questions of economic policy. Bringing together in informal session twenty-two finance ministers who represent the whole membership, it has had an influence both on the institutions—most recently in insisting on the importance of environmental factors in development lending—and on the quality of the political consensus between capitals.

Critics of the Bank and IMF would add a final dimension that marks them out: their susceptibility, situated as they are in Washington, to American influence. The geographical factor, while important, works in two directions: while conscious of their proximity to Capitol Hill, the two organizations also influence U.S. policy as does no other part of the United Nations—including the Security Council. The speed with which the Reagan administration's early attacks on both institutions turned into the Baker plan illustrates the point, and it could be argued that their emphasis on the importance of market-based economic reforms in developing countries was a response not so much to political pressures as to an emerging conventional wisdom about the limited efficacy of state planning and control. If the wind from Capitol Hill blows particularly freshly on them, it has the merit of reminding them that in the last resort and within the terms of their articles, they are political institutions, tools as well as generators of government policies.

The critical review of Bank and IMF policies carried out in 1981 by the Reagan administration was only part of a much broader political reassessment of U.S. interests in multilateral cooperation. It is to American demands for reform of the rest of the United Nations—the first to be politically driven, and the catalyst for a new Western activism that is needed in the 1990s more than ever before—that we return in the next chapter.

American disaffection with the United Nations was not new, but the declared scope and radicalism of the across-the-board review, announced in 1981, of U.S. participation in UN organizations appeared to go beyond criticisms of the UN's inefficiency and irritation at its politicization, to question its place both in U.S. policy, and in the global networks of multilateral cooperation. If the questions raised by the Reagan administration, grounded in conservative distrust of "world government" and a reassertion of American power, lent strength to the essentially diversionary theory of a "crisis of multilateralism," they also forced governments and secretariats to rethink the case for institutions that they had for too long comfortably supposed would, if they did not exist, have to be invented. The new, activist U.S. approach to the United Nations in the 1980s altered the time frame for discussing reform; it could no longer be addressed at junior level as tomorrow's problem. U.S. criticisms, and the prolonged bipartisan support in the U.S. Congress for the withholding of U.S. dues, opened up questions about the "value" of the rest of the United Nations—questions that the Bretton Woods organizations, operating as they did within the marketplace, had been constantly required to answer, but to which the other global institutions had hitherto been relatively immune.

8. THE CHALLENGE FROM WASHINGTON

THE NEW AMERICAN AGENDA

The most surprising aspect of the Reagan administration's decision in 1981 to undertake an iconoclastic survey of U.S. participation in United Nations organizations was that the United States had not taken action earlier. There was nothing particularly novel or radical about most of the Reagan team's criticisms of the United Nations. Concern about the abuse of UN forums and resources, about double standards with regard to Soviet and U.S. actions and the constant pillorying of the United States, about political jobbery, lax administration, budgetary irresponsibility, and lack of accountability had been enunciated before in milder terms both by the United States and other Western governments, and had prompted, as we have seen, earlier campaigns for reform. American impatience with Western "appeasement" of the Third World majority dated back at least to Daniel Patrick Moynihan's short tenure of the post of U.S. permanent representative to the UN in the mid-1970s.

The radicalism of the Reagan approach lay not in its complaints, but in its open questioning of the value of these global institutions to the United States. It had hitherto been U.S. policy to seek reform within the context of a firm commitment to multilateral diplomacy. (The U.S. withdrawal from the International Labor Organization between 1977 and 1980 was only an apparent exception to this rule. The State Department had resisted the decision, but the AFL-CIO and the American Chamber of Commerce were so opposed to continued U.S. participation that, given the ILO's unique tripartite character, withdrawal was unavoidable. In announcing it, President Carter had been careful to emphasize that "the U.S. remains ready to return whenever the ILO is again true to its proper principles and procedures."[1])

The Reagan administration, by contrast, brought to its review a clearly articulated distrust of "world government" and international regulation—an extension to foreign policy of its emphasis in domestic affairs on a reduced role for government and greater reliance on the play of market forces. Its attitude to the United Nations also reflected a shift in the national mood, extending far beyond conservative circles, toward the reassertion of U.S. military and economic power, and of the "values of the free world." U.S. support for organizations whose members attacked these values and whose activities reinforced state control over markets could, the new administration asserted, no longer be taken for granted.

The implications of this shift were not immediately grasped abroad, in part because while the general stance was clear enough, the initial articulation of accompanying policies was hesitant and self-contradictory. It was not until June 1982 that the State Department came up with the five guiding principles for U.S. policy: restoration of U.S. influence in UN forums; active defense there of democratic values; more jobs for Americans in UN secretariats; steep cuts in the number of UN meetings and conferences (estimated by the U.S. mission in New York at eleven thousand a year in New York and Geneva alone); and zero growth in UN budgets.

These less than homogeneous criteria were applied to an official review of all UN "agencies" to which the United States belonged—ninety-six separate bodies, according to Gregory Newell, the then U.S. assistant secretary for international organization affairs. Some of these—a zinc study group or the management committee for a couple of lighthouses for which the United Nations was responsible—were so small as to suggest that the real reason for including them was to give the impression that the United States was overcommitted to multilateral cooperation. Two-thirds of them were, however, subjected to quite serious scrutiny. Where the conclusions suggested that they failed to meet the new U.S. criteria for participation, "consultations" with the secretariats followed, the principal themes of which were U.S. demands for a clampdown on budgetary growth and on the politicization of debates and programs. By 1983 the ILO, the International Telecommunications Union (ITU), the UN Environment Program (UNEP), the International Atomic Energy Agency (IAEA), and UNESCO had thus been reviewed. And in the summer of 1983 a far more detailed probe, involving some five hundred people inside and outside government, began with regard to UNESCO, which the State Department found in its initial review to be the most flagrant case of policies and activities "inimical to U.S. interests."

The reviews were, however, relatively low profile and attracted the attention of only a handful of UN civil servants and a few officials dealing with international organizations in other countries. Even among this expert minority, opinion was divided as to whether the wind from Washington was a temporary squall to be weathered, or the harbinger of a lasting change of climate. The U.S. Treasury's parallel review of the multilateral development banks served clear warning of the new administration's antipathy to all forms of state intervention. What was not clear was how far these various reviews were intended to prepare the grounds for demands for policy reform, or whether their real purpose was to provide ideological justification for U.S. withdrawals. Even within the administration, the line between criticisms of the actual functioning of the global organizations, and ideological hostility to multilateral diplomacy, was not always clearly drawn.

Public attention, both in the United States and abroad, focused on the performance in the Security Council and the General Assembly of the new U.S. permanent representative, Jeane Kirkpatrick. An academic whose theories on the distinctions between the (redeemable) nature of authoritarian dictatorships and the (irredeemable) character of totalitarian ones first brought her to President Reagan's attention, she gathered in New York a team largely composed of political appointees who shared her determination to reassert U.S. interests with "neither bluster nor appeasement."

Kirkpatrick believed in taking rhetoric seriously. UN votes matter, she argued, because they "affect both the image and the reality of power in the UN system and beyond it." The confrontational tone of debates at the United Nations had, in her view, heightened rather than eased international tensions. She demanded "fair treatment" for the United States as a matter not simply of moral justice, but of political necessity. When the Soviet Union was never criticized by name and "the U.S. and its friends are subjected to harsh and often unfair attack," she testified to Congress in 1985, "the U.S. appears to be devoid of influence, and associations with it become undesirable if not dangerous." The United States, she argued, should take account of UN votes in its bilateral diplomacy, adopting a system of penalties and rewards. She persuaded the State Department to adopt the tactic first suggested by Moynihan in 1975: U.S. ambassadors were instructed to make formal protests in capitals whenever representatives of "friendly" states made hostile speeches or voted against the United States in Turtle Bay.

In New York, Kirkpatrick gave early proof of an unusual directness of approach. In September 1981, ninety-three governments endorsed a UN resolution accusing the United States of being a threat to global peace and prosperity. Immediately she wrote to the UN ambassadors of each to ask why they had done so. *Time* magazine characterized this calling to account, departing as it did from Western conventions about not offending the nonaligned majority, as "letter bomb diplomacy." It was intended by Kirkpatrick to advertise that the United States would no longer be party to what she described, with contempt, as a Western policy of "preemptive capitulation."

In this she faithfully reflected the administration's belief that the West, through its addiction to "consensus politics," had betrayed the UN Charter—by failing to insist on strict adherence to it by the UN's membership, as the condition of the industrialized democracies' continued participation in, and financing of, the organization. The United States, announcing its determination to confront the double standards that tarnished the UN's image, had little sympathy for the politics of "the art of the possible": reasonableness had got the West nowhere.

"The founders," President Reagan reminded the General Assembly in 1983, "intended this body to stand for certain values, even if they could not be enforced, and to condemn violence, even if it could not be stopped . . . governments got in the way of the dreams of the people. Dreams became issues of East versus West. Hopes became political rhetoric. Progress became a search for power and domination." The polarization of the UN had, he said, undermined its worth; what was required was an end to bloc voting and "a true nonalignment of the United Nations." The United States was committed to the founders' ideal of "a world . . . where the rule of law would prevail, where human rights were honored, where development would blossom." Conjuring up a vision of member states voting freely, their decisions based on the merits of issues in "a great, global town meeting," he exhorted his audience to "regain the dream the United Nations once dreamed."

This was Reagan at his populist best, deliberately using images—like that of the global town meeting—to recall the hopes expressed at San Francisco in 1945 by such respected members of the U.S. delegation as Senator Arthur S. Vandenberg. U.S. public opinion may have been his main target, but he was also out to appeal to the feeling of ordinary men and women in many countries that "we, the peoples," in whose name the Charter created the United Nations, had been betrayed by the cynicism of governments.

Reagan's more immediate audience was by this point aware that these words were not just hortatory platitudes. Even his reminder that the UN had been intended "to strengthen the bonds of civility among nations" was a way of emphasizing that the United States was no longer prepared, as Kirkpatrick had put it, to tolerate "name-calling"—a demand for civility intended to cover genuine disagreements as well as the gratuitous insults of which the United States had over the years become a target. And there was more than a hint that by not tolerating, the United States might well mean not staying around—as an incident only a few weeks earlier had suggested. Because of the shooting down by Soviet military of a South Korean civilian airliner, the United States had refused to allow the Soviet delegation arriving for the General Assembly to use Kennedy airport. In protest at this technical breach of the headquarters agreement between the United States and the UN, a group of Third World and Eastern bloc governments threatened to relocate the UN General Assembly and Security Council outside the United States. Charles Lichtenstein, Kirkpatrick's deputy at the Security Council, replied that the United States would put no impediment in their way and would be at the dockside waving. This off-the-cuff sally drew no disclaimer from Washington and even elicited murmurs of sympathy from the White House.

The United States was not only demanding "civility" and respect. It sought changes of substance as well as rhetoric. And on this count, the achievements of U.S. policy had, by the time of Reagan's speech, been negligible—even on such bell-weather issues as restraint in budgetary growth, and in the treatment of Israel. On the issue of runaway UN budgets, at least, the West was by this time united. In 1981, all the dozen Western governments that financed three-quarters of the UN's regular spending had agreed to the U.S. target of zero growth in UN budgets—except the Scandinavians, and even they were unhappy about the UN's rate of budgetary expansion. In November 1982 the Soviet Union, ever in harmony with the West when it came to money, joined the United States and Great Britain in a démarche to the secretary-general to insist on budgetary stringency. The General Assembly treated this demand with its customary contempt. The following month, against the opposition of all the major donors, it voted through a 10 percent increase in the UN's current budget. The pattern was similar in most of the UN's specialized agencies.

The United States was similarly rebuffed over its insistence on an end to the victimization of Israel. In 1981, Kirkpatrick had to threaten to walk out of a conference convened by the UN High Commissioner for Refugees (UNHCR) in Geneva to raise funds for African refugees, taking with her about $300 million in proffered assistance, in order to prevent the exclusion from the meeting of Israel, an important donor to UN refugee programs, on the insistence of Arab governments whose aid to refugees was almost nonexistent. The following year both houses of Congress passed resolutions requiring the administration to suspend U.S. participation in any UN body that "illegally expelled, suspended, denied its credentials, or in any other manner denied [Israel's] right to participate," and to withhold U.S. contributions. Even this clear warning had had no impact. In 1983, Israel was excluded from Third World talks on economic cooperation at the UN Conference on Trade and Development (UNCTAD); had its credentials rejected at the International Atomic Energy Agency; and avoided the same fate at the International Telecommunications Union only after three weeks of united Western resistance. Even after the United States suspended its participation in the IAEA in protest, it took the personal intervention of the secretary of state, George Shultz, to prevent a repeat performance at the General Assembly itself.

It had, quite simply, not been understood that the United States was serious. Governments did not realize that exasperation over the constant attacks on U.S. policies and over the abuse of voting majorities to force through programs that it had consistently opposed and for which it paid a quarter of the costs—an exasperation that had been accumulating in Washington for years—had finally crystallized into revolt. This was partly attributable to the enclosed and artificial political culture that had developed in UN forums. States had acquired the habit of mentally divorcing their conduct at the UN from "real" politics and thus assumed that those governments that elsewhere exercised influence and power could there be ignored, or even insulted, with impunity. Third World governments, in particular, tended to be misled by their own rhetoric: they had for so long cast the United States in the role of opponent to the wishes of "the international community" that the qualitative change in the character of its opposition went almost unnoticed.

Even in Western capitals, opinion was divided on the nature, and the importance, of the change in U.S. policy. The support that the administration might have expected to summon on issues of principle was to some extent blunted by its own rhetoric. Its new, uncompromising comportment was widely interpreted as a manifestation of conservative neo-isolationism, essentially destructive and therefore to be resisted. The UN, in this reading, was being treated as a political football, the target of a raw America-first philosophy in which the public posture of reforming zeal masked narrow petulance and a frank disregard of Third World sensibilities and of broader Western interests in conciliation and dialogue.

The "political football" theory was seductive because it deflected attention from the complaints to the complainant. It was consonant with a long-standing conventional assumption that the United States, as a superpower, did not need the UN. Its criticisms, on this reading, were a mask: the real problem was not the failings of the global institutions, but Washington's ideological distrust of what some right-wing American columnists called "globaloney." The United States was succumbing to the perennial temptation to unilateralism created by its own power.

Certain American actions in the early 1980s, outside as well as inside the UN, lent this theory credibility. Less than a fortnight after Reagan's inauguration the new budget director, David Stockman, proposed not only to phase U.S. contributions to the multilateral development banks down, or even out; he also suggested that the United States cut its foreign aid from $8 billion to $5.4 billion, link it firmly to U.S. "security and military concerns," and use it "to encourage selected countries to develop economic and political systems compatible with U.S. interests." The primary effect of these proposals, according to Stockman, "would be to eliminate or reduce U.S. participation in a range of multilateral organizations which are not responsive to U.S. policy concerns."[2] These ideas were firmly opposed by the Treasury, by Kirkpatrick, and by the new secretary of state, Alexander Haig, who argued that they represented a U.S. "withdrawal from the world." But what struck outsiders was the fact that they had been presented well in advance of any review of the actual performance of these organizations.

A year later, transatlantic relations were severely strained by the Siberian gas pipeline affair, when the United States imposed an embargo on supplies of equipment to the Soviet Union that applied not only to U.S. companies, but to their subsidiaries in Western Europe and to foreign companies using U.S. equipment or manufacturing components under license from U.S. firms. To Western European governments (whose companies stood to lose contracts worth more than $3 billion) this action was another example of the primacy of ideology over cooperation or even—given the extraterritorial reach of the U.S. embargo—accepted principles of international law.

There was also a strong suspicion that the U.S. stance had more to do with domestic than international politics. One decision in 1984, to cut off U.S. funding for the UN Fund for Population Activities, an agency that the United States had launched and had until then enthusiastically supported, followed a vociferous election-year campaign by right-wing antiabortion groups and coincided with the Republican party convention.

Finally, there was uncertainty over the extent to which U.S. policy on the UN was formed within the government itself, or was shaped by conservative think tanks and lobbyists. Early in 1982—prior to the State Department's review—one of the most influential of these, the Heritage Foundation, had launched its own "UN Assessment Project." It started from the premise, formulated by its vice president Burton Yale Pines, that "a world without the UN would be a better world."[3] During and after the Reagan administration, the Heritage project published well over a hundred reports and briefing papers on the politics and institutional malfunctioning of the UN and its agencies, and organized dozens of working groups and round-table discussions that brought together academics, diplomats, and congressmen.

Constantly questioning the value of U.S. membership in organizations where its values and policies were attacked, the foundation set out to radicalize the debate on institutions that, it insisted, had too long been treated as untouchable. Its *leitmotif* was that "time may be running out for the United Nations, and time may be running out for the United States at the United Nations." Entering into detail only on selected targets, the project launched a broad-brush attack on "the all too common characteristics of the Secretariat and other UN bureaucracies: inefficiency, cronyism, high pay, lavish expense accounts and even corruption and illiteracy." It accused the UN bureaucracy of "cheating . . . the poor nations of the Third World" with biased advice and "research . . . manipulated to confirm the premises of the New International Economic Order" and to prejudice governments against multinational corporations. It criticized the UN for pursuing a "crusade against the free enterprise system" through support for the NIEO, by propagating redistributive economic theories and by multiplying international regulatory regimes.

The vehement tone of many of its reports made it easy to dismiss the project as high-profile, undifferentiated, UN-bashing in support of a bigoted unilateralism. The foundation's undoubted influence with the White House and on Capitol Hill encouraged the European tendency to treat the new American approach to the UN as a passing fashion, a response to domestic pressures, which would be tempered gradually to the realities of the West's minority status and limited influence within the United Nations. The UN's more venal apologists used the existence of the project as evidence that the UN's difficulties were simply the product of a Heritage conspiracy. UNESCO's director-general, Amadou Mahtar M'Bow, sought for example to attribute the withdrawal of the United States and Great Britain from that organization entirely to the Heritage Foundation's machinations and its manipulation of the Western press. In this instance, it is true that a Heritage paper on UNESCO published in 1983 played an important part in the U.S. decision to give notice. But it also happened to be a detailed and accurate indictment, prepared with inside knowledge of the organization by Owen Harries, a former Australian ambassador to UNESCO.

Pines himself claimed that the Heritage project did a service both to the United States and to the UN, which could "only be saved by being reformed," and it did open up a number of serious issues and articulate some widely felt frustrations. And some of its work (for example, on UNESCO, on the FAO in Rome, and on the functioning of the General Assembly) was extremely well informed. Nor was its impact wholly negative. The foundation lobbied vigorously for U.S. contributions to the International Fund for Agricultural Development, a small and well-run UN body created in Rome in 1974 expressly to help small-holder farmers in the Third World. Some of its roundtables on UN reform brought together some of the UN's ablest, because most realistic, defenders—men such as Tommy Koh, Singapore's permanent representative to the UN for fifteen years and president of the final, critical stages of the Law of the Sea Conference.

Crassly reductivist as were many of its arguments, and unjustified as were some of its attacks, the Heritage Foundation succeeded in pressing the case for radical reform not only because it was marshaling the U.S. administration along paths that the president found congenial, but because its criticisms reverberated well beyond conservative circles. It mustered facts and raised ethical as well as management questions that should have stirred the supporters of multilateral cooperation to action long before. It publicized much that was outrageous: the abuse of funds; the use of the United Nations for espionage by the Soviet Union; examples of sharp practices and absurd decisions by UN executives. It reported, for example, the UN secretariat's decision in 1986, citing the need to make economies, not to print complete translations of an account by the UN's own rapporteur of atrocities committed in Afghanistan by Soviet forces and the Kabul government—and pointed out that a few months later it spent $250,000 printing a message from Czech academics and students, complete with nearly a hundred pages of signatures, congratulating Mikhail Gorbachev on his Reykjavik summit proposals.[4] Whatever the doubts about its ultimate aims, the Heritage Foundation's activism did much to demonstrate that a realistic case, going beyond platitudes, had now to be made for the global organizations.

Neither the revival of unilateralism in the United States, nor indifference to the UN, nor conspiracy theory, adequately explained the Reagan administration's stance. There may have been a kernel of truth in each of these convenient hypotheses, but the United States did not need to develop an activist policy toward the UN in order to assert its interests and, in Reagan's phrase, to "walk tall." It could simply have ignored it, as, in practice, did many governments publicly committed to multilateral diplomacy. If the United States chose the path of confrontation and insisted on articulating demands for reform as a condition of its continued participation, this was at least in part because it had traditionally taken the UN more, not less, seriously than most other Western governments (and, in practice, many in the developing world). The Reagan administration's insistence on reasserting U.S. power and moral eminence at the UN, was not, as was sometimes asserted, a "break with the past": it represented the radicalization of traditional U.S. policy.

A SPECIAL RELATIONSHIP

Americans, while disapproving, often vehemently, much that takes place there, have never quite buried the UN in the peace of indifference. The diplomatic fortunes of the United States at the UN have never ceased to touch the U.S. public's sense of the country's international standing. This is, paradoxically, not unrelated to the nation's sense of itself as set apart by geography, by its immense natural resources, and by historical predilection: it is this that makes membership of the UN a conscious commitment to internationalism by the United States. The U.S. wartime decision to take the leading role in creating the UN reversed the isolationism of the interwar years, symbolized for Europeans, in particular, by Congress's refusal to sanction U.S. membership of the League of Nations. The drama of that decision has been kept alive by its veto power in the Security Council, by the location of the UN's political forums in New York; and, with unfortunate effects, by the continuing confrontations there and elsewhere in the UN over Washington's support, often in isolation, of Israel.

The importance of the General Assembly and the Security Council as barometers of the U.S. relationship to the UN has to do with more than simple geographical proximity. From the outset, the United States attached particular importance to the UN's "opinion-forming" role. For President Eisenhower, who once described the UN as "the moral conscience of mankind," the General Assembly was "a place where the guilt can be squarely assigned" and an arena for "international presentation and rebuttal"—notably, and unsurprisingly in the 1950s, of Soviet policies and actions.[5] The commitment to the UN, which perhaps reached its high point with Eleanor Roosevelt's impassioned involvement in drafting the Universal Declaration of Human Rights in 1948, has always been associated with the sense that the UN is worth supporting because it embodies and projects U.S. values. In 1945, the United Nations offered the United States an honorable platform for the exercise of its global influence and power—and its considerable philanthropic energies. The UN was the perfect vehicle for what Shirley Hazzard has characterized as a "concept of the 'international' [which] was—as it continues to be—at best a sort of benign unilateralism through which American policies would work uncontested for everybody's benefit."[6]

In the period of U.S. ascendancy at the United Nations, American initiatives were in fact consciously benign, and to a notable extent disinterested. From the Baruch plan of 1946, which proposed that the raw materials of which atomic weapons were made should be placed under international control and U.S. atomic weapons stockpiles thereafter destroyed, to President Truman's Point Four program and the launching by President Kennedy of the first UN Development Decade in 1960, and in the creation of the World Bank's International Development Association, the UN Development Program, and the World Food Program, U.S. influence and finance were decisive. Whether these initiatives, several of which contributed to the diffusion of UN activities, were ultimately beneficial, is another matter: the intentions behind them were honorable—as was the U.S. commitment to the process of decolonization. That commitment may have been subconsciously reinforced by the country's confidence in its ability to influence the increasingly fragmented postcolonial world; but it was conceived in a spirit of altruism, as part of the agenda of freedom and of upholding the rights of the powerless.

As for U.S. support for multilateral cooperation in the economic and social domains, this remained remarkably constant. Even President Nixon, whose contempt for the UN as political vehicle was absolute, conceded its usefulness for what he called "global challenges"—population planning, management of the oceans and the environment, the prevention of hijacking, control of drug trafficking, and cooperation in outer space—not at the time an unreasonable summary of the global organization's areas of comparative advantage. And Henry Kissinger, capable as he was of telling Samuel de Palma, then U.S. assistant secretary for international organization affairs, "don't bother me with that UN crap,"[7] still came up with proposals (like the international resources bank he suggested at the UNCTAD IV meeting in Nairobi in 1976), which would have altered the tone and substance of North-South economic relations, had Third World governments had the imagination to take them up.

Not all American attention to the UN had been beneficial. The declamatory style of UN debates, and the destructive use of its forums for the cross-ventilation of propaganda rather than exchanges of ideas, originated in the period of the Cold War. When U.S. ascendancy at the UN—in terms of votes, finance, and even the deployment of the moral energies of democracy—was unquestioned, it placed an emphasis on propaganda victories that the United States and its allies had, later, cause to regret. The tactic of repeatedly compelling the Soviet Union, the minority superpower, to resort to its blocking veto at the Security Council—thus exposing its pariah status in the "international community"—was one that could be, and later was, exploited against the West.

The Reagan administration's perfectly proper objections to the cynical abuse of the UN international civil service by the Soviet Union, which had for years treated it as employment agency and cover for large numbers of KGB and GRU operatives, also struck those with a sense of history as somewhat ironic. It was, after all, the United States that had initially flouted the stipulation, set out in Article 100 of the Charter, that "the staff shall not seek or receive instructions from any government or from any other authority external to the Organization." (That this was a point of cardinal importance to the authority of the United Nations had been recognized by the UN Preparatory Commission, which had firmly rejected a Yugoslav proposal that a citizen's appointment to UN secretariats should be subject to the consent of his or her government.) The United States began systematically to violate this all-important principle within four years of the UN's founding—although by his own admission, it was the first UN secretary-general, Trygve Lie, and not the U.S. government who set the ball rolling.

Lie records that in 1948, he had begun to worry whether, in the haste of early recruitment, the UN Secretariat had hired any American Communists. First he tried informal approaches to the U.S. government. When these elicited no response, he submitted, in August 1948, a list of 377 American staff members due to attend the UN General Assembly in Paris "with the request that the usual passport enquiries be made"—hoping, his memoirs record, to receive information that would "furnish a basis for investigation."[8] He got back forty-two "adverse reports." In June 1949, Lie approached the FBI through a senior UN executive, Byron Price, asking it to supply him with "any derogatory information on American applicants for UN positions."[9] Within three months of that approach, as Shirley Hazzard has recorded in detail in *Defeat of an Ideal*,[10] the U.S. State Department and the UN Secretariat concluded a secret agreement under which all American members of the New York secretariat would be screened without their knowledge. This agreement later became public in the course of the hearings conducted on the "Activities of United States Citizens Employed by the United Nations" by a Senate subcommittee chaired by Senator Pat McCarren.[11]

On December 2, 1952, a federal Grand Jury in New York, which had been investigating communist activities both at the UN and in the United States, reported that "infiltration into the United Nations of an overwhelmingly large group of disloyal United States citizens," was threatening the security of the United States.[12] The Grand Jury issued no indictments. But it demanded that the United States institute clearance procedures, and the government obliged by issuing U.S. Executive Order 10422, which applied thereafter to all U.S. citizens seeking employment anywhere in the UN.

This rule not only violated the spirit of the UN Charter but, as a U.S. court ruled thirty years later, contravened the U.S. Constitution: investigations into a citizen's loyalty interfered, the judgment said, with his right to "unfettered employment with an international organization" and infringed his or her "associational and other First Amendment rights."[13]

Instead of protesting, Lie positively welcomed the order "as giving help I had sought for years." He permitted the FBI to establish an interrogation office on the third floor of the UN building and to install fingerprinting equipment in the basement. And he further cooperated with this McCarthyite witch hunt by dismissing many American employees who declined to cooperate with the FBI's enquiries. Other staff, non-Americans, were also "invited" to the FBI office. The final irony was that, throughout these years of anti-Communist hysteria, the only UN employees to be insulated from FBI probes were—for obvious reasons—Soviet bloc nationals.

This whole episode, which led to the unjustified dismissals of dozens of UN staff and the suicide of the UN's American legal adviser, Abraham Feller, and which, with the creation of the International Organizations Employees Loyalty Board of the United States, spread to all the UN's specialized agencies, had a lasting impact on the character of the UN's secretariats. It established a precedent for government lobbying over staff appointments and promotions and established an informal practice, inimical to the independence of the international civil service, according to which candidates for senior UN jobs were expected to have their governments' backing. The trauma of those years also established habits of political circumspection in the UN's bureaucracies, which stifled innovation and nurtured conformity.

It also damaged the reputation of the United States in a period that otherwise reflected well on its commitment to multilateralism. Senator William Fulbright was later to muse that, in the first two decades of the UN's history, "having controlled the United Nations for many years as tightly and as easily as a big-city boss controls his party machine, we had got used to the idea that the United Nations was a place where we could work our will."[14] But in broad terms, except for the FBI investigations, the work had been creditable. In congressional hearings in 1985, Jeane Kirkpatrick maintained that "the United States lost its influence in the United Nations in the mid-60s. And for 20 years, the United States was not fairly treated inside the United Nations. The democracies generally lost their dominant role to other blocs in the mid-60s. And with that, the United Nations lost its capacity to work for constructive purposes."[15] Such a straightforward equation of U.S. influence with the value of the body it influenced is not a bad example of Shirley Hazzard's "benign unilateralism" hypothesis; but her claim contained at least a measure of truth.

The low point in U.S. influence, when—as Kirkpatrick said on the same occasion with some revelatory exaggeration—"the United States sunk slowly to a position so impotent and isolated . . . that we could not even protect ourselves against the attacks of arrogant dictators who are dependent on us for help," did in practice coincide with the fragmentation of UN activities and a serious decline in the ability of secretariats and member states to exercise the discrimination between areas of possible agreement and areas of deadlock on which the UN's effectiveness and credibility depended.

On March 17, 1970, the United States cast its first veto in the Security Council. In the decade that followed, a certain measure of unease, amounting almost to culture shock, permeated U.S. debate about its standing in the UN General Assembly and its international profile in general. A country accustomed to seeing itself as a liberating and progressive force was finding itself pilloried as an imperialist aggressor—and pilloried not only by its established opponents but by respectable factions among its allies and by a substantial and vocal public within its own borders. Successive U.S. administrations had to grapple with the breakdown of domestic consensus over the Vietnam War and the U.S. "incursion" into Cambodia, with "moratorium" marches in Washington and hostile press analysis culminating in the leak of the Pentagon Papers, while contending in international forums with the challenges to U.S. power and values articulated "new orders" by Third World governments in the name of politics.

The United States's isolation at the UN caused pain and anger. There seemed, as Kirkpatrick was to argue much later, something deeply illogical about the hostility with which the United States was treated in the body it had consciously shaped in its image. True, she conceded, the numbers of nations had trebled since 1945, and most were "unrich, undeveloped, and unhappy" and lacking "experience in the ways of democratic Western liberal values." But that should not have led automatically to attacks on the United States—quite the contrary, in fact, since "their two over-riding concerns are and have been decolonization and development . . . both . . . subjects where the United States is on exactly the same side. . . . We were the first new nation. . . . We have never been a colonial nation. . . . Development? We almost invented development assistance."[16] This was, as we have seen, a misreading of the new nations' priorities, but an understandable one: these were, after all, what Third World speakers at the UN *claimed* were their objectives.

The United States was not, of course, on "the same side" in the new politics then being articulated at the UN, which used development, decolonization, and redistribution of wealth as convenient tools with which to attack the dominance of Western ideas and economic influence. The United States was above all isolated in its indignation in the face of this challenge. Most Western governments reacted with a certain fatalism, tinged with a somewhat paternalistic welcome for the new world of multiple national voices. In the United States, by contrast, politicians, government officials, and academics responded with a torrent of congressional hearings, presidential task forces, and reports by think tanks and study groups devoted to "the future of the United Nations," discussing both the need for institutional reform and new multilateral approaches to global problems such as hunger and the management of the environment.

This debate persisted through periods of official indifference. In 1970, the U.S. permanent representative to the UN, Charles Yost, suggested to President Nixon that to mark the UN's twenty-fifth anniversary (a banal affair that still, in contrast with the fiasco of 1985, did produce a commemorative declaration) he should set up a presidential commission to consider "strengthening" the UN. Nixon agreed. Yost then submitted twenty-five names to the White House, which "sent back a completely different list distinguished by their political value to Nixon and their lack of knowledge of the UN."[17] The fifty-member commission chaired by Henry Cabot Lodge nonetheless produced a serious report, presenting ninety-six recommendations in the areas of peace and international law; economic, social, and environmental questions; and organizational and structural reforms. The only one to be implemented—significantly, under a threat from Congress to take unilateral action if it were not—was the negotiated reduction, from 31.52 percent to 25 percent, of the U.S. contribution to UN budgets. What was still more revealing was that the United States was unable to persuade its European allies, through the Lodge commission, to join in a search for UN reform.

In 1976, as U.S. support for the UN plummeted in the wake of confrontations over a New International Economic Order and, above all, of the General Assembly's resolution 3379 of 1975, which equated Zionism with racism, an Atlantic Council working group was convened under the now retired Yost. The UN, the Council concluded, was now dominated by groups that were asserting themselves "in ways that could lead to disorder and dangerous confrontation." The "basic consensus on political values," needed for serious discussion in the global forums had evaporated.

Resolutely internationalist, the group shrank from the implications of this conclusion, resting its case instead on the platitude that the UN's "imperfections" were the fault of its member states and unanimously recommending that the United States stay in the UN. En route to this conclusion it did, however, give serious thought to the possible reduction of Western financial contributions, the introduction of weighted voting, selective boycott of debates, and partial or complete withdrawal. It agreed that the UN—or more specifically, the UN's political forum, on which it had principally focused—was useless for harmonizing policy between Western nations and "only marginally useful in bridging the East-West gulf." For "concrete action on economic, financial or technical policy" the group advocated reliance on smaller bodies. Strengthened regional coalitions, it felt, could take on more of "the international agenda," and there was a case for "a new concert of the free industrialized nations." Above all, "fixed doctrine about 'working within the UN system' (or 'avoiding the UN') should not stand in the way of practical movement."[18]

Ambassador Moynihan's perception of the UN as "a dangerous place" was beginning to take hold among its natural supporters in the United States. Some of the questions that would resurface under Reagan were already being posed: the difficulty of reconciling Western interests with proposals that were "patently illegal, outrageous, or destructive of compromise"[19] was beginning to be understood. And with these questions went closer scrutiny of mismanagement, corruption, and irresponsible programming in the secretariats. Meanwhile, ironically enough, U.S. government policy was simultaneously being reshaped by the new Carter administration in a conciliatory mold.

President Carter reasoned that the United States had lost international standing as a result of the debacle in Southeast Asia, and could only regain it by visibly demonstrating its attachment to justice and decency, by restoring ethical standards to U.S. foreign policy, and, at the UN, by adopting a conciliatory stance that would contrast as sharply as possible with Moynihan's confrontational style. Carter's choice as U.S. permanent representative was the Reverend Andrew Young, a man publicly committed to putting the United States "on the right side of the moral issues of the world," such as apartheid and Rhodesia, and who tended to assume that where values clashed, there must be something wrong with the Western position. In Washington, the new assistant secretary for international organization affairs, Charles William Maynes, asserted that everything in U.S. multilateral policy had now changed: "the *style*," through Young's "energetic efforts to cultivate leaders in the Third World;" "the *substance* . . . through our recognition that the United Nations is a vital ingredient in the world's business. . . . The *funding* aspect . . . [in that] we have tried to reverse 10 years of decline in American [voluntary] contributions."[20]

Young later recalled with special pride that "during the entire time I was there, we didn't have any embarrassing, condemning resolutions in the Security Council at all, and we had very few in the General Assembly, mainly because we talked to people and we negotiated reasonable language."[21] His deputy, James Leonard, gave as an example of U.S. success its work with the nonaligned, at the first UN Special Session on Disarmament in 1978, "on this great document that they produced . . . which they attached a totally disproportionate importance to." The United States, he said, had decided to "help"; and "in the end we were able to compromise everything—fine language—and it came out as a consensus document."[22] This is what Maxwell Finger, a long-serving member of the U.S. mission to the UN, once described as "the business of making the obnoxious into the meaningless."[23] And, since Carter's honorable ambition of demonstrating through flexibility the depth of the U.S. commitment to the UN and to building, in Young's words, "bridges to the developing world" met with no reciprocal softening of nonaligned positions, Young's readiness to negotiate "reasonable language" contributed to the slow legitimization of views that were inimical to the West.

There was, moreover, more than a touch of paternalism about the Carter administration's approach. Maynes believed that the United States should be "a sympathetic but tough parent, or brother, towards the UN. You don't give this dependent child everything it wants, because it will abuse the affection and the attention. It needs to be both disciplined and supported."[24] Such benign condescension was hardly consonant with making the UN "a vital ingredient in the world's business." There was, in practice, more drift than discipline in U.S. policy, above all at the General Assembly, where the Carter administration failed to translate its genuine commitment to the UN into effective support for the reforms advocated by the group of experts chaired by Richard Gardner,[25] or to open debate on the serious question raised by groups like the Atlantic Council about the future of multilateral cooperation. Failing to address the reasons for the UN's declining stature, administering placebos in the interests of harmony, it managed, against its stated intentions, to take the UN less, not more, seriously than had previous administrations.

The extent of U.S. appeasement of the Third world majority in this period should not however be exaggerated—particularly when its stance on a number of issues (for example, its refusal to allow the inclusion of the Bretton Woods organizations in the agenda for "global negotiations") is compared with those of some of its European allies. European diplomats continued to criticize the United States for pressing confrontation too far, and for refusing to recognize the limits to Western influence. Carter carried out the U.S. decision to leave the International Labor Organization (ILO), and took it back into membership in 1980 only after a number of reforms had been implemented. The United States suspended payments to UNESCO in protest against the exclusion of Israel from the Arab regional group, and joined forces with Britain to fight off some of the most obviously threatening UNESCO proposals for international regulation of the media (although it greatly reduced the impact of this display of firmness by joining in the unanimous reelection of M'Bow in 1980). Carter rightly persisted in negotiating the Camp David accords in the teeth of majority condemnation from the General Assembly. And the United States made serious efforts, against much Third World opposition, to improve the quality and even-handedness of the UN's performance in protecting human rights.

But the general drift of Carter's approach to multilateralism was toward damage limitation, dressed in the language of a campaign to win hearts and minds. Kirkpatrick may have exaggerated in describing this as a period of "pre-emptive capitulation," but the Carter style suggested compromise even where the United States remained firm in practice, and this lent to U.S. policies an aura of well-intentioned incoherence. It was against the background of this atypical phase in U.S. multilateral diplomacy that the uncompromising stances of the incoming Reagan administration acquired some of their shock value.

Style and Substance

In practice, these stances were themselves neither entirely coherent nor, for that reason, easily translatable into policies. The administration insisted on the paramount importance, in Reagan's words, of "the rule of law"; but its antipathy to international regulation was a key factor in its rejection of the Law of the Sea Convention, the most ambitious framework for extending international law yet devised in the history of the UN. The United States set out to fight double standards and to establish benchmarks of principle, while insisting that the yardstick of its attitude to given global institutions would be the U.S. national interest: these objectives were not necessarily consistent. Reagan argued, correctly, that the polarization of the UN had undermined its "worth," and his officials campaigned against the introduction of extraneous political questions into debates on technical issues. But to fight back, through a robust defense of "the values of the Charter" and the interests of the Western world, was inevitably to intensify this polarization. Washington's new intolerance of fudged agreements, while salutory, raised the political temperature.

The Reagan agenda for reform was all-embracing, ranging from the quality of management to the content of programs, from the distortion of UN mandates to the mismatch between voting power and financial contributions; but it was unevenly implemented. The United States inveighed against the corruption and mismanagement in UNESCO but, until late in Reagan's second term, turned a blind eye to failings quite as gross in the Food and Agriculture Organization (FAO), giving the impression that its quarrel with UNESCO was ideological and that, in the absence of such factors, it would tolerate venality. It assaulted, quite rightly, the practices of nepotism and vote- buying that had grown up in the international secretariats, yet demanded more jobs in them for U.S. citizens. It pressed consistently and successfully for a more effective multilateral trading regime: but its advocacy of new powers for the GATT was made against the background of threats, some of which it implemented, to take unilateral action against its trading partners. It declared the politics of consensus bankrupt, while seeking to exploit the mechanisms of consensus to give Western governments something akin to a veto in matters of budgetary growth. It stressed the importance of firm Western positions; but its allies complained that U.S. policy had never been more unpredictable.

What most of them meant was that, with its contempt for the routines of negotiation geared to the art of the possible and its insistence that if business continued as usual the United States might withdraw from some or all parts of the United Nations, U.S. multilateral diplomacy under Reagan was thoroughly destabilizing. Indeed, it was: and it was this, as much as any single element of U.S. policy, that gradually changed the whole tone of discussion about the UN and its agencies, and opened a debate on the future of the postwar machinery for international cooperation. Successive U.S. administrations had complained that U.S. allies left it to fight alone against resolutions or programs to which they too objected, that they declined to use their diplomatic skills and their not inconsiderable influence either to resolve confrontations or to face them squarely. Now, by declaring its freedom to formulate, and act on, its own diagnoses, Washington challenged them to pull together, or risk U.S. dissociation from a wide range of multilateral undertakings.

The aggressiveness with which the administration embarked on its campaigns caused disquiet even among those of its allies who were prepared to give more critical scrutiny to UN organizations. It was one thing to make common cause in crying halt to certain UN activities and management practices, and in contesting the processes by which the Third World abused its voting majority. But few governments wished to be too closely identified, even in a good cause, with an administration whose overall objective they suspected to be the destruction of institutions it had no intention of replacing with other forms of international collaboration. Washington's apparent lack of a positive agenda reinforced the impression that the United States was basically out to create circumstances that justified the untrammeled unilateral pursuit of its national interests.

The American U-turn on the Law of the Sea Convention was a case in point. In 1966, President Johnson, foreseeing the dangers of "a race to grab and hold the land under the high seas," sought to forestall it by securing global agreement that "the deep seas and ocean bottoms are and remain the legacy of all human beings." The United States proceeded to encourage the train of thought that led the UN in 1970 to declare the oceans—the seas and seabed beyond the limits of national jurisdiction—"the common heritage of mankind." The United States entered into agreement with the Soviet Union on the opening of international negotiations, based on that principle. These began at the UN in 1973, on a fully multilateral basis.

By the time Reagan took office the objective had been actively pursued by four administrations, and negotiations on the convention—an enormously complex document containing more than three hundred articles and dealing with everything from the protection of dolphins to the rights of submarines to pass submerged through straits and territorial waters—were nearly complete. In 1980, the United States had joined the consensus agreeing on an "informal text" of the whole, subject to some final adjustments. Ninety percent of its provisions were strongly in the interest of any major trading and military power, although the governments of virtually all the industrialized countries had reservations about the international regime the convention laid down for mining the rich deposits of minerals on the deep ocean bed. In the form proposed in 1980, most believed this regime to be so cumbersome and restrictive as to be unworkable. They had nonetheless agreed that it was time to conclude negotiations; the package as a whole was satisfactory, and they hoped that the details of the mining regime could be improved when they proceeded to set up the International Seabed Authority to be established under the convention.

Such resignation to unsatisfactory ambiguity seems, in retrospect, remarkable. The mining regime was no mere appendage to the Law of the Sea convention: it was its heart. It represented a trade-off that gave the major powers secure rights of commercial and military navigation, in return for their agreement to share the profits from seabed mining—for which they alone were likely to develop the technology and muster the required finance. It was not only profits they were to share. In an unprecedented contractual relationship between private enterprise and the United Nations, an International Seabed Authority would issue companies with operating licenses, in return for which they would be obliged to offer to the authority "parallel" mining sites that they had identified. The authority would mine these on behalf of the United Nations, using technology made available to it by the private consortia.

The concept of international taxation of mining operations and the system for "parallel mining" by the UN had been proposed in 1976 by Henry Kissinger. Like Johnson, he believed that without international control the scramble for the strategically important minerals on the ocean beds would generate political tensions and "eventually, military conflict." The mining consortia were opposed to the terms of the convention, objecting both to the obligatory transfer of technology and to the "extortionate" mining fees to be exacted by the UN. But by 1981, the industry was also broadly agreed that only an international regime would give them the secure title to sites without which, a survey by the U.S. General Accounting Office had confirmed, no bank would be willing to lend the billions involved.

But in March of that year, on the eve of what was supposed to be the final negotiating session and without a word of warning even to its closest allies, the United States announced in a nine-line press release that its delegation could not proceed pending a comprehensive interagency review not only of every provision of the convention, but of the principles underlying it. The announcement was greeted at the UN with loud dismay, but it was quietly applauded by industrialists and by some diplomats. In the view of the principal British negotiator, the United States was "doing something unheard of—which it should have done a long time ago—which is to say we won't have it." The initial assumption was that the decision had been taken on technical grounds.

This was a misreading: the administration's opposition was ideological. For Reagan personally, the idea of a supranational mining authority was anathema. Conservative American critics found a receptive ear when they argued that the convention subjugated U.S. industry to international regulation in the cause, as William Safire put it, of "global socialism." The deep sea mining provisions, they contended, created an embryonic form of world government and set dangerous precedents for international taxation and the compulsory transfer of technology. The Seabed Authority would be the first international organization with income independent of governments—and potentially, as mining developed, financially autonomous. The United States needed no one's permission to go out and mine the seabed. And the supposed bargain was false: customary law provided for most of the rights of navigation embodied in the convention and nobody, in the real world, was going to blow the Sixth Fleet out of the water.

The Law of the Sea negotiations hung fire for nearly a year while administration conservatives and pragmatists argued over the review. In January 1982, Reagan committed the United States to further negotiations on the basis of six principles. The treaty must set no "undesirable precedents"; must set no production ceilings; must not compel technology transfers; must guarantee U.S. companies access to sites; must give the United States effective veto powers over the convention's operation; and must not be capable of amendment without Senate approval. According to its deputy, Leigh Ratiner, the U.S. negotiating team went back to the UN with instructions "to convert the treaty into a 'frontier mining code.'"[26] But, as Ratiner himself was later to record, these instructions were less clear-cut than that would imply. Influential members of the administration, led by Edwin Meese, wanted no further truck with the convention. Ratiner, who believed that agreement could have been reached on U.S. terms, claimed that the instructions from Washington were aimed at preventing agreement—and preventing the negotiation of improvements that might have encouraged other Western governments to sign the convention. "The primary U.S. objective," in his view, "was the eradication of ideological impurity"—an impression reinforced by the U.S. team's introduction, at the eleventh hour, of a fat "green book" of U.S. conditions that gave the president's six points the most restrictive possible interpretation.

The convention was put to a vote at the end of April 1982, the first in an eight-year negotiating history in which all decisions had been reached by consensus. The result was 130 in favor, 4 against (including the United States but no other Western government). West Germany and the United Kingdom—which were in fact just as adamantly opposed to the seabed mining provisions as was the United States—figured among the seventeen abstainers; France and Japan did not. In July, Reagan announced the United States's final decision not to sign: despite "many positive and very significant accomplishments," his six principles had not been met. That was true, but Ratiner was probably right when he said that the real question was more fundamental. At the National Security Council meeting on June 29 at which that decision was taken, Reagan was reported by a participant to have paid little attention to the detailed arguments, doodling for much of the time on a pad. But at the critical moment, he intervened. "You know," he ruminated, "we're policed and patrolled on land, and there is so much regulation, that I kind of thought that when you go out on the high seas you can do what you want."[27]

As in the review of U.S. policy toward the multilateral banks, what rankled most with other countries was this tone of distaste for multilateral order. The Law of the Sea negotiations had been among the most sober and workmanlike ever conducted under UN auspices. They were also seen as a test case for the expansion, by common consent, of international law. For the sake of a convention to which they attached enormous symbolic importance, the Group of 77 had made unusual efforts to accommodate U.S. concerns in the final round, including an offer open to all U.S. consortia of preferential licenses as "pioneer investors." But this did not overcome the key sticking points, technology transfer and taxation. It is doubtful whether at that late stage the seabed provisions could have been modified radically enough to make them viable. What mattered more than such practical concerns (particularly since, for both technological and economic reasons, seabed mining lay some distance into the future) was the evidence that apparently technical reservations were in reality reservations about international regulation in general. The more the Group of 77 insisted on the importance of the precedent being set, the deeper these became—not just in Washington, but in London and Bonn, which were also to decline to ratify the convention. Yet the great bulk of this vast structure of international law was solidly in Western interests. And once the convention was poised to come into force, which it finally did in 1994, the majority of states—including virtually all "straits states"—declared that they intended to challenge American and British assertions of the validity of customary law for freedom of navigation.[28]

What the Reagan administration's reversal of position on the Law of the Sea Convention most clearly indicated at the time, however, was its determination to accept nothing about the United Nations as given. But it was not until December 1983, three months after Reagan's address to the General Assembly, that the implications of U.S. policy finally became clear. The trigger was Washington's formal notice of U.S. withdrawal from UNESCO. The shock with which this announcement was greeted, in Western as well as Third World capitals, in UNESCO and in other UN secretariats, says more about prevailing attitudes to the UN than it does about the United States. It was common knowledge that, even by UN standards, UNESCO was appallingly, and corruptly, managed. Its director-general had packed its management with his cronies, used its funds for patronage, and sustained a nine-year ideological war against the West. He had used an organization created to promote the free exchange of ideas as a launching pad for attacks on Western "cultural imperialism" and politicized practically every area of its activities, even the combating of illiteracy and the protection of ancient monuments. Within the secretariat he had created what a departing assistant director-general for human rights, a distinguished Mexican, described as a "bureaucratic terrorism which has led to total intellectual suffocation."[29]

Ambassadors to UNESCO who attempted to criticize the content of its programs, to demand investigations of waste and suspected fraud, to question the probity of M'Bow's hiring practices, or to contest the rapid growth in the agency's opaquely presented budget were rudely rebuked in public, and thereafter found the director-general's door closed to them. Some found themselves recalled home. The Reagan administration itself received similarly short shrift. When Gregory Newell visited M'Bow in June 1983, in the company of the U.S. permanent representative, Jean Gerard, to tell him that, having calculated the increase in his proposed 1984–85 budget at 25 percent, the United States would not tolerate it, M'Bow lost his temper, telling them that they could not treat him "like an American black who has no rights."[30] The shoddiness of UNESCO's work had meantime become a byword in the UN. By any standard, it had retreated so far from its original purposes as to have become an obstacle to international cooperation.

Yet, while it was privately welcomed by several Western governments as creating decisive pressure for reforms, the U.S. decision was given little public support. It was held to be a mistake—under whatever provocation—to withdraw from any UN organization: the proper course was "to work for reform from within." When efforts during 1984 to forestall the U.S. departure by introducing reforms came to nothing, the United States was blamed by many of its Western allies. The Third World, they argued, could not "make concessions" under duress. This assumed, of course, that any reform of a UN organization constituted a concession from the very countries that stood to benefit most if it were properly focused and better run. Only the Dutch and British governments responded by laying down criteria for reform and warning that their own participation in UNESCO would depend on the results.

In giving the statutory twelve months' notice of withdrawal in December 1983, the United States had stated that UNESCO was the "worst case" and that its decision did not presage withdrawals from other UN organizations. But in March 1984, citing problems that "parallel . . . our experience in recent years in UNESCO" with the politicization of debates, with budgetary growth, and with "statist theories" and "compulsory transfer of technology," the United States demanded a radical overhaul of UNCTAD.

The discussion paper in which the U.S. mission in Geneva set out its criticisms of UNCTAD emphasized that these were "clearly applicable to other elements of the UN system."[31] The paper declared the United States to be "committed" to making multilateral economic cooperation for development function effectively. It addressed "abuses of the process" of North-South dialogue, and the role played in its degeneration by a "willingness to agree to language, and indeed in some cases to appear to be negotiating on substance, for purely 'political' purposes." Agreements reached on that basis, it said, were "leading to unfulfillable expectations and thereby contributing to the deterioration of the climate." As for the UNCTAD secretariat, U.S. criticisms embraced its management, the quality of its research, its interpretation of its mandate, and the manner in which it conducted its business. They included "technically deficient and biased" documents, "wasteful and duplicative programs, questionable financial management, and an inadequate flow of information" to governments, which consequently found it "virtually impossible . . . to make rational decisions on the work program." The organization had ignored requests from the UN General Assembly to set up an internal evaluation unit; and it had failed to identify programs that were "completed, obsolete, of marginal utility or ineffective."

There was no disputing the substance of the U.S. case. When the United States first raised it at a meeting of the OECD's North-South group that January, several European colleagues openly wondered why it was bothering about an organization that had ceased to do any useful work. Once it presented the paper, however, several of the ambassadors in Geneva, including the British, accused the United States of negativism. A European Community response, drafted by the French, admitted the need for reform but said that Western initiatives "should in no sense be considered as a 'war machine' against the G-77 or a questioning of UNCTAD's role" and added pointedly that "it is indispensable that the United States play a role commensurate with its importance and responsibilities. Withdrawal under one form or another, neglect being a form of withdrawal, would damage the organization and international economic cooperation in general."[32]

The real argument was over U.S. intentions. The U.S. deputy assistant-secretary for international economic affairs, Gordon Streeb, claimed that its criticisms were wholly constructive, and that the United States intended to give UNCTAD until the end of 1985 "to pull its act together." But, he said, other countries would "just have to meet our concerns, and take it on trust that in an improved climate we should be more prepared to talk." The United States did not want to leave UNCTAD (which, as Streeb knew, was legally impossible to do: since it was not a specialized agency but came under the umbrella of the UN in New York, the United States would simply put itself in arrears on its obligatory contributions to the UN's central budget if it withdrew from UNCTAD and refused thereafter to pay for it). It would therefore try for reform, and "then take a decision on the next step—and that decision is wide open."[33] At the core of Washington's "concerns" about UNCTAD was not its inefficiency, but its prevailing ideology, which the United States characterized as "paternalistic statism." Streeb openly acknowledged that the United States wanted "to shift UNCTAD's ideology more to the market-place, away from pushing state intervention, exaggerating the roles of governments and multiplying international codes and regulations."

UNCTAD's secretary-general, Gamani Corea, admitted that the organization had lost its élan and was marking time. But he accused the United States—in terms that revealed the extent to which UNCTAD's secretariat had come to see the organization as an advocate of Third World positions—of "wanting us to be less of a nuisance, not to pester the West." It would, he said, continue to do so because the West was "not doing enough."[34]

Just how unproductive this "pestering" had become was illustrated by the 1983 UNCTAD conference in Belgrade, which had ended in the usual stalemate over Third World spokesmen's demands for vastly increased Western aid, and for Western commitments on issues, such as debt relief, which the West considered to be the preserve either of the Bretton Woods institutions or the Paris Club. During that meeting, a serious rift developed between the United States and its European allies. Washington had proposed a new North-South trade round, from which developing countries in general stood to gain and to which they in fact agreed, at the GATT, three years later. But at the same time, it had tried to get the most prosperous (and protectionist) Third World governments, such as Brazil and South Korea, to agree in principle to "graduate" from the Generalized System of Preferences, which exempted developing countries from reciprocity in tariff-cutting negotiations. This eminently reasonable proposition was not only resisted by the countries concerned—supported, in the name of Third World "solidarity," by the Group of 77. The Europeans, for whom a new North-South trade round would mean pressures to lower some of their more indefensible trade barriers, happily joined in criticizing Washington's "incomprehension of the Third World."

In the same spirit, they now criticized U.S. efforts to turn back the clock on "new order" politics at the UNCTAD as unrealistic. The United States returned serve, reserving the harshest criticisms in its discussion papers for its Western allies who it said, needed "to take a firmer, more forthright, and less patronizing attitude" in negotiation. "As long as we continue to accept radical and non-serious proposals as bases for negotiation," it argued, "the more the serious and moderate elements will continue to be shunted aside." The West should be frank about Group of 77 and UNCTAD proposals, should offer alternatives to those which were "gratuitously contentious or economically unsound," and should, if these were rebuffed, refuse to negotiate on the original texts. Failure to react did not prevent confrontation; and uncritical acceptance, "followed by negotiations that lead to artificial results, can and should be regarded by the developing countries as a sign that the developed countries do not take them seriously." The West should henceforth refuse to negotiate on "coercive measures"—such as international codes for shipping or pharmaceuticals industries or rules for the transfer of technology.

Few U.S. initiatives on the UN attracted more hostility—or achieved as much. By the time its next conference convened in 1987, UNCTAD was still far from establishing a contemporary role for itself, but at least it had begun the search. It had cut its documentation by almost half and improved its quality, and it was endeavoring to capitalize on its interdisciplinary mandate to promote discussions rather than negotiations. The seventh UNCTAD, trimmed to three weeks from the customary six, restricted itself to seeking broad agreement on ways to "reactivate" growth and development. The Group of 77 platform, an eighty-seven-point shopping list drafted by Cuba demanding more aid, loans and debt relief, new commodity agreements, and a new global trading order, was quietly set on one side. The final document, although anodyne to a fault, did contain an acknowledgment by Western governments of their duty to pursue "policies to promote stable, sustainable, noninflationary growth," and to open their markets to Third World exports; and by Third World governments, which for once did not blame their countries' poor economic performance on external factors, of the "primary responsibility" of each country for its own development. The Western group acknowledged that debt reschedulings had to be flexible enough to permit governments to plan ahead, and that debt management in general required more innovative approaches. In marked contrast to the confrontations of Belgrade, the conference agreed that restrictive trade and business practices in *all* countries hampered Third World growth. And, despite the Soviet Union's unexpected decision to join the Common Fund for commodities—which was almost certainly motivated by Mikhail Gorbachev's determination to be seen to be playing a "positive" role in the UN rather than by any enthusiasm for the Common Fund itself—there was a marked shift away from emphasizing commodity price controls. UNCTAD, it was finally recognized, would do better to advise governments on ways to improve their processing and marketing, and reduce their dependence on small baskets of commodities. The seventh UNCTAD may not have been the "new beginning" called for by Mahbubul Haq, Pakistan's planning minister of the day and a former senior World Bank official, but it represented a retreat from what Haq had called "the merciless bashing of the North." Dennis Goodman, the State Department official heading the U.S. delegation, later assessed it—with a tinge of regret—as "positive enough to have made it impossible for us to go ahead with getting the organization scrapped."[35]

THE WASHINGTON TEA PARTY

By 1984, at the end of the first Reagan term, the impact of these disparate U.S. initiatives, and of the changed tone of its dealings in the UN General Assembly, had begun to show. In some of the more prudent UN bureaucracies, more care was being exercised both in budgetary growth and in the formulation of programs. External factors—principally the desperation induced in many developing countries by the combination of recession and debt overhang in the early 1980s—had helped to tone down the combativeness of UN debates. But the overall effect of U.S. policies toward the UN would probably have been minimal, had not the U.S. Congress begun to withhold U.S. dues to UN organizations.

The practice predated the Reagan administration. The Kemp-Moynihan amendment of 1979 had prohibited the administration from paying the U.S. share of UN funds for liberation movements, such as the Palestine Liberation Organization. But the sums involved had been minor (and dwarfed by nonpayments to the UN by other states, notably the Soviet Union). The Kassebaum-Solomon amendment of 1985 to the Foreign Relations Authorization Act was in a different league. It compelled the administration to cut its payments to UN organizations by 20 percent, unless and until they changed their budget-fixing methods, which then in most organizations gave countries contributing, between them, less than 1 percent of the budget an absolute majority over the sixteen that contributed over 80 percent. The amendment demanded that countries be given a say proportionate to the size of their contributions—an apparently straightforward insistence on weighted voting in budgetary matters that reflected a much broader discontent not only with the increases in UN budgets, which had, in cash terms, nearly doubled in a decade, but with the way the money was spent.[36]

Nancy Landon Kassebaum, the Kansas senator who initiated the proposal—which was approved in the Senate by 71 votes to 13—was neither an isolationist, nor hostile to the United Nations. But she had been scandalized by the General Assembly's majority decision, at the height of the Ethiopian famine, to authorize the building of a $73 million conference center in Addis Ababa—a decision opposed by the U.S., Dutch, British, and Luxembourg governments. The U.S., she said, was thus bound to pay out $18.5 million to enable African governments "to stand on the twenty-ninth floor and watch the rest of the country starve." And she shared the perception of many members of Congress that the UN bureaucracy was bloated (which it was) and overpaid (which, by 1985, most of its junior and middle-ranking staff had ceased to be). One highly publicized incident brought that long-standing complaint to the surface. Brian Urquhart, a UN under-secretary who had been with the organization since the beginning, retired, took a third of his pension, as he was entitled to do, in capital—and was immediately reappointed as a consultant. The capital sum was large, reflecting his seniority and exceptional length of service; so it would have been had he belonged to the State Department, on which the UN pension fund was modeled.[37] Such niceties were lost on Congress, for which the case—a by no means isolated instance of costly UN "consulting contracts" for retired senior officials—appeared to demonstrate the need to curb the UN's profligacy by resort to the ancient principle of "no taxation without representation."

The effect of the amendment was to compel the U.S. administration to default on its legal obligations to the UN. The impact on the UN General Assembly was predictable. Initially, there was outrage; but as the message sank in that the UN now had to choose between bankruptcy and budgetary reforms, it agreed on December 18, 1985, to set up an eighteen-member "Group of High-Level Intergovernmental Experts to Review the Efficiency of the Administrative and Financial Functioning of the UN." The group, whose mandate[38] was confined to the UN Organization and its dependencies, excluding the specialized agencies, held sixty-seven meetings, and, the following August, issued a report[39] that was extremely critical of the secretariat, whose structure it found top-heavy and plagued by "diffuse lines of authority, accountability and communication." It recommended reducing the staff by 15 percent, eliminating a quarter of the UN's eighty-seven posts at under- and assistant secretary-general level, trimming staff benefits, and consolidating its nine political and eleven economic and social departments. And it tried, but failed, to agree on a new basis for drawing up and voting on the UN's budget.

By the time it reported, the Kassebaum-Solomon amendment was not the only threat to U.S. funding of the UN: there was also the Gramm-Rudman legislation to impose ceilings on the U.S. budget deficit. Between them, these two pieces of legislation appeared to reduce U.S. payments by 70 percent rather than 20 percent. The administration, which at first formally opposed the Kassebaum amendment on legal grounds, although it was well pleased by the leverage it provided, had bowed to Congress and cut $42 million from its fiscal 1987 request for the UN's central budget. By the autumn of 1986, the congressional appetite for cuts had grown. The House proposed cutting the $212 million assessment by $126 million. And in the Senate, a proposal to withhold *all* U.S. contributions until the president could certify that Soviet espionage at the UN had been eliminated, and with it, the Soviet practice of requiring its nationals in the Secretariat to pay the USSR a proportion of their salaries, was defeated only by a narrow margin. It was with great difficulty that the administration managed to pay the UN, which came close to bankruptcy as the year ended, $100 million. The administration was by now compelled to plead with Congress to release funds for the organization whose profligacy and inefficiency it had so severely castigated.

The severity of the congressional backlash brought home to other governments that the U.S. sense of injury was real, and that the UN was considered dispensable as an instrument of foreign policy. Some, at least, of the members of the Group of 77 abruptly realized, in the words of a senior UN official, that "they could not afford to alienate those who paid [for the UN] to the point where survival of the organization would be in jeopardy."[40] As Javier Pérez de Cuéllar himself acknowledged, this political dimension affected more than debates on Capitol Hill. Governments, he said that September, did not see the UN as "viable or credible." The 1986 General Assembly was finally stirred to respond, if not to the broader problem, at least to meeting U.S. demands on the financial side. Under the pressure of cash constraints it set up a special commission to consider the Group of 18's proposals, which would ordinarily have been pigeonholed. And a "gentleman's agreement" was worked out for controlling the regular UN budgets.

Resolution 41/213, adopted on December 19 (three weeks after the General Assembly was supposed to have finished work) was greeted by Reagan as a "sweeping" and "historic" step. That it was not. The resolution was a compromise designed to give major donors effective control while leaving the final decision on UN budgets—as laid down in the UN Charter—with the General Assembly. It also attempted to give governments more influence over UN spending. It required the secretary-general to provide the UN's twenty-one-member governmental Committee for Program and Coordination (CPC) with a detailed, costed plan, the year before the biennial budget came up for approval.

The CPC would submit comments, which the secretary-general was to take into account when drawing up the formal budget the following year. That was in turn to be reviewed by the CPC and by the Advisory Committee on Administrative and Budgetary Questions (ACABQ), another body of experts nominated by governments but serving in their personal capacity. The point of these elaborate procedures was first, to provide for governmental scrutiny at an early stage; and second, to increase the authority of the CPC and ACABQ. These two bodies, on which major contributors were well represented, were to decide on the budget by "consensus." Thereafter, by implication, their decisions were to be rubber-stamped by the General Assembly.

This principle of common consent was an attempt, without moving formally to weighted voting, to meet congressional demands. As a senior U.S. official commented, it was "a formula which gives Malta and the United States a veto on spending—and people can lean on Malta more easily than they can lean on the United States." The two committees were also to set limits to budgetary "add-ons," and to the size of the UN's contingency fund, both of which had been tools used by the General Assembly to increase spending. The U.S. administration responded by promising to seek the resumption of U.S. payments. Congress, which remained skeptical, insisted on tying U.S. payments to presidential "certification" that reforms were being implemented, and by setting its appropriations to the UN in New York for fiscal 1988 and 1989 at $144 million, only two-thirds of its assessed dues. Its skepticism was justified by events: the CPC failed, in September 1987, to agree on the UN's 1988–89 budget, which was passed by vote that December with the United States, Japan, and Australia abstaining.

Having discovered the leverage it could exert, Congress was reluctant to relinquish its hold. The new conditions it attached to U.S. payments, valid until September 30, 1989, permitted the administration to pay only 40 percent of congressional appropriations in the first instance. The next 40 percent would be forthcoming only if the president declared that the "consensus" mechanism was working—and was being "respected by the General Assembly." In the case of a UN specialized agency, the administration was required to certify that "substantial progress" had been made toward budgetary processes in which "sufficient attention is paid to the views of the United States and other member states who are major financial contributors to . . . assessed budgets." The president would also have to certify that the reductions in ordinary and senior staff—15 percent and 25 percent, respectively—recommended by the Group of 18 were on schedule, and that the UN was enforcing the principle that no more than half of the UN employees from any country should be hired on short, fixed-term contracts. (This was directly aimed at the Soviet Union, which regularly "rotated" its nationals, treating them, in violation of Articles 100 and 101 of the Charter, as an extension of the Soviet government. But as we shall see, it was not necessarily a constructive way of dealing with the appalling quality of much of the UN's staff.) The final 20 percent remained subject, even after presidential certification, to a joint veto by House and Senate.

The virtue of these conditions was that they prevented the UN secretariat and its member governments from declaring the crisis over and returning to business as usual. The leverage was genuine. The drawback was that it gave undue prominence to the financial dimensions of what had originally been a much broader, more policy-based American challenge to global organizations. And for some years after that, U.S. contributions to the UN were effectively pegged by the domestic agreement on the U.S. deficit, which limited increases in spending the following year, 1988, to 2 percent across the board.

By this time, the administration was becoming concerned that U.S. arrears were nearing the point at which it could forfeit its voting rights at the UN. In February 1988 the U.S. permanent representative asked Congress to vote these back dues—on the ground that "the initial shock of our withholding created the impetus for reform" but that reform would be "unlikely to take full effect in an organization paralyzed by financial instability." Richard Williamson, the State Department's new assistant secretary in charge of international organizations, told Congress that, with the exception of the FAO, most UN agencies had now met congressional requirements on budgeting.[41] Most had complied with the principle of consensus, ensured special representation for major donors, and set ceilings for the development of future budgets. Governments were gradually reasserting control over secretariats, which could be required to present program priorities and submit budgets to an item-by-item review.

In practice, full funding was not in prospect: by the time the Reagan administration left office in January 1989, the United States owed $520 million in accumulated arrears to the UN and its specialized agencies. The United States was to resume full funding only in 1990—and even then in principle rather than in practice. Since there was no prospect, in 1988, of paying even the current dues in full, the United States was forced, for the first time, to think through its priorities with regard to the UN. In the spring of 1988, it divided UN organizations into four categories for funding purposes. The first comprised the thirty smallest multilateral organizations, which were considered "technical and generally effective"; they were to receive 100 percent funding. In a second category came larger organizations—the International Telecommunications Union, "of over-riding strategic importance and recognized effectiveness"; and the International Atomic Energy Agency (IAEA), the World Health Organization (WHO), the World Meteorological Organization (WMO), the International Civil Aviation Organization (ICAO), and the GATT, considered "particularly effective, well-managed and of critical importance." They, too, were eligible for full funding. A third cluster included organizations that the administration would have liked to fund fully and that were thought to serve U.S. interests, but that did "not command the same level of . . . attention" or offer "the same level of effectiveness": among these were the ILO and the UN Industrial Development Organization (UNIDO). Into the last category went the UN itself and the FAO, which were described as "organizations which have been the least responsive to United States calls for budgetary controls or other U.S. concerns." Contributions to the FAO had been entirely suspended in calendar 1987, and the UN had received only 75 percent of the sum appropriated by Congress in 1988. There was a difference between this review and the one with which the Reagan era had begun. The first review had been launched with the aim of evolving a radical new U.S. strategy for global organizations; the second was in essence dictated by financial constraints. The difference reflected a change in official thinking. By 1988, the enthusiasm even for selective withdrawals from parts of the UN had become muted—partly by external factors (most notably improved relations with the Soviet Union, which was pushing for an expanded role for the UN), partly through simple loss of élan. The Reagan challenge, which looked at first as if it would either transform or destroy them, had become no more than a pendant to the problem of reforming the global institutions. Even so, it had exerted for a time the most powerful single pressure for reform in the UN's history, even redefining the terms in which reform could henceforth be described. More governments were prepared to ask where, and even whether, the global institutions furthered their national interest. And this was healthy: the relative immunity of the UN from such down-to-earth considerations had been a factor in its marginalization.

PLAYING THE GAME

The next chapter in U.S. policy seemed likely to be written in terms of continued, if critical, membership of UN institutions. While admitting that the United States had not yet formulated its participation in positive terms, a senior official argued in 1988 that the Reagan administration had at least achieved "a far-reaching change of tone in the conduct of UN business." That was the more important, he conceded, because

> on the larger [political] game, we can't get out, can't leave our real interests undefended. It is not true that the damage done when we aren't there is damage we don't have to worry about. The Europeans don't conduct this game very well without us. So if we are not getting out, we have to play the game well. That is why we have shifted the emphasis, to insist that the game has to be fair, that there must be constitutional restraints to see that nobody abuses their power, compensatory structures to enforce a certain respect for the minority.[42]

His point about "constitutional restraints" had implications that, however, reached well beyond linking voting rights to financial contributions, or the "manageability" of organizations that then had at least 160 theoretically equal governors and was soon to have many more—or even institutional streamlining, badly though the global organizations stood in need of it. The main and by no means securely anchored "outcome" of U.S. nonpayments—the establishment of a procedure for setting budgets by common consent—did no more than provide a tool for imposing zero growth. What was now needed was a careful review of the factors that underlay the West's determination to put a ceiling on UN spending, with a view to directing money where it would most usefully be spent. The unilateral actions taken by the Reagan administration and the U.S. Congress had underlined the need for more serious reflection about what types of global cooperation were possible or desirable—and whether there might not be merit in an *à la carte* approach that singled out the best UN "investments."

Such a process would require much closer collaboration between the key donor governments. A beginning was made in the last year of the Reagan administration. The

United States and Great Britain, as cochairmen of the Geneva Group of the main Western contributors to UN budgets, obtained the backing of Japan, West Germany, Canada, and Australia for a series of policy reviews, to include the quality of programs as well as management questions. The aim was to maximize Western capacity to influence UN activities, by reactivating an aspect of the group's original mandate, the monitoring of "program development," which had been allowed to lapse. The paper prepared by the cochairmen for the meeting in March 1988, which launched this initiative, differed in another important respect from previous Geneva Group custom. Drafts had been circulated for discussion by the missions based in Geneva, and by bureaucrats in capitals; but the final text, instead of seeking consensus, included all proposals that had broad support without trying for unanimity.

In addition to the main paper, individual governments produced studies on different aspects of the problems facing the UN. The British dealt with "political malaise," the Italians with the familiar question of overlapping mandates and duplicated efforts, Canada with possible strategies for involving governments in the identification of priorities by secretariats, and West Germany with ways to compel organizations to set aside contingency funds to protect them against nonpayment of contributions and currency fluctuations.

This was a promising start, and a distinct improvement on the Geneva Group's previous concentration on zero growth and its half-hearted and unimplemented agreement to impose a two-term limit on UN executive heads. But the catalysts for this advance on damage limitation were negative. The first was the realization by U.S. allies that in the absence of more far-reaching reforms to the UN, it would be difficult to get Congress to authorize payment of U.S. dues. The second was that the limitations to a purely reactive strategy had been exposed by the fact that the West had failed to impose change on the UN Food and Agriculture Organization. The FAO's director-general, Edouard Saouma, had been reelected in November 1987 for a third term, although the West had what it thought was a good (and African) candidate and although France was the only notable maverick in an otherwise unusually united and firm Western front. It was a humiliating end to a confrontation that had been building up for nearly a decade.

Since the latter part of the 1970s, shifting Western coalitions had made periodic attempts to control the FAO's spending, curb its empire-building, and find out how it spent its money. Saouma had circumvented them all. His task had been made easier in the early years by Western division, and lack of persistence. In 1981, the year the Geneva Group adopted the principle of zero growth, six of its eleven members voted for or abstained on an FAO budget based on 8.5 percent real growth. And the dissenting governments, in a repeat of the Western performance at UNESCO a year earlier, had then joined the unanimous decision to give Saouma a second term. They did so even though it was by then clear that, as Richard Gardner put it from the perspective of a veteran of UN reform and former U.S. ambassador to Italy, "the UN system's capacity to deal with food issues [was] threatened" by the West's bad relations with Saouma in particular, and by the general chaos created by the involvement of no fewer than twenty-nine different UN organizations in food and agriculture.[43]

The policy issues would have been difficult to address even with a cooperative director-general and a united Western front. And the West was no match for Saouma even at the tactical level. Saouma's method for dealing with criticism was counterattack—not, as a rule, in person, but through speeches that his secretariat drafted and gave Third

World delegates to produce as their own. Their rewards were jobs in the secretariat, consultancy contracts, or allocations to their countries of funds from the Technical Cooperation Program, a pool of FAO money on which no detailed accounts were provided and which was disbursed at the director-general's discretion.

The African famine of 1984–85, which exposed the inadequacy of an "early warning system" set up by the FAO after the Sahel famine of 1973–74, prompted a second effort at reform. The FAO stood indicted on two counts. The first was that its systematic advocacy of massive food aid, while popular with African governments, had deepened African dependence on food imports even in normal years. The second was that its penchant for putting countries on the FAO list of "calamity-affected" states, when they were known by Western donors to have had good or near-normal harvests, had destroyed its credibility as an assessor of impending famine. In 1984, the FAO had put twenty-four African countries on this list; yet in Ethiopia, where famine really threatened, the warning system failed. The first realistic FAO assessment of Ethiopia's food needs was produced only at the end of 1984, nine months after the Ethiopian government had launched its first international appeal and well after the BBC's harrowing October broadcast from Korem, north of Addis Ababa, had rung alarm bells around the world. And it was the same in Sudan. In May 1984, the U.S. embassy in Khartoum estimated that half that year's harvest would be lost due to drought, and started massive shipments of emergency food aid; yet five months later, the country still did not figure on the FAO's crisis list.

The FAO had never been thought of as an emergency relief unit. But it was supposed to provide reliable information, and it had not only not done so, but had ignored warnings from its member governments. The Canadians, for one, had tried in vain to convince Saouma of the gravity of the situation in Ethiopia in the late spring of 1984, when Ottawa unilaterally doubled its food shipments to that country. They then learned from the head of Ethiopia's Relief and Rehabilitation Commission that at a meeting in June 1984, the FAO director-general had indicated to him that cooperation with Ethiopia would be difficult unless the government agreed to recall its junior delegate to the FAO, Tesema Negash, whose "loyalty" to the organization was considered "unsatisfactory" by Saouma. The suspicion that the director-general was prepared to put politics before the relief of suffering was compounded by his refusal, until it was clear that the FAO's rival emergency appeal had no support, to cooperate with the Office for Emergency Operations in Africa set up by the UN at the end of 1984. At the FAO General Conference in 1985, a sustained barrage of criticism both of the handling of the African emergency, and of the way in which the FAO was run, came from Canadians, Scandinavians, and British delegations. And for the first time, some of these criticisms were echoed by a small handful of African delegates.

The whole scandalous business outraged the Nordic countries, which in 1986 officially informed Saouma that they were launching a major joint assessment of the FAO's operations and future direction. Saouma refused to cooperate. The Scandinavians then joined forces with other Western countries in the Camberley group—an informal coalition of a dozen countries seeking radical reform of the FAO, convened on the initiative of Great Britain and Canada and named after the location outside London of its first meeting.

This group established some important precedents for Western policymaking in the UN context. It was composed of senior home-based officials, to keep it free of the pressures exerted on missions to the FAO in Rome. It excluded those Western governments—France and, until 1987, the United States (whose ambassador to the FAO at the time,

Millicent Fenwick, was an ardent Saouma supporter[43])—which were not thought to be committed to reforms. It carried out serious analyses of the organization's failings, coordinated the findings carefully, and prepared a long-term strategy for reforms.

All this careful preparation failed, at the 1987 FAO conference, either to prevent Saouma's reelection by a resounding majority, or to secure serious reforms. The much-respected Scandinavians, acting for the group, put forward a proposal to subject the FAO's operations and policies to external scrutiny. That was sidetracked by the conference majority, and a demand by the United States, a midnight convert to the reformers' camp, that governments should be involved in the preparation of budgets and should approve them by "consensus," was roundly rejected. A new budget was then voted through against United States, Canadian, Australian, and British opposition—prompting Britain and Canada, traditionally firmly opposed to nonpayment of UN dues, to delay their contributions by a calendar year. At the invitation of scandalized Nordic countries, who had expected their excellent standing with most developing countries to carry the day, the Camberley group reconvened early in 1988. But the experience had demonstrated that reform would require a long campaign and fresh strategies—and at the FAO, they recognized that serious work would have to wait until 1993, the next opportunity to remove Saouma.

So in 1988, the question was how, short of nonpayment of dues, which was illegal, or threats to withdraw, which few countries were prepared to contemplate, Western governments could exert leverage. They evidently needed more detailed analyses of the organizations' performance and a strategic view of their potential uses. The point had been driven home not only at the FAO but at UNESCO, where in the near absence of Western strategic thinking, reforms attempted in 1984 had achieved almost nothing and where, in 1988, the occasion to persuade the new director-general, Federico Mayor of Spain, to carry out a thorough housecleaning was being missed. Western governments proved unwilling either to put real effort into salvaging UNESCO, or to decide that it was of no consequence and draw the appropriate conclusions. Only in the GATT, as the Uruguay Round got under way after 1986, was there solid evidence of a general will to improve the functioning of a "global" organization—and the GATT was neither fully integrated into the United Nations, nor, although its membership swelled rapidly as the round proceeded, a universal forum.

As for New York, the small window of opportunity created by financial crisis was steadily being filled with the cotton-wool of procedural argument over minor incremental changes. The Special Commission set up to carry on the work of the Group of 18 had wasted endless time in fruitless debate on trimming the government committee structures at the UN. It wound up its "work" in May 1988 with, in the measured view of the Nordic countries

> a report characterized by a conspicuous lack of agreement, especially between the group of industrialized countries and the group of developing countries. There were differences of opinion on the orientation of reforms, in addition to which the developing countries were unwilling to commit themselves to any discussion of reform as long as the U.S. withheld its assessed contributions. There was agreement in principle that several bodies should be abolished or merged with other bodies. But there were differences of opinion in both groups as to which bodies should be affected. . . . Developing countries made it a condition [of any reforms] that membership of ECOSOC should

> be universal, a condition that was unacceptable to the industrialized countries (and many developing countries as well). Several member states have declared that the process must continue. But the support for reforms has so far been insufficient.[45]

In the Geneva Group, the United States soldiered on, arguing that much could still be done at the level of officials. In each agency, it suggested, the group could set up a working party of the most experienced permanent representatives to assess the organization's strengths and weaknesses, analyze its programs, and plot future strategy. A UN-wide scale of Western priorities could then be drawn up, taking into account each organization's ability to contribute to cooperation in given areas, and adjusting financial support accordingly. That made sense. If the bureaucrats were to convince their political masters that new approaches to the global organizations might be worth backing, they would have to map out some reasonably clear ideas about what these organizations had to offer.

Even then, action would depend on reducing the frictions between Western governments, whose approaches to multilateral diplomacy differed widely. The Reagan administration had been successful in opening up, and radicalizing, Western debate on the global organizations; but there was no doubt that its approach had exacerbated long-standing transatlantic tensions over the proper approach to multilateralism.

There was, first, the problem of differing styles. When they heard the United States insisting, rightly, on the importance of principles, of fidelity to the Charter's affirmation of enlightened consistency in the conduct of human affairs, Europeans tended to react with skepticism and embarrassment to what they saw as a rallying of the language of morality to the service of U.S. power.

It is a broad but fair generalization to say that Americans take rhetoric in such forums more seriously than do Western Europeans, who, for example, tend to abstain on resolutions they find repugnant, unless they expect them to have significant consequences. Insofar as there is an identifiable European trait, it is to prefer what will work to what ought to be; Europe's political traditions are marked by a strong disinclination to couple diplomacy with morality. There are exceptions to this, of course, that take the Europeans themselves by surprise: in 1989, Ayatollah Khomeini's *fatwa* against the author Salman Rushdie, an international murder warrant, so flagrantly violated human rights and international law that European reactions were speedy, unanimous, and only slowly eroded by the desire of governments such as Germany to land fat Iranian contracts. Traditionally, however, Europeans have responded to the diet of UN rhetoric with markedly greater *sangfroid* than has the United States.

Among Europeans, the British have taken the UN General Assembly relatively seriously. But their definition of seriousness differs from the Americans'. In 1975, for example, within a week of the adoption of the UN resolution declaring Zionism to be "a form of racism," Ivor Richard, the British permanent representative to the UN, bluntly criticized Ambassador Moynihan's denunciation of this singularly repugnant statement as unduly moralistic. Britain, said Richard, treated the UN as "a major instrument of her foreign policy"—but it was realistic. The art was *not* "to take on those countries whose political systems and ideology are different from mine. . . . There is nothing whatever to be gained by ideological disputations of the most intense sort which one is probably going to lose anyway or at best end up with a rather unsatisfactory intellectual statement. My function is to use the United Nations, not to purge it."[46] For Richard, the most significant aspect of the Zionism-equals-racism vote was not what the resolution said, but that the vote pointed to the emergence of cracks in the alliance between the Africans and the Asians. Contempt for facts and deliberate insults evidently did not, for Richard, detract from the value of the United Nations as an instrument "to use."

When Western Europeans admit a moral dimension to multilateral diplomacy, it has traditionally been of an intrinsically different kind, based loosely on four tenets: that morality resides more in the acceptance of difference than in insistence on universal values; that the West's moral capital rests in part on its readiness to acknowledge its imperfections—whether seen through the prism of its colonial past or from the standpoint of economic inequalities; that European states that no longer possess significant global power should be reticent in propounding moral absolutes; and that moral stances are of limited use in seeking agreement between more than 180 states. There is a reluctance to admit that the erosion of the Charter's principles might weaken international cooperation. Insistence on defending "mere words" appears to most European diplomats arrogant, and doomed to failure.

This difference of perspective has been at times so marked as to give the impression that "European policy," insofar as there is such a thing, is largely about mitigating the excesses in UN forums of Europe's embarrassing friend, the United States. This was a fairly constant theme from the time of John Foster Dulles, and the resurgence under President Carter of the "moral dimension" in U.S. policy, ridiculed in Europe as "open mouth diplomacy," was greeted with some embarrassment. Reagan's very different moral call to arms embarrassed too, but differently: it appeared altogether too Manichean for comfort, too rigidly intolerant, for example, of any argument that did not accept the most intimate link between liberty and free enterprise. Even though by the end of the 1980s Reagan, while no intellectual, had come to seem ahead of his time—as the language of the marketplace gained currency from Accra to Ulan Bator and the Soviet empire he had called evil dissolved—the mantle of moral crusade in which his policies had been clothed diminished some of the support that Western Europeans might have been expected to give to arguments with which most of them quite largely agreed.

The contrast can of course be overstated. The actions of Western governments differ less from the United States than does the rhetoric with which they present them. U.S. governments are not immune to the double standards they deplore—expressing their devotion to the ideals of the Charter while pursuing bilateral or regional policies that are at variance with them. There are *chasses gardées*: the United States prevented Vietnam from being debated at the Security Council, and Central America is to a large extent an American diplomatic fiefdom—but then, much the same might be said of France in relation to Francophone Africa. Britain, after its brilliant marshalling of international support at the UN over the Falklands, had no compunction about rejecting subsequent UN involvement in Anglo-Argentinian relations. But it remains broadly the case that, for much of the time since 1945, Washington has doubted the seriousness of its allies' multilateral diplomacy: while they, for their part, have wished that the United States could refrain from expressing its own seriousness in moral imperatives. Under the strain of the direct Third World challenge to Western interests at the UN, these irritations became more acute. Europeans were inclined to distrust the somewhat greater U.S. willingness to pursue objectives more ambitious than damage limitation, attributing it either to great-power arrogance, or to naivete.

Substance as well as style militated against a unified Western stance. Countries' national interests differed along with their size, their geographical location, and their separate histories. For West Germany and Japan, losers in the war and (along with the more detached Italians) latecomers to the UN, membership offered proof of international respectability and a theater in which to manifest their now-impeccable world citizenship. Their apparent reluctance to use the weight that their immense economic power could have given them in global forums was a source of irritation to the United States—although Washington took time to adjust to the idea of increased Japanese status in the Bretton Woods institutions, finally endorsing it only in 1990.

For the French, the UN remained an essentially Anglo-Saxon set of institutions—"ce machin," General de Gaulle had contemptuously called the UN, a thingamajig to be used but never relied on. France's attitude was most clearly exemplified by its reaction to the crisis at UNESCO. Virtually every member of the French government and establishment maintained a sphinxlike silence as UNESCO disintegrated in the shadow of the Eiffel Tower. The reason is not hard to find: UNESCO did not have to be well or even honestly run to be an effective tool of Francophone policy, an extension of France's cultural (and political) "mission civilisatrice." And above all, France had no interest in quarreling with a Senegalese director-general.

To many governments, in the West as well as the developing world, the Reagan challenge had come more as a threat than an opportunity. Even the "Anglo-Saxon club" was far from united on the subject. It was, for example, a matter of special pride to Canada that *its* segment of North America was capable of productive dialogue with the developing world. Canada's diplomats could be forthright and tenacious in specific cases; but it attached as much importance to its bridge-building image as did the Scandinavians.

Yet the Reagan challenge nevertheless had its effect. The international response to the congressional withholding of funds was surprisingly muted: it was tacitly acknowledged that it had helped to force the pace of necessary change. Japan's unexpected insistence on the creation of the Group of 18 in 1985 to investigate the UN's financial and administrative problems certainly reflected its prominence as a donor (it overtook the Soviet Union in assessed contributions to the UN the following year, to lie in second place after the United States). Yet it is unlikely that Japan would have shed its customary reticence in a different climate.

The unilateralist fervor with which the Reagan administration launched its revolt against what it saw as the defeatism of the West in the face of degenerate institutions and the "tyranny of the majority" exercised in their forums had subsided by 1988. But by then, the prospects for a collective Western approach had improved. The "relevance" of the global organizations was no longer a taboo subject; it was a shared concern. Even if the habit of considering the United Nations synonymous with multilateral diplomacy, and therefore sacrosanct, remained deeply rooted in the political and bureaucratic consciousness, a spirit of iconoclasm was abroad. The small or neutral countries, for which the UN was actually as well as formally a pillar of national foreign policy, had been genuinely afraid that to attempt fundamental reforms would, should the attempt fail, fatally weaken structures they knew to be fragile. Yet it was a group of these countries, the Scandinavians, who were to emerge from this period as the impassioned advocates of far-reaching reforms to the development activities of the UN, which they funded with a generosity out of all proportion to their size and wealth.

Meanwhile, shifts in Soviet policy—and developments in Eastern Europe—were beginning to undermine the ancient alibi for inaction—the excuse that the sterility of so much UN debate mirrored the sorry state of mankind. In this less rigid world, there was fresh scope for assessing what organizations of states could realistically offer, in the context of a new modesty about the domestic roles of the state. Imagination is generally slow to catch up with change, and policy slower still. But the Reagan challenge had acted as an accelerator, and at the right moment. The 1990s were to present the UN with unlooked-for opportunities. But so deeply ingrained are the bad habits and institutional follies of nearly half a century that new variants on the old interplay between governments and institutions clearly cannot bring about its regeneration. The United Nations will be hard-pressed to adapt to a suddenly very fast-changing global polity.

IV

BEYOND UTOPIA

9. Ways Ahead: The Options

Points of Departure

Efficiency is not, of course, the only criterion by which the United Nations should be assessed. Treated, to borrow from La Rochefoucauld, as "the tribute which vice pays to virtue," to affirm commitments to certain moral codes, the UN serves a purpose even in the absence of a common interpretation of the vocabulary. However unedifying may be the spectacle of the "international community" giving polite audience to dictators calling for "a new humanitarian order" (as did Imelda Marcos while she and her husband were still rifling the Philippines both of money and of elementary human rights), hypocrisy is a dynamic force for the modification of government policy. However inadequately the United Nations Commission for Human Rights performs, it remains at least a potential point of pressure on governments. The world would be marginally worse off without some such mechanism, and here the slenderest marginal benefit may be worth defending.

But when hypocrisy extends to the substance of multilateral cooperation, and broad "strategies" for sustainable growth, the promotion of literacy, or the management of debt gloss over deep-seated differences as to the desirability or relevance of a particular course of action, global organizations become part of the problems they were created to address. This reflexivity has been exacerbated at the UN by organizational aggrandizement, where ambitious UN barons assert their "stake" in a particular problem in order to expand their empires. Governments in turn have fed this process by demanding the launch of global campaigns, even when they are far from agreed either on their objectives, or the resources required. Conferences then foster rigidity rather than flexibility in national positions; paper commitments devalue the process of conciliation. Governments with the capacity to act look elsewhere.

The rhetoric of multilateral diplomacy will always be somewhat more fulsome than the substance. That governments use the United Nations only when the limitations of a unilateral or regional approach outweigh the frustrations involved in activating global machinery should be obvious, and untroubling. That some governments exploit it as a platform from which to blame "external factors" for their domestic problems is not surprising, given the intractability of the political and economic dilemmas confronting so many states. That they continue to use it, out of habit, even where they are no longer convinced of the comparative advantages of acting multilaterally, should be seen as a profoundly troubling symptom of debility. When, as began to happen in the 1980s and will be even more the case in the 1990s and beyond, they are increasingly improvising alternatives for negotiation and cooperation, even where an issue clearly has global implications and the UN provides, in theory, the appropriate vehicles, it can paradoxically be a healthy sign, because it means that governments are putting the objectives of cooperation before institutional niceties.

When the five permanent members of the Security Council (and, in particular, the United States and the Soviet Union) began regular consultations over regional disputes in 1987, the United Nations appeared to be recovering some of its long-lost prestige—an impression naturally promoted by the UN secretary-general, who proclaimed in his 1988 annual report on the "Work of the Organization" that "the vessel has come within sight of large sections of the shore."[1] Such confidence was, to say the least, premature. The major powers *were* working better together and that, as Javier Pérez de Cuéllar said, created "new possibilities for successful action by the world body." But they remained "possibilities." In practice, as he acknowledged, most of the diplomatic running in the period in question, from Afghanistan to Namibia, had been made outside the UN. There was nothing inherently wrong with this, but the fact remained that *within* the United Nations, progress on these regional conflicts would still at that time have been impossible. "The United Nations," the secretary-general stated, "does not seek, and was never meant to seek, any kind of diplomatic autarky"—a welcome assertion and one much at odds with the rhetoric of decades. What mattered, he said, was that diplomacy between governments "should help realize the aims that it has defined" so that "all relevant points of diplomatic contact and influence in the network of multilateral relationships can be coherently drawn upon to achieve the objectives of peace."

So far, so good. But he went on to say that the United Nations offered all countries, great and small, a forum where they could "take a lead in framing the universal agenda, draw attention to new concerns and new ways of solving problems." Such exaggeration does the United Nations no service.

We have passed the point at which governments can be expected to treat with respect either exhortations to take seriously forums and procedures that they find self-canceling, or statements, such as the above, that they do so. Pretensions outstripping its capacities can only bring the machinery into contempt. Even Pérez de Cuéllar, while confident that "the crucial role of the Organization in the political sphere" had been reestablished, recognized that, as he euphemistically put it, "the question of how best to utilize its capacity to find integrated solutions to economic and social issues in all their aspects still remains subject to debate."

Even supposing this to be a valid objective—no *national* government would make such grandiose claims—it bears little relation, as we have seen, to the actual use governments make of the global forums. Even as a political experiment, the concept of universality has lost much of its momentum. Governments are tempted to bypass forums that have grown to unmanageable size and that lack ideological cohesion or judicial common ground—hence, in the 1990s, the relative downgrading of the General Assembly, to be discussed in Chapter 11, in the context of the increase in great power cooperation. And the UN's relevance to economic and social cooperation has, in the broad-brush terms employed by the secretary-general, become marginal at best. The donor governments have begun, quite reasonably, to ask whether the expenditure of national energies on today's complex web of organizations and interminable succession of conferences is justified. An enterprise on a far more modest scale would still preserve those parts of the UN that they routinely use—its regulatory service agencies such as the International Civil Aviation Organization, offices for humanitarian assistance such as that of the Office of the UN High Commissioner for Refugees (UNHCR), or the Bretton

Woods institutions—and those, like the Security Council, which they will use to reinforce bilateral diplomacy or, *in extremis*, when that breaks down.

The renewed efforts in the 1980s to make UN secretariats more efficient and accountable, and to give the major contributors more weight in budgetary decisions, did not address the UN's most pressing need for economies: those at the conceptual level. Cutting the quantity of cloth without redesigning the coat is a policy with obvious limitations. What, then, given the lessons of past experiments, are the possible ways forward?

It could be argued that once UN organizations find "new, relevant themes—such as the connections between employment, adjustment and growth—the institutional problems will arrange themselves."[2] But it is difficult, for a number of reasons, to escape "institutional problems." The first is the legacy of distrust. When Francis Blanchard sought in 1987 to revitalize the International Labor Organization (ILO) with this theme, he explicitly, and logically, envisaged closer collaboration between the ILO and the International Monetary Fund (IMF). But to a number of governments, led by the United States, Great Britain and West Germany, this looked suspiciously like a bit by the ILO to step outside its mandate, and Blanchard's plans were politely interred. Second, even the most auspicious themes require organizations capable of converting them into coherent work plans. The sectoral character of UN specialized agencies, and the hallowed practice of involving every member state equally in the endorsement of policy, militate against such coherence. Finally, it is hard to ensure that grand designs such as Blanchard's can be made equally relevant to countries as disparate as Burma and Brazil. Even where problems are global, solutions, *pace* the secretary-general's ruminations in 1988, rarely are.

Yet at the same time, it is undoubtedly true, as Blanchard maintained, that "there is no hope of a debate which centers on UN management leading to the recommitment of major donors, without which the UN cannot operate."

National policymakers need some starting point from which to tackle this chicken-and-egg dilemma about the future of the United Nations within the larger framework of multilateral diplomacy. Four possible options are sketched out in the following pages, principally with the major donors in mind. These are the governments that have the responsibility for thinking through fresh approaches because, for all their minority status in voting terms, they have the capacity to act on them.

The first approach could be described as opting out, the second as structural reform, the third as façade management, and the fourth as a policy of selective action, building on what works best. None is wholly exclusive of the others. Even opting out would imply some degree of structural reform of the machinery for international cooperation, to provide a new framework. Building on what works would involve a judicious counterpoise of façade management and selective opting out. The chances are that a policy of façade management would lead gradually toward opting out, and conversely, that if selective action scored some clearly identifiable gains, that would help to create a climate in which structural reforms appeared more attainable. They are sketched here as alternative models of possible points of entry. The eventual shape of multilateral cooperation will be determined by the angle of approach.

OPTING OUT

This is not, in this century, a course politicians are likely to follow, but it is becoming less and less unthinkable. In the 1980s, for the first time, governments left individual UN organizations, not in order to create pressures for reform, but because they regarded membership as a pointless waste of money: Singapore left UNESCO on that ground in 1985, Australia gave the UN Industrial Development Organization (UNIDO) notice in 1987, and Great Britain came within a whisker of withdrawal a few years later. Some clubs, such as the International Telecommunications Union (ITU), are indispensable. But nobody doubts that these clubs—with the single exception of the Security Council—would survive, UN or no UN; and there is a strong case for arguing that they would function better as free-standing entities.

Major powers still feel that by wholesale withdrawal they would be shirking their international responsibilities; small powers still cling to the belief that there is safety in numbers. But for how long? The 1990s ushered in a new optimism about the UN as a political organization; but there persists an undercurrent of skepticism about the utility of much of the rest of the universal machinery, and the doubts are not confined to conservative or unilateralist circles. The perceptions of the UN as "fragile, ancillary and problematic," a contract about whose "survival, let alone its efficiency, there is some doubt,"[3] go back more than a quarter of a century. Calls for "far more radical pruning . . . of the central global institutions than is today being contemplated," and the abandonment of an "inefficient universalism" that drains the manpower resources of small states and encourages the rich to go elsewhere, are no longer controversial.[4] Blunt assertions that governments should "let it sink"[5] are still the exception, but in the absence of a serious revitalization of the UN's claims to governments' allegiance, the allure of such absolute propositions could eventually overcome routinized pieties and political inertia.

The governments on whose membership the UN depends for its survival might then argue that the Charter had become a minority document. The basis for universal associations of nation-states no longer existed: there was neither a genuine common commitment to such fundamental premises for the organization of society as the separation of powers, respect for basic human rights, and the rule of law; nor a common capacity to live up to those commitments through effective national institutions. In such circumstances, they might argue that reliance on the UN to keep the peace was a dangerous fiction. Deprived of its sheet anchors, "universality" had become a hindrance to the effective containment of conflict and to control of other areas of friction. Both in the Security Council and the General Assembly, the involvement of all states in all conflicts, even those in which they had no conceivable direct interest—encouraging Botswana to pronounce on Afghanistan or Fiji on the rights of Palestinians—complicated the search for solutions. Discreet pressures on belligerents by coalitions prepared to pool their credit with the respective parties stood at least as good a chance of success as megaphone diplomacy by "the international community." Assistance in resolving internal conflicts, effecting transitions from dictatorship to democracy, and even disengaging exhausted belligerents, could be provided with less fanfare by observer groups or peacekeeping forces chosen by coalitions capable of extracting the assent of the contending parties.

Proponents of opting out might argue that Western governments had no conceivable interest in paying for organizations in which it was heresy to suggest that a country's role should reflect its influence in the world outside, in which the application of double standards weakened respect for human rights, in which the values that inspired their creation were continually attacked, and in which the intrusion of controversies extraneous to the agenda sabotaged the pursuit of cooperative activities. They might conclude that the removal of the UN umbrella was unlikely to weaken the authority of international standards and agreements: countries would adhere to them where it was in their interest to do so, much as before, and umbrellas that collapsed in the rain conveyed a false sense of security. They might argue that with fewer "global missions" and vague catchall objectives such as "human resources development," the world would be freer to form *ad hoc* coalitions for specific tasks. They might, finally, reason that their membership in the UN served to legitimize the illegitimate. It conveyed international respectability on governments whose usurpation of power made a nonsense of the concept of national self-determination and which, in any serious interpretation of the Charter, ought to be pariahs; and financing of UN development programs, far from being neutral and humanitarian, reinforced the grip of repressive and corrupt elites on their subjects' lives.

Many politicians think some of these things some of the time already. The line of least resistance, whether damage-limitation or budget-capping, begins to look inadequate at best, and ultimately corrupt and wasteful of time and talent. The prospect of continuing to court vilification by the majority for attempting to ensure that these organizations provide their members with better services gradually loses its appeal. Those who can choose are likely to canvass multilateral or bilateral alternatives with increasing candor. And these alternatives do exist, actually or potentially. During the years when debates on South Africa ran to stereotype inside the UN, outside the UN Western assistance to enhance the economic well-being of the nine "front-line" states within the Southern African Development Coordination Conference (SADCC)[6] was developing solid momentum—not that this prevented the beneficiaries from rising at the UN to pillory the West for its failure to impose still tougher sanctions on South Africa. The European Community's Lomé conventions were more effective in cushioning impoverished Asian, Caribbean, and Pacific exporters against the effects of commodity price fluctuations than was UNCTAD's Integrated Program for Commodities. There is no reason why new clubs should not form, on the lines of the European Union's "association agreements" with Eastern European states, in which membership carries clearly understood obligations as well as benefits.

A policy of opting out would put the burden on the "functional" secretariats to justify their existence by demonstrating their capacity to provide tangible services. None, in this scenario, would be considered *necessarily* irreplaceable: even the functions of the UN High Commissioner for Refugees could in theory be assumed by the International Committee of the Red Cross, acting in close conjunction (as it already does) with the international army of voluntary organizations. The ICRC has developed considerable expertise in responding to both emergency and long-term humanitarian needs.

Advocates of opting out would argue that the universal human rights machinery has degenerated into farce, as governments avoid condemning one another's behavior for fear of seeing the spotlight turned on them. They would echo the Nobel address of Alexander Solzhenitsyn, who as far back as 1970 was arguing that what we have "is not a United Nations Organization, but a United Governments Organization [which] thanks to the venal prejudice of the majority of its members . . . jealously guards the liberty of certain nations and neglects the liberty of others;" which fails to investigate "private grievances—groans, cries and entreaties of simple, humble individuals, insects too tiny for such a large organization to concern itself with"; and which, having produced the Universal Declaration of Human Rights has failed "to make endorsement of it an obligatory condition of membership, and thus . . . left ordinary people at the mercy of governments not of their choosing."[7] They would contend that membership of UN human rights commissions and committees involves an unacceptable degree of compromise and that regional commissions would make at least as much impact as global ones. They would argue, for example, that insofar as Turkey's record on human rights improved during the 1980s, this was prompted by fear of being thrown out of the Council of Europe and its ambitions to join the European Community, rather than by the remoter prospect of being condemned by "the international community." What really stings governments, they might add, is the publicity attracted by such groups as Amnesty International, whose reports, unlike UN documents, are up to date, accessible, and devoid of diplomatic circumlocution.

A "world without the UN," to borrow the Heritage Foundation's polemical catchline, could, paradoxically, develop into a less fragmented world. The doctrine of sovereign equality would lose some of its gilt, and countries too small or sparsely populated to sustain the paraphernalia of a modern state would be encouraged to weigh the advantages of federation with their neighbors that they now dismiss. Regional cooperation would become a more serious business because it would become unavoidable. Development cooperation would be put on a more realistic basis, relying on consultations between customers and suppliers at country or regional level and involving not only governments but the growing pool of managerial talent and self-help associations.

A strategy of opting out would aim to elaborate a new network of multilateral cooperation—purpose built, with memberships varying according to subject matter. It would take a more reticent view of the role of governments and, where governmental cooperation was essential, would seek to make it both more focused and more capable of tackling problems cross-sectorally. With respect to international security, it would accept that in most circumstances, countries rely not on the UN but on regional alliances and bilateral agreements. It would, however, see the need for a "fail-safe," but would not necessarily look to the Security Council to provide it, preferring concentration within a narrower circle than that provided by the UN framework. The risk of an initial boycott of such a club by some powerful countries would be acknowledged; but some of these, it would be argued, were by no means "like-minded"; and, given their national interest in being part of the "big league," boycotts would in any case be of short duration. A council that included the major global or regional players would find applicants knocking at its door. And, since council debates would be held in private, members would be less inclined to play to the gallery. The common instinct for survival would outlast the UN: governments would devise alternatives to the law of the jungle and, because membership of such a council or of *ad hoc* working groups set up by it would be based on the capacity to contribute to the resolution of disputes, the alternatives would in practice work better.

As a strategy, opting out would still carry considerable risks, not least because it would only work if major donor governments were sufficiently united to make the break with the past decisive. A world with half, or more than half, a UN could prove distastefully unstable. Most politicians would prefer to try to make what exists work better, on the ground that a church full of unbelievers is still preferable to schism. The abatement of the Cold War is further incentive to giving the UN a second chance. But opting out has to be included in the range of possible policies because the expanded opportunities for cooperation make it even less likely that failure will be tolerated indefinitely: the need for effective international management is already creating momentum outside the UN. It is not inconceivable that the UN's constituency could one day disappear.

Structural Reform

At the opposite end of the spectrum lies root and branch reform. Institutional complexity and ossified negotiating procedures are preventing the UN from working effectively, and most governments know it. The diagnosis is not invalidated by the dismal record of past failures to simplify and streamline. Bland general statements about "revitalizing growth, development and trade" are of little use to governments struggling with the effects of domestic mismanagement, accumulated debt, or global recession; and the same is true of the forest of underfunded miniprograms so characteristic of the UN. Somewhere between the excessively holistic and the stubbornly compartmentalized a balance must be struck. That means finding ways of reducing the artificiality of UN debates and putting the vast amount of data stored in the bowels of its multiple bureaucracies to practical use as a resource base.

In theory, and at the safe distance of capitals, many policymakers agreed with the new wave of reports[8] that, in the 1980s and early 1990s, stressed that, without structural overhaul, the UN cannot hope to provide either useable channels for dialogue or a coherent mix of services. They agreed, too, that it was more than time to take a hard look at the UN's operational activities, unkindly but accurately encapsulated by Mort Rosenblum as "a tangle of egos grappling for power under the same blue banner."[9] And they were beginning to acknowledge the need for more systematic and professional management of the UN's operations in the field of international security, although for obvious historical and political reasons, this was an area in which the "structuralists" were still feeling their way. But even in a climate of greater optimism with regard to the Security Council, proposals for structural reform have to contend with the sense of "system failure" surrounding the generality of UN organizations. So long as politicians suspect that the most thoroughly prepared reform package is liable to be diluted to the point where it becomes as irrelevant as the structures to which it is addressed, they will fight shy of radical reform.

The most ambitious of these blueprints was the work of Maurice Bertrand, the retired chief inspector of the UN's Joint Inspection Unit (JIU). His scheme for a "third-generation" United Nations, to be given strategic direction and coherence by a ministerial council and an administrative commission modeled on that of the European Community, has all the appeal of intellectual order, of a quintessentially French variety. It made some headway among academics and diplomats. But it ran up against all the familiar problems of the specialized agencies' constitutional prerogatives and, at the political level, assumed an unrealistic degree of shared ground about the purposes of global forums. Not long after the publication of *A Successor Vision*, the report produced by the United Nations Association of the United States that was based on his ideas, Bertrand himself acknowledged that his proposals had "no chance at all of being implemented now," and could be considered only in the context of a break with the past. A complete break was necessary, he insisted, because "improving the system is impossible, there are too many interests involved," and "trying for a halfway house would produce the worst of all worlds."[10]

The more modest proposals for structural reform circulating in the 1990s have, as before, been New York- centered. They involve, at the minimum, merging the governmental bodies—ECOSOC, UNCTAD, and the Second and Third Committees of the General Assembly—that deal with broad economic and social issues. They also consider it indispensable to consolidate the Secretariat machinery for economic and social affairs into a single interdisciplinary think tank. A brain is not much use unless it can reach the nerve ends. So there would need to be, in addition, some sort of global "summit machinery" small enough to explore contentious issues flexibly, and high-powered enough to outline frameworks for collaborative action by governments and to indicate what contributions were expected from UN secretariats. These ministerial summits would have three purposes. They would set agendas for UN debates. They would seek to improve nations' understanding not only of the international impact of their policies, with a view to encouraging consistency, but also of the way different areas of policy relate to one another. And they would aim to bring the UN's fiefdoms under broad policy control.

Emphatically as all structural reformers, from Jackson onward, insist that they are decentralizers at heart, structural reform would radically modify the polycentric autonomy that exists today. Key elements would be central appointment of the agencies' directors-general and even, in some versions, the appointment of a paramount economic secretary-general; and joint priority-setting, within the framework of the new ministerial guidelines and in the context of a consolidated UN budget. Auditing and evaluation would be undertaken by a single independent body. The functions of the specialized agencies would come under review in the context of a major reappraisal of the UN's technical assistance machinery, which would also involve radical surgery on UN-affiliated programs and organizations, such as the UN Development Program (UNDP) and UNICEF. All development funds would be controlled by a single agency.

It is on the overhaul of this "operational" machinery that structural reform places most emphasis—because it is here that the anarchy is greatest and that most money is spent: its reform is the key to making the machine "governable." These proposals have been accompanied in the 1990s by ambitious blueprints—such as *An Agenda for Peace*,[11] the 1992 report with which Boutros Boutros-Ghali made his policy debut as UN secretary-general—for enhancing the UN's capacity to contribute to international security. And indispensable to the whole design, as indeed it would be to any policies aimed at equipping the UN for the next century, is a thorough overhaul of the international civil service. Some of these ideas have been around for decades and have already been described in more detail in preceding chapters. Some of them, notably the Nordic UN Project, have entered the Western policy loop in the 1990s.

The essence of the structuralist approach is that most if not all the ingredients of political and institutional reform are linked. It is no use having economic summits if the agencies ignore what they say. It is no use having interdisciplinary think tanks if there is no governmental machinery capable of giving their recommendations political impetus. It is no use devising integrated strategies for tackling environmental degradation or the causes of mass migration if they are implemented in a remorselessly sectoral and uncorrelated manner. You cannot make sense of budgetary priorities for a hundred legally separate UN entities. You cannot make sense at all, if more than 180 governments are involved at all stages of decisionmaking. And therein, as always, lies the rub. Experts may agree; but more than 180 states will not—above all if reform implies some sacrifice of the hallowed principle of sovereign equality.

In the long term, it is hard to see how the UN can survive without some such revolutionary assault on the *status quo*. Hence the continuing fascination which structural reform exerts not just on academics, but on some of the most farsighted and experienced analysts of multilateral cooperation, including many with years of "inside" experience. Ideas which stubbornly refuse to die despite repeated rejection—such as the demand, put forward in many plans, for an International Development Authority—must reflect more than passing fashion. Beginning in the late 1980s, the emphasis of structural reform started shifting away from traditional preoccupations with more efficient interagency coordination and program implementation—reflecting a growing conviction that this would never be achieved until the strengths and limitations of global organizations had been redefined.

Some of these proposals would fit into any nonfatalistic policy conspectus. But in the short term, and above all *as a point of entry*, structural reform remains a nonstarter. It carries with it too great a weight of past failure, and the conditions for failure still obtain. It relies on negotiation. The great slough of despondency between diagnosis and cure is peopled, much as before, by intergovernmental committees and secretariats jealous of their prerogatives. Structural reform assumes a degrees of positive assent as to objectives as well as means, and these have only just begun to be explored by a handful of diplomats, academics, and international civil servants.

The prospect of actually negotiating yet another structural reform package brings vividly to diplomats' minds the ritual, ideological, and political hurdles that would have to be vaulted even to secure outline agreement, never mind ensure that this time, agreements were implemented. A politician who agreed that structural reform was not only logical but would confer real practical benefits would still ask: How do you get from here to there? The mighty shifts in the geopolitical landscape, which will be explored in the concluding chapters, may bring the answer a little closer. But until it is possible to map the route clearly, politicians will leave wholesale reorganization of the UN out of their calculations.

FAÇADE MANAGEMENT

To most politicians, façade management would seem the intelligent way to live with a marginal UN. It would accept that, on the record of four decades, the UN was incapable of reform and that, great power concertation in the Security Council somewhat apart, the goal had, if anything, receded since Sir Robert Jackson penned his monumental Capacity Study. It would adjust expectations accordingly. The maintenance of a few irreplaceable functions—Conor Cruise O'Brien's "ritual at the brink," the use of the blue flag for humanitarian purposes and (manpower permitting) for selected peacekeeping operations, the international regulation of certain activities—justifies playing the game. Since the game, however, had its insurmountable limitations, there would be little point in alienating secretariats and the habit-bound majority either by selective withdrawals from UN organizations or by brandishing brooms in the Augean stables. Façade managers would view the UN General Assembly and the agencies' general conferences as diplomatic exercises which committed nobody, useful for nourishing the self-esteem of small and powerless countries but otherwise without consequence. They would exploit their marginal uses—the opportunities they offer for bilateral meetings, or for putting pressure on governments guilty of particularly blatant violations of the Charter—and would accept that acting out the fiction of sovereign equality had a mildly therapeutic effect. In the spirit of Churchill's soothing admonition to Stalin at Yalta (to allay his objections to the notion of equal voting rights for Albania and the Soviet Union), they would assent to the proposition that "the eagle must allow the little birds to sing, without troubling itself over the contents of their song."[12]

They would argue that the "damage limitation" of the past was a time-wasting exercise and counterproductive in two ways: spending weeks turning obnoxious language into meaningless jargon irritated the "little birds" and ended up anyway by compromising Western principles. Refusing, therefore, to be drawn, they would spend little effort on negotiating resolutions, and decline to participate in debates on issues extraneous to the business of a conference or where positions were diametrically opposed. They would vote according to national interest, never joining a "consensus" with which they were not in agreement. And they would give no explanations of vote.

Both at the UN and in each agency, façade managers would continue to argue the case for better management and more financial transparency, without illusions as to the probable result. They would routinely vote against budgets that involved real growth. But they would pay their assessed dues, on the general premise that the UN's curate's eggs were not so expensive that they could not afford to buy them for their good parts, while declining to swallow the bad. Façade management would commit no energy to sorting out the UN's hierarchies, establishing clear orders of priorities or creating more effective mechanisms for dialogue. Such initiatives, they would reason, however meticulously conceived and skillfully pursued, stood not the faintest chance of being executed. Better passivity than nervous tinkering at the margins. They would assume that even if individual organizations improved their performance, the changes would not amount to a qualitative difference—and that even marginal improvements would overwhelmingly depend on the personal characters and talents of the chief executive, rather than on any external pressures, however well coordinated. They would therefore, as basic insurance against runaway maladministration and extreme politicization, take the choice of chief executives seriously—a radical departure, it should be noted, from traditional practice—but thereafter would burn no midnight oil scrutinizing their performance.

Façade managers would, however, review their voluntary contributions to UN programs. They would continue to maintain support for the handful that reflected vital national interests, such as the International Atomic Energy Agency's (IAEA) efforts to prevent the proliferation of nuclear weapons, and those that were conspicuously successful—the AIDS program for example, or the multiagency campaign against river blindness—and for such aspects of refugee care as could not be handled by private voluntary organizations. But they would divert most of these funds to other channels, assuming that, since most Third World heads of state valued the UN as a propaganda platform rather than for its practical contributions to development, increased bilateral assistance would more than compensate diplomatically for their reduced support for UN-based "development" activities. Their involvement in these would be minimalized and, where they felt the need to work through multilateral channels, they would resort to nonuniversal forums such as the Development Assistance Committee of the OECD, the European Community and the Western economic summits; or channel cooperation through the Bretton Woods institutions and regional development banks.

But they would say as little as possible about their actions. They would never repeat the gaffe of the former Australian prime minister Malcolm Fraser, who at a particularly frustrating juncture of the Uruguay Round negotiations announced that governments had better "accept that the multilateral trading system under GATT has failed" because "it is not equipped to deal with today's problems."[13] They might increasingly rely on one-on-one settlements of trade disputes or on regional trade agreements, but they would pay lip service to the continuing importance of a nondiscriminatory global trading regime. As for the other UN regulatory organizations, they would continue to use them, but would adopt a conservative, skeptical attitude to the elaboration of any conventions that went beyond what was strictly required for the predictable ordering of international activities.

The Security Council would, in this approach, be considered essential as contingent insurance. Since, however, it would also be considered as liable to aggravate tensions as to relieve them, it would be sparingly used. Extreme prudence would be urged on the secretary-general—should that, unexpectedly, be necessary—in the name, of course, of safeguarding the prestige of his office. No expectation would be entertained, or encouraged, that the UN could usefully intervene in such sensitive matters as Arab-Israeli relations, but its mediation and peacekeeping functions would be maintained as useful stopgaps.

Essentially, façade management would operate on two assumptions: that the marginalization of the UN is a fact of life, and that the course of action that would least disrupt the serious business of international diplomacy would be to leave the shell intact. Policymakers would argue that all governments are perfectly well aware that this business is still shaped by the "spheres of influence . . . alliances . . . balances of power . . . the special arrangements by which, in the unhappy past, the nations chose to safeguard their security or to promote their interests," which, on his return from Moscow in 1943, Cordell Hull rashly predicted would be rendered obsolete by the United Nations. But they would consider it tactless—and possibly damaging to those "special arrangements"—to insist on the fact.

The agnostic's role is less taxing than the atheist's or the true believer's. Façade management, as the intelligent approach to minimalist conservation, would still represent a distinct improvement on most governments' current policies, with their tendency to oscillate between energetic flurries of micromanagement of the secretariats, and the flaccid compromises of damage-limitation. Nor would it be a soft option if consistently pursued. It would, for example, require a self-denying ordinance on the negotiation of paper compromises. And that would run against the grain of diplomatic training: arguments over squared brackets and modifying subclauses have an allure for professional bureaucrats that few politicians, and no layman, can hope to understand. But it would be even harder to ensure a common front for this approach than for structural reform. It is difficult enough to ensure consistency for positive purposes. It is still harder where the policy, however realistic it may appear, is fundamentally negative.

SELECTIVE ACTION

This approach is essentially pragmatic. It, too, would take it as a given that, at least until a sufficient number of Third World leaders saw an irresistible advantage in giving up the pleasures of rhetorical politics *and* were prepared to exert enough discipline on their negotiators to stop them behaving like free-lance prima donnas, systemic reform of the UN was out of the question. It would calculate that grappling with the worst-run institutions, the most intractable areas of confrontation, and the most unmanageable forums represented the least promising route to reform. It would make the most of subglobal vehicles for cooperation, official and unofficial. But because it would recognize that the uses of global dialogue go beyond maintaining international regulation of the mails and the airwaves or keeping in place a face-saving arena for the exercise of political brinkmanship, it would select the parts of the UN that it was possible to take seriously, and try to augment their capacity to cope with the larger dimensions of political and economic friction and social adjustments to rapid change.

Such a strategy would dispense with certain illusions—above all, the idea that governments ought to have "a UN policy," rather than different policies, depending on the kinds of cooperation that were called for. It would argue that the criteria for judging the efficacity of most UN organizations had become thoroughly skewed by the emphasis on "development"—that most of them were not, or should not be, in business to provide "public goods" such as jobs, education, or—save in emergency—food. It would judge them on their performance as clearinghouses for information, as places for exchanges of views, as catalysts for ideas, and—but only where common action was indispensable or common regulations were needed—for intergovernmental negotiation.

Selective action would start with decisions on what most needed to be accomplished. Where the UN could contribute, the aim would be to build on excellence, relying on those organizations that could take the weight. By breaking down or ignoring institutional prerogatives based on sectoral "mandates," it would restore flexibility and pragmatism to the conduct of essential global business. Policymakers would hope that the "demonstration effect" of success in the better-run parts of the UN would improve prospects for eventual reform of some of the others. But they would recognize that stretching the capacities of the best would not reform the worst—and would accept the implications, abandoning the conventional view that nonparticipation in programs or organizations of doubtful utility was a form of moral turpitude or a dereliction of international duty.

At the same time, there would be no attempt to embark on intergroup negotiations to abolish parts of the machinery—on the ground that, at least until working alternatives were in place and probably even then, the process would be self-canceling. The strategy would work by attrition. The considerable overlap between UN mandates means that there is more scope for selectivity than might appear. And, given a basic decision to concentrate on objectives rather than on institutions, there is room for maneuver on the financial side. Arguments over the "regular" UN budgets, contributions to which are based on an agreed scale of assessment and are mandatory, have tended to obscure the fact that about three quarters of the *overall* budget of the UN and the agencies directly affiliated to it, and around half those of the autonomous specialized agencies, are made up of voluntary contributions, mainly from the dozen governments that form the Geneva Group.

The total sums involved in the UN, excluding the World Bank and the IMF, are of course very small. Apart from peacekeeping and the care of refugees, the UN and its affiliates and the specialized agencies were spending between them around $5.5 billion a year in the early 1990s, of which $2 billion derived from obligatory contributions—the membership dues, as it were.[14] But of the rest, nearly a third of UN spending is voluntarily funded. That sum could, in theory, be reallocated by donors, either within the UN or in favor of non-UN organizations. In practice, some of it is earmarked for spending, such as food aid delivered by the World Food Program. Nonemergency food aid, a thoroughly questionable item of voluntary expenditure, is likely to prove incurably addictive until Western food surpluses decline and, as most of it is provided in kind, this form of aid would not necessarily be replaced by its cash equivalent. But the remaining voluntary contributions are large enough, as a proportion of UN spending, to give Western governments considerable leverage without needing to renege on their legal obligations or to embark on lengthy negotiations over structural reform. A policy aimed at stripping New York of its great tangled forest of "operational units," while simultaneously compelling the specialized agencies to concentrate on their original functions as clearinghouses for information and research and as promoters of dialogue, could achieve its ends through the power of the purse.

Once the "output" of the United Nations ceased to be measured in terms of the quantity of technical cooperation projects it was able to "deliver"—the verb, commonly used, illustrates the top-down approach to these field programs—the pressure to improve the quality of its statistical and analytic services would increase. Financial discipline would be easier to impose. Because there would be less scope for specialized agencies to claim that their field programs involved them in "administrative overheads"—routinely calculated at 20 percent of program costs rather than the already too generous 13–14 percent allowed for by the UNDP—links between manpower and objectives would be easier to determine.

Restoring the "talking-shop" function to center stage would not by itself improve the quality of the talk, but if Third World governments ceased to regard all UN secretariats as sources of grants free of policy conditionality, and no longer approached meetings as recipients, issues would be more likely to be discussed on their merits. There would also be more incentive to reach agreement when the success or failure of a particular conference hinged on the progress made, to quote the Charter, in "harmonizing the actions of nations," rather than in stimulating direct action by the UN. Some of the artificial underpinnings of North-South confrontation would be eliminated. Secretariats would be forced to reestablish their credentials as catalysts inspiring action by others, as pipelines for ideas and as forums in which governments increased their understanding of one another's problems.

To argue that a major, though not exclusive, aim of selective action should be to get rid of the UN-as-aid-machine is not be anti-aid, or antimultilateralism. It is simply to recognize that UN technical cooperation has marginal impact, exacerbates interagency rivalries, is outmoded both in conception and in its methods, adds to the UN's institutional and functional fragmentation, and aggravates North-South tensions. Nor is it negative. A policy of building on what works would exploit those organizations that had demonstrated their comparative advantage. It would use the Bretton Woods institutions, including the new World Trade Organization (WTO) due to open for business in 1995, for trade, financial and monetary issues, economic analysis, and the marshalling and transferring of multilateral development funds. It would insulate the political debating forum in New York, by declining to finance the gamut of economic and social programs to which the UN's political as well as its "functional" machinery is now so disproportionately devoted. Concentrating multilateral aid and investment in the development banks would compel the major specialized agencies to create new identities for themselves.

This would, paradoxically, require the agencies to reinvent their original functions. A simple return to the tasks set them in 1945 would not suffice, because the most complex problems facing national policymakers are cross-sectoral. In concentrating on their original roles, therefore, two or more of them would often need to pool their expertise to provide the right of guidance. They would also need to establish much closer relations with outside research centers and professional organizations. And these initiatives would have to come from the secretariats: governments can encourage change but would be foolhardy to attempt to negotiate agreement on such institutional transformations. The process would almost certainly be slow; where, as for the environment, it seemed important to improve the quality and exchange of technical research, a faster route might be to establish new autonomous research centers, on the lines of the mainly Western-funded Consultative Group for International Agricultural Research.

Finally, in a few areas, selective action might require major institutional innovations—outside the UN as well as within its framework. The 1990s will call for strategic decisions, for example, on the most productive ways of dealing with environmental questions that, because environmental diplomacy is inherently intrusive, would seem to require a global umbrella yet could lead in global forums to a repetition of the worst excesses of North-South confrontation. The UN should be anything but marginal to disaster relief and humanitarian emergencies, but UN disaster relief coordination has itself been such a disaster that ways may have to be found to rely less on the UN. And the containment of conflict, in the turbulent post-Cold War world, will require much more serious thinking about ways to mesh Chapter VIII of the UN Charter, which calls for the active involvement of regional organizations in security matters, with the work of the Security Council. The task of maintaining patterns of growth that are both adequate to alleviate poverty and sustainable down the generations has some unmistakably global dimensions. The question for a policy of selective action is how to minimize frictions and correlate policies, in the absence of anything approximating to an "international community." The "survival" of the UN is, and ought to be, a subordinate consideration.

THE OPTIONS IN CONTEXT

Which approach politicians take will depend on their interpretation of the conflicting trends in international relations and in public attitudes. The old multilateralism, based on a functional division of labor and the association of roughly comparable nation-states, has not survived the confrontations of the era of decolonization: the "little birds" have driven the eagles away. We are living with the wreckage of world-order politics—of the original variety that attempted to contain frictions and promote cooperation through the observance of commonly accepted principles and rules, and of the Third World politics of the "new orders" that challenged their validity. The exaggerated claims that have echoed through UN forums, the agencies' sectoral squabbles, and the undisciplined expansion of economic and social programs under the UN's umbrella have made it an awkwardly inflated and institutionally cumbersome instrument. You do not ride out to establish a new "world order" on the back of a dinosaur. In addition, organizations based on the principle of sovereign equality and noninterference in countries' internal affairs are increasingly ill qualified to handle issues that transcend frontiers, or to address the problems of states incapable of sustaining domestic order or of feeding their people.

Yet economic interaction and political fragmentation, two major postwar phenomena, make the reconstruction of multilateral cooperation essential. For all its political and ideological fissiparousness, an increasingly integrated world is shaping, exposing the limitations of national autonomy even as nationalism and micronationalism take on fresh and venomous life in a world freed of the dreary certainties of the Cold War.

Public understanding of these conflicting pressures has dramatically increased in the quarter-century since the Club of Rome's predictions of physical *Limits to Growth* and Barbara Ward's eloquent manifesto, *Only One Earth*, popularized the concerns that made the 1970s a decade of intense speculation about the consequences for "spaceship earth" of economic growth and the imminent, unstoppable doubling of the global population. Even for the least internationally aware, these issues were dramatically highlighted by the Sahel drought and famine of 1968–74 and the global grain shortage, which coincided with the worst of that crisis. And the interconnectedness of national economies was brought home to millions by the 1973 Arab oil embargo and subsequent quadrupling of oil prices.

The initial reaction was in many ways remarkably outward-looking. There were world order projects, "global 2000" reports, and the Brandt commission's "program for survival." UN secretariats sprouted millennialist manifestos—health for all, food for all, a world employment program—setting targets for the year 2000. Even Henry Kissinger was sufficiently stirred by what Stanley Hoffman called the "flickerings of 'universal consciousness'"[15] to proclaim in 1974 the "bold objective: that within a decade, no child will go to bed hungry; that no family will fear for its next day's bread and that no human being's future and capacity will be stunted by malnutrition." Kissinger based this extraordinary pledge on the objective fact that the necessary technical knowledge existed. But ten years and billions of dollars later, as famine ravaged the Horn, Africa proved once again that technology can do little in the absence of supporting policies. Drought in 1984 simply reduced food production per head in Africa to a level it would have reached a few years later, even with normal rains; before the drought, one African in five were living on imported food. And just under twenty years later, millions were dying in Sudan and, in a first and controversial experiment in armed humanitarian intervention, U.S. Marines headed for Somalia to avert the starvation of hundreds of thousands of victims of armed anarchy there.

But if the landing on the moon, illustrating technology's enormous peaceful potential, seemed a giant step forward for mankind, the photographs of the globe seen from space powerfully symbolized the vulnerability of a planet that satellite communications technology was putting in dramatically instant touch with itself. Groups of environmentalists flourished, and found political expression for the first time in the various "green" parties of Western Europe. Global conferences on population and the environment generated near panic about the depletion of nonrenewable resources—and helped to engender simplistic demands for zero growth in the West to curb the destructive consumerism of the rich and for a radical redistribution of wealth to meet the "basic needs" of the poorest. As stagflation in Western economies, with rising unemployment, then gave people a taste of what zero (and, in many Third World countries, negative) growth might actually feel like, political economists turned to emphasizing policies that maximized the advantages of global interdependence. As the Brandt report was to put it, the coexistence of idle factories in the North and unsatisfied demand in the South pointed to the sense and necessity of global bargains.

These factors combined in the 1970s to put strong pressures on governments to act in concert—just as the political and institutional bases for such cooperation were increasingly being thrown into question. The propriety of a universalist system of values was challenged by "new orders" politics, by the Dag Hammarksjöld Foundation's call for "another development" free of Western hegemony, and by a guilt-ridden Western emphasis on diversity, pluralism, and cultural "authenticity." A brutal dimension was added to these liberal doubts. The notion of the existence of an international community, whose members belonged in a common moral universe, was challenged by the collapse of once-prosperous Uganda under Idi Amin Dada's politically and culturally illiterate tyranny; by the horrors of Cambodia's Year Zero; by the open contempt of the Ayatollah Khomeini's fundamentalist revolution for basic international rules governing diplomatic immunity, religious freedom, or due process; and by the large following the Ayatollah attracted, partly for that reason, among the dispossessed of Islam. The rationale for global cooperation in the Brandtian mode was that sovereignty was a myth of limited validity, since governments could not assure the safety and prosperity of their citizens in isolation. Yet the 1974 Charter of the Economic Rights and Duties of States was the most uncompromisingly absolutist assertion of the primacy of sovereignty to have been produced in the modern era. By the 1980s, the basic continuum between ideas of political and social organization necessary to intergovernmental cooperation could hardly be said still to exist. Nations even resorted once again to chemical warfare, taboo for sixty years. Millions of refugees, fleeing *en masse*, were testimony to forms of conflict and social upheaval not foreseen by the Charter, and to the absence of a shared commitment to "the dignity and worth of the human person."

So what could be called a massive expansion of the perceived "global agenda" coincided with growing skepticism as to whether cooperation was possible, given the intractable realities of political, economic, and cultural heterogeneity. Such were the incongruities and tensions between the UN's members that it seemed increasingly unlikely that universal intergovernmental organizations could be a functioning locus of policymaking—a pessimistic assessment that the degeneration of what passed for debate at the UN did everything possible to confirm. The contrast between what was needed to manage the consequences of economic integration and the poor functioning of the international machinery seemed unbridgeable.

To these contradictions should be added a third element of disjunction in public attitudes. Governments are expected to join forces to meet challenges that, whether they concern drug trafficking, global warming, or the consequences of rapid population growth, are increasingly global—yet to do so through institutions whose legitimacy is based on national sovereignty and that are thus, in terms of these phenomena, anachronistic. They are expected to offer some degree of predictability in a world where the magnitude of global financial flows set obvious limits to their powers even to manage their currencies. Yet at the same time, partly as a result of the severe economic and social dislocations of the 1970s and 1980s, popular faith in the ability of governments to order either their national societies or the global dimensions of change has declined — in Africa as in Western Europe and the United States, in Eastern Europe and the former Soviet Union as in Latin America or even Vietnam. Governments everywhere are cutting their public sectors and modifying their ideas about the appropriate scope for state intervention. Their publics are demanding more sophisticated governmental management of the global commons, but rejecting the domestic micromanagement that has been the stock in trade of most bureaucracies.

The Bretton Woods institutions apart, this massive reassessment of the role of the state, central to the "structural adjustment" of national economies to transnational competition, has been barely reflected in the vast majority of UN endeavors. Programs that continue to be based on welfare state objectives that rely on the operation of a *dirigiste* or even command economy kind can only reinforce the UN's credibility gap.

None of these developments makes it any easier to assess the cost-benefit ratio of the different approaches to multilateral cooperation sketched out above. Even to have set these four options out as though they were on an equal footing is in some way misleading: the point of indicating what they might involve is not to suggest that politics is a precise art, or that alternatives can be neatly packaged, but to underline the need for some identifiable starting position from which to fit the UN into the broader multilateral context.

Opting out is worst-case thinking. It may come to that in the end, and it therefore pays to give it thought. It also provides a point of reference against which to consider other possibilities. Structural reform, its utopian opposite, looks no less accident-prone today than it has been throughout the UN's history. The second preambular paragraph of the General Assembly resolution[16] on the "restructuring and revitalising of the United Nations in the economic, social and related fields" of December 20, 1993, is unintentionally eloquent. In what is claimed to be an incomplete list, it refers to no fewer than fifteen previous General Assembly resolutions on this subject, reaching back to Resolution 57 of December 11, 1946. Jonathan Swift's tailors of Laputa had a methodologically impeccable system for measuring a man for a suit of clothes using abstract geometrical calculations, but they were incapable of producing a suit which fitted. And in Laputa, they had the advantage of agreed rules of calculation. Façade management is also logical, as a response to the breakdown of the universalism of 1945, but it is an inadequate formula for addressing the enlarged global agenda just alluded to—and wholly incommensurate to the fresh hopes engendered by the crumbling of the Iron Curtain.

It will be the argument of the concluding chapters that selective action, a policy of building on what works, is worth trying. It represents an avenue between the somewhat patronizing and largely counterproductive game of damage limitation, and the structural blueprints that have an awkward tendency to meet their nemesis in *ad hoc* committees. Its success will, of course, obviously depend on some skillful façade management—in the positive sense of active efforts to persuade Third World capitals that for the West to concentrate on key objectives and switch funds accordingly is in everybody's interest. But, and this is cardinal, action would not depend on first eliminating all opposition; the agreement of all would not be necessary to make a start. Nor would such a policy even require absolute unanimity among donor governments; the agreement of a few major countries to act in concert would create the momentum for change.

Consisting as it must of multiple decisions, selective action would imply using a mix of tools, global and subglobal, and its objectives would not necessarily be centered on the UN. The next chapter will discuss the broad dimensions of such an approach, always in the knowledge that these are themes with many variations. The first will be the transformation of multilateral development cooperation; the second, approaches to tighter financial and managerial discipline; the third, the management of disasters and of what could be called the new economic and social agenda of a more promising "new world order." The inescapable implication of this approach is that the UN would end up doing less, and that there would be less of the UN. But this is a necessary condition for its reestablishment as a cluster of centers for dialogue, for the reinforcement of its focus on conflict resolution, and for the rediscovery of its catalytic potential in economic and social affairs. It is a condition for the restoration of its authority.

10. The Discriminating Buyer's UN

The Uses of Leverage

Experience teaches that governments cannot manage the global organizations. They should not need to. The responsibility for devising programs and methods of work capable of eliciting assent and even enthusiasm properly belongs to the secretariats. That does not mean that governments, particularly those that provide the lion's share of UN finance, are impotent. Where secretariats falter, they can provide political leadership. As consumers of UN services, it is broadly up to governments to convince the UN's many agencies that, to survive, they will have to learn to market their "products" effectively, not only to government ministries but to a wide variety of users. Without seeking to usurp the managerial function, governments can establish priorities.

They will be successful, however, only if they concentrate on objectives rather than institutional frameworks. About the institutions themselves, they should be more iconoclastic. Because nearly a billion people are malnourished, for example, it does not necessarily follow that the Food and Agriculture Organization (FAO) should be given more money; an equally valid conclusion might be that the FAO had not provided the appropriate policy advice in agricultural development, and that funds might be better spent elsewhere. To make more effective use of their financial leverage, donor governments will have to start by developing reasonably clear and consistent priorities for multilateral action, and yardsticks against which to judge the likely capacity of individual agencies—both UN and non-UN—to help achieve these goals.

There are obvious incentives for Western governments to make such an effort in the 1990s, beginning with the strains inflicted on their national budgets for international cooperation by the urgency of promoting stability in the post-Soviet world and by the seemingly limitless "opportunities" that, in a more flexible geopolitical environment, have opened out for humanitarian and peacemaking intervention. Such action may no longer be constrained by the superpower confrontation of the Cold War, but any early euphoria about the post-Cold War "peace dividend" has rapidly given place to the realization that the aftermath of the dissolution of the Soviet empire could well prove as fraught as was that of the Ottoman and Austro-Hungarian empires which confronted the League of Nations; and it is not only on the Eurasian landmass that the "new world order" resembles a "new world disorder." In addition, there are new demands on international cooperation, to arrest and reverse environmental degradation or to find compassionate means to address the huge escalation in mass migration, by people driven either by terror or by economic misery. These are challenges that will require far more sophisticated dovetailing of national policies with international strategies than has been needed simply to channel traditional development aid. Environmental diplomacy is particularly delicate, because inherently intrusive; devising more effective international monitoring of nuclear capabilities and the trade in missiles, equally urgent, will be even more so.

There are greater opportunities, too, for more effective multilateral cooperation. The industrialized West is no longer as isolated as it was in demanding value for money of UN agencies and programs: many of the Asian and Latin American countries that now contribute more substantially to the UN have come to share that objective. And finally, the political conditions for international cooperation have been transformed by the ripple effects of political as well as economic liberalization, penetrating as far afield as Africa and Mongolia. Financial muscle could be decisive in effecting reforms; and to use it will be imperative because old habits die harder in the United Nations than elsewhere, as the routinized litanies of complaint echoing through the General Assembly's special conference on development in 1990 and the first session of the new Committee on Sustainable Development in 1993 made painfully apparent.

Spurred by the Nordic countries' critical evaluation of the UN development machinery,[1] published in 1991, Western governments began once again in 1992 to try to win agreement by the General Assembly to strip the "system" down. The chances are that these efforts, which will be discussed later in this chapter, will fail in the 1990s as surely as they did in the three preceding decades—if by success one means the effective mobilization of scarce resources behind precise objectives with clear time frames, and not merely the amalgamation of a few committees, shorter speeches, and a bit of agenda trimming. The lesson of the past is that the more reforms depend on multilateral negotiation, the more liable each step becomes to dilution and self-cancellation. It would be simpler, and more effective, for donor governments to leave pointless or ineffective activities that are financed by voluntary contributions to die of attrition, rather than to put endless effort into getting 160 or so other states to agree to their cancellation.

However carefully focused, new policies will not be effectively implemented by UN secretariats without a serious overhaul of the ways they recruit, promote, and monitor the performance of their staffs. The indispensable accompaniment to modernizing internal management is competent independent evaluation and auditing of UN organizations. The UN needs "daylight" rules on accountability just as urgently as it needs "sunset" rules on jettisoning ancient program baggage. A system of impartial assessment would not, by itself, improve the performance of the secretariats; but it would provide a factual basis for assessing the capacities of different institutions with a view to channeling funds to the most effective of them—or outside the United Nations altogether, if that seemed more likely to yield results.

So long as we persist in conceiving the UN as a "system," fatalism may be appropriate. But the polycentric organization of the global organizations, the considerable autonomy they exercise, gives governments opportunities to circumvent institutional obstacles. The useful need not, indeed should not, wait on the ideal. Piecemeal action, backed by the power of the purse, could have a salutary demonstration effect. It needs to be recognized once and for all that, save for certain discrete tasks, "harmonizing" the activities of the different UN agencies is beyond the power of governments. The alternative is to make a reality of competition, rewarding effectiveness and penalizing incompetence. The probable result of such an approach, if carried out with reasonable consistency (unanimity is too much to hope for) by groups of powerful governments, would be *à la carte* use of the United Nations. The most essential and/or effective organizations would be built up. Instead of wasting effort on reforming the most incompetent or least relevant, the activities of these could and should be firmly pruned—either by agreement, or by necessity, as a consequence of reduced funding. The focus would be on activities, not institutions. Only where absolutely essential to fill gaps in international cooperation need new mechanisms be put in place, and these might be created, as appropriate, inside or outside the UN.

A somewhat low-key start along this route was made at the end of the 1980s, when the donors' Geneva Group embarked on a program of agency-by-agency assessments of the UN and the group's cochairmen, Great Britain and the United States, began to canvass the hitherto unthinkable notion of transferring funds from weaker to more effective organizations. By 1994, members of the group were conducting detailed in-house studies of a clutch of organizations—United Nations Environment Program (UNEP), United Nations Conference on Trade Development (UNCTAD), the Office of the United Nations High Commissioner for Refugees (UNHCR), the UN's regional Economic Commission for Europe (ECE)—and were investigating the UN's human rights machinery. It had also broadened its purview, formerly confined to the specialized agencies, to cover the UN in New York. But these initiatives were still geared more to institutions than to objectives. The Geneva Group's effectiveness was, moreover, handicapped by its low profile. When the Americans, in late 1991, sought to raise the Geneva Group's political profile, the Europeans took fright, arguing that this was, after all, just an informal club of the rich, had no official "standing," and should therefore avoid being provocative. The Americans retreated; but however excellent the proposals formulated by officials meeting in private session, it was difficult to see how their adoption was to be secured without the determined, public intervention of their political masters. The heads of UN agencies are political animals with a well-documented record of ignoring national civil servants. More radicalism was required—as one powerful government had already begun to argue some years earlier.

The call to rethink strategies toward the global forums had issued from the most unexpected quarters: the Soviet Union. Mikhail Gorbachev's proposals in 1987 for reinforced cooperation within a "global system of international peace and security" will be discussed in the next chapter. What here concerns us is that they explicitly included "economic security." Western governments reacted skeptically, naturally enough, since outside a handful of its client-states the Soviet Union contributed little or nothing to Third World development. But the relationships between wars and poverty, demographic pressures and environmental degradation, or even "debt and democracy" were hard to deny. And within a few years, the concept of "economic security" was in practice to move to center stage, though not as Gorbachev had envisaged. First came the political liberation of most of Eastern Europe after 1989—and the consequent demands on Western wealth to help reconstruct their economies. All forms of Western development aid, whether bilaterally or multilaterally channeled, rapidly came under scrutiny: however ministers might insist that aid to Eastern Europe would not be at the expense of their traditional clients, value for money was now a serious consideration, not just a formal requirement. The competition for funds was too intense for waste to be tolerable. Further, having set political conditions for aid to Eastern Europe, it was hardly logical to continue assisting politically oppressive and unaccountable governments elsewhere—or, by extension, to put up with enforced levies against aid budgets, voted through by Third World majorities for UN organizations that continued unquestioningly to bankroll ill-conceived or even spurious projects.

The international agenda was thus already undergoing profound changes when, on Christmas Day, 1991, Gorbachev became the first Soviet leader to leave office without being removed by Communist party coup or the grim reaper. He was also the last: his resignation set a personal seal on the dissolution of Soviet Union, the end of a regime he had struggled for seven years to revitalize and, for the time being at least, of a "union" he had fought to the last to preserve. He left a world truly transformed, though not yet into a pattern that could inspire confidence; as he bitterly commented, the old system had fallen apart before a new one could be shaped. That may have been in the nature of the system. But as James Baker observed, in calling for a "grand coalition" to repair the economic devastation communism had left, "great empires rarely go quietly into extinction." The world beyond, to which Gorbachev had offered not just cohabitation but cooperation, was largely unprepared for life beyond containment of the superpower that appeared abruptly to have evaporated. The United Nations seemed at one level more central to the global reordering in prospect than it had been for years, thrust into the headlines by Iraq's invasion of Kuwait and called on to mount more peacekeeping operations in the years immediately after the crumbling of the Berlin Wall in 1989 than it had been in the whole of its previous history. But in Baker's "grand coalition" the UN, with the notable exceptions of the International Monetary Fund (IMF) and the World Bank, was an irrelevance. And in the new debate on "good governance" and democratic reforms in the developing world, a debate joined by increasingly vocal groups of these countries' own citizens, the UN was almost equally marginal.

In the overcharged agendas of the turn of the century—those of new opportunities, those of the "new disorder"—there will be a premium on what works, and Western governments need to make it much clearer than they have so far done that the global organizations are under serious pressure to adapt, and to tap whatever support can be mustered for change, whether among other governments, UN secretariats, or the large spectrum of nongovernmental organizations (NGOs), research centers, and companies with international interests. Greater realism is also needed about what global cooperation can achieve. Predictability and reciprocally binding agreements are necessary for the conduct of much international business—rules can reduce friction and common standards benefit all. The inflation of the regulatory agenda is, however, counterproductive: and before "green diplomacy" becomes deeply afflicted with the giganticism it has shown signs of developing since the 1992 "Earth summit," that message needs to be got across. In many environmental questions, informal conciliation may be more productive than attempts to negotiate restrictive legal straitjackets.

A firm prejudice in favor of multilateral cooperation is perfectly compatible with a candid acknowledgment that much UN activity no longer responds to current needs and that, in any case, cooperation in some fields might not best be furthered through global organizations or, even, by intergovernmental bodies. It is compatible with withdrawing support for these activities—or withdrawing from individual organizations that persist in attaching priority to them, though that is a matter for each government to decide: participation is a matter of sovereign choice. The parts of the UN that prove incapable of adapting ought, in any serious modernization of policies, to be left to subsist on the budgets provided by the governments that abet their secretariats in resisting reforms—who might well be numerous, but impecunious. That would release funds for the most indispensable organizations and those that showed most potential, and would also make money available for the creation, where this was unavoidable, of new bodies. But what is needed is concentration of effort, not the creation of new machinery; global cooperation has already been sufficiently blighted by the proliferation of agencies. Governments have an opportunity in the 1990s to be seriously engaged, perhaps more seriously than before, in multilateral cooperation; but if their participation in the global organizations is indeed to be serious, it must discriminate between the indispensable services the UN can offer, and the surplus baggage acquired over nearly half a century.

TRANSFORMING DEVELOPMENT

By 1990, the fortieth anniversary of the start of UN technical cooperation programs, some Western governments were in fact beginning to think about alternative uses for their aid money. That June, Lynda Chalker, the British minister for overseas development, delivered an uncompromising speech to the UN Development Program's (UNDP) governing council that contained an oblique threat to withdraw from UN development programs. There was, she said, "a troubling and rising dissatisfaction with the impact of much UN and UNDP assistance" and, if they were "to continue to spend our money through the UNDP," they had to change their attitudes and methods. Britain's three conditions for continued support for the UN agencies' field programs were "an end to bickering over rival claims to competence" and "an end to empire-building" by the agencies and by UNDP itself; vastly improved teamwork to mobilize all UN resources effectively within recipient countries; and "proper standards of planning back-up," preferably country-focused, and for "identifying, appraising *and monitoring* and *evaluating* programs and projects" (Chalker's emphases). These conditions would have to be met by the time the new UNDP five-year program cycle began in 1992.

Turning to the UNDP itself, Chalker demanded a much tougher, more "hands-on" attitude to dialogue with recipients about the uses to which money was put, "properly concerted" with donor governments and "especially the World Bank." The heart of technical cooperation, she added, was "the creation of good governance, sound and efficient institutions," and "intelligent management." The UN should be working on "concentrated programs of institutional revival," and that message needed "to be passed right down the line" and reflected in a switch from projects to programs for recovery, which should be based on clear strategies. UNDP would need to change its managerial structure and alter its own "skill mix." And it must develop a clear idea of the services it needed from the UN agencies, insist on their compliance, "and monitor that it is getting what it pays for—or rather, what we pay for through it."

The bluntness of this attack on the UNDP's senior management, and on the whole project-based approach of the UN agencies, was intentional. So was the ostentatious reference to a 1992 deadline. To the UNDP Council, Chalker said only that failure to move rapidly, and radically, would "not be in the interests of the recipients, the donors or the UN itself." But in another speech that day, she confirmed that if the UN agencies failed to "signal that they are capable and willing" to respond, the time had come to ask: "Who is left to pick up the gauntlet as we enter the second millennium?" And in an interview published in the *Times* on June 7, she said that donors would continue their support "only if the system as whole adapts and is seen to be delivering the goods."

Said a senior British official four years later:

> We all knew that the 1992 deadline wasn't going to happen. But what it reflected was real enough. Simply put, finance was really beginning to bite at our end. European Community aid spending was rising exponentially and cutting into the total available for bilateral aid, we were obliged to pay our dues to the regular UN budgets, and so we started to look hard at whatever multilateral spending was discretionary. That led to UNDP, UNFPA [the UN Fund for Population Activities,] and UNICEF, and the more we looked, the less impressed we were."[2]

Britain was far from alone in concluding that automatic support for UN technical assistance had to end; but what began to give such discontents a political focus, displacing the work in the Geneva Group, was the publication, in 1991, of *The UN in Development*,[3] a report backed by a damning series of field studies of UN operations that was produced by the Nordic countries—which between them paid for nearly 45 percent of the UN's "operational activities for development."

The report acknowledged the gloomy fate of previous efforts at UN reform, above all in the economic and social spheres. It discussed with remarkable frankness the damage done to the specialized agencies' "standard-setting, research and information roles" by their "excessive concentration" on technical cooperation. The Nordic governments expressed "mounting concern" that the agencies had become project-dominated "to the detriment of their important original functions and their ability to carry out new ones." They called on them to reduce their involvement in aid projects, "increasing their role in upstream activities such as sectoral analysis and advice." Yet at the same time, they acknowledged that field studies[4] for the Nordic project had found that even when it came to policy analysis in their own sectoral specializations, the agencies' capacity had "gone beyond the point of no return;" with the possible exception of the World Health Organization (WHO), they were at best capable of acting at "subsector level." Their "center of excellence" functions had "migrated to the development banking system." The World Bank's expertise in education now exceeded that of UNESCO, for example, and its team of environmental experts surpassed, in number and qualifications, anything available in the UN. And even at project level, the "speed and reliability" of the agencies' work had "declined significantly during the 1980s."

There were two reasons for this "migration of tasks" to the banks, the report found. The first was that in order to maximize the impact of their investments, the international financial institutions had made institution-building, particularly in the area of economic management but also in social policy, a priority for the 1990s. The second reason was "one of default: the fact that the UN agencies have not been able to deliver the necessary technical assistance in fields such as education, health, energy, environment or agriculture has forced the IFIs [international financial institutions] to get involved in these areas too." They were fast becoming "dominant multi-sector development agencies, with large capital resources and with great power to prescribe policies."

Yet having diagnosed the disease, the report shrank from drawing the logical, although radical, conclusions. Quite the opposite: it argued that "it would be a great loss to the world in general and the developing countries in particular, if the vast UN system for development cooperation were allowed to slide into marginalization." The UN, it said without explaining why this could not be achieved by other means, embodied a precious idea, that of "a development partnership between industrialized and developing countries." The task must now be to identify "complementary" roles for the specialized agencies, without restricting the activities of the development banks. And the "relative decline in the role of the UN development organizations must be reversed."

"No issue," the report acknowledged, "has been discussed so much and with so little result as coordination of the UN's activities. . . . There is no central management and it is unlikely that there ever will be." Yet to give UN development efforts "critical mass," it proposed to seek "collaboration within the framework of the pluralistic UN system . . . a functional and rational division of labor"—and to do so by "restructuring the central organs of the UN, ECOSOC in particular," to include some form of International Development Council to conduct "high-level policy debate" that would involve ministers, and whose views and recommendations would, the report hoped, therefore "carry weight." It called—yet again—for departmental mergers at the UN in New York to create an undisputed center of economic and social policy. And finally, although the report admitted that "the World Bank is considered by many to be the most effective institution for the coordination of multilateral assistance," instead of accepting this, it proposed as an "urgent" task "to revitalize and reaffirm the role of the UNDP as a major and potentially effective instrument of multilateral development cooperation." The report argued that, as the hub of UN technical cooperation, the voluntary basis of funding for UNDP should be replaced by a new, more automatic system of negotiated pledges.

The UN seemed condemned to relive history. In 1992, soon after Boutros Boutros-Ghali settled in as the new secretary-general, restructuring proposals began to trickle down from the thirty-eighth floor. By the year's end, the General Assembly had again agreed—in principle—on the familiar agenda of streamlining debates in New York and reducing duplication of effort in the UN by "strengthening" ECOSOC. Principle was painfully translated, by December 1993, into a long General Assembly resolution on the well-worn theme of "restructuring and revitalisation of the United Nations in the economic, social and related fields."[5]

Truth should not be sought in such documents, Western diplomats comforted themselves. No matter that it was the opposite of the case that the UN had "a unique and paramount role in the promotion of international cooperation for development," as the resolution proclaimed. Getting this document through at all had been "very, very painful," according to a leading Western negotiator, "so we swallowed a lot of garbage for the sake of the things we wanted done." The Group of 77 had been deeply suspicious that the purpose of the exercise was to reduce donor contributions to UN development programs (they got a vague promise to increase them)—and to link UN assistance, for the first time, to policy reforms in the recipient countries, which was anathema. They had signed in the end only because several developing countries were convinced that the money for these UN programs would otherwise dry up.

Building on the Nordic report, a group of Western governments—with little real input from the United States—had drawn up a four-tier agenda. The first tier was, once again, ECOSOC reform; the second, overhauling the management of UN programs in New York; the third, tackling the management of the specialized agencies; and the fourth, about which they said little in public, was to get rid of uncooperative UN executives. Needless to say, what the Third World countries signed up to was hardly a revolution. They did agree to a formal "division of labor" between ECOSOC and the General Assembly, which looked deceptively tidy. For ECOSOC, topics were formally grouped into categories for annual, biennial, or triennial consideration—although this still did not stop any delegation from demanding "the discussion of any specific issue" if it chose. And they agreed to "high-level segments" of ECOSOC debates, open to ministers of all member states, to consider selected "policy themes" and "provide the United Nations system with cross-sectoral coordination and overall guidance on a system-wide basis." The council was even, it was agreed, to refrain from reopening substantive debates already held in its subsidiary committees—again, unless "one or more Member States" so requested. Finally, the resolution did contain, and this was the most bitterly contested Western objective, agreement on cutting the membership of the governing bodies of the UNDP and other programs subordinated to New York's authority—not to eighteen, as the Nordics wanted, but to thirty-six members. These new executive boards were to meet four or five times a year (again, the Nordics wanted weekly sessions, as at the World Bank, but this was considered too much to expect the Group of 77 to accept). They would, the donors hoped, exert more effective control—and set a precedent for similar improvements to the "governance" of the specialized agencies.

In the real world, however, the West was depending on political factors to effect real change. There was a fresh drive to get rid of ineffectual or obnoxious chief executives, in New York and the specialized agencies; and to convince their successors that unless they came up with solid reforms, the donors were at last determined to walk away. This was nothing if not overdue. Insiders at the UN blame governments—and above all, influential governments—for settling for less than they should with respect to the most senior appointments. The criticism is justified. In the history of the United Nations, not one UN secretary-general has been appointed because he was expected to provide outstanding leadership. Grey, safe men were positively sought out. (In Dag Hammarskjöld, the five permanent members simply made a mistake of judgment: they thought the man to be the very model of the modern faceless bureaucrat.) We do not yet know whether the Americans and the Russians selected Kurt Waldheim because they had particular reason to be convinced that his secret past would render him exceptionally pliable, or whether his character alone was enough to reassure them that, as Shirley Hazzard has written, he would be "proof against every occasion of a larger kind."[6] But Waldheim certainly fitted smoothly into the role set from the moment he was inaugurated, when he pronounced that this was a job in which "one has to know the limits."

Where the UN secretary-generalship is concerned, it might be argued that Cold War politics intervened; yet elections to other top positions have been handled just as cynically by the West, and in organizations, such as the FAO, of which the Soviet Union was not even a member. With energetic canvassing by Western governments, world-class figures might have been persuaded to stand for the director-generalship of UNESCO in 1987—men who might, even at that late stage, have conceivably arrested its decay. But instead of trying to build support around Enrique Iglesias (the energetic Uruguayan foreign minister who later became the head of the Inter-American Development Bank), or Prince Sadruddin Aga Kahn, a respected former UN High Commissioner for Refugees, they let the charming, unimpressive Spanish biochemist Federico Mayor slide into place almost by default.

UNESCO's management slowly improved, although Mayor signally failed to make the clean sweep of M'Bow's cronies that should have been his first step, or to have the accounts ruthlessly vetted. It was therefore unsurprising that the senior external consultant on the international panel called in to monitor UNESCO reform, Knut Hammarskjöld, found that staffing remained subject at all levels to "unethical pressures." But management was only part of the problem: this was above all a case when dropping a few controversial programs was not enough. Some UNESCO ventures, such as its promotion in 1993 of Islamic schools in Sudan—where the government was not only waging war against Christians in the south but refusing to educate children in any language other than Arabic—were straight out of the old mold. And although Mayor came into office promising that UNESCO would concentrate on its role as catalyst, "making yeast, not bread," bread, in the form of underfunded miniprojects, continued to be its staple product. What UNESCO needed to recapture, above all to respond to the needs of post-Communist societies and to the isolated and vulnerable voices of intellectual dissent abroad in Africa, was something of the spirit of the interwar Organization for Intellectual Cooperation. It needed to become a *real* talking shop, but it had yet, in Hammarskjöld's view, to rid itself of "the historically conditioned proliferation of activities, often confusing and unclear."[7] He was duly elected for a second term despite, or because of, his timidity as a reformer. And in 1994, the Clinton administration held out the prospect that the U.S. would rejoin—a triumph of political correctness over common sense.

In UNESCO and the FAO, indecision may partly be explained by contempt for the organizations (and the West *did* make an effort in 1987 to find a challenger for Edouard Saouma, although in 1993 they proved utterly disorganized, fielding a plethora of Western candidates rather than uniting behind an able Australian who stood a plausible chance of election). But after years of demanding more effective coordination from the UN—a futile campaign, but that is beside the point here—Western governments made little effort to insist on the appointment of an outstanding candidate when the job of director-general for economic cooperation and development fell vacant in 1989. Political lethargy at such crucial junctures did nothing for Western credibility in pressing for reform.

The case of the WHO, which had been considered by Western governments to be relatively well run under Halfdan Mahler and to do irreplaceable work, is even more depressing. The West's critical mistake was to do far too little in 1988 to stop the election of Dr. Hiroshi Nakajima as Mahler's successor, although not one government thought him of sufficient stature for the job, and he was rapidly seen to display "a lack of interest or of ability in forming broad policy goals."[8] Two years later, Dr. Jonathan Mann resigned as head of the WHO's Global Program on AIDS, citing Nakajima's "systematic interference" with its management and lack of commitment to its objectives. Although Mann was highly respected, particularly for the speed with which he had assisted governments to devise preventive strategies and his skill in eliciting the participation of voluntary organizations, and although his departure was in addition acknowledged to be only the most visible symptom of WHO's sudden contagion with the UNESCO disease, protest was minimal. A British minister even opined that it would be inappropriate to intervene in "an internal staff matter, just a question of personalities."[9] But by 1992, this "question of personalities" had assumed dimensions that could not be ignored, as Nakajima traveled the world seeking reelection.

The United States and the European Community, alarmed by the speed with which WHO was losing its reputation for forward planning and sound administration and by the slump in staff morale, sought to induce the Japanese to persuade "their" man not to seek another term; when that failed, they backed a rival, an Algerian neurosurgeon, Muhammad Abdelmoumene. When it came to the WHO board in January 1993, Nakajima won the nomination, by 18 votes to 13, but so strong was the circumstantial evidence that both he and the Japanese government had exerted improper influence on the vote that the United States and the European Community urgently requested the British National Audit Office (NAO)—a body with long experience of UN agencies—to conduct a special audit. The NAO found that Dr. Yugi Kawaguchi, a Japanese promoted to be the WHO director of planning by Nakajima, had recently allocated five contracts of up to $150,000, disregarding WHO procedures for processing contracts, to individuals or institutions represented on the board. Japan had invited other board members to Japan shortly before the vote and, according to U.S. State Department officials, had threatened to cut its imports from two countries with board representation and made known to others that Japanese aid to their country happened currently to be under review. The NAO evidence, together with a report by the internal auditor that confirmed these findings, was presented to that May's World Health Assembly. Yet with both his probity and professional ability publicly in question, Nakajima was reelected by 93 votes to 58, becoming the first WHO director-general not to have been elected unanimously. This was after an acrimonious debate[10] in which several African and Asian delegates backed a Bolivian charge that the West's attack was really aimed at developing countries, which it was insulting by suggesting that they were easily corruptible. "We either had to cave in over Nakajima's second term," one delegate commented, "or it was World War III with the Japanese."

Admitting defeat at the WHO, Western officials nonetheless insisted that there really was a new strategy. They pointed to indications that it was working at the United Nations Industrial Development Organization (UNIDO), whose new Mexican director-general, Mario Y Campos, had sacked all eight of his deputies, promised a root and branch review of its mandate, and even promised to establish just what, in "the field" where it had extensive offices, the organization actually *did*. They were delighted that a respected environmentalist, Gustave Speth, had taken over from Draper as UNDP administrator. At UNICEF, Western governments pointed out that the Group of 77 had given its full support when they toughened the terms of reference for an external management review. And they were rightly encouraged by the International Labor Office's success, initially under the pressure of "zero growth," in pruning its staff of dead wood and by the imaginative, forward-looking strategy being pursued by its director-general Michel Hansenne. But they privately admitted that for many governments, this was the UN's last chance to get its development act together; and the jury was still out.

These reforms aimed at getting the UN's economic and social machinery to do the same things better are, however, almost certainly on the wrong track. They still depend on coordination, albeit in a looser form, and on the top-down allocation of funds. They do not address "projectitis," which, as the Nordic report noted, has destroyed the specialized agencies as "centres of excellence." The sectoral division of funds for technical assistance has stimulated empire-building, fragmented the efforts of what are after all small organizations, and seriously distorted the UN's work, both in the specialized agencies and in New York itself. The conventional wisdom behind the 1993 reforms seemed still to be geared, as it had been in the late 1980s, to "strengthening" the UNDP "to assist governments to impose the necessary discipline on the Agencies" of the UN. If governments took that approach seriously, they would indeed logically aim to fuse the UNDP, UNICEF, the World Food Program, and the UN Fund for Population Activities (UNFPO) into a UN Development Authority. And, as a review of the specialized agencies had commented in 1987,[11] this implied faith that "the level of expertise available to the UNDP to manage development funds [could] match that of the World Bank, and [that] the contributors to these funds would tolerate this degree of centralization" and that the agencies would bring their activities into line. The conventional wisdom, then as in the 1990s, was also that none of this will happen.

A break with this "system" would be more likely to bring about the modernization the UN needs. And the point of departure should be that since competition is ingrained in the way the UN operates, the power of the purse should be used to make this genuine and open competition. What is needed is a demand-led, manpower-planning approach aimed at encouraging developing countries to make better use of the skilled manpower already available in the domestic marketplace. Through the creation of a genuinely open market in technical cooperation, developing countries could draw on a pool of grant finance to "buy" in the technical advice they need on the basis of competitive tenders.

The poorest countries, those eligible for low-cost International Development Association loans, could have access to a common pool of funds, either to finance the training of their own nationals, or to "purchase" external advice. They would be encouraged to use the money to improve the skills of their own people, but where they needed to buy in advice, their governments would invite bids on an open market, in which the UN agencies with relevant expertise would have to compete with national aid agencies, private consultants, and voluntary agencies. Power would be transferred to the customers. Since they could obtain these grants to pay their own nationals, they would be more likely to consider whether the much costlier services of expatriates were indispensable, whether they were getting the best available, and whether outside expertise would increase their own future capacity to run things independently. Bleak necessity is already compelling governments in the poorest countries to improve their policies and make better use of their neglected "human capital." And they are becoming more realistic about the actual cost of finance from whatever source (including aid). Many of them have begun to recognize that relying on "free" expatriate advice, provided on an *ad hoc* basis for specific projects and often with scant regard for economic priorities, has actually retarded the national "institution-building," which was supposed to be the point of the whole exercise. The artificial division between technical assistance and capital investment that is such a marked feature of UN field programs is, moreover, manifestly absurd in countries attempting ambitious market reforms.

This would deprive the specialized agencies of any monopoly claims to execute projects in "their" sectors. If they wished to stay in the technical assistance business, they would be forced to market their services, competing for contracts instead of operating a cartel. They have to establish their preeminence as specialists in a competitive world. There would, at the least, be a sharp reduction in the number of underfunded miniprojects and pointless five-day "training" seminars characteristic of UN field programs. The empire-building rivalries between agencies that defeat, and always will, the coordinators' best efforts would of necessity gradually give way to genuine, market-based competition. And the global organizations would have to rediscover their roles in terms of the services they could perform for their whole memberships, not just their Third World "clients." Competitive tender, within the framework of a consolidated pool of grant funds, would not abolish UN field programs. They would survive, on a self-financing basis, insofar as there was a demand for them. But their working methods would certainly have to be overhauled. What would be involved is best illustrated by the experience of George Kanawaty, who, as head of the International Labor Organization's training department in the 1980s, made it the first UN unit routinely to bid for World Bank contracts.

It took Kanawaty, who describes himself as an Egyptian product of American business school, six months to obtain ILO clearance to bid for work in this way—and two years to train the ILO's finance department to pull bids together within six weeks and be prepared to cut tenders in order to land contracts. "You can imagine," he says, "what it means to the UN to put somebody on a plane within 24 hours of hearing that a job is on offer, and to conduct business by telephone and fax instead of the 2nd class mail. But it concentrates the mind to be competing with Bechtel."

His division had to learn to work with ministers who had never heard of the ILO. Traditionally the ILO's area offices work largely through labor ministries. Kanawaty's teams were dealing instead with the prime minister's office, the ministries of industry, planning, construction, and even agriculture and education—the people who actually make decisions about training and employment. Kanawaty admitted to losing as many bids as he won, adding wryly that UN organizations are somewhat restricted when it comes to "sweetening" contracts. But he reckoned that

> without these contracts, and the experience of selling our services we have acquired, we would have been out of the training business. Thirty or forty years ago the ILO was providing training institutes; we were a specialty store. Now countries want more diverse products: courses in managing food distribution or machine tool repair, accountancy colleges or training for the disabled. We have had to become a supermarket. It means a totally different attitude to finding out what governments, and employers, want.[12]

Despite the internal resistance initially encountered by Kanawaty, in the mid-1980s the ILO was one of the few specialized agencies attempting to think through the implications for its work of the diminishing role of the state. A report by the then director-general Francis Blanchard, in 1986[13] to the ILO's tripartite membership of governments, employers' organizations, and trade unions drew their attention to the constituency they did *not* represent: the twelve hundred million "potential workers" outside the organized labor force. It explicitly asserted that to continue to emphasize legislation and the promotion of formal labor standards—the ILO's traditional armory—would stifle the dynamism and creativity of the really poor. The ILO had, in Blanchard's view, been "successful—some people would say too successful—in promoting workers' rights. But what about all those poor devils beyond all the laws we can devise?"[14] The ILO needed "new techniques to give free enterprise—perhaps I should have said free initiative—its head," encouraging street vendors and fish dryers "to organize better the jobs they create themselves." But no institution that works through governments or even organized labor, which customarily treats people in the "informal" sector with hostility, is well placed to foster such self-help. UN projects are, typically, run by (and often for) the powers that be. By emphasizing the need to help the poor assert their rights against tissues of privilege and hierarchy, the ILO was reaching beyond its traditional clientele. And, since it could reach the poor neither through its existing tripartite membership, nor by direct action, the report recognized that it would need to work indirectly, establishing contacts with grass-roots activists, churches, and young people with skills but no jobs ready to implement locally devised strategies of self-help. It implied, in the words of an ILO rural development manager, "tackling poverty by turning the aid industry upside down." The new strategy "would have to be slipped past the powers that be, and carried out not by them—or by us for that matter—but by locals, because they know their terrain and have far more at stake than expensive foreign experts." The ILO could best help by persuading recipient governments, and individual aid donors, of the futility of an organized, top-down approach to generating the multiple, necessarily small-scale initiatives that together would dynamize the informal economic sectors.

This is the sort of rethinking the West should be out to encourage. One approach open to donor governments would be to create a new grant "window" of the World Bank, stipulating that through the Bank's International Finance Corporation, private sector employers would also have access to it for help with manpower training. Donors could monitor the use recipients made of this pool through the Bank's Consultative Groups. A country's eligibility for grants could be determined through studies of its manpower and training needs and linked with its adjustment programs. Small World Bank teams could work with national ministries as they already do on these programs, while taking care actively to involve private sector employers. Their task would be to assess the skills the country was producing, where it needed to build them up, and how to make the most cost-effective use of external advice.

The idea is not particularly revolutionary. Early in the 1980s, at a seminar in the Hague, the late George Arthur Brown—until 1993 the UNDP's associate administrator—proposed merging the UNDP with the World Bank as its technical assistance affiliate. This would, he argued, bridge the artificial gap between human and capital investment, enhance efficiency, and, because of the Bank's prestige with donors, attract more money then a free-standing UNDP. Under the Bank's competitive tender rules, UN specialized agencies would no longer be able to claim the right to execute UNDP-funded projects in their sectors. Brown later, diplomatically, "mislaid" this speech, and in 1985[15] explained that he had changed his mind. The proposal, he said, was politically impossible.

Were any such plan to be submitted to a vote of the UNDP's members, he would of course be right. Few developing countries would be likely to endorse shifting UNDP funds to an organization in which weighted voting operated, even if the result was likely to be more efficient use of the money and an increase in the donor governments' contributions. Indeed, one source of Third World attachment to the UNDP (and to the specialized agencies' field programs which absorb most of its money) is that controls over this project aid have been relatively feeble. Pork barrels create bonds of collusion and opportunism, and many recipient governments would make common cause with the agencies to resist a World Bank takeover. But even under new management, an agency whose brightest executives (Brown was not alone) believe that it perpetuates a superannuated model of development cooperation, and that it would be better off merged with the World Bank, makes a poor focus for reform. A *negotiated* transfer of funding may be out of the question, but there is no inherent reason why such a plan would have to be negotiated, since these funds are voluntarily provided. The power of the purse would here be decisive. And change need not come about overnight. The transfer of Western contributions to the new window need not, and almost certainly would not, be effected unanimously, or at a stroke. Nor would the creation of the World Bank channel require the abolition of the UNDP, or of the agencies' operational activities, since they could stay in business to the extent that they could market their wares.

Matters are moving in that direction, as the Nordic report acknowledged. It believed that the specialized agencies' involvement in technical assistance ought increasingly to be "organized on a contractual basis, with payment for services rendered," giving "due recognition" to their independent status—and also to "the fact that today the expertise required for development activities is often more readily found in institutions outside the system."[16] The view that the agencies should compete, and that "those who are demonstrably more creative and efficient should be rewarded with increased funding and growth, while those whose structures fail the test will find their resource base dwindling," was not yet official policy, the report noted. But it had "an increasing number of adherents as an organizational philosophy in line with the thinking of market economists."

An early decision by key Western governments to transfer these "operational" resources to the Bretton Woods institutions would yield immediate dividends. First, by switching a whole class of funds to the organizations likely to use them most effectively, the West would provide an example of what was meant by policies of positive discrimination. The other organizations would be compelled to concentrate on their original functions as centers for the exchange of information, catalysts for ideas, and forums for policy dialogue. This would be a process not of reform in the traditional sense, but of creative deconstruction. But it would also require some serious rethinking in the West, where donor governments have been as cynical as any recipient in playing the project game, frequently lobbying quite shamelessly for those that would benefit their exporters and provide jobs for their expatriate experts. For years, they found it convenient to maintain that the UNDP itself was relatively well managed—an assertion based in willful myopia—declining even to ask why the UNDP deemed countries such as Saudi Arabia, Brunei, and Qatar to be eligible for grant aid. For years, they ignored the problem of the low caliber and lack of experience of many UNDP representatives—especially in the poorest countries, which most need high-quality advice and are most vulnerable to the selling pressures of rival UN agencies. They also ignored a steady flow of Joint Inspection Unit (JIU) reports drawing attention to the lax evaluation of the use of UNDP funds—which was due partly to the low standing of the UNDP officers, and partly because those doing the assessing (the UNDP representative, the recipient government, the UN "executing agency," and the consultants hired in) had an obvious interest in claiming success, or in using evidence of failure to make a case for further "rescue" funding.

Even in the 1980s, they pretended to take seriously the UNDP's new National Technical Cooperation Assessments and Programs (NATCAPS), which were supposed "to help governments identify, assess and rank their human resource needs . . . and provide the basis for more rational allocation of funding from all sources,"[17] but which, according to a senior OECD official, served merely to "collect a list of technical assistance projects and publish it as a strategy." Most UNDP resident coordinators, this official added, saw their job as "getting on with local governments," with the result that the UNDP was considered in many Third World capitals as a comforting soft touch in austere times; and the West had been content to leave matters there because "ministers don't give a damn."

Western governments insisted in 1994 that this attitude had completely changed. They held out the prospect of a compromise, under which the World Bank and the UNDP would work together on an across-the-board reassessment of the purpose of technical cooperation—and that UNDP, apart from providing services in technology transfer to middle-income countries, would in the future concentrate on the poorest. But that is still no reason to locate such a facility in New York—or a justification for the preservation of UNDP as a free-standing agency. And not all the reasons for the donors' anxiety to "reform" UNDP were exactly edifying. The truth was that UNDP continued to be a convenient one-stop shop for the Nordics. And the West was doing rather well out of doing good. As Gustave Speth pointed out in a letter to *The Times* in 1994, "UK aid channeled through UNDP is a good investment for Britain. In recent years, for every pound given to UNDP, the UK has received a return flow of nearly £2 spent on British expertise, equipment and training."[18] It was not exactly encouraging that UNDP's supposed new broom was putting forward, as a reason for continuing British support for UNDP, the argument that it was a useful gravy train for donors.

With only minimal extra staffing, the World Bank could do the job. And one effect would be to modernize the aid business. "Hard" technical assistance—feasibility or engineering studies, typically carried out by consulting firms rather than intergovernmental agencies—would continue to be in demand. As the emphasis switched to local management, the future of project officers would be much less certain. The main losers, apart from UN bureaucrats, would be the international, mostly Western, experts profitably employed in consultancy work for the UN. They constitute a powerful lobby, and they would of course object. But they would not lose their jobs overnight, rationalization is long overdue, and there are already signs of consumer resistance: Gambia's minister of agriculture once publicly accused the FAO of "bombarding" his country with consultants. Once the emphasis switched to the development of an integrated approach to manpower planning, bilateral donors and the World Bank itself would have to situate their own offers of technical assistance within these new frameworks.

Many senior World Bank staff accept this. One of its most experienced experts on Africa professes himself "aghast that the attitude to technical assistance in Africa hasn't changed in twenty years—years in which Africa's national capacities have been transformed. The question is how to stop governments from taking the lazy way out, hiring in outsiders instead of running things with their own people." There is no discipline like realistic costing. It is also increasingly acknowledged in Washington that the Bank's own "soft" technical assistance—project managers, visiting experts—has largely been wasted money. One Bank vice president describes it as "always the least well scrutinized part of a loan. It is often thrown in to compensate for the lack of sufficiently rigorous prior analysis of the conditions affecting a project. It exists essentially because of the huge lobby for it; and most consultants in Africa are primarily interested in their next assignment."[19] What applies to Africa could be evenly more sharply stated of countries with large numbers of educated young people who are underemployed or unemployed.

There are two more substantive objections to opening "field programs" to market competition. The first is that the global agencies' field activities would almost certainly shrink, and that once deprived of these and the "field presence" that goes with them, they would become ivory towers remote from the quotidian needs of developing countries. But they are *already* remote, and this need not in any case be so. An intelligent attitude to secondment—through which the agencies could, by recruiting them on short-term contracts, tap the local knowledge of developing country nationals while giving them access to international data and comparative ajpproaches—would produce more effective "feedback" than the mass of project reports that, even when not doctored, gather dust unread at their headquarters. After all, research centers outside the UN do high-quality work without resort to the far-flung quasi-ambassadorial presence of "resident coordinators." The World Health Organization, whose remit in disease prevention and the control of epidemics has always given it a "fireman's" field role, has put its best work into promoting strategies for primary health care, and this policy focus has increased its standing. (Its more project-focused regional offices have always been held in less esteem.) The International Fund for Agricultural Development, a pioneer of innovative approaches to rural credit and low-cost assistance to poor farmers, has virtually no "field presence."

The second objection—which has also been raised against the concept of a UN Development Agency—is that to concentrate funds and organizational responsibility for multilateral technical assistance in one agency would foster monopoly and bureaucratic gigantism. This argument needs to be taken more seriously. Although the World Bank is the most respected of the multilateral development organizations, it has made spectacular mistakes, particularly with respect to environmental questions but also in rural development. So great is the scope for error in the extraordinarily complex business of promoting, and managing, economic and technical change that it is imperative to sustain a multiplicity of approaches.

The answer to this, of course, is that pluralism is not in danger. The UN is only part of a multilateral industry, whose research and development divisions are found in universities, governments, multinational corporations and foundations which, in the private voluntary organizations, has developed a flourishing boutique division. Individual donor and recipient governments have never been reticent about criticizing Bank (or IMF) initiatives with which they disagree and, unlike most other UN agencies, whose boards have—as the West now complains—tended to act as rubber stamps, the Bank and the IMF are under permanent scrutiny from active and generally well-qualified executive directors. Rivalry between UN agencies, each out to defend its sectoral monopoly while grabbing an ever-larger share of projects, hardly promotes pluralism anyway. Agency salesmen are more likely to confuse ministers, particularly those of small countries, than to offer them genuinely broader choice. It is not through "field presence" that the necessary degree of intellectual competition is maintained. The successful campaign mounted in the 1980s, principally by UNICEF, to get the IMF to pay more attention to the effects of policy reforms and economic retrenchment on the poorest sectors of society was generated by headquarters think tanks. This sort of pressure, the creatively subversive questioning of methods and policy assumptions, would be more effective if UN organizations were seen to be genuinely disinterested. And UN agencies that developed Kanawaty's customer-conscious approach would find their markets. The essence of the entire concept is antimonopolistic.

Breaking with the custom of seeking prior agreement for new policies would certainly exacerbate North-South tensions at the UN, at least in the short term. But once it began functioning, developing countries would find that the new system worked to their advantage, and not only because competitive tender would provide better value for money. The Bank has leverage with donor governments that other UN agencies do not possess and, once charged with overall responsibility for multilateral technical assistance grants, could use that leverage to insist that donors apply more rigorous standards when offering their bilateral technical assistance and transfers of technology. The Bank would be far more difficult than the UNDP for Western governments to use as a machine for export promotion and job agency for their nationals, all disguised as aid.

Such a revolution remains extremely unlikely, certainly unless the United States becomes more actively and intelligently engaged in this debate than seemed likely in the early years of the Clinton administration. But it would assist in the task of identifying the comparative advantages of the UN's specialized agencies in "the third millennium." Stripping the "political" UN in New York of most of its development baggage would simplify and concentrate its work. The scope would be greatly reduced for "the dissipation of money in tiny enclaves of activity which are a law unto themselves"—a criticism made of the New York machine by the head of a specialized agency that applies at least equally to the agencies themselves. And the time is propitious for change. The 1980s have been called the "lost decade for development," and it is true that in many countries, principally in Latin America and Africa, the already wretched living standards of the poor further declined, creating intense and widespread suffering. But the conclusion is nonetheless too pessimistic. Governments that had squandered their own resources and those they had borrowed were confronted with economic recession just as those debts fell due and new loans were drying up; and this forced them to learn critical lessons about the conditions required to sustain development and the roles of governments in creating them. These were not, moreover, purely economic lessons. More and more governments were forced to recognize—formally, if not by changing their ways—that people cannot help themselves, and put their considerable entrepreneurial energies to good use, in a climate of corruption, political repression and censorship, and disrespect for the rule of law. The 1980s established the links between political and economic freedoms. No such period should be described as "lost." The lost decades had, if anything, been those in which patronage and mismanagement flourished, lubricated by flows of inadequately monitored aid.

This was also the decade that, at one extreme, demonstrated conclusively that development was possible. Countries such as South Korea, a "basket case" only thirty years earlier, joined the ranks of the industrialized world, and membership of what might be called the "northern South" grew exponentially. At the other extreme were countries, principally in Africa, whose governments had run entire economies as spoils systems for their small elites, and were now forced by economic and social collapse to take their producers seriously, and to do so as enablers rather than supreme actors. There was no escaping the correlation between economic prosperity and competitiveness, on markets rendered increasingly international by technological change.

Putting the UN's "operational" activities on a competitive, self-financing basis would help to reduce confusion about the types of functions that global organizations can reasonably be expected to perform. Depriving the agencies of their field empires would not, of course, bring about a transformation in the quality of their statistical and analytical work, so essential if the secretariats are to recover their international standing and to promote genuine dialogue in their fields. But such a move would compel them to base their claims for support on their achievements in these areas. It would force them to ask what, in a world in which governments themselves are subject as never before to competition from other economic and social actors, the organizations that bring governments together and thus will inevitably be subject to similar competition can still achieve. It would concentrate the energies of the UN on those aspects of the international agenda for which cooperation between governments remains indispensable, and where they need the mediating touch of common institutions.

Shaking Out the Bureaucracy

The UN's bureaucracy must however shed its scales before the global organizations can hope to identify, let alone concentrate on, their areas of comparative strength. As presently structured, the machine remains as incapable of governing itself as it was when Jackson described it in 1969 as a "prehistoric monster." Priority-setting is a phrase as overworked as it is, for most UN managements, meaningless: the enormously detailed line-item budgets they churn out provide a mass of small print for "governing bodies" to wrangle over, but bear no resemblance to a coherent program of work with definable "end products." Beginning with UNESCO, governments sought to impose some semblance of long-term strategic planning through six-year medium-term plans, but succeeded only in adding to the paperwork and locking in the obsolete. After a year at the UN attempting to introduce management reforms the former U.S. attorney-general Richard Thornburgh observed to Boutros Boutros-Ghali in 1993 that the UN's own medium-term plan was "simply useless . . . a document which no one does (or in all candor, should) read or refer to" and "a gross misallocation of scarce talent."[20] And if talent is scarce, that is largely thanks to the UN's "common system" for the international civil service. A monster of unwieldy centralism that stifles initiative, rewards mediocrity, encourages featherbedding, and bedevils any effort at intelligent recruitment, it can best be compared with Gosplan, the monolithic center of the command economy in the former Soviet Union.

Competence and integrity cannot be externally manufactured. But the UN's slide into irrelevance will not be arrested unless it modernizes its management practices, planning procedures, financial controls, evaluation systems, communications, training, and personnel policies. To assume that it will do so on a "systemwide" basis is, to put it mildly, optimistic. In the 1990s some UN secretariats, conscious that those governments with other clubs to turn to are increasingly prepared to rely on what works best, have begun to put their houses in order. But they cannot be expected to recruit the most talented to their staffs, and use their talents effectively, when they are enmeshed in the "jobs-for-life" culture and the rigid grading systems of the UN's fossilized staffing arrangements.

For years Western governments have complained about the lack of accountability prevailing in UN organizations, but in practice they have tolerated a degree of opacity that would be considered totally unacceptable for any civil service in a democracy. The Geneva Group's "zero-growth" policy has been the nearest they have come to sanctions, but this negative policy has had only limited success in compelling secretariats to cooperate in discussing management practices and opening the books. Inadequate internal auditing and slipshod evaluation procedures have not only shielded inefficiency, waste, maladministration, and downright fraud; they have deprived the UN's member states of the information they need to identify the organizations' weaknesses—and strengths. Regular but far from comprehensive external auditing is carried out by national auditing offices, hired by the individual UN agencies themselves on a contractual basis. This system is open to abuse, since the contracts are lucrative, and agency heads have been known (at the FAO and UNESCO, for example) to discourage overzealous inquiries by hinting at their cancellation or nonrenewal. But even the most scrupulous external examinations, which down the years have soberly recorded flagrant examples of mismanagement and malpractice, have frequently been ignored. Internal auditors' offices tend to be inadequately staffed, both in number and competence, even where their members are not thoroughly cowed by the powers that be. The UN's Joint Inspection Unit, created in 1968, has made some inroads on bureaucratic malpractice. But the JIU, a creature of the UN General Assembly which appoints its staff of inspectors, is too small—and too amateur, since the General Assembly has taken to offering inspectorates as "plums" to retiring diplomats rather than to experts in finance or administration—to provide the kind of service that would restore public confidence in the UN's running of its affairs. Its best reports are formidable, but the worst (a notorious example was a report on "managing works of art in the United Nations") have made the JIU itself a target for reform.

Evaluation and *auditing* are dry words. But like undemocratic governments, organizations that are unaccountable finish up by being irresponsible if not corrupt, unresponsive to opportunities, and unintelligible to the public. Even were the UN's various "governing" bodies capable of performing this function effectively—as, manifestly, most of them have not been—they should be concentrating on general policies, and have neither the competence nor the manpower to conduct detailed scrutinies even were secretariats to hide less from them. Regular public scrutiny, far from intruding on the UN management's "right to manage," would make effective management possible: ignorance of the organizations' activities is by no means confined to governments. Quite as importantly, proper evaluation would give hope to those within UN secretariats who have courageously reported failures, incompetence, and even corruption, only to find their reports gather dust and their careers mysteriously blighted.

No serious review of UN organizations can ignore this question and no amount of exhortation—as the years have proved—can compensate for the lack of routine inspection under established rules of "open government." It has always been open to Western governments to do something about this, by insisting on and if necessary financing a proper system of genuinely independent evaluation and auditing. Evaluation should not be confined to discrete, agency-by-agency assessment, but should be extended to assess the capacity of UN organizations, singly or in groups, to perform particular tasks, and would require built-in procedures requiring the UN bureaucracies to respond to criticisms. So ingrained is the collusion between the permanent representatives to these organizations and the secretariats that a majority for such an initiative among the UN membership would be difficult though not impossible to muster. But many UN staff members would welcome more rigorous scrutiny, as they would modern management structures.

When Boutros Boutros-Ghali took office in 1992, he promised sweeping management reforms to establish clear lines of responsibility, a proper career structure and a systematic attack on fraud and inefficiency. He made a promising start on streamlining the UN's top-heavy directorate (where more than forty officials reported directly to the secretary-general) receiving wide praise for promptly scrapping a quarter of these posts, amalgamating some departments, and creating new ones charged with overhauling the management. But within a few months, he was creating new top-level posts and by 1994, nearly fifty under- and assistant-secretaries-general were again reporting directly to the thirty-eighth floor. He promised a wholesale reform of the UN's finances, budgeting, and program planning, and created a new Office for Inspections and Investigations headed at assistant-secretary-general level by a respected functionary, Mohamed Ali Niazi. Niazi found, however, that the management advisory services and internal audit staffs placed under him, in an amalgamation of four existing units, represented in microcosm one of the very problems he was charged to inspect. Only a tiny minority of his staff turned out to be properly trained auditors, there was virtually no training allowance in his budget, and he had powers neither to parachute people in from other divisions or from outside the UN, or to insist on the transfer or dismissal of the incompetents he had inherited.

In 1994, governments weighed in, with the United States leading demands for the creation of an independent body, headed by a UN inspector-general, with broad authority for evaluation, audit, and investigation, reporting annually to the secretary-general and the General Assembly. The plan put forward by the U.S. mission to the UN envisaged a much larger staff, up to one hundred in the first instance, "selected on the basis of strict standards of competence through competitive examination in the fields of auditing, financial or management analysis, public administration, investigations and law"—but also "on the basis of equitable geographic distribution." The post was duly created in the summer of 1994, at the level of deputy secretary-general—the *quid pro quo* being the Clinton administration's agreement to pay in full the substantial arrears that had by then accrued in U.S. payments to the UN peacekeeping budget.[21] This was at least a start. The new plan stood a better chance than previous proposals because the entire system for assessing contributions to the regular UN budget—under which bankrupt Ukraine was, absurdly, being charged more than ten times Saudi Arabia—was simultaneously being reviewed, and Washington was making no secret that its readiness to continue as the largest contributor was contingent on agreement.

But it was only a start, because the inspector-general's remit extended only to the UN Organization, although the Americans hoped—against all experience—that his authority would in time be extended to the UN's specialized agencies. For these, the shortest cut might still be to enlarge the JIU corps of inspectors, while insisting that the General Assembly accept the nomination of candidates by the UN's Advisory Committee on Administrative and Budgetary Questions (ACABQ), which by convention is composed of experts from member states. The JIU could continue to concentrate on management and value for money in the broad sense, but work with a panel of external auditors who could in the first instance be drawn from the staffs currently contracted to individual UN agencies, but whose remit would cover all the specialized agencies. The work of these two staffs, while distinct, could be mutually reinforcing—above all if, instead of being presented to UN chief executives, their reports were submitted directly to governing boards, and made available for public inspection. An integral part of their work would be published follow-up reports saying which of their recommendations had been applied, and with what results; and which had been ignored. Groups of ten or more states should be entitled to ask either body to conduct special investigations, footing the bill if these involved recruiting extra staff. The difficulties of setting up such a system would be considerable. It would be opposed by many senior UN executives. But those who refused to cooperate could be left with no doubt that their organizations faced the prospect of reduced Western funding (or even, possibly, Western withdrawals).

You still cannot move mountains with lousy shovels. Nor can you expect innovation from demoralized staff trapped in rigid hierarchies, or from managers lumbered with unqualified personnel who have been hired thanks to political jobbery or because their passports fit the requirements of "equitable geographical distribution." The quality of UN staff is the question on which governments (often while negotiating contracts for their nationals under the table) are most critical, most hypocritical, and most fatalistic. The final report of the international panel on UNESCO cited earlier concluded with some comments on "ethics in management of international organizations," which, as it said, applied across the board:

> It is a sad and frustrating experience to see how in the sensitive area of staff—high and low—unethical pressures are applied—contrary to agreed rules of the game—to obtain advantages of [a] political, personal or prestige nature, by promoting openly and behind the scenes the cause of preferred individuals—international civil servants. These practices do not serve to inspire in the public . . . respect and confidence in international governance. They also render difficult the maintenance of morale and high standards among even the most conscientious international civil servants . . . these practices appear to have become, in some cases, a matter of national policy.[22]

There is, admittedly, a chicken-and-egg aspect to the question of staff quality: good recruits will be increasingly difficult to attract to, and retain in, organizations out of touch with the world they exist to serve. And governments have themselves been guilty of worse than collusion with the UN's patronage system. The superpowers early set an appalling example: the Soviet Union's cynical disregard for the requirement of Article 100 of the UN Charter that staff should be "responsible only to the Organization" was paralleled, for thirty-three years from 1953 to 1986, by the U.S. government's inexcusable official screening of all American applicants for UN posts, a hangover from the McCarthy witchhunt era. But from a purely administrative viewpoint, the "international civil service" is a disgrace: lacking a career structure worthy of the name, inflexible, underskilled and overmanned, and alien to the concepts of productivity or rewards for exceptional merit.

These defects have been extensively documented, in a series of reports by the JIU dating from 1971 and by expert groups appointed by governments, in testimony from serving and retired staff members, and in indignant protests by congressional committees. There have been two standard responses. Proposals have been drawn up, some of them radical and detailed, for the reform of the international civil service; these have been watered down by intergovernmental committees and then ignored (with impunity) by UN executives. Alternatively, the axe has been brought out, setting ceilings on staff numbers and restricting pay increases under the "common system" whereby the UN fixes remuneration and working conditions.

Even as a counsel of despair, the axe has been an ineffective weapon. For a start, staff numbers can easily be disguised under "temporary" contracts or by paying consultants out of operational overheads. (In 1984, for example, the FAO's personnel director claimed that the agency's payroll was 7,000. Yet the FAO's own computer put the number at 8,729;

and the budgetary experts of the United States and Canada calculated that the true figure was 9,730.) Hiring freezes, arbitrary ceilings on staff numbers, and cuts through attrition tend to be counterproductive. The ones to go (as happened under the 15 percent staff cut imposed on the central UN secretariat under the 1986 "reform package") are those with the best prospect of employment elsewhere, or relatively new recruits who do not have permanent contracts. Boutros-Ghali's hiring freeze at the UN in 1992 was followed up better than before by Thornburgh, who conducted a post-by-post review aimed at redeploying staff to areas of shortage, but it affected only seventy-four posts. This exercise barely touched, as Thornburgh was to note, the "defects . . . in nearly every aspect of present personnel practice"—haphazard recruitment, nugatory training programs, promotion procedures so complicated as to be "nearly unworkable," and those for discipline and dismissal subject to "seemingly interminable appeals processes." And, as he drily noted, the secretary-general's pledge that no staff members would lose their jobs through restructuring had "hamstrung efforts to increase productivity." Expensive as severance payments were, he advised, the cost of keeping on incompetent and unqualified staff was far greater. There was, however, no response to his plea that "managers simply must be permitted to terminate those not measuring up to 'the highest standards of competence, integrity' contemplated by the Charter."[23]

If the effect of reform through "attrition" is to increase the proportion of dead wood in the tree, the wage freezes beloved of donor governments are almost equally unsatisfactory. They seldom make life uncomfortable enough to drive out the incompetents at the top—those who, as a perceptive study of the politics of UN staffing observed as far back as 1974, have often been placed there by governments "as insurance against unwanted Secretariat action,"[24] or who have attained their position through systematic inertia, unquestioning conformity, or as trusted henchmen of agency barons. And the penalty of freezing salaries is that rates for junior grades become uncompetitive; by the 1990s, even the best-run UN agencies were having genuine difficulty in attracting young people with skills in demand elsewhere.

The regulations drawn up by the International Civil Service Commission have come to hamper initiative without preventing corruption. The UN's common grading system compels each organization to pay the same salaries to staff in a given grade (apart from minor, and still centrally determined "post adjustments" to reflect cost-of-living differentials in different capitals), leaving almost no leeway for merit awards. The original argument in favor of this common system was that it would create a corps of able international administrators who could move between agencies, since they all operated under the same rules. In practice, such mobility is the exception, not merely between agencies but even within them: people may stay in the same division for their entire career. The system of permanent contracts, intended to promote political and intellectual independence, has also misfired. It has failed to ensure that UN staff give their undivided loyalty to "the Organization" or, equally significantly, to prevent the creation of a corporate culture in which the chief executive—the secretary-general at the UN and the directors-general in the agencies—is in practice the focus of loyalty, rather than the institution he serves. The pursuit of these coveted permanent contracts promotes subservience, their attainment complacency tempered only by the knowledge that any UN civil servant may have his or her contract terminated by the relevant chief executive "in the interest of the organization." Yet for all the theoretically absolute power of chief executives in personnel matters, such rigidities have been built into the system as to make hiring, promotion, and, above all, firing a permanent nightmare for managers genuinely concerned with quality and flexibility.

Before they hire, divisional managers are required, as one of them bitterly records, to "report on all candidates and all *potential* candidates, making it incredibly difficult to get the person you want—even if that person is not then disqualified by the personnel department for lack of seniority."[25] Such systems positively invite circumvention. But they are most often bent in order to accommodate political appointees, rather than to make room for exceptional talent. Once hired, the performance of UN civil servants is vetted annually—in theory, at least. In practice, 80 percent of staff at UN headquarters consistently receive "A" ratings and 90 percent are "positive"; and the pattern is similar elsewhere. Candid assessments are inhibited, to put it no more strongly, by the fact that staff can vet their assessments and insist on complicated and time-consuming rebuttal procedures.

As to firing, the UN secretariats are at once absurdly overprotected, and subject to arbitrary executive decision. In the latter category, some of the most flagrant examples date back to the McCarthy years, discussed in Chapter 8, which victimized hundreds directly and indirectly and intimidated many more. (Some of the victims did not even have the satisfaction of knowing that the reason for their dismissal was political: Shirley Hazzard cites the case of sixty UN employees dismissed in 1952 "as part of an 'efficiency survey' . . . the records of which were then immediately destroyed."[26] But such cases are exceptions: as a general rule, staff are extremely difficult even to downgrade, never mind to dislodge. According to one frustrated senior UN official, "Once somebody has a permanent contract, they have to be practically convicted of robbing the till to be fired and even that is not always enough. The disciplinary procedures are so complicated that even in the most blatant case, it is simpler to resort to the quiet golden handshake."[27] All this makes nonsense of the concept of a *career* civil service; what is left is the concept of *permanence*, reinforced by pressures from staff associations that (partly for lack of satisfaction on other counts) have made security of tenure their obsession. For the vast majority, a job at the UN is a job for life.

Since overcentralization is an integral part of the problem, a centrally devised solution is unlikely. Yet few governments, even in the 1990s, even in the West, are ready to contemplate the erosion of the "common system." In the first place, they are under the illusion that this colossally wasteful and inefficient system is cheap. At the UN, one European foreign ministry's management expert argued in 1994, the staff cost 80 percent of the budget; "if we were to lose the constraints of the common system, individual agencies would start paying the going rate and costs would go through the roof." To the thought that cash limits could take care of that problem, he reacted with incredulity.

> But that would mean firing a lot of people. And that's just not on. You have to remember that staffing is a highly emotive question at the UN— not just for the staff, but for governments, who want jobs for their nationals. And efficiency cannot be the sole criterion; equitable geographic distribution of posts is a fact of life, and if directors-general were free to fire incompetents, where is the guarantee that they would respect national quotas?

The resistance goes beyond treating the UN as though it were an international employment agency, and logic rarely enters in. An official who acknowledged that the

Bank and IMF had combined a high degree of competence with a reasonable, if not mathematical or formally required, spread of nationals working for them added that at the lower levels their staff "tend to be American or American-trained." Even if this were cause for serious concern, it is equally true that secretarial and blue-collar grades are extensively filled by Italians at the FAO in Rome, and by French people at UNESCO. Another argued that to maintain the unity of the UN, it was important to protect the generic nature of the international civil service. The principle of parity of pay and conditions between, say, a P2 grade at UNEP in Nairobi and his equivalent at the ILO in Geneva must, he said, be maintained. He admitted that transfers from one to the other almost never happened, but argued that it would be "wholly unacceptable" for staff in the parts of the UN, such as peacekeeping in 1994, which were "the flavor of the month" to be paid more than the same grades at UNESCO.

The final lines of defense are first, that there is nothing wrong with the common system per se, but that any system can be only as good as the body that controls it. At the most, it is conceded that there might be some need to create a new exceptional employment category within the common system, to enable the UN to compete in the international market for specialists in keen demand such as economists or logistics experts. The priorities, in this view, should be to improve the working of the International Civil Service Commission, to introduce new management techniques based on "best practice" for recruitment, retention and motivation, and to insist on "line responsibilities" within devolved budgets. As for salaries, governments of the poorer countries are still queueing for jobs for their people; and even if the UN cannot attract really high flyers, it can easily ensure, with a few improvements to techniques for staff assessment that admittedly would only "tinker at the margins," that a good half of its employees are "perfectly respectable."[28]

Yet even within this shrunken perspective on modernization, even within this frank acceptance of the second best, the defenders of the common system are hard-pressed to explain why and how the "system" might be induced after all these years to loosen the sinews of patronage and dismantle some of its treasured perks and restrictive practices. When countries in every continent, even Africa, have been forced by the financial burdens of inefficient bureaucracies or by the requirements of international competitiveness into the business of "reinventing government," they have no business issuing the UN with such certificates of immunity from change—above all when they purport to be working hard on UN reform.

A more fruitful approach might be for donor governments to encourage reform by force of example, rewarding whatever agency takes a convincing lead in modernization. They should invite chief executives to make use of their extensive powers, and hold them directly accountable for the quality of their management. To that end, they should support those agency heads who wanted to break away from the "common system" and operate, within the cash limits of agreed overall budgets, personnel policies emphasizing flexibility, and incentives. Not a few might respond with enthusiasm to the new freedom to manage this would give them.

The World Bank and the IMF, which continue to recruit able people, pay them the "going rate," and exact high levels of performance from them, have consistently refused to have anything to do with the common system. The best-run UN agencies chafe under it and would gladly opt out, and they deserve backing from Western capitals. The mold might well be broken by the GATT, where a working group was set up in March 1994 to settle the administrative and financial questions involved in converting it from a "general agreement" into a World Trade Organization (WTO). GATT's director-general, Peter Sutherland, made no secret of his belief that the new WTO should be taken out of the common system.

As a "provisional" body, the GATT was in a sense half in, half out of the UN, and little scarred by the UN diseases of bureaucratic aggrandizement and dreams of empire. But as a fully fledged organization, Sutherland feared infection. His ambition was to associate the new WTO not with the UN in New York but with the IMF and the World Bank—achieving the original aims of the founders at Bretton Woods to create a trio of financial and trade institutions. The WTO must, he argued, be able to establish itself early as an undisputed center of excellence, and must therefore be free to hire the best talent available.

If the GATT succeeded in opting out of the common system, the dominoes might start to fall. The Universal Postal Union, an institution far older than the common system that was already virtually self-financing by the 1990s, could follow suit, as could the International Telecommunications Union. These are UN minnows, but opting out of the common system would be a logical accompaniment to the new management techniques actively being introduced at the ILO by Michel Hansenne, its director-general since 1989. This formed part of an ambitious strategy to modernize and relaunch the ILO on its seventy-fifth anniversary in 1994, and to "move away from the caution, the prudence, the safety-first attitude that too often characterizes the ILO's work" and that, in his view, could "lead to intellectual sterility and irrelevance." Like Sutherland, Hansenne saw closer cooperation with the international financial institutions as an integral part of his drive to give the ILO greater intellectual authority, diversify its sources of funding, and speed up its responses to requests—which were coming particularly thick and fast from the former Communist countries—for immediately relevant, practical policy advice.[29]

Any organization that broke with the common system would come up against a further question: whether the concept of a permanent international civil service was still viable. Any international bureaucracy needs a core of "career" staff, however small. But much more use could be made, as a matter of deliberate policy, of secondment. This would indeed be indispensable for organizations that pursued Hansenne's aim to "profit from the widest range of knowledge and experience," drawing in "experts from government departments . . . other than labor ministries, from international organizations dealing with economic and social matters, from nongovernmental organizations with different specializations, and from universities and research institutes."[30] The Soviet Union's deployments of its nationals (many of them from the KGB) on rotating contracts in the UN has given secondment a bad name. But secondment could be the most attractive and direct route to enlivening UN secretariats, provided recruits were brought in not just from national bureaucracies, but from industry, universities, private voluntary organizations, and even—to inject some *glasnost* and professionalism into UN information services—the media. The point would be to diminish, through cross-fertilization, the distance between the global organizations and the constituencies they are supposed to serve. Greater reliance on secondment, through deliberately short-term contracts understood by both sides to be renewable only in exceptional circumstances, would improve mobility and flexibility and introduce some real competition into the secretariats. By matching talents to jobs, it would reduce the pressure for "equitable geographical distribution" of posts in favor of the "efficiency, competence and integrity," which the UN Charter intended to be "the paramount consideration" (Article 101).

Secondment might even, in practice, sustain geographical diversity without sacrificing standards. It is not difficult to see why. The smallest and poorest countries tend to be shortest of skilled people. But through secondment, such people could gain international experience without being permanently lost to the domestic resource base. Governments might in such circumstances be more inclined to recommend their most promising young and middle-range people for UN jobs. They might, though this may be too much to hope, gradually cease to regard the UN exclusively as a source of permanent meal tickets for friends and relations, or as a means to rid themselves of awkward critics.

The argument against secondment is that people's loyalties would remain with their countries, not the organization. That objection might look stronger were it not that this disembodiment is in practice pretty fictional: links with, and loyalties to, capitals flourish among even the most distinguished permanent international civil servants. But the objection could in part be met by emphasizing recruitment from the private sector, rather than national bureaucracies, coupled with a policy of neither seeking governments' approval of candidates nor permitting them to vet appointments.

An agency that "opted out" of the common system would still have to offer the permanent core staff reasonable security of tenure. After a probationary period, that might mean renewable six-year contracts. A career structure would have to include elements normal in any business, but almost unknown in the UN, such as proper management and retraining courses. Once out of the common system, executives would be free to introduce merit awards as incentives, and to pay more for skills in particularly high demand. They would also be free to negotiate severance payments for staff whose performance was satisfactory but whose skills were no longer required (attrition, the standard UN procedure, is no way to achieve turnover that reflects staffing needs). Where disciplinary procedures were used for unsatisfactory work, staff should have recourse to speedy and clearly independent arbitration panels, whose decisions both sides would be bound—contrary to existing practice—to accept.

Such reforms could not be imposed by governments; but that need not inhibit the donors from making it plain that organizations that resist the concept of staff mobility and merit-based pay cannot hope to remain relevant, and would be less likely to attract support. They could draw attention to the powers of the chief executives and their attendant responsibilities to manage their staffing effectively. And governments could do one more thing to improve the secretariats: abandon the pretense that where the top jobs are concerned, political pressures are not applied. These jobs should be frankly recognized as "political" posts—and their tenure limited accordingly. Of course, governments will bid for these positions for their nationals; but carefully drawn job descriptions, advisory panels, and search committees could help to ensure that they at least put forward genuinely well-qualified candidates.

Above all, and although it is at least equally important to take the initial appointments of UN executives a great deal more seriously, a single-term rule for chief executives would reduce the temptation for them to bow to political pressures in making appointments or to use the offer of plum posts to purchase reelection. Many Western governments would concede that the mismanagement, low staff morale and performance, and waste of which they complain can often be traced not to the powers possessed by UN executives, but to the quality of those who exercise them—and that only in extremely rare instances has quality of leadership not suffered in the pursuit of reelection. This is an area in which Western diplomatic influence has been too little tested. So long as the constitutions of particular organizations (including, of course, the UN in New York) contain no impediments to reelection, mere statements of policy by the Geneva Group will change nothing. Changes to constitutions to lay down, say, a single six-year term, could be introduced only gradually because they would in practice require the support of the chief executive concerned (and that would probably be forthcoming only on the understanding that the changes would not apply to the present incumbent). That is no reason not to set such an objective. If global organizations are to be proof against improper pressures from member states, their heads must have considerable executive freedom. But time and again, the reelection campaigns of executive heads have marked the point at which freedom turned into license. Absolute power corrupts, but it is the prospect of losing it that corrupts absolutely: single terms would be a blow for probity.

HUMANITARIAN CHALLENGES

Most people, most of the time, give the United Nations little thought. The exceptions are when wars break out, when people are starving, or when typhoons, volcanic eruptions, earthquakes, or floods inflict massive disruption and loss of life. In these emergencies, neither politics nor doctrines of national sovereignty cut much ice with ordinary people. No matter how rebarbative a country's government, sympathy reaches out to the victims; and no matter how chaotic the situation, people have come to expect—and will often generously donate to—a swift humanitarian response. During the Cold War years, when publics had ceased to expect much of the UN in the way of keeping the peace, they continued to look to it to help the victims of war and disaster, and often to blame it when humanitarian crises were tardily or inadequately tackled. Yet even in this field, where there is an evident need for some body that can coordinate the efforts of individual governments and private charities, a certain skepticism has crept in. When disasters strike, most people give money not to the UN but to the Red Cross, to charities, to relief funds set up by their own governments, or even (as in Armenia in 1989 or following the earthquake in the Indian state of Maharashtra in 1993) to special accounts opened by the government of the afflicted country.

This perception of the UN's inadequacy was heightened from the mid-1980s by its catastrophically tardy response to famine in Ethiopia, Sudan, and much of the Horn. But within a few years, there was no disguising the serious strains placed on all systems, public and private, national and international, by an exponential increase in the scale and number of disasters primarily caused by man. "Little" wars in poor countries had long been part of the "normal" world, to a degree that would have horrified the UN's founders. Even those that inflicted such indescribable suffering on civilians as the vicious fighting between Liberia's repellant warlords, or the war waged on Sudan's Christian-animist south by Islamic dictators in Khartoum, aroused horror and pity but few demands for UN policing. But toward the end of the 1980s, the UN was increasingly drawn into emergency relief in war zones, from Angola and Mozambique to Bosnia; and the UN came under justified criticism when its agencies pulled out of Somalia early in 1991, leaving the International Committee of the Red Cross (ICRC) and private agencies such as Save the Children to handle what was fast becoming an acute famine. And for more than a decade, doubts had been building about the capacity of the UNHCR and the international regime for refugees based on the 1951 covenant to cater to the hugely increased number of people forced to flee their homes.

To what has been described as the "semipermanent humanitarian emergency" of "a Fourth World"[31] were added, in the 1990s, the instabilities of the post-Communist one. The humanitarian mission is daunting in range, reaching beyond disaster prevention and relief to embrace forced migration, environmental devastation, and consumption of and trade in drugs, the gold of the poor. Because national frameworks are inadequate to deal with these menaces, multilateral cooperation is essential. Western governments have an unavoidable duty to make the most of whatever organizational and financial resources are available—unavoidable because the poorest and most vulnerable are the first victims of waste. And this means that where the United Nations proves incapable of providing coherent organizational leadership for international efforts, multilateral alternatives will have to be developed—beginning with disaster relief.

The impact of any disaster is enormously magnified by poverty. Drought does not lead to famine in the United States. Earthquakes devastate shantytowns far more frequently than they shake the houses of the rich. Countries that are resource poor, environmentally fragile, and ill governed are "prone to breakdown"[32] and tend to be least capable of responding when disaster strikes. Their governments also, unfortunately, tend to be among the world's tetchiest. That ought to make the United Nations the ideal instrument for mobilizing international assistance: the "international community" is a useful cover for foreign aid that comes almost exclusively from the industrialized world. The UN's administrative havoc in this field has, however, been so great that each time catastrophe strikes, fresh expedients have to be devised to overcome its paralysis. Disaster relief is admittedly an inexact science, but it is not as inexact as the UN has made it. The problem with the UN is not money (generally forthcoming for such crises). It is incoherence, timidity toward governments that obstruct relief operations, interagency feuds, reliance on paper commitments to pool funds and expertise that have repeatedly broken down just when the need is greatest.

Randolph Kent's study[33] of international disaster relief is a considered, compassionate, and pessimistic assessment of the whole sorry history of *ad hoc* expedients and what he politely calls "institutional insecurities." He points out that it took the Nigerian civil war (which claimed, without UN intervention as peacekeeper, perhaps a million casualties and which was one of the prime post-1945 examples of man-induced famine), the Peruvian earthquake, and the combination of war with natural disaster in Bangladesh—all of which occurred between 1967 and 1971—"to bring the simmering issues of the United Nations' role in emergency operations to the boil." Unproductively on the boil it has remained. Since 1971, no fewer than ten UN disaster units have been created, each exerting its claim to be treated as contact point, fund-raiser, coordinator, and assessor, each with a mandate in excess of its capacities. Alongside these are at least a dozen national disaster units, and an increasingly sophisticated, relatively well coordinated and flexibly managed assortment of voluntary organizations.

From 1971 to April 1992, UN disaster relief and humanitarian assistance was in theory directed by the Office of the United Nations Disaster Relief Coordinator (UNDRO), set up after two years of General Assembly debate to "mobilize, direct and coordinate relief" in response to requests from a "stricken country." In practice, UNDRO rarely managed to act even as traffic policeman, let alone the focus for action. While voluntary organizations welcomed and actively assisted the creation of UNDRO, the established UN agencies resented it as an interloper, and gave it the cold shoulder. The 1973–74 Sahel famine operations were coordinated (at least on paper) by a specially created unit set up in the FAO. In November 1974, the General Assembly passed resolution 3243 calling for measures to "strengthen" UNDRO, the main result of which was a hiring binge at headquarters. In 1980, when the Joint Inspection Unit published[34] an unprecedentedly severe report on all aspects of UNDRO's work, the staff had grown from an original six to fifty, and the annual budget from $330,000 in 1971 to $3.6 million.

The first draft of this report, subsequently bowdlerized, recommended abolishing UNDRO, and what the inspectors found makes it easy to see why this was their first reaction. UNDRO was not "in actual fact" mobilizing or coordinating UN relief. Since it was "strengthened" in 1975, it had been seriously involved in only a tenth of disasters, and in ten out of forty-eight emergencies since 1976 had confined itself either to sending out a few alert notices or to providing a few thousand dollars' worth of emergency cash. To meet its "information-sharing" responsibilities, UNDRO had set up a fine coordination center and operations room, with sophisticated telecommunications, but the center was "empty for long periods of time" and used "chiefly as a stop for UNDRO visitors." Three-quarters of the situation reports it had issued on disasters were unworthy of the appellation, amounting to a maximum of four short telexes. Records of the relief channeled by governments and international organizations, where UNDRO issued them at all, were sketchy and months late. Two high-frequency radio sets, purchased for emergency field use, had been used only once (and unsuccessfully) in 1976 before being put in storage. The organization had never compiled lists of relief supplies immediately available in donor countries or of the needs of disaster-prone countries—partly because its data bank was being compiled by one part-time clerk. Its library was rarely used, and had no catalog or way of dealing with enquiries. Where disaster preparedness was concerned, UNDRO's impact had been "hardly discernable." It senior staff were constantly traveling, but almost never in disaster areas: three-quarters of their trips were to seminars and to donor capitals. The organization's general sense of priorities was illustrated by its plans to install air-conditioning in the communications center, although the two clerical staff who had occupied desks there had been transferred to another office. UNDRO, the report concluded, had no authority as a coordinator, had developed no strategy for disaster relief operations, was almost useless as an information center, and had done little or nothing "to reduce waste and inefficiency in relief administration." The inspectors' final report, acknowledging the view of many officials that UNDRO should be abolished, recommended halving its staff, restricting its brief to "sudden natural disasters," handing over disaster coordination in the field to the UNDP, and relying on an interagency Emergency Assistance Committee to synchronize the UN's response.

The agencies were delighted. Not so governments, which in defiance of this evidence of failure reaffirmed UNDRO in 1982 as the "focal point" for UN coordination and again agreed to "strengthen" it. Little changed. Asked, in June 1984, what it had done to alert the world to the Ethiopian famine, UNDRO replied that it had sent out three round-robin telexes; by October, the number had risen to six.[35] In Africa in 1984–85, as in Bangladesh in 1971 (when after a chaotic start by the UN, Sir Robert Jackson's brilliant work with a tiny staff won the complete trust of governments and voluntary agencies and helped to salvage the UN's reputation), the UN was once again compelled by public outcry to improvise. Late in 1984, the secretary-general set up a small UN unit, staffed with the sharpest operators the UN could muster, to knock sense into the UN's barons, galvanize governments, and get emergency relief flowing. The Office for Emergency Operations in Africa (OEOA) was headed by the UNDP administrator of the day, Bradford Morse. A former congressman, he led the diplomatic assault, leaving the practical hustling to a Canadian businessman, Maurice Strong.

The OEOA broke rules, bullied, and cajoled, using the UN flag where useful and bypassing the UN where necessary. Pulling people in on secondment from UN agencies and recruiting others from outside, the OEOA resembled a team with remarkable speed, not to mention a computerized information base that let donors know what was needed, where, and how it could get there. In Ethiopia, it got the Polish, West German, and British air forces to run a joint airlift. Because it had the enthusiastic support of the major donors and voluntary organizations, it managed to operate not only in the face of opposition from UNDRO and the FAO, but without the backing of the UN General Assembly's majority. Then, after twenty-two months, the OEOA was disbanded. In the report[36] Strong submitted to the secretary-general in 1986 on the lessons to be drawn from the OEOA's experience, he stated that "it would clearly be better for the United Nations not to have a permanent organization than to have an organization with mandated responsibilities but without the capacities and credibility to discharge them effectively." Existing without acting, it was likely to impose "a heavy cost in terms of human lives as well as in terms of the credibility of the United Nations."

True to form, the General Assembly proceeded solemnly to affirm, yet again, the importance of strengthening UNDRO. But the General Assembly was not alone in its inability to look failure in the face. Even somebody with the experience of Prince Sadruddin Aga Khan was still arguing in 1987 for UNDRO's retention. In a report for the UNA-USA panel,[37] he acknowledged that UNDRO's lack of leverage, its limited manpower, its "information-management capability . . . outdated, even by the standards of other UN agencies" and its small scale prevented it from fulfilling its mandate. But he argued that no other UN body could take on the job and that "to follow up even legitimate criticism of UNDRO by dissolving the office *would be to set a politically inexpedient precedent for other UN bodies in a similar position*" (emphasis added).

But what were the options if even the most useless unit had to be protected, if for no other reason, in order to avoid a "politically inexpedient precedent" and when (as was the case with UNDRO) governments could neither withdraw from membership nor decline to fund it because the organization in question was funded through the budget of the "political" UN, and nonpayment would breach legal obligations? Western governments could impose retrenchment by stopping the voluntary contributions that provided half UNDRO's budget. But this would neither solve the institutional problem nor, more importantly, improve the handling of emergencies. The UN response was twofold. In March 1987 the secretary-general created ORCI, a unit for "research and the collection of information," attached to his office. This was intended to provide an early warning system and stimulate action in the case of "manmade disasters." In December 1989, the General Assembly drew up an "International Framework of Action for the International Decade for Natural Disaster Reduction"[38] and called on the secretary-general to "strengthen further" the UN's capacity to organize humanitarian assistance.

In April 1991, the Kurdish refugee crisis in northern Iraq, when 1.9 million fled Iraqi government forces, graphically exposed the need for more radical cures. The Kurdish operation set a precedent for armed humanitarian intervention whose enormous importance for the future will be discussed in the concluding chapters. What concerns us here is the criticism the UN again attracted for the agencies' lumbering inefficiency, "the lack of inter-agency coordination and the lack of leadership provided by the UN system to the numerous other agencies (donor, NGO and intergovernmental) involved in the response."[39] Seventy percent of the refugees made it across the frontier to Iran, where they were admirably treated by local authorities and the Iranian Red Crescent; but the rest, trapped in high altitudes and icy weather on the Iraqi side of the Turkish frontier, would have frozen or starved without a large-scale Western military operation that the UN was painfully slow to complement.

That July in London, in an unprecedented move, the annual Group of 7 summit insisted on the designation of a "high level official answerable only to the UN Secretary-General" to coordinate future international emergency operations. The British and Germans followed this up with a draft resolution for the 1991 General Assembly, which after watering down by the Group of 77 resulted[40] in the creation of such a post, and also of a $50 million Central Emergency Revolving Fund (CERF), to be voluntarily financed. But even then, the omens were not encouraging. In the first place, what the Group of 7 had had in mind was a new supremo, second only to the secretary-general, with the rank of deputy; what they got was an addition to the ranks of under-secretaries-general. Second, his new Department of Humanitarian Affairs (DHA) was given a small New York office but relied for most of its manpower on "a strengthened" UNDRO, still based in Geneva. Jan Eliasson, the Swedish diplomat who took the post in April 1992, set up some new coordination mechanisms before resigning, dispirited, late in 1993. The truth was that, while Eliasson had some marginal clout, the new DHA-UNDRO did not pay the UN pipers—the CERF was no more than a fallback facility, to be reimbursed by the agencies from funds they raised directly from donors—and they had no intention of letting it call the tune.

It is time lessons were learned. If the UN cannot provide the framework that the voluntary agencies and the governments that provide relief agree is needed, alternatives should be considered. The report issued by the UN secretary-general in 1971 that led to UNDRO's establishment[41] could usefully be disinterred for guidance. This report stated bluntly that "the principal organs equipped for international emergency relief are and will continue to be the League of Red Cross Societies, other voluntary organizations and church groups, and Governments . . . the United Nations System is not geared for action of this kind, nor is it realistic to suppose that, given its structure, it could become so." Where the UN could help, without "raising false hopes," would be in promoting national disaster prevention and control measures; in assembling computerized data on conditions in disaster-prone countries (including the state of national preparedness to cope) and on potential sources of assistance; finally, it could assist in negotiating with recipients, as well as countries through which supplies would have to pass. The report proposed a small unit of three professional officers and three assistants, attached to the secretary-general's office, to be supplemented at need and at very short notice to deal with particular emergencies. It assumed that actual relief operations would be conducted by those equipped to act.

There are solid reasons to return to some version of this modest and more feasible division of labor. There will always be some confusion in the early stages of emergency relief, but it could be greatly reduced. Where disasters strike in relatively peaceful countries, most assistance is in practice provided government to government; the roles of UN agencies and international voluntary organizations tend to be marginal. Where there is conflict and/or obstruction by the authorities, the UN's role is likely, save in exceptional circumstances, to be hampered by protocol (it was for eight years inactive in Afghanistan, and between 1984 and 1991, voluntary organizations are estimated to have channeled 80 percent of the relief that reached war-torn Ethiopia and Eritrea). But even where the UN umbrella is politically advantageous or even indispensable, so heavily dependent are UN agencies, the Red Cross, and even many voluntary agencies on donor responses to their appeals that the donors need only to employ what Jackson called the "stabilizing effect of the power of the purse" to impose a reasonable degree of order. And it is surely within the West's capability to coordinate the use of the money, and the equipment and relief supplies that go with it.

To do that outside the UN would not preclude using UN organizations, but *would* limit the agencies' power to obstruct operations by quarrels over turf. Given the real need for multilateral coordination, one possible approach would be to call on the development center of the OECD. There would be two virtues in making the OECD the coordinating hub for emergency relief. The first is that the countries that belong to it provide the overwhelming proportion of disaster relief funds, and are the home bases of the most experienced international charities. Other rapidly industrializing countries are likely to follow Mexico, admitted in 1994, into OECD membership. Secondly, unlike the UN, the OECD is accustomed to operating through mixed working groups which bring together its own secretariat, government representatives, and experts from the private sector. Such an umbrella could easily be used to harmonize the efforts of OECD members and representatives of other governments contributing significantly to a particular emergency, the European Commission (which set up its own humanitarian office in 1992), voluntary agencies including the International Committee of the Red Cross and the League of Red Cross Societies—and, as and when this "core" of those principally involved in relief requested, experts from the UN agencies. The UN would still be needed in some instances to mediate with the governments of affected countries; but it is unlikely that the secretary-general or the Department of Humanitarian Affairs would ignore a joint request for such mediation by OECD governments and private charities.

The working groups could be supported by a small OECD secretariat, whose job would be not only to deal with sudden disasters, but to coordinate the logistics and planning required for the increasingly long-term business of caring for refugees. It could also stimulate an urgently needed debate on what policies and arrangements can best address the increasingly vexed problem of helping people who have fled war, famine, and social breakdown but who remain inside their own countries. On conservative estimates, there were twenty-five million "internally displaced" people at the beginning of 1994, and the Rwandan crisis alone added a million more within that country's borders. As the UNHCR itself stated forcefully in its first-ever *State of the World's Refugees* report in 1993, no reassessment of multilateral humanitarian aid can evade the increasingly untenable position of the UN with regard to these people.

The Office of the United Nations High Commissioner for Refugees was created in 1950 to handle short-term crises, notably to protect and assist people in Europe displaced by World War II and by Communist persecution. It was to supervise the building of emergency shelters for refugees, protect their rights (including, in particular, the right to refugee status), and help them to resettle in another country if they were unable to return home. That mission has been expanded, since the 1960s, to deal with long-term refugee problems: in many parts of Asia, Africa, and Central America, there are refugee camps that have been in existence for years. The UNHCR's overall responsibility for providing food, clothing, schools, shelter, and medical care for these semipermanent settlements has generated a number of serious conflicts of interest. The primary duty of the UNHCR is to protect refugees: a task liable to bring his office into conflict with governments. But the UNHCR's operational role in the routine victualling and maintenance of refugee settlements requires good working relationships with governments—both those in which the camps are located, and the donors who provide the wherewithal. There is a further problem. The UNHCR's mandate is increasingly artificial because—at least in theory—it is only permitted to assist people once they have crossed national frontiers. This limitation leaves the internally displaced in a humanitarian no-man's-land and stimulates international migration, since hundreds of thousands cross boundaries not because they are fleeing political persecution in the strict sense but because that is the only way to obtain relief in desperate circumstances. These are people the international system has failed, victims of conventions that permit their leaders to refuse foreign intervention on the grounds of sovereignty and, often, national security, when all that is actually threatened by outside involvement is their freedom to abuse their own subjects.

For some time, it has also been clear that the UNHCR is overwhelmed by the scale of the problems with which, *faute de mieux*, it has to deal. In 1984, the UN's external auditors identified serious administrative shortcomings. Examining nine hundred deliveries to refugees camps, for example, worth $54 million, they discovered that 86 percent of these were not covered by receipts. In an effort to introduce leaner, more accountable, and more decentralized management, the donor governments elected Jean-Pierre Hocké, a graduate in business administration and director of operations for the International Committee of the Red Cross, to succeed the idealistic but unmanagerial Poul Hartling in 1986. Three years later, Hocké was forced to resign, leaving behind an organization deeply in the red and at odds with governments, the media, and itself.

Hocké's approach to refugee "management" put the UNHCR's role in question as never before. Essentially, he tried to handle the consequences of the massive migrations of the 1970s and 1980s by treating refugees not as individuals but as problems to be "solved," *en bloc*, principally by sending them back whence they came. When voluntary agencies protested that refugees' rights were being ignored, he and his close aides responded that it was time to recognize that many refugees were not "political"—individuals, that is, with a well-founded fear of persecution within the meaning of the relevant international covenants. They were either economic migrants in pursuit of a better life, or peasants uprooted by war or natural disasters who would be perfectly content to be repatriated provided they were helped to resume their normal lives. He had a point, but so did his critics when they argued that nothing should erode the rights of refugees as individuals to claim asylum, or to have their fears of returning home properly addressed. And, in the view of senior staff members and of respected voluntary agencies, Hocké's reorganizations of the UNHCR dangerously downgraded the protection of refugees. Symbolically, he renamed the HCR's division for refugee protection the division of refugee law and doctrine; and the new emphasis was on repatriation, but without the HCR's traditional insistence that it should be voluntary. Feeling within the organization ran high, and when Hocké advised cutting food rations for Ethiopian refugees in Djibouti who declined to "choose" to go home, his staff revolted. Meanwhile, controversies spread over the UNHCR's failures, from Suriname to the Thai frontier with Cambodia, to intervene on behalf of refugees. Governments became more confident that they could expel refugees, as Turkey did many Iranians, without having to worry about protests from the UNHCR. The British and Hong Kong governments, perceiving in Hocké an intellectual ally, sought the HCR's endorsement for forcible repatriation of Vietnamese boat people from Hong Kong on the ground that they were not *bona fide* refugees—a program into which limited safeguards were eventually inserted only because of the HCR's heavy dependence on funding from the United States, which (blithely disregarding the fact that at the time it was turning back destitute Haitian boat people on the high seas) was implacably opposed to the policy.

The immediate cause of Hocké's departure was a Danish allegation that he had misused a special fund for refugee education for first-class travel and entertainment. This was, at the least, a serious error of taste and judgment at a time when the HCR's deficit amounted to 10 percent of its budget, all other staff travel had been cut to the bone, and Hocké had warned donor governments that basic refugee welfare was at risk. But his failure to speak out for refugee rights was more serious, putting in question as it did the basic principle of *nonrefoulement*. Nothing could have been more damaging to the HCR's sense of its special responsibility for refugees, of the special claims stateless persons have on the international community, as the temptation thus to "solve" refugee problems. The High Commissioner ought to exist to fight what had, by the late 1980s, become known as "compassion fatigue," not to align himself with it.

His successor, Sadako Ogata, did much to restore the HCR's moral integrity. But regardless of the identity of the High Commissioner, such controversies are likely to become more acute as large-scale migration becomes the typical pattern of asylum seeking. By 1994, some ten thousand people a day, the equivalent of the population of a small market town, were fleeing their homes, and forty-two million people, one for every 130 on Earth, were displaced or in exile. In the middle of that year, and within the space of weeks, more than a third of Rwanda's entire population spilled pell-mell into Tanzania, Burindi, and Zaire—terrified masses that no civilian organization could hope to feed and shelter. Many sought what shelter and safety they could find within their own borders: in Bosnia, southern Iraq, or parts of the former Soviet Union, that almost certainly meant continued danger as well as destitution. Others, increasingly unwelcome, sought asylum abroad. The refugee's problems had not greatly changed, but this huge escalation in numbers had changed "the refugee problem." A thirty-five-hundred-year-old tradition of asylum, an acceptance of the duty to protect foreign victims of persecution that had been honored by Hittite kings every bit as ruthless as any modern dictator, was verging on breakdown. As individuals, people still responded generously to the plight of refugees. But as societies, particularly in the West, they were slamming the door: expelling asylum-seekers known to be in danger or at best, interpreting the 1951 UN convention on refugees so as to admit the smallest possible number.

Factors are at work that no amount of handwringing will alter. In an age of mass migration—some one hundred million in the 1990s were living outside the countries in which they were born—the prosperous West will be increasingly reluctant to distinguish between those whose lives and freedoms are in danger and the "huddled masses" of "economic migrants yearning for a decent living." Ideological considerations played a role too: the enemy of my enemy is my friend, and the West had extended welcome mats to refugees from Communist regimes that they were not prepared to extend to those from ex-Communist or non-Communist countries. And the more restrictive immigration policies became in the 1980s, the more bogus asylum claims soared, weakening public support for genuine asylum-seekers.

Most modern refugees were, moreover, unlikely to be fleeing individual persecution in the narrow sense of the 1951 convention. More typically, they were victims of the disintegration of the social order, of economic collapse, or of internal wars in which they had often been deliberately targeted through scorched earth policies, ethnic persecution, or "ethnic cleansing." And many of them were fleeing almost simultaneously, in huge numbers of anything up to half a million, from Togo to Benin or Ghana, from Burma to Bangladesh, from Iraq to Iran. For the poor countries who had taken in most of 1993's total of 18.2 million refugees, these influxes were creating severe economic, environmental, and even political problems. Even in Western Europe, applications for asylum had surged from 30,000 a year to 825,000 in 1992, costing Western European taxpayers $7 billion and putting governments under intense pressure to be seen to be "in control" of the asylum process. However strong the temptation for governments to brush individual suffering aside, the destabilizing impact of these massive refugee crises could not be ignored: in the former Soviet Union alone, seventy-two million were living outside the republics of their ethnic origin, discrimination against minorities was rife, and these tensions were exacerbating secessionist trends.

Yet the machinery for dealing with what Gil Loescher has called "complex emergencies"[42] has evolved barely at all since the 1950s. The methods of international charity were still being applied, case by case and mostly after the fact, with little serious thought being given to preventive political action. By 1994, UNHCR's annual spending was three times that in 1989, and it was working beyond the limits both of its institutional capacities and its original mandate—which had certainly never included the ferrying of relief through battle lines, as in Bosnia. The more key HCR personnel find themselves constantly redeployed to deal with emergencies, the more difficult the organization will find it to offer policy guidance and long-range planning for dealing with the changed nature of refugee problems. It has responded to criticisms of its slow responses to crises by setting up emergency response teams, but it has never had a particularly strong procurement and logistical capacity—and it might not be as wise as it might seem to insist that it acquires one.

Above all, HCR is not, and should not become, another development agency. There is a case for relieving the HCR of its involvement in logistical support for refugee settlements, once the initial crisis has passed and the camps are on a care and maintenance basis. That would help the agency to concentrate not just on refugee protection, which is its primary responsibility, but on providing a clearinghouse for an urgently required multilateral debate on developing new techniques of crisis prevention, mediation, properly funded and protected repatriation schemes, and the refugee dimensions of postwar rehabilitation of shattered countries. Long-term refugee maintenance could be taken over by the voluntary agencies to whom in practice the HCR already subcontracts much of the work, and the UN's World Food Program could be given full responsibility for coordinating and supplying both emergency and long-term food relief. Were disaster relief to be placed under an OECD organizational umbrella, the same mechanism could help to coordinate the funding and servicing of refugee settlements.

The argument against such a division of labor is that the UNHCR acquires leverage with host governments by providing physical assistance to refugees—that its efforts to enforce compliance with the 1951 convention were a miserable failure until the Ford

Foundation came up with the first million dollars for refugee welfare, and would again fail once the capacity to bribe governments into good behavior was taken away. But that leverage works in two directions. A clearer focus on refugee rights would help the UNHCR to concentrate on more effective preventive strategies, on securing host governments' respect for the obligations of asylum, and on engaging Western governments in developing a concept of "temporary asylum" for victims of conflict. Where repatriation is a genuine possibility, the High Commissioner would be better placed to mediate credibly between governments if it were crystal clear that HCR's sole concern was the welfare of the people whose fate was being negotiated and had nothing to do with reducing the HCR's workload. The Commissioner could pay more attention to monitoring situations likely to produce refugees, and persuading "exporting" governments to take remedial action. As a humanitarian observer, the HCR could provide early warning of situations liable to send people fleeing across borders.

Finally, although the ICRC has the experience and training to work in internal conflicts and HCR should not in principle be called on to do so, it might be possible to consider extending its mandate to the protection of the internally displaced. Clarifying the High Commissioner's role might thus, in the longer run, help to strengthen the UN's role in promoting and, above all, enforcing respect for human rights in general. If mass migrations are to be prevented, the strongest of links is required between the observation of human rights and refugee flows. This will be equally important for refugee repatriation; the HCR has only a minimal capacity to monitor the safety of those who return under repatriation agreements, and systems of protection need also to be developed for those who return spontaneously.[43] The links between human rights violations and mass migrations, within countries or across international frontiers, needs to be consistently addressed. There is no escaping the connection between refugee protection and the UN's broader role as a guardian of human rights.

Citizens' Causes

The UN has created an impressive body of international human rights law since 1945, an achievement of which something lasting and valuable might yet be made. But as guardian of its own Charter and covenants it has performed lamentably, and publics know it. The plethora of UN human rights mechanisms includes the notoriously venal UN Commission on Human Rights. Its membership is composed of government representatives appointed by ECOSOC, on the basis of recommendations from regional groups that all too frequently nominate such notorious human rights abusers as Libya, Sudan and Iraq. Not surprisingly, it has spent at least of a third of every session down the years on Israel and South Africa.[44] Its subcommission on the prevention of discrimination and protection of minorities started life as a body of independent, and largely impotent, experts, but was gradually stuffed with ambassadors and envoys whose independence of their governments was purely formal. Then there are the review committees set up under UN conventions, of which the Human Rights Committee is the best known; the third, fourth, and sixth committees of the UN General Assembly; and the UN Secretariat's center for human rights in Geneva. The keystone was finally added in 1994, with the appointment of a UN high commissioner for human rights. In addition, the performance of governments with respect to labor conventions is vetted by "peer group" committees at the ILO; and a modest committee of UNESCO's governing board investigates (in secret session) violations of the human rights of scholars, writers, and scientists.

The common denominator of all these bodies is that they inspire little awe in governments, and consequently little respect among the public. Almost fifty years after the Universal Declaration of Human Rights, enforcement remains an aspiration, and the UN's "shaming mechanisms" are shamelessly manipulated by governmental alliances. Until its invasion of Kuwait, for example, Iraq could count on nonaligned countries' support to escape condemnation for the gassing in 1988 of thousands of its Kurdish citizens, an act of genocide.

An Oxford academic has argued that too much could never be expected of any system involving governments—that "where states themselves are the judges of others' human rights records, we should not be surprised if a kind of freemasonry operates among them, making them reluctant to call each other names in public in case such a policy were to rebound to their disadvantage."[45] But in the 1990s there is less excuse than before to accept that where states are the problem, states are not going to provide the answers, to look to regional bodies for enforcement, and otherwise to rely on private organizations such as Amnesty and the increasingly effective cluster of Human Rights Watch groups to exert pressure on governments, and leave it at that.

While regional approaches may now work in Europe, East as well as West, and may be the most reliable formula for the Western Hemisphere, reliance on them would condemn the citizens of many countries in Africa and Asia to perpetual second-class status. When individual Asians and Africans, drawing hope and courage from Eastern Europe's liberation, are finding their voices, the temptation to abandon efforts to establish and enforce universal standards should be firmly rejected. Such standards are not only basic to the maintenance of international law—which is meaningless if it is not universally applicable. Increasingly, they are recognized as essential underpinnings of sustainable, and sustained, development. The economic, as distinct from the moral and political, case for respecting human rights and democratic freedoms is still more controversial than careful analysis of modern history suggests it should be. Since the late 1980s, the debate has been distorted by the fashionable tendency to cite China's headlong growth and the success of "disciplined" Asian countries such as Malaysia or Singapore as evidence that authoritarian rule is more "efficient" than democracy. India—a democracy, but significantly for years a country in which government maintained tight controls over the economy—is often contrasted with China to demonstrate that political freedoms can be a drag on economic growth. But not only does this ignore recent evidence of the ruinous impact of communism, or the fact that the world's richest countries are those with the longest and most securely entrenched histories of respect for human rights and that the poorest tend typically to be poor also in civil liberties. It neglects the economic benefits of the rule of law—of secure property rights, of contracts protected by an independent judiciary; and above all, of the confidence people have in democracies that these economic rights and freedoms will not arbitrarily be taken away from them.[46]

The case for a universalist, as opposed to a "regional" and by implication relativist, approach has lost none of its force since 1948. But it has constantly to be made and remade. In the 1990s, there is some encouragement to be drawn from several developments within the UN bodies dealing with human rights. In 1992, for example, the Human Rights Commission issued a resolution condemning Equatorial Guinea—its first public statement on a sub-Saharan African country other than South Africa—and followed up the next year with resolutions on Zaire, Somalia, and Sudan. And in 1994, by including anti-Semitism in a declaration on contemporary forms of racism, the commission finally ended a shameful silence: in half a century, the UN had never explicitly condemned anti-Semitism.

For millions in Eastern Europe, 1989 seemed the year when the future began and for democratic governments, the hope was that Moscow's sudden anxiety to present itself as a champion of the rule of law would change the climate sufficiently in the 1990s to make possible a more systematic attempt to enforce compliance by governments with their international legal obligations. The UN's World Conference on Human Rights in Vienna of 1993, the first since the Tehran conference in 1968, must have seemed a marvelous idea when preparations were launched in 1990. But the high hopes of a new global commitment to strengthen the enforcement of human rights were severely jolted before the conference started. Largely thanks to the UN habit of setting up regional preparatory conferences before global gatherings, the arguments that did so much to discredit the UN in the 1970s and 1980s promptly resurfaced. The Asian group reopened the old arguments about the universality of human rights, arguing that their application must be modified to take into account national "particularities"—differing traditions and social customs. As usual, this was the work of a small number of governments, but it included, disturbingly, not just the usual suspects—China, Burma, Iraq, and Syria—but relatively prosperous and "moderate" Malaysia and Indonesia. They proceeded to lecture the world that Asia's economic success demonstrated the soundness of putting the rights of "society" before those of the individual.

The outcome at Vienna demonstrated all too clearly that ideological confrontations over the meaning as well as the individual and collective dimensions of human rights, and their universal character, discussed in earlier chapters, have not disappeared as a result of the transformations in Eastern Europe. The final document held firm on the question of universality. Defeat on that score would have been a colossal setback: cultural differences could cover a multitude of sins ranging from the denial of women's freedom to exercise their human rights, or the mutilating practice of genital infibulation, to the death sentences imposed in Iran on persons professing religions other than Islam. But Vienna was in many ways a step backward: the final document was remarkably reticent on the rights to freedom of expression and religion, while endorsing an "inalienable right to development." The oddest thing about this was that the West had fought off this particular addition to the canon of rights throughout the 1970s, when the support of the Eastern bloc made this to some extent a Cold War issue, only to crumble when it had become purely a claim by the "South" against the North. The extent to which this "right" was in fact perceived as a claim by poorer states against the rich was demonstrated by the demand for debt relief appended to the Vienna text. The liberal dilemma dies hard. The West with difficulty fought off the inclusion of a statement that the free flow of information was permissible only if it was "objective, responsible and impartial"—conditions allowing almost unlimited scope for censorship. The North-South confrontations on human rights will outlast the Cold War, although the standard-bearers for "difference" are increasingly found in Asia and the Islamic world rather than Africa and Latin America.

The conference did, however, agree at long last on the creation of a UN high commissioner for human rights, who was appointed in 1994. The argument for a human rights commissioner, first put forward in the 1960s by Costa Rica, has long been that there is an obvious need to offer victims of human rights violations an ultimate recourse where other bodies fail to act. An individual could also initiate investigations more readily than the UN's committee system. Provided a human rights commissioner's commitment to the principle of universality is unwavering, his independence is absolute and his authority clear-cut, this could do much to focus the commission's agenda and bring some efficiency, as well as prestige, to the UN Center for Human Rights. A commissioner would would not disband the governmental freemasonry but, when it is already showing signs of becoming less monolithic, he could further tilt the balance in favor of "the peoples of the United Nations" in whose name the UN Charter was drawn up. Against that, in no area of the UN's activities would the wrong appointment inflict more damage. The powers subsequently conferred by the General Assembly on the first commissioner, José Ayala Lasso of Ecuador, were worryingly ambiguous, although his mandate contained a robust affirmation of the duty of states to promote and protect all fundamental human rights "regardless of their political, economic and cultural systems." Immense vigilance will be required. But human rights was clearly established at the outset of the 1990s as one of the very small group of large questions on which governments are beginning to catch up with their citizens' needs and convictions. It is one of the few cases where institutional innovation is overdue and worth attempting.

The pressures exerted by citizens have been still more effective in setting the pace where the environment is concerned. Principally but by no means exclusively in the industrialized world they have, both as lobbyists and consumers, compelled both business leaders and politicians to incorporate a "green" dimension into a wide range of investment decisions. The speed with which policies are evolving indicates that effective multilateral cooperation need not wait on the perfection of organizational arrangements. The modesty of existing global mechanisms for tackling environmental problems may even, paradoxically, have been helpful: this has been an area in which the UN started out lightly burdened with institutional baggage. It should be a priority for Western policy to ensure that this remains the case.

By the sluggish standards of international diplomacy, the world has responded with extraordinary dispatch to counter the life-threatening damage to the ozone layer, and to move on to the vastly more complex task of countering excessive global warming. Part of this has been due to luck, part to the inventive strategy devised by the Cinderella of the UN agencies, the UN Environment Program (UNEP)—a strategy that has done much to repair its image. The luck was that the test case, the protection of the stratospheric ozone layer, was of all environmental threats the easiest to counter. The strategy was to get governments first to agree, as they did at UNEP in Vienna in 1985, to a "framework convention" that committed them to do little more than conduct accelerated research—and then to follow up with protocols committing them to action. The speed with which governments moved is nonetheless remarkable. In 1987, some of them agreed under the first Montreal protocol to freeze immediately, and halve by 1998, production and use of chlorofluorocarbons (CFCs), the chemicals mainly responsible for ozone depletion. This was only two years after scientists first detected a hole in the ozone layer over Antarctica, and before there was any certainty that commercially viable alternatives to CFCs could be developed. Two years later, in 1989, when only thirty-one governments had ratified the protocol, eighty nations led by the United States and the European Community concluded that this target was already inadequate and agreed on total elimination of these chemicals by the end of the century. In this they were following the lead of all the main CFC manufacturers. By 1990, some Western countries supported a target date of 1997; and for once, target setting was followed as the decade wore on with active programs to implement them.

There were contributing factors. The first is that although CFCs, halons, and other ozone-depleting chemicals had been deemed indispensable to producing a wide range of basic goods such as refrigerators and air-conditioners, the number of companies manufacturing them was small, and had every incentive to develop less harmful substances before developing countries started their own production. Industry therefore responded still more rapidly than governments. The second is that phasing out CFCs and halons was a relatively cheap proposition—estimates in 1990 were in the range of $5 billion for the chemicals industry, and $100 billion for their industrial customers—compared with tackling other sources of environmental degradation. The benefits were comparatively evident, the dangers of inaction accepted, and success so obviously depended on countries working together that industrialized countries were prepared to offer developing countries special dispensations, aid, and technological help to switch to to the use of nonozone-depleting chemicals in order to secure their agreement in principle.

The third was unusually creative interaction between national and international forms of mediation. In March 1989, the British government hosted an international conference, linked to the Montreal protocol and under UNEP's auspices, aimed at persuading the developing countries to collaborate in banning CFCs in return for Western aid and technology to help them bypass CFCs in favor of less harmful substitutes. Many of the 113 participating governments arrived in London in no mood to be told by the handful of industrialized countries responsible for three-quarters of global CFC consumption that, for the sake of the world, they should forgo using chemicals needed for refrigerators just as mass domestic markets for these products were beginning to develop. But instead of turning into a North-South confrontation, that meeting ended with solid indications that, provided help to develop alternatives was forthcoming, a global ban stood a good chance of being implemented. Fifteen months later, a follow-up conference in London was convened, this time aimed not only at tightening targets but moving to implementation, including an international fund to induce countries such as China and India to sign the protocol.

These meetings were good examples of the flexible use of UN institutions, both augmenting UNEP's prestige and endorsing its concentration on brokering conventions, rather than acting as a project aid agency. Banning a handful of chemicals, however widely used, was however child's play compared with the task of limiting the emissions of other "greenhouse gases" that trap the sun's heat within the atmosphere: carbon dioxide, methane, and nitrous oxide. The complexity of the problem, the scientific uncertainties about the extent as well as the probable impacts of the global warming phenomenon, and the economic and social costs of action, were bound to test the UN's capacity for realistic global bargaining as no other issue had done. When negotiations began at the World Climate Conference in October 1990, science had no economically viable alternative to the use of fossil fuels for transport and most forms of power generation, no ready answers to methane pollution. The basis of common interest, so clear in the case of the ozone layer, was less easily established. Even if the scientists' assessments proved accurate, the penalties for inaction would be unevenly distributed.

Global warming might produce rises in ocean levels, which threatened the livelihoods of a third of mankind, those living within forty miles of the sea, and might even obliterate low-lying deltas and some island states. Yet warmer, wetter weather might also benefit the Canadian and northern Eurasian grain belts, and large producers of fossil fuels had to be convinced that it was in their interest to sign up to international treaties that would cut global demand. In advance of conclusive scientific evidence, governments would inevitably be loath to put current economic growth at risk for future, intangible, benefit, to relinquish sovereignty in economic decisionmaking, or to embark on "environmental accounting" in all areas of economic activity.

"Green diplomacy" was still in its infancy. Yet the intensification of public demands for preventive and palliative action put governments under strong pressure to make progress. People in the industrialized world increasingly recognized that population pressures, increased energy consumption, and deforestation in the developing world affected them intimately. Those in the Third World were gradually realizing that the poor would be the first to suffer from environmental mismanagement. Calls for "strengthening" the UN to meet these challenges began to surface. The first proposals of the kind were put forward in March 1989 at a meeting of twenty-four governments at the Hague convened by France and the Netherlands. This meeting suggested the establishment of an executive global body with powers to enforce sanctions against polluters, to seek damages from violators of international environmental codes, and to give the UN General Assembly a legislative role.

This was not a positive move, and it was one that was to have consequences later. The environmental challenge is political, not institutional; the task is the conciliation of different interests rather than the construction of complex bureaucracies. (Should codes of practice in different areas be agreed, for instance, the International Court of Justice is already empowered to arbitrate in environmental disputes.) But it was already clear that, because both preventive and remedial action would impinge directly on people's lifestyles and even living standards, the environment was a prominent potential source of fresh North-South friction. "Eco-imperialism" was already, by 1990, becoming a Third World watchword. As Margaret Thatcher acknowledged at an international conference on the ozone layer in 1989, their governments suspected that "countries which have already industrialized, and have caused the greater part of the problems we face . . . expect others to pay the price in terms of *their* people's hopes and well-being."[47]

This the West acknowledged, in principle, without having yet given serious thought to devising ways of sharing technology without infringing on the intellectual property rights of private industry. Western governments did, however, see the need for a special fund to compensate developing countries for the "incremental" costs of managing the global commons. These were investments countries agreed to incur because of their benefit to mankind, even though in a domestic context the costs might outweigh the benefits: such as the extra costs to Brazil of protecting its tropical rainforests, to China of switching to nonfossil fuel sources of energy when it had massive coal reserves, or to other countries of building more expensive power plants to reduce carbon dioxide emissions. In September 1989, France and Germany proposed the establishment of a separate funding "window" of the World Bank, expressly to fund projects to control global warming, protect biological diversity, and prevent further pollution of the oceans and depletion of the stratospheric ozone layer. To some environmental lobbyists, the suggestion sounded as constructive as inviting the tiger to become a herbivore. The antigrowth environmental school had seen more threat than promise in the creation of the Bank's new environmental division in 1987, and in 1989 it was only beginning to establish its "green" credentials even among those who accepted the need to reconcile care of the environment with economic growth. Besides, the green lobbies perceived clearly that the Global Environmental Facility (GEF), which divided responsibilities between the Bank, the UNDP, and the UN's existing Environment Program, was designed to forestall the creation of a new bureaucracy.

But the idea of relying on the Bank to serve as the operational complement to UNEP's scientific and standard-setting work made practical sense. UNEP'S role in the GEF was primarily to ensure, through the Scientific and Technical Advisory Panel which it serviced, that the work of the GEF was consistent with agreed objectives; the UNDP's focus was to be "capacity building" and preinvestment studies; and the Bank, as repository of the Trust Fund, was in charge of implementing investment projects. Four years later, despite criticisms of aspects of its mandate and operation, the Bank's Global Environment Facility had established itself among professionals as the major international mechanism for financing environmental cooperation. But by this time, the political UN was grabbing hold of the ball.

In 1987, the World Commission on Environment and Development chaired by Gro Harlem Brundtland, the Norwegian prime minister, had issued its report, calling for comprehensive strategies to promote "sustainable development."[48] In 1990, the Inter-Governmental Panel on Climate Change reported that immediate cuts were needed, worldwide, in the output of the main greenhouse gases even to stabilize their concentration in the atmosphere. Scientists were increasingly in accord that, if only as insurance against worst-case projections, an international convention was needed on climate change. The UN duly launched into another of its global extravaganzas, the UN Conference on Environment and Development (UNCED) which, attended by 178 government delegations, over fourteen hundred NGOs, and eight thousand journalists, opened after more than two years of intensive international negotiations in Rio de Janeiro in June 1992. Its organizer, Maurice Strong, modestly billed it in advance as "the most important meeting in the history of humanity."

Such mammoth set pieces of global diplomacy have one virtue, which is to concentrate governments' minds. Their characteristic vice is to compensate for the absence of a genuine meeting of minds by agreeing, on the vaguest of terms, to grandiose strategies there is no hope of carrying through. Rio differed in important respects from the UN conferences of the 1970s. First, East and West had similar stakes in progress. Second, this was the first time in the UN's history that the North, which consumes four-fifths of the world's resources and accounts for most of its emissions, was the *demandeur*, seeking the agreement of developing countries to adopt more environmentally friendly policies than the rich had employed at comparable stages in their growth. Third, the conference before it had two conventions—on climate change and the protection of biological diversity—prenegotiated and thus open for signature.

Both documents were flawed. The convention on biodiversity's provisions on technology transfer and intellectual property rights over genetic research drove a coach and horses through international patent law. The climate convention, which attracted sufficient ratifications by 1994 to enter into force, committed rich countries to draw up detailed plans to returning their greenhouse gas emissions to 1990 levels by 2000, while requiring the poorer countries merely to make lists of the sources of their greenhouse gas emissions. But both were landmarks on the way to more careful, and more equitably shared, custodianship of the planet. By contrast, Strong's team headed into the stratosphere of wishful thinking with Agenda 21, a list nearly eight hundred pages long of 150 programs, divided into twenty-four-hundred tasks. To this program of action, the UNCED secretariat had attached an *annual* pricetag of $600 billion a year, and a demand that the West should finance this through grants or soft loans to the tune of an annual $125 billion—more than double the existing total of official development assistance. Worse still, Agenda 21—accepted by the usual "consensus" by countries that had absolutely no intention of handing out checks on this scale—was landed in the lap of the General Assembly through a Commission on Sustainable Development (CSD) to be established by ECOSOC.

No worse fate could be wished on environmental diplomacy than to be thus handed to a 1970s-type UN Committee of the Whole (with, this time, the addition of more than five hundred NGOs). The CSD was supposed to be a high-level forum for monitoring Agenda 21's progress, with annual ministerial sessions and an initial three-year work-plan running to 1997. At its first session, in June 1993, it promptly lapsed into the depressingly familiar pattern of North-South confrontation. The North was determined not to write a blank check, the South was out to prevent any form of environmental conditionality being attached to aid. Nobody could agree on a definition of "sustainable development," nor was there genuine accord on the subjects the commission's working groups should address. The Group of 77 insisted that it would discuss only two topics—how to finance Agenda 21, and technology transfer. The Group of 77 won, but only on paper: Western governments had no intention of allowing the UN to take strategic decisions, as the Group of 77 demanded, on the use of IMF and World Bank funds. A new green route had been opened into the old arguments about the relationship of the UN to the Bretton Woods organizations. And the relationship of this talking shop to the work of the GEF and of UNEP itself had been left wide open.

As an operational organization, UNEP has been weak, but that does not necessarily matter. The service it can best perform is to build on the negotiating precedents it has set, to bring experts together, and to help in the circulation of information. Thanks to the collaboration of the remote-sensing research laboratory of NASA (the U.S. National Aeronautics and Space Administration), private industry, and the University of Geneva, its capacity to provide an international data network has been transformed. The University of Geneva handles data capture, analysis, and distribution for UNEP's GRID (global resources information database), while UNEP draws on the findings to draft recommendations to governments. This system is a model of the kinds of collaboration with the outside world that UN agencies need to develop. But if UNEP provides an adequate vehicle, along with the World Meteorological Organization, for promoting further research and providing a forum for negotiations, there will still be pressures for a new agency to serve as UNEP's operational complement. Where governments have the capacity to finance and manage cooperative environmental programs themselves, UNEP can act as a catalyst. It did so in the Mediterranean, where (again initially through a framework convention) UNEP designed a program with incentives for each country in the region and, through skillful mediation, helped to depoliticize the question of marine pollution. What began as a UNEP venture became a self-managed joint venture involving all the littoral states, including such enemies as Israel and Syria. But UNEP, by common consent, has neither the authority nor the expertise to work effectively with governments that have no such capacity, particularly as the environmental agenda grows. The GEF, however, could easily be built on, and the Bank's country reports are becoming an effective tool for for environmental accounting and planning.

Environmentally friendly development will work only in the context of such cost-benefit analyses. The lesson of national as well as international experience is that an environmental watchdog is useful only insofar as it can influence economic decisions as it were from the inside, rather than working for an environmental "add-on" to economic decisionmaking. And practical politics, *pace* Agenda 21, suggest that what will work best is a step-by-step approach, starting with the actions that cost least. Energy conservation is undramatic, but would make a solid practical contribution to slowing the pace of global warming, and here virtue would clearly be its own reward. Where the Bank can make an impact on industrialized countries' multilateral policies is in aid and joint investment policies and sensible technology sharing—the last of which will be an indispensable ingredient of any global compact. This is likely to be an increasingly important ingredient of Western cooperation with the horrendously polluted countries formerly within the Soviet empire.

As for the North, which contributes most to global warming, its governments will take environmental conservation steadily more seriously, not because of the UN but in response to strong popular demand. This is likely to be an increasingly important ingredient of Western Cooperation with the horrendously polluted countries formerly within the Soviet Empire. The temptation to create a new global environmental institution should be resolutely resisted—not because strategic cooperation is not important, but because in the crowded environmental agenda of the 1990s it would be a time-consuming irrelevance. In practice, every gain will be dependent on countries working together—no government will readily take unilateral action to curb carbon dioxide emissions, which could affect the competitiveness of national industries—and a continued global dimension is thus indispensable. But the UN is perilously close to damaging its potential for good in this vital field by succumbing to the virus of unreality.

By contrast, the equally global challenge of combating drug trafficking and abuse would seem to require a stronger institutional base, either inside or outside the United Nations. Efforts to combat drug trafficking stretch back to the time of the League of Nations, but politically, the conditions for international cooperation were more promising at the start of the 1990s than for decades. The old arguments between "producing" countries in the Third World and "consuming" countries in the West had lost their force for two reasons. With the spread of synthetic drugs manufacture in the United States and Western Europe, production had ceased to be a "southern" problem; and governments in developing countries had come to realize that their own people had become important new market targets for traffickers. An OECD report[49] drew attention in 1987 to the spread of Third World drug addiction. In Malaysia, even though drug trafficking carried the death penalty, the proportion of addicts in the population had grown to three times the level obtaining in the United States. Pakistan, which had no heroin addicts in 1978, had more than three-hundred thousand ten years later.[50] In Colombia, where a coca cigarette cost no more than a piece of chewing gum, the market price was still high enough to make coca far more profitable for peasants than other crops were. The consequences, in both hemispheres, of the drugs trade had also ceased to be confined to social and economic destruction. The drug cartels challenged political stability in Central America, bringing Colombia at one stage close to civil war with the Medellin barons.

The result was a new readiness in the West to take curbing demand very seriously, and in the Third World, to tackle all links in the chain between producing peasants and consumers. The first fruit of this consensus was the 1988 UN convention against illicit traffic, including provisions for extradition of traffickers, confiscation of assets, and the criminalization of money laundering and controls on exports of chemicals needed for refining. That was followed in February 1990 by agreement at the UN General Assembly on a global program of action, intended to bind states to specific actions to fight the drugs trade and to submit their policies to regular multilateral scrutiny.

Yet the machinery for putting these political initiatives into effect was so appallingly ineffective that the British were, in desperation, seeking to bring drug abuse and trafficking to the Security Council, on the ground that this had become a threat to international peace and security. UN efforts were divided between the Economic and Security Council, responsible for policy, the intergovernmental Commission on Narcotic Drugs, which reported to it, the Division of Narcotic Drugs servicing the commission, the International Narcotics Control Board (a quasi-judicial body charged with monitoring compliance with conventions), and the UN Fund for Drug Abuse Control. The appointment of a UN drugs coordinator (with limited powers, and then over only two of these agencies) was merely, according to Giuseppe de Gennaro, director of the Fund for Drug Abuse Control, to add coordination to the paperwork—the round of committees and seminars—which already absorbed most of these bodies' time and much of the UN's slender drugs budget. "The real goal of the UN," he remarked in desperation, had become "the procedures" of running these different agencies.[51]

Merging all these UN activities was one option, favored by most governments, although many senior UN officials continued to argue that that there was nothing wrong with these overlapping miniagencies that a large injection of funds would not cure. The funding for UN drug-control activities has indeed always been derisory, set against the power of a transnational industry in illicit drugs estimated to be worth well over $500 billion—second only to the international arms trade. But the UN would have to make a much better case for more generous funding. And what may in fact be needed is a novel approach.

Global though the problem may be, not all countries are equally plagued by illicit drugs. The most profitable approach might therefore be to set up not just a new agency, but a new type of agency: not a traditional UN agency based on universal membership, but an organization that involved the countries most seriously engaged in combating this multifaceted problem. Membership in such an organization would carry obligations as well as rights, with explicit provision for sanctions for noncompliance. Obligations could include the ratification of existing UN conventions on narcotic drugs and psychotropic substances, of the 1987 convention on trafficking, and commitments to work with other members on extradition, intelligence sharing, and the provision of information to bodies such as Interpol. Members would also agree to abide by World Health Organization guidelines on new addictive substances.

In return, developing countries' governments would have access to information, policy advice, and, where necessary, money. The organization, whose core budget would inevitably be provided by the industrialized countries (both East and West) would not have an operational role, but could assemble *ad hoc* teams of acceptable nationalities to assist countries requiring help. Finance could be generated through agreements to enact national legislation empowering governments to seize the assets of drug traffickers. Countries whose per capita GNP exceeded a certain level could make a scaled proportion of these assets available to the agency's trust fund; poorer governments could undertake to use them to buy advice and to strengthen national enforcement capacities and for drug-related education and development programs. For governments too deeply penetrated by the drugs business to enact such legislation and survive, the laws could be gradually phased in.

Such an agency could operate on fresh principles, drawing on OECD practice to work through joint committees composed of secretariat officials and governmental, police, and private sector experts. Political direction could be provided, on the Bretton Woods model, by executive directors in constant session and short annual ministerial meetings. As a consortium of seriously committed governments, it could help to establish awareness of the continuum of interests that has rendered "donor" and "recipient" categorizations irrelevant, and bring together the different strands—crop substitution, interdiction of supplies, confiscation of drug traffickers' assets, public education and the rehabilitation of addicts, and international conventions—of a necessarily integrated set of strategies.

No general model for the future evolution of multilateral cooperation, or of the UN's role, will have been found in these pages. The argument is rather that there cannot be one. The emphasis is on an empirical, piecemeal approach, and the purpose of these examples is to indicate some starting points that could help carry debates and action beyond the generalizations of "reform of the UN," exploiting the variety of its many mansions. Little attention has been paid to the worst-run UN organizations, the focus of all too much effort already. In these, little is likely to come of institutional reforms. Governments (and others) would be more profitably engaged in exploring the kinds of cooperation in, say, education and science they expect to need in the twenty-first century, and what machinery for it would be workable. There is nothing about the piecemeal that precludes radicalism: deliberate bypassing of an institution could in certain circumstances be a positive step toward more effective multilateralism. The UN cannot be immune from decisions to write off losses.

The two large tasks for multilateral diplomacy just alluded to, environmental management and the war against illicit drugs, will be tackled both inside and outside the UN. That is partly because countries at every stage of development and political sophistication find it difficult to use the global institutions as centers for dialogue: where the outcome really matters, they will take out insurance in other forums. That aspect has only been touched on obliquely here, but is one reason why, in talking about steps to rebuild confidence in multilateral cooperation, the focus has been on those changes least reliant on multilateral negotiation, and on those organizations least affected by the degeneration of global dialogue and therefore most capable of meeting widely acknowledged needs. Skepticism about the value of its forums remains a serious obstacle to the modernization of the United Nations and its capacity to survive in the twenty-first century. Because the breakdown is procedural as well as ideological, East-West détente will not suffice to cure the malaise. There is already some some evidence that the emergence of a genuinely northern—as opposed to "northwestern"—club makes some Third World governments thoroughly uneasy, and could generate new forms of North-South confrontation.

This problem has always been most conspicuously present in the Security Council and the UN General Assembly. Yet paradoxically it is in the "political" UN, where the paralysis had been greatest, that the prospects have suddenly and unexpectedly appeared to improve. Beginning in 1986–87, as a direct consequence of "new thinking" in Moscow, the possibility of collective action to prevent and contain armed conflicts, dormant for decades, became a proposition to be taken seriously. Within seven years, the proposition was being "field-tested" on so many fronts that the UN was cracking under the strain. It is to an assessment of these developments, and their significance for the broader multilateral agenda, that we now turn.

11. ANOTHER "NEW WORLD ORDER"?

"THE SCOURGE OF WAR"

So deeply rooted is the belief that the United Nations—both as neutral guardian of international law and as political embodiment of the collective will—exists to prevent bloodshed that, although so much of the UN is otherwise engaged, the reputation of the entire global machinery oscillates according to its failures and successes as peacekeeper and peacemaker. So powerful is the resonance of the Charter's proclaimed determination "to save succeeding generations from the scourge of war" that it continued to echo loudly in the public mind through four decades in which the UN proved manifestly incapable of preventing close to 150 conflicts, including more than 125 in the Third World, which cost some 22 million lives.[1] Hence the surge of public excitement in autumn 1990, when the Security Council responded to Iraq's invasion of Kuwait by invoking the enforcement provisions of Chapter VII of the Charter.

As we shall see later, Operation Desert Storm owed in the end little to the Chapter VII rules for enforcing collective security. The American-led international coalition was neither assembled on the order of the Security Council nor sent into action under the UN flag. After the event, the UN secretary-general himself emphasized, in a speech to the European Parliament, that this was "not at all a victory for the United Nations, because this war was not its war. It was not a United Nations war."[2] But for the public, these were technicalities. What mattered was that the world was at last prepared to unite against aggression and sanction the collective use of force to uphold international law, and that those exerting the military force were ready, even anxious, to use the UN as their source of legitimacy.

The notion that the UN was necessarily paralyzed by the Cold War always seemed less compelling to ordinary citizens than it did to diplomats and other "insiders." They sensed that the UN was less than ingenious in picking its way through political minefields, and hardly proactive in preventive diplomacy; and that successive secretaries-general had been singularly reticent about testing the large freedom of initiative accorded them under Article 99 of the Charter. Down the years, early expectations that the UN would "make war on war," compelling nations to settle their disputes peacefully, punishing aggression and providing a collective framework for national security, were tempered and some "failures" came to be accepted, however reluctantly, as givens. Few people would now take seriously the proposition that the UN could prevent World War III if the world's most powerful states, with or without nuclear weapons, were bent on fighting. The UN was intended to prevent this from happening by *accident*, by providing a golden bridge for the superpowers to retreat across—as it in fact did in the Cuba crisis of 1962 and in the Middle East in 1973.

But through the years of paralysis at the UN, people persisted in believing that it was created to prevent, not merely to contain or to mop up after, other types of conflict. They continued to expect the UN not only to offer exhausted combatants a collection of safety nets and face-saving devices for ending wars, or to provide police forces for troubled frontiers, but to deter governments from taking up arms in the first place. Where conflicts did break out, they expected the UN to intervene, not merely to await the dawn of sense on the part of one or more of the combatants. They continued to believe in collective deterrence, the collective preservation of peace.

Governments meanwhile put their security eggs in other baskets, but continued to pretend that an "effective" UN was their dearest ambition—at least, when speaking at the UN. Few conflicts were unaccompanied by Security Council resolutions. But it is much harder to disguise nonperformance in the maintenance of peace than it is in matters of economic and social cooperation. Time frames are shorter, outcomes quantifiable in terms of physical devastation and numbers of maimed and killed, and anxiety sharpens vigilance. When Security Council resolutions are ignored, when appeals by the UN secretary-general fall on deaf ears, it is generally in situations that are making headlines. Each outbreak of war drives home the message that the UN "has failed in its primary task" of creating "a new world order in which every state derives its security from the collective strength of the whole."[3]

The theory of collective security rests on more than enforcement—the power of the UN to make war on war-makers. It embraces diplomatic vigilance and internationally backed conciliation to prevent disputes from escalating into conflict, the promotion of international security (indirectly, by tackling economic and social roots of conflict, and directly, through making forces available to act as trip-wires along troubled frontiers), peacemaking, and peacekeeping. By the mid-1980s the UN could still claim, through the secretary-general's "good offices," some relevance in conciliation and peacemaking, and UN peacekeeping units were policing some of the most persistent trouble spots on the globe. But both in conflict prevention and conflict management, the UN seemed to be irretrievably marginalized. Chapter VII of the Charter, which in 1945 had seemed the UN's most important innovation, was a dead letter. Unable to call on the standing military reserves that member states had been expected to make available to the Security Council under Article 43—because the relevant agreements had never been negotiated—the UN had no deterrent powers. Its peacekeeping forces were a makeshift device, generally mobilized when disputes had already got out of hand. Even as trip-wires, they were inadequate, since they could be stationed only with the assent of both parties in a dispute, could be removed at the whim of either, and were empowered to shoot only in self-defense. These police forces were better than nothing, but they had nothing to do with collective enforcement of peace.

How far the emphasis had by then shifted from collective security was illustrated by Javier Pérez de Cuéllar's definition in 1987 of a UN secretary-general's "priorities." First, he listed "disarmament, particularly nuclear disarmament"—thus putting at the forefront the area in which the UN had least influence. Next came bringing relief to victims of human rights abuses. Third, he put addressing "the shaming disparity of living standards" between North and South, and fourth, "rallying" the world's response to natural and manmade disasters. The prevention of conflict and punishment of aggression simply did not figure.[4]

The UN had indeed responded to its failures to keep the peace by switching the spotlight to the other side of the security coin: disarmament. The ostentatious pursuit of the swords-into-ploughshares ideal—symbolized by a huge bronze sculpture outside its Turtle Bay headquarters—became the substitute for effective police action. For three decades after 1959, when the General Assembly first adopted Khrushchev's call for "general and complete disarmament under effective international control," this became a perennial and time-consuming feature of the General Assembly's agenda—and the one most stubbornly divorced from reality.

The emphasis on disarmament was in fact a complete distortion of the intentions of the UN's founders, who had the failure to rearm to confront Nazi Germany sharply in mind when they were drafting the Charter. The experience of the League of Nations between the wars had, they believed, demonstrated that it was pointless to exhort states to disarm when they had legitimate reasons to fear for their security. Disarmament could be dangerous, unless it was linked to an effective system of collective security. And such a system, moreover, could only provide adequate insurance if sufficient military resources were available to the collectivity. The Charter therefore made the Security Council responsible for devising "a system for the *regulation* of armaments" (emphasis added). The UN General Assembly was merely empowered to make recommendations, always bearing in mind the maintenance of international security, on "principles governing disarmament and the regulation of armaments." The accent was on extreme caution.

What little of UN disarmament debate has not been pure charade has been rankly hypocritical. The UN's successive "disarmament decades," its special sessions on disarmament, and the World Disarmament Campaign launched in 1982 were in fact far more concerned with asserting the sovereign equality of states than with disarmament. They were about the "right" of all states to be involved in nuclear disarmament: on the ground that, in the words of Pérez de Cuéllar himself, a negotiating "process by which a responsibility that belongs to all nations is monopolized by a few—the responsibility of assuring the survival of humanity"[5] was unacceptable. This focus on nuclear disarmament was of course mighty convenient for the majority of governments. It kept the spotlight off the much more unpopular subject of conventional arms spending.

By the third UN special session on disarmament, in the summer of 1988, global arms spending exceeded $1 trillion a year. Four-fifths of that was in the industrialized north, but in the north at least, negotiations on arms control were by then beginning to evolve—outside UN auspices—into the first serious programs of disarmament. There was no such progress in developing countries, whose governments were by that time spending on average a third of their national incomes on their military machines—a far more impressive share of their resources than those expended by the nuclear powers. And when the 1988 session convened, much of that hardware was in use, either to repress dissent among Third World citizens or to fight twenty-five major Third World wars—of which seventeen were civil wars and only half a dozen involved the troops of third countries. The five permanent members of the Security Council—Roosevelt's global policemen—were moreover the Third World's armorers, supplying 83 percent of global arms exports.

In the industrialized world, peace had been maintained since 1945—albeit at great cost to the citizens of the countries that found themselves on the wrong side of the "Yalta divide." It rested on nuclear deterrence, on Western acquiescence in the Soviet

Union's imperial hegemony in Eastern Europe, and on two thoroughly nineteenth-century institutions, the regional military alliances of NATO and the Warsaw Pact. These arrangements closely approximated the system of "exclusive alliances, and spheres of influence, and balances of power," which President Roosevelt had claimed would be superseded by the United Nations. And it was outside the UN that advances on this state of heavily armed peace were achieved—through bilateral superpower arms control agreements and through the 1975 Helsinki Final Act and the years of patient follow-up negotiations.

The "Helsinki process" began in early 1970s as a modest venture with apparently irreconcilable objectives. The Soviet Union participated because Leonid Brezhnev wanted a forum to legitimize Soviet dominion over the Eastern bloc and confirm the division of Germany. The West hoped to elicit formal undertakings to respect human rights from the East's Communist rulers. No government, even when the Final Act was signed, expected greatness to be thrust on the Conference for Security and Cooperation in Europe (CSCE). Yet the process had introduced genuine novelty: the Final Act's linkage between security, economic cooperation, and civil and political rights seriously eroded the doctrine of nonintervention in countries' internal affairs, and this—however cynically—was accepted by the Soviet government and its satellites.

When the Iron Curtain finally vanished in 1989, the UN's last military enforcement action dated back to the Congo operation of the early 1960s. Largely due to bitter Soviet opposition, that prolonged and somewhat inconclusive intervention had created an acute political and financial crisis for the organization, and such operations seemed unlikely to be mounted again. The UN's last major success in managing a grave threat to international security had been in 1973, following Egypt's attack on Israel. The Security Council obtained a cease-fire and the positioning of a UN observer force between the warring parties, enabling the United States and the Soviet Union to back away from an extremely dangerous military confrontation. But the eventual peace between Egypt and Israel was the result of President Anwar Sadat's dramatic decision to fly to Jerusalem and the active American mediation that followed. The Camp David accords brokered by President Carter, and the multinational military monitoring force for the Sinai that was set up under them, were not only reached outside the United Nations but were vociferously condemned by most of its members. Under pressure from the rest of the Arab League, both Kurt Waldheim, then UN secretary-general, and the Security Council itself had refused either to redeploy UN peacekeeping units to monitor Israel's withdrawal or to provide the Sinai peacekeeping force requested by Egypt and the United States.[6]

Elsewhere, UN peacekeeping forces kept some conflicts on ice: in Kashmir, on the Golan Heights, in Cyprus, to a limited degree in southern Lebanon. But by 1986 Brian Urquhart, the UN's long-serving executive in charge of peacekeeping, had concluded that the UN could at best freeze conflicts or contain their impact; it could seldom prevent and more seldom still resolve them. This reactive, piecemeal, patch-and-mend service seemed a poor substitute for anticipatory, preventive mediation and a mile removed from collective deterrence or punishment of aggression. Where had the UN been in the summer of 1980, when any halfway informed newspaper reader could see the danger of war breaking out between Iran and Iraq? When Iraq indeed invaded that September, the Security Council had done worse than sit on its hands. The resolution it eventually issued, a week late, failed clearly to condemn Iraq's aggression and did not even call on it to withdraw from Iranian territory. The implication seemed clear:

where an unpopular state was the victim of aggression—and where important oil supplies were at stake—international law would be ignored.

In Urquhart's view, the weakness of the Security Council was central. It had failed to create "a benevolent international framework to assist combatants to resolve their differences and to provide the necessary protective apparatus" without which "it is often impossible for the parties to a conflict that is violent, deep-rooted and complex to make progress on their own and in the open."[7] The conventional explanation for the UN's loss of authority was that the Security Council—not to mention the whole collective security apparatus—could only work in the context of superpower agreement. But this could only be half the story. In periods of détente, the superpowers had found it easier to cooperate outside the UN than inside, where the temptations to play to the gallery were irresistible. And if this was true, did it not put in question the notion of "collective" decisionmaking—either in peacekeeping (which the UN secretariat was careful to keep under its own control) or in deterring conflict? How much real use was the "stage of world opinion," if what was said on it bore little relation either to the capacity to act, or to governments' policies within the closed corridors of national chancelleries?

Three main factors had eroded the UN's capacity to keep the peace to the point where there was little but theater left. First, the concept of collective military enforcement of Security Council resolutions had indeed been rendered inoperative by the Cold War. But even had it been put in place, the UN machinery was designed for traditional, declared, interstate wars, not for the types of conflict—wars of liberation, civil wars, transfrontier guerrilla operations, and even *jihad*—which had been most prevalent since 1945. Second, UN peacekeeping forces, the device invented to circumvent Cold War constraints, had an obviously limited role. Strictly noncombatant and normally deployed only with the consent of both parties to a conflict, the "blue berets" tended to be not only *ad hoc* forces, but to be the result of *ex post* mediation, typically interposed only as fighting died down. Finally, the wider involvement of the whole UN membership, dating from the Uniting for Peace General Assembly resolution employed to circumvent the Soviet veto during the Korean War, had diluted the Security Council's authority.

General Assembly resolutions on the Middle East, southern Africa, or Central America had locked the UN into positions and commitments that, often biased against one of the parties, reduced its credibility as impartial mediator and, therefore, the secretary-general's freedom of maneuver. If the Cold War had rendered Chapter VII of the Charter unusable, the universalization of "responsibility" for security drastically reduced the Security Council's utility as a "Chapter VI" body for mediating in disputes or recommending terms for settlement. The Security Council itself began to reflect a similar tendency, often turning into a mini-General Assembly as states with no standing in a particular dispute took to declaring their "interest" and therefore their right to address the Council. Group of 77 caucusing on the Security Council meant that meetings could be delayed for days or even weeks, effectively until agreement had been reached by all Third World countries, whether members or not: the council had become another tool of bloc politics.

On paper, the Charter's provisions for collective security were relentlessly elitist. Designed to deter aggression by the threat of joint action, the Security Council's decisions under Chapter VII were made by only a handful of states but were binding on the "international community." Less a guarantee of world peace than an attempt to institutionalize and codify cooperation between the principal wartime allies, these arrangements owed more to the Concert of Europe than to the League of Nations. The major powers were not intended to stay clear of disputes. On the contrary, they were intended to combine their forces to resolve or contain them, using individual influence where their writs ran, concerting strategy, jointly enforcing peace where persuasion failed. The five permanent "veto" powers were to be supported in this by the other members of the Security Council, who it was intended would be elected (under Article 23) on the basis of their capacity to contribute to collective enforcement. Security Council offers of mediation under Chapter VI were expected to carry weight with governments because it could impose, and enforce, penalties against the recalcitrant.

Had this formula held, there is no reason why the Security Council should not have been able to mediate in at least some of the secessionary and civil wars of the following half-century. Where it determined that international peace was threatened, it was open to the Council to override the strictures against intervention in states' internal affairs contained in Article 2.7 (just as, in practice, it became generally accepted that *apartheid* in South Africa destabilized the whole Southern African region—a standard that did not however apply to the murderous wars in Sudan and the Horn). But once that elitism was eroded, and large numbers of states became involved in the collective security and peacemaking machinery, the council became paralyzed. Most of the states involved in these small destructive wars had only a tenuous hold on order at home. For such governments, the protection of the principle of nonintervention—sanctions against a handful of scapegoat countries excepted—was far more important than the abstract benefit of the peaceful settlement of somebody else's war.

Between 1983 and 1985, at the secretary-general's prompting, the Security Council explored remedies for its loss of authority. Without serious results: the minor procedural changes agreed were no solution to the problem of its "democratization"—the wide involvement in its decisions of states without power to act. The council had become a sounding board rather than a decision-making body. Even its landmark resolutions—such as 242 and 338 on Israel or 435 on Namibian independence—were landmarks more because they were formally backed by both superpowers than because there was an immediate prospect of their being called into play. Most Security Council resolutions were appeals to governments to exercise restraint. The few that called for action tended, significantly, to transfer the responsibility for implementation to the secretary-general. There was much grave talk about the need for better early warning systems, when the real problem was not ignorance, but unwillingness to act. In many instances, the disputes in question were all over the newspapers; and even where this was not so, intelligence was useful only if the Security Council was prepared to act on the information. This was eloquently demonstrated two years later. In 1987, at the Palestine Liberation Organization's request, the secretary-general brought to the council's attention the bitter fighting in Lebanon's refugee camps. The Lebanese government invoked national sovereignty. The president of the council invited views. There followed five minutes of total, embarrassed silence.

The UN's remaining claims were that, even if it could not bring the great powers together do the policing job Roosevelt had had in mind, it had served—and might yet serve again—to keep the superpowers apart; that the secretary-general's "good offices" helped to keep conflicts under review and to remind antagonists of the negotiating option; that peacekeeping forces under the UN flag still looked marginally easier to organize than similar options outside its framework; and that the UN had the nuclear nonproliferation treaty, a partial nuclear test ban, and agreement on the peaceful uses of the seabeds and outer space to its credit. But even some of these achievements seemed in jeopardy. Despite solid superpower support for nonproliferation, backed by the International Atomic Energy Agency's monitoring systems, at least fourteen more states were believed to have developed nuclear weapons already or to be on the verge of production. France was continuing to test in the Pacific. And research by both superpowers into strategic defense, following Reagan's "Star Wars" initiative, appeared likely to render the treaty on the peaceful uses of outer space a dead letter.

The recurrent pantomime of UN deliberations on nuclear disarmament had to some extent been offset by progress in specific areas of arms control by the misleadingly named UN Conference on Disarmament. This forty-nation working group, helped perhaps by being located in Geneva rather than New York, showed that agreements could be reached without waiting for the eagle and the bear to embrace. A convention outlawing the production and stockpiling of chemical weapons, vitally needed to supplement the ban on their use, which had been in place since 1925, was tantalizingly close.

But even here, skeptics might well question the value of such a deal, when Iraq was using chemical weapons in the battlefield and incurring, for this gross breach of a sixty-year-old taboo, no more than ritual Security Council condemnation. The proliferation of advanced military technologies was speeding up; several countries—already including China, Brazil, Argentina, Egypt, and India—were developing medium- and long-range missiles and, since all these countries were keen to maximize their foreign exchange earnings, many more were likely soon to possess these highly destabilizing weapons. But the old protest that the West was out to "disarm the unarmed" still made it impossible to talk at the UN about controlling either traffic in arms or access to such technology (or so the West and the Soviet Union, whose arms industries made enormous export profits, maintained with perhaps more outward show of frustration than real regret).

Governments, meanwhile, were resorting to other methods of containing conflict. Commonwealth forces, not the UN's, monitored the cease-fire and elections which led to Zimbabwe's independence in 1980. The United States intervened unilaterally in Grenada in 1982—an action that, while welcomed by the Grenadians themselves, was stirringly condemned by the General Assembly (in a vote joined by Washington's European allies) as a violation of international law comparable to the Soviet Union's occupation of Afghanistan—for which the Soviet Union had yet, ironically, to be criticized by name in the UN. The Security Council had admittedly speedily and forthrightly condemned Argentina's invasion of the Falklands in 1982, and demanded Argentina's withdrawal, and at first it had seemed that the UN might take center stage. But unanimity rapidly dissipated. The British did not press for economic sanctions because they knew there would be a Soviet veto. Unbacked by anything more than verbal condemnations, the secretary-general's efforts at mediation failed to impress the Argentinian junta. It was left to a British task force to prize Argentina out. In Lebanon, following Israel's brief invasion in 1982, a Western multinational force was assembled to try to impose peace—only to retreat in disorder after terrorist attacks on U.S. and French troops. Even for mediation, governments looked outside the UN: it was the Pope who mediated the dispute over the Beagle channel between Argentina and Chile.

Regional remedies were also sought. In Central America in 1983, it was the Contadora Group of Mexico, Colombia, Venezuela, and Panama, not the UN, that braved American disapproval to come up with a peace plan. Indian troops arrived in Sri Lanka to police the Tamil insurgency and, with more success, to suppress a domestic coup against the government of the Maldives. The countries of the Association of Southeast Asian Nations (ASEAN) tried fitfully to find a solution for Cambodia. Australia, alarmed by U.S. intelligence that China, Taiwan, both Koreas, Vietnam, and Burma had begun to develop chemical weapons, began efforts to put a regional ban in place without waiting for the UN.

Much of this activity was consonant with the Charter's recommendation that disputants should, before approaching the Security Council, exhaust regional or other subglobal remedies available to them.[8] But in practice it reflected growing skepticism about the council's usefulness even as an ultimate resort. And skepticism was justified. In theory, regional organizations had a clear call on the global body, if need arose. In 1981, the Organization of African Unity (OAU), in a promising departure from its chronic immobility in the face of crisis, agreed to send a peacekeeping force to monitor the withdrawal of Libyan troops from Chad. Having assembled the troops but lacking the money to pay for the operation, the OAU appealed that December to the Security Council for financial backing. The council took four months to respond, and then effectively declined to cooperate. Instead, it set up a voluntary fund—the time-honored UN way of saying no. The OAU was told, in essence, that the United Nations would not finance what it did not control. By this time the civil war in Chad had resumed in earnest and the opportunity was lost. The UN, it appeared, was prepared neither to act nor to help others to do so. Collective security, even at arm's length, seemed dead in the water.

THE WIND FROM THE EAST

Suddenly, in the spring and summer of 1988, a cluster of the world's most intractable disputes began almost simultaneously to look soluble. On February 8, Mikhail Gorbachev announced that on May 15, Soviet troops would begin a total withdrawal from Afghanistan, which they would complete the following February, provided Pakistan first assured the Afghan government that it would stop arms reaching the *mujahideen*. The future government of the country would be a matter for the Afghans themselves. On April 14, the seemingly hopeless "proximity talks" between Pakistan and Afghanistan (in which the UN's negotiator, Diego Cordovez, had spent six years shuttling between adjacent rooms trying to broker a settlement between two parties that refused to meet) duly crystallized in an agreement guaranteed by both superpowers. The Soviet pullout began on schedule.

Then, on July 18, after a year of stalling, Iran abruptly accepted Security Council resolution 598, which called for a ceasefire in the eight-year Gulf War, followed by withdrawals to the two countries' international frontiers and peace negotiations. The Security Council, setting aside its pro-Iraq bias, leant on Baghdad to drop its last-minute extra preconditions and hostilities ceased—all in the classic context of a UN resolution, UN-sponsored peace talks and the dispatch to the frontiers of a UN Military Group. In southern Africa, where U.S. mediation had all decade appeared to be getting nowhere, the prospect that the decade-old UN resolution 435 on Namibian independence might be implemented, and even that Angola's civil war might end, became more than a glimmer in the eyes of a handful of African politicians. Vietnam began withdrawing from Cambodia, and as regional negotiations on Cambodia's future picked up élan, Margaret Thatcher pledged herself to involve a newly impressive Security Council. The outlines of a compromise to end the thirteen-year-old war in the western Sahara seemed to be taking shape, and a thaw in Greco-Turkish relations gave rise to optimistic predictions that years of inconclusive UN mediation over Cyprus might finally yield results.

Some of this optimism was premature—the peace talks between Iran and Iraq, for example, got nowhere for the next two years, only to be concluded overnight and without UN mediation in August 1990, when Saddam Hussein needed to free his forces for the battle in Kuwait—but there was still real and unexpected progress. The predisposition to believe that the UN was capable of beating swords into ploughshares revived almost overnight. Encomia of Pérez de Cuéllar, whose grey manner, low profile, and evident inaptitude for administrative reform had singularly failed to inspire enthusiasm up to that point, began to fill diplomats' discourse and newspaper commentaries. The political skills of a man of whom it had been said that "he wouldn't make waves if he fell out of a boat" were suddenly found by Vernon Walters, then U.S. permanent representative to the UN, to have been capable of revitalizing the organization. Senior correspondents, hastening to New York, hailed the transformation, lamenting the "often unfair criticisms of [the UN's] effectiveness, of its bureaucracy or of the radical political poses struck by many of its members." The *New York Times*, which remarked that great powers found "this unwieldy forum indispensable" when they wanted to resolve conflicts, abruptly discovered that progress toward budgetary and staffing reforms had been "indisputable" and called on the U.S. government to resume full funding. And in Great Britain, a normally iconoclastic columnist invited the public to consider the stirring prospect that the UN had "blearily aroused itself from two decades of chicanery and corruption, wiped the mud from its eyes and found itself called upon to fulfill a real live role."[9]

The truth was more complex—and both more and less banal than appeared. No great wind of change had blown through the corridors of the organization itself. On the contrary, the staff cuts that had been forced on the UN by cash shortages had been so mishandled that instead of ridding the secretariat of the incompetent and corrupt, they had deprived it of much of its most promising younger talent. On the program front, there had been no serious pruning, and negotiations on reducing the number of intergovernmental committees had just ended in deadlock. For all that the UN appeared to be moving toward center stage, the critical shifts in the geopolitical compass had not taken place because of the UN and it was far from clear that this spate of diplomatic "successes" was to its credit.

But if the signs in 1988 were therefore somewhat misleading, that did not mean that optimism was unjustified. The prospects for cooperation between the five permanent members of the Security Council, both in handling regional conflicts and, just possibly, in collective deterrence, were better than for forty years. The five-power collaboration that, in July 1987, had produced resolution 598 on the Iran-Iraq war was beginning to look like more than an ephemeral conjunction. Yet the United Nations was profiting as an ancillary to the plot rather than as leading actor in this drama. The catalyst for change was external. What was altering the rules of the international game was the radical overhaul of Soviet foreign policy. This was as rapid as it was far-reaching. As recently as 1985 the Australian ambassador to the UN, Richard Woolcott, had approached Oleg Tryanovsky, his Soviet counterpart, to find out whether Moscow would support ideas to improve the Security Council's mediating and conflict-prevention functions. Although these included nothing earthshaking—UN fact-finding missions, ways of bringing states in dispute into informal Security Council consultations before a resolution was adopted—Tryanovsky gave him the cold shoulder. Yet within a year, the Soviet Union was embarking on a high-profile campaign for innovations across the board, and championing a new enhanced role for the UN in crisis management.

The early Soviet steps were easily taken for old policies in new guises. At the 1986 General Assembly, arguing logically enough that the political and economic causes of international friction were linked, Soviet diplomats floated their first draft of a "comprehensive system for international peace and security." Since, however, this "fresh approach" also insisted on the total abolition of nuclear weapons as the precondition for promoting collective security through the UN, Western diplomats saw it in a new and subtler version of Khrushchev's call for "general and complete disarmament." But in January 1987, Soviet officials proved unexpectedly accommodating in the five-power consultations on Iran-Iraq; and in April, the Soviet Union not only voted to extend the mandate of the UN peacekeeping force in south Lebanon (UNIFIL), but also offered to pay its share of future costs.

This small step was genuinely revolutionary. For forty years, the Soviet Union had refused to have anything to do with peacekeeping. Ever since the deadlock in the Military Staff Committee (MSC) in 1948, every UN military deployment, from Korea to Cyprus, had either had to circumvent a Soviet veto or—a token contribution to the UN force patrolling the Golan Heights apart—to be content with Soviet abstention coupled with a flat refusal to pay its legally due share of the costs. And this was followed on October 16 by Moscow's announcement that it had not only paid off its arrears to the UN's regular budget, but was ready to honor its debts for past peacekeeping operations "without exceptions." The sum, close to $200 million, included the Congo operation it had so bitterly opposed back in the 1960s.

Confirmation that a completely new Soviet strategy was evolving had been provided in the previous month. On September 17, 1987, in an article published, exceptionally, in both *Pravda* and *Izvestia* to make sure that its importance was grasped abroad, Gorbachev himself spelt out Kremlin thinking on the UN. Entitled "The Reality and Guarantees of a Secure World," this article relaunched the proposal for a comprehensive approach to security in the context of an unambiguous Soviet commitment to multilateral diplomacy. To be sure, Gorbachev began by stressing the Soviet objective of complete nuclear disarmament, emphasizing that a "system of all-embracing security . . . could become a reality only if all means of mass annihilation were destroyed." But he went on to argue that "the sphere of the reasonable, responsible and rational organization of international affairs" was expanding and that while the Soviet Union accepted that "any attempts to influence the development of countries which are 'not one of our own' should be ruled out . . . at the same time the world community cannot stay away from inter-state conflicts." In Europe, he suggested building on the Helsinki accords by evolving an East-West doctrine of "military sufficiency" as the basis for balanced mutual disarmament. At the global level, he proposed to strengthen the Security Council and to make of the UN "a multilateral center for lessening the dangers of war" by exploiting the extensive powers conveyed on the Security Council by the Charter.

Gorbachev suggested annual meetings at the foreign minister rather than the diplomatic level—taking place not just in New York but in the capitals of any of the five permanent members, or in "regions of friction and tension." The council's cooperation with regional organizations could, he said, be "considerably expanded" in "the search for a political settlement of crisis situations." The five permanent members "could become guarantors of regional security" and should, with this in mind, establish hotlines to UN headquarters. They could use the Security Council to set up "a mechanism for extensive international verification of compliance with agreements to lessen international tension, limit armaments and for monitoring the military situation in conflict areas." This should include intelligence monitoring (by implication, by the five), the results of which would be made available to the UN to provide "an objective picture of the events taking place, to timely detect [sic] preparations for hostilities, impede a sneak attack, take measures to avert an armed conflict, prevent it from expanding and becoming worse." Wider use should be made of UN observer and peacekeeping forces. And the Security Council should turn more frequently to the International Court of Justice for opinions on international disputes, with the permanent members setting an example by recognizing the Court's "mandatory jurisdiction." (This last point was, again, revolutionary: the Soviet Union had consistently rejected compulsory jurisdiction by the Court, on the ground of the absolute juridical supremacy of the socialist state.) Looking further into the future, Gorbachev also called for collective measures to guard against nuclear piracy, and "drastic intensification" of cooperation against terrorism, possibly through a UN investigative tribunal.

The economic dimensions of this new Soviet strategy were more hazily sketched and—partly because Gorbachev remained a convinced Communist, partly because he was no economist—less sure in their touch. He acknowledged that consensus on "the concept of the new world economic order" was hard to achieve, but could not bring himself to jettison a slogan that the Soviet Union had exploited since the early 1970s. He was silent on the subject of development cooperation, except in terms of the familiar disarmament/development link, dwelling instead on the alleviation of Third World debt (an almost cost-free policy for the Soviet Union). In calling for "a global strategy of environmental protection and the rational use of resources," he buried this admirable goal in the jargon of the command economy and the five-year plan. Yet in sum, the Gorbachev article was a dramatic break with forty years of Soviet policy toward the West and, by extension, toward the UN. And it was certainly far more ambitious than anything emanating from Western capitals.

A good deal of fumbling went into putting all this into practice. In the General Assembly following the publication of Gorbachev's article, the main Soviet effort went into gaining acceptance of a revamped version of its 1986 draft resolution—now grandly dubbed a Comprehensive System of International Peace and Security (CSIPS). As things turned out, it had a rocky ride, ending in a vote that split the membership straight down the middle.[10] The British and Americans led a campaign designed to persuade the nonaligned that the Soviet Union was trying to rewrite the Charter. This was almost certainly untrue and would have been completely out of character—the Soviet Union had always been a rock-ribbed conservative on the subject of Charter revision—but Soviet diplomats were handicapped by their inability to explain just why a fresh "comprehensive" policy was needed to supplement it. Skepticism about the Kremlin's real intentions was, in addition, reinforced by the continuing Soviet emphasis on nuclear disarmament, nuclear-free zones in South Asia and the Middle East, a "Zone of Peace" in the Indian Ocean, and the need for treaties on "nonuse of force" and "nonuse of nuclear weapons"—all of them variants on familiar Soviet themes. Western diplomats complained that, when pressed to explain what they were seeking to achieve with many of the new proposals, Soviet diplomats retreated into platitudes or said that they were, frankly, still working on the small print.

The short answer was that in detail, the Kremlin did not quite know. Its diplomats, immensely skilled as they were at exploiting UN procedures and Third World sensibilities in order to discomfit the West, were feeling their way to a new language of conciliation. Much was not thought through. The week after Gorbachev's article appeared, the secretary-general invited the five permanent members to what by all accounts was a wholly convivial lunch—itself an unthinkable event only a couple of years earlier. There the Soviet foreign minister, Eduard Shevardnadze, electrified his colleagues by abruptly proposing the revival of the long-moribund Military Staff Committee—a proposal publicly reiterated on October 15 in a BBC interview by his deputy, Vladimir Petrovsky.

The truth was that, far from being a carefully premeditated step, this suggestion resulted from a conversation about peacekeeping only five days before the lunch between Petrovsky and Brian Urquhart, recently retired from the UN. "I mentioned the MSC," Urquhart recalls, "and mentioned that it had originally been intended to discuss disarmament regularly as well as to coordinate military enforcement under the Charter. Petrovsky said, what a wonderful idea—and his tone made it pretty clear that he had really never heard of the MSC until we talked. And to my amazement its revival was suddenly a Soviet proposal."[11]

Soviet diplomats were far from speaking with one voice. Old habits of blaming Third World poverty on "imperialism, racism, and Zionism" died hard in a foreign service where the *nomenklatura* was still solidly entrenched. Westerners were rightly skeptical when Soviet diplomats excused a virtuoso exhibition of "old thinking" by one of their colleagues by saying that now that *glasnost* had come to the Soviet Union, everyone was free to speak his mind. But with foreign policy in the melting pot, there was some truth in this. And many Soviet decisions, such as its donation—having contributed almost nothing to famine relief in 1985—of 250,000 tons of wheat to Ethiopia in January 1988, were evidently intended to demonstrate its *bona fides*. However vague the Kremlin's promises to fund multilateral aid programs, Soviet insistence that it approached economic cooperation in the understanding that "no social structure or economic model is perfect" ended years of confrontation in that field.

Soviet attitudes to the UN secretariat also changed radically—at least in theory. In the summer of 1988 Moscow abruptly announced that it no longer insisted on filling its UN "quota" of secretariat jobs by secondment and that Soviet citizens were now free to accept permanent UN employment. This removed, in principle, a longstanding bone of contention with the West (and an obstacle to the resumption of full U.S. funding to the UN). Petrovsky summed up the new approach:

> We were wrong not to pay for peace-keeping operations. We are paying up. We were wrong towards international civil servants. Now we accept permanent contracts. We consider that the whole of the UN Charter should be fulfilled, not just the parts we like. We were wrong to oppose an active role for the Secretary-General. . . . We need a stable structure for international affairs, and we see the United Nations as a major way of achieving it.[12]

In this torrent of Soviet proposals, more than sixty by one count, the puzzle for the West was where and what to take up. Some of them were old ones rehashed; others—on peacekeeping, the International Court of Justice and the Military Staff Committee—were new but had not been elaborated in any depth. The CSIPS proposal, with its echoes of "global negotiations," NIEO politics, and the disarmament/development linkage, was as formulated a nonstarter for the West. Yet the concept of economic security, stressing the links between poverty, environmental degradation, and political instability, was squarely within the received wisdom of the Western development community. Soviet diplomats, moreover, were disarmingly diffident about the proposals. They insisted that they were completely open to suggestions and even urged Sir Crispin Tickell, the then British permanent representative to the UN, to rewrite anything in their draft his government objected to and generally to help them put the resolution in a form that would attract Western support. Tickell declined.[13]

What stands out in retrospect is how frank senior Soviet diplomats actually were about the thinking behind this ferment. Petrovsky's speech to the UN's second committee in October 1987 was more candid than he was given credit for. Given the Soviet track record, it is not surprising that few were prepared to take on trust his assurances that Moscow's new approach was predicated not "on a desire to gain victory in the rhetorical competition or in the propaganda exercise, and even less so on philanthropy," but on the Soviet Union's need for "a secure future" in which economic and environmental as well as military threats were reduced. But Petrovsky was perfectly serious about "reaching agreement on measures that would make the process of economic interdependence manageable and ensure predictability and stability," and easing the Soviet "integration into the world economic system."[14] And Shevardnadze's team almost certainly *was*, as Petrovsky claimed, rereading every line in the Charter in the search for new opportunities for five-power cooperation. All this was part and parcel of the new foreign policy that Shevardnadze, with Gorbachev's backing for most of the time, was struggling to put in place—a policy that went far beyond modernizing the doctrine of "peaceful coexistence." The centerpiece was improving relations with the West, but the new Soviet leadership also saw the United Nations as one way of giving institutional form to this "new thinking," in ways which would commit not only the West but the Soviet foreign and military establishments. A vigorous UN policy was one way of "making *perestroika* irreversible" in foreign affairs.

More mundanely, the Kremlin sought to use the UN to present the strategic retrenchment on which it was necessarily embarked as a global strategy for peace and cooperation. Late in July 1988, Shevardnadze recalled every Soviet ambassador to Moscow for a three-day conference of more than a thousand diplomats, ministers, military top brass, academics, and party officials. Coexistence, he announced, "must not be equated with class struggle" and confrontation between the capitalist and socialist systems was "no longer the decisive factor." Foreign policy was about economics, "the ability to advance people's welfare at a fast pace through the use of the latest achievements in science and engineering." The Soviet Union had "failed to use all the possibilities for preventing the emergence of the Iron Curtain, for lowering the level of confrontation and curbing the arms race."[15] There could have been no clearer repudiation of Andrei Gromyko's thirty-year reign as Soviet foreign minister—as Yegor Ligachev, the party's ultraconservative chief ideologue, promptly objected, arguing that the Soviet Union must never deviate from "the class character of international relations."[16] This accusation stuck and was a factor in compelling Shevardnadze's resignation in 1990. But for the time being, Shevardnadze had not only Gorbachev but economic necessity on his side. It was all too obvious that the Soviet economy was near-bankrupt and that Moscow urgently needed to disengage from expensive regional entanglements, modernize its economy, and put its relations with the important economic powers on a stable and cordial footing.

This required, first and foremost, accelerating the thaw in relations with the United States. Discussions between the United States and the Soviet Union on regional tensions, initially included alongside disarmament on the agenda for bilateral summits only on Ronald Reagan's insistence, now meshed perfectly with Soviet priorities. The UN, in this scheme of things, was not only a useful additional mechanism to help the Kremlin disengage and a display cabinet for its new cooperative image, but a form of multilateral insurance with which to buttress its new bilateral diplomacy.

But for that the Soviet Union badly needed to reengage U.S. interest in the UN. That was in large measure the point of the great public importance Gorbachev and Shevardnadze were now attaching to the organization. As a Scandinavian diplomat monitoring the Soviet Union's new UN policy put it:

> They may not know what they are doing, but they are doing the right things—from their own point of view, but also to the UN's benefit. The impulse is partly negative. They thought at first that the U.S. would fail in its go-it-alone foreign strategy and would lose influence by taking a tough line in multilateral forums. But the U.S. has been doing quite well. So the conventional wisdom that the Russians are exploiting a vacuum at the UN is ill-founded: what has happened is that the Russians have become alarmed by the possibility of an American retreat from multilateral cooperation. They need the U.S., *nolens volens*, and they also need it fettered by multilateral commitments—because the essence of the new thinking in the Kremlin is that the U.S. may be strong enough to operate a unilateral policy, but they are not. So what we are seeing is a charm offensive, not to fill a vacuum, but to coax the U.S. back into harness.[17]

And this reading was borne out the following year, when Moscow quietly abandoned the CSIPS proposal in deference to U.S. opposition. Instead, for the first time ever, the Soviet Union and the United States cosponsored a General Assembly resolution on strengthening the UN's effectiveness in maintaining international peace and security and improving economic, social, cultural, and humanitarian cooperation. The text was utterly bland. The fact of cosponsorship was what was important, as Petrovsky and the U.S. assistant secretary for international organizations, John Bolton, jointly emphasized. The resolution, they said, was intended to demonstrate that the recent agreement between James Baker and Eduard Shevardnadze in Wyoming to work together in the UN would be energetically implemented. Their efforts for reform were "an attempt to explore an area of mutual advantage." They would begin close cooperation not only in the Security Council, but "throughout the United Nations system to promote budgetary reform and the elimination of duplication of effort . . . to depoliticize its proceedings and promote an atmosphere of realism and practicality." They intended this resolution "to offer an example to other member states . . . to set aside the tendentious polemics that have been too common in the United Nations in the past."[18] (The initiative made no headlines. There was little in yet another "motherhood" resolution at the General Assembly to prompt them. But it was a more important harbinger of things to come than was realized.)

The fact was that the UN was the only forum available to the Soviet Union to project itself as a superpower. The main thrust of Moscow's policy toward the UN was thus inevitably concentrated on the part of its machinery that most closely reflected the realities of global power: the Security Council. The Kremlin was wearying of the game of General Assembly resolutions—however it might now serve its interests to show as an active and constructive participant in these debates. Its aim was to make the Security Council a force to be reckoned with—not excluding, Soviet officials were already insisting, resort to its powers of enforcement under Chapter VII. Forty years late, Moscow was discovering the attractions of Roosevelt's concept of the "four policemen": projecting itself through the UN as a peacemaker was a means to reassert a presence in areas, such as the Middle East, where it had been progressively marginalized. The new thinking did not mean that the Soviet Union was renouncing its claims to global influence, only that it was modernizing the forms they took. And in this search for a "constructive" role, it was displaying a sophistication it had not previously thought necessary to expend on multilateral diplomacy. Whether or not the Soviet Union was in fact becoming a *status quo* power, its determination to project itself as such changed the equations at the UN.

Under the UN Umbrella

As Laurence Sterne brilliantly described in *Tristram Shandy*, causal explanations do not always help narrative to progress and may even lead in the opposite direction from the observable thread of events. The new Soviet policy began to be closely watched by diplomats and commentators who also noted that Soviet practice was naturally driven by more self-interested calculations than was suggested by the Kremlin's formal presentations of this policy. The wider public observed a "renaissance" of the United Nations, and tended to credit either the organizations's mediators or Western diplomatic skills for the speed with which hitherto intractable disputes now became negotiable. So it was with the Soviet Union's abrupt renunciation of its Afghan adventure early in 1988.

Since 1979 the General Assembly, albeit naming no names, had annually condemned "foreign intervention" in Afghanistan. But neither these resolutions nor the UN's six-year effort at mediation weighed heavily in the Soviet decision. The Afghan war was expensive, but the economic and military costs of a decade's fighting against ill-armed guerrillas were nothing compared to the long campaigns to subdue Central Asia first under the Czars and then by the Soviet leadership. Belated U.S. and British assistance to the *mujahideen*—particularly the supply of Stinger and Blowpipe missiles—increased Soviet costs and casualties. But that was important chiefly because it reinforced the case for disengagement being advanced for political reasons by Soviet reformers. The old debates about whether Russia was a Western or Asian power revived almost from the beginnings of *glasnost*. Reformers believed good relations with the West, and the United States in particular, to be indispensable to modernizing Soviet society and economic life. They knew that in reaching out to the West, the strongest card the Soviet Union possessed was the offer of "partnership" in resolving regional disputes—and that this partnership was also the best way of enlisting U.S. support and face-saving UN machinery to extricate the Soviet Union from regional entanglements that it had become essential to shed. From that perspective, they believed the Afghan intervention to be the Soviet Union's worst foreign policy blunder since the invasion of Czechoslovakia in 1968. Internally, they were arguing that intervention had been a political miscalculation, an effort to impose socialism on a country that "was not ready" for it. It helped their case against the hard-line factions in the Soviet military that it was also looking more and more like a military miscalculation.

The decision to get out was the fruit of *perestroika*, not external pressure, a unilateral decision that would have been taken even had the UN not existed. Even Moscow's demand for a political settlement was cosmetic—as was shown by the agreement between Moscow and Washington to continue to arm their respective clients on the basis of "positive symmetry" that accompanied the UN-brokered Geneva accords of which they were joint guarantors. This was no peace settlement, but a device to internalize the conflict, leaving Afghans to fight it out themselves—which they continued to do with considerable ferocity as the Soviet troops went ahead with their withdrawal and for long after its completion. The superpowers gave their blessing to further UN mediation and to an ambitious program for refugee resettlement and economic reconstruction—to which Moscow promised to contribute generously. But there was no doubt that what the Kremlin cared about was speedy disengagement; the existence of a UN negotiating forum was merely a bonus it was glad to exploit. Subsequent collaboration between the United States and the Soviet Union rapidly settled into a pattern of bilateral negotiation between the superpowers, with the results presented to the UN for legitimization. Where the Soviet Union could not pretend to equal partnership, it sought to establish its *bona fides* with Washington by offering constructive support. The Reagan-Gorbachev summit in May 1988 set a firm target for Namibian independence, which by implication committed the Soviet Union to securing the withdrawal of Cuban troops from neighboring Angola—a linkage on which the U.S. administration had been insisting through eight years of apparently hopeless mediation between South Africa, Angola, and Cuba. Within three months of that summit the American negotiator, Dr. Chester Crocker, had secured the basis for a settlement. Many factors contributed, not least white anxieties in South Africa about the increasing human and financial costs of holding on to the territory following an impressive Cuban assault in southern Angola that summer. But Moscow's firm warnings to Cuba and Angola that it was no longer prepared to bankroll the presence of fifty-seven thousand Cuban troops made it possible for the Americans to increase the pressure on Pretoria.

When Namibia finally achieved independence in 1990, this was to all appearances a victory for the UN. The transition was presided over by a substantial UN monitoring force, under the time-hallowed UN Resolution 435 of 1978. Yet the UN could never have brought South Africa to the table, never mind brokered an agreement. At the time of the 1988 superpower summit, it was twenty-two years since the General Assembly had declared South Africa's occupation of Namibia illegal, twenty-one since it had established a UN Council for Namibia to "administer" a territory to which UN representatives could not even gain access, and a decade since South Africa had accepted 435 in principle. This was an example of what closed-circuit secret negotiations, as opposed to megaphone diplomacy at the General Assembly, could achieve—above all when backed by economic and military pressure, commodities in which the UN had rarely been effective at dealing.

Money and superpower cooperation, not the UN, were also behind the Vietnamese withdrawal from Cambodia, which paved the way for protracted negotiations on an internal peace settlement. Cambodia's long ordeal had reflected credit neither on the West, which dismissed Vietnam's claim to have rescued Cambodians from the unspeakably atrocious tyranny of the Khmer Rouge in 1978, nor on the United Nations. With Western support, the General Assembly refused to recognize the Hang Semrin government installed by Hanoi. That might have been defended on the ground of upholding international law—there was little doubting its puppet status—had Cambodia's seat been left empty. But instead, it continued to be awarded to the Khmer Rouge, albeit formally as part of a coalition headed by the former ruler (and occasional Khmer Rouge prisoner) Prince Norodom Sihanouk. The United Nations thus continued to recognize a regime that was not only not in *de facto* control of the country, but that had when in power murdered a higher proportion of its civilians than any peacetime government in the UN's history. Vietnam in turn, with Soviet backing, had ignored nine UN resolutions calling for its withdrawal and a government of national reconciliation. In 1987, however, Moscow had begun to exert pressure on Hanoi, setting in motion an unsteady gavotte between the Hang Semrin government and Prince Sihanouk. Tacitly acknowledging the Khmer Rouge as a common problem, Cambodia's other warring factions set out to find ways to meet the UN demands to fulfill "the right of the Kampuchean people to determine their own destiny" without returning them to the grip of terror. And Moscow had leverage to exert: Vietnam, in hideous financial straits, could only sustain its expensive occupation of Cambodia thanks to an annual $2 billion subvention from the Soviet Union. The Kremlin now served notice that the game was no longer worth the drain on its coffers and the damage to its relations with China, the principal armorer to the Khmer Rouge, and with the United States. With Vietnam's withdrawal, the route was open for the five permanent members to lead the exhaustive peacemaking negotiations that culminated in the Paris Agreement of August 1991, and to the deployment thereafter of the largest force ever fielded by the United Nations to supervise a cease-fire, set up a transitional UN administration, help refugees to return, and organize the democratic elections for a new government which, to the surprise of almost every participant in the mission, were successfully conducted in 1993.

The real catalyst for the revival in public confidence in the United Nations that began during 1988 was, however, the cease-fire in the Gulf after eight years of a grisly war of attrition between two medium-sized oil exporting powers. There could be no more ironic disfunction between cause and effect than the credit given to the UN for the end of the fighting, or the talk about the UN's rediscovery of its role that accompanied the announcement. Even before Iraq's next aggression put it into even darker perspective, the Iran-Iraq war counted as the UN's most significant and dangerous security failure.

Iraq had violated international law both by its initial act of aggression in 1980 and by its subsequent resort to chemical weapons. Its invasion of Iran presented a clear threat to international peace under the Charter, yet the Security Council dithered for days and then failed to condemn the aggressor. By using chemical weapons in violation of the 1925 Geneva Convention, it broke a taboo so strong that it had held even during World War II. Yet Iraq ignored six Security Council denunciations of this offense, confident that none of its chief bankrollers and arms suppliers—Kuwait and Saudi Arabia, France and the Soviet Union in the forefront—was prepared to agree to any sanctions that might imperil its continued prosecution of the war. War against a pariah state such as Iran, even after the use of banned weapons, was manifestly condoned.

The Security Council's bias owed something to its members' anxiety not to upset the Arab oil exporters, and much to Iran's own conduct. Donald McHenry, the U.S. permanent representative, stated bluntly that if Iran needed the Security Council's assistance, it had better abide by the earlier Security Council resolution condemning the seizure and detention of hostages from the U.S. embassy in Tehran. The major powers may have failed to anticipate the scale of the conflict; more pertinently at the time, the Americans at least shared Iraq's hope that a sharp military defeat would cause the downfall of the Khomeini regime. The council's permanent members took six years to start serious work on finding ways to end the war—and when they did, the spur was fear of victory by Iran, then at the gates of Basra. And when, after six months, the five finally put Resolution 598 in place, they were so taken by the novelty of five-power cooperation that none was prepared to insist on enforcing the decision through economic sanctions or a full-scale military embargo, since to do so might expose cracks in the painfully wrought consensus. Had an embargo been agreed, it would have been imposed on Iran for refusing to accept 598, but not against Iraq for initiating the war and being the first to use chemical weapons.

By the time the guns fell silent, up to a million had been killed, industrial and urban infrastructure wrecked, and magnificent monuments such as Isfahan's Friday mosque damaged. The two countries had spent well over $400 billion on the war effort, and the warships of the United States, the Soviet Union, and several Western European nations had been drawn into the Gulf. The conflict ended, what is more, not because of any great international effort but because Iran had no real choice.

Iran's acceptance of Resolution 598 on July 18, 1988, took all players by surprise. There had been some indications that factions favoring a diplomatic solution were gaining the ascendancy in Tehran. Earlier that month, Iran had ended its seven-year boycott of the Security Council. But the conventional wisdom was that the war would drag on until after the Ayatollah Khomeini's death—an interpretation compatible with Iran's heated demands earlier that month that the Security Council not only condemn the United States for its accidental shooting down of an Iranian airbus on July 3 but call for the withdrawal of foreign naval forces from the Gulf. The old man took the decision he described as "more deadly for me than taking poison" because Iran was economically, militarily, and physically exhausted. Its forces, critically short of *matériel*, had in the space of a few months been forced by Iraq almost to the pre-1980 frontiers, recruitment was encountering resistance, and dissension within the leadership threatened to destabilize the country after Khomeini's death. Iran's easiest way out was to treat, through the UN, with the international community—and invoke its protection against Iraq. The Security Council could thus finally claim to have exerted some influence. But the fact remains that this was a classic case of international aggression, tailor-made for the Security Council as few conflicts had been since 1945, a destructive war prosecuted in defiance of logic in a particularly sensitive area of the world—an area moreover in which both superpowers were anxious to avoid confrontation. Yet it took the council seven years to put together a resolution to end this war, and it was even then unable to agree how to enforce it. The unspoken common interest in preventing Iran from claiming a triumph had taken precedence over upholding the Charter. The only mitigating factor in this history of a UN failure is that it could be argued that Iran's decision to accept 598 rather than, say, Islamic mediation owed most to the diplomacy of the secretary-general, who, in the year after 598 was adopted, sought to persuade Tehran that he and his office could be trusted to act impartially, even if the Security Council could not.

The eventual unanimity of the superpowers on 598 was significant mainly because it could be built on in the future. The chief contribution to the cease-fire by the five permanent members—forcefully supported by Saudi Arabia and Kuwait—was to impress on Iraq in the days following July 18 that nobody was prepared to permit it to set fresh conditions for a cease-fire now that it needed one less than Iran. And the contempt in which President Saddam Hussein continued to hold the Security Council was made evident within weeks. In August 1988, even as UN observers were fanning out along the Iran-Iraq cease-fire lines, he turned with renewed vigor to the massacre and wholesale deportation of Iraq's large Kurdish community. And he again unleashed chemical weapons—killing an estimated five thousand Kurds in the village of Halabja. The UN saw nothing; the military observers were not allowed north. And even when it was presented with incontrovertible evidence of this attack, the UN said little. The Security Council again denounced the use of chemical weapons, but did not even mention the Kurds. Moscow continued to supply Iraq with arms, but the West behaved little better, continuing to furnish Saddam with militarily applicable technology, generous credits, and precursor chemicals for his "pesticides" factories.

No Cold War alibi can seriously be adduced in justification. The UN, an institution intended to prevent any recurrence of the horrors of Nazism, had sunk to the point where the nonintervention clause of the Charter became a defense against law and conscience, even when confronted by a blatant violation of the sixty-three-year-old Geneva Convention banning the use of these weapons. *Kristallnacht* was also an internal affair. The West's readiness to blink at Iraqi violations of international law, a pattern set in 1980 and increasingly reinforced by the belief of Arabists in foreign ministries that Iraq had become too powerful to quarantine, led directly to the invasion of Kuwait in 1990. Saddam calculated his risks, concluded he ran none, and acted accordingly. Of all auguries for a "revived" United Nations at the end of the 1980s, the ending of the Iran-Iraq war was the least propitious. Only in the new closeness with which the veto powers worked together did it represent the opening of a new chapter; in most respects it was the improvised, and largely discreditable, end to an old one.

Yet none of this meant that the public perception of a UN "renaissance" was merely naive. Within only a few years, what had seemed an unshakable antagonism between the superpowers had given place, in dispute after dispute, to good-faith joint efforts at conciliation. Eastern Europe's headlong abandonment of communism in 1989, the peaceful dissolution of the Warsaw Pact and the unification of Germany transformed the postwar scene—not only in Europe but in the developing world. Repressive governments could no longer bank on the protection of one or other rival bloc; the collapse of seemingly impregnable Communist regimes emboldened other peoples to demand accountable, democratic forms of government. The two most important "global policemen" were at least beginning to do the job Roosevelt intended, not as he had envisaged by means of armies, but by combining their influence to force combatants to sheathe their swords. Although this had yet to be reflected in Third World attitudes to the UN—beyond a certain amount of grumbling about "bipolar triumphalism" in the Security Council—the dissolution of the Eastern bloc spelled the end for the concept of nonalignment as a "third force." However little these transformations owed to the UN, the UN could not fail to be affected by them. And so it proved on August 2, 1990.

A "COMMON POWER TO KEEP MEN IN AWE"

Hobbes wrote that a state of war is defined not necessarily by fighting, but by the absence of this "common power." Saddam Hussein apart, the one thing on which there was universal political agreement throughout the six months it took to drive his troops out of Kuwait was the importance of establishing the United Nations, then and in the future, as the fount of "common power." Each government had its more immediate reasons for acting through the UN, some of which were sketched in the introduction to this book. For the Americans, necessarily providing the bulk of the manpower and weaponry for the military effort, reference to the UN helped to broaden the military coalition to twenty-eight countries, hampering Saddam's efforts to depict the conflict as one between Iraq and the United States. For the Arab members of this coalition, for all of whom Iraq's defeat was a strategic imperative, UN sanction was a useful cover behind which to side with unbelievers against an Arab neighbor and member—for all the Iraqi regime's secularism—of the Islamic *umma*. In Western democracies, emphasis on the importance of supporting the UN relieved opposition parties of the "duty to oppose." For Gorbachev and his increasingly harried foreign minister, Eduard Shevardnadze, the UN's authority was an indispensable counterweight in dealing with hard-liners who objected to close cooperation with the United States in a war the Soviet Union could not control, and who argued that the Soviet Union had no business forsaking Iraq, a treaty ally. For Cuba, the lone voice of consistent opposition in the Security Council, the UN was a stick with which to beat the West for forging a military coalition outside UN command. For the Germans and Japanese, it justified financial contributions to the war effort. And for politicians who believed that the world should rely on sanctions alone to bring about Iraq's withdrawal, strict compliance with the letter of the Charter was a respectable platform from which to plead their case.

The impression deliberately given of UN "leadership" was, as noted in the introduction to this book, misleading. In the days immediately following Iraq's invasion, the Security Council was of critical importance. The invocation of Chapter VII, the unambiguous demand for immediate and unconditional Iraqi withdrawal, the commitment "to restore the authority of the legitimate Government of Kuwait," the imposition within four days of mandatory sanctions—these first two resolutions[19] created a legal straitjacket that reduced almost to zero the room for compromise with Iraq. The third, Resolution 662 of August 9, required Saddam not only to withdraw his troops but to acknowledge that his annexation of Kuwait had "no legal validity." Would-be mediators in the months that followed, from Jordan's King Hussain to Kurt Waldheim, from Gorbachev's special envoy Yevgeni Primakov to the UN secretary-general, were constrained by this legal framework. The first lesson of the Gulf crisis was that the Security Council was at last capable, at least in exceptional circumstances, of an unambiguous response to aggression. It was "good," said Shevardnadze at the end of September to the General Assembly, "that we are calling aggression by its proper name" and prepared "to punish its perpetrator." More than good, it was historic for Moscow to be taking the lead, as Shevardnadze did on this occasion, in calling for the judgment of war crimes by an international tribunal, in laying squarely on Baghdad responsibility for "a great war" that could break out at any moment, and in insisting that "if the illegal occupation of Kuwait continues," the UN would indeed use force.

But having set the stage, as it were, the UN followed rather than led the action. There was universal reluctance to accept that Iraq's action had dragged the United States and the allies it mustered into what President François Mitterrand was to call "the logic of war." But from the first, the great powers understood that the ball was firmly in their court. The silence of Iraq's Arab neighbors in the aftermath of the invasion was testimony to that. In most Middle Eastern countries, the press was not even allowed to report the news when it happened; only Syria, Iraq's sworn enemy, issued a forthright condemnation.

A glance at the map, and the briefest scrutiny of the forces they could muster, was explanation enough. On August 6, the day the UN imposed sanctions on Iraq, the U.S. defense secretary, Richard Cheney, was already in Saudi Arabia requesting permission to airlift troops. The next day, President Bush ordered the first U.S. contingents to Saudi Arabia. His "line drawn in the sand" was not only against a feared Iraqi attack on the kingdom. It was already clear that economic sanctions would be enforced only with military backing: how else would Saudi Arabia risk cutting Iraq's oil pipeline? There was still hope that an unprecedently well-coordinated and comprehensive operation to choke off Iraqi imports, exports, and access to Kuwaiti and Iraqi assets abroad would convince even Saddam that he had no choice but to withdraw. The alternative was a military operation on a scale not seen since Vietnam—and one that would need at least the tacit blessing of the Soviet Union and China. But the need to protect other states in the region against possible Iraqi attack and relieve them of pressure to make peace with the aggressor meant that the ink was not dry on Resolution 661 imposing sanctions before a parallel military operation had begun—outside Chapter VII. The legal basis for the movement of U.S. and then other nations' troops to Saudi Arabia and the Gulf was Article 51 of the Charter, which provides for individual and collective self-defense. This action was independent of the Security Council. The practical applicability of Chapter VII to a military enforcement action was thus in doubt from the beginning, despite the emphasis placed by everybody concerned on the cardinal significance of the precedent set by invoking it.

The "no rewards for aggression" rule laid down in the Security Council's early resolutions meant, baldly, that Iraq could have only two incentives for abandoning Kuwait: the complete collapse of its economy, or the certainty of a punishing military defeat. However dependent Iraq was on imported food and goods, the logic of the Security Council's chosen weapon, sanctions, was untenable in the twentieth century, in the sense that no country was prepared to see Iraqis starve: the cruelty of medieval sieges was an unthinkable method of enforcing the rule of law. And nothing less, it rapidly became apparent, was likely to impress a dictatorship insulated from hardship and accustomed to running a war economy. Yet the aim of Chapter VII is action short of force, if possible; the UN secretary-general made no secret of his belief that to resort to military action would be a failure for the United Nations.

Above all, the military articles of Chapter VII posed enormous problems. Under Chapter VII, member states are required to make forces available to the Security Council, which the council may call on if it decides to use force—provided that it invites the contributing state to join it in deciding how these are to be used. The council is responsible for making "plans for the application of armed force," with the assistance of the Military Staff Committee. That committee, composed of commanders from the five permanent members, is responsible under Article 47 "for the strategic direction of any armed forces placed at the disposal of the Security Council." Before embarking on any of these steps, moreover, the Security Council must determine whether the measures already taken (sanctions, in this instance) "would be inadequate or have proved to be inadequate."

The utter impracticability of such a procedure in most situations of actual conflict scarcely needs spelling out. In dealing with Iraq it would have been paralyzing, even if the council had had—as, thanks to the Cold War, it had not—standby forces available to call on. To begin with, months of preparation were required to deploy forces in the Gulf on the scale required; there was no conceivable way that waiting until the Security Council decided that sanctions had failed or might fail made military sense. Second, the idea that the entire Security Council—including, in 1990 and 1991, Cuba and Iraq's ally Yemen—should be charged with the planning was simply frivolous. And even if China abandoned its reservations about the use of force, strategic control by the five permanent members would have been a recipe for military disaster. (The Americans agreed to give President Gorbachev advance warning of the eventual counterattack, only to discover that the Soviet ambassador in Iraq was instantly ordered to warn Saddam and failed only because he was unable to secure an audience. Under collective strategic control, there could have been no such thing as secure intelligence.)

The second lesson of the Gulf crisis was therefore that, although five-power coordination might theoretically be possible for some small policing operations in the future, the Charter's "teeth" were too blunt for modern warfare. This was evident as early as August, long before either the United States or its allies were committed to a counteroffensive against Iraq. By August 13, there was firm evidence that Iraq was seeking to defy economic sanctions. Yet it took until August 25 for the Security Council to authorize naval enforcement of a blockade, and the sanction would probably not have been forthcoming had not the United States and Great Britain already ordered their ships in the Gulf to use force. The Security Council in effect endorsed action already taken under Article 51, thereby agreeing in principle that the council could authorize military action it did not control. Although a precedent had been set for this in the case of Rhodesia, when the British Beira patrol operated as an independent force with the council's blessing, it took considerable pressure by the Americans on the Soviet leadership to win their assent to such an "enabling" resolution in the Gulf.

The Soviet Union, which had seen the crisis as an opportunity to reactivate the Military Staff Committee, had been insistent that military action should take place only under full UN control. Looking beyond the Gulf, the Kremlin was anxious to lay down rules for its involvement in any future enforcement action under the UN by establishing the principle of equal partnership. China voted for Resolution 665 only on the "understanding" that since the text contained no reference to the use of force, the authorized "measures commensurate to the specific circumstances" would not include armed enforcement of sanctions.[20] The negotiation of this masterpiece of ambiguity had been as tortuous as this Chinese interpretation of the text implies. No clearer warning could have been given of the difficulty the United States and its allies would encounter if they sought Security Council approval for a full-scale military counteroffensive.

By the time that sanction was sought on November 29, in a modified form that again left the initiative to individual member states, Saddam had done everything conceivable to harden the resolve of waverers: by taking foreign hostages, Soviet as well as Western and other civilians; by ruthlessly pillaging Kuwait and torturing its citizens; by rejecting numerous ploys devised by Soviet and other mediators to provide him with a dignified exit from Kuwait, now renamed as Saddam Iraq's nineteenth province. Early in November, James Baker had reached agreement with King Fahd on military command and control. The provisions of this agreement, joint U.S.-Saudi command in Saudi Arabia and U.S. command in Kuwait and Iraq, confirmed both that the Americans were becoming resigned to a military operation and that they intended to act under Article 51 of the Charter. Three days later, on November 8, Bush announced that two hundred thousand more troops were being sent to the Gulf, nearly doubling U.S. strength there, in order to give the allied coalition offensive capability.

Publicly, the Bush administration, backed by the British, maintained that there was no legal requirement to seek further explicit sanction by the Security Council: Article 51 was a sufficient basis under international law for a counteroffensive. There was support from an unexpected quarter. On November 9, Javier Pérez de Cuéllar warned that if it were to seek a Security Council resolution under Chapter VII of the Charter, the coalition could forfeit the right to act under Article 51. His point was that Article 51 proclaimed the "inherent right" to individual and collective self-defense, but only "until the Security Council has taken the measures necessary to maintain international peace and security." That left open to interpretation whether these measures were adequate, but implied that this was for the Security Council, not individual states, to decide. Action under "Article 42 would be the normal thing, but 51 as well can be applied," the secretary-general opined, "and that is what makes things a little complicated for those who want to apply 51 or 42. They have to be very careful from a juridical point of view."[21] But even this careful formulation understated the difficulties, for what the coalition needed was a Security Council decision under Chapter VII on the use of force, which yet authorized action under Article 51 instead of invoking the cumbersome procedures provided for in Chapter VII—thus maximizing the UN's authority as legitimator, without involving it directly in enforcement.

For all the Western members of the coalition, a military counteroffensive without explicit Security Council sanction would have created immense political difficulties at home—above all in the United States, where the Gulf crisis had reawakened the constitutional feud between Congress and the White House concerning the legal authority to wage war. But a failed attempt to obtain Security Council authority would be politically, if not legally, still more disastrous. American and British insistence on the legal validity of acting under 51 was intended to increase their leverage in the intensive diplomatic consultations now in train, but it was also a form of insurance. Neither wanted to be forced to draw on that insurance, however, and in the fortnight that followed, the United States invested all its prestige in gathering the necessary Security Council votes. Baker consulted all the fourteen other governments except Cuba, some of them many times, and both he and Bush exploited to the maximum the Soviet Union's anxiety to be seen to be acting as a partner in upholding international law.

Even so, when Bush met Gorbachev in Paris for the summit of the CSCE on November 19, the Soviet president was still insisting that peaceful pressures and negotiation must be given more time. Not until November 27, two days before the Security Council vote, did Gorbachev give public backing for the use of force as a last resort. But that decision once taken, the Soviet Union cosponsored the resolution and brought its influence to bear in Peking to persuade China to abstain rather than use its veto. The United States was the president of the Security Council that month, and Baker convened it at foreign minister level for only the fourth time in the UN's history to emphasize the gravity of the moment and secure a speedy decision. Resolution 678, passed with only Cuba and Yemen voting against and China abstaining, was a triumph for U.S. diplomacy: its effect was to give the coalition blanket authority "to restore international peace and security in the area," with no restrictions on the means employed. That the Soviet Union should have cosponsored such a resolution (making it politically impossible for China to use its veto in isolation) was, even in this exceptional context, extraordinary. But the United States had also yielded ground, ceding to the Soviet Union's insistence on what Shevardnadze called a "pause of goodwill" of forty-seven days before the resolution took effect. The deadline, January 15, gave the coalition only a narrow leeway in deciding the moment to strike before climatic conditions in the Gulf put its forces at grave disadvantage.

The following day, to underline the political intent behind that "pause," Bush offered Saddam direct talks. By the time the air offensive was launched on January 16, Iraq had been besieged by processions of would-be mediators. Some of them, such as President Mitterrand's unofficial emissary Michel Vauzelle, who suggested as late as January 6 that everything was possible provided Saddam "makes certain gestures," came close to offering him diplomatic rewards merely for promising to withdraw. On January 9, Baker met Tariq Aziz, the Iraqi foreign minister, in Geneva—a date far closer to the deadline than the United States had initially accepted. After six hours of talks, Aziz emerged to announce that he had refused to take delivery of a letter from Bush to Saddam, giving a rambling press conference in which he mentioned neither the word *withdrawal* nor the existence of Kuwait.

On January 13, the day following the late, close, vote by the U.S. Congress in favor of using force, Pérez de Cuéllar flew to Baghdad. This was only his second round of talks with the Iraqi leadership since August 2, and his first direct discussion with Saddam. The first round, with Aziz in Jordan at the end of August, had been described by both men as the start of a "long haul to peace" but had in fact yielded nothing. Since that point, the secretary-general's absence from the stage had been one of the notable features of months of diplomatic maneuvering. Pérez was able by virtue of his office to take along suggestions that, without departing from the Security Council script, offered Iraq dignified means to retreat. Since August 12, Saddam had linked Israel's occupation of the West Bank and Gaza strip with his obliteration of Kuwait—not because he intended to relinquish the emirate but because he saw this as a way to divide the coalition and split Arab opinion. Without countenancing explicit "linkage" between these cases, Pérez was in a position to point out that Middle East peace conferences had been part of the UN agenda for years, and that the UN had constructive ideas on longer-term regional security. When Pérez saw Saddam, after a considerable wait in Baghdad, he found him "very serene," fatalistic about what he had already dubbed "the mother of all battles"—and totally unprepared to withdraw from Kuwait.

Yet even this did not deter Gorbachev from issuing a last-minute appeal for the prolongation of diplomatic efforts, or France from asking the Security Council to approve a peace offer for its foreign minister, Roland Dumas, to take to Baghdad. This last-minute plan (formulated with more than half an eye to French interests in the Maghreb, where there was much popular support for Saddam) was launched on the evening of January 15, only a few hours after President Mitterrand had agreed with the British prime minister, John Major, that there could be no question of postponing the deadline. The plan called for an Iraqi withdrawal under a clear timetable, to be monitored not by the coalition's forces but by UN and Arab observer contingents, nonaggression guarantees for Iraq, and a Security Council guarantee that it would convene an international conference on the Palestinian question after Iraq withdrew. The plan had no hope of being accepted, but neither the United States nor Great Britain wanted to be in the position of using its veto, and both were furious that France had garnered support for it from ten of the council's members, including not only China and the nonaligned but

Austria and Belgium, leaving only Romania joining the British, American, and Soviet opposition.

Failure is an orphan, success has many godfathers, as the saying goes. The diplomatic maneuvering continued through the first, air-based phase of Operation Desert Storm, which was launched before dawn broke in the Gulf on January 16. As late as February 18, the Soviet Union offered Iraq a peace plan that would have rescinded all Security Council resolutions, including that which declared its annexation of Kuwait null and void, if Iraq accepted Resolution 660 and withdrew to the position its forces occupied on August 1—an offer Iraq accepted on February 21 after initial attempts to haggle, prompting the United States to lay down its own, tougher conditions the following day. Although the Soviet offer would have left Kuwait as fully exposed to Iraqi intimidation as it had been in August and would have enabled Saddam to claim a resounding diplomatic victory, Pérez de Cuéllar hailed it as "a unique opportunity" for peace.[22] The wavering ceased only with the unexpectedly decisive and swift land offensive, when Iraq's attempts to obtain a cease-fire on its own terms got short shrift from all five permanent members.

Once Bush (not the UN) had ordered the suspension of hostilities on February 27, Resolutions 686 and 687 laying down the terms for a cease-fire were as free of ambiguities as had been the original resolutions of August 1990. The leeway that 686 gave the coalition, rather than the council, to determine whether Iraq was complying with the conditions for a cease-fire attracted opposition from some Third World members (and another Chinese abstention); the conditions themselves did not. The definitive cease-fire resolution, adopted on April 3, was the longest and most detailed in the council's history. It provided for Iraqi reparations; the destruction or removal of its chemical, biological, and nuclear weapons capacity; and the maintenance of a strict arms embargo. But there were two omissions. There was no reference to calling the country's leadership and military officers to account for crimes under the Geneva conventions; and, in an echo of the council's inaction two years earlier, there was no reference to the butchery by Saddam's forces of Iraqi Shias and Kurds who had risen in revolt against Baghdad.

During the war, President Bush had explicitly called on the Iraqi people "to take matters into their own hands" and oust Saddam;[23] in Great Britain, John Major had expressed the hope that they would do so. The great throngs of Iraqis who were now, with the support of some Iraqi troops, attempting this in some two dozen cities and hundreds of villages in southern Iraq expected allied assistance. There was none. Loyalist Republican Guard troops sent from Baghdad to crush the rising in the southern city of Basra passed unhindered within range of the coalition's guns. To the north, hundreds of thousands of Kurds were fleeing in terror to the Iranian and Turkish borders. Turkey closed the frontiers, and complained to the Security Council that Iraq's "inhuman repression" was a threat to international peace and security. France called for a resolution condemning Iraq and demanding that Baghdad open peace talks with the rebels and give foreign aid missions unhindered access. Within weeks of apparent triumph "the political and moral authority of the United Nations" was, as President Mitterrand said, once again in question.

This time, the Security Council just managed to rise to the challenge. After three days of negotiation, Resolution 688 was passed on April 5. It passed only by 10 votes to 5, one more than the minimum required. The Soviet Union's initial objections to involving the UN in Iraq's "internal affairs" were overcome. Not so China's or India's.

They abstained and Cuba, Yemen, and Zimbabwe voted against. The text was a weak one. It gravely recalled Article 2.7, the Charter's "nonintervention" clause, and the commitment of all states to Iraq's "sovereignty, territorial integrity and political independence." But it characterized "the repression of the Iraqi civilian population" as "a threat to international peace and security," ordered Iraq to call an immediate halt and expressed "the hope . . . that an open dialogue will take place to ensure that the human and political rights of all Iraqi citizens are respected." It appealed to all states and humanitarian organizations to provide relief to the victims and insisted that Iraq provide access and all necessary facilities for these operations. There was no provision for enforcement (beyond the deliberate reference to a threat to international peace).

For all its modesty, Resolution 688 made history in a way that not even the series of resolutions concerning Iraq's aggression against Kuwait had done. This was the first time that the United Nations had formally determined that the international community had a right to intervene to stop the intolerable persecution by a government of its own subjects. For the first time, the Security Council recognized that common humanity might occasionally take precedence over the doctrine of nonintervention. But the difficulty of securing passage of the resolution, and the manner in which it was implemented, also illuminated some of the obstacles the UN's political and organizational machinery would have to overcome if the Security Council was to build on the undoubted if imperfect success of Iraq's expulsion from Kuwait.

The bald fact is that left to the UN, thousands more Kurds would have died. When what was clearly needed was a humanitarian enforcement operation, different in character from a standard UN relief operation, Pérez de Cuéllar insisted that to carry relief into Iraq would require Saddam's approval. That would have handed Baghdad an internationally financed food aid weapon. The Kurds would have stayed in the mountains rather than submit to being herded into "secure" ghettos under Saddam's control. Moreover, Pérez planned to wait until a UN "fact-finding mission" dispatched to Baghdad had reported back to New York. Had his views prevailed, Resolution 688 would have been stripped of its path-breaking potential. He was preempted by a British initiative later that month, somewhat reluctantly agreed to by Bush, to create "safe havens" for the Kurds under the military umbrella of nine thousand U.S., British, French, and Dutch troops in a broad swathe of northern Iraq that would be declared out of bounds to Iraqi troops.

The logistics of mounting such a rescue with the requisite speed were almost certainly beyond the UN's capacities in any case. Sites with adequate water supplies had to be identified in the plains, reachable by rapidly deployed, adequately protected, and efficiently supplied convoys over rough roads from Turkey; people weakened by hunger had to be reached (largely by air-dropped leaflets), persuaded that they would be safe from attack, and helped down from the mountains along protected routes. But in military terms, this was a relatively modest operation. It was borne of political embarrassment and public outrage. It was carefully presented as a stopgap before the UN could take over. It ducked certain legal niceties. It was prematurely wound up. And it failed to shield the Shia refugees from Saddam's merciless revenge in southern Iraq; they were offered only the protection of a tiny UN observer unit within a "demilitarized zone" under Iraqi control. But it set an important precedent. And, far from putting the allies on a "collision course with the UN," as the UN team in Baghdad complained, Operation Provide Comfort gave Saddam a strong incentive to comply with Resolution 688 and agree to a UN relief effort throughout Iraq. Significantly, this was forthcoming only after he had tested the allies' resolve by sending heavily armed security forces to Zakho, withdrawing them after an ultimatum. Saddam was to continue to frustrate the operation as far as he dared, denying visas to UN relief workers and the UN guards who took over from the military, and even planting bombs on UN aid convoys. But the "safe haven" concept was sufficiently maintained to provide the Kurds with a genuine measure of protection, whereas in southern Iraq, the failure to create such a haven exposed the Shias and marsh Arabs to continued savage persecution and the UN relief effort dwindled almost to nothing.

The second lesson to be drawn from the closeness of the vote over Resolution 688 was that the cohesiveness of the Security Council, which had been achieved only in unprecedented circumstances and through the most intensive U.S., British, and French diplomacy, was almost certainly an ephemeral phenomenon. Few wars take the form of one state swallowing another whole, as Iraq did Kuwait and, with that drama formally if not actually over, the council was already showing signs of reverting, if not to its former state, at least to its penchant for phony decisions. This was to be amply confirmed in the next few years, as resolutions on Bosnia and Somalia that were more substitutes for policy than reflections of agreed strategies poured out of New York.

The Gulf War should, moreover, have left the Western permanent members with few illusions about the likelihood that China could indefinitely be dissuaded from using its veto.[24] In northern Iraq, they had wisely contended that explicit Security Council sanction was not indispensable provided an action was clearly in defense of international law, including humanitarian law and the Geneva conventions predating the UN. There will be occasions, even in the post-Cold War world, when the UN is paralyzed, whether by China, a newly assertive Russia, or by what might be called the "sixth veto," the blocking power which the requirement of mustering a minimum of nine favorable votes gives the nonpermanent members.

Faced with the strong possibility that the council would block Operation Provide Comfort, the West improvised; its governments need better understandings in place for the occasions when they will need to do so again. In addition, the difficulty of forging consensus among the council's existing fifteen members should have put all thought of expanding it firmly on the back burner. Instead, in June 1993, the Clinton administration announced that it intended to do just that.

Every politician makes rash campaign pledges, and every politician attaches importance to meeting them if they look relatively cost-free, but this was one the Clinton team should, at the very least, have shelved. Possibly it thought to make U.S. policies at the UN more "manageable" by responding to the growing restiveness in the General Assembly about its "loss of authority" now that the Security Council was functioning better. Certainly, it worried about the continued readiness of Germany and Japan to pay the collective security piper if they did not call the tune. Perhaps, since Washington had not obtained the prior agreement of the other four permanent members, which had the power to veto any proposal involving revision of the Charter, this was never more than an exercise in public relations. If so, it was singularly ill-timed, since the United States was at loggerheads with France and Great Britain over Bosnia and with France on trade and hardly needed another furious Transatlantic argument with the two allies most likely to contribute forces to collective actions and most likely also to take a global view of their broader interests. On no count was this initiative properly thought through.

The United States was determined, said Madeleine Albright, Clinton's permanent representative to the UN, not to "sacrifice the council's newfound effectiveness on the altar of reform." But Germany and Japan were great powers and the council must represent the "real world." In the real "real world," however, Germany and Japan were giants hobbled in the exercise of military power. Not only did their postwar constitutions place severe inhibitions on the use of their armed forces; their people overwhelmingly approved of these constraints. So strong was this pacifist sentiment that, as the whole tenor of their domestic debates and their leaders' pronouncements during the Gulf War had confirmed, both governments would have difficulty not only in contributing forces to collective enforcement actions, but in voting for any decision to use force. Leaving aside the anxiety that any projection of Japanese military power would still generate among its Asian neighbors, the time to consider adding these countries to the permanent membership was surely after, not before, their domestic laws and the sentiment of their voters permitted them to commit troops to combat overseas. In theory, the "German question" might be subsumed in the condensing of the French and British seats into a single European Union seat, but that assumed the existence of a genuinely common EU foreign and security policy. The U.S. experience over Bosnia should have been enough to warn Washington against hastening the day. Claims by India, Brazil, Nigeria, and Egypt were moreover the inevitable corollary of this proposal—as were counterclaims, should these be advanced, by Pakistan, Mexico, or Kenya. To this further dimension, the Clinton administration appeared to have given even less reflection.

Changing the Charter would in any case be a complex, time-consuming, and certainly contentious venture. In the context of the new opportunities for more effective UN action, it presents itself as a diversion from the main political task. If reform of the Security Council is to be on the agenda, the purpose should be to make it more, not less, incisive in its decisions and better able to follow them through. Reforming zeal would be better directed toward the neglected potential of Article 23, which stipulates that the nonpermanent members should be elected on the basis of their ability to contribute to "the maintenance of international peace and security." And this will be especially important if the UN is to develop the capacity to handle not just the modest peacekeeping operations of the Cold War years, but the vastly more complex, ambitious, and militarily risky undertakings it has been called on to perform since 1989.

For major conflicts, the only form of collective security that seems likely to work in practice is the delegated version adopted in the Gulf. It may or may not be under the UN umbrella: the Gulf case suggests how rarely such a mobilization would receive the support of the Security Council. The "Kuwait precedent," under which the Security Council tacitly subcontracted responsibility for enforcement to a U.S.-led coalition, provided for the clearly defined command structures, and indispensable protection of military intelligence, essential to modern warfare. But collective security should be defined more widely than resort to war on the scale of the 1991 counteroffensive. Collective deterrence, policing actions or even—as in Cambodia—administrative bridging operations while the structures of civil order are restored are promising ground for the UN in a "new order." But even for much smaller operations, the line between peacekeeping with the consent of all parties, and peace building or enforcement in conditions where at least some of the parties are hostile, is likely to be much more blurred than in the past. And this means that for the security of their own nationals, the publics of the countries called on to provide the bulk of the fighting troops will demand more professionalism than the UN secretariat can muster. Governments will continue to dump problems they do not wish to deal with in the UN's lap. But in the absence of better UN procedures for dealing rapidly and effectively with threats to security, the trend toward resorting to the UN when they actually want something done is likely to be of brief duration.

It would have been astonishing if, by 1994, the UN's peacekeeping capacity had not been creaking. The problem was not just the increase in the number of demands, from thirteen between 1946 and 1988 to twenty-one since then. Many of the new operations (Cambodia alone involved more than twenty-five thousand civilian and military personnel and cost some $2 billion) were on an entirely new scale of magnitude, and eleven of them were highly complex, with political and economic dimensions that were miles removed from the traditional "cook and look" patrols along established ceasefire lines. But UN peacekeeping had long been a seat-of-the-pants affair—politically, financially, and organizationally. The unfortunate UN contingent in Lebanon had to make sense of three mutually incompatible Security Council mandates; the peacekeeping budget had been permanently in arrears, and the UN could not even find the money to stockpile such basics as blue helmets in advance. As for the UN's tiny peacekeeping department, suffice it to say that the Cambodia operation was sketched out by a Nigerian desk officer in an afternoon (as a NATO officer, who arrived in New York in 1993 armed with eleven fat briefing books on procedures for launching limited airstrikes in Bosnia, was electrified to discover).[25] The standard lag between a request for a peacekeeping force and its deployment was sixty to ninety days in the early 1990s, and delays were getting longer, not shorter.

At the end of 1993 this Rube Goldberg setup was formally responsible for operations involving some seventy-five thousand troops and a $3.6 billion budget. Following Boutros Boutros-Ghali's publication in 1992 of his ambitious *An Agenda for Peace*, minor improvements had been effected at UN headquarters, including an embryonic military planning cell and—for the first time—a continuously manned "situation room" staffed mainly by military officers seconded to the UN by governments. But this was clearly only a start.

In November 1993, a brainstorming session in the peacekeeping department, attended by some of the West's most senior military planners, had no difficulty in compiling an agreed wish-list—beginning with the need for clearly set political and military objectives. Field commanders needed to be appointed early, given a say in the planning of the operation, and there must be unity and integrity of command (a point brought home in Somalia, when the commander of the Italian contingent refused to rescue Pakistani UN troops under fire until he had obtained clearance from Rome). They must not be reduced to begging for reinforcements—which meant that since troops had to be rotated, every operation required earmarked reserves. There must be close cooperation between the military and civilian arms of a mission (including UN agencies). The UN needed to be able to call on adequately trained and equipped troops—as one of the generals present put it: "The First Combined Harvesters won't do." There was a need for training in UN operations, including disaster relief, and for a common forces' manual to increase the operational compatibility of forces drawn from anything up to thirty countries. While giving field commanders full operational control, steady strategic direction was required from New York.

And in the absence of any of these factors, they concluded that the UN's best bet was to rely on what already worked, at least for Chapter VII missions, subcontracting operations either to a national command or to a military organization such as NATO, with other countries' contingents taking their drills from that core force. But as the Bosnian operation demonstrated, this was no guarantee of a smooth military operation unless the subcontracting was total. In 1994, NATO finally agreed with the UN that it would carry out air-strikes if so requested by the UN Protection Force (UNPROFOR). Tactical airstrikes were militarily useless, as UNPROFOR's military commanders on the ground made clear, unless they could be summoned instantly—within thirty minutes. But the UNPROFOR commander in Bosnia was required to contact the UNPROFOR commander for the whole of former Yugoslavia, who was based in Croatia; and he in turn had to get the approval of Yasushi Akashi, the secretary-general's civilian representative in former Yugoslavia, before word could be passed down the line to the NATO command. Time and again, because the relevant authority was physically uncontactable, strikes were authorized only after an interval of three hours or more and then had to be aborted because the Serbs had by then moved their guns. On other occasions, notably when Bosnian Serb forces were closing on the UN "safe area" of Gorazde, Akashi turned down UNPROFOR requests because he was in the middle of negotiating yet another "cease-fire," which was not in the event honored. The result was humiliation for the UN, embarrassment for NATO—and death for civilians who could have been protected.

Collective action coordinated by a "revitalized" Military Staff Committee might find favor with Moscow, but finds no takers in Western military establishments. The official reason is that all five permanent members may not be involved in a peacekeeping operation, but the real reason is almost certainly that no Western government wants to be obliged to bring Russia, let alone China, into all future strategic direction of UN operations. There could be a role for the MSC in the five-power consultation, which is needed, at a senior level and on a regular basis, to control sales not only of arms but of missile technology and precursors for chemical weapons: one of the more embarrassing lessons of the Gulf crisis was the ease with which Iraq had obtained all these, even from states like Great Britain which had placed a formal embargo on exports liable to add to Iraq's military capacity. Without much more professional military input, the new UN arms register set up on Great Britain's suggestion in 1991 was contributing nothing to human knowledge that was not available from the Stockholm International Peace Research Institute (SIPRI) in Stockholm or from Jane's defense statistics and military directions. Such a role for the MSC is foreseen in the Charter, and would be the more appropriate given the serious anxieties about arms sales from the former Soviet Union, and the already-dominant position of the five permanent members in the arms trade. But it is hard to see the MSC providing any other service, except possibly that of an informal "risk assessment agency" for the secretary-general, pooling unclassified or only moderately sensitive information. That might have uses, but mainly as a "confidence-building" measure between the permanent five.

It is probably correct, as a study by Cambridge University's Global Security Program[26] concludes, that for some time to come and for all large-scale operations, "the military aspects of UN peace support operations will continue to be implemented only through the agency of militarily competent states . . . or regional organizations." But that would imply, as the authors say, reducing the Security Council to "a licensing authority—a relationship also characterized as 'the UN issues the warrants and the U.S. makes the arrests'." What then, if the United States decides not to play sheriff?

Under the Clinton administration, this was anything but an academic question. During the 1992 presidential election campaign, Clinton had been an enthusiast for collective security, even advocating the creation of a UN Rapid Deployment Force to act as a trip-wire on threatened borders, to combat terrorism, and to protect the civilian victims of civil wars. He promised that the UN would be central to a new U.S. security policy "that builds on freedom's victories in the Cold War." A new U.S. strategy for peacekeeping was in fact prepared for publication in October 1993—only to be sent back at the last minute to the drawing board after the disastrous military operation in Mogadishu in which eighteen U.S. soldiers were killed. Although the troops in this particular operation had been under U.S., not UN, command, the Clinton administration had been quick to blame the UN. The predictable consequence was that Clinton was abruptly faced with a fierce domestic backlash against U.S. involvement in UN military operations.

Partly in consequence, when Clinton finally signed the long-awaited strategy paper the following May, it was cautious in the extreme. Presented as the administration's "policy on reforming multilateral peace operations,"[27] it imparted a flavor not of reforming zeal, but of retreat in the face of unwelcome expansion in the task of sustaining "world order." Negatives littered the pages: "The U.S. does not support a standing UN army, nor will we earmark specific U.S. military units for . . . UN operations. . . . It is not U.S. policy to seek to expand either the number of UN peace operations or U.S. involvement in such operations." Unless such operations were "linked to concrete political solutions . . . they normally should not be undertaken." It presented checklists of questions that would need to be answered before U.S. troops were committed that, while sensible enough in themselves, were so exhaustive as to reinforce the impression that they would only rarely be made available. It contained constructive proposals for strengthening the UN peacekeeping department's planning, logistics, and command-and-control capabilities, including the concept of a civilian reserve corps that could serve as a pool of "external talent" for the management and execution of UN peace operations. And it offered (on a reimbursable basis) to provide U.S. facilities for training. But it finessed the question of the degree to which U.S. forces that participated in UN operations would remain under U.S. control. In theory, the Clinton paper accepted that while U.S. troops would always be under the command of the president—a concept "covering *every aspect* of military operations and administration," U.S. forces could for specified purposes, including "unity of command," be placed under foreign officers in UN operations. Yet even then, U.S. commanders of such units wold "maintain the capability to report separately to higher U.S. military authorities." There was, the administration claimed, no intention of using these conditions "to subvert the operational chain of command. Unity of command remains a vital concern." It was hard to see how it could do otherwise, in practice. Only in its clear recognition that the growth in demand for UN peace operations called for a more distinctively military perspective on their planning and organization did the Clinton policy mark a clear step forward.

Chester Crocker, the U.S. secretary for African affairs in the Bush administration who had negotiated the Namibia settlement, complained that

> Up to now, U.S. policy toward UN peace operations has been a haphazard patchwork of funding shortfalls and financial threats, basic ignorance of the relationship between peacekeeping mandates and the resources required to carry them out, periodic bouts of UN bashing and a pervasive reluctance to recognize the political effects of U.S. conduct on those who

> may be engaged in (or targets of) UN peace operations. These unhappy facts lead even America's friends to question U.S. competence in shaping security mechanisms.[28]

To this charge, the new strategy provided only the most tentative of answers.

In the event of a semidetached stance by the leading military powers, it was hard to see ways in which UN peace operations could be significantly strengthened. One possibility, the Cambridge study cited above suggests, would be for the Security Council to use its blanket powers to set up subsidiary organs under Article 29 of the Charter, to create three new committees. The aim would be to enable the council to exercise political control of peacekeeping, but without impinging on the operation autonomy of UN field commanders.

A military committee, representing the chiefs of staff of all Security Council members, would advise the Security Council on the military implications of a decision to commit forces, and on the appropriate rules of engagement. Governments that contributed forces to each operation would form a force contributors' panel, the aim of which would be to protect the interests of their military contingents. The task of the third committee, a "strategic core group" half of whose members would be drawn from each of the first two, would be to reconcile the Security Council's political objectives with the military requirements of the governments contributing forces. All three would be able to draw on a professional UN military staff, drawing heavily on seconded personnel from capitals to ensure that it was sufficiently expert.

The goal of reinforcing the visible international legitimacy of UN security operations—and of countering the impression in small countries that they are being subjected to a great power condominium—is hard to fault. Some such structuring may be needed in the longer term, above all if countries are to accept humanitarian intervention as part of the UN's remit. The UN's function of collective legitimization was important in the Gulf, and will continue in many circumstances to be so. But combining military effectiveness with collective political control will be inordinately difficult. The risk that a military committee of all Security Council members would soon start to insist first on laying down military strategy, then on imposing tactical decisions by remote control, would be enough to give any national military authority second thoughts about committing troops. It lingers in the collective memory that in the Congo in the 1960s, the UN force was able to launch its military operation to "reintegrate" Katanga only by engineering a breakdown in communications with UN headquarters—and with the Security Council, where the Soviet Union would have vetoed the offensive. But these objections would have to be overcome if the UN were, as Brian Urquhart suggested in 1993,[29] to form its own rapid-deployment force of UN volunteers.

There are strong arguments for such a force. Even where the political backing can be summoned, the UN has little ability to deter aggressors or to intervene at a very early stage in conflicts because it cannot move troops at a moment's notice. Urquhart calls, rather as did candidate but not President Clinton, for a force of international volunteers, able "to fight hard to break the cycle of violence at an early stage in low-level intensity but dangerous conflicts, especially ones involving irregular missions and groups." It is highly possible that, had the UN deployed just such a force in Bosnia when the Serbs refused to accept that country's independence referendum, the war in former Yugoslavia might have been contained to Croatia. The first attacks were launched in eastern Bosnia by tiny undisciplined squads of "weekend warriors" and adventurers from Serbia under the command of the notorious Serb troublemaker, Arkan, and these would have been no match for "a relatively small but highly trained force, willing and authorized to take combat risks." Such troops could in theory be deployed on one side of a border at the request of a government fearing attack, without the consent of the other party to a worsening dispute. Governments would still worry about command and control, but at least they would not be putting "our boys" in harm's way. These would be troops who had volunteered for service under the UN, and not therefore men for whom they had national responsibility.

Such a force, even a small one, would not come cheap. Governments cutting back their national defense budgets would need much persuading that they would get value for money from a UN "army of mercenaries" that would have to be trained, billeted, and armed with the expensive panoply of a rapid-reaction force. Not to mention the possibility put forward by General Olosegun Obasanjo, the former Nigerian president, that the UN might be embarrassingly swamped by the mass of would-be UN legionaries and by their lop-sided national mix: "In some countries of the south, the entire national defense force would volunteer in order to get out of the morass of their national situation, while volunteers may be entirely unavailable from a country in the north whose participation is of utmost importance."[30] But recruitment is not the real problem: with military forces being cut back in both East and West, and superbly trained non-Western forces such as the Gurkhas who served in the British army being disbanded, highly trained manpower was never more readily available for international service than in the 1990s.

Until the UN's peacekeeping budget was put on a more rational footing, however, the Urquhart proposals seemed destined to remain a visionary gleam. Negotiations finally opened in 1993 to distribute the costs of peacekeeping more rationally. The existing system of expecting the five permanent members to pay a premium on their normal rates of assessment seemed fair enough—although the Clinton administration was out to reduce the U.S. assessment from 31.7 percent to 25 percent by 1996, and Congress had signaled its reluctance to pay more than that after fiscal 1995—but the rest of the peacekeeping rating scale had become an absurdity. Group C (less developed countries) paid only 20 percent of the rate at which their hardly excessive contributions to regular UN budgets were assessed, and the least developed 10 per cent of their minuscule UN assessment ratings. Peacekeeping is one area where the UN indubitably requires more money as well as more efficiency, and since Group C included by 1994 at least fifteen states with *per capita* incomes well above the average, fairer burden sharing was evidently overdue.

The Clinton administration proposed that with more equitable burden-sharing, it would support the (eminently sensible) concept of a unified budget for all UN peace operations, and an increased revolving fund of $500 million (although Washington was careful to stress that this must be financed by voluntary contributions). Potentially far more significant was the announcement that henceforth, the United States would divide responsibility for UN peace operations between the Department of State and the Department of Defense. State would continue to instruct the U.S. mission in New York, and would be the "lead agency" and source of funding for conventional peacekeeping operations. But for all those that were likely to involve combat, whether or not U.S. combat units were involved, Defense would assume control, and take over responsibility for funding.

This was the first explicit acknowledgment by any leading power that it was only logical to treat UN peace operations, at least where there was an element of enforcement, as an integral part of the burden of national defense. Its novelty was only slightly dulled by the U.S. insistence that these costs would, of course, be reimbursable by the UN—as in theory had always been the case—unless the president personally issued a waiver. In the case of the United States, at least in the atmosphere of hyper-caution prevailing in the Pentagon in the mid-1990s, there was a risk that this would diminish rather than strengthen American readiness to commit troops to multilateral operations. But in the longer run, it opened up the prospect of a more professional approach to multilateral military operations. Other countries could be expected to follow suit, and outlays that were large in relation to diplomatic budgets would bulk less heavily as a proportion of national military spending.

That could, in time, lead to a more serious assessment of Urquhart's plan. It had the great merit of highlighting the obvious truths: that UN forces are almost always needed long before they can be deployed, are often undermanned and underequipped when they do arrive; that civilians often pay the costs of these delays in blood; and that once the situation on the ground has deteriorated, much larger forces are required than would otherwise have been needed. But governments would back such a scheme only if they were confident that politically and militarily feasible systems of command and control could be put in place. If there was more than a touch of circularity about the burgeoning debate on UN peace operations in the 1990s, it was not only because the territory was relatively unfamiliar, but because some fairly basic questions about the willingness of the West to place its security eggs in the UN basket were far from being resolved.

The rebirth of the "political" UN will start from the head: as a vehicle for a "new world order" that strengthens the rule of law, the hard political truth is that it will be effective only insofar as it attracts the commitment of the major powers. The General Assembly is likely to be marginal in this process. In the first place, it shows no signs of being capable of streamlining an agenda stuffed with trivia, overlap, and pointlessly contentious or thoroughly obsolete items. And that will remain so as long as "the right of every member state to place any item on the agenda, no matter how parochial or trivial, continues to be sacrosanct,"[31] and the president annually elected on the Buggins' turn rota acts not as a speaker of the house, but as a pampered king-for-a-day. If strategic direction is provided by the industrialized powers in a modern version of the Concert of Europe, Third World objections will be raised. But these may be muted by the ambitions of many industrializing countries to join the northern "club"; and when more than forty UN member states have smaller populations than Kuwait, they have a vested interest in a more effective system of cooperative, if not exactly collective, security. As for sub-Saharan Africa, that great bloc of militantly one-nation/one-vote states, it would have most to lose if the UN slipped quietly back into impotence and alternative circuits for managing instability had to be devised. The UN has been marginalized in most of the world's killing fields since 1945. It will continue to be so, unless its members can agree on some basis for effective international control of the wars that most typically ravage the poorest countries.

It will, obviously, take more than Olympian collaboration between the major powers to drag the UN into the twenty-first century. The UN, as this book has emphasized, has purposes far broader than the prevention of conflict, and most of the rigidities, inefficiencies, and bureaucratic malformations that plague it are not merely the product of political malevolence and will not be solved by political will. In the words of a senior international civil servant,

> Within the UN, we continue to talk about throwing responsibilities at governments who cannot act any more because they are not sure quite how, and at institutions which cannot assume their responsibilities because they are acting in isolation. States are losing sovereignty, but they are reluctant to yield it. The UN, instead of guiding the transition, is the last refuge of their illusions.[32]

Events may be conspiring to increase our reliance on international organizations, and the constitutional purposes of the UN remain examples of supreme enlightenment. But with the UN's new prominence in a post-Cold War world has come more active scrutiny of its performance and actual potential. The scene is set against the traditional comedies of the General Assembly, the unrealism and time wasting of UNESCO, and the diplomatic universe of resolutions that have little bearing on reality. For all the increased prestige with which the UN emerged from the Gulf crisis, it emerged unprepared both politically and institutionally for the more complex demands of crisis management to which the emerging concept of humanitarian intervention was to give rise. It emerged, too, into a competitive world. The UN will only be one component of a "new world order."

12. An Improbable Phoenix

Security's Novel Dimensions

"Rarely can an empire have risen or declined so rapidly." The bleak verdict in the *Financial Times*[1] reflected profound public disillusion, and disquiet. In April 1994, the UN "safe area" of Gorazde was in flames, as Bosnian Serbs continued to pound the town in defiance of both the UN and NATO. In New York, the Security Council had just interrupted its emergency debate on Bosnia in order to pass a hurried vote on Rwanda. Faced with the collapse amid wholesale slaughter of the peace agreement between the Rwandan government and the rebel Rwandan Patriotic Front that the UN was there to monitor, the council ignored the pleas of the International Red Cross and opted to pull almost all UN troops out of the country. The international experiment in humanitarian intervention, which appeared to promise so well in 1991 when Western armies moved to protect the Kurds in Iraq and when twelve thousand U.S. troops provided swift and efficient help to Bangladesh in the wake of a killer typhoon, appeared to be collapsing in ignominy and embarrassment for NATO, the West, and the United Nations itself. The symptoms of wavering resolve had been evident since at least October 1993, when less than a hundred armed thugs on a quayside in Haiti had brought about the humiliating retreat of the *USS Harlan County* and the suspension of the UN's plans for the restoration of democracy there.

These were untested approaches to international order, in which single instances of success or failure could do no more than fit small pieces into the jigsaw of a *terra incognita*. But the temptation was to conclude that the West had been foolish even to think of circumventing the twin taboos against intervention that had operated for most of the UN's history. The first taboo, against the alteration of international boundaries, had been paralleled by another, almost equally strong, against challenging too insistently what went on within a state's borders. For half a century, it had seemed obvious that these taboos were less a function of peaceful assent to common rules and institutions than a survival pact made necessary by the upheavals of decolonization and, above all, by the Cold War.

This had seemed to necessitate a tacit agreement that the UN Charter could not be taken too literally. Governments endorsed conventions outlawing genocide and torture: but more in the hope that they would deter internal repression and contempt for law than with the intention of intervening even where, as in Idi Amin's Uganda or Cambodia's Year Zero, persecution was on a nationwide scale. During the Cold War, the doctrine of nonintervention served as a cover for containing ideological rivalries, in the Third World as in Europe. But it was also an alibi for neglecting internal brutalities ranging from the Syrian massacre at Hama to a long list of civil wars. Even when millions of refugees poured across international borders in consequence, no thought was given to activating the Charter provisions governing threats to international peace and security. Only in the case of South Africa was the suppression of the great majority of the population by a government committed to *apartheid* deemed to constitute such a threat: and even then, the response was confined to the imposition of economic sanctions.

It was always open to the UN to intervene in gross and destabilizing instances of persecution; the prohibition against intervention in a state's internal affairs contained in Article 2.7 is partly overridden by Article 34, which provides that "the Security Council may investigate any dispute, or any situation which might lead to international friction or give rise to a dispute." It can recommend settlements; and it can, in extremis, turn to Chapter VII. It was not the law, but the desire of all governments to preserve their internal freedom of action, which conspired in favor of silence over even the grossest and most systematic abuses of human rights. That, and the fear of superpower confrontation.

The geopolitical constraints had weakened after 1989. The Security Council was able to muster an unprecedented degree of agreement on the importance of containing instability and limiting civilian suffering. But the UN seemed little more capable than before of consistent decisionmaking, let alone of enforcing its decisions. Governments almost seemed to be regretting the disappearance of the Cold War alibi. As the demands for intervention in low-intensity conflicts and humanitarian disasters multiplied, Western politicians were increasingly appalled by the implications, for their armed forces and their national treasuries, of accepting the admittedly reduced military and political risks involved in converting a *droit d'ingérence* from an attractive theoretical legal hypothesis into a working defense of the rule of law.

But however great their misgivings, the political and economic mutations that the concept of sovereignty is undergoing in the 1990s cut off the lines of retreat. To abandon the doctrine of territorial integrity would be to open the floodgates to chaos: one has only to think of the hundreds of African "states" that could result from a purist interpretation of the doctrine of self-determination. Given the delicacy of external interventions to promote peaceful settlements, nonintervention is likely for solid practical reasons to remain the norm. Yet in the new international climate, nonintervention will be increasingly harder to defend to the public. It will take more than the end of the Cold War to eliminate double standards in human rights. But it has greatly enlarged the arena of the possible, publics know it, and governments will be forced to respond. There is a further consideration, which is that non-intervention may also be increasingly incompatible with political stability.

Most of the "nation-states" created in the twentieth century contain groups, sometimes dozens of them, with different ethnic, cultural, linguistic, or religious affinities. And where "national" identities do not coincide with established political maps, dissatisfied or repressed minorities have responded to the liberalization of the political climate by appealing for international assistance to defend their cultural and political rights. Questions familiar to the League of Nations, whose covenant sought to promote tolerance within multiethnic states by endorsing the concept of minority rights, became anything but academic as the new Europe of the 1990s struggled with resurgent nationalism and simultaneous political, social, and economic revolutions. Everywhere, the Westphalian traditions of tolerance, which since the end of the Thirty Years War until the age of totalitarianism had mitigated the consequences of diversity within the European "nation state," came under tremendous strain. Worldwide, there had never been such a high degree of consensus on the importance of human rights as there was in the 1990s; yet in Europe, where the concept was born, there was mounting confusion. Western governments might entertain some private nostalgia for the crude and cruel certainties of the Cold War, but to meet the expectations placed in them as "victors," and to contain the turbulence that followed, they were condemned to experiment.

The collapse of communism in Europe as an organizing principle for industrialized society was an affirmation of the superiority of democratic pluralism and open markets that found a receptive global audience. In particular, it undermined the claims to legitimacy of one-party (or, which is in many cases more accurate, one-man) regimes, as a succession of African dictators rapidly discovered. But what might be called the "post-Yalta instability" that accompanied the collapse of authoritarianism and the weakening of what had been known as the "balance of terror" also extended far beyond central and eastern Europe and the volatile successor states to the Soviet Union. Some of this loosening of taboos had wholly benign consequences. Outside Europe, the United States, with the tacit assent of the Soviet Union, blessed the first serious infraction of the rule that colonial boundaries could not be changed[2] when it supported Eritrea's right to secede from Ethiopia as part of the civil war settlement. But storm clouds lowered over Europe itself.

The United Nations had already begun to develop embryonic concepts for dealing with this new turbulence. In 1987, a group of French jurists and voluntary agencies had started to press for a *droit d'ingérence*—a right to intervene—in international law. They put the idea to a conference cosponsored by Médecins du Monde at the Université de Paris-Sud, with President François Mitterrand in the audience. After initial opposition from the Quai d'Orsay, France began to lobby for this right to intervene—albeit strictly on humanitarian grounds—at the UN. On December 8, 1988, the General Assembly adopted the first, vague resolution. All Resolution 43/131 did was recognize the role of nongovernmental organizations in "natural disasters and similar emergency situations" and acknowledge the need for them to have "access to victims." But two years later, this time with Moscow as cosponsor, a further resolution, 45/100, provided for access corridors through war zones for humanitarian aid workers and supplies.[3] These two innocuous resolutions (which already had the merit of giving voluntary aid organizations some official standing with "host" governments) had, of course, no legal force. But they paved the way for Security Council Resolution 688 of April 5, 1991, which did. Saddam Hussein's new attack on Kurds (and Shias) was declared a threat to international peace and security. And this, as noted in the previous chapter, made international legal history.

The subsequent dispatch of Western troops to provide "safe havens" in northern Iraq owed nothing to the support of the UN secretariat. As secretary-general, Javier Pérez de Cuéllar made no secret of his opposition on legal grounds, while conceding the "moral and humanitarian" case for action. The troops, he said, should be sent only with Baghdad's permission. And he set the same conditions, later in the year, for replacing the multinational contingent with a UN peacekeeping force or a UN civilian armed guard for the camps that had been established. Other UN officials, however, were already urging a more activist stance. James Jonah, then UN assistant secretary-general in charge of its Office for Research and Collection of Information—a unit created in the 1980s to serve as an early warning system for the secretary-general—had proposed in 1989 that the UN should develop a capacity to intervene in grave humanitarian emergencies even without the cooperation of the "host" government.

His idea was that governments should make available standing military units, specially trained and equipped for such emergencies. Where governments (or insurgents) refused to admit the need for help or to cooperate with relief agencies, he proposed that the Security Council should issue an order requiring them to let relief reach the victims. Supplies would then be guarded by these military contingents, which would also be able to assure the logistics. In practice it was expected that a Security Council order would generally be enough to secure a government's compliance, if the alternative was an infringement of its sovereignty. Jonah's proposal was borne of the frustrations experienced by aid agencies struggling to prevent another famine in Ethiopia in 1988–91. But Sudan's refusal in 1990 even to admit the existence of famine had, once again, delayed relief operations by more than six months and condemned thousands to starve. The modification of the international convention that help must wait on a formal request by the government concerned, and that the distribution of relief must be formally under its sovereign control, was clearly overdue.

But within the UN Secretariat, there was a marked reluctance to accept the idea that the scale of some natural disasters might call for a military response. Jonah's report was quietly shelved, and in 1991 it was Western governments, keen to build on Security Council Resolution 688 for future humanitarian emergencies, which made the running. The Western economic summit in London in July 1991 declared that where emergencies were attributable to "violent oppression" by a government, the UN and its agencies would "consider similar action" to that taken in northern Iraq. Stating that "the international community cannot stand idly by in cases where widespread human suffering from famine, war, oppression, refugee flows, disease or flood reach urgent and overwhelming proportions," the London communiqué placed the *droit d'ingérence* squarely on the international agenda.

What all this supposes, however, is an extension of the writ of international law to the righting of terrible wrongs inside countries rather than merely between them—not just the wrongs created by callous governmental neglect of the consequences of a natural or manmade catastrophe, but those deliberately inflicted by governments on particular communities or, as in the case of Pol Pot or of Rwanda's ruling clique in 1994, on an entire people. It implies the use of power, economic pressure but also military power where necessary, to influence and even to counter a country's internal policies. It implies that borders may, in certain extreme circumstances, be permeable and that sovereignty may be treated as conditional. But who is to decide when human suffering has, in the words of the London communiqué, "reached urgent and overwhelming proportions"? And what safeguards can prevent such interventions being a cover for less than disinterested ambitions?

Ideally, Western governments were agreed, the *droit d'ingérence* would be enforced under Security Council supervision—which could include the imposition of sanctions against recalcitrant governments and agreed terms of reference for the deployment of military contingents. But even in 1991, there was little reason to suppose that the Security Council's speed of action over Iraq would be repeated in such grey areas of diplomacy. International legitimation should always be sought where this is feasible, but not where the price of "due process" would be too high in human lives—as would have been the case in Northern Iraq had the Western allies waited for the secretary-general to unpurse his lips. The United Nations is a fabulously conservative organization, not least because so many of its members have so much to hide, but also because an activist interpretation of the Charter has been politically impossible for most of its history.

Just as Iraq's invasion of Kuwait was the first test of the changed balance of power in the wake of the Cold War, so Iraq postwar provided the laboratory in which just intervention in a country's internal affairs could be given its first trial since the victorious Allies had taken over postwar Germany and Japan. The international community's "war aims," as laid down in Resolutions 660 through 678, were strictly limited to reversing aggression. But, beginning with the cease-fire terms imposed by Resolution 687, postwar Iraq was treated almost as a ward of the United Nations. The UN was empowered to secure compensation for Iraqi war damages to Kuwait and other countries affected by its aggression, and to oversee the destruction of its nuclear, chemical, and biological weapons stocks and production facilities. The Iraqi government initially treated UN inspection teams with contempt and lied about its capacity. The consequence was a further unanimous Security Council resolution, in August 1991, which insisted on full disclosure and gave UN teams unimpeded access to any part of the country, including the right to use their own helicopters and aircraft and to use their own communications, even in code. Iraq was banned from producing vaccines and required to open all health facilities to inspection. And when Iraq demanded authorization to resume exports of oil to pay for food and medicines, Resolution 706 directed the UN secretariat to set up an escrow account into which all revenues would be paid, to organize purchases of essential supplies, and to monitor their distribution within Iraq. Part of this revenue was to finance the destruction of proscribed Iraqi weaponry, to meet claims under the Compensation Fund, and to cover the cost of returning looted property to Kuwait—all of which Iraq was obliged to pay for in full. To all these measures, Cuba was alone among the Security Council to dissent.

The actions of President Saddam Hussein's forces after the cease-fire did, however, contribute heavily to the formulation of this severely interventionist response. In the immediate aftermath of the war, the Security Council provisions on the destruction of Saddam's illegal arsenals and missiles and the Compensation Fund apart, the Western coalition was out to emphasize that there was no intention of intervening in Iraq's domestic affairs. Even in this extreme case, domestic butchery was treated with extreme circumspection. The tourniquet was tightened because Iraq's conduct made it clear that its compliance with the terms of the cease-fire would have to be enforced—and seen to be enforced, lest the coalition's decision to call a military halt be interpreted as weakness and the deterrent effect of the war to liberate Kuwait be lost.

Intensive, patient Western diplomacy went into rallying the support of the Security Council's Third World members for this succession of resolutions—diplomacy lasting nearly five months. With sanctions in place, time could be afforded. And Iraq's offenses against international law, both in invading Kuwait and in violating the conventions against chemical and biological weapons and its obligations under the Nuclear Non-Proliferation Treaty, were so serious that the most resolutely "noninterventionist" government could hardly make a case against exceptional measures. The other main interventionist experiments of the early 1990s—in Cambodia, Somalia, and former Yugoslavia—were harder tests both of doctrine, and of Western resolve.

Chance dictated that each of these operations differed so markedly that they presented, between them, something close to a topography of the accidented landscape the UN was exploring. Despite its huge scale and unprecedentedly ambitious remit, the United Nations Transitional Authority in Cambodia (UNTAC) was patterned most closely on traditional UN peacekeeping operations, and—perhaps more by luck than because of the relatively familiar nature of the operation—came closest to success. Somalia was an unambiguous case of a country without a government, in which armed anarchy had generated famine: it was, or seemed to be, a "pure" case for humanitarian intervention. Had it been launched much earlier—as it could have been for Bosnia-Herzegovina, if not for Croatia—the UN Protection Force (UNPROFOR) operation in former Yugoslavia might have turned into an encouraging experiment in the preventive use of force. Instead, it turned into an uneasy hybrid between humanitarian intervention to patch the wounds of a war in midcourse and an attempt to use a military presence to bolster the prospects of negotiated political settlements. What all three had in common was the large demands they placed on manpower, money, and—the commodity in shortest supply—the preparedness of the main contributing powers to stay the course when the going got rough.

When it was formally set in action with the signing of the Paris agreement in October 1991, the UN mission in Cambodia was perceived as the first serious test of President Bush's "new order." The road to a peace settlement had been long and tortuous. The original focus of diplomatic effort had been to persuade Cambodia's four warring factions—the Phnom Penh government installed by Vietnam, and the theoretically united opposition composed of forces loyal respectively to Prince Norodom Sihanouk, to the Khmer Rouge, and to the non-Communist Khmer People's National Liberation Front—to agree to share power, pending elections. When it became clear that this would not work, the Australians came up with a plan in 1989 for the UN to take over Cambodia pending elections—not merely by monitoring a cease-fire but by playing a role in governing the country. But this implied unanimity between the five permanent members of the Security Council; and China, which armed and bankrolled the Khmer Rouge, insisted that this must have the assent of their protégés.

The way out of this impasse was jointly charted, as so often during the Bush years, by the United States and the Soviet Union. In the summer of 1990, James Baker and Eduard Shevardnadze agreed to short-circuit diplomatic niceties: in a reversal of its policy since the Vietnam War, the United States agreed to talk directly to Hanoi about a Cambodian settlement; and both superpowers agreed that if China could not or would not bring the Khmer Rouge into line, they would if necessary jointly guarantee a deal between the other parties. Peking began to negotiate seriously, and the road opened to a settlement guaranteed by all five, under which a "supreme national council" of all factions was to "embody Cambodian sovereignty" while the UN took effective charge. It was to demobilize and disarm the combatants, provide an interim administration, repatriate 370,000 refugees, and create a "neutral political environment" for internationally supervised elections, provisionally set for March 1993.

This was as close as the UN had come to being handed an impossible mission. The UN was being asked to take full responsibility for the transition from war to democratic peace, in a country driven back to almost medieval conditions by two decades of war and the genocidal reign of terror of the Khmer Rouge between 1975 and 1978, a country that was one vast minefield and whose treacherous tropical terrain was riddled with bandits as well as guerrilla armies. It was assumed, correctly, that this would require more than ten thousand UN civilians and as many more military. Yet although there was nothing unexpected about the timing of the Paris agreement, almost nothing was ready. The Security Council had yet to authorize UNTAC's creation; it had agreed only to send a 268-strong reconnaissance team to Cambodia and wait for its reports. Almost no money had been pledged.

In such a heavily militarized country—there were believed to be 150,000 fighters in the field—it was little short of miraculous that the Khmer Rouge failed to sabotage the entire peace process in the dangerous vacuum before the UN finally arrived in sufficient force the following spring. It came close enough to doing so after UNTAC's deployment. The peace process gave the Khmer Rouge a foot in the door. By May 1992, its leadership had decided that they had everything to lose by demobilizing and contesting the elections. Complaining (with some evidence on its side) that the UN had failed to wrest control of the civil administration from the Phnom Penh authorities, the Khmer Rouge set about kicking down the house the UN was trying to construct. It refused to demobilize, and the UN had no mandate to compel it to comply. Khmer Rouge troops blocked UN access to areas they controlled, mounted a campaign of terror in the countryside, boycotted meetings, and attacked UN forces.

With twenty-two thousand troops, administrators, and police from forty-four countries in Cambodia, the UN's authority was on the line. Between then and May 1993, when elections were finally held, there were many points at which it seemed that the mission was turning into the UN's most expensive and politically consequential failure. What saved it was the decision, for which Chinese support was secured, to call the Khmer Rouge's bluff. The Security Council insisted on pressing ahead with elections on the appointed date, with or without Khmer Rouge participation. Assisted by hundreds of volunteers from dozens of countries, UNTAC was remarkably successful in registering voters, training fifty thousand Cambodian poll workers. As important, the UN kept the voters relatively well informed, directly through the vitally influential UN radio network and indirectly by protecting the freedom of the Cambodian press. It was still a gamble: Yasushi Akashi and General John Sanderson, the civilian and military heads of UNTAC, were under considerable pressure up to the last minute to postpone the polling, for fear that the elections would just be the prelude, as they had been in Angola, to the resumption of civil war.

They were vindicated by the determination of the Cambodians to defy both the military threats of the Khmer Rouge and the considerable intimidation of voters by the Phnom Penh government. Of those eligible, 95 percent registered, and people trudged miles to election rallies; voter turnout on the day was 90 percent, even though the Cambodians who turned up at polling stations fully expected them to be targeted by Khmer Rouge guerrillas. Resolve, in the event, paid off: the Khmer Rouge shelled some polling stations and attacked some voters walking to them, but decided against an all-out military attack. The success of the elections offset UNTAC's failure to disarm the combatants. Within a few months, Cambodia had a government, a new constitution that restored Sihanouk to his throne as the new king, and, although war with the Khmer Rouge continued in parts of the country, a chance to start healing itself. The UN operation in Cambodia was no copybook exercise; extravagance, fraud, undiscipline, and disorganization marked every stage, particularly of the civilian mission. Its failure to create a properly functioning civil administration left Cambodia deeply vulnerable to corruption and administrative chaos after the UN's departure—the factors most likely to reignite civil war.

But for all that, it went some way to redeeming the international silence during and after Year Zero; and it contained some lessons for the future. UNTAC had luck on its side. But it also had a detailed treaty framework to refer to, actively supported by all five members of the Security Council; its military and civilian commands had clear authority to get on with the job, and worked well together most of the time; and in Sihanouk it had, as William Shawcross has pointed out, "an overarching figure . . . a court of last resort to whom all the parties turned."[4]

All these elements were absent in Somalia. For Brian Urquhart, the international operation that got off to a delayed and faltering start early in 1992 was "an object lesson in what to avoid in future."[5] But insofar as this was true, it was not because the tragedy in Somalia presented a more intractable problem for outside intervention; in many ways, when the U.S. military first became involved in December 1992, it stood a better chance of succeeding than the rescue mission for Cambodia. Up to that point, the record of the UN had been a miserable chapter of neglect compounded by error. When Siad Barre, the Somali President whose twenty-one-year dictatorship succeeded in turning practically the entire country against his rule, fled Mogadishu in January 1991, the UN relief agencies fled too. For more than a year, voluntary agencies such as the International Committee of the Red Cross (ICRC) and Save the Children, which did not, were left to tend the wounded and stave off famine as best they could. Their repeated requests for decisive international action to save the country from the total collapse of civil society were ignored. The UN stuck to its rule of providing emergency relief only at the request of a country's government; and Somalia had no government. In July 1992, the UN finally dispatched fifty unarmed observers to Mogadishu, followed by the United Nation's Operation in Somalia (UNOSOM), a five-hundred-strong UN military contingent which was first denied entry to the country by Somali warlords and then humiliatingly confined to barracks: the grim joke was that it needed to pay Somali gunmen to protect it. Boutros Boutros-Ghali blamed the Security Council for the slowness of its response, but his office had taken weeks to respond to the council's request for a plan of action and when it came, it was inadequate.

In April 1992, shortly after becoming UN secretary-general, Boutros-Ghali had indeed sent an outstanding envoy to Somalia. Muhammad Sahnoun, an Algerian of exceptional courage, possessed the diplomatic finesse and deep understanding of Somalia's complex tribal allegiances that could have brought about a political settlement. Diplomats and aid workers in Somalia considered him their greatest asset. But in October, Boutros-Ghali sacked him: with the death toll from starvation reaching three-hundred thousand, Sahnoun had openly criticized the "lousy" performance of the UN's specialized agencies.

It was no moment for such pettiness. Both the UN and the voluntary agencies had been reduced to begging and bribing the rival warlords who had usurped the traditional clan authorities for permission to save their countrymen from starving. The warlords were making fortunes out of this protection racket, paid for mounting guard on convoys from which they continued to loot the goods anyway: four-fifths of the food and medicine reaching Somalia was being hijacked, as Boutros-Ghali himself admitted. At the end of 1992, when President Bush offered a U.S. force of up to twenty-eight thousand troops—provided the UN would give them a mandate to fight their way through any attempt to obstruct the flow of humanitarian aid—a million Somalis had fled the country, and a quarter-million more deaths were expected by the new year.

That December, when the advance party of the Unified Task Force (UNITAF) swarmed unopposed into Mogadishu under the arc-lights of television crews, the U.S. intervention seemed to mark another new departure for the UN. Far from being ill defined and ambiguous, the aims of Operation Restore Hope were extremely simple, and extremely clear. That was not what was wrong with it. Bush was anxious to ring-fence the U.S. commitment for domestic reasons, but there was nothing inherently mistaken about the limited scope of its mission. There was no harm either, provided the United States was in practice prepared to be flexible, about limiting the length of UNITAF's duration. But to make the anticipated time frame public made no sense other than in terms of U.S. public opinion: to announce your departure almost before you arrive is not a way to intimidate warlords. The stated U.S. purpose was not to bring about a negotiated settlement, but to create a "secure environment" for aid operations: in the undiplomatic parlance of one senior U.S. official, the troops' job was to "shoot to feed." Colin Powell, the then U.S. chairman of the Joint Chiefs of Staff, likened the operation to sending in the cavalry, which would hand over to the UN sheriffs once order was restored. But the essence of this analogy was that U.S. troops were capable, as the UN would not be, of disarming Somalia's clan armies and teenage gangs. Their job, without rounding up every Kalashnikov in the country, was to render Somalia "policeable" by disarming the rival factions and finding and destroying the heavy weaponry littering the country.

Operation Restore Hope saved hundreds of thousands of lives; but in this key task, it failed. The initial impact of the arrival of U.S. tanks was electric: the Somalis were clearly convinced that force would now be met with immensely superior force, and the armored trucks and guns disappeared almost overnight. But instead of pressing home their advantage, U.S. diplomats, anxious not to be too deeply drawn in, preferred to buy off Somalia's warlords, who had everything to lose by peace, when they should have arrested these men for the war crimes they had committed under the Geneva conventions. Not only that, but the United States allowed each of them to keep his armed entourage, preserving the warlord culture. This was seriously to damage the chances of bringing together Somalia's traditional clan elders, whose authority the warlords had usurped, in a government of national reconciliation. They failed to impound the arsenals and destroy the heavy weaponry. Somalis, most of whom had lost family members to gunmen or starvation, would have supported a short war for a long peace, but that would have entailed risks that the commanders of this uniquely formidable UN force proved not prepared to take.

When the United States handed over to the much less heavily armed second UN Operation in Somalia (UNOSOM II) in May 1993, it had imposed order in much of the country and aid was reaching those in need. But as Washington's decision to leave a rapid reaction force in place tacitly acknowledged, they had not created the conditions for Somalia to be policed by lightly armed units, mostly in unprotected vehicles. Conventional peacekeeping in the middle of a giant arms dump is impossible. UNOSOM II's tough mandate from the Security Council, for which it was undermanned and seriously underequipped, spelled out in plain language what still remained to be done: it was to be peace enforcer, disarmer, humanitarian logistics unit, and political conciliator in one. The Americans left a fuse trailing in the Somalian scrub, and it took only a month for General Farrah Aidid, the Somali warlord holed up in the southern part of the capital, Mogadishu, to set it alight with the deliberate ambush on June 5 of a Pakistani contingent of UN peacekeepers in which twenty-three were killed and more than fifty wounded.

This was a calculated provocation aimed at undermining the UN's authority. The Security Council responded, unanimously, by ordering UNOSOM to bring those responsible to justice. The decision is hard to fault: a weak reaction to this calculated, and unprecedented, attack on UN troops would have jeopardized not only UNOSOM II, but the authority of UN peacekeeping worldwide. Where the UN erred was in then allowing the pursuit of Aidid to obscure the *raison d'être* of the Somalia mission. To rely on U.S. airpower for this purpose was no substitute for equipping UN forces to regain full command of the capital's streets: it was used because UNOSOM troops lacked the military cohesiveness and strength to reimpose order in southern Mogadishu. The ensuing manhunts, which culminated in the disastrous operation of October 3—under direct U.S., not UN, command, and in which eighteen U.S. Rangers and many Somalis died—were not only militarily chaotic, with officers from different national units literally ringing home for instructions, but ultimately became a substitute for a strategy to prevent a return to armed anarchy.

The October fiasco was a watershed. President Clinton, after pledging that the United States would respond with "firmness and steadiness of purpose," more than doubled the U.S. presence in Somalia; but, in a pattern that was becoming all too familiar in the Clinton presidency, undermined the impact of this decision by simultaneously announcing that all U.S. troops would be withdrawn by April 1994. Robert Oakley, the U.S. diplomat whose earlier decision to let Aidid and his rivals keep their armed retainers had crippled the demobilization strategy, was sent back to Somalia in a fruitless attempt at a quick diplomatic fix. Within weeks, under U.S. pressure, the UN was to alter course, to pursue a policy of appeasing General Aidid: a strategy unlikely to assist the process of rebuilding either the traditional hierarchies of clan power or the modern machinery of government.

When the last U.S. soldier withdrew in March 1994, much of Somalia was still in the grip of armed bandits, and UNOSOM was conducting sorties from heavily fortified barracks. There was a severe cholera epidemic in Mogadishu—symptom of failures on the humanitarian front—and the UN was far from forging agreement on a new government. Two internationally sponsored conferences of the fifteen main Somali factions, in March 1993 and March 1994, had produced paper agreements but nothing more. A less publicized failure was that the UN, preoccupied by the extended military confrontation, had paid insufficient attention to the structural rehabilitation of the country. And, although it was by now evident that it would take considerable time before Somalia ceased, in the fullest sense of the term, to be a failed state, there was little enthusiasm for taking the country into UN trusteeship. Article 78 of the Charter, it was argued, precluded the institution of a UN trusteeship in a country that was already a UN member. But since it was three years since Somalia had possessed a government, there was scope here for a constructively flexible interpretation of the Charter. Military failures and political embarrassment had dampened the ardor to innovate, just when innovation was clearly called for.

Cynics suspected in 1992 that the Pentagon was happy to deploy troops in Somalia because it promised spectacular political results for minimal military risk—and because it would ease the pressure from Europe to deploy U.S. ground forces in the Balkans. From the outset of Operation Restore Hope, there had been anxiety that a lack of U.S. staying power in Somalia would lead to an ambiguous outcome, and that this would serve as a deterrent when it came to dousing the far fiercer fires in former Yugoslavia. By the end of 1992, the fighting that had flared briefly in Slovenia in the summer of 1991, then subjected a third of Croatia to the horrors of what came inaccurately to be called "ethnic cleansing" and the systematic bombardment of civilian populations, had engulfed Bosnia-Herzegovina. The humanitarian relief effort was faltering, millions were homeless, and the inadequacy of the piecemeal, incremental international response was at last beyond gainsaying. The need for a tougher approach to avert the dangers of a widening war in southern Europe was equaled only by the reluctance of the European Community and above all of the United States to become further embroiled.

If Somalia was an example of a strategy badly implemented, there was a strategic limbo where former Yugoslavia was concerned. This was a humanitarian intervention dictated by a massive failure of preventive diplomacy. Each step toward intervention in the Balkans was reactive; and because the outside world was following, rather than attempting to shape, events there, its reluctance to be drawn in had the paradoxical effect of imposing an escalating external involvement almost by default. Humanitarian intervention was coupled with shifting diplomatic expedients that bore almost no relation to what was happening on the ground, and eventually with hesitant gestures toward enforcing the peace. What was thought to be Western Europe's problem, a classic case for testing Chapter VIII of the Charter, became a threat to the credibility of the Security Council, a hazard to the future of NATO, and the fulcrum for a painful examination of the cohesion of "the West" itself.

There could, admittedly, hardly have been a worse moment than 1991 for Tito's federation to disintegrate, although the trend had been well in evidence since 1987, when the Serbian communist party chief, Slobodan Milosevic, launched his campaign for the "reunification of the Serbian state." European governments were thoroughly aware of the fragility of Tito's construction, a federation forged in the aftermath of savage internecine fighting between Serbs and Croats during World War II in which far more Yugoslavs had died at each other's hands than had been killed by German divisions. They understood the explosive potential of a resurgence of Serbian irredentism in a land with six official languages, twenty nationalities, and three main religions. But in the late 1980s, when the fears of other Yugoslav nationalities might have been eased by the negotiated construction of a loose confederation with externally monitored guarantees of minority rights, all eyes were turned to eastern, not southern, Europe.

Since the confrontation between Serbia and Croatia was political as well as nationalistic—Croatia, and Slovenia, abandoned communism in free elections while Milosevic grafted nationalism onto communism—there was a tendency to interpret events there in the light of the struggles between democrats and the Communist old guard elsewhere in Eastern Europe. Insofar as it had a policy, the European Community sought to underpin the federal government in Belgrade. The map of Yugoslavia provided some justification for this: in every republic, with the exception of Slovenia, populations were so intermingled that a "clean" division along the old republican borders was impossible. But the EC—and Washington—continued to do so long after it was clear that real power in Belgrade resided not with the federal authorities, but with Serbia. And the EC's counsels were divided. The two guiding principles of the 1975 Helsinki Final Act—respect for human rights on the one hand, territorial integrity and the inviolability of frontiers on the other—were brought into confrontation with each other in the Balkans. The Germans, conscious of their own recent unification, contended that it was hard in *principle* to argue that the sanctity of boundaries must always take precedence over "nationhood." Great Britain and France saw clearly that such arguments, in this supremely volatile area, spelled nothing but trouble, but put little diplomatic energy into reconciling the increasingly irreconcilable.

The feat might have been achieved as late as 1990; determined diplomatic mediation might still have secured a nonviolent divorce settlement. But attention was inevitably riveted on the Gulf. Pleas from the Conference for Security and Cooperation in Europe (CSCE) to all parties to resolve their differences were all that were forthcoming until June 1991, when—a week after James Baker and Jacques Delors had separately inveighed against secession—Slovenia and Croatia declared their independence and the federal army rolled onto the streets of Ljubljana.

From its Lisbon summit, the European Community abruptly dispatched the "troika"—Italy, Luxembourg, and the Netherlands, which were the past, present, and future holders of the EC's rotating presidency—to mediate, proclaiming that "the hour of Europe has struck." The phrase was all too revealing: to compensate for the EC's utter disarray in the Gulf War, disintegrating Yugoslavia was to be the testing bed for the EC's vaunted new common foreign policy. The envoys were to broker a ceasefire and a political settlement based on the delayed implementation of Slovenian and Croatian independence. Confidence in the moral authority of the EC was high. But the pressure was misdirected: the whole thrust of EC diplomacy should have been on Milosevic, who should have been told unequivocally at that stage that Serbia's choice was between accepting a new southern Slav community of sovereign republics, or unsplendid and impoverished isolation: and that sanctions would follow attempts to hold the federation together at gunpoint as surely as night followed day. Most seriously of all, the EC's eagerness to test its mettle caused it to ignore the obvious case for involving the Security Council early: with Serbia, Russian influence could have been decisive; and if Moscow had been drawn in, President Bush's thankful relinquishing of the burden to the EC would have been swiftly rethought.

From these early failures flowed others. EC mediation succeeded mainly in demonstrating that cease-fires were not worth the paper they were written on. Lord Carrington's admirably logical peace plan was the first of many to be doomed because there were no credible sanctions to back it up. EC monitors, an ill-thought-out compromise between mediation and peacekeeping—a Dutch proposal in September 1991 to send thirty-thousand peacekeepers was vitiated by the impracticality of its plan to put these under the umbrella of the totally unequipped Western European Union—succeeded merely, and then only partially, in chronicling the progress of the war in Croatia. In September, the UN imposed an arms embargo on Yugoslavia, the only real significance of which was that the Security Council formally declared the fighting there to be a threat to international peace. Boutros-Ghali, concerned to draw attention to Somalia, complained that the West was allowing itself to be obsessed by a "rich men's war," a foolish statement that was also a gross exaggeration. The truth was that Western governments, whose forces would be required to make the deployment of peacekeeping forces to a heavily armed war zone credible, had just ended Operation Desert Storm and were in no mood for fresh commitments.

By the time the first UN Protection Force (UNPROFOR) was deployed after months of delay, in Croatia in 1992, the "demilitarized zone" they were to protect was effectively under Serb control. The UN mission was in theory to impound the heavy weaponry, to provide the protective umbrella under which, reversing "ethnic cleansing," survivors could return to their burnt-out homes, and to create the conditions for a resumption of civil authority that reflected the pre-war population mix. In practice, the UN presence merely froze the battle lines, useful but marginal to the strategic priority of containing the war in order to create space for winding it down. Had the UN's political antennae been properly tuned to the Balkan crisis, it would have deployed the first peacekeepers not just to Croatia, but to Bosnia-Herzegovina as a preventive trip-wire.

Desperate to avoid being dragged into the war, the Bosnian president, Alia Izetbegovic, had formally appealed to the UN to make the republic a demilitarized zone. Cyrus Vance, the UN's envoy, supported his request, and with good reason: the demography of the republic was like a leopard skin, with Orthodox Serbs, Catholic Croats, and Muslims living cheek by jowl in every village and most urban apartment blocks, and intermarriage even more common than elsewhere in former Yugoslavia. Croatia's president Franjo Tudjman and Serbia's president Slobodan Milosevic had already discussed carving up the republic. Once fighting started there, it would be appallingly difficult to disentangle the combatants or to limit war's destruction. And so it was to prove, once Serb irregulars had crossed into eastern Bosnia that summer. By August 1992, when the UN Security Council, acting under Chapter VII of the Charter, unequivocally affirmed "the sovereignty, territorial integrity and political independence of Bosnia and Herzegovina," the belated reiteration of the principle that borders must not be altered by force had a singularly hollow ring. Bosnian Serbs controlled 70 percent of the republic, Bosnian Croats had seized a sizable slice of Herzegovina, Sarajevo was under siege, and Western publics were sickened by atrocities, including appalling detention camps, they had not thought to see again in Europe. Their governments responded by promising to use "all necessary measures" to secure the flow of humanitarian relief; but the mandate for the enlarged UN force dispatched to Bosnia that autumn was given narrowly defensive rules of engagement that were transparently minimalist.

No Western government was prepared for the heavy military commitment implied by a policy of forcing humanitarian aid through roadblocks, let alone one of actively protecting civilian populations under attack. Instead, sanctions were applied on Serbia, and military pressure was ratchetted up so slowly that it had barely any impact on the course of the fighting. The West talked about deploying a full-scale peacekeeping force—once a peace settlement had been reached and all sides were committed to military disengagement: but these very preconditions undermined the peace negotiations being conducted by Cyrus Vance and Lord Owen, the joint UN-EC team of negotiators. The Bosnian Serbs were given no incentive to surrender territory. On the contrary, a filibuster at the negotiating table enabled them to consolidate their conquests. By the summer of 1993, Western disarray was complete, with the EC publicly at loggerheads with the Clinton administration over Washington's fitful demands for an end to the arms embargo against the Bosnians and the use of airpower against the Serbs, coupled with a refusal to commit any ground troops until peace had been achieved. At the UN, they sought to paper over their disagreements by declaring six "safe areas" in Bosnia, but UN resolutions by this stage could not change the grim equations on the ground or camouflage irresolution: the Serbs had no reason to believe in Western determination to make these areas genuinely safe from attack—and indeed, the wording of the resolution carefully avoided the word *havens*, to distinguish it from the serious protection extended to the Kurds in Iraq.

Not until February 1994, by which time the Security Council had issued around fifty resolutions concerning former Yugoslavia, did UN forces under a new commander threaten—successfully—to force their way past a Serb roadblock. Almost simultaneously, a credible threat, and limited use, of NATO airpower was brought into play. Seriously challenged for the first time, the Bosnian Serbs stopped the shelling of Sarajevo and withdrew their heavy weaponry: a retreat that was made easier for them by some fancy Russian diplomatic footwork, but that suggested that similar action could have been effective at the very beginning. Within a month, American diplomacy had succeeded in brokering agreement between the Bosnian government and Bosnian Croats on a federation in the parts of Bosnia-Herzegovina they controlled. The momentum was promptly interrupted. Instead of capitalizing on this first real success, the Clinton administration performed another of its diplomatic somersaults. At the end of March, the United States refused at the last minute, on grounds of cost, to vote for a Security Council resolution authorizing the dispatch of a further eighty-five hundred UN troops to Bosnia—and simultaneously hinted that Sarajevo had been a special case and that attacks on other "safe areas" would not prompt a NATO response. Days later, William Perry, the U.S. defense secretary, flatly stated that the United States would not intervene to prevent one of them, Gorazde, being overrun. The indecisive reaction of Western governments, NATO, and the UN to the Bosnian Serb assault on Gorazde, which promptly followed, revealed how far policy still was from coherent direction. But the conjunction of force and diplomacy had at last briefly been tried, and shown to work. With the United States and Russia finally edging toward cooperation in the search for a diplomatic solution, the frictions between the major military powers that had bedeviled both the military and political responses to the Bosnian tragedy seemed in sight of resolution. But it was all tragically late.

The fears expressed by Boutros-Ghali that Bosnia would be "the UN's Vietnam" overrode the fear that should have preoccupied Western leaders fully as much: that Bosnia would prove to be the UN's Munich. The claims that this was purely a civil war were elaborate fictions. The Serbs, in Belgrade as well as Bosnia, were able with impunity to flout the elementary obligations enjoined on all member states under the Charter, and compounded that by repeatedly frustrating the efforts of the UN to relieve civilian suffering in the areas of hostilities. As George Kennan commented,[6] "There could have been no behavior more fundamentally contrary to the first principles of the UN Charter, not to mention the provisions of international law and the laws of war, than the persistent artillery bombardment over weeks and months on end of the helpless civilian populations of entire cities."

Yet this was still a relative, not an absolute, failure. As in Somalia, armed peacekeepers were absolutely crucial to the delivery of food and medicine, saving hundreds of thousands of lives. For a start, whatever the dedication of the ICRC, the UN High Commissioner for Refugees (UNHCR), and voluntary organizations, only sappers could have kept the tortuous tracks through the Bosnian mountains open. The concept of armed humanitarian intervention may not suffer terminal damage as a result of the all-too-conspicuous confusion that dogged this effort at a combined humanitarian and peacekeeping operation. But the damage done was certainly considerable. The UN resorted to bluff in Bosnia, sternly laying down the law and then failing to provide the means to make its authority felt, and its bluff was repeatedly called. Aggression was seen to pay and, although France, Great Britain, and Russia all committed ground troops to the "humanitarian" effort, governments that were capable of the firepower required to intimidate the aggressors were seen to lack both organization and resolve. Only in Macedonia, where a few hundred U.S. soldiers were quietly deployed, was preventive diplomacy given a military dimension. The first serious experiment in "contracting out" collective security to a regional organization—in this case NATO, the world's most powerful—demonstrated the imperative need to work out clear rules for this new game: and to accept that such interventions cannot be militarily cost-free.

When things go wrong, politicians are inevitably tempted to conclude that national interest in the maintenance of the rule of law is an unaffordable luxury. The power is mainly in Western hands, and the ending of the Cold War means that the West is free to an unprecedented degree to try to protect people from the excesses of their rulers. The "rules," in a sense, exist: in the Charter's preamble. But just as in wars between states, the need for an enforcer of last resort was given powerful reaffirmation in the second Gulf war, so jurisprudence will need to be developed for external mediation in internal conflicts and for human rights violations of less formal intensity but equally brutal consequence. If the UN proves too hidebound, coalitions for this purpose will develop outside it, even though external interventions will be a last resort, considered as proof of failure to take less drastic preventive action. Preventive diplomacy, accordingly, is likely to take more decisive forms. Similarly, political conditions for aid are likely to become generally accepted Western practice, and the international supervision of elections increasingly routine.

Meantime, management of what Douglas Hurd dubbed the "new disorder" will be an uncertain business. There were few more vivid instances of this than the case of Rwanda in 1994. The first reaction, as we have seen, was to pull out all but a token UN presence, leaving the ICRC almost alone to protect the few it could from a massacre that claimed at least half a million lives within a matter of weeks. Next, the Security Council agreed to bolster the UN presence—a resolution passed without any idea of where the more than 5,000 troops to be sent were to come from, or how they were to be equipped. Eyes turned to African governments, the least capable of any to mount a rapid deployment. Then President Mitterrand, declaring that every hour mattered, abruptly announced the dispatch of a French force—wholly separate from the UN military effort. For French politicians, this was a case of France—alone in the Western world—assuming its humanitarian responsibilities. The trouble was that France could hardly pretend to be neutral in Rwanda: on successive occasions, since 1990, it had supplied arms, advisers, and even troops to help the government of President Juvenal Habyarimana fend off advances by the Rwandan Patriotic Front. France's decision to intervene coincided with the RPF's imminent military victory, and appeared suspiciously like an attempt to shore up the self-proclaimed government that had taken power after Habyarimana's assassination in April. This mainly Hutu regime had instigated the massacres of the Tutsi minority, and France, particularly when its troops failed to arrest the ringleaders, appeared to have intervened on the side of the criminals for its own reasons of *Realpolitik*. Yet so appalling were conditions in Rwanda that the Security Council blessed the French operation—and when the French contingent withdrew that August, largely in response to international questioning of France's motives, it did so against a background of appeals from the UN to stay.

In many instances, the *droit d'ingérence* will be treated with suspicion, seen as an outwardly benign mask for a new form of neoimperialism. In the case of France in Rwanda, this was more than half-true. But that should not deter Western governments from developing the doctrine—or from modifying the rules, provided they do so in the spirit of the Charter. In practice, this may mean that these rules have more often than not to be tested outside the UN, in a pragmatic accumulation of case law to bring international diplomacy into line with decreasing public tolerance for "domestic" brutality. The sights of Western governments may have been lowered by the experiences of Somalia and former Yugoslavia, which will linger in the mind when the successes in Namibia and Cambodia fade. But in a world where domestic terror is almost instantly translated to the screen, governments will be unable to resist the domestic pressure to use what power they have to relieve suffering; peace is steadily more indivisible. If they want to minimize the use of military means, they will have to be steadily more imaginative about using the other stabilizers at their command: the collective development of preventive diplomacy and the stake in peace that derives from the integration of economic activity across national frontiers.

Global Stabilizers

For all the turbulence that accompanied the breakup of the Soviet empire, the abatement of the Cold War created fresh opportunities to develop more sophisticated "stabilizers" for a world in rapid and highly uneven evolution, where no problem, even tyranny, is purely domestic. But simultaneously, it inclined Western governments to relax their vigilance against growing threats to world peace from nations that they had for years been accustomed to consider of secondary importance. A symptom of this was the West's extraordinary decision, in March 1994, to dismantle the secretive seventeen-nation Coordinating Committee for Multilateral Export Controls (COCOM), which for four decades had operated a legally enforceable system of controls on exports of militarily sensitive technology, without putting in place any convincing alternative machinery. The argument for winding up COCOM was that it was an obsolete remnant of the Cold War. With each government now free to decide what technology it wished to control, instead of being legally obliged to submit decisions on export licenses to joint scrutiny in COCOM, the new emphasis was to be on information sharing, to detect suspicious patterns of technology purchases by suspect regimes.

Institutions are not in themselves stabilizers; but what this decision implied was a weakening, for reasons of commercial advantage, of Western determination to control nuclear proliferation at an early stage, by depriving hostile or dangerous regimes of the means to manufacture nuclear and other weapons of mass destruction. The timing was singularly unfortunate: that same week, the United Nations had suffered a disturbing reverse, when the threat of a Chinese veto had prevented the Security Council from issuing an ultimatum to North Korea to end its year-long refusal to submit its nuclear installations to inspection by the International Atomic Energy Agency (IAEA).

North Korea was the test case for the IAEA's tougher new inspection rules, activated after the UN's highly intrusive postwar inspections in Iraq revealed the extent to which that country had for years hoodwinked the outside world. Pyongyang's defiance of the IAEA was not only a stark illustration of the difficulty of getting a nearly or possibly nuclear power to give up a clandestine program; it was a reminder of the growing ease of access to the technology required for nuclear and other weapons of mass destruction. With the number of suspected nuclear weapons aspirants reaching into double digits, a period of relative certainty was ending. The spread of ballistic missiles—more than a thousand had been fired in the Iran-Iraq war—was more rapid still, and some of these missiles could be equipped to carry chemical or nuclear warheads. As for chemical weapons, the hopes reposed in the Chemical Weapons Convention, which was opened for signature in January 1993, were being tempered by testimony from Russian scientists that the Russian military was continuing to develop new chemical and biological weaponry.

The dismantling of COCOM would have mattered less had the international machinery for controlling proliferation inspired more confidence. But the Missile Technology Control Regime, an essentially Western affair, lacked enforcement powers; so did the Australia Group (for chemical weapons) and the Nuclear Suppliers' Group, and none of these dealt with the control of dual-use technology that could be used to develop highly sophisticated conventional weapons. The nuclear power industry was, in addition, notoriously as reluctant to give prominence to the dangers of proliferation as it was to acknowledge the scale of international assistance required to prevent potentially catastrophic accidents at the ill-designed and poorly maintained nuclear energy plants in Eastern Europe and the republics of the former Soviet Union. Until the mid-1980s, this attitude had infected the work of the IAEA itself. Established in 1957, the agency was given to emphasizing its mission to promote the diffusion of peaceful nuclear technology, putting too little emphasis on building up the efficiency of its inspection procedures under the safeguards regime that constituted the UN's early warning system under the 1968 Nuclear Non-Proliferation Treaty.

Some of the IAEA's shortcomings were attributable to the Cold War. Although the Soviet Union was formally a firm advocate of containing the spread of nuclear weapons, in practice it did much to hobble the IAEA's work. Moscow's insistence, for example, on imposing full IAEA safeguards on the large Japanese and German nuclear energy industries so distorted its activities that, as Thomas Graham has pointed out,[7] "70 per cent of the IAEA safeguards budget is expended on the monitoring of facilities in Western Europe, Canada, and Japan, all countries that present virtually no proliferation concern." The presence on the IAEA's governing board of states—such as Syria, Libya, or Pakistan—that were actively seeking to develop nuclear weapons hardly contributed to effective monitoring: their main aim was to use the IAEA as a channel for the acquisition of nuclear technology while minimizing the effectiveness of its inspection procedures.

This has begun to change. After the accident at Chernobyl in 1986, the IAEA became far more active in nuclear safety; and in the early 1990s, it began to confront the problem of proliferation much more forcefully. Before the Gulf War, the agency confined its inspections to facilities declared by governments; since then, it has activated its powers to conduct special inspections of undeclared material in any state that is a party to the NPT, and also to inspect facilities long before they become operational. Governments refusing to permit these intrusive inspections face an IAEA reference to the Security Council for noncompliance with the treaty. But these reforms, vitally necessary as they are, involve increased expenditure. And despite their obvious strategic interest in nonproliferation, Western governments subjected the IAEA to the same zero budgetary growth policy that they have applied to the UN since the early 1980s. By the early 1990s, the safeguards budget had remained static in real terms for a decade, although the number of nuclear facilities subject to inspection had more than doubled.

The IAEA is one of the global institutions that would have to be reinvented if it shut up shop. Only a global institution could hope to operate in countries such as Iran. But the IAEA cannot deal with all the problems of proliferation—and each instance of successful nuclear cheating places a further question mark over any regime that depends on the consent of a government within an international treaty framework. Governments *may* eventually come to perceive nuclear weaponry as a barren investment, even if rogue states cling to the clandestine production of chemical weaponry. But meantime, this is one of the areas in which cooperation outside the UN, both for preventive measures and for contingency planning, is both underdeveloped and urgently needed—and where subglobal networks of the key players are essential as an active complement to the services performed at global level. And conversely, in any selective strategy for using the UN to best advantage, the strengthening of the IAEA would figure prominently. Precisely because it is a multilateral vehicle, the IAEA cannot be part of initiatives where secrecy is imperative (after the Gulf War, a defecting Iraqi nuclear scientist reported that the experience he had acquired as an IAEA safeguards inspector in Japan was invaluable to the Iraqi military program). But a discriminating buyer would nonetheless put money on the IAEA's expertise, access, and powers of investigation.

The nuclear issue, both civilian and military, acquired fresh urgency in the 1990s not just from the spread of technology, but from the disorder affecting almost every aspect of political, military, and economic life in Russia and its neighboring republics. Russia's admission, in 1993, that it had thwarted the departure of a planeload of Russian nuclear scientists to North Korea was a chilling reminder of the risks of a brain drain to countries prepared to pay handsomely for conventional as well nuclear military technology. In 1994, a series of arrests in Germany pointed to a sharp increase in the smuggling of Russian plutonium and uranium. The difficulty of finding new careers in the civilian economy for the highly skilled manpower at the heart of the Soviet military-industrial complex highlighted the vital importance of arresting the dramatic collapse of these postcommunist economies.

In any assessment of the business of global diplomacy at the century's turn, the unprecedentedly complex task of economic and political stabilization in Russia and its neighbors in the Eurasian landmass would assume in most eyes an absolute priority. Yet to this process, the United Nations could be relevant only in narrowly defined senses. Politically, there is no doubt that Moscow, at least in the Gorbachev and early Yeltsin years, attached considerable value to permanent membership of the Security Council. It was both a channel for regular backstage communication and for the testing of "new thinking" about the uses of power; and an important vehicle for affirming that the dissolution of empire was not incompatible with claims to superpower status. The importance of the Security Council, as psychological reassurance and as a ready-made form of linkage in an extremely delicate phase of the Soviet and Russian revolutions, should not be underestimated. But *qua organization*, most of the UN machinery was irrelevant to the giant task of clearing up the industrial, social, and environmental wasteland left by communism. In theory, these political transformations should have rejuvenated the UN's Economic Commission for Europe (ECE). In practice no politician, from East or West, even thought of giving it an enhanced role. For Eastern Europeans and some of the republics of the embryonic Commonwealth of Independent States, the CSCE served as a transitional instrument for political cooperation; but for Eastern Europe at least, the magnets for the longer term were the European Union and NATO.

Of the global institutions, only the International Monetary Fund (IMF) and the World Bank were sought out by both East and West as indispensable mediators in the transition from centrally planned economies under state ownership to market economies based on private property rights. Admittedly, the readiness of Western governments to give the Bretton Woods duo a central role was not entirely based on admiration for their track record in structural adjustment. They marked the fiftieth anniversary of Bretton Woods in 1994 by demanding an in depth review of the functioning and remits of both institutions. But, above all in a period of Western recession, their ability to provide loans that did not impact directly on national treasuries or require congressional authorization was extraordinarily convenient. Governments had a strong political interest, too, in distancing themselves—particularly with respect to Russia—from the tough bargaining over the conditions for providing external financial assistance that lay ahead.

At the end of 1991, when the Soviet Union collapsed, Russian industrial output had fallen 19 percent within a year, its share of the Soviet budget deficit was 31 percent of Russian gross domestic product, and even though the dying Gorbachev government had raided $10 billion from deposits in the state bank owned by foreign and Russian companies, the new Russia had foreign reserves of just over $20 million. With the shops empty and city-dwellers facing serious food shortages, it was a case of total economic collapse. Beginning with the lifting of price controls in January 1992, Russia lurched over the following two years from a command-based to a money-based economy, succeeded in privatizing more than eighty thousand enterprises, and drew back, just, from the precipice of hyperinflation. At the end of 1993, Russia's reformers lost the Russian parliamentary elections. Western politicians, whose foreign policy establishments were accusing them of failing to give sufficient support to reforms, blamed the IMF and the Bank, and it was true that of the roughly $18 billion that the Group of 7 had agreed in 1993 that they could lend Russia, only some $2 billion had actually been disbursed that year. It was equally true that legislative chaos, coupled with the Russian central bank's resort to the printing presses, had so undermined the reformers' best efforts that the agreed conditions for disbursement had not been met. The criticism was that the conditions set by the IMF had been unrealistic: that it had put far too much emphasis on deep cuts in the budget deficit, for which the reformers had now paid the political price, instead of providing transitional loans and grants to help the government pay its bills.

The assumption was that Russia was too large, too important, and in too desperate an economic plight to be subjected to the normal disciplines of structural adjustment. Shock therapy had been talked about so much that publics, in Russia and the West, assumed that it had been administered too harshly. But Russia's leading economic reformers themselves argued that the therapy had barely begun: at the end of 1993, despite considerable progress in reducing the budget deficit and building up foreign exchange reserves, subsidies to loss-making state enterprises still cost the Russian government more than defense and education put together. Had the IMF been willing to relax its conditions for releasing funds, many Russian economists themselves argued, the money would in practice have financed the status quo, merely prolonging the agony of transition and spurring further capital flight.

What *had* been demonstrated was that in the absence of a domestic consensus on reform, the leverage of external agencies on a country as powerful and administratively chaotic as Russia was severely limited. There had, for example, been no real progress on developing a social safety net, which was critical to the next stage of reforms and for which the World Bank had offered $500 million. The problem was that the Russian finance ministry could not decide whether it wanted to borrow the money. An equal sum was available for agriculture, but there was deadlock within the government over whether or not to privatize collective farms. There were similar problems in the oil sector, and in housing. Yet for all the halting nature of the policy dialogue, the involvement of the

IMF and the Bank had offered the reformers, in Russia as in central and Eastern Europe, a degree of political cover for unpopular but essential policies. The Bretton Woods institutions had a degree of political visibility that the Western private sector could never have acquired, even where it was ready to lend or to invest without waiting on the IMF's imprimatur. Reforms in Russia were far from entrenched, but they were no longer, as they had been only two years earlier, as vulnerable as a spider's web in a cloudburst. Western governments could, had they put goodwill toward the West before value for money, have provided more in the way of direct grants and loans. They could, above all, have done more to open their markets to Russia and the countries of Eastern Europe: and by 1993, the clearest indication that these governments were irreversibly committed to the market economy was that the maintenance of protectionist barriers was the failure for which they chiefly reproached the West.

The conversion of governments the world over to free trade as a vital economic lubricant was one of the most encouraging international mutations of the 1980s. In a short list of "stabilizers" for tomorrow's world, few things are more important. Only in the context of a binding, nondiscriminatory global regime will regional trading blocs remain "open" and fulfill their potential as poles of growth. The GATT, one of the least visible of the international bodies created in the 1940s, was not even an institution: it was simply a center, and a provisional one that was always in theory intended to be superseded by a full-blown organization, for policing mutual trade agreements. Yet the record of this small secretariat in bringing real prosperity to millions far outshone that of most UN agencies; its championing and refereeing of an open trading system underpinned a long and mutually enriching postwar global boom. But at the beginning of the 1980s, these achievements were in danger of erosion. The majority of developing countries relied on high tariff barriers behind which to shield inefficient domestic industries; and in the industrialized world itself, there was an ominous weakening of the liberal postwar trading system in favor of "managed" trade. When the Uruguay Round of trade negotiations was launched in 1986 under the auspices of the GATT, the GATT system, which was intended to impose consistency, predictability, and liberalism on its members' trading policies, was in serious trouble.

The initial damage had been done in the 1960s, when the GATT strayed from the principle of nondiscrimination by bowing to developing countries' demands for "special and differential status." This permitted them to maintain their own trade barriers while benefiting from open markets in the industrialized world. The concession backfired on its intended beneficiaries in two ways. For protected developing country industries, it reduced the incentives to compete. And, beginning with the Multifiber Arrangement for textiles and clothes, it prompted a backlash in the industrialized world. By the mid-1980s, Western governments had imposed a barrage of nontariff barriers on most of the other sectors—such as steel, footwear, and, notably, processed food—where developing countries had a comparative advantage. Mercantilism had bred mercantilism, and the Western countries held the best bargaining chips. The reluctance of such leading developing countries as South Korea, India, and Brazil to lower their tariff barriers was used by Western governments, alarmed at the sharp rise in domestic unemployment, to justify a battery of "voluntary" export restraint agreements, "temporary safeguard" measures, and dubiously based antidumping actions. More than half of global trade was taking place outside the GATT regime. The West was veering toward the development of arrangements within the industrialized world, from which the countries already finding it hardest to compete would be excluded.

It seemed an unpropitious moment to launch the most ambitious attempt since the GATT's founding to modernize and rewrite the world's trading rules. The Uruguay Round was a conscious decision to halt a ruinous cycle of beggar-my-neighbor protectionism, but its ambitions went further. The aim was to modernize the GATT by bringing under its rules two sectors that had always been excluded: agriculture and services. The United States made clear from the beginning that it saw this as a test of the GATT's ability to remain relevant to the world trading system; failure, U.S. officials said, would force the United States to rely on unilateral pressure to prise open markets. The round involved fifteen separate negotiations, ranging from tropical products and textiles to institutional reform of the GATT, but services and agriculture offered the most dramatic gains — and were the most contentious.

The round, scheduled to end in 1990, dragged on interminably, with negotiations ending only in December 1993. In these seven years, one of the most dramatic evolutions in global negotiation to have taken place since 1945 occurred. Developing countries, most of which had entered the round as confirmed protectionists, became some of the most vocal advocates of liberalization. Mexico, which had not even been a member of the GATT, began to put itself forward as a country that had once been a focal point for world trade and now aimed to be a center in which East and West, North and South, would converge.[8] Before the Round ended, it had fulfilled part of that ambition, with the ratification of the treaty creating a North American Free Trade Area with Canada and the United States. Even India had by then ended its long love affair with autarky, and was fast dismantling trade barriers. Agreement on rules for trade in services, worth at least $600 million a year to the industrialized countries, had seemed impossible in 1986; by 1990, it was no longer the main obstacle to agreement. The principal difficulty lay with agriculture, and here the quarrel was not between North and South, but between the industrialized countries.

Every Western economic summit solemnly reiterated that the reform of farm trade was overdue. When the Round began, the twenty-four members of the OECD were supporting their agricultural industries to the tune of $225 billion a year. The estimated costs to farmers in developing countries of these policies was an annual $26 billion, partly thanks to a system of export subsidies that depressed world market prices, and partly thanks to import barriers. Four years later, the OECD bill had risen to $300 billion. In the European Community, voters paid twice over for the Common Agricultural Policy: as taxpayers, and as consumers paying well over world prices for food. No market-rigging distortion in the Third World competed in scale or comprehensiveness with this staggeringly inefficient system. An Australian study in 1988 estimated that abolishing the OECD systems of farm support would cut the U.S. budget deficit and its balance of payments deficit by $40 billion each, and finance the creation of over a million new industrial jobs in the European Community.[9] The United States, no slouch at subsidizing its own farmers, came into the round with a Zero-2000 proposal, to abolish all production and trade subsidies by the end of the century, with only rural income support permissible. The EC and Japan, seemingly impervious to warnings from U.S. trade officials that the EC's stance not only threatened the entire Uruguay Round but could be "the beginning of the end of multilateralism and the GATT,"[10] refused to contemplate ending subsidies or to set any timetable for reducing them.

The deadlock nearly brought about the collapse of the Round in 1990, when the EC was universally blamed for putting the global trading system at risk. It took until late 1992 for a compromise between the United States and the EC to be hammered out, and even then, the risk that it would be unraveled because of French objections persisted until the final hours of negotiation a year later. The frustration of the other players gave rise to the first effective issue-based coalition to have surfaced in quasi-universal negotiations. The Cairns Group of fourteen agricultural exporters included countries as disparate as Canada, Hungary, Fiji, and Brazil.[11] Broadly in the U.S. camp, the group acted as a pressure point on the Europeans; and by doing so, helped to enlarge the constituency not only for the Round, but for the broader objective of creating a World Trade Organization (WTO) with a status akin to that of the Washington Bretton Woods institutions.

The final result of the Uruguay Round was less than ideal; the text signed at Marrakesh in March 1994 bore the scars of the protracted and unedifying arguments over corn gluten, shipping monopolies, and audiovisual protectionism between the United States and the European Union. It was still, if ratified, a political achievement of the first importance—both in terms of the sweeping scope of the agreements reached, and as an affirmation of a vital principle. When the Round began in 1986, the GATT was widely viewed as a rich men's club; by the time it was concluded, it had become a magnet for reformers and a symbol of economic integration. The wartime labor of the imagination by the handful of men who created the Bretton Woods system was finally brought within sight of completion. At a time of almost equal political uncertainty and of unparalleled technological change, the need for a more powerful international regime was accepted by nearly 120 governments. World trade policy had crossed an important threshold.

A World Trade Organization should be a people's weapon, properly used. Its rules protect them from powerful domestic interest lobbies, which their governments find slightly easier to resist collectively than apart. But, partly because trade negotiations use the misleading term *concessions* when barriers are lowered, the benefits of free trade are not always apparent. Consumers are apt to complain about "floods of cheap imports," when these in fact raise their living standards; to look at the dole queues in Detroit without appreciating that protectionism against Japanese car imports, while it may shorten these lines for a time, does so at a cost (in the 1980s) of $100,000 for every job temporarily saved. Transforming the GATT was essential to the realization of the twenty-first century's economic and technological potential. The most immediate effect of the deal closed in December 1993 was to lift the threat of trade wars, which was damaging business confidence and, consequently, investment. But by 2005, the GATT secretariat's estimate was that the volume of trade would be 12 percent higher than it would have been without an agreement.

The principal reservation about the creation of a WTO is that the GATT—partly because of its provisional character—has been remarkably immune to bureaucratic sclerosis: it is lean, and dynamic because lean. There is a risk—and U.S. pressure in this direction was already apparent at Marrakesh—that the transformation of a "general agreement" into a fully fledged organization could lead to the overloading of its agenda with contentious new issues, such as environmental and labor standards, pushed by powerful Western lobbies whose commitment to free trade is open to doubt. But the multilateral system needed strengthening. The WTO will not only have tougher and speedier machinery for settling trade disputes; the reviews of the trading performance of individual countries, which the GATT began to produce in 1988 as a step toward preparing for the WTO, will make it harder for governments to fall short of their obligations. Breaking with the UN's "common system" would, as argued in Chapter 10, provide some safeguard against bureaucratic mediocrity, with the rigidities that engenders. Meetings of trade ministers ought, in principle, to have as high a profile as the annual Bank/IMF meetings. The challenge for the WTO will be to involve multilateral corporations and investors in the GATT's work, and to build strong domestic constituencies for liberal and nondiscriminatory trading rules.

The importance of preventing growth-inhibiting exclusive regional deals does not mean that trading patterns will not change over the next decades. Open-ended trading agreements between smaller groups of countries are already developing. A strong international regime is the best insurance that they will indeed be open ended—free for others to join—and nondiscriminatory. Trade is genuinely a matter for governments because they set the rules. Unwatched by other governments able to point to the rulebook, they have an historical tendency to set them to the disadvantage of the majority of their citizens: the power of protectionist lobbies distorts political judgment.

Stabilizers for the volatile worlds of capital flows and financial services may be a different matter. Banking is beginning to be regulated on a worldwide basis, through capital adequacy accords negotiated between governors of the leading central banks. And it will only be a matter of time before there is an international regime for the securities industry. "Uniform trading, accounting, capital and disclosure standards for major markets and institutions" are recognized by such influential market participants as Henry Kaufman of Salomon Brothers as essential, if major disruption on global markets operating around the clock is to be prevented. The market-makers need such regulation; this is a case of experience creating political will.

The hallmark of tomorrow's forms of dialogue will be careful attention to detail, progress toward reasonably well-defined and achievable objectives, and growing realism about what governments can, and cannot, expect to control. Differing perspectives are useful. The Greek poet Archilochus observed that foxes know many things and the hedgehog knows one big thing; in the business of making the world "safe for diversity," foxes are better equipped than hedgehogs. The powerful will pay attention only to those global organizations that take this rich world of cooperation into proper account.

But with increasing mobility of capital have come new kinds of trading competition. Wide ranges of manufactured goods compete not on the traditional basis of price advantage, but on product differentiation, style, and marketing. Countries short of investment and technology have been unable either to develop the industries that have been at the forefront of trade expansion, or to participate in the trade flows within the advanced industrial sectors. They have also lost out in the active trading between the subsidiaries of a typical multinational corporation. There may, in the post-Cold War world, be some scope for pragmatic experiments with dialogue on economic policy within the United Nations, however, as one way of ensuring that the concerns of these "outsiders," who are excluded from the flourishing multilateral networks developing between the world's more prosperous countries, are taken into account. Several groups in the late 1980s[12] put forward proposals for an Economic Security Council, whose authority in economic and social questions would parallel that of the Security Council. The idea was that such a body would have limited membership, with permanent seats for states or regions of major economic importance—the U.S., Japan, the EC, and—reflecting their potential rather than actual economic importance—Russia and China. The rest of its fifteen to twenty seats could be allocated on a rotating basis, on principles similar to those used to select members of the interim and development committees for the World Bank and IMF. The body would be ministerial, rather than part of the UN's diplomatic machinery, a political center operating as something of a hybrid between the European Union's Council of Ministers and the Western economic summits.

An Economic Security Council has obvious attractions. It would bring into play at global level the economic weight of Japan and, through the EC, Germany. A small and authoritative council could provide high-level political direction to deal with major natural or manmade disasters. And the dismal debut of the Commission for Sustainable Development suggests that something of the kind may be needed for environmental diplomacy. Such a council could provide a much-needed political filter for global dialogue, able to decide how, when conditions seemed to be ripe for multilateral negotiations, these might best be organized.

But the UN has some way to go before it sheds its image as a theater for pseudo-decisions, and the likely pressures to make an economic security council answerable to the General Assembly would be a disincentive to its creation. The lesson of the 1992 UN Conference on Environment and Development (UNCED) in Rio de Janeiro is not encouraging: no sooner were preparations placed under the aegis of the General Assembly than they began to take on an aura of unreality. Even if Western governments were persuaded, in principle, of the value of a manageable forum for "soft" economic and social policy questions such as international migration, drugs or the environment, they will rightly do nothing to weaken the forums they do trust. And for economic policy, these are the IMF and the World Bank, and their own clubs—the Western economic summits and the OECD. The structural rigidities of the United Nations remain a formidable obstacle to its use.

THE SHIFTING PARADIGM

To think back to Roosevelt's voyage to Yalta is to realize how automatic has come to seem the schedule of regional tours, international conferences, and summits that bulks out the diaries of ministers of foreign affairs, finance, trade, and industry of even medium-sized countries. The density and variety of international dialogue greatly exceed anything the architects of the United Nations could have anticipated, and most of it is multilateral in character. The most restricted of these encounters has a broader dimension—even bilateral summits have invisible participants, just as agreements reached there influence larger gatherings. A government's domestic political standing is increasingly profoundly and publicly connected with its success in handling the matter-of-fact business of managing interdependence.

This new multilateralism is driven by what is, not what ought to be. It responds to the globalization of banking and financial markets, the transnational integration of investment and manufacturing strategies by the major corporations, and the increasing vulnerability of each national body politic to political, environmental, or economic mismanagement elsewhere. As with all efforts to adjust to extremely rapid change, the building of these new networks of debate, competition, and cooperation is a halting and unevenly successful process, but it is continuous and multifaceted. And it is flexible, taking account both of an individual country's level of integration with the international economy and, still more importantly, of the need to involve the commercial and financial actors whose decisions increasingly constrain governmental choices. The UN will continue, selectively, to be used for the maintenance of international peace; but for purposes of economic and social cooperation, it will have to hook up with the "hot circuits" of multilateralism—international banking and financial flows, regional trading partnerships, chambers of commerce, and research centers.

Governments in the late twentieth century must balance diminished sovereignty with a lively sense of nationhood. The language of politics is still couched in terms of national units, and national interest, but these interests can be served only by coming to terms with an increasingly transnational world. The meaning of economic integration is that corporations and financial markets are leaving behind the nineteenth-century concept of international relations, to operate across frontiers. The switch by large manufacturers from international trade to direct foreign investment and multicountry production is one symptom of this "globalization"—albeit a selective globalization that tends to bypass countries without attractive domestic markets or developed regional trading networks. Governmental organizations that are remote from this real world of political constraints and economic opportunities are not much use to politicians.

The political machinery of cooperation, based as it is on the nation-state, has to take into account these wider dimensions of global change. If the new multilateralism is largely subuniversal, this will not so much dignify a retreat from the global dimensions of policy-making as imply a recognition that the principles on which the existing global organizations operate are impractical. The romantic view that all interests coincide and all countries are equally to be involved in decisions because all are affected may have some Platonic allure, but has little relevance to political or economic life. And, with the partial exception of the International Labor Organization (ILO), the financial, corporate, and intellectual communities are barely tolerated in UN forums—and then only as "nongovernmental observers." Since outside the UN, governments have to take these constituencies into account, this helps to explain the gap between what they say at the UN and what they do outside. Even the World Bank and the IMF, much the most innovative in this respect, have yet to integrate the private sector adequately into their operational planning and consultative mechanisms—although the Bank's International Finance Corporation, a joint investment corporation to promote the development of the private sector in developing countries, was expanding its activities by the late 1980s to offer advice on company restructuring, the development of local stock markets, and the development of an underwriting service to enable creditworthy Third World companies to borrow direct on the international capital markets.

A senior Scandinavian official describes this aloofness as

> the UN's most insuperable credibility gap. We sit there, paper tiger governments, discussing principles and theories. They, meanwhile, have created their own economic space, where they talk about how to make things work. Our discussions are falling behind in this new, fascinating world, because these corporations are creating multilateralism and we are still playing with what it might, in a properly ordered world, mean. There is a role for governments, but it is only by working with and through the market approach that we can discover the market imperfections which need to be addressed.[13]

The government-oriented bias of most UN activity is one reason why the driving impulses of the new multilateralism are coming from outside the global frameworks. New geographical, functional, and organizational coalitions are forming—and reforming, for the strongest characteristic of these groups is their fluidity.

The war to drive Iraq out of Kuwait put the fashionable theses about the decline of U.S. power of the late 1980s into perspective, but paradoxically emphasized how greatly any future Pax Americana would depend on supporting coalitions. The active involvement of other countries was a precondition of U.S. public support for U.S. engagement in the Gulf. The U.S. war effort was financed largely from allied contributions, and had to be: the U.S. budget deficit was heading toward $350 billion as the war ended. The United States, heavily dependent on foreign investors and financial markets, cannot afford to shoulder alone what George Bush once called "the hard work of freedom." The coalition must include the marketplace, too, since even the most powerful governments have understood the limits of the traditional tools of macroeconomic policy. The postindustrial revolution is well launched. Access on a global scale to instantly processed information is having a profound effect, not only on individual lives but on the world economy, and political institutions are beginning to catch up with these changes. Rules are needed to provide fairness and predictability, but the scope for effective government intervention has to be finely judged.

It is difficult to assess the future of the United Nations organizations without taking these transformations into account. Regional cooperation is being redefined in the light of them, in ways that will profoundly influence what demands are made on global structures. So is international negotiation. What may be emerging is a "multilateralism of the North." But the "North" is simultaneously being forced to redefine itself not only in East-West terms, but in response to a growing continuum of interest between the old industrialized world and energetic newcomers. Previous assumptions about the technology gap are becoming rapidly outdated by the globalization of research and development networks, by transnational agreements between companies and between branches of the same company that give developing countries' companies direct access to data, markets and finance, patents, and consultancy services. The quantum leap in communication flows and the tendency of corporations to maximize different countries' comparative advantage in a "global market" further reduce geographical barriers to technological innovation. The artificiality of "North" and "South" is giving way to a practical distinction between insiders and outsiders, hot circuits and cold. And the outsiders, immensely disparate in most respects, have this in common: for want of alternatives, they rely more than others on the universal forums. Yet these are of limited practical use to them. The remarkable growth of regional and interregional cooperation between the richer countries—networks that involve not just governments but businessmen and bankers—has created emerging patterns of reciprocity from which the poor are largely excluded. Governments in the most dynamic economies are wrestling with the disruptive effects of the transition to a world driven by microchips and telecommunications, and are disinclined to include mere passengers, countries outside the mainstream, in their joint efforts to adjust.

Ironically, this has not been without benefit to the poorest countries. In some ways their special needs are being more firmly addressed. There was considerable progress in the 1980s, for example, toward forgiving or sharply reducing sub-Saharan Africa's unpayable official debt. The most isolated countries were those that were not "basket cases" and did not qualify for emergency packages, yet that were neither sufficiently important to be included along with the newly industrialized countries in the new clubs, nor sufficiently indebted to make their recovery vital to the international financial system. These middle-range countries had always formed the backbone of the Group of 77 and—Algeria, for example, or Peru—had been the principal advocates of a New International Economic Order. They could with justice argue that Western debt strategies were chronically shortsighted, more like muddling on than muddling through, and that if Third World countries continued to repay interest and capital at a rate far exceeding the flows of new finance, this would threaten not only their own stability but the health of the global economy. But they had little collective weight and no serious forum in which to band together. (In such matters as these, the General Assembly is not serious.) And where private flows were concerned, the leading corporations were already patterning their investment according to the emerging American, European, and East Asian trading blocs. During the 1980s, when multinational companies tripled their worldwide stock of foreign direct investments, 80 percent of capital flows were within these three regions. By the end of the decade, the developing countries' share of private investment had fallen from 25 percent to 18 per cent—and of that, nearly three-quarters went to five East Asian and four Latin American countries. The least-developed countries' share of this Third World total was 0.7 percent. Although investment picked up considerably in the early 1990s, it was still fairly heavily concentrated on a few rapidly developing countries. The bleak message for those on the outside was that unless they could link up with one of these "poles of growth," economic reforms alone might not be enough to attract foreign capital.

Meanwhile, the traditional regional organizations—the Organization of African Unity (OAU), the Organization of American States (OAS), and even the more narrowly focused Asia Pacific Economic Cooperation (APEC) forum—are either stagnating, or evolving at a snail's pace. With northern multilateralism developing in ways that have nothing to do with the old "bloc" definitions, those outside the charmed circles have to establish afresh their claims to be recognized as partners in dialogue. The new multilateralism works outward from small circles, like ripples on a disturbed lake. "Global dialogue" may be effective only to the extent that smaller groups sharing particular interests have first discussed a given issue. This is not new, but is only now beginning to be recognized. The modernization of global structures, where this is possible at all, may have to work through the modernization of subglobal mechanisms, governmental and private.

On the most favorable assumptions, the dynamic growth of groups of middle-income countries could accelerate South-South trade. The hope is that as the more advanced industrializing economies integrate successfully into the global economy, they will exercise a "pull" effect, much as Asia's growing number of "tigers" have on countries in the Pacific region. And the communications revolution should increase access to knowledge and skills, speeding up intraregional shifts in comparative advantage in ways that would assist the poorest to compete in the international marketplace. But there is another, less optimistic projection. The speed of technological and industrial change could further complicate the initial processes of economic "take-off," leaving the poorest on the bottom rungs of an even longer ladder. Their dependence on commodity exports may become still more of a handicap as developments in biotechnology make the industrialized world's output less commodity intensive. Middle-income producers such as Mexico, Indonesia, and Malaysia have been modernizing and cutting production costs, squeezing more traditional producers out of these staple markets. And, above all in Africa, rapidly growing populations put enormous pressures on land, health and education facilities, job markets, and urban centers, greatly complicating the difficult task of adjustment.

In the postwar generation, albeit with generous external finance and assisted by very rapid growth in global trade, countries like South Korea broke through odds that seemed as formidable. And South Korea, unlike some of the poorest countries in the 1990s, did not have considerable natural wealth—although natural resources (take copper, for example) are no longer the automatic base of wealth they once were. There were no *inevitable* basket cases in these decades. Blessed were the microstates of the East that took to microcircuits: in theory at least, why should not barren Djibouti or tragically anarchic Haiti be one day of their number? Yet a study of the odds suggested that the future does not belong to the countries that will enter the twenty-first century poor.

Technology is "heating up" the world in other, more positive ways that still put new strains on established institutions. The process of "structural adjustment," at first thought of as a finite program of reforms to streamline and modernize a country's administration and liberalize its economy, is now seen as a necessary constant. To change as rapidly as did Western European countries in the 1950s would be not much better than treading water in the 1990s. The pyramid gets taller, and consequently wider at the base. Even in the industrialized world, the race is to the innovative, not the merely productive, and this has created profound changes in official thinking about the priorities for government action. Gone, in practice, is the goal of full employment; governments are thinking instead about tomorrow's jobs, emphasizing public investment in frontier technologies while they move to "free up" the current working environment through reforms to tax regimes and financial markets. "Flexible" labor markets may be essential, but some will benefit and some will not. Within every country, there is considerable fumbling and uncertainty about where and how to compensate the dropouts from the information society. On a global scale, we are still more perplexed: how can we help the "marginalized"? One of the most difficult challenges for bodies dedicated to multilateral cooperation will be to harness the opportunities created by technical change to enhance the prospects for those outside the mainstream. But institutionalized global dialogue on such matters will become a realistic possibility only when and if the UN wins back its long-lost reputation for political responsibility and organizational effectiveness, bridging the gap between global rhetoric and the pragmatic incrementalism of the world outside its corridors.

There is a sense in which the colossal institution-building effort of the past half-century may have weakened our natural radar. There is an understandable temptation to let an institution be, simply because it exists, even when it is neither efficient nor honorable nor even safe to do so. We need international institutions, but we need to cooperate in more flexible and sensitive ways than we have come to do in many of them. If the United Nations is to be relevant to the rule-making and management problems of the twenty-first century, its organizations face an enormous task of adaptation: to sub-universal approaches to problem solving, and to working with wider constituencies. And some will fail. That does not matter. The polycentric structure of the UN should be treated as an asset, not a defect, because the considerable autonomy enjoyed by different organizations enables the best of them to innovate. The myth of the UN "system," as we have seen, has been worse than a misdescription of the way these organizations actually function: it has been an obstacle to making the best of what exists. Coordination has been the pursuit of utopia masked in the language of the boardroom; what the best of these organizations require is encouragement to set fresh route maps of their own, to experiment, and to question every facet of their current operations. They need to be freed of the conceptual carapace of the utopian construct, the systemic ideal.

Outside the UN, we have begun to innovate—through special task forces, through regional and subregional associations, through the commercial networks for which cooperation is, happily, not a luxury but a banal necessity, through increasingly courageous human rights organizations. As national networks become richer, they complement the flourishing international dimension. And this approach to world order, inductive and spreading in concentric circles, seems more likely to set the pattern of the twenty-first century than global plans of action that are like uncut jigsaws, grand strategies that are imposed from the top and rarely stand the test of implementation at local level. We should not be concerned if a good deal of the political and economic machinery of the 1940s looks, in these conditions, in need of more than cosmetic surgery. That is not a reason for jettisoning all of it, but it is a reason for applying to these organizations the same criteria we would apply to any national institution, for insisting that the United Nations be judged by competitive standards.

This more realistic view of global organizations is in prospect. It is only a question of time. Already, a generation gap is apparent in thinking about multilateralism. The United Nations bulks large for those now nearing retirement, for whom its creation marked the rebirth of the rule of law, and even of those in midcareer, who were brought up to regard it as the guarantor of what limited stability the postwar world has known. But younger generations have diminished expectations for the power of governments to organize their lives and are considerably more skeptical about the desirability of their doing so. The original animating impulses behind the myth of the United Nations make us reluctant to jettison what was created, and this is prudent. But it would be mistaken to assume that the global agenda of a "new world order" necessarily requires global initiatives, international bureaucracies, or the guiding hand of the state. The withering away of the state may be as remote as the end of history, but the civil society through which it operates is vastly more dynamic, and more complex, than the world of the United Nations yet allows.

The preoccupations, the "great general questions," may remain constant. But myths can outlive the temples of their cult. In a world transformed since 1945, so long as UN forums are perceived as intractable hidebound clubs of diplomatic generalists, bent on asserting the dignity of 180-plus stubbornly separate sovereignties, increased public awareness of the need for effective cooperation could paradoxically erode public support for the global organizations. It is not just a question of refusing to accept the old excuse that the UN is "only the mirror of mankind." It is a question of a spreading, and largely salutory, challenge to the right of governments to shape the mirror in the first place.

Events may conspire to create richer tissues of multilateral cooperation, without precipitating the reforms of which the UN stands so deeply in need. The universal character of the global organizations will need to be modified—through steering committees, weighted voting, selective participation in negotiations, and so on—if they are to function; but such measures to improve efficiency will not be enough to assure them a future. They have to overcome the skepticism of the young, for whom World War II or colonialism or even the Holocaust has diminished resonance, but who do care about fairness, are many of them passionately concerned about the destruction of the environment, who believe in the indivisibility of human rights and who see the toleration of atrocities as an abdication of responsibility. Directly or indirectly, as a result of the communications revolution, pressure is being put on governments by citizens who are more aware of these rights, and more able to compare the records of their leaders with those of others. In Africa, the fall of each dictator weakens the throne of another. Seen in Rangoon, television images of life in Thailand hold out, in all its relativity, the promised land. Generations that have grown up with incompetent and unaccountable dictatorships are not fooled by "international development strategies," or impressed by a United Nations that is seen to protect the rights of rulers against the ruled.

Issue-based coalitions are beginning to emerge, inside and outside the UN. The test for the global organizations will be to make the most of them. It may be that the reassessment by the major powers of the UN's collective security functions,[14] coupled with a more sophisticated approach to international stability, will begin to weaken the foundations of sovereign autonomy on which the global organizations are so unrealistically constructed. And that may make it possible to integrate the UN's activities more closely with those of the other multilateral circuits that criss-cross the world. And some at least of the UN organizations may rediscover their original, creatively subversive role as hairshirts for governments, reminding them of their domestic and international obligations and subjecting their conduct to independent scrutiny. But it will not be the end of multilateralism if they do not. Neither pessimism nor optimism about institutions should obscure the matter-of-factness with which we have come to accept the realities—the tensions as well as the opportunities—of interdependence.

Thomas Kuhn has observed that the great changes that sometimes occur in science take place when an old paradigm of scientific thinking is, through experimental discovery or another means of analysis, replaced by a new one.[15] Before that "paradigm shift" occurs, the solutions to problems may run in circles, on the tracks of the old model. Beyond it, a new form of thought must shape itself. Human institutions, multiple, diffuse, and shapeless as they are, hardly lend themselves to such formal analysis. But it is reasonable to ask whether or not a kind of watershed may be close, a point at which institutions that seem to frame present realities may very quickly seem to belong to the past. Not that they will vanish, or like legendary states wither away, but that they will no longer suggest political means that we can creatively use. The developments sketched in this chapter are at best uncertain indications. By no means do all of them point away from the global institutions. But they do point to a rapid process of experimental discovery, however piecemeal in character, through which a new multilateral world is being constructed. The paradigm shift has not fully declared itself. A fuller understanding of that world lies in future. But the laboratory has about it the excitement and tension of imminent discovery.

Notes

Introduction

1. The legal standing under the Charter of the UN operation in Korea has been a matter of academic controversy. The first two Security Council resolutions on the Korea crisis, 82 of June 25, and 83 of June 27, 1950, calling on the North Korean forces to withdraw and (after President Truman decided to dispatch troops to defend the south) on members of the UN to provide the Republic of Korea with military assistance, were technically recommendations only, not binding orders. They were passed (9–0 and 7–1, with Yugoslavia abstaining) only thanks to the temporary boycott of the Security Council by the Soviet Union. The third resolution in this series, 84 of July 7, was also a recommendation. It *recommended* that states providing "military force and other assistance" under previous resolutions put them under unified U.S. command. But the key clause, paragraph 5, "*authorizes* the unified command . . . to use the United Nations flag in the course of operations." This would seem to justify the contention that the multinational force was operating with the explicit sanction of the Security Council, which had in effect "contracted out" the military command. Resolution 84, technically still in force in 1994 (because fighting was ended only under an armistice), bears a generic similarity to the type of Security Council authority given the U.S. intervention in Somalia in 1992, and the French intervention in Rwanda in 1994.

2. DuPont in fact set itself, in 1988, a more stringent timetable for ceasing production of these chemicals than had been agreed by governments in the 1987 United Nations Environment Program convention on protecting the ozone layer. Consumer pressure produced industrial decisions on environmental standards in the late 1980s and early 1990s that were frequently ahead of legislation, a trend likely to be maintained.

3. Secretary-general's statement to the Preparatory Committee for the fortieth anniversary of the United Nations (United Nations, SG/SM/3563 ANV/153, May 31, 1984).

4. Ibid.

5. Earl of Lytton, ed., *First Assembly: The Birth of the United Nations Organization* (London: Hutchinson, 1946), p. 26.

6. Maurice Bertrand, "Some Reflections on Reform of the United Nations," Joint Inspection Unit Report, JIU/REP/85/9 (Geneva, United Nations, 1985). The author requested a copy of this report, at the United Nations, on October 24, 1985, knowing it to be in print. She was told that it had not yet been printed, but obtained a printed copy the same day from a diplomatic mission. The report, which called for a "third generation" world organization, made some impact among Western and other governments, including the Soviet

Union, but was treated by senior UN officials with almost universal hostility. The quotation here is from para. 48, p. 16.

7. The consequent endless cycle of resolutions "recalling," "reiterating," and often in large part simply repeating previous resolutions—which makes up a high proportion of the business with which delegates occupy themselves in the General Assembly and other UN "governing" bodies—prompted one experienced Asian diplomat flatly to assert, at a closed seminar in England in 1988, that "the UN is brain-dead."

8. Sir Karl Popper, *The Open Society and Its Enemies* (London: Routledge & Kegan Paul, 1952), vol. 1, chap. 9.

9. Ibid., vol. 1, p. 159.

10. Ibid., pp. 164–65. It should be added that Popper's reflection on the value with which the injection of reason, responsibility, and humanitarianism could endow the "dangerous enthusiasm," which he found common to Plato and Marx for "the apocalyptic revolution which will radically transfigure the whole social world," was set out in terms of principle—not of specific institutions such as the United Nations, which he saw as being "inevitably" the result of compromise.

CHAPTER 1

1. Alfred Zimmern, *The League of Nations and the Rule of Law*, 1918–1935 (London: Macmillan, 1936), p. 1.

2. F. S. Northedge, *The League of Nations* (Leicester: Leicester University Press, 1986), p. 51.

3. Zimmern, *League of Nations*, p. 192.

4. The Four Freedoms, formulated by Roosevelt in his State of the Union address to Congress on January 6, 1941, were freedom of speech and expression, freedom of religion, freedom from want, and freedom from fear (the last through "a worldwide reduction of armaments").

5. Lend-Lease was the act under which Congress was persuaded by Roosevelt, after bitter debate, to authorize supplies of arms, food, and services to any country whose defense was deemed by the president vital to the security of the United States. Aimed primarily at helping Great Britain, it was introduced in March 1941 and continued after U.S. entry into the war. By 1945, it extended to thirty-eight nations including the Soviet Union. Some $8 billion of the $41.1 billion cost was offset by Allied assistance to U.S. troops abroad later in the war. The act gave the president discretion to accept repayment in any form he deemed acceptable: most of the balance became, in fact, an outright gift. The Atlantic Charter was a joint declaration by Churchill and Roosevelt on August 14, 1941, after a five-day meeting aboard warships in the North Atlantic. In effect a statement of war aims, it was not so formally because of U.S. nonbelligerency at the time. It committed them to respect self-determination and the sovereign right of self-government; to promoting equal access for all to trade and raw materials; to promoting economic progress and social welfare; to a peace enabling nations to live within their borders without fear or want; and to disarming the aggressors pending the establishment of a security system. The charter was incorporated in the Declaration of the United Nations of New Year's Day 1942, signed by forty-six governments.

6. Roosevelt's predilection for joint policing of the world—by the United States, Great Britain, the Soviet Union, and (a reflection of personal attachment to its national struggle rather than considerations of *realpolitik*) China—survived well into the early planning phases for a global organization. The Moscow conference of October 1943 issued a four-power

declaration on "general security," which, inter alia, committed the Four Policemen to "joint action" to maintain peace and security "pending the re-establishment of law and order and the inauguration of a system of general security." This survived in the UN Charter itself in the "transitional security arrangements" provided for under Article 106.

7. H. G. Nicholas, *The United Nations as a Political Institution* (Oxford: Oxford University Press, 1959), p. 63.

8. Ruth B. Russell, *A History of the United Nations Charter: The Role of the United States, 1940–45* (Washington, D.C.: Brookings Institution, 1958), p. 963. Much of the detail on the deliberations of the wartime committees and their composition draws on this uniquely authoritative work.

9. It did not, in practice, last long enough to produce a European peace treaty. For fourteen years—until 1959—foreign ministers of the United States, USSR, Great Britain, and France met at intervals in fruitless efforts to draw up such a document. No peace conference ever convened.

10. Winston Churchill, *Triumph and Tragedy* (London: Cassell & Co., 1953), p. 400.

11. Russell, *History of the United Nations Charter*, p. 215.

12. United Nations Charter, Article 1.

13. Ibid., Article 63.

14. David Mitrany, *A Working Peace System* (London: Royal Institute of International Affairs, 1943).

15. The United Nations Educational, Scientific, and Cultural Organization; the Food and Agriculture Organization; and the World Health Organization. (Only UNESCO carries "UN" in its title and acronym.) UNESCO and the WHO were more ambitious outgrowths of forms of cooperation that had existed under the League of Nations. UNESCO replaced the nongovernmental, and much respected, International Institute for Intellectual Cooperation established in 1925.

16. United Nations Charter, Article 1.3.

17. United Nations Charter, Article 61.

18. Earl of Lytton, ed., *First Assembly: The Birth of the United Nations* (London: Hutchinson, 1946), p. 26.

19. Ibid., p. 45.

20. Nicholas, *United Nations as a Political Institution*, p. 124.

21. Preamble to the UN Charter.

22. Maurice Bertrand, *Refaire l'Onu!* (Geneva: Editions Zoe, 1985), p. 28. Bertrand argued in this book that the primacy of the political approach to maintaining peace put the emphasis on the sphere in which states were most reluctant to yield sovereignty, and was therefore fundamentally mistaken: A fresh approach would stress building peace on the basis of economic and social cooperation.

23. Lytton, *First Assembly*, p. 35.

24. Winston Churchill, "Sinews of Peace" (speech given at Westminster College, Fulton, Missouri, March 5, 1946). Full text printed in the the *Times*, London, March 6, 1946.

CHAPTER 2

1. The United Nations in New York means, to most people, the Security Council and the General Assembly. Some are familiar with the existence of ECOSOC and the International Court of Justice, also a Charter body. Reality is more complex. An idea of the

range of activities and organizations generated in New York may be suggested by the following lists of the more important:

Bodies Formally Related to the UN Economic and Social Council (ECOSOC)

- Five regional economic commissions:
  - Economic and Social Commission for Asia and the Pacific (ESCAP)
  - Economic and Social Commission for Western Asia (ESCWA)
  - Economic Commission for Africa (ECA)
  - Economic Commission for Europe (ECE)
  - Economic Commission for Latin America and the Caribbean (ECLA)
- Commission for Sustainable Development (CSD)
- International Narcotics Control Board (INCB)
- United Nations Capital Development Fund (UNCDF)
- United Nations Children's Fund (UNICEF)
- United Nations Conference on Trade and Development (UNCTAD)
- United Nations Development Program (UNDP)
- United Nations Environment Program (UNEP)
- United Nations Fund for Drug Abuse Control (UNFDAC)
- United Nations Fund for Population Activities (UNFPA)
- United Nations High Commissioner for Refugees (UNHCR)
- United Nations Research Institute for Social Development (UNRISD)
- United Nations Special Fund (UNSF)
- United Nations Special Fund for Land-Locked Developing Countries
- World Food Council (WFC)
- World Food Program (WFP) (joint direction of UN secretary-general and FAO director-general)

Special Bodies and Programs of the United Nations

- United Nations Center for Human Settlements (HABITAT)
- United Nations Disaster Relief Office (UNDRO)
- United Nations Institute for Disarmament Research (UNIDR)
- United Nations Institute for Training and Research (UNITAR)
- United Nations International Research and Training Institute for the Advancement of Women(INSTRAW)
- United Nations Relief and Works Agency for Palestine Refugees in the Near East (UNRWA)
- United Nations University (UNU) (joint UN/UNESCO control)
- United Nations Volunteers (UNV)

2. **United Nations Specialized Agencies**
   - Food and Agriculture Organization (FAO)
   - International Atomic Energy Agency (IAEA)
   - International Civil Aviation Organization (ICAO)
   - International Fund for Agricultural Development (IFAD)
   - International Labor Office (ILO)
   - International Maritime Organization (IMO)
   - International Telecommunications Union (ITU)

- International Union for the Protection of New Varieties of Plants (UPOV)
- United Nations Educational, Scientific, and Cultural Organization (UNESCO)
- United Nations Industrial Development Organization (UNIDO)
- Universal Postal Union (UPU)
- World Health Organization (WHO)
- World Intellectual Property Organization (WIPO)
- World Meteorological Organization (WMO)
- World Tourism Organization (WTO)

Bretton Woods Group

- International Bank for Reconstruction and Development (IBRD) (the World Bank)
- Affiliated Agencies of IBRD:
  - International Center for the Settlement of Investment Disputes (ICSID)
  - International Development Association (IDA)
  - International Finance Corporation (IFC)
  - Multilateral Investment Guarantee Agency (MIGA)
- International Monetary Fund (IMF)
- General Agreement on Tariffs and Trade (GATT). Inaugurated in 1947, the GATT was not strictly speaking a UN agency but a compact between governments, pending the creation of an
- International Trade Organization (ITO). This prospect only materialized with the conclusion of the Uruguay Round of GATT trade negotiations in 1993, the provisions of which included the establishment of a
- World Trade Organization (WTO). GATT and UNCTAD jointly run the
- International Trade Center (ITC)

3. Maurice Bertrand, "Some Reflections on Reform of the United Nations," Joint Inspection Unit Report, JIU/REP/85/9 (Geneva, United Nations, 1985), p. 8.

4. Gunnar Myrdal, *Beyond the Welfare State* (London: Duckworth, 1960), p. 271.

5. "Reporting to the Economic and Social Council," Joint Inspection Unit Report, JIU/REP/84/7 (Geneva, United Nations, 1984).

6. The principal "service," or nineteenth-century-type, organizations are the International Telecommunications Union, the Universal Postal Union, the International Maritime Organization, the World Meteorological Organization, the International Civil Aviation Organization, the World Intellectual Property Organization, the International Atomic Energy Agency, and—hybrid that it is—some parts of the World Health Organization.

7. Douglas Williams, *The Specialised Agencies and the United Nations: The System in Crisis* (London: C. Hurst & Co., 1987), p. 64.

8. *UN Bulletin*, December 1, 1951, p. 446.

9. Williams, *Specialised Agencies*, p. 152.

10. UN doc. E/1470, 1949; ECOSOC resolution 324, 1950.

11. Thomas W. Graham, "The International Atomic Energy Agency: Can It Effectively Halt the Proliferation of Nuclear Weapons?" in *United States Policy and the Future of the United Nations* (New York: Twentieth Century Fund Press, 1994), p. 109.

12. UNESCO 23C/5, 1985, especially subprogram XIII.2.2. and paragraph 13415.

13. Williams, *Specialised Agencies*, p. 52.

14. Interview with Seymour Maxwell Finger, 1985.

15. "Measures for the Economic Development of Under Developed Countries," UN Department for Economic Affairs, New York, 1951, p. 87, cited in Bernard D. Nossiter, *The Global Struggle for More* (New York: Harper & Row, 1987).

16. "Generation: Portrait of the UNDP 1950–85," United Nations Development Program, New York, 1985.

17. *Development Cooperation*, 1986 Report (Paris: Organization for Economic Cooperation and Development, 1987), p. 22.

18. United Nations Development Program, doc. DP/1987/WG/WP.4 (New York, December 31, 1986), para. 31.

19. Robert Cassen et al., *Does Aid Work?* (Oxford: Oxford University Press, 1986).

20. Unattributable interview, New York, 1990.

21. Transcript of UNESCO director-general's reply to UNDP representative, at UNESCO Executive Board, 1986: "Je ne permets à qui que ce soit de critiquer quoi que ce soit."

22. *The United Nations in Development: Reform Issues in the Economic and Social Fields, a Nordic Perspective*, final report by the Nordic UN Project (Stockholm: Almqvist & Wiksell International, 1991), p. 53.

23. *World Bank News* 13, no. 7 (February 17, 1994): 1.

24. Letter from R. van Branteghem, *Economist*, May 16, 1987.

25. Conversation with the author, 1986.

26. *United Nations in Development*, pp. 62–63.

27. N. Hirschorn in Richard Cash, eds., *Child Health and Survival: The Unicef GOBI-FFF Programme* (London: Croom Helm, 1987). Cited in James Le Fance, *Chattering International: How UNICEF Fails the World's Poorest Children* (London, the Social Affairs Unit, Research Report 19, 1993).

28. Dr. Jacques Diouf, "A Reinvigorated FAO to Meet the Challenge of Hunger in the 90s and Beyond" (paper distributed to FAO member governments, 1993), pp. 7–8.

29. Ralph Atkinson in a CBC interview for "The Fifth Estate," November 4, 1986.

30. An IFAD official, a former UNDP resident representative, with long experience of the elephants in their trampling grounds.

31. A leitmotif, for example, of Timothy Raison's calls for reform of UNESCO when he was British minister of overseas development. The persistence with which Western governments insist that UN organizations should deploy more staff from headquarters to "the field" probably has more to do with the perception that they are doing little good in headquarters than with any very clear idea of what these staff would actually do if redeployed.

32. *Development Cooperation*, p. 100.

33. Unattributable interview with senior UN policy planner, 1987.

34. United Nations Charter, Article 1.4.

CHAPTER 3

1. Anthony Parsons, "Waffle, but Still Worthwhile?" the *Times*, London, October 6, 1984.

2. Maurice Bertrand, "Some Reflections on Reform of the United Nations," Joint Inspection Unit Report, JIU/REP/85/9 (Geneva, United Nations, 1985), p. 16.

3. The Lebanese intervention (author's translation): Records of the UNESCO Twenty-first General Conference, vol. 3, p. 483, and M'Bow's speech of welcome to Sekou Touré were cited in two brilliant analytical articles by Professor Pierre de Senarclens of the University of Lausanne: "Jalons pour une étude psycho-politique du processus de decision

au sein d'une organisation intergouvernementale à vocation universelle: le cas de l'Unesco" (draft) and "Fiasco at Unesco: The Smashed Mirror of Past Illusions," *Society*, September-October 1985.

4. As Brian Urquhart, former UN under-secretary-general for special political affairs, characterized it in an interview for Adam Platt's article, "United Nations: Time of Judgement," *Insight*, November 17, 1986.

5. David Mitrany, *The Functional Theory of Politics* (London: London School of Economics, 1975), pp. 6–7.

6. The Covenant of the League of Nations, Article 5, stated that unless it was "otherwise expressly provided in this Covenant . . . decisions at any meeting of the Assembly of the Council shall require the agreement of all the Members of the League represented at the meeting." Since Articles 10, 11, and 16, the key "enforcement" clauses in the Covenant, contained no such express provision, aggressors could and did argue that their assent must be obtained to any sanctions the League might impose. Oddly enough, Article 15, which dealt with the League's power to establish the facts in a dispute, did take the precaution of excluding the parties to a dispute from the right to vote.

7. Peter Calvocoressi, "The Withering of the UN and the International Extension of the Rule of Law" (Harold Leventhal Memorial Lecture, Columbia University, New York, 1984).

8. Sheila Harden, ed., *Small Is Dangerous: Micro States in a Macro World*, David Davies Memorial Institute report (London: Frances Pinter, 1985), p. 18; UN doc. S/9836, 1970.

9. Peter Calvocoressi, *World Order and New States* (London: Chatto & Windus for the International Institute for Strategic Studies, 1962).

10. Harden, *Small Is Dangerous*, p. 1.

11. Conor Cruise O'Brien: *To Katanga and Back* (London: Hutchinson, 1962), p. 17.

12. This official, one of the UN's foremost education experts, argues that because sovereignty has long become more important than action to the majority, reforms directed toward improving negotiating mechanisms are doomed. A nonaligned citizen with considerable experience in Africa, he stresses the attachment of new states to words as ends in themselves.

13. Conor Cruise O'Brien, *The United Nations: Sacred Drama* (London: Hutchinson, 1968), p. 287.

14. Pakistan's speech on that occasion is recalled by Arthur J. Goldberg, then U.S. permanent representative to the UN, in Linda M. Fasulo, *Representing America* (New York: Praeger, 1984), p. 101.

15. United Nations Charter, Article 2.7.

16. Thomas Franck, *Nation against Nation: What Happened to the UN Dream and What the U.S. Can Do about It* (New York: Oxford University Press, 1985), p. 125.

17. Recollections in 1985 of Dragoljub Najman, who had been the UNESCO official charged with maintaining—which effectively meant creating—the Congo's national education system during the Congo operation.

18. O'Brien, *Sacred Drama*, pp. 137–38.

19. Theo van Boven, "1984 and Human Rights" (Minority Rights Group Annual Lecture, London, February 23, 1984).

20. Franklin D. Roosevelt, "War—and Aid to Democrats," State of the Union message to the U.S. Congress, January 6, 1941.

21. A Western government's legal expert, at a conference held at Ditchley Park, Oxfordshire, U.K., June 17–19, 1988.

22. William F. Buckley, *United Nations Journal* (London: Michael Joseph, 1975), p. 257.

23. Seymour M. Finger, *Your Man at the UN: People, Politics and Bureaucracy in the Making of Foreign Policy* (New York: New York University Press, 1980), p. 258.

24. Richard Schifter, "The United States Government's Commitment to Human Rights" (address to the Council of the Americas, Washington, D.C., June 3, 1981). President Bush's reaction to the massacre of Tiananmen Square in 1989 was also, by comparison with the outrage felt by ordinary Americans, statesmanlike to a fault: National interest here, however, was reinforced by the administration's belief that it would not help those fighting for democracy in China by slamming the door on its government.

25. Blaine Harden, "Moi Calls Trip 'Success,' Rejects Critics," *International Herald Tribune*, February 18, 1987.

26. Verbatim statement by Ambassador Rajai-Khorassani of Iran to the Third Committee of the Thirty-ninth UN General Assembly, December 7, 1984.

27. Scott Sullivan, "A Sad Mockery of Human Rights," *Newsweek*, February 28, 1983.

28. Ben Whitaker, "Reforming the Human Rights Structure of the United Nations," report issued by the Minority Rights Group, London, 1983.

29. "Alternative Approaches . . . for Improving the Effective Enjoyment of Human Rights and Fundamental Freedoms," General Assembly Res. 32/130, UN doc. A/32/45, 1978.

30. Statement by the chairman, Kenneth Dadzie of Ghana, "Report of the Committee on the Review and Appraisal of the International Development Strategy for the Third United Nations Development Decade," UN General Assembly Official Records, suppl. no. 48, UN doc. A/40/48, 1985.

31. Bertrand, *Some Reflections on Reform*, p. 18.

CHAPTER 4

1. Heads of State or Government of Non-Aligned Countries (Declaration made at Ninth Conference, Belgrade, September 4–7, 1989). Recorded as UN doc. A/44/551 S/20870, September 29, 1989.

2. Daniel P. Moynihan and Suzanne Weaver, *A Dangerous Place* (Boston: Little, Brown, 1978), pp. 132–33.

3. Richard L. Jackson, *The Non-Aligned, the UN and the Superpowers* (New York: Praeger, 1983), p. 213.

4. *Reflections on the Future of Multilateral Cooperation: The ILO Perspective*, report of the director-general, International Labor Conference, Seventy-third sess., Geneva, 1987, p. 5.

5. Quoted in Edward Mortimer, *Roosevelt's Children: Tomorrow's Leaders and Their World* (London: Hamish Hamilton, 1987), p. 112.

6. Jackson, *The Non-Aligned, the UN and the Superpowers*, p. 101, makes the point that for Sikkim and Bhutan, "comparable Himalayan Kingdoms," UN membership was the "margin of survival." Bhutan, which joined the UN in 1971 and the Non-Aligned Movement in 1973, retained a theoretical independence; India annexed Sikkim while it was still preparing its application for UN membership. In the sense that the fiction of sovereignty is more important than the fact, this is valid: Bhutan, now a fictional state if ever there was one, is undoubtedly glad to have this tenuous claim on hypothetical existence.

7. John Foster Dulles, address to Iowa State University, June 9, 1956; reported in *New York Times*, June 10, 1956.

8. Paul Mosley, *Overseas Aid: Its Defence and Reform* (London: Wheatsheaf Books, 1987), pp. 25–27.

9. UN General Assembly Res. 1785 (XVII) (New York, 1962).

10. The Group of 77's Joint Declaration said: "The developing countries regard their own unity . . . as the distinctive feature of this Conference . . . an indispensable instrument for securing the adoption of new attitudes and new approaches in the international economic field."

11. See especially *Towards a New Trade Policy for Development*, report by the secretary-general of UNCTAD, Geneva, 1964.

12. Fundamental Texts of the Fourth Conference of Heads of State or Governments of Non-Aligned Countries: Algiers Charter and Economic Declaration, Algiers, 1973.

13. At UNCTAD V in Manila. The rumor was immediately started by Algerian and other OPEC diplomats that the United States had put Costa Rica up to it; untrue, but it illustrates the liability of any state breaking ranks to be pilloried as a stooge of imperialism. Costa Rica's motivation was simple economic distress.

14. UN General Assembly Res. 3201 (S-VI) (New York, 1974).

15. Bernard D. Nossiter, *The Global Struggle for More* (New York: Harper & Row, 1987), p. 58.

16. "Zaire: Ouverture des travaux du Conseil Général de l'UPZA [Union de la Presse de Zaire]," AZAP/PANA dispatch, Kinshasa, August 1, 1986.

17. German Carnéro Roque, "L'Information dans le Tiers Monde," *Le Monde Diplomatique*, August 1976. Partly on the strength of this article, Carnéro Roque was hired by UNESCO's communications division.

18. A clear statement, by one of the Eastern bloc's most articulate theorists, is in the essay by Professor Wolfgang Kleinwachter of the Karl Marx University, Leipzig, "Aims and Principles: International Information and Communication—A Global Problem," in *New International Information and Communication Order, A Sourcebook* (Prague: International Organization of Journalists, 1986). In pp. 107–10, Kleinwachter sets out the "seven fundamental principles" of international law that should be applied to the new information order. Kleinwachter's activities in this field continued after the unification of Germany. He was prominent in the lobbying by the International Association for Mass Communication Research at the 1993 UN Conference on Human Rights in Vienna, for international recognition and codifying of the "responsibilities" of journalists.

19. Sinnathamby Rajaratnam, justifying legislation enabling the Singapore government to penalize foreign publishers found to be "engaging in the domestic politics of Singapore." *Financial Times*, November 3, 1986. Singapore was still persisting with this policy in 1994. As for Malaysia, Prime Minister Mahathir Muhamed imposed trade sanctions against British companies in 1994 retaliation for reporting by British media investigating a series of dubious aid and trade deals in Malaysia by the British government which he considered offensive to "Asian values."

20. Stockhom International Peace Research Institute *1987 Yearbook on World Armaments and Disarmament* (Stockholm, June 1987).

21 "The UN and International Security," in *United Nations, Divided World*, ed. Adam Roberts and Benedict Kingsley (Oxford: Clarendon Press, 1988), p. 145.

22. Jackson, *The Non-Aligned, the UN and the Superpowers*, p. 159.

23. Formula setting the mandate for "restructuring" the UN agreed at the Seventh Special Session of the UN, Part VII, final text. United Nations, New York, 1975.

24. Heads of State or Governments of Non-Aligned Countries (Declaration at the Sixth Conference, Colombo, 1976).

25. Thomas G. Weiss, *Multilateral Development Diplomacy in Unctad: The Lessons of Group Negotiations 1964–84* (New York: St. Martin's Press, 1986).

26 For a summary of this debate, see UNCTAD Bulletin no. 229, February 1987, and the (more revealing) press release TAD/INF/1985, UNCTAD, Geneva, February 12, 1987.

27. Statements by Richard Kauzlarich (United States) and Muchkund Dubey (India/Group of 77) during debate on UNCTAD's role in the UNCTAD Trade and Development Board, TAD/INF/1969, UNCTAD, Geneva, March 26, 1985. Italics added.

28. Discussion with the author in Geneva, June 1986.

29. *Journal de Genève*, July 5, 1985.

30. *Reflections on the Future of Multilateral Cooperation*, see note 4, supra., p. 4.

CHAPTER 5

1. *Defining Purpose: the UN and the Health of Nations*, final report of the United States Commission on Improving the Effectiveness of the United Nations (Washington, D.C.: U.S. Government Printing Office, September 1993).

2. Western European foreign service official, in an unattributable interview, June 1987. While acknowledging that the crisis was not budgetary but concerned the question of "what the UN is for," he argued that the UN's track record forced the West to confine its creative energies to managing what Conor Cruise O'Brien called the "ritual at the brink" (referred to in Chapter 3).

3. Definition of liberalism in the *Oxford English Dictionary*, complete microedition, 2 vols.

4. Meeting in London, at one of those peculiarly British events in which the most unexceptionable and certainly nonsensitive views are aired only on condition that neither the speaker nor the institution at which it is held is identified.

5. Preamble to the United Nations Charter.

6. In a private meeting in New York in March 1987 between editors and members of the Committee on Information.

7. UN General Assembly Res. 59(1) (New York, December 14, 1946), preamble.

8. UN General Assembly Res. 127(ii) (November 15, 1947), on "False and Distorted Reports." For a detailed discussion of these early debates, see Clare Wells, *The UN, UNESCO and the Politics of Knowledge* (London: Macmillan, 1987).

9. See note 6, above.

10. Rose Sue Bernstein, U.S. alternate representative, speaking at the UN Committee on Information on July 2, 1987. Recorded in press release 36(87) issued by the U.S. Mission to the UN. Deadlock continued in the UN Special Political Committee in 1988.

11. Frantz Fanon, *Les Damnés de la Terre* (Paris: Maspèro, 1961). Quotations are from the English translation, *The Wretched of the Earth* (London: Penguin, 1969).

12. A. M. Rosenthal, "A Korean Tang of Liberty Spices the Winds of Asia," *International Herald Tribune*, July 21, 1987.

13. Altaf Gauhar, ed., interview with Jan Pronk, former Dutch minister for development cooperation (1973–77), in *Talking about Development* (London: Third World Foundation, 1983), pp. 181–211.

14. Charles Yost, "How U.S. Harms Human Rights Policy," *Christian Science Monitor*, August 26, 1977.

15. Speaking at a UN colloquium on the theme "Is Universality in Jeopardy?" Geneva, December 1985.

16. Stephen P. Marks, "Emerging Human Rights: A New Generation for the 1980s?" Stoffer Lectures, *Rutgers Law Review* 33 (1981): 435–52.

17. See, for example, Draft Declaration on the Right to Development; note by secretary-general; resolution adopted by the UN High Commission on Human Rights on March 14, 1985 by roll call vote; draft declaration A/40/277 E/1985/70 presented to the 1985 UN General Assembly.

18. Kenneth Adelman and Marc Plattner, "Western Strategy in a Third World Forum," *Atlantic Quarterly*, Fall 1983, pp. 81–93.

19. Swiss diplomat formerly responsible for Swiss UN policy, in unattributable briefing, July 1987.

20. Douglas Williams, *The Specialised Agencies and the United Nations: The System in Crisis* (London: C. Hurst & Co., 1987), p. 120.

21. Interview cited in note 2 above.

22. Sir John Thomson, then U.K. permanent representative to the UN, speaking in Los Angeles, February 1985.

23. Speaking in final plenary of UNESCO General Conference, Belgrade, 1980. Author's notes, not official UNESCO record.

24. The first move was at UNESCO's General Conference in Sofia, Bulgaria, in 1985. The speech quoted was by the USSR delegate at the 126th session of the Executive Board of UNESCO, May 1987.

25. Gunnar Myrdal, "Realities and Illusions in Regard to Inter-Governmental Organizations," L. T. Hobhouse Memorial Trust Lecture no. 24, February 25, 1954 (London: Oxford University Press, 1955), p. 10.

26. Gunnar Myrdal, *Beyond the Welfare State* (London: Duckworth, 1960), p. 202.

27. See note 15 above.

28. Peter Calvocoressi, "A Problem and Its Dimensions," in *To Loose the Bands of Wickedness: International Intervention in Defence of Human Rights*, ed. Nigel Rodley (London: David Davies Memorial Institute of International Studies & Brassey's, 1992), p. 10.

29. Sir Robert Jackson, *A Study of the Capacity of the UN Development System* (Geneva: United Nations, UNDP/5, 1969), vol. 1, p. 3.

30. This, ironically, was the same ambassador who argued on the same occasion that the West had all the cards and was "feeble" if it didn't win. See note 4, above.

31. Unattributable briefing by a Scandinavian permanent representative to the FAO, September 1985. At the FAO, Western governments did in fact agree to suspend voluntary contributions to field programs shortly after this interview, out of frustration at the opposition in the Secretariat to reforms. But the Scandinavians weakened the effect of this joint policy by continuing to fund "ongoing" FAO projects—and they continued to press for still larger contributions to UN technical assistance programs, notably in the Nordic UN Project's proposals published in 1991 and in subsequent negotiations at the UN.

32. Gérard Blanc, "La Face Cachée des Organisations Internationales," in *Les Organisations Internationales entre L'Innovation et la Stagnation*, ed. Nicolas Jecquier (Lausanne: Presses Polytechniques Romandes, 1985), p. 252.

33. Douglas Williams, "The UN and Its Specialised Agencies: A System under Strain" (address to the British House of Commons All Party Parliamentary Group on Development, February 2, 1987).

34. Senior career official, U.S. State Department International Organizations department, in an unattributable briefing, 1989.

35. Top policymaker in the Canadian International Development Agency, unattributable conversation, November 1985.

36. CIDA official, 1990.
37. See note 31, above.
38. Unattributable briefing during ECOSOC meeting, Geneva, 1985.
39. Daniel P. Moynihan and Suzanne Weaver, *A Dangerous Place* (Boston: Little, Brown, 1978), p. 12.
40. Founded, significantly, in 1964—the year of the first UNCTAD meeting—the group's members in 1994 were Australia, Canada, France, Germany, Italy, Japan, Netherlands, Spain, United Kingdom, United States, and Sweden, which had just opted for full membership rather than observer status.
41. At private seminar for officials and academics on the future of the United Nations, 1990.

CHAPTER 6

1. Sir Robert Jackson, *A Study of the Capacity of the UN Development System* (Geneva: United Nations, UNDP/5, 1969), vol. 1, p. 3.
2. In 1988, a typical year, the members of the Development Assistance Committee of the OECD financed $3.47 billion—94 percent—of the $3.61 billion technical assistance expenditure of the UN (excluding the international financial institutions); 89 percent of this was in voluntary contributions. *The United Nations in Development: Reform Issues in the Economic and Social Fields*, a Nordic Perspective, final report by the Nordic UN Project (Stockholm: Almqvist & Wiksell International, 1991), p. 84.
3. Jackson, *Study of the Capacity of the UN Development System*, vol. 1, pp. 49–52.
4. Robert Muller, speaking at a colloquium organized at the Palais des Nations in Geneva in December 1985 on the theme "Is Universality in Jeopardy?" The formal papers presented to this meeting are available from the Department of Economic and Social Information, UN, Geneva.
5. Marten Mourik, Netherlands ambassador for international cultural cooperation, lecture at the Netherlands Association for International Affairs, the Hague, December 4, 1985.
6. Second Report of the Ad Hoc Committee of Experts to Examine the Finances of the United Nations and the Specialized Agencies, A/6343, UN General Assembly, July 19, 1966, p. 11.
7. Article 5.1 of the Statutes of the Joint Inspection Unit, JIU/1 UN, Geneva, 1978 ed.
8. Here and passim, Jackson, *Study of the Capacity of the UN Development System*.
9. Seymour Maxwell Finger, in conversation, 1985.
10. *1985—and Towards the 1990s* (New York: UNDP, October 1986).
11. Lester Pearson, *The Crisis of Development* (New York: Praeger, 1970).
12. *United Nations in Development*, pp. 70–71.
13. Comment by a member of the UN secretariat who was intimately involved with the later "restructuring" exercise of the 1970s and with developing coordination machinery for UN programming.
14. Jackson's comment to the author, 1986.
15. UN General Assembly Res. 3343 (XXIX) (New York, December 17, 1974).
16. A/32/pv.109, p. 6, UN, New York.
17. "A New United Nations Structure for Global Economic Cooperation: Report of the Group of Experts on the Structures of the United Nations System," EC/AC.62/9 (New York, United Nations, May 28, 1975).

18. Res. 3362 (S-VII), sect. VII, para. 1, (New York, 1975).

19. Pierre de Senarclens, *La Crise des Nations Unies* (Paris: Presses Universitaires de France, 1988), p. 157 (author's translation). Text of the Charter of Economic Rights and Duties of States, adopted by majority vote against the opposition of the U.S. and many other Western governments: Res. 3281 (XXIX) (New York, 1974).

20. Report of the Ad Hoc Committee on the Restructuring of the Economic and Social Sectors of the United Nations System, UN General Assembly A/32/34 (New York, United Nations, 1978).

21. Ronald I. Meltzer, "Restructuring the United Nations System: Institutional Reform Efforts in the Context of North-South Relations," *International Organization*, University of Wisconsin, no. 32.4 (Autumn 1978): 1009.

22. The agency heads flatly refused to permit the director-general to stand in for the UN secretary-general as chairman of the Administrative Committee on Coordination (ACC): in their view, he ranked far below them. (See Paul Taylor, *International Organization in the Modern World* [London: Frances Pinter, 1993], p. 135.) The office was effectively abolished in 1992—in order, naturally, to improve the efficient coordination of UN development activities.

23. Douglas Williams, *The Specialized Agencies and the United Nations* (London: C. Hurst & Co., 1987), p. 54.

24. Nicol Davidson and John Renninger, "The Restructuring of the United Nations Economic and Social System: Background and Analysis," *Third World Quarterly*, Spring 1982, p. 1009.

25. This happened at a committee meeting to review the UN's International Development Strategy in 1985.

26. Samuel de Palma's comment to the author, 1985.

27. "British Policy towards the United Nations," Foreign Policy Documents no. 26, Foreign and Commonwealth Office (London: Her Majesty's Stationery Office, 1978).

28. Cited by Shirley Hazzard, *Defeat of an Ideal* (London: Macmillan, 1973), pp. 212–13.

29. The "checklist" was appended by Muller to his address to the thirty-third annual assembly of the International Press Institute in Stockholm, May 1984. His claims at the Geneva meeting on UN staff qualifications ignored the findings of numerous reports by the UN's Joint Inspection Unit.

30. Brian Urquhart, *A Life in Peace and War* (London: Weidenfeld & Nicholson, 1987), p. 108.

31. "The UN—Its Staff—Its Future" and "Thirteen Proposals for the Future" (UN Staff Association, Geneva, 1986).

32. Interview with FAO division chief, July 1984.

33. Respectively, the then president of the World Bank, director-general of the ILO, and managing director of the IMF. The anecdote was provided unattributably by one of the participants at the meeting.

34. Quoted by M. S. Swaminathan, director-general of the excellent International Rice Research Institute, in a speech accepting the General Foods World Food Prize, Washington, D.C., October 6, 1987.

35. Cited in Edward Mortimer, *Roosevelt's Children* (London: Hamish Hamilton, 1987), p. 359.

36. Urquhart, *Life in Peace and War*, pp. 352–53.

CHAPTER 7

1. IMF Departmental Memorandum 80/17, February 1980, and World Bank 1981 *World Development Report*, cited by Dr. Tony Killick, "Disequilibria and Adjustment in Developing Countries" (paper prepared for joint IMF/Overseas Development Institute seminar, London, October 1981). Paper available froms Overseas Development Institute, London.

2. Stanley Please, *The Hobbled Giant: Essays on the World Bank* (London: Westview Press, 1984), p. 25.

3. Unattributable interview, 1988.

4. Elliot Berg (coordinator), *Accelerated Development in Sub-Saharan Africa: An Agenda for Action* (Washington, D.C.: World Bank, 1981).

5. "Assessment of U.S. Participation in the Multilateral Development Banks in the 1980s" (consultation draft, Department of the Treasury, Washington, D.C., September 1981), pt. 4, p. 1.

6. August 20, 1981, earlier draft of the above.

7. "Assessment," final report (Washington, D.C., Department of the Treasury, February 1982), p. 87.

8. Please, *Hobbled Giant*.

9. Unattributable conversation with World Bank official. There was throughout the 1980s considerable anxiety in-house about the structural adjustment programs: concern on the one hand that they should not be allowed to degenerate into blank balance-of-payments checks, and on the other that the Bank was not equipped for detailed on-the-spot monitoring. It was also argued that if there had not been failures—as there had certainly been—in the SAL program it would indicate that the Bank had not been sufficiently ambitious. The purpose of SALs, to promote "the steady addressing of institutional issues" by governments and business leaders in recipient countries, could not, it was argued, yield results overnight. By the end of the decade, however, the Bank was looking for a middle road between seeking adjustment of the entire economy of a country and the project-by-project approach, by selecting aspects of economic management requiring policy reform.

10. Presentation to a high-level meeting of the Development Assistance Committee of the OECD, Paris, December 1986.

11. Willi Wappenhans, senior vice president for administration of the World Bank, discussing the thinking behind the World Bank reorganizations in 1987.

12. "Reorganizing the Bank: An Opportunity for Renewal, Report to the President from the Steering Committee on the Reorganization of the World Bank" (Washington, D.C.: World Bank, April 6, 1987).

13. Speech by Jacques de Larosière, Philadelphia, 1984.

14. Unattributable discussion with senior World Bank official, 1988.

15. Unattributable discussion with World Bank official, 1988.

16. Michael W. Bell and Robert L. Sheehy, "Helping Structural Adjustment in Low-Income Countries," *Finance & Development* (Washington, D.C.: World Bank/IMF, December 1987).

17. *Sub-Saharan Africa: From Crisis to Sustainable Growth* (Washington, D.C.: World Bank, November 1989).

18. "Getting Results: The World Bank's Agenda for Improving Development Effectiveness" (Washington, D.C:. World Bank, 1993), p. 7.

CHAPTER 8

1. Walter Galenson, *The International Labor Organization: An American View* (Madison: University of Wisconsin Press, 1981), pp. 111–39.

2. The document, leaked in January 1981, is cited in Righter, "Haig Wins Round in Fight to Keep Aid Policy Intact," *Sunday Times*, London, February 1, 1981.

3. Burton Yale Pines, ed., *A World without the UN: What Would Happen If the UN Shut Down* (Washington, D.C.: Heritage Foundation, 1984), p. xix.

4. Juliana Pilon, "No Wonder the United Nations Hurts," *New York Times*, July 6, 1987. Pilon was a Heritage Foundation analyst.

5. Seymour Maxwell Finger, *Your Man at the UN* (New York: New York University Press, 1980), p. 80.

6. Shirley Hazzard, *Defeat of an Ideal* (London: Macmillan, 1973), p. 9.

7. Finger, *Your Man at the UN*, p. 197.

8. Trygve Lie, *In the Cause of Peace: Seven Years with the United Nations* (New York: Macmillan, 1954), p. 389.

9. Ibid., p. 387.

10. See Hazzard, *Defeat of an Ideal*, esp. chap. 2, for a detailed "insider's" account of the impact of McCarthyism on the UN.

11. Activities of United States Citizens Employed by the United Nations: Hearings before the Subcommittee to Investigate the Administration of the External Security Act and Other Internal Security Laws of the Committee of the Judiciary, U.S. Senate, 82d Cong., 2d sess., 1952 (including appendix D.2).

12. Quoted in Julian Behrstock, *The Eighth Case: Troubled Times at the United Nations* (Lanham, Md.: University Press of America, 1987), p. 21.

13. U.S. District Court of Massachusetts, *Ozonoff v. Bersak*, Civil Action No. 71-1046-MC. Judgment, September 6, 1983. Cited in ibid., p. 10.

14. *New Yorker*, January 8, 1972.

15. Testimony of Jeane Kirkpatrick before the Senate Foreign Operations Subcommittee of the Senate Appropriations Committee, March 25, 1985.

16. Linda M. Fasulo, *Representing America* (New York: Praeger, 1984), p. 285.

17. Finger, *Your Man at the UN*, p. 202.

18. Charles W. Yost and Lincoln P. Bloomfield, *The Future of the UN: A Strategy for Like-Minded Nations* (Boulder, Colo.: Westview Press, 1976).

19. Ibid.

20. Address to the Association of American University Women, December 1977.

21. Interview in Fasulo, *Representing America*, p. 233.

22. Ibid., p. 247.

23. Ibid., p. 62.

24. Ibid., p. 259.

25. See the account of the restructuring exercise at the UN, Chapter 6.

26. *Foreign Affairs*, Summer 1982.

27. Interview with unattributable National Security Council source, July 1982.

28. By then, however, the Clinton administration had abtained the G-77's agreement to radical modifications of the seabed mining regime. These, it proclaimed in the summer of 1994, tallied sufficiently with the six principles to permit U.S. accession to the

convention. The prolonged American hold-out had paid off—disproving the cliché, beloved of diplomats dealing with the UN, that absentees have no influence.

29. Resignation letter by Dr. Rodolfo Stavenhagen, 1982.

30. Author's discussions with Gerard and Newell, January and February 1984.

31. "U.S. Paper on North/South Dialogue and UNCTAD" (unpublished discussion paper circulated to UNCTAD member states by the U.S. mission in Geneva, March 1984).

32. "Amélioration possible du processus de négociation pour le Dialogue Nord-Sud: Position de la Communauté Européene" (unpublished paper, March 22, 1984).

33. Discussion with the author, March 1984.

34. Discussion with the author, March 1984.

35. Interview with David Goodman, March 1988.

36. Section 143 of the Foreign Relations Authorization Act, fiscal years 1986 and 1987, p. 21.

37. Senator Kassebaum raised the case in her Senate speech putting forward the amendment, though without mentioning Urquhart by name. At the time, she believed the payment to have been improper, as well as large, but subsequently acknowledged that she had been misinformed.

38. UN General Assembly Res. A/40/237 (New York, December 18, 1985).

39. Report of the Group of High-Level Intergovernmental Experts to Review the Efficiency of the Administrative and Financial Functioning of the United Nations, General Assembly Official Records, 41st sess., supp. 49, A/41/49 (New York, United Nations, 1986).

40. Göran Ohlin, "The United Nations Contribution to the Improvement of the Human Condition" (unpublished mimeograph, January 1991).

41. Williamson's testimony to the Foreign Affairs Subcommittee on Human Rights and International Organizations of the House of Representatives, February 23, 1988.

42. Senior Reagan administration official, in unattributable discussion, March 1988.

43. According to a highly critical 1981 survey by the World Food Council, which was completely ignored.

44. Saouma flattered the doughty but eccentric Fenwick assiduously. She was touched, she told the author in one of many long discussions in Rome, by the attention to detail of a man who despite all his weighty responsibilities, had the kindness to send her regular flowers, and who "told me that he reads and rereads every word I have ever uttered on the terrible drama of hunger in the world."

45. *The United Nations in Development: Reform Issues in the Economic and Social Fields, a Nordic Perspective*, final report by the Nordic UN Project (Stockholm: Almqvist & Wiksell International, 1991), p. 38.

46. Cited in Daniel P. Moynihan and Suzanne Weaver, *A Dangerous Place* (Boston: Little, Brown, 1978), p. 213.

CHAPTER 9

1. Annual report of the UN secretary-general on the "Work of the Organization," United Nations, New York, 1988.

2. Interview with Francis Blanchard, director-general of the International Labor Office, in 1986. Blanchard proceeded in November 1987 to call the first multiagency meeting on

this theme, using the ILO's tripartite structure to involve governments, employers, and union leaders from some twenty countries. It was effectively boycotted by all major donor governments except France, Italy, Canada, and Australia.

3. Peter Calvocoressi, *World Order and New States* (London: Chatto & Windus for the International Institute for Strategic Studies, 1962), p. 69.

4. Miriam Camps, *Collective Management: The Reform of Global Economic Organizations* (New York: McGraw-Hill, 1981), p. 55.

5. Charles Krauthammer, "Let It Sink," *New Republic*, August 24, 1987.

6. The members of the awkwardly acronymed SADCC, created in 1980, are Angola, Botswana, Lesotho, Malawi, Mozambique, Swaziland, Tanzania, Zambia, and Zimbabwe.

7. Alexander Solzhenitsyn, *One Word of Truth: The Nobel Speech* (London: Bodley Head, 1971), p. 12.

8. Among these were Maurice Bertrand, "Some Reflections on Reform of the United Nations," Joint Inspection Unit Report, JIU/REP/85/9 (Geneva, United Nations, 1985); Final Panel Report of the United Nations Management and Decision-Making Project of the UNA-USA, *A Successor Vision: The United Nations of Tomorrow* (New York: United Nations Association of the USA, 1987); and *The United Nations in Development: Reform Issues in the Economic and Social Fields, a Nordic Perspective*, final report by the Nordic UN Project (Stockholm: Almqvist & Wiksell International, 1991).

9. Mort Rosenblum and Douglas Williamson, *Squandering Eden: Africa at the Edge* (New York: Harcourt Brace Jovanovich, 1987).

10. In conversation with the author, 1988.

11. Boutros Boutros-Ghali, *An Agenda for Peace: Preventive Diplomacy, Peacemaking and Peacekeeping: Report of the Secretary-General Pursuant to the Statement Adopted by the Summit Meeting of the Security Council on 31 January 1992* (New York: United Nations, Department of Public Information, July 1992).

12. Quoted by Pierre de Senarclens in *Yalta* (Paris: Presses Universitaires de France, 1984).

13. Malcolm Fraser, "Australia: Two Centuries and Much Yet to Do," *International Herald Tribune*, January 26, 1988.

14. Since exact totals change from year to year, these figures present no more than orders of magnitude. They do not, for that reason, take account of emergency spending cuts imposed by the withholding of U.S. contributions and by other member states' arrears. Governments' enthusiasm for the UN's expanded peacekeeping role in the late 1980s did not extend to paying for it. The UN peacekeeping forces won the Nobel Peace prize in 1988. In March 1989, on the eve of the major Namibia operation (trimmed on the insistence of the five permanent members of the Security Council), more than half the members of the United Nations were in arrears with their contributions to peacekeeping. Of the $372 million then owed, the Soviet Union's arrears accounted for $143 million and those of the United States for $103 million. The United States resumed payment in full of its regular contributions to the UN in 1990 (apart from its share of funding for the Division of Palestinian Rights and the Office of Ocean Affairs and the Law of the Sea, which it had consistently refused to finance). It also began to pay off arrears, which at the peak of the U.S. "taxpayers' revolt" had accounted for about 80 percent of UN debt, at a rate of some $40 million a year. The will to pay did not, however, generally increase with the public acclaim for the UN's "renaissance" in the 1990s: At the end of 1992, when its reputation was at a forty-year peak, eighty-eight states were in arrears in payments to the regular budget, fifty-two

of them by more than a full year. And by mid-1994, the United States owed close to $1.2 billion, largely because of late payment of peacekeeping assessments.

Regular UN budgets are financed by assessed contributions from member states, based on an approximation of member states' ability to pay. Since a ruling by the International Court of Justice in 1962 that peacekeeping should be considered a regular expense of the UN, peacekeeping has been paid for through a separate assessment, mission by mission apart from a small (and recent) revolving startup fund voted by the General Assembly. For peacekeeping, the five permanent members (Group A) pay a premium on their ability-to-pay standard assessment, which means that the United States, for example, is assessed at 25 percent for the regular budget and 30 percent for peacekeeping. Group B (developed countries) pays at the same rate as their regular budget assessments. Group C (less developed) pays 20 percent of their regular assessment and Group D (least developed) only 10 percent. Since by the early 1990s Group C included at least fifteen states with above-average per capita incomes, this system is overdue for revision.

Humanitarian and development programs are funded essentially by voluntary contributions. These now exceed contributions to the regular budget of the United Nations Organization and its affiliates, and vary between just under and just over half of most specialized agencies' total budgets.

Of a $5.5 billion total, the UN and its affiliates accounted in the late 1980s for $3.5 billion, excluding peacekeeping, and the specialized agencies for $2 billion—a dramatic illustration of the proliferation of economic and social programs around the "political" United Nations. The proportions, and the sums involved, were similar in the mid-1990s, once enormously increased costs for refugee crises were stripped out of the totals.

It is precisely because the sums involved are so small that the dispersal of funds between thousands of studies, technical assistance programs, and separate units is a recipe for waste. Dividing responsibility for drug abuse control, for example, among an intergovernmental commission, and expert group, and two United Nations units, one in Vienna and one in New York, with less than $3 million basic budget to split between them, was hardly a way to maximize impact.

For a readable and expert summary of the way spending is allocated in the United Nations and its affiliates, see the paper prepared by Maurice Bertrand for the UNA-USA Management and Decision-Making project referred to in note 8 above, entitled "The UN in Profile: How Its Resources Are Distributed" (New York, United Nations Association of the USA, 1986). A later breakdown, which however excluded the specialized agencies, was provided in *Financing an Effective United Nations: A Report of the Independent Advisory Group on UN Financing* (New York: Ford Foundation, 1993).

15. Stanley Hoffman, *Primacy or World Order: American Foreign Policy since the Cold War* (New York: McGraw-Hill, 1978), p. 242.

16. UN General Assembly Res. 48/162 (New York, December 20, 1993).

CHAPTER 10

1. *The United Nations in Development: Reform Issues in the Economic and Social Fields, a Nordic Perspective*, final report by the Nordic UN Project (Stockholm: Almqvist & Wiksell International, 1991).

2. Unattributable interview, 1994.

3. *United Nations in Development.*

4. See, for example, *Effectiveness of Multilateral Agencies at Country Level: Case Study of Eleven Agencies in Kenya, Nepal, Sudan and Thailand* (Copenhagen: DANIDA, 1991).

5. UN General Assembly Res. 48/162 (New York, December 20, 1993).

6. Shirley Hazzard, *Countenance of Truth: The United Nations and the Waldheim Case* (New York: Viking, 1990), p. 73.

7. Appendix 4 to the Fifth Report of the British House of Commons Foreign Affairs Committee on *Membership of UNESCO* (London: Her Majesty's Stationery Office, August 2, 1993).

8. Leon Gordenker, "The World Health Organization: Sectoral Leader or Occasional Benefactor?" in *U.S. Policy and the Future of the United Nations* (New York: Twentieth Century Fund Press, 1994), p. 171.

9. Interview with the author, cited in Righter, "Make These Fiefdoms Prove Their Worth," *The Times*, London, March 31, 1990.

10. Nigel Hawkes, "West Fails in Bid to Topple Health Chief Hiroshi Nakajima," *The Times*, London, May 6, 1993.

11. Douglas Williams, *The Specialised Agencies and the United Nations: The System in Crisis* (London: Hurst & Co., 1987), pp. 79–80.

12. Interview with Kanawaty, Geneva, 1986.

13. *The Changing World of Work: Major Issues Ahead*, report of the director-general to the ILO General Conference (Geneva, June 1986).

14. Interview with Francis Blanchard, June 1986.

15. Discussion with author, New York, 1985.

16. *The United Nations in Development*, pp. 55–57.

17. UNDP World Development Annual Report, 1987 (New York, 1987), Table, "Distribution of UNDP Resources, 1972–91," pp. 30–33.

18. Letter, *The Times*, London, March 18, 1994.

19. Unattributable interview, 1991.

20. Richard Thornburgh, internal memorandum to the UN secretary-general on the progress of UN restructuring (unpublished document, March 1993), pp. 16–17.

21. The person appointed to this post, with strong U.S. backing, was a German career diplomat, K. T. Paschke; the inspector-general was to report directly to the UN secretary-general, but could not be dismissed without the assent of the UN General Assembly.

22. *Membership of UNESCO*, Appendix 4.

23. Thornburgh memorandum, p. 9.

24. Seymour Maxwell Finger and John Mogno, *The Politics of Staffing the United Nations Secretariat* (New York: Ralph Bunche Institute, 1974).

25. Unattributable interview, UN, New York, 1988.

26. Hazzard, *Countenance of Truth*, p. 19.

27. Unattributable interview, Geneva, 1988.

28. Unattributable interview with European foreign service official, 1994.

29. *Defending Values, Promoting Change, Social Justice in a Global Economy: An ILO Agenda*, report of the director-general to the International Labor Conference (Geneva, ILO, 1994).

30. Ibid., p. 77.

31. *A Successor Vision: The United Nations of Tomorrow*, report of a UNA-USA panel chaired by Elliot Richardson (New York, UNA-USA, September 16, 1987), p. 73.

32. Ibid.

33. Randolph C. Kent, *Anatomy of Disaster Relief: The International Network in Action* (London: Frances Pinter, 1987).

34. "Evaluation of the Office of the United Nations Disaster Relief Coordinator," Joint Inspection Unit Report, JIU/REP/80/11 (Geneva, United Nations, October 1980).

35. Author's enquiries to UNDRO, June and October 1984.

36. "Report of the Working Group on Incorporation of OEOA's Experience and Capacities into the Permanent Structure of the United Nations," attached to interoffice memorandum by Maurice Strong to the secretary-general (September 22, 1986).

37. Prince Sadruddin Aga Khan, "Improving the Disaster Management Capability of the United Nations," report prepared for the United Nations Management and Decision-Making Project of the UNA-USA (New York, UNA-USA, January 1987).

38. Annex to UN General Assembly Res. 44/236 (New York, December 22 1989).

39. "Recent Changes in the International Relief System," Overseas Development Institute briefing paper (London, ODI, January 1993).

40. UN General Assembly Res. 46/182, "Strengthening the Coordination of Humanitarian Emergency Assistance of the United Nations" (New York, December 19, 1991).

41. Comprehensive report by the secretary-general, E/4994, ECOSOC, UN, New York, May 31, 1971.

42. Gil Loescher, "The United Nations, the United Nations High Commissioner for Refugees, and the Global Refugee Problem," in *United States Policy and the Future of the United Nations* (New York: Twentieth Century Fund Press, 1994), p. 139.

43. Gil Loescher, *Beyond Charity: International Cooperation and the Global Refugee Crisis* (New York: Oxford University Press, 1993), pp. 203–4.

44. Morris B. Abram, "The United Nations, the United States and International Human Rights," in *U.S. Policy and the Future of the United Nations* (New York: Twentieth Century Fund Press, 1994), p. 120.

45. R. J. Vincent, *Human Rights and International Relations* (Cambridge: Cambridge University Press/Royal Institute for International Affairs, 1986), p. 94.

46. Fascinating fresh research into the relations between human rights, democracy, and development was being carried out in the early 1990s. For an evocative summary, see "Democracy and Growth: Why Voting Is Good for You," *Economist*, August 27, 1994.

47. Margaret Thatcher, opening address to the UNEP Conference on the Ozone Layer, London, March 5, 1989.

48. *Our Common Future*, report of the World Commission on Environment and Development (New York: Oxford University Press, 1987).

49. "The Role of Development Assistance in Narcotics Addiction in Developing Countries" (Paris, Organization for Economic Cooperation and Development, 1987).

50. Including opium, U.S. estimates in 1987 put the total number of addicts in Pakistan at nearly half a million.

51. Interview with *The Times*, London, July 20, 1990.

CHAPTER 11

1. Data drawn from Ruth Leger Sevard, *World Military and Social Expenditures* Stockhom International Peace Research Institute (SIPRI) 1989.

2. Speech by the UN secretary-general to the European Parliament, April 18, 1991.

3. Professor Sir Michael Howard, "The UN and International Security," in *United Nations, Divided World*, eds. Adam Roberts and Benedict Kingsbury (Oxford: Oxford University Press, 1988), p. 45.

4. Javier Pérez de Cuéllar, "The Role of the UN Secretary-General," in *United Nations, Divided World*, eds. Adam Roberts and Benedict Kingsbury (Oxford: Oxford University Press, 1988), pp. 73–74. (He did not amend this list for the 2nd edition, published in 1993.)

5. Pérez de Cuéllar, ibid.

6. Following the Security Council's refusal to authorize a peacekeeping force (on May 18, 1981), an outstandingly successful Multinational Force and Observers (MFO) operation was rapidly assembled. Under a Norwegian commander, it deployed U.S. civilian observers and contingents from nine countries. For a detailed account, see Richard W. Nelson, "Multinational Peacekeeping in the Middle East and the United Nations," *International Affairs* 61, no. 1 (1984).

7. Brian Urquhart, 1986 Alistair Buchan Memorial Lecture, *Survival* 28 (September-October 1986).

8. United Nations Charter, Article 33.

9. See, inter alia, Christopher Thomas, "Friend to the World's Enemies," *The Times*, London, July 28, 1988; Andrew Gowers, "Steering a Surer Course at Last," *Financial Times*, August 5, 1988; editorial, "A Better United Nations," *New York Times*, July 23, 1988; Simon Jenkins, "UN Struggles Happily from Its Swamp," *Sunday Times*, London, July 24, 1988.

10. UN General Assembly Res. 42/93 (December 7, 1987). Votes were 76 for; 12 against; 63 abstentions; 7 absent.

11. Urquhart in discussion with the author, March 1988.

12. Petrovsky in an interview with Flora Lewis, *International Herald Tribune*, July 7, 1988.

13. Tickell, interview with the author, March 1988.

14. Statement by Vladimir Petrovsky to the 2nd Committee of the UN General Assembly, October 7, 1987.

15. Quoted by Quentin Peel in "The Foreign Face of Perestroika," *Financial Times*, July 29, 1988.

16. In a speech a week later.

17. Interview, March 1988, New York.

18. Press release 202, New York, November 3, 1989, USSR permanent mission to the UN.

19. Res. 660 (August 2, 1990), passed by 14 votes in favor with Yemen not participating in the voting; Res. 661 (August 6, 1990), passed by 13 votes in favor, 0 against, Cuba and Yemen abstaining.

20. See excerpt from Chinese delegate's speech to the Security Council, *The Kuwait Crisis: Basic Documents*, Cambridge International Documents Series (Cambridge: Grotius, 1991), vol. 1, p. 121.

21. Secretary-general's briefing for correspondents, reported to *The Times*, London, by James Bone (quotations unpublished).

22. Secretary-general's news conference, New York, February 20, 1991.

23. Speech by President Bush to the American Academy for the Advancement of Science, February 15, 1991: "But there's another way for the bloodshed to stop, and that is for the Iraqi military and the Iraqi people to take matters into their own hands to force Saddam Hussein the dictator to step aside and to comply with the UN and then rejoin the family of peace-loving nations."

24. Prior to 1994, China had in fact been more sparing in its use of the veto than the other four permanent members. The record was: Soviet Union 114 (mainly between 1946 and 1956); U.S. 69 (mainly between 1976 and 1990); Britain 30; France 18 and China only 3. (Adam Roberts and Benedict Kingsbury: "The UN's roles in International Society": *United Nations, Divided World*, op. cit., 2nd edition, 1993, p. 10–11.) But the use of the veto has

historically reflected a state's degree of isolation at the UN (not necessarily coterminous with isolation in the world outside); and on that basis, and given its obsessive fidelity to the principle of non-intervention, the number of China's vetos could be expected to rise if the Security Council maintained its more interventionist profile.

25. Unattributable briefing by senior NATO officer, 1994.

26. Dr. Jim Whitman and Commander Ian Bartholomew, "Collective Control of UN Peace Support Proposals," Global Security Program, Cambridge University, *Security Dialogue*, March 1994.

27. The Clinton administration's Policy on Reforming Multilateral Peace Operations (Presidential Decision Directive No. 25); text released by the U.S. State Department, May 1994.

28. Chester A. Crocker, "How to Restore Public Confidence in the Necessary Art of Peacekeeping," *International Herald Tribune*, May 10, 1994.

29. In *New York Review of Books*, June 10, 1993; see also the extensive correspondence this prompted in the issues following, on June 25 and July 15 1993.

30. Letter, *New York Review of Books*, July 15, 1993.

31. Ronald A. Spiers, "Reforming the United Nations," in *U.S. Policy and the Future of the United Nations* (New York: Twentieth Century Fund Press, 1994), p. 29.

32. Conversation with Dragoljub Najman, assistant director-general of UNESCO until 1983, later director of the Inter-Action Council.

CHAPTER 12

1. Bruce Clark, "Idealism Gives Way to Disenchantment," *Financial Times*, April 19, 1994.

2. In his essay on "Non-Intervention, Self-Determination and the 'New World Order,'" Professor James Mayall states that the doctrine of *uti possidetis* was first applied in Central and South America, but was adopted with regard to Africa by the International Court of Justice and thereafter was deemed to have general application. Under it, states undertook not to challenge the boundaries they inherited from colonial rule. *International Affairs* 67, no. 3 (July 1991).

3. For an account of this French initiative, see Mario Bettati, "When It Is the World's Business," *International Herald Tribune*, April 19, 1991. Bettati was one of the originators of the proposal, which was firmly supported by France's then minister for humanitarian affairs, Bernard Kouchner.

4. William Shawcross, "Cambodia Peacemaker Faces Tougher Balkan Test," *Times*, London, February 18, 1994. Shawcross, whose book *The Quality of Mercy* (London: André Deutsch, 1984) is required reading for anyone concerned with emergencies and disaster relief, believed that Akashi's principal success in Cambodia was to retain Chinese support throughout the transition.

5. Brian Urquhart, "Who Can Police the World?" *New York Review of Books*, May 12, 1994.

6. George F. Kennan, "The Balkan Crisis: 1913 and 1993," *New York Review of Books*, July 15, 1993.

7. Thomas W. Graham, "The International Atomic Energy Agency: Can It Effectively Halt the Proliferation of Nuclear Weapons?" in *U.S. Policy and the Future of the United Nations* (New York: Twentieth Century Fund Press, 1994).

8. Speech by Fernando Solana, Mexican foreign minister, to a meeting of the Pacific Economic Cooperation Council in Singapore, May 1991.

9. Dr. Andy Stoeckel, "Macro-Economic Consequences of Farm Support" (Canberra, Center for International Economics, 1988).

10. For example, Daniel Amstutz, addressing a conference in Munich on agricultural reform. *Financial Times*, May 12, 1988.

11. Members of the Cairns group were Argentina, Australia, Brazil, Canada, Chile, Colombia, Fiji, Hungary, Indonesia, Malaysia, Philippines, New Zealand, Thailand, and Uruguay.

12. Maurice Bertrand,"Some Reflections on Reform of the United Nations," Joint Inspection Unit Report, JIU/REP/85/9 (Geneva, United Nations, 1985). *A Successor Vision: The United Nations of Tomorrow*, report of an UNA-USA panel chaired by Elliot Richardson (New York, UNA-USA, September 16, 1987).

13. Conversation during conference at the Ditchley Foundation, Oxfordshire, 1988.

14. This will be an evolving, continuous process. The huge expansion in UN peacekeeping operations was a source of gratification to the permanent Security Council members in 1992, when at a special UN summit they asked Boutros Boutros-Ghali to map out his expansive *Agenda for Peace*. By the summer of 1994, they were close to the view that this erstwhile cottage industry had far outgrown either the UN's management capacity, or their own readiness to finance it, and were preparing for a new 'peacekeeping summit' in 1995 (James Bone: "UN to Hold Peacekeeping Summit," *Times*, London, August 8, 1994). Such shifts in the pendulum were likely to continue.

15. Thomas S. Kuhn, *The Structure of Scientific Revolutions*, 2d ed. (Chicago: University of Chicago Press, 1970).

INDEX

Abdelmoumene, Muhammad, 272
Abortion, 216
ACABQ (Administrative Committee on Administrative and Budgetary Questions), 233, 282; inefficiency, 48
ACC (Administrative Committee on Coordination), 171, 172, 181, 389n. 22; inefficiency, 47–48
Accountability, 54–56, 280–83; international civil service, 11; specialized agencies, 48; and UN budget, 160
"Activities of United States Citizens Employed by the United Nations," 219
Adelman, Kenneth, 133–34
Administrative Committee on Coordination. *See* ACC
Adoula, Cyrille, 79
Advisory Committee on Administrative and Budgetary Questions. *See* ACABQ
Afghanistan, 45, 85, 294; and media guidelines, 139; and Soviet Union, 217, 317, 318, 325–26
AFL-CIO, 211
Africa, 34, 45, 85, 101; and communications revolution, 376; decolonization, 99; development programs, 194, 202; economic collapse, 17, 93–94, 188–89, 279; famine, 46, 71, 237, 259; and FAO, 180; and France, 240; and Group of 77, 105; and human rights, 299, 300; population growth, 374; technical assistance, 277; and UNDRO, 291; UN votes, 67; and World Bank, 193, 200
African Capacity Building Foundation, 207
Afro-Asian meeting (Bandung), 99–100
Afro-Asian Peoples' Solidarity Organization, 100
Agenda 21, (UN Conference on Environment and Development, 1992), 305
Agenda for Peace, An (Boutros-Ghali), 252, 339
Agricultural trade reform, 367–69
Aidid, Farrah, 355–56
AIDS, 148–49, 271
Akashi, Yasushi, 340, 353, 398n. 4
Albright, Madeleine, 337–38
Algeria, 101, 106, 108; decolonization, 99
Algiers summit, 107–9, 111, 112, 116
Amazon development scheme, 201
American Chamber of Commerce, 211
Amin, Idi, 107, 259
Amnesty International, 18
Angola, 81, 326
Anticolonialism, 93, 100
Anti-Colonialist Charter, 73
Anti-Imperialist League, 100
Anti-semitism, 300
Apartheid, 111, 316, 348
APEC (Asian Pacific Economic Cooperation), 373
Aquino, Corazon, 84
Arab League, 314
Arab oil embargo, 107, 258
Argentina: debt management, 204; military technology, 317; trade negotiations, 101–2
Arkan, 343
Armenia, 289; ESAF loans, 205
Arms sales, 340
ASEAN (Association of Southeast Asian Nations), 318
Asia, 1, 15, 99; and human rights, 299, 300

Asian Pacific Economic Cooperation forum (APEC), 373
Association of Southeast Asian Nations (ASEAN), 318
Atlantic Charter, 26, 378n. 5
Atlantic Council, 222, 223
Atomic weapons, 218
Attlee, Clement, 13–14, 37
Australia, 248; and conflict containment, 318; and OECD, 367; and UN budget, 236
Australia Group, 363
Austria: and Cambodia, 352; and Gulf War, 335
Aziz, Tariq, 334

Baghdad, 113–14
Baghdad Pact, 100
Baker, James, 200, 210; and Cambodia, 352; and former Yugoslavia, 358; "grand coalition," 266; and Gulf War, 332, 333, 334; and Shevardnadze, 324
Balfour Declaration, 13
Balkans, 4, 356
Bandung principles, 99–100
Bangladesh, 297; and UNDRO, 291
Barre, Siad, 354
Baruch plan, 218
Baya, Ramazani, 112
Belgium: and Congo peacekeeping mission, 78, 80; and Gulf War, 335
Belgrade summit, 100, 101, 103
Ben Bella, Ahmed, 102
Benin, 297
Berg, Elliot, 195
Berlin Wall, 94
Bertrand, Maurice, 70–71, 377–8n. 2, 379n. 22; on UN ineffectiveness, 14; and UN reform, 157, 158, 251
Bertrand report (1985), 47, 87–88
Bettati, Mario, 398n. 3
Bevin, Ernest, 38
Bhutan, 384n. 6
Biological weapons, 351; and Russia, 363. *See also* Chemical weapons
Black, Eugene, 190
Blanc, Gérard, 143
Blanchard, Francis, 119–20, 157, 181, 182, 392–3n. 2; ILO report, 274; and ILO revitalization, 247; and multilateral cooperation, 98
Bloc politics, 20, 105
Bokassa, Jean Bédel, 84
Bolton, John, 324
Bonaparte, Napoleon, 29, 31
Bosnia, 338, 339–40, 342–43, 347; intervention in, 18; refugees, 296
Bosnia-Herzegovina, 352, 357; intervention in, 359–60
Boumedienne, Houari, 107, 108, 109, 111, 112
Bouteflika, Abdelaziz, 116
Boutros-Ghali, Boutros, 252; *An Agenda for Peace*, 339; and Bosnia, 360; and former Yugoslavia, 358; management reforms, 280, 281–82; personnel practice, 284; and Somalia, 354
Boven, Theo van, 82, 83
Boyd Orr, Lord, 163
Brady, Nicholas, 204
Brady plan, 188
Brandt report, 259
Brazil, 118, 338; and agricultural trade reform, 368; Amazon development scheme, 201; debt management, 205; development programs, 208; and environment, preservation of, 303; military technology, 317; Polonoroeste scheme, 194
Bretton Woods conference, 31, 36
Bretton Woods Group, 381n. 1
Bretton Woods institutions, 44, 60; and decolonization, 98; effectiveness, 51; and Gardner report, 171, 173; and Japan, 241; and nonaligned movement, 109; reform, 18–19; and Russian economic reform, 364–66; and Third World majority, 223. *See also* IMF; World Bank
Brewster, Havelock, 118, 179
Brezhnev, Leonid, 107, 314
Britain. *See* Great Britain
British National Audit Office (NAO), 272
Brown, George Arthur, 275
Bruce, Stanley, 32, 33
Bruckner, Pascal, 128
Brundtland, Gro Harlem, 304
Buckley, William, 84

Burkina Faso, 59
Burma: and chemical weapons, 318; and human rights, 297, 300
Burundi, 81, 99, 296
Bush, George, 4, 372; and Cambodia, 352; and former Yugoslavia, 358; and Gulf War, 3, 10, 331, 332–33, 335, 397n. 23; and Hussein, Saddam, 334; and Kurds, 336; and "new world order," 121; and Somalia, 354–55; and Tiananmen Square massacre, 384n. 24
Bush administration, and Gulf War, 330–37
Byrnes, James, 28, 40–41

Cairns group, 368; members, 398n. 11
Cairo summit, 102, 103
Camberley group, 145–46, 237–38
Cambodia, 81, 85, 221, 259, 339; intervention in, 352–54; and Vietnam, 318, 326–27
Camdessus, Michel, 148, 181, 203
Camp David accords, 223, 314
Campos, Mario Y, 272
Canada, 241; and agricultural trade reform, 368; and FAO, 138, 144, 176, 237–38, 284; and IAEA, 363; and NAFTA, 367; and UN budget, 235–36
Capacity Study, 160–69
Carrington, Lord, 358
Carroll, Lewis, 71
Carter, Jimmy, 240; and Camp David accords, 314; and ILO, 211; and UN reform, 174–75
Carter administration: and human rights, 130, 223; and IDA, 197; policy toward UN, 222–24
Cassen, Robert, 61
Center-periphery theory, 104–5
Central America, 240; and conflict containment, 317–18; drug trafficking, 307
Central Emergency Revolving Fund (CERF), 293
CFCs. *See* chlorofluorocarbons
Chad, 81, 318
Chalker, Baroness (Lynda), 267–68
Charter of Economic Rights and Duties of States, 76, 106, 170, 259–60
Charter of the United Nations. *See* United Nations Charter
Chemicals: and environment, 6–7; and ozone layer, 301–2
Chemical warfare, 260
Chemical weapons, 317, 318, 351, 362–63, 364; and Iraq, 327, 328–29
Chemical Weapons Convention, 363
Chenery, Hollis, 191
Cheney, Richard, 331
Chernobyl, 363; and IAEA, 51
Cheysson, Claude, 84
Chile, 85, 135, 317; debt management, 204–5; and nonaligned movement, 107
China, People's Republic of, 1, 13, 117, 189, 303, 384n. 24; and Bandung meeting, 99–100; and Cambodia, 352; and chemical weapons, 318; and Group of 77, 116–17; and Gulf War, 331, 332, 333, 334, 335, 337; and human rights, 82, 84, 299, 300; and Khmer Rouge, 327; military technology, 317; and North Korea, 362; and Security Council, 27, 29; and UN Charter, 27; and UNHCR, 296; UN membership, 73; UN votes, 67; and Waldheim, Kurt, 56
Chlorofluorocarbons (CFCs), 6, 301–2. *See also* Environment, preservation of
Cholera, 356
Chun Doo Hwan, 129
Churchill, Winston, 30, 41, 42, 253; and Atlantic Charter, 378n. 5; and organization of UN, 26
Civil servants, on UN reform, 177–81
Civil service, UN, 283–89; and secondment, 287–88
Civil war, 68
Clausen, Tom, 199
Clinton administration, 279; and Bosnia-Herzegovina, 359–60; and collective security, 340–41; and peacekeeping missions, 282, 343–44; policy toward UN, 121; and Security Council, 337–39; and Somalia, 356–57; and UNESCO, 270
Club of Rome, 258
COCOM (Coordinating Committee for Multilateral Export Controls), 362, 363

Cocos Island, 116
Collective rights, 86
Collective security, 2, 6, 26–31; and Clinton administration, 340–41; definition, 338–39; and Gorbachev, 17; nonfunctioning, 10–11; and Soviet Union, 320–25; theory, 312–13; and UN Charter, 16
Collective self-reliance, 111
Colombia: and conflict containment, 317; drug trafficking, 306–7
Colombo summit, 96, 117
Colonialism, 93, 100, 105, 110–11; and fourth nonaligned summit, 107. *See also* Decolonization
Comintern Congress of Oppressed Nationalities, 100
Commission on Narcotic Drugs, 307
Commission on Sustainable Development (CSD), 305, 370
Committee for Program and Coordination. *See* CPC
Commodities price index, 118
Commodity price management, 119
Common Agricultural Policy, 367
Common consent, 233, 235
Common Fund, 117, 118, 230
Common system, UN, 280, 283, 284–87, 288, 369
Commonwealth of Independent States, 364
Communications: revolution, 372, 373, 376; and Third World, 112–14
Comoros, 75
Compensation Fund, 351
Comprehensive System of International Peace and Security (CSIPS), 321, 322–23, 324
Conable, Barber, 181, 200–2
Conference on Human Rights in Vienna, UN, 18
Conference on Security and Cooperation in Europe (CSCE), 15, 314, 358, 364
Conflict, containment of, 10, 151, 317–18
Congo, 101; peacekeeping mission in, 14, 29, 68, 78–80, 81, 158, 342
Congress (U.S.): and IDA, 197; and ITO, 186; and taxpayer's revolt, 175, 183; and UN dues, 210, 232–35
Consensus, 138–40, 166, 238
Constitution (U.S.), 220
Consultative Groups, World Bank, 199
Coolidge, Calvin, 16
Coordinating Committee for Multilateral Export Controls (COCOM), 362, 363
Cordier, Andrew, 79
Cordovez, Diego, 318
Corea, Gamani, 115, 229
Costa Rica, 108, 385n. 13; and human rights, 301
Council of Europe, 250
Covenant of the League, 28, 383n. 6; and UN Charter, 25, 27
CPC (Committee for Program Coordination), 233; inefficiency, 47–48
Croatia, 342, 352, 357, 357–59
Crocker, Chester, 326, 341–42
Cruise O'Brien, Conor, 75, 80
CSCE (Conference for Security and Cooperation in Europe), 314, 358, 364
CSD (Commission on Sustainable Development), 305, 370
CSIPS (Comprehensive System of International Peace and Security), 321, 322–23, 324
Cuba, 13, 326; and Gulf War, 3, 330, 333, 336; and human rights, 84; and Iraq, 351; and nonaligned movement, 100, 102, 107
Cuban missile crisis, 77
Cultural imperialism, 107, 112
Cultural pluralism, 18
Cultural sovereignty, 127
Cyprus, 314, 319; peacekeeping mission, 158
Czech Republic, 209

Dada, Idi Amin, 107, 259
Dadzie, Kenneth, 118, 170, 172, 181
Dag Hammarksjöld Foundation, 259
Damage limitation, 136, 138, 261
Debt management, 196–210
Decade for Women, 135
Declaration and Program of Action on the Establishment of a New International Economic Order (NIEO), 170
Decolonization, 41, 67, 94, 98–99; and multilateralism, 258; and nationalism,

20; and UN membership, 73, 74; and U.S., 97, 218. *See also* Colonialism
Defeat of an Ideal (Hazzard), 219
Deforestation, 303
Delors, Jacques, 358
Denmark, 175
de Palma, Samuel, 174; and Kissinger, 218
Department of Humanitarian Affairs, UN, (DHA), 293
Department of International and Social Affairs, UN, 172
Dependencia theory of economics, 106, 111
Development Committee, World Bank, 60
DHA (UN Department of Humanitarian Affairs), 293
Dia, Mamadou, 74
Diouf, Jacques, 62
Directors-general, UN: abuse of technical assistance, 59; accountability, 54–56
Disarmament, 124, 223; and UN Charter, 29–30; UN deliberations on, 313, 317
Disaster relief, 290
Does Aid Work? (Cassen), 60, 61
Domestic information system, 109
Draper, William, 167, 181
Drug addiction, 306–7
Drug trafficking, 17, 306–8
Dulles, John Foster, 100, 240
Dumas, Roland, 334
Dumbarton Oaks conference, 27, 30, 36, 37
Dunkel, Arthur, 56
DuPont Chemicals, 6, 377n. 2

Earth summit (1992), 121, 135
Eastern bloc, 189; collapse, 20, 329
Eastern Europe, 150; economic reform, 208–9; and human rights, 18; modernization of economy, 20; nuclear technology, 363; versus Third World, 188
East Timor, 81
EC. *See* European Community
Echeverría, Luis, 106, 107, 111, 125
ECLA (Economic Commission for Latin America and the Caribbean), 63, 103
Economic and Social Council, UN. *See* ECOSOC
Economic Commission for Europe (ECE), UN, 364
Economic Commission for Latin America and the Caribbean (ECLA), UN, 103
Economic cooperation: approaches to, 32–34; and Cairo summit, 102
Economic Council, UN, proposal for, 35–36
Economic integration, 371
Economic ministry, 150
Economic Security Council, 369–70
ECOSOC, 103, 134, 156; bodies related to, 380n. 1; and Capacity Study, 162–63, 168; formation, 32; functions, 36–38; and Gardner report, 169–70, 173; inefficiency, 47; proliferation of activities, 52–54; reform, 269–70; task of, 43–44; and UN budget, 158–59, 160; unmanageability, 48–49
Egypt, 338; and Israel, 314; military technology, 317
Eisenhower, Dwight, 100, 218
Eliasson, Jan, 293
Emergency alert system, 46
Energy conservation, 306
Energy consumption, 303
Energy price indexing, 114
Enhanced structural adjustment facility (ESAF), 205–6
Environment, preservation of, 17, 259, 301–6; and chemicals, 6–7; and World Bank, 201
Environment conference in Stockholm (1972), 135
EPTA (Extended program of technical assistance), 57
Equatorial Guinea, 299–300
Eritrea, 294, 348
ESAF (Enhanced Structural Adjustment Facility), 205–6
Ethiopia, 27, 81, 118, 231; and Eritrea, 348; famine, 289, 294, 350; and FAO, 237; and OEOA, 292; and UNDRO, 291
Ethnic cleansing, 357
European Commission, 294
European Community (EC), 13, 15, 142–43; and agricultural trade reform,

367–68; and CFCs, 301–2; and former Yugoslavia, 357–59; and Turkey, 250; and UNCTAD, 229; and WHO, 272
European Economic Community, 101
European Free Trade Area, 101
European Union, 364
Extended program of technical assistance (EPTA), 57

Façade management approach, 253–55, 261
Fahd, King, 332
Falklands, 240, 317
Fanon, Frantz, 128–29
FAO, 145–46, 178, 224, 234, 277; and African famine, 46, 237; British policy toward, 144, 237–38; and Canada, 138; constitution, 56; cooperative action, 53; efficiency, 175–76; establishment of, 33; inefficiency, 88, 180; interagency rivalry, 63; personnel practice, 283–84; purpose, 43–44; reform, 119, 134, 236; and Scandinavia, 387n. 31; staff management, 286; task of, 51–52; technical assistance activities, 61, 62–63; and UNDP, 60
FBI, 220
Federal Reserve Board, 196
Feller, Abraham, 220
Fenwick, Millicent, 237, 392n. 43
Field programs of technical assistance, 56–63, 88; failure of, 201; impetus behind, 64. *See also* Technical assistance
Fiji, 368
Finger, Maxwell, 166, 223
Five-power veto, 25, 28, 72–73
Food and Agriculture Organization. *See* FAO
Ford Foundation, 298–99
Ford Motor Company, 190
Foreign investment, 7; and nonaligned movement, 108–9
Foreign Relations Authorization Act, 231
Four Freedoms, 25, 378n. 4
Four Policemen, 26, 378–9n. 6
France, 27, 101, 237–38, 240, 360, 361; and environment, 303; and former Yugoslavia, 358; and freedom of information, 127–28; and Gulf War, 334–35, 337; and humanitarian intervention, 18, 348; and human rights, 84, 130–31; and Iran-Iraq war, 327; and nuclear weapons, 317; and peacekeeping missions, 14, 158; policy toward UN, 145, 241; and seabed mining, 227; and UN budget, 159
Franck, Thomas, 79
Fraser, Malcolm, 254
Freedom of information, 126, 146
Free market, and OPEC, 109
Free press, 113, 146
Free trade, 366–69
French film industry, 128
Fulbright, William, 220
Functional cooperation, 25, 43; doctrines of, 33–35
Fyodorov, Boris, 208

Gabon, 84
Gaidar, Yegor, 208–9
Gambia, 74, 277
Gandhi, Mahatma, 182
Gardner, Richard, 156–56, 169, 223, 236
Gardner report, 169–74
GATT, 20, 44, 101, 103, 105, 238; and Fraser, Malcolm, 254; and ITO, 187; and Reagan administration, 224; reform, 366–69; staff management, 286–87; U.S. funding, 234. *See also* Uruguay Round and World Trade Organization
Gaulle, Charles de, 241
GEF (Global Environmental Facility), 304, 306
General Accounting Office (U.S.), 159, 226
General Agreement on Tariffs and Trade. *See* GATT
General Assembly, 43, 44, 102–3, 126–27, 214, 218, 220–21, 232–33, 325; and Algiers summit, 116; and Bretton Woods institutions, 116–17, 183, 185; "consensus," 166; credibility, 315; and disarmament, 29–30, 313; functions, 36–37; and Gardner report, 169–73; and Great Britain, 239;

inefficiency, 46–47; and JIU, 281; nomination of candidates, 282; procedure, 68–70; reform, 344; resolutions, 139, 378n. 7; and UN budget, 49, 159–60; and UNCED, 370; and UNCTAD, 229; and UNDRO, 292. *See also* specific resolutions
Generalized System of Preferences, 105, 230
Geneva Group, 149, 235–36, 239; assessment of UN, 265; zero-growth policy, 280
Gennaro, Giuseppe de, 307
Georgia, 205
Gerard, Jean, 175, 228
Germany, 239, 303, 338; and former Yugoslavia, 357; and Gulf War, 330; and IAEA, 363; and League of Nations, 30
Getachew, Medhin, 118
Ghana, 79, 207, 297
Giscard d'Estaing, Valéry, 84
"Global 2000," 259
Global Environmental Facility (GEF), 304, 306
Global negotiations, 116–17
Global Program on AIDS, 271
Global Security Program, Cambridge University, 340, 342
Global warming, 6, 303, 306
Golan Heights, 314
Goldberg, Ruth, 339
Goodman, Dennis, 231
Gorazde, 347, 360
Gorbachev, Mikhail, 11, 31–32, 217, 326; and Afghanistan, 318; and collective security, 320–25; and Common Fund, 230; and economic security, 265–66; and Gulf War, 330, 332, 333, 334; policy toward UN, 17, 96
Gordon-Lennox, Lord Nicholas, 139
Governments: and global organizations, 263–65; versus secretariats, 87–89; and UN reform, 156, 181
Graham, Thomas, 363
Gramm-Rudman legislation, 232
Great Britain, 13, 34, 101, 134, 139, 147, 150, 227, 265, 267–68; and Bosnia, 360; and CFCs, 302; and drug trafficking, 307; and Falklands, 240, 317; and FAO, 237–38; and former Yugoslavia, 358; and General Assembly, 239; and Gulf War, 3, 332, 334, 337; and human rights, 84–85; and Lend-Lease Agreement, 378n. 5; and Malaysia, 385n. 19; and OEOA, 292; policy toward UN, 145; and Soviet Union, 321; and UN budget, 214, 235; and UN Charter, 27; UN dues, 238; and UNESCO, 140, 175, 223; and UNHCR, 296; and UNIDO, 248; UN membership, 74; and World Bank, 204
Great Depression, 31
Greco-Turkish relations, 319
"Green diplomacy," 266, 303
Grenada, 317
GRID (global resources information database), 305
Gromyko, Andrei, 323; policy at UN, 96
Group of 5, 192, 209
Group of 7, 209, 293; summits, 15
Group of 10, 192
Group of 18, 156, 180–81, 232–33, 241
Group of 24, 192
Group of 77, 76, 116–19, 146, 232, 305, 373, 385n. 10; erosion of solidarity, 142; formation, 101; and Gardner report, 171–74; and nonaligned movement, 105; and Nordic report, 269–70; and OPEC, 111; and poplation growth, 135–36; and SDR, 192; and seabed mining, 227; as voting bloc, 104–5, 115, 134, 139–40
"Group of High-Level Inter-governmental Experts to Review the Efficiency of the Administrative and Financial Functioning of the UN," 232
Guinea, 71
Gulf War, 2–4, 10, 12, 80–81, 121, 329–37, 364, 372; intervention in, 351; and resolution 598, 318; superpower collaboration, 11

Habitat conference (1976), 135
Habyarimana, Juvenal, 361
Hague conference (1989), 11
Haig, Alexander: and Stockman, 215; and Third World foreign aid, 197
Haiti, 347

Haitian boat people, 296
Halons, 302
Hamengku Buwono IX, 55
Hammarskjöld, Dag, 79, 80, 177; appointment, 270; and Bretton Woods institutions, 186
Hammarskjöld, Knut, 270
Hang Semrin government, 326–27
Hansenne, Michel, 272, 287
Haq, Mahbubul, 231
Hart, Baroness (Judith) 146
Hartling, Poul, 295–96
Havana Charter (1948), 170
Hazzard, Shirley, 218, 219, 220, 270; and McCarthy era, 285
Helsinki Final Act (1975), 113, 314, 357
Helsinki watch groups, 18
Heritage Foundation, 216–17
Hocké, Jean-Pierre, 295–96
Hoffman, Paul, 58, 165
Hoffman, Stanley, 259
Hoggart, Richard, 55
Howard, Sir Michael, 115
Hull, Cordell, 26, 27, 32–33, 36, 255
Humanitarian assistance, 289–98
Humanitarian intervention, 18, 68, 78, 347–48, 349–51; and Somalia, 259. *See also* Intervention; Non-intervention
Human rights, 11, 18, 81–87, 151, 294, 296, 298–301, 299; and Carter administration, 130, 223; collectivization of, 86–87; Guinea, 71; and new orders politics, 131–34; and nonintervention, 82, 347–48; and Philippines, 245; protection of, 68; and role of UN, 18; and Third World, 125–34; and Turkey, 249–50; and UN Charter, 25, 31–32
Human Rights Commission, 83, 84, 85
Human Rights Watch, 18
Hungary, 368
Hurd, Douglas, 361
Hussain Ibn Talal, King, 330
Hussein, Saddam, 2, 319, 329–37, 351

IAEA, 49; and Chernobyl, 51; inspections, 362–64; and Israeli exclusion, 214; and nuclear nonproliferation, 317; proliferation of activities, 53; and U.S. funding, 234; U.S. review of, 212
IBRD (International Bank for Reconstruction and Development), 31, 36, 187, 201
ICAO. *See* International Civil Aviation Organization
ICRC (International Committee of the Red Cross), 249, 289, 294, 298; and Bosnia, 360; and nonintervention, 81; and Rwanda, 361; and Somalia, 354
IDA (International Development Association), 58, 101, 201; and Capacity Study, 162; creation, 163, 190, 218; and nonaligned movement, 109; and sub-Saharan Africa, 205; U.S. contributions to, 197, 198
Iglesias, Enrique, 270
ILO (International Labor Office), 32–33, 120, 135; and Blanchard, 247; and human rights, 82; and Kanawaty, 274; purpose, 43–44; reform, 19; staff management, 287; task of, 51–52; technical assistance activities, 61–62, 63; and U.S. funding, 234; U.S. withdrawal from, 211, 212, 223
IMF (International Monetary Fund), 20, 31, 36, 116–17, 186–90, 371; and Capacity Study, 167; debt management, 196–210; and Gardner report, 170; and ILO, 247; influence of, 185–86; purpose, 51; reorganization, 191–93; staff management, 286; transformation, 183–84; and weighted voting, 74. *See also* World Bank
India, 20, 75, 78, 190, 338; decolonization, 99; development programs, 208; and Gulf War, 335; and human rights, 299; military technology, 317; and Narmada Dam scheme, 201; and Sikkim, 384n. 6; trade barriers, 367
Individual rights, 86
Indochina, 101; decolonization, 99
Indonesia, 81, 118; and Bandung meeting, 99–100; decolonization, 99; and human rights, 300

Indonesian islands, 201
Information sovereignty, 113
Integrated Program for Commodities (IPC), 117, 118
Interagency rivalry, 17, 46, 49, 53; and technical assistance programs, 63, 161; and UNDP, 58
Interbloc confrontation, 171
Inter-Governmental Panel on Climate Change, 304
International Atomic Energy Agency. *See* IAEA
International Bank for Reconstruction and Development. *See* IBRD
International Civil Aviation Organization (ICAO), 51; autonomy, 44; and U.S. funding, 234
International civil servants, 17
International civil service, 177, 280; reform, 11; staff quality, 283–89
International Civil Service Commission, 284–85, 286
International Commission on Environment and Development, 304
International Committee of the Red Cross. *See* ICRC
International Court of Justice, 11, 40, 321
International Decade for the Eradication of Colonialism, 4, 76
International Development Association. *See* IDA
"International Framework of Action for the International Decade for Natural Disaster Reduction," 292
International Fund for Agricultural Development (IFAD), 217, 278; and weighted voting, 74
Internationalism, 217–18
International Labor Office. *See* ILO
International law: development of, 11, 18; and Gulf War, 2, 3; and Law of the Sea, 224, 227; and NIEO, 110; and Siberian pipeline, 215
International Monetary Fund. *See* IMF
International monetary stabilization fund, 26
International monetary system, 106, 192
International Narcotics Control Board, 307
International Organizations Employees Loyalty Board of the United States, 220
International Organizations (IO), U.S. Department of, 144
International Red Cross, 347
International Rice Research Institute, 60
International Seabed Authority, 225
International taxation, 226
International Telecommunications Conference for Technical Negotiations on the Allocation of Radio Frequencies (WARC), 123
International Telecommunications Union (ITU), 123; and Israeli exclusion, 214; staff management, 287; and U.S. funding, 234; U.S. review of, 212
International Telegraph Union, 50
International Trade Organization. *See* ITO
International Year of Peace, 115
Intervention: and Cambodia, 352–54; and former Yugoslavia, 357–61; and Gulf War, 351; and Somalia, 354–57; and UN Charter, 329, 337–38. *See also* Humanitarian intervention; Nonintervention
IO (International Organizations), U.S. Department of, 144
IPC (Integrated Program for Commodities), 117, 118
Iran, 3, 77, 85, 239; and human rights, 85; and Kurds, 293; refugees, 296, 297
Iranian Red Crescent, 293
Iran-Iraq war, 314, 319, 327–29; ballistic missiles, 362
Iraq: and chemical weapons, 328–29; and human rights, 298, 300; intervention in, 68, 349, 351; and Kurds, 292–93, 359; and Kuwait, 2–4, 299, 329, 351; military capacity, 340; nuclear inspection in, 362; refugees, 296, 297; Republican Guard, 335
Islam, 7, 259; and human rights, 300
Islamic schools in Sudan, 270
Israel, 85; and Egypt, 314; and ITU, 123;

and Lebanon, 317; UN treatment of, 214
Italy, 241, 358
ITO (International Trade Organization): and Gardner report, 170; purpose, 186–87
ITU. *See* International Telecommunications Union
Izetbegovic, Alia, 359

Jackson, Sir Robert, 142, 155, 174, 177, 181, 182; and Bangladesh, 291; Capacity Study, 160–69; on Sikkim and Bhutan, 384n. 6; and UN reform, 157, 158
Japan, 28, 48; and agricultural trade reform, 367; and Bandung meeting, 99; and Bretton Wood institutions, 241; and Group of 18, 241; and Gulf War, 330; and IAEA, 363; and seabed mining, 227; and Security Council membership, 338; and UN budget, 235–36; UN membership, 241; and WHO, 272; and World Bank, 190
Java, 201
Javits, Jacob, 95
JIU (Joint Inspection Unit), 48, 87–88; creation, 159; inefficiency, 281; reform, 282–83; report on UNDRO, 291
Johnson, Lyndon, 225
Joint Inspection Unit. *See* JIU
Jonah, James, 349–50
Judeo-Christian model, 18

Kanawaty, George, 274–75
Kashmir, 78, 314
Kassebaum, Nancy Landon, 231, 392n. 36
Kassebaum-Solomon amendment of 1985, 231–32
Katanga, 78–79, 80, 342
Kawaguchi, Yugi, 272
Kemp-Moynihan amendment of 1979, 231
Kennan, George, 19, 360
Kennedy, John F., 101; UN Development Decade, 218
Kent, Randolph, 290
Kenya, 84–85, 207, 338; decolonization, 99
Khan, Sadruddin Aga, 270, 292
Khartoum, 237, 289
Khiary, Mahmoud, 79
Khmer People's National Liberation Front, 352
Khmer Rouge, 326–27, 352–53
Khomeini, Ayatollah, 85, 239, 259, 328
Khrushchev, Nikita, 77, 313
Kirkpatrick, Jeane, 126, 133, 212–14, 220–21; and Carter administration, 223; and Stockman, 215
Kissinger, Henry, 95–96; and Hoffman, Stanley, 259; and nonaligned movement, 107; policy toward UN, 218–19; and seabed mining, 226
Kleinwachter, Wolfgang, 385n. 18
Koh, Tommy, 217
Korean War, 3, 377n. 1
Kouchner, Bernard, 398n. 3
Kurds, 359; and chemical weapons, 329; and Gulf War, 335, 336, 337; refugee crisis, 292–93
Kuwait: and Iran-Iraq war, 327; and Iraq, 2–4, 299, 319, 329, 351
Kyrgyztan, 205

Lang, Jack, 127
Larosière, Jacques de, 196, 203
Lasso, José Ayala, 301
Latin America, 15, 99, 101, 103, 279; debt management, 203–5; economic collapse, 93–94, 188–89; and human rights, 300; and nonaligned movement, 102; and Palestinian rights, 111; and Prebisch theory, 105; and World Bank, 190
Law of the Sea Conference, 217
Law of the Sea Convention (LOSC), 224–27
League of Nations, 17, 25, 38–39; failure of, 29–30; and human rights, 31; and international civil service, 177; membership in, 73; and minority rights, 348; purpose, 72; successes, 32–33; U.S. membership, 218
League of Red Cross Societies, 293, 294
Lebanon, 70–71, 314, 316, 339; and Israel, 317
Lend-Lease Agreement, 26, 378n. 5
Lenin, V. I., 100, 113
Leonard, James, 223

Lewis, Arthur, 58
Liberal democracy, 97
Liberal economics, 106
Liberal internationalism, 123
Liberia, 142, 289
Libya, 81; and Chad, 318; and human rights, 298; and IAEA, 363; oil royalties, 106
Lie, Trygve, 219–20
Liechtenstein, 73
Ligachev, Yegor, 323
Limits to Growth, 258
Literacy programs, 62
Lodge, Henry Cabot, 221
Lodge commission, 221
Loescher, Gil, 297
Lomé conventions, 133, 249
Lumumba, Patrice, 78–79, 80
Lusaka, Paul, 13
Lusaka summit, 102
Luxembourg, 73, 358

Maastricht Treaty on European Union, 7
Macedonia, 360–61; and ESAF loans, 205
Macmillan, Harold, 101
Maharashtra, 289
Mahathir, Muhamed, 385n. 19
Maheu, René, 137
Mahler, Halfdan, 56, 119, 148, 271
Major, John, 334, 335
Malaria, vaccine, 60–61
Malawi, 207
Malaysia, 385n. 19; drug addiction, 306; economic growth, 373–74; and human rights, 299, 300
Maldives, 74; and conflict containment, 318
Malta, 160
Manchuria, 27; and League of Nations, 28
Manila, 147
Mann, Jonathan, 271
Marcos, Imelda, 245
Margan, Ivo, 147
Marks, Stephen, 131–32
Marshall Plan, 58, 187
Marsh Arabs, 337
Marxism, 96, 97
Mass migration, 296–98
Mayall, James, 398n. 2
Maynes, Charles William, 222–23
Mayor, Federico, 89, 176, 238, 270–71
M'Bow, Amadou Mahtar, 60, 120, 137–38; corruption, 55–56, 228; and Heritage Foundation, 216; reelection, 71, 147–48, 176, 223; and Sekou Touré, 382–3n. 31; and UN reform, 175
McCarren, Pat, 219
McCarthy era, 220, 283, 285
McHenry, Donald, 327
McNamara, Robert, 125, 133, 183, 201; and development aid, 190–91, 194
Media, 113; American, 127–28; Third World guidelines, 139
Meese, Edwin, 226
Mensah, Moise, 176
Mexico, 20, 338; and conflict containment, 317; economic growth, 373–74; foreign debt, 196–97; and GATT, 367; and human rights, 84; OECD membership, 294
MFO (Multinational Force and Observers), 396–7n. 6
Micronationalism, 74, 258
Microstates, 59; voting, 72–77
Middle East, 85, 95, 182
Middle East Supply Centre, 34
Military Staff Committee (MSC), 28, 29; and Gulf War, 331, 332; and Soviet Union, 320, 322, 340
Milosevic, Slobodan, 357, 358, 359
Mining, seabed, 224–27
Missile Technology Control Regime, 363
Mitrany, David, 50, 56, 161, 170; and functional cooperation, 33–35; on politics, 44; on sovereignty, 67
Mitterrand, François, 84, 334; and Gulf War, 330; and humanitarian intervention, 348; and Rwanda, 361
Mobutu, Joseph, 79
Mobutu, Sésé Séko, 84, 131
Mogadishu, 341, 354–56
Moi, Daniel Arap, 84–85
Monnet, Jean, 101
Montreal protocol, 301, 302
Morse, Bradford, 56, 292
Moscow conference (1943), 26, 35, 378–9n. 6

Mosley, Paul, 102
Mourik, Marten, 158, 176
Moynihan, Daniel Patrick, 95, 147, 211, 222, 239
MSC. *See* Military Staff Committee
Muller, Robert, 178–79, 389n. 29
Multifiber Arrangement, 366
Multilateral cooperation, 5, 6, 15, 149–51, 245; and consensus, 138–40; and humanitarian assistance, 290; and liberal internationalism, 123; and non–UN organizations, 20; opportunities for, 264, 266–67; and Reagan administration, 210; U.S. support for, 218
Multilateral diplomacy: approaches to, 239–41; and Reagan administration, 212, 224
Multilateralism, 1, 5, 119–20, 370–72, 375–76; and Carter administration, 223–24; and decolonization, 258; and inefficiency, 183–84; versus sovereignty, 19; U.S. commitment to, 220
Multinational Force and Observers (MFO), 396–7n. 6
Museveni, Yoweri, 84
Myrdal, Gunnar, 48, 75, 141–42

NAFTA (North American Free Trade Agreement), 367
Nairobi, 85
Najman, Dragoljub, 137, 383n. 17
Nakajima, Hiroshi, 148–49; election, 271–72
Namibia, 318, 326
Narmada Dam hydroelectric and irrigation scheme, 201
NASA, 305
Nasser, Gamal Abdel, 102
NATCAPS (National Technical Cooperation Assessments and Programs), 276–77
Nationalism, 41, 258; and decolonization, 20; erosion of, 35; and voting majority, 75
National sovereignty, 5, 260; erosion of, 35
National Technical Cooperation Assessments and Programs (NATCAPS), 276–77
NATO, 11, 101, 314, 364; and Bosnia, 340, 360, 361
Negash, Tesema, 237
Nehru, Jawaharlal, 100, 105
Neocolonialism, 93, 110, 111; and Fanon, Frantz, 129
Netherlands, 130; and environment, preservation of, 303; and former Yugoslavia, 358; and UNESCO, 175
Newell, Gregory, 175, 212, 228
New International Economic Order. *See* NIEO
"New orders," 93–98, 109–14
New World Information and Communication Order. *See* NWICO
New world order, 10
New Zealand, 103
Niazi, Mohamed Ali, 282
NIEO (New International Economic Order), 94, 103, 111, 117, 125, 170, 171; and Blanchard, 120; creation, 107; 1975 Declaration, 133; and Group of 77, 373; and international law, 110; and Kissinger, 95–96; need for, 185; and Prebisch theory, 105
Nigeria, 81, 338; development programs, 208
Nixon, Richard, 106, 187; policy toward UN, 218–19; and Yost, 221
Nkrumah, Kwame, 93
Nonaligned movement, 76, 99–104, 105; and Third World solidarity, 107
Nonaligned summit: Algiers, 107–9, 116; Belgrade, 100, 101, 103; Cairo, 102, 103; Colombo, 96, 117
Nonintervention, 7, 68, 77–81; and human rights, 82, 347–48; and UN Charter, 336. *See also* Humanitarian Intervention; Intervention
"Non-Intervention, Self-Determination and the 'New World Order'" (Mayall), 398n. 2
Nordic UN Project, 61–62, 156, 252; report, 268–69, 276
North Africa. *See* Africa
North American Free Trade Agreement (NAFTA), 367
North Korea: and chemical weapons, 318; nuclear inspection in, 362; nuclear technology, 364

Norway, 75, 117
Nossiter, Bernard, 111
NPT (Nuclear Non-Proliferation Treaty), 316–17, 351, 363
Nuclear confrontation, 100
Nuclear disarmament. *See* Disarmament
Nuclear Non-Proliferation Treaty (NPT). *See* NPT
Nuclear proliferation, 362–64
Nuclear Suppliers' Group, 363
Nuclear technology, 363
NWICO (New World Information and Communication Order), 112–14, 115; New information order, 126–28
Nyerere, Julius, 108; on IMF, 193

Oakley, Robert, 356
OAS (Organization of American States), 373
OAU. *See* Organization of African Unity
Obasanjo, Olosegun, 343
OECD (Organization for Economic Cooperation and Development), 15, 59, 61, 117; and agricultural trade reform, 367; and Capacity Study, 168; Development Assistance Committee, 102; and development financing, 64–65; disaster relief, 294; and drug addiction, 306; and Stern, Ernest, 200; technical assistance finance, 388n. 2
Office for Emergency Operations in Africa (OEOA), 63, 291–92
Office for Inspections and Investigations, 282
Office for Research and Collection of Information, 350
Ogata, Sadako, 296
Only One Earth (Ward), 258
OPEC (Organization of Petroleum Exporting Countries), 107, 108, 111; and free market, 109; and IMF, 192–93; oil embargo, 107, 258
OPEC Special Fund, 117
Open market, 273–79
Operation Desert Storm. *See* Gulf War
Operation Provide Comfort, 336, 337
Operation Restore Hope, 354–56
Opting out approach, 247–50, 260
Oral rehydration therapy (ORT), 62
ORCI, 292
Organization for Economic Cooperation and Development. *See* OECD
Organization for Intellectual Cooperation, 270
Organization of African Unity (OAU), 148, 176, 318, 373
Organization of American States (OAS), 373
Organization of Petroleum Exporting Countries. *See* OPEC
ORT (oral rehydration therapy), 62
Ottawa, 237
Overseas Development Administration, U.K., 144
Owen, Lord, 359
Ozone layer, 6, 301–2, 303, 377n. 2

Pakistan, 77, 78, 95, 318, 338; and Bandung meeting, 100; drug addiction, 306; and IAEA, 363; and Somalia, 339
Palestine, 85, 94
Palestine Liberation Organization (PLO), 135, 231, 316
Panama, 317
Parallel mining, Law of the Sea, 226
Paris Agreement (1991), 327
Paris Club, 205
Parker, Dorothy, 16
Parsons, Sir Anthony, 68–70
Peace Corps, 101
Peacekeeping missions, 10, 45; and Clinton administration, 282, 341, 343–44; and Congo, 29, 68, 78–80, 81, 342; and Soviet Union, 320; strengthening, 342–43; and UN budget, 14–15, 158–59, 393–4n. 14; UN capacity for, 339
Pearl Harbor, 26
Pearson report, 167
Pentagon Papers, 221
Pérez de Cuéllar, Javier, 12–14, 56, 83, 178, 232, 246, 312–13; and Gulf War, 3, 333, 334, 335, 336; incompetence, 47, 319; and Iraq, 349; reelection, 148; on UN ineffectiveness, 15, 19; and UN reform, 180–81
Pérez Guerrero, Manuel, 117, 170

Permanent contracts, UN, 284–85, 287
Perry, William, 360
Peru, 107
Petrovsky, Vladimir, 322, 323, 324
Peyrefitte, Alain, 129
Philippines, 147, 245; and human rights, 84
Phnom Penh, 352–53
Pines, Burton Yale, 216
Piniés, Jamié de, 12–13
Pisani, Edgard, 130, 131
Pitcairn Island, 116
Please, Stanley, 194
PLO. *See* Palestinian Liberation Organization
Plutonium, 364
"Point 4" strategy. *See* Truman
Poland, 30, 85; economic reform, 208; and OEOA, 292
Pol Pot, 350
Pollution, 135. *See also* Environment, preservation of
Polonoroeste scheme, 194
Popper, Sir Karl, 21, 378n. 10
Population growth, 303; African, 374; and Group of 77, 135–36
Powell, Colin, 355
Prebisch, Raúl, 103–5, 125
Preston, Lewis, 207–8
Price, Byron, 219–20
Primakov, Yevgeni, 330
Proliferation of activities, 52–54
Protectionism, 31
Pyongyang, 362

Racism, 93, 100, 105, 110, 222, 239–40; and Zionism, 76, 107
Radio frequencies, allocation of, 50
Raison, Timothy, 382n. 31
Rajaratnam, Sinnathamby, 385n. 19
Rangoon, 376
Ratiner, Leigh, 226–27
Reagan, Ronald, 128, 197, 240, 317, 324; on General Assembly, 213; and human rights, 84
Reagan administration, 149, 219 224–27; and Bretton Woods institutions, 188–89, 209–10; inquiry into IMF, 197–99; multilateral diplomacy, 124, 212, 239; policy toward UN, 178; review of UN, 211–17; UN funding, 140, 231–35; UN reform, 235–42; withdrawal from UNESCO, 227–28
"Reality and Guarantees of a Secure World, The," (Gorbachev), 320–21
Red Cross, 289, 294
Redistribution with Growth (Chenery), 191
Refaire l'Onu! (Bertrand), 379n. 22
Refugees, 260, 336, 337; Kurds, 292–93; management of, 295–98
Regan, Donald, 197
Regional cooperation, 372
Report on the World Social Situation, 147
Reykjavik summit, 217
Rhineland, 27
Richard, Ivor, 239
Right to development, 132–33
Ripert, Jean, 172
Roosevelt, Eleanor, 218
Roosevelt, Franklin Delano, 5, 6, 34, 50, 378–9nn. 4; and human rights, 82; and ILO, 32–33; and organization of UN, 25–26, 30; and Soviet Union, 28; and UN Charter, 26–27
Roque, Carnéro, 385n. 17
Rosenblum, Mort, 251
Rosenthal, Abe, 129–30
Rotberg, Eugene, 202
Royal Institute of International Affairs, 33
Ruding, Onno, 148
Rushdie, Salman, 85, 239
Russell, Ruth B., 30
Russia: and Biological weapons, 363; and Bosnia, 360; domestic problems, 1; economic reform, 208–9, 364–66; modernization of economy, 20; and MSC, 340; multilateral diplomacy, 149. *See also* Soviet Union
Russian Central Bank, 208
Russia's Choice, 208
Rwanda, 5, 294, 347, 350, 361; refugees, 296
Rwandan Patriotic Front (RPF), 361

Sadat, Anwar, 314
SADCC (South African Development Coordination Conference), 248, 393n. 6

Safire, William, 226
Sahara, 319
Sahel famine, 237, 258, 290–91
Sahnoun, Muhammad, 354
SAL program, 390n. 9
Salvador, 107
Sanctions, 3; and Gulf War, 330, 331; and human rights abuses, 350
Sanderson, John, 353
San Francisco conference (1945), 30, 40, 68, 98
Saouma, Edouard, 46, 55–56, 175–76; criticism of, 178; and Fenwick, Millicent, 392n. 43; inefficiency, 180; reelection, 176, 236–38, 270
Sarajevo, 359
Sartre, Jean-Paul, 129
Saudi Arabia: and Gulf War, 3, 331, 332; and human rights, 84; and Iran-Iraq war, 327; and OPEC, 111
Save the Children, 289, 354
Scali, John, 76
Scandinavia, 145–46, 241; and FAO, 237–38, 387n. 31; and UN budget, 214; and UNESCO reform, 88–89
Schifter, Richard, 84
Scientific and Technical Advisory Panel, 304
Scranton, William, 84
SDR (special drawing rights), 114; creation, 192
Seabed mining, 224–27
SEATO, 100
Secondment, 287–88
Secretariat: criticism of, 232; status, 39
Secretariats, 87–89, 119, 264; accountability, 280–83; control of, 68; effectiveness, 6; executive independence, 65; inefficiency, 17, 97–98; power of, 69; role of, 50–51; and UN reform, 156–57, 175, 181–82
Secretaries-general: appointment, 270; incompetence, 47; power, 39
Secret ballot, 76–77
Sectoralization, 38
Security Council, 121, 214, 218, 327–29, 357–61, 362, 377n. 1; and Cambodia, 352–54; and Clinton administration, 337–39; and conflict prevention, 318–19; creation, 26–30; and disarmament, 313; and drug trafficking, 307; and Gulf War, 2–4, 80–81, 330–37; ineffectiveness, 314–18; intervention policy, 7, 68, 348–51; need for, 77; resolutions, 142, 182; and Russia, 364; and Rwanda, 361; and secretary-general, 39; and Somalia, 354–57; and Soviet Union, 28–30, 51, 219, 319–25; and UN membership, 73–74; U.S. veto, 220; and Vietnam, 240. *See also* specific resolutions
Security Council's Standing Committee on Admissions, 73
Sedou, Amadou, 55
Selective action approach, 255–78, 261
Self-determination, principle of, 78, 80, 98; and Echeverria, 106
Senarclens, Pierre de, 170
Serbia, 343, 357–59
Service organizations, 381n. 6
Shaming, collective, 70
Shawcross, William, 354, 398n. 4
Shevardnadze, Eduard, 322, 323, 324; and Cambodia, 352; and Gulf War, 330, 334
Shia refugees, 336, 337
Shultz, George, 214
Siberian gas pipeline affair, 215
Sihanouk, Norodom, 327, 352, 353, 354
Sikkim, 384n. 6
Singapore, 75, 248, 385n. 19; and human rights, 299; and UNESCO, 175
SIPRI (Stockholm International Peace Research Institute), 340
Slavery Convention (1926), 31
Slovenia, 357–59
Small Is Dangerous (Harden), 74–75
Solidarity. *See* Third World solidarity
Solzhenitsyn, Alexander, 85, 249
Somalia, 4, 289, 339, 352, 358; and human rights, 300; intervention in, 18, 68, 78, 259, 354–57
"Some Reflections on Reform of the United Nations" (Bertrand), 377–8n. 2
South Africa, 326; and Amin, 107; apartheid, 316, 348
South African Development Coordination Conference (SADCC), 248, 393n. 6

Southeast Asian Treaty Organization. *See* SEATO
South Korea: and chemical weapons, 318; economic growth, 279, 374; and Soviet Union, 51, 214; student demonstration, 129–30, 384n. 24; and UNDP, 61
Sovereign equality, 27, 75–76, 88, 95, 97; and colonialism, 111; and Gardner report, 174; and Mitrany, David, 33–34
Sovereignty, 67; and foreign investment, 7; and human rights, 82–83; versus multilateralism, 19
Soviet empire: collapse, 10; UN membership, 72
Soviet Union, 11, 13, 21, 94, 100, 189, 233, 246, 314; and Afghanistan, 139, 317, 318, 325–26; blocking veto, 219; and Cambodia, 352; civil service staff, 283; and economic security, 265–66; espionage, 217, 232; and former Yugoslavia, 358; and Gulf War, 2–4, 330–37; and human rights, 31–32; and Iran-Iraq war, 328; and Kirkpatrick, 213; and Latin America, 101; and Lend-Lease Agreement, 378n. 5; and peacekeeping missions, 14, 158; policy toward UN, 17, 96; and Reagan, 128; and resolution 1514, 73; and seabed mining, 225; and secondment, 287; and Security Council, 28–30, 219, 319–25; Siberian pipeline, 215; and South Korea, 51, 214; and UN budget, 156, 159, 214; and UN Charter, 27; and UNESCO, 141, 176; and Vietnam, 326–27
Soviet Union, former, 6; and IAEA, 363; nuclear technology, 363; refugees, 296, 297
Special drawing rights (SDR), 114, 192
Specialized agencies, 5, 39–42, 380–1n. 1; accountability, 48; and Capacity Study, 163; management reform, 282; purpose, 50–51
Special Program for Research and Training for Tropical Diseases. *See* TDR
Special UN Fund for Economic Development (SUNFED), 101
Speth, Gustave, 272, 277
Sprinkel, Beryl, 197
Sri Lanka, 317–18
Stalin, Joseph, 30, 32, 82; and Security Council, 29
Stanleyville rebellion, 80
"Star Wars," 317
State Department (U.S.): draft constitution, 35, 36; and ILO, 211; IO, 144; review of UN, 212
State of the World's Refugees (report), 294
Stern, Ernest, 200
Stockholm International Peace Research Institute (SIPRI), 340
Stockman, David, 197, 215
Streeb, Gordon, 229
Strong, Maurice, 292, 304–5
Structural adjustment, 114, 202, 205, 207, 260, 365, 374, 390n. 9; loans, 195, 199
Structural reform approach, 250–53, 260–61
Subcommission on the Prevention of Discrimination and Protection of Minorities, 83
Sub-Saharan Africa, 59, 189; development programs, 194; economic collapse, 195, 205–7
Sub-Saharan Africa: From Crisis to Sustainable Growth (World Bank report), 189, 206–7
Successor Vision, A, 251
Sudan, 81, 237, 259; famine, 289, 350; and human rights, 298, 300
Sukarno, 102
Sullivan, Scott, 85
SUNFED (Special UN Fund for Economic Development), 101
Supranational mining authority, 226
Sutherland, Peter, 56, 287
Switzerland, 143–44
Syria, 13; and Gulf War, 330; and human rights, 84, 300; and IAEA, 363

Taiwan, 318
Tajikistan, 205
Tamil, 318
Tanzania, 61, 205–6, 296
TDR, 60–61

Technical assistance, 64, 88, 201; and Capacity Study, 160–68; and Great Britain, 267–68; and OECD finance, 388n. 2; and open market, 273–79; proliferation of, 56–63; reform, 272–73; and UN budget, 159; and World Bank, 195–96
Technical Cooperation Program, FAO, 236–37
Technology, 225–26, 373, 374; sharing, 306, 372
Tehran conference (1943), 26–27
Thailand, 376
Thant, U, 74, 103
Thatcher, Baroness (Margaret), 303, 318
Third World, 45, 93–98, 105–9, 125–34, 215, 303; and Bretton Woods institutions, 185, 187, 191; and Capacity Study, 160–68; and communications, 112–14; debt management, 203; decolonization, 98–99; drug addiction, 306–7; and FAO, 176; and Gardner report, 170, 171, 173; and IDA, 197, 198; media guidelines, 139; and NWICO, 112–15; process of organization, 98–105; and radio frequencies, 50; technical assistance, 57–62, 64; and UN budget, 156, 159, 160; and UNDP, 59; and UN reform, 157, 175. *See also* NIEO
Third World forums, 151
Third World majority, 110, 134–42, 174, 223
Third World Solidarity, 20, 76, 107, 118, 151; erosion of, 142
Thompson, Sir John, 81
Thornburgh, Richard, 280, 284
Tiananmen Square massacre, 384n. 24
Tickell, Sir Crispin, 323
Tito, Josip Broz, 100, 102, 105, 116, 357
Togo, 297
Tokyo, Bank of, 201
Touré, Sekou, 71, 84, 382–3n. 3
Trade reform, 366–69
Transfer of technology, 225–26
Treasury (U.S.), 26; IMF inquiry, 197–99; review of development banks, 212; and Stockman, 215
Treaty of Versailles, 25, 30
Truman, Harry, 100, 101, 377n. 1; and ITO, 186; Point 4 strategy, 100, 218
Tryanovsky, Oleg, 319–20
Tshombe, Moise, 78
Tubman, William, 142, 165–66
Tudjman, Franjo, 359
Tunisia, 112
Turkey, 296; and Bandung meeting, 99; development programs, 208; and Gulf War, 335; and human rights, 249–50
Tuvalu, 73

Uganda, 76, 81; and Amin, 107; collapse, 259; and human rights, 84
Ukraine, 209
UN Commission on Human Rights, 245; membership, 298–300
UN Committee of the Whole, 305
UN Committee on Information, 128
UN Conference on Disarmament, 317
UN Conference on Environment and Development (UNCED), 94, 304–5, 370
UN Conference on Human Rights in Vienna (1993), 300
UN Council for Namibia, 326
UNCTAD (UN Conference on Trade and Development), 48, 103–6, 115–19, 218, 385n. 13; and Gardner report, 170, 171, 173; and Israeli exclusion, 214; reform, 181; U.S. criticism of, 228
UNDA (UN Development Authority), 169, 191; and Gardner report, 170
UN Decolonization Committee, 73, 116
UN Development Decade, 87, 101, 218
UNDP (UN Development Program), 43, 172, 269; British policy toward, 144; and Capacity Study, 160–68; and Chalker, Lynda, 267–68; creation, 105, 218; policy of, 57–62; propaganda, 45; round tables, 199; and UN budget, 159; and World Bank, 191, 275–77
UNDRO (UN Disaster Relief Organization), 290–93
UN Economic Commission for Latin America (ECLA), 63
UNEP (UN Environment Program), 301–6, 377n. 2; cooperative action,

53; and Gardner report, 170; U.S. review of, 212
UNESCO (UN Educational, Scientific and Cultural Organization), 51–54, 60, 70–71, 120, 140, 144, 283, 379n. 15; and France, 241; and freedom of information, 127–28, 146; and Heritage Foundation, 216; and Hoggart, Richard, 55; and information sovereignty, 113; Israeli exclusion, 223; and media guidelines, 139; and Najman, Dragoljub, 137; propaganda, 62; purposes, 43–44; and Raison, 382n. 31; and Reagan administration, 224; reform, 119, 238, 270; and Scandinavia, 88–89; Singapore withdrawal, 248; staff management, 286; U.S. review, 212; U.S. withdrawal, 140–41, 227–28. *See also* M'Bow, Amadou Mahtar
UN Fund for Drug Abuse Control, 307
UN Fund for Population Activities, 216
UNHCR (UN High Commissioner for Refugees, Office of the), 143, 249; and Bosnia, 360; capability, 289; creation, 300–1; and Kirkpatrick, 214; and nonintervention, 81; problems, 295–98; purposes, 294–95
UN Human Rights Center, 82
UNICEF, 45, 272; and Gardner report, 169; and IMF reform, 278; propaganda, 62
UNIDO (UN Industrial Development Organization), 105, 117; and Australia withdrawal, 248; reform, 272; and U.S. funding, 234; and weighted voting, 74
Unified Task Force (UNITAF), 355
UNIFIL (UN Interim Force in Lebanon), 320
Unilateralism, 216; 217
UN in Development, The, 268
UN Industrial Development Organization. *See* UNIDO
UN Interim Force in Lebanon (UNIFIL), 320
UNITAF (Unified Task Force), 355
United Kingdom. *See* Great Britain
United Nations: complexity, 43–46; dues, 72, 210, 232–35, 238; fortieth anniversary, 12–14, 178; 38–40; management reform, 282; membership, 72–75, 241; in New York, 379–81n. 1; as organization, 38–39; organizations of, 8–9; politicization, 93, 94; polycentrism, 38, 43–46; and population, 135–36; and postwar security system, 10–11; purpose, 12, 72; reform, approaches to, 247–61; special bodies and programs, 380n. 1; political football theory, 215; population conference in Bucharest, 135–36
United Nations budget, 49, 156, 160, 214, 393–4n. 14; and peacekeeping missions, 14–15, 158–59; and Reagan administration, 214; reform, 235–41; U.S. contribution, 221
United Nations Charter, 5, 10, 12–13, 16, 25, 219, 239; Article 1, 136; Article 2, 27; Article 2.1, 74; Article 2.7, 18; Article 37, 78, 316, 336, 348; Article 18.1, 74; Article 23, 27, 28, 316, 338; Article 29, 342; Article 34, 348; Article 41, 3, 333; Article 43, 25, 312; Article 47, 29, 331; Article 51, 3, 29, 331, 332, 333; Article 55, 51; Article 56, 31, 82–83; Article 78, 356; Article 99, 39, 79, 81, 311; Article 100, 219, 233, 283; Article 101, 186, 233, 287; Article 106, 379n. 6; Chapter VI, 315, 316; Chapter VII, 10, 28, 29, 78, 311, 312, 315, 325, 331, 332–33, 333, 348, 359–60; Chapter VIII, 357; Chapter IX, 31–32, 37; drafting, 26–30, 31–38; erosion of principles, 240; and five-power veto, 72–73; and Gulf War, 2–4; and human rights, 18, 82, 86; and intervention, 77–81, 329, 337–38, 347–48; and Kirkpatrick, 213; as minority document, 248; and new orders politics, 122, 126, 131; and Soviet Union, 321–22; specialized agencies, 39–42; and UN membership, 74–75
United Nations Resolutions: Resolution 32/130, 86; Resolution 32/197, 172,

173; Resolution 41/213, 233; Resolution 43/131, 349; Resolution 45/100, 349; Resolution 57, 261; Resolution 84, 377n. 1; Resolution 242, 316; Resolution 338, 316; Resolution 435, 316, 318, 326; Resolution 598, 318, 319, 328; Resolution 660, 335, 351; Resolution 661, 331; Resolution 662, 330; Resolution 665, 332; Resolution 678, 333, 351; Resolution 686, 335; Resolution 687, 335, 351; Resolution 688, 335, 336, 337, 349, 350; Resolution 706, 351; Resolution 1514, 73; Resolution 3243, 291; Resolution 3379, 222; Resolutions, 69, 139, 378n. 7
United States: and agricultural trade reform, 367–68; and Camberley group, 237–38; and CFCs, 301–2; and China's UN membership, 73; and decolonization, 97; domestic problems, 1; drug manufacture, 306; and ECOSOC, 134; and FAO, 284; and freedom of information, 127–28; Grenada invasion, 317; and Gulf War, 3–4, 372; and Iran-Iraq war, 328; and Macedonia, 360–61; and M'bow reelection, 71; McCarthy era, 283; and Soviet Union, 246, 321; and Third World, 96; and UN Charter, 27; UN dues, 72; and UNESCO, 140–41, 175, 223; and UN fund transfer, 265; UN membership, 74; and WHO, 272. *See also* specific administrations
Universal Declaration of Human Rights, 5, 18, 82–86, 113, 125, 127; and Echeverría, 106; and new orders politics, 122; and Roosevelt, Eleanor, 218
Universalist approach, 299
Universality, 6, 246; and human rights, 300
Universal Postal Union (UPU), 20–21, 36, 40; purpose, 50; staff management, 287
UNOSOM (UN Operation in Somalia), 354–56
UN Preparatory Commission, 219
UNPROFOR (UN Protection Force in former Yugoslavia), 340, 352, 358
UN Rapid Deployment Force, 341
UN Relief and Rehabilitation Administration (UNRRA), 34, 161, 162
UN Relief and Works Agency (UNRWA), 143
UN Research Institute for Social Development (UNRISD), 43
UN Special Session on Disarmament (1978), 223
UN Staff College, 164, 166
UNTAC (UN Transitional Authority in Cambodia), 352–54
Uranium, 364
Urquhart, Brian, 231; criticism of UN, 179; and decolonization, 98; peacekeeping proposal plan, 342–43, 344; and Security Council, weakness of, 314–15; and Somalia, 354; and Soviet Union, 322; and UN obsolescence, 182–83
Uruguay Round, 20, 56, 128, 187, 366–68. *See also* GATT
U.S. Climate Analysis Center, 53
U.S. Executive Order 10422, 219
USS Harland County, 347
Utopianism, and Popper, Karl, 21

Vance, Cyrus, 359
Vandenberg, Arthur S., 213
Vauzelle, Michel, 334
Venezuela, 317
Vietnam, 106, 221, 240; and Cambodia, 318, 326–27; and chemical weapons, 318; and McNamara, 190
Vietnamese boat people, 296
Volcker, Paul, 196, 200
Voting, 67, 231, 233; and microstates, 72–77; and secret ballot, 76–77; and blocs, 134; and Group of 77, 104–5, 115; and majority, 75, 76–77, 174; abuse of, 214–15; use of, 134–42

Waldheim, Kurt, 56, 148, 169, 172; appointment, 270; and Egypt, 314; and Gulf War, 80–81, 330; incompetence, 47
Walters, Vernon, 319
War crimes: former Yugoslavia, 11; and Gulf War, 330

Ward, Barbara, 258
Warsaw Pact, 11, 314
Weighted voting, 74, 231, 233
Weiss, Thomas, 117
Western economic summit (1991), 350
Western Europe: drug manufacture, 306; and IAEA, 363; and World Bank, 190
Western European Union, 358
West Germany, 13; and OEOA, 292; and seabed mining, 227; and UN budget, 235–36; UN membership, 241. *See also* Germany
WFC (World Food Council): and African famine, 46, 71; interagency rivalry, 63; and UNDP, 59
Whelan, Eugene, 71
Whitaker, Ben, 85–86
WHO (World Health Organization), 49, 145; and AIDS, 148–49; and damage limitation, 136; and drug addiction, 307; management, 271–72; purposes, 43–44; reform, 19; successes, 278; task of, 51; technical assistance activities, 60, 61–62; U.S. funding, 234
Williams, Douglas, 137
Williams, Maurice, 63
Williamson, Richard, 234
Witte, Barthold, 139
WMO. *See* World Meteorological Organization
Woolcott, Richard, 319–20
World Bank, 20, 46, 47, 116–17, 201, 303–4; adaptability, 186–89; Articles of Association, 193; budget evaluations, 55; and Capacity Study, 162, 166, 167; debt management, 196–210; and Gardner report, 170; and IDA, 101; influence, 185–86; and McNamara, 125, 183, 190–91, 201; poverty programs, 193–96; and private sector, 371; purpose, 51; staff management, 286; structural adjustment, 390n. 9; and UNDP, 275–77; U.S. inquiry, 197–99; and weighted voting, 74. *See also* IMF
World Climate Conference (1990), 302
World Disarmament Campaign, 313
World Employment Conference, 135
World Food Council. *See* WFC
World Food Program, 218, 297
World Health Assembly (1983), 119
World Health Organization. *See* WHO
World Meteorological Organization (WMO), 305; cooperative action, 53
World Trade Organization (WTO), 44, 187, 368–69; staff management, 287
Wretched of the Earth, The (Fanon), 128–29
WTO. *See* World Trade Organization

Yalta, 30
Yaoundé conference (1980), 114
Year Zero, 259, 354
Yeltsin, Boris, 11, 208–9
Yemen, 3, 333, 336
Yost, Charles, 130, 221–22
Young, Andrew, 222–23
Yugoslavia, 100, 219
Yugoslavia, former, 11, 68, 142, 342, 356; intervention in, 357–61; and UNPROFOR, 352

Zaire, 84, 131, 207; and human rights, 296, 300
Zero growth, principle of, 235, 236
Zero-2000 proposal, 367
Zimbabwe, 336
Zimmern, Sir Alfred, 25
Zionism, 111, 222, 239–40; as racism, 76, 107